PASTOR, CHURCH & LAW

VOLUME FOUR

Liability & Church and State Issues

RICHARD R. HAMMAR
J.D., LL.M., CPA

ISBN-10: 0-917463-48-X
ISBN-13: 978-0-917463-48-8

Published by Your Church Resources
Christianity Today International
465 Gundersen Drive
Carol Stream, IL 60188
(630) 260-6200
www.ChristianityToday.com
www.YourChurch.net
www.ChurchLawToday.com

Edited by: Marian V. Liautaud
Cover design by: Dean Renninger
Interior design by: Mary Bellus

Printed in the United States of America

This publication is designed to provide accurate and authoritative information in regard to the subject matter covered. It is sold with the understanding that the publisher is not engaged in rendering legal, accounting, or other professional service. If legal advice or other expert assistance is required, the services of a competent professional person should be sought. *From a Declaration of Principles jointly adopted by a Committee of the American Bar Association and a Committee of Publishers and Associations.*

*To my beloved wife Christine,
and our children.*

PASTOR, CHURCH & LAW
Volume Four

TABLE OF CONTENTS

Preface

Over the past several decades, the number of laws and regulations enacted by legislative and administrative agencies of federal, state, and local governments have increased enormously. Inevitably, questions have arisen as to the application of these laws and regulations to religious organizations. After all, it is one thing for a statute to apply to a local dry cleaner or fast food restaurant. But it is quite different to apply the same law to a church, since churches are protected by the First Amendment guaranty of religious freedom as well as similar provisions in state constitutions.

How far, then, can government go in applying legislation and regulations to religious organizations without violating the First Amendment? The amenability of religious organizations to some regulation is not seriously disputed. For example, few protest the application to churches of laws and regulations prohibiting fraud in the sale of securities, requiring donated funds to be expended for the purposes represented, protecting copyright owners against infringement, or prohibiting activities that cause physical harm, property damage, or material disturbance to others. Similarly, churches routinely comply with municipal building codes and zoning regulations in the construction of worship facilities. In short, most churches have acknowledged that religion should not be used as a means of avoiding laws and regulations that are designed to protect the life, health, or safety of members of the public, or that impose fair and reasonable obligations upon those activities of churches that are not intrinsically religious.

But some attempts by the government to regulate the activities of churches are more objectionable. For example, should the government have the authority to invalidate any gift to a church simply because it was contained in a will or deed executed within a prescribed time prior to the donor's death? Should the government have the ability to regulate a church's solicitation of funds? Or, should the government have the authority to apply anti-discrimination requirements to churches? Such governmental assertions of authority are opposed by many churches as unreasonable intrusions into the life of the church. While many of these issues have been addressed in previous chapters, in this volume we will look at additional examples of government regulation of church activities and available exemptions from such law.

Along with studying the laws that apply to churches and other religious organizations, in this volume you'll also examine the liabilities churches face as a result of specific acts and omissions.

To illustrate, churches can be vicariously liable for the negligence of employees committed within the course of their employment under the legal principle of *respondeat superior*, a concept that is explained and applied in various case studies. Churches also may be liable on the basis of negligence in the selection, retention, or supervision of employees and volunteer workers. In recent years, some courts have found churches liable on the basis of a breach of a fiduciary duty for injuries occurring on their premises or in the course of their activities. With every liability, chapter ten places a special emphasis on "risk managementiópractical ways your church can reduce its risk of legal liability.

Chapters 11, 12, and 13 delve into constitutional history and our courts' views on First Amendment freedoms. Since the United States Supreme Court is the highest court in the federal judicial system, its pronouncements have the ultimate authority. An interpretation of the Constitution by the Supreme Court becomes the supreme law of the land until the court reverses itself or until a constitutional amendment is ratified that alters the Court's interpretation. The importance of Supreme Court interpretations of the First Amendment religion clauses should thus be apparent.

Can persons engage in religious "witnessing" or proselytizing in residential neighborhoods on a door-to-door basis? Can persons use public parks for religious meetings? Under what circumstances can voluntary prayers be uttered on public property? Can a city display a cross or nativity scene on public property during the Christmas season? Can a court display a picture of the Ten Commandments? Can the federal government constitutionally print the national motto "In God We Trust" on all of our nation's currency? What activities are included within the term "religious"? What activities are excluded? Such questions present the courts with difficult choices. We conclude Volume 4 with a review of the application of the First Amendment religion clauses in several contexts.

Government
Regulation of Churches

Legal Briefs

With the ever-increasing amount of legislation imposed by federal, state, and local governments, questions have arisen as to the application of these laws and regulations to religious organizations. After all, it is one thing for a statute to apply to a local dry cleaner or fast food restaurant. But it is quite different to apply the same law to a church, since churches are protected by the First Amendment guaranty of religious freedom as well as similar provisions in state constitutions.

> "After all, it is one thing for a statute to apply to a local dry cleaner or fast food restaurant. But it is quite different to apply the same law to a church, since churches are protected by the First Amendment guaranty of religious freedom as well as similar provisions in state constitutions."

How far, then, can government go in applying these laws to churches and ministries without violating the First Amendment? The willingness of religious organizations to comply with some regulation is not seriously disputed. For example, few protest the application to churches of laws and regulations prohibiting fraud in the sale of securities. Essentially, federal and state laws regulate the offer and sale of securities for the protection of the investing public. In general, an organization that issues securities must register the securities, and the persons who will be selling the securities, with state and federal agencies. In addition, federal and state laws contain a broad prohibition on fraudulent activities in the sale of securities. Churches are exempt from some of these requirements in some states. However, they remain subject to the prohibition of securities fraud in all fifty states, and under federal law.

The government also protects copyright owners against infringement, which has significant relevance and benefit to churches. In short, most churches have acknowledged that religion should not be used as a means of avoiding laws and regulations that are designed to protect the life, health, or safety of members of the public, or that impose fair and reasonable obligations upon those activities of churches that are not intrinsically religious.

But when does the government cross a line? For example, should the government have the authority to invalidate any gift to a church simply because it was contained in a will or deed executed within a prescribed time prior to the donor's death? Should the government have the ability to regulate a church's solicitation of funds? Or, should the government have the authority to apply anti-discrimination requirements to churches?

Many churches oppose these kinds of governmental assertions of authority as unreasonable intrusions into the life of the church. Some of these issues have been addressed in previous chapters. In this chapter, we'll take a look at additional examples of government regulation of church activities, and available exemptions from such laws. As you read the text, attempt to formulate a rule that will define those instances in which government regulation of church activities may be warranted.

Introduction

The amenability of churches to some governmental regulation is not seriously disputed. For example, few would protest the application to churches of laws prohibiting fraud in the sale of securities, requiring donated funds to be expended for the purposes represented, protecting copyright owners against infringement, or prohibiting activities that cause physical harm, property damage, or material disturbance to others. Similarly, churches routinely comply with municipal building codes and zoning regulations in the construction and location of worship facilities.

There is much less agreement concerning the *degree* to which churches should be subject to governmental regulation. The United States Supreme Court has observed:

> The [First Amendment] embraces two concepts—freedom to believe and freedom to act. The first is absolute but, in the nature of things, the second cannot be. Conduct remains subject to regulation for the protection of society. . . . It is clear that a state may by general and non-discriminatory legislation regulate the times, the places, and the manner of soliciting upon its streets, and of holding meetings thereon; and may in other respects safeguard the peace, good order and comfort of the community, without unconstitutionally invading the liberties protected by the [First Amendment]. . . .

> Nothing we have said is intended even remotely to imply that, under the cloak of religion, persons may, with impunity, commit frauds upon the public. Certainly penal laws are available to punish such conduct. Even the exercise of religion may be at some slight inconvenience in order that the state may protect its citizens from injury.[1]

Laws affecting churches consistently are upheld by the courts if they (1) are neutral and of general applicability, (2) avoid excessive governmental entanglement

---

[1] Cantwell v. Connecticut, 310 U.S. 296 (1940). Similarly, the Supreme Court has concluded: (1) "[E]ven when [an] action is in accord with one's religious convictions, it is not totally free from legislative restrictions. The conduct or actions so regulated have invariably posed some substantial threat to public safety, peace or order." Sherbert v. Verner, 374 U.S. 398, 403 (1963), quoting Braunfeld v. Brown, 366 U.S. 599, 603 (1961). (2) "The mere fact that the petitioner's religious practice is burdened by a governmental program does not mean that an exemption accommodating his practice must be granted. The state may justify an inroad on religious liberty by showing that it is the least restrictive means of achieving some compelling state interest. However, it is still true that the essence of all that has been said and written on the subject is that only those interests of the highest order can overbalance legitimate claims to the free exercise of religion." Thomas v. Review Board, 450 U.S. 707, 718 (1981). (3) "Conscientious scruples have not, in the course of the long struggle for religious toleration, relieved the individual from obedience to a general law not aimed at the promotion or restriction of religious beliefs. The mere possession of religious convictions which contradict the relevant concerns of a political society does not relieve the citizen from the discharge of political responsibilities." Minersville School District v. Gobitis, 310 U.S. 586, 594-595 (1940) (Justice Frankfurter).

with religion, (3) are the least restrictive means of accomplishing the intended result, and (4) require no judicial determination of the validity of religious belief. To illustrate, the courts consistently uphold reasonable governmental regulation of church securities offerings, labor practices, construction projects, fundraising schemes, child-care and nursing-care facilities, and private schools. One court, in rejecting a religious organization's claim to immunity from governmental regulation on the ground that it was engaged in "God's work," observed that "no court has ever found that conduct, by being so described, is automatically immunized from all regulation in the public interest."[2]

Key point. *Laws that are not neutral toward religion, or that are not of general applicability, must be supported by a compelling government interest in order to be consistent with the First Amendment guaranty of religious freedom.*[3]

The application of many laws and regulations to religious organizations has been addressed in previous chapters. These include:

- child abuse reporting laws[4]

- the regulation of church counselors[5]

- nonprofit corporation law[6]

- state and federal reporting requirements[7]

- zoning[8]

- building codes[9]

- landmarking legislation[10]

- eminent domain[11]

- workers compensation[12]

---

[2] Securities and Exchange Commission v. World Radio Mission, Inc., 544 F.2d 535, 539 n.7 (1st Cir. 1976).

[3] *See generally* chapter 13, *infra.*

[4] *See* § 4-08, *supra.*

[5] *See* § 4-10, *supra.*

[6] *See* § 6-02, *supra.*

[7] *See* § 6-04, *supra.*

[8] *See* § 7-06, *supra.*

[9] *See* § 7-08, *supra.*

[10] *See* § 7-10, *supra.*

[11] *See* § 7-11, *supra.*

[12] *See* § 8-07, *supra.*

- immigration law reporting requirements[13]

- Title VII of the Civil Rights Act of 1964[14]

- the Age Discrimination in Employment Act[15]

- the Americans with Disabilities Act[16]

- the Fair Labor Standards Act (federal minimum wage and overtime pay)[17]

- the Employee Polygraph Protection Act[18]

- the Occupational Safety and Health Act[19]

This chapter will address the application of additional federal and state laws and regulations to religious organizations.

Regulation of Charitable Solicitations

§ 9-02

Key point 9-02. *Several states have enacted laws regulating the solicitation of charitable contributions. These laws generally do apply to solicitations of contributions by churches from their members. However, in some cases, they may apply to churches that use professional fundraisers, or that actively solicit contributions from nonmembers.*

1. State Charitable Solicitation Laws

Several states have enacted laws regulating the solicitation of charitable contributions. The purpose of such laws is "to protect the contributing public and charitable beneficiaries against fraudulent practices in the solicitation of contributions for purportedly charitable purposes."[20] The IRS has made the following observations concerning the purpose of such laws:

According to the Fall 1998 issue of the Internal Revenue Service Statistics of Income Bulletin, between 1975 and 1995 the number of tax-exempt organizations more than doubled to 1,200,000, their assets increased by

---

[13]   *See* § 8-04, *supra.*

[14]   *See* § 8-12, *supra.*

[15]   *See* § 8-13, *supra.*

[16]   *See* § 8-14, *supra.*

[17]   *See* § 8-08, *supra.*

[18]   *See* § 8-18, *supra.*

[19]   *See* § 8-19, *supra.*

[20]   Larson v. Valente, 456 U.S. 228 (1982).

312 percent to $1.9 trillion, and their revenue increased by 380 percent to $899 billion. The nonprofit sector's growth in assets and revenue significantly outpaced the country's 74 percent growth in Gross Domestic Product in the same period.

The astonishing growth of the tax-exempt sector reflects the significant contributions charitable organizations make to society. They perform many important functions that would otherwise need to be performed by government or not at all. Unfortunately, the charitable community is no different than any other sector of the economy in that it also has its share of unscrupulous individuals who seek to profit by defrauding innocent donors out of their hard-earned income and, in some cases, their lifetime savings. These fraudulent schemes harm not only contributors who respond in the mistaken belief they are helping charitable causes, but also the charitable community, as each new scandal hurts every legitimate charitable organization by increasing skepticism in the giving public. The states have the difficult, but essential, tasks of protecting their citizens from charlatans who prey on their charitable natures while challenging them to recognize that we all benefit when worthy charitable organizations are generously supported. Their role is even more critical when major government cutbacks shift the responsibility for relieving many of society's burdens to the charitable sector.

> "The astonishing growth of the tax-exempt sector reflects the significant contributions charitable organizations make to society. They perform many important functions that would otherwise need to be performed by government or not at all."

To protect their residents and legitimate charitable organizations, approximately 40 states have enacted charitable solicitation statutes. Although specifics vary, state statutes usually require organizations to register with the state before they solicit the state's residents for contributions.

State solicitation statutes generally serve two important purposes. First, they allow the public to get basic information about organizations asking for contributions so donors can make better, more informed charitable giving decisions. . . . The second, and equally important, purpose state solicitation statutes serve: they help protect state residents from charitable solicitation fraud and misrepresentations. Although most charitable organizations are fine, worthy organizations that deserve to be generously supported, unfortunately, many are fraudulent, employ deceptive solicitation practices, or mislead the public by submitting false or inaccurate Forms 990.[21]

---

[21] K. Emerson, *State Charitable Solicitation Statutes*, 2001 IRS EXEMPT ORGANIZATIONS CONTINUING LEGAL EDUCATION.

The typical statute requires designated charitable organizations to register with a state agency prior to the solicitation of contributions within the state, and imposes various reporting requirements. These statutes ordinarily give the state authority to revoke the registration of any charitable organization upon a finding that the organization has engaged in a fraudulent or deceptive practice, or that it has expended more than a prescribed or "reasonable" amount of solicited funds for administrative and fund raising costs, and that the public interests so require.

Key point. *A few states have not yet enacted laws regulating the solicitation of charitable contributions.*[22]

Key point. *Many states have laws requiring registration and regulation of "professional" fund raisers. The validity of such laws was called into question by the United States Supreme Court in a 1988 ruling in which the Court struck down a North Carolina statute requiring professional fund raisers to be licensed by the state, and establishing maximum administrative fees and expenses that could be charged.*[23]

Most state laws that regulate the solicitation of charitable contributions exempt religious organizations.[24] Some restrict the exemption to religious organizations that are exempt from the requirement of filing annual information returns (Form 990) with the IRS.[25] A few states have enacted the Uniform Supervision of Trustees for Charitable Purposes Act.[26]

The application of state charitable solicitation laws to religious and charitable organizations has been challenged in a few important cases. In *Larson v. Valente,*[27] the United States Supreme Court invalidated a section of the Minnesota Charitable

---

[22] For an updated summary of state charitable solicitation laws in all 50 states, visit the Giving Foundation USA website.

[23] Riley v. National Federation of the Blind, 108 S. Ct. 2667 (1988).

[24] *See, e.g.,* CAL. GOVERNMENT CODE §§ 12583 et seq. ("any religious corporation or organization that holds property for religious purposes"); FLA. STAT. § 496.403 ("bona fide religious institutions"); Ga. Code § 43-17-2 (any religious organization that conducts religious worship and is exempt under section 501(c)(3) of the federal tax code); KY. REV. STAT. § 367.660 ("solicitations by a religious organization for funds for religious purposes such as maintenance of a house of worship, conduct of services, and propagation of its faith and tenets"); MD. CODE ANN. § 6-102(c) (a "religious organization, a parent organization of a religious organization, or a school affiliated with a religious organization" that does not employ a professional fundraiser and "has in effect a declaration of tax-exempt status from the government of the United States"); N.J. REV. STAT. § 45:17A-26 ("any religious corporation, trust, foundation, association, or organization"); OHIO REV. CODE § 1716.03 ("any religious agencies and organizations, and charities, agencies, and organizations operated, supervised, or controlled by a religious organization"); OKLA. STAT. title 18, § 552.4 ("organizations incorporated for religious purposes and actually engaged in bona fide religious programs, and other organizations directly operated, supervised, or controlled by a religious organization"); PA. STATS. title 10, § 162.3 ("any bona fide duly constituted religious institutions and such separate groups or corporations which form an integral part of religious institutions, provided that: (i) such religious institutions, groups or corporations are tax exempt pursuant to the Internal Revenue Code of 1986; (ii) no part of their net income inures to the direct benefit of any individual; and (iii) their conduct is primarily supported by government grants or contracts, funds solicited from their own memberships, congregations or previous donors, and fees charged for services rendered").

[25] *See, e.g.,* ALASKA STAT. § 45.68.120(a)(1).

[26] CAL. GOVERNMENT CODE §§ 12583 *et seq.*; 760 ILL. COMP. STAT. 55/1 *et. seq.*; MICH. COMP. LAWS § 14.251 *et seq.*; OR. REV. STAT. § 128.610 *et seq.*

[27] 456 U.S. 228 (1982). The Court invalidated § 309.515-1(b) of the Minnesota Statutes.

Solicitation Act that exempted from registration only those religious organizations receiving more than half of their support from members. The Court emphasized that "the clearest command of the Establishment Clause [of the First Amendment] is that one religious denomination cannot be officially preferred over another,"[28] and concluded that "the fifty percent rule . . . clearly grants denominational preference of the sort consistently and firmly deprecated in our precedents."[29] Such a law, observed the Court, must be invalidated unless (1) it is justified by a compelling governmental interest, and (2) it is "clearly fitted to further that interest." The "tripartite" establishment clause analysis formulated by the Court in the *Lemon* case[30] was deemed inapplicable in this context, since that analysis was "intended to apply to laws affording a uniform benefit to *all* religions, and not to provisions, like the . . . fifty percent rule, that discriminate among religions."[31]

The Court acknowledged that the State of Minnesota had a significant interest in protecting its citizens from abusive practices in the solicitation of funds for charity, even when the solicitation was conducted by religious organizations. However, it rejected the state's contention that the 50 percent rule was closely fitted to further that interest.

Would a state charitable solicitation law requiring *all* religious organizations to register be constitutionally permissible? Such a law obviously would avoid the "denominational preference" that tainted the Minnesota statute. The Supreme Court even observed in *Larson* that it was not suggesting that "the burdens of compliance with the Act would be intrinsically impermissible if they were imposed evenhandedly."[32] This more difficult question was addressed in 1980 by the Supreme Court of North Carolina in the *Heritage Village* decision.[33]

The Supreme Court of North Carolina, in striking down a state charitable solicitation law exempting all religious organizations except those whose financial support came primarily from nonmembers, concluded that the First Amendment (to the United States Constitution) prohibits any state from subjecting religious organizations to the administrative requirements of a charitable solicitation law. The Court noted:

> For a statute to pass muster under the strict test of Establishment Clause neutrality, it must pass the three-prong review distilled by the Supreme Court from "the cumulative criteria developed over many years": First, the statute must have a secular purpose; second, its principal or primary effect must be one that neither advances nor inhibits religion . . . ; finally the statute must not foster an excessive government entanglement with religion.[34]

---

[28] *Id.* at 1683.

[29] *Id.* at 1684.

[30] Lemon v. Kurtzman, 403 U.S. 602, 612-13 (1971). The *Lemon* case is discussed in chapter 12, *infra*.

[31] *Id.* at 1687. While the Court concluded that the tripartite test of *Lemon* was inapplicable, it nonetheless observed that the Minnesota statute did not satisfy that test.

[32] *Id.* at 1688.

[33] Heritage Village Church and Missionary Fellowship, Inc. v. State, 263 S.E.2d 726 (N.C. 1980).

[34] *Id.* at 731.

The court concluded that the first part of the Supreme Court's three-prong test was satisfied, since the Act had a valid secular purpose of protecting the public from fraud. It found, however, that the Act violated both the second and third elements since it inhibited certain religious groups and constituted an impermissible governmental entanglement with religion. As to the second element, the Court observed:

> The Act grants an exemption from the licensing and reporting requirements to a broadly defined class of religious organizations. . . . The proviso, however, which immediately follows in the same section denies the benefits of the exemption to those religious organizations which derive their financial support "primarily" from contributions solicited from "persons other than their own members" . . . . [T]he *effect* of the proviso is to alter the original exemption's religious neutrality. The result is a qualified exemption which favors only those religious organizations which solicit primarily from their own members. The inescapable impact is to accord benign neglect to the more orthodox, denominational, and congregational religions while subjecting to registration those religions which spread their beliefs in more evangelical, less traditional ways. This the state may not do.[35]

As to the third element of the test, the Court observed:

> Considerations of the excessive entanglement between church and state threatened by the Act's substantive requirements additionally compels us to conclude that plaintiffs may not constitutionally be denied an exemption. . . . Should plaintiffs or any other religious organization be subjected to the full panoply of strictures contemplated by the Act, we would be faced with precisely the sort of "sustained and detailed administrative relationships for enforcement of statutory and administrative standards" that have been repeatedly condemned by the Supreme Court.[36]

Both the *Larson* and *Heritage Village* decisions were based on the establishment clause. Neither court directly addressed the applicability of the First Amendment's free exercise of religion and free speech clauses in analyzing the constitutionality of applying charitable solicitation laws to religious organizations. The free exercise and free speech clauses have been relied upon by several courts in invalidating municipal charitable solicitation ordinances.[37] In 1980, the Supreme Court observed in the *Village of Schaumburg* decision:

> Prior authorities, therefore, thoroughly establish that charitable appeals for funds . . . involve a variety of speech interests—communication of information, a dissemination and propagation of views and ideas, and the

---

[35] *Id.* at 732-33.

[36] *Id.*

[37] *See* Village of Schaumburg v. Citizens for a Better Environment, 444 U.S. 620, 632 (1980).

advocacy of causes—that are within the protection of the First Amendment. Soliciting financial support is undoubtedly subject to reasonable regulation but the latter must be undertaken with due regard for the reality that solicitation is characteristically intertwined with informative and perhaps persuasive speech seeking support for particular causes or for particular views on economic, political, or social issues, or for the reality that without solicitation flow of such information and advocacy would likely cease.[38]

Such reasoning buttresses the conclusion reached in *Heritage Village*. Not only would a state charitable solicitation law that applies to religious organizations be constitutionally suspect under the establishment clause, but it also would clash with the free exercise and free speech clauses.[39]

As the Supreme Court noted in *Larson*, a state unquestionably has a significant interest in protecting its citizens from abusive practices in the solicitation of funds for charity. However, such an interest alone does not determine constitutional validity. The state must also demonstrate that its charitable solicitation law is "closely fitted to further the interest that it assertedly serves."[40] The Court noted in *Village of Schaumburg* that "the Village may serve its legitimate interests, but it must do so by narrowly drawn regulations designed to serve these interests without necessarily interfering with First Amendment freedoms."[41]

Can a state serve its legitimate purpose of preventing fraud in the solicitation of funds by religious organizations in a less drastic way than by registration under a charitable solicitation law? The answer clearly is yes. In an analogous case, the Supreme Court in the *Village of Schaumburg* decision observed that the government's legitimate interest in preventing fraud can be served by less intrusive measures: "Fraudulent misrepresentations can be prohibited and the penal laws used to punish such conduct directly."[42] Another court has noted that less restrictive alternative means of fulfilling the government's interests include "enforcement of existing laws against fraud, trespass, breach of the peace, and any other substantive offenses which might be committed. The [government] may adopt appropriate registration and identification procedures to protect its

---

[38] *Id.* at 632.

[39] In 1990 the Supreme Court observed that the compelling government interest test is triggered if a neutral and generally applicable law burdens not only the exercise of religion, but some other First Amendment right (such as speech, press, or assembly) as well. Employment Division v. Smith, 494 U.S. 872 (1990). The Court observed: "The only decisions in which we have held that the First Amendment bars application of a neutral, generally applicable law to religiously motivated action have involved not the free exercise clause alone, but the free exercise clause in conjunction with other constitutional protections, such as freedom of speech and of the press . . . ." In other words, if a neutral and generally applicable law or governmental practice burdens the exercise of religion, then the compelling governmental interest standard can be triggered if the religious institution or adherent can point to some other First Amendment interest that is being violated. In many cases, this will not be hard to do. For example, the First Amendment guaranty of free speech often will be implicated when a law or governmental practice burdens the exercise of religion. The same is true of the First Amendment guarantees of free press and assembly.

[40] 456 U.S. 228 (1982).

[41] 444 U.S. at 637.

[42] *Id.*

residents against wrongdoing by spurious solicitors."[43]

In summary, the *Heritage Village* decision strikes a reasonable balance of the competing interests of church and state. It frees religious organizations from entangling administrative supervision by the government; it acknowledges that the government remains capable of asserting that a particular organization is not in fact a bona fide religious organization entitled to exemption; it does not insulate religious organizations from civil lawsuits or criminal penalties; and it recognizes that the solicitation of funds for the support of religious organizations is often an expression of religious faith.[44]

A similar result has been reached in the related context of securities regulation. Most state securities laws, while designed primarily to prevent fraud, exempt religious organizations from the securities registration requirement. Religious organizations are not exempted from the anti-fraud provisions of such laws, and thus they remain liable for fraudulent conduct even though they are exempt from registration. Further, the state is free to deny an exemption to religious organizations that have engaged in fraud in the past or that are not bona fide religious organizations. Such a balance between the competing interests of church and state serves as a model for the related contexts of state and municipal charitable solicitation laws. The government's interests can be served by less restrictive means than registration.

2. Municipal Charitable Solicitation Laws

Several cities have enacted ordinances regulating the solicitation of charitable contributions. These ordinances often are similar in content and purpose to state laws, and contain an exemption for religious organizations that meet certain requirements. For example, some cities exempt religious organizations that are exempt from federal income taxation. Other cities exempt properly authorized solicitors of established and organized churches or other established and organized religious organizations, organizations conducting a solicitation among their own membership, solicitations in the form of collections or contributions at a regular assembly or service, and any church which solicits funds for religious purposes. Some cities require religious organizations that use professional fund raisers to register under a charitable solicitation ordinance.

The constitutionality of applying charitable solicitation ordinances to religious organizations has been challenged in several cases. In *Village of Schaumburg*,[45] the Supreme Court struck down an ordinance prohibiting the solicitation of contributions by charitable organizations that did not use at least 75 percent of their receipts for charitable purposes. The ordinance excluded solicitation expenses, salaries, overhead, and other administrative expenses from the definition of "charitable purpose." The Court conceded that charitable appeals

---

[43] Alternatives for California Women v. County of Contra Costa, 193 Cal. Rptr. 384, 392 (Cal. App. 1983).

[44] *See, e.g.,* Heffron v. International Society for Krishna Consciousness, 452 U.S. 640 (1981); Village of Schaumburg v. Citizens for a Better Environment, 444 U.S. 620, 637-39 (1980); Murdock v. Pennsylvania, 319 U.S. 105 (1943); Heritage Village and Missionary Fellowship, Inc. v. State, 263 S.E.2d 726, 734 (N.C. 1980).

[45] *See* note 37, *supra.*

for funds involve a variety of speech interests that are within the protection of the First Amendment, and that any ordinance interfering with such interests would be constitutionally valid only if it (1) served a compelling governmental interest and (2) was narrowly drawn to serve that interest without necessarily interfering with First Amendment freedoms.

The Court acknowledged that a city has a substantial interest in protecting the public from fraud, crime, and undue annoyance. However, it concluded that a municipal ordinance banning solicitations by any charity that did not expend more than 75 percent of solicited funds for charitable purposes could not be upheld, since the city's legitimate interests could be "better served by measures less intrusive than a direct prohibition on solicitation."[46] The Court also noted that there was no evidence that "organizations devoting more than one-quarter of their funds to salaries and administrative expenses are any more likely to employ solicitors who would be a threat to public safety than are other charitable organizations."[47]

In summary, the *Village of Schaumburg* decision may be reduced to the following two principles: (1) The right to solicit funds for religious and charitable purposes is protected by the First Amendment's free speech clause, and (2) this right is not unconditional, but may be limited by a municipal ordinance if the ordinance (a) serves a compelling government interest and (b) is narrowly drawn to serve that interest without unnecessarily interfering with First Amendment freedoms.

Village of Schaumburg has been followed in several other cases.[48] In most of these decisions, municipal ordinances attempting to regulate charitable solicitations were invalidated. The courts generally concede that a city has a legitimate and substantial interest in preventing fraud, crime, and undue annoyance, but they often conclude that a particular charitable solicitation ordinance too broadly serves that interest since other, less restrictive, alternatives exist which serve the same interest. The Supreme Court in *Village of Schaumburg* noted:

> Frauds may be denounced as offenses and punished by law. Trespasses may similarly be forbidden. If it is said that these means are less efficient and convenient than . . . deciding in advance what information may be disseminated from house to house, and who may impart the information, the answer is that considerations of this sort do not empower a municipality to abridge freedom of speech and press.[49]

---

[46] *Id.* at 637.

[47] *Id.* at 638.

[48] *See, e.g.,* Chiu v. Plano Independent School District, 339 F.3d 273 (5th Cir. 2004); ACORN v. City of Frontenac, 714 F.2d 813 (8th Cir. 1983); ACLU v. City of Las Vegas, 466 F.3d 784 (9th Cir. 2006); Pacific Frontier v. Pleasant Grove City, 414 F.3d 1221 (10th Cir. 2005); United Youth Careers v. City of Ames, 412 F.Supp.2d 994 (S.D. Iowa 2006); Pennsylvania Public Interest v. York Township, 569 F. Supp. 1398 (M.D. Pa. 1983); NAACP Legal Defense and Educational Fund, Inc. v. Devine, 567 F. Supp. 401 (D.D.C. 1983); Taylor v. City of Knoxville, 566 F. Supp. 925 (E.D. Tenn. 1982); Optimist Club v. Riley, 563 F. Supp. 847 (E.D.N.C. 1982); Los Angeles Alliance for Survival v. City of Los Angeles, 993 P.2d 334 (Cal. 2000); People v. World Church of the Creator, 760 N.E.2d 953 (Ill. 2001); State v. Dean, 866 N.E.2d 1134 (Ohio App. 2007); State v. Gold, 850 N.E.2d 1218 (Ohio App. 2006).

[49] 444 U.S. 620, 639.

In conclusion, a municipal ordinance purporting to regulate the solicitation of funds by some or all religious organizations should presumptively[50] be unconstitutional unless the city can demonstrate that the ordinance serves a legitimate and compelling interest *and* that this interest cannot effectively be protected by less intrusive, more narrowly drawn, alternatives.

Several courts have concluded that the availability of private causes of action for fraud and trespass, together with penal prohibitions of such conduct, sufficiently protect a city's legitimate interests in safeguarding its citizens from abusive charitable solicitations by religious organizations.

A city also of course may make a determination that a particular "religious" organization is spurious and therefore not entitled to an exemption, and it is free to deny an exemption to otherwise bona fide religious organizations that have been proven to have engaged in frauds upon the public.[51] Further, any municipal charitable solicitation ordinance exempting only some religious organizations from registration would be suspect under the establishment clause, since some religious groups are singled out for favored treatment while others are not. All of these factors indicate that most charitable solicitation laws cannot constitutionally be extended to religious organizations.

Certainly any charitable solicitation law that gives a licensing body or official effective discretion to grant or deny permission to solicit funds for religious purposes is likewise unconstitutional:

> The solicitation of funds for religious purposes is protected by the First Amendment. Any law restricting the exercise of such rights must do so with narrow, objective and definite standards. If a certificate is required for one to solicit funds for religious purposes, the discretion of the official granting the certificate must be bounded by explicit standards. If the decision to issue the certificate "involves appraisal of facts, the exercise of judgment, and the formation of an opinion," the ordinance violates the First Amendment. Ambiguities in the application process which give the licensing official effective power to grant or deny permission to solicit funds for religious purposes is likewise unconstitutional. In other words, it is not enough that an official is directed to issue the license forthwith; if the official may deny the application because of unclear requirements in the application process, the law is unconstitutional. Laws allowing an investigation into the financial affairs of religious institutions have been held unconstitutional as an impermissible entanglement of the affairs of church and state. Finally,

---

[50] *See, e.g.*, Pennsylvania Public Interest v. York Township, 569 F. Supp. 1398, 140 (M.D. Pa. 1983) ("because the ordinance impinges on the exercise of free speech, it is presumptively unconstitutional").

[51] *See* Larson v. Valente, 102 S.Ct. 1673, 1689 n.30 (1982):

Nothing in our opinion suggests appellants could not attempt to compel the Unification Church to register under the Act as a charitable organization not entitled to the religious-organization exemption, and put the Church to the proof of its bona fides as a religious organization. Further, nothing in our opinion disables the State from denying exemption from the Act, or from refusing registration and licensing under the Act, to persons or organizations proved to have engaged in frauds upon the public.

any prior restraint on the exercise of First Amendment freedoms must be accompanied by procedural safeguards designed to obviate the dangers of prior restraint.[52]

The Supreme Court has held that the fund raising activities of religious organizations, "like those of others protected by the First Amendment, are subject to reasonable time, place, and manner restrictions."[53] It is doubtful that these restrictions are of any practical relevance in the context of charitable solicitations by religious organizations. One court specifically held that the Supreme Court's decision in *Heffron* "has a rather narrow applicability" because of its "somewhat unusual factual situation" involving solicitation at a state fair.[54] The court observed that "the flow of the crowd and demands of safety are more pressing in the context of the fair."[55] The Supreme Court's decision in *Village of Schaumburg* strongly intimated that "time, place and manner" restrictions do not justify regulation of charitable solicitations.[56]

Limitations on Charitable Giving

§ 9-03

Key point 9-03. *Historically, several states had laws limiting the right of persons to leave gifts to religious organizations within a specified time prior to their death. In recent years, these laws have been struck down by the courts in nearly all states.*

In the past, several states had laws limiting the right of persons to leave property to religious organizations by a will or deed executed within a specified period prior to death. The purpose of such laws (often called "mortmain" laws) was to prevent "deathbed" gifts to religious organizations by persons who might be unduly influenced by religious considerations.[57] The California Supreme Court explained the purpose of an early state mortmain law as follows: "It is that a man's fears or superstition, or his death-bed hope of purchasing a blissful immortality, shall not be allowed to influence the disposition which he may thus make

> Mortmain = the possession of real property in perpetuity by a corporate body (as a church)

---

[52] Taylor v. City of Knoxville, 566 F. Supp. 925, 929 (E.D. Tenn. 1982).

[53] Heffron v. International Society for Krishna Consciousness, Inc. 452 U.S. 640, 647 (1981).

[54] Pennsylvania Public Interests v. York Township, 659 F. Supp. 1398, 1402 (M.D. Pa. 1983).

[55] Id.

[56] 444 U.S. 620, 639-640 (1980).

[57] The name "mortmain" derives from two Middle English words meaning "dead hand". The idea is that a decedent continues to exercise posthumous influence over the property he or she owned while living.

of his property, to the injury of his heirs."[58]

More generally, such laws were intended to protect a donor's family from disinheritance due to charitable gifts made either without proper deliberation or as a result of "undue influence."

Several states enacted mortmain laws. One commentator noted that "in 1970, eleven American jurisdictions still had mortmain statutes: California, District of Columbia, Florida, Georgia, Idaho, Iowa, Mississippi, Montana, New York, Ohio, and Pennsylvania," but that "all of them have since been repealed or held unconstitutional."[59]

To illustrate, the Florida Supreme Court struck down a state mortmain law that permitted certain heirs to challenge gifts made to churches and other charities in a will executed within six months of a person's death.[60] Prior to this ruling, Florida law permitted a spouse or "lineal descendent" to challenge a will of a decedent who died within 6 months after executing a will leaving all or part of his or her estate to a religious or charitable organization. An elderly Florida resident executed a will leaving most of her estate to a charity. The woman's will left only a token gift to her sole surviving daughter since the daughter "has not shown or indicated the slightest affection or gratitude to me" and since "I have contributed substantially during my life for her education and subsequent monies I have been required to expend primarily due to her promiscuous type of life." The woman died two months later, survived only by her daughter. The daughter immediately challenged her mother's will on the basis of the state law permitting lineal descendants to challenge charitable gifts made in their parents' wills if executed within six months of death. The charity opposed the daughter's action on the ground that the state law violated the constitutional guaranty of the "equal protection of the laws." A trial court agreed with the charity, but a state appeals court agreed with the daughter.

The case was appealed to the state supreme court, which ruled that the state law was unconstitutional. The court began its opinion by observing that statutes restricting charitable gifts originated in feudal England "as part of the struggle for power and wealth between the king and the organized church." As feudalism declined, the justification for these laws became the protection of surviving family members against disinheritance caused by the undue influence of religious organizations. In rejecting this rationale, the court observed that "it is unreasonable to presume, as the statute seems to do, that all lineal descendants are dependents, in need, or are not otherwise provided for."

The court emphasized that state law has ample protections against undue influence and fraud that can be used by disinherited family members without the need for a specific statute. Further, the court observed that "the charitable

---

[58] In re Lennon's Estate, 92 P. 870, 871 (Cal. 1907). *See generally* A.H. Oosterhoff, The Law of Mortmain: An Historical and Comparative Review, 27 U. Toronto L.J. 257, 267 (1977) ("some . . . legislators expressed a distrust of the clergy and a belief that a failure to control conveyances in trust for charitable uses would result in a renewal of death-bed vigils on the part of ambitious clerics").

[59] J. Sherman, *Can Religious Influence Ever Be "Undue" Influence?* Brooklyn L.R. vol. 73:2, p. 579 (2008). This article contains an excellent analysis of mortmain laws.

[60] Shriners Hospital v. Zrillic, 563 So.2d 64 (Fla. 1990).

gift restriction fails to protect against windfalls by lineal descendants who have had no contact with the decedent but who may benefit from the avoidance of a charitable gift." Since the statute was not "reasonably necessary to accomplish the asserted state goals," it violated the state constitution. Further, the statute violated the federal and state constitutional protections of the "equal protection of the laws," since it treated gifts made to charitable and religious organizations within six months of death less favorably than other gifts without any rational justification. The fact that a gift is made within six months of death is not in itself sufficient proof of undue influence, noted the court, since most gifts made within six months of death are not the product of undue influence and some gifts made more than six months prior to death are. Accordingly, the six-month rule was arbitrary and treated charities less favorably than other citizens or organizations without adequate justification.

One dissenting justice cautioned that the law might still serve a valuable purpose in appropriate cases: "Surely one would have to say that, had the [decedent] succumbed to a television evangelist's call to be with the Lord by delivering her property to his church and thus leave unprotected a physically handicapped child, a rationale basis for the statute would exist." In conclusion, note that the court observed that there are only three other states that have laws invalidating charitable gifts made within a specified time prior to death—Georgia, Idaho, and Mississippi.

In another significant decision, the Supreme Court of Pennsylvania struck down a state law invalidating any testamentary gift for religious or charitable purposes included in a will executed within 30 days of the death of the donor.[61] The court reasoned that the fourteenth amendment to the United States Constitution, which prohibits states from denying to any persons the "equal protection of the laws," requires that statutory classifications must be "reasonable, not arbitrary, and must rest upon some ground of difference having a fair and substantial relation to the object of the legislation, so that all persons similarly circumstanced shall be treated alike."[62] The Pennsylvania statute, concluded the court, divided donors into two classes, one class being composed of donors whose wills provided for charitable gifts and who died within 30 days of executing their wills, and the other of donors who either made no charitable gifts in their wills or who survived the execution of their wills by at least 30 days. Gifts made by a donor in the first class were nullified by the statute, while gifts made by donors in the second class were permitted.

Such a classification, concluded the court, violated the fourteenth amendment's equal protection clause and therefore was impermissible:

Clearly, the statutory classification bears only the most tenuous relation to the legislative purpose. The statute strikes down the charitable gifts of one in the best of health at the time of the execution of his will and regardless of age if he chances to die in an accident 29 days later. On the other hand, it leaves untouched the charitable bequests of another, aged and suffering

---

[61] In re Estate of Cavill, 329 A.2d 503 (Pa. 1974).

[62] Id. at 505.

from a terminal disease, who survives the execution of his will by 31 days. Such a combination of results can only be characterized as arbitrary.[63]

The court also observed that although the legislative purpose was to protect a donor's immediate family, the statute sought to nullify testamentary gifts to charity even where the donor left no immediate family. Protection of distant relatives with whom a donor may have had little if any contact during his life was not consistent with the statute's purpose, the court concluded.

Other courts have reached similar results. A District of Columbia statute invalidating any gift to a clergyman or religious organization made in a will executed less than 30 days prior to a donor's death was struck down on the ground that it arbitrarily discriminated against clergymen and religious organizations. A court emphasized that the law did not invalidate gifts to nonreligious charitable organizations that were in an equal position with religious organizations to influence a donor.[64]

One judge has observed that laws limiting the right of religious organizations to receive testamentary gifts are invalid if they are based on a desire to prevent clergy from influencing the dying by holding out "hopes of salvation or avoidance of damnation" in return for generous gifts to further the practice of religion. Such an objective "is precisely what the 'free exercise' of religion clause of the First Amendment forbids, for it is premised upon the assumption that such representations are false and hence Congress can enact safeguards against their effect."[65] Another court held that a state's adoption of the Uniform Probate Code by implication repealed a law limiting testamentary gifts to charity.[66]

The repeal of such statutes has the salutary effect of abolishing the irrebuttable presumption that certain gifts to charity are the product of undue influence, and of compelling disinherited heirs to prove undue influence in order to invalidate testamentary gifts to charity.

Federal and State Securities Law

§ 9-04

Key point 9-04. *Federal and state laws regulate the offer and sale of securities for the protection of the investing public. In general, an organization that issues securities must register the securities, and the persons who will be selling the securities, with state and federal agencies. In addition, federal and state laws contain a broad prohibition on fraudulent activities in the sale of securities. Churches are exempt from some of these requirements in some states. However, they remain subject to the prohibition of securities fraud in all fifty states, and under federal law.*

---

[63] *Id.* at 505-06.

[64] Estate of French, 365 A.2d 621 (D.C. 1976), *appeal dismissed*, 434 U.S. 59 (1977).

[65] *Id.* at 625 (Reilly, C.J., concurring).

[66] Matter of Estate of Holmes, 599 P.2d 344 (Mont. 1979).

1. In General

Laws regulating the sale of securities have been enacted by the federal government[67] and by all 50 states.[68] The term *security* is defined very broadly by such laws. The Uniform Securities Act, which has been adopted by a majority of the 50 states, defines a *security* as

> a note; stock; treasury stock; security future; bond; debenture; evidence of indebtedness; certificate of interest or participation in a profit-sharing agreement; collateral trust certificate; preorganization certificate or subscription; transferable share; investment contract; voting trust certificate; certificate of deposit for a security; fractional undivided interest in oil, gas, or other mineral rights; put, call, straddle, option, or privilege on a security, certificate of deposit, or group or index of securities, including an interest therein or based on the value thereof; put, call, straddle, option, or privilege entered into on a national securities exchange relating to foreign currency; or, in general, an interest or instrument commonly known as a "security"; or a certificate of interest or participation in, temporary or interim certificate for, receipt for, guarantee of, or warrant or right to subscribe to or purchase, any of the foregoing. The term:
>
> (A) includes both a certificated and an uncertificated security;
>
> (B) does not include an insurance or endowment policy or annuity contract under which an insurance company promises to pay a fixed [or variable] sum of money either in a lump sum or periodically for life or other specified period;
>
> (C) does not include an interest in a contributory or noncontributory pension or welfare plan subject to the Employee Retirement Income Security Act of 1974;
>
> (D) includes as an "investment contract" an investment in a common enterprise with the expectation of profits to be derived primarily from the efforts of a person other than the investor and a "common enterprise" means an enterprise in which the fortunes of the investor are interwoven with those of either the person offering the investment, a third party, or other investors; and
>
> (E) includes as an "investment contract," among other contracts, an interest in a limited partnership and a limited liability company and an investment in a viatical settlement or similar agreement.[69]

This definition is broad enough to include many instruments utilized in church fundraising efforts.

---

[67]   Securities Act of 1933, 15 U.S.C. §§ 77a-77aa.

[68]   Nearly 40 states have enacted all or significant portions of the Uniform Securities Act.

[69]   UNIFORM SECURITIES ACT § 102(28).

Securities laws were enacted to protect the public against fraudulent and deceptive practices in the sale of securities and to provide full and fair disclosure to prospective investors. To achieve these purposes, most securities laws impose the following conditions on the offer and sale of securities:

1. registration of proposed securities with the federal or state government in advance of sale

2. filing of sales and advertising literature with the federal or state government

3. registration of agents and broker-dealers who will be selling the securities

4. prohibition of fraudulent practices

The federal Securities Act of 1933 exempts "any security issued by a person organized and operated exclusively for religious, educational, benevolent, fraternal, charitable, or reformatory purposes and not for pecuniary profit, and no part of the net earnings of which inures to the benefit of any person, private stockholder, or individual."[70] Similarly, the Uniform Securities Act, which has been adopted by most states, exempts from registration:

[A] security issued by a person organized and operated exclusively for religious, educational, benevolent, fraternal, charitable, social, athletic, or reformatory purposes, or as a chamber of commerce, and not for pecuniary profit, no part of the net earnings of which inures to the benefit of a private stockholder or other person, or a security of a company that is excluded from the definition of an investment company under Section 3(c)(10)(B) of the Investment Company Act of 1940; except that with respect to the offer or sale of a note, bond, debenture, or other evidence of indebtedness issued by such a person, a rule may be adopted under this [Act] limiting the availability of this exemption by classifying securities, persons, and transactions, imposing different requirements for different classes, specifying with respect to paragraph (B) the scope of the exemption and the grounds for denial or suspension, and requiring an issuer:

(A) to file a notice specifying the material terms of the proposed offer or sale and copies of any proposed sales and advertising literature to be used and provide that the exemption becomes effective if the administrator does not disallow the exemption within the period established by the rule;

(B) to file a request for exemption authorization for which a rule under this [Act] may specify the scope of the exemption, the requirement of an offering statement, the filing of sales and advertising literature,

---

[70] Section 3(a)(4).

the filing of consent to service of process complying with Section 611, and grounds for denial or suspension of the exemption; or

(C) to register under Section 304 [pertaining to registration by qualification].[71]

Note that this language gives state legislatures some flexibility in crafting a religious exemption. States may require religious organizations to file a notice with the state securities commission describing a proposed offer of securities, with the exemption becoming effective within a specified time if the securities commission does not object to the offer. Or, states may require religious organizations to file a more formal request for recognition of exemption, subject to such terms as the state legislature chooses to impose. States are also free to make their exemption of religious organizations automatic, or to provide no exemption of any kind (and thereby require religious organizations to pursue registration of their securities offerings).

An official comment by the drafters of the Uniform Securities Act states:

Section 201(7) provides statutory authority for the states to adopt rules with respect to notes, bonds, debentures and other evidences of indebtedness issued by nonprofit organizations. Each state may adopt different rules tailored for various types of nonprofit debt offerings, (e.g., local church bond offerings, national church bond offerings, church extension funds, charitable gift annuities). For states that do not wish to provide an automatic exemption from registration for a particular type of nonprofit debt instrument or offering, Section 201(7) creates three categories of regulatory review that may be required by rule: (a) exemption by notice filing, (b) exemption by state authorization, and (c) registration by qualification. These categories are consistent with the manner in which many states currently review different types of nonprofit debt securities.

Key point. *All securities laws subject churches and other religious organizations to the antifraud requirements. Churches therefore must not assume that any securities that they may offer are automatically exempt from registration or regulation. Church securities always will be subject to some degree of regulation. The question in each case is how much.*

In the minority of jurisdictions in which a church must register its securities, registration ordinarily is accomplished by filing a *registration statement* with the state securities commission setting forth the following information:

---

[71] *Id.* at 201(7). *See generally* Horner & Makens, *Securities Regulation of Religious and Other Nonprofit Organizations,* 27 STETSON L. REV. 473 (1997).

- ☐ the issuer's name, address, and form of organization;

- ☐ the state or foreign jurisdiction and date of its organization;

- ☐ the general character and location of its business;

- ☐ a description of its physical properties and equipment;

- ☐ the name, address, and principal occupation of each officer and director for the previous five years;

- ☐ the amount of securities of the issuer held by each officer and director;

- ☐ the remuneration paid to each officer and director during the previous 12 months and estimated to be paid during the next 12 months, directly or indirectly, by the issuer;

- ☐ the capitalization and long term debt of the issuer;

- ☐ the kind and amount of securities to be offered;

- ☐ the proposed offering price or the method by which it is to be computed;

- ☐ the estimated aggregate underwriting and selling discounts or commissions and finders' fees, or anything else of value to accrue to the underwriters or finders in connection with the offering;

- ☐ the estimated amounts of other selling expenses, including legal, engineering, and accounting charges;

- ☐ the estimated monetary proceeds to be received by the issuer from the offering; the purposes for which the proceeds are to be used by the issuer;

- ☐ the estimated amount to be used for each purpose;

- ☐ the order or priority in which the proceeds will be used for the purposes stated; the amounts of any funds to be raised from other sources to achieve the purposes stated;

- ☐ the sources of the funds;

- ☐ a description of any pending litigation, action, or proceeding to which the issuer is a party and that materially affects its business or assets, and any litigation, action, or proceeding known to be contemplated by governmental authorities;

- ☐ a copy of any prospectus, pamphlet, circular, form letter, advertisement, or other sales literature intended as of the effective date to be used in connection with the offering;

- ☐ a specimen or copy of the security being registered, unless the security is uncertificated;

- ☐ a copy of the issuer's articles of incorporation and bylaws or their substantial equivalents;

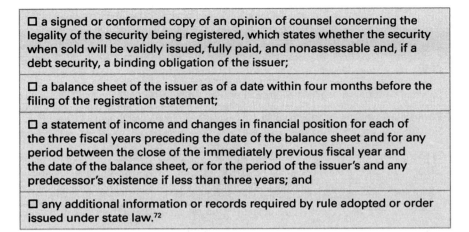

☐ a signed or conformed copy of an opinion of counsel concerning the legality of the security being registered, which states whether the security when sold will be validly issued, fully paid, and nonassessable and, if a debt security, a binding obligation of the issuer;

☐ a balance sheet of the issuer as of a date within four months before the filing of the registration statement;

☐ a statement of income and changes in financial position for each of the three fiscal years preceding the date of the balance sheet and for any period between the close of the immediately previous fiscal year and the date of the balance sheet, or for the period of the issuer's and any predecessor's existence if less than three years; and

☐ any additional information or records required by rule adopted or order issued under state law.[72]

The method of registration described above is referred to as registration by *qualification*. Most states also provide for registration by *coordination*. Churches will rarely if ever utilize registration by coordination, since this method assumes registration of an issuer's securities under the federal Securities Act of 1933 and churches are exempt from registration under this Act.

The registration statement ordinarily is prepared on a form provided by the state securities commission. Considerable effort has been expended to standardize securities laws and related forms among the 50 states. Most states now permit issuers to register their securities on a uniform application developed by the American Bar Association. This uniform application is called Form U-1.

Generally, the filing of a registration statement with a state securities commission constitutes registration of the security unless the commission objects to the registration statement within a prescribed period. A state securities commission retains the authority to suspend or revoke a registration of securities on the basis of a variety of grounds, including fraud, unreasonable commissions, illegality, omission of a material fact in the registration statement, and willful violation of any rule, order, or condition imposed by the securities commission.[73] Registration of securities generally is effective for one year, although some state laws stipulate that a registration will expire when the securities described in the registration statement have been sold.

Most securities laws that exempt church securities from registration also exempt churches from the requirement of filing sales and advertising literature with the securities commission. Again, churches must not assume that they are exempt from the filing requirement, since some state securities laws contain no such exemption. Furthermore, even if a church is exempt from the requirement of filing its sales and advertising literature with a state securities commission, it may be deemed to have entered into fraudulent transactions with investors if at

---

[72] Uniform Securities Act § 304.

[73] *Id.* at § 306.

or before the time of a sale or an offer to sell it does not provide each investor with a prospectus or offering circular containing sufficient information about the securities to enable an investor to make an informed investment decision.

The North American Securities Administrators Association (NASAA) has issued the following three guidelines pertaining to securities issued by religious organizations[74]:

(1) Church Bonds

In general, these guidelines require certain basic information on the cover page, and in addition require a full description of the history and operations of the church; the church's prior borrowing experience; risk factors associated with investment in the church's securities; how funds will be held during the offering period; anticipated use of proceeds; current financial condition of the church, accompanied by financial statements for the past three years; the church's properties; the type and amount of the securities to be offered, including interest rates, maturity dates, payment dates, and paying agent; the plan of distribution; pending or threatened legal proceedings against the church; tax aspects of ownership of the church's securities; and the church's leadership.

(2) Guidelines for General Obligation Financing by Religious Denominations

These guidelines address debt securities offered by denominational agencies that are used to provide resources to affiliated churches and institutions in the form of grants or loans. In general, these guidelines incorporate many of the same standards that are contained in the guidelines for local church securities offerings. They also contain guidelines for evaluating the strength of a loan fund. The guidelines are accompanied by the following explanation: (Rich: It seems like something is missing here. Did you mean to add the explanation?)

(3) Church Extension Fund Securities

These guidelines define a church extension fund (CEF) as follows: "A not-for-profit organization affiliated or associated with a denomination, or a fund that is accounted for separately by a denomination organized as a not-for-profit organization, that offers and sells notes primarily to provide funding for loans to various affiliated churches and related religious organizations of the denomination for the acquisition of property, construction or acquisition of buildings and other related capital expenditures or operating needs."

An official comment accompanying the guidelines provides the following clarification:

> General obligation financing by a CEF is different in its purposes and operation than the one-time offering of Church Bonds by an individual church or congregation to finance the construction of a single, specific church building or other related capital improvements, in which all of the securities are repaid within a set period of time. CEF notes are sold for

---

[74] The guidelines are available on the NASAA website (www.nasaa.org).

various terms and at varying interest rates and the offerings are normally continuous in nature to provide an ongoing source of financing to the various affiliated churches and related organizations. In order to maintain the CEF as a permanent resource for the affiliated churches and related organizations, repayments of principal on loans made by the CEF are continuously reinvested in new loans to affiliated churches and related organizations.

A CEF should be a single purpose organization or fund with most of its activities related to raising and managing funds for the purpose of making capital loans to its affiliated churches and related organizations, and it should either be incorporated and operated separately from the denomination and its affiliated churches and related organizations, or its accounting records should be maintained separately. Assets of the CEF should be used primarily for the purpose of financing building projects or property acquisitions for affiliated churches and related organizations. If the CEF is a separately incorporated entity, it normally is not liable for any debts arising from other unrelated activities or programs of the denomination or its affiliated churches and related organizations.

The primary indebtedness of CEFs is the outstanding notes. A significant number of investors reinvest with the CEF when their notes mature. Due to the continuous nature of the offerings and the fact that the funds are not designated for specific capital projects, special repayment provisions, including a sinking fund or trust indenture, for the purpose of making payments on principal or interest due on notes, are normally unnecessary and inappropriate.

It is important to observe that most states require that persons who sell or offer to sell securities be registered with the state securities commission. Registration involves submitting a detailed application[75] and, in most cases, the successful completion of a securities law examination. A few states that exempt the securities of religious organizations from registration do not exempt persons selling or offering to sell such securities from the salesman registration requirements.

2. Securities Fraud

No state securities law exempts religious organizations from the antifraud provisions. The antifraud provisions of the Uniform Securities Act are set forth in section 501:

It is unlawful for a person, in connection with the offer, sale, or purchase of a security, directly or indirectly:

(1) to employ a device, scheme, or artifice to defraud;

(2) to make an untrue statement of a material fact or to omit to state a

---

[75] Most states accept the uniform Form U-4 prepared by the National Association of Securities Dealers. *See generally* § 4-07, *supra*.

material fact necessary in order to make the statement made, in the light of the circumstances under which it is made, not misleading; or

(3) to engage in an act, practice, or course of business that operates or would operate as a fraud or deceit upon another person.

This section is substantially the same as section 17(a) of the federal Securities Act of 1933. Section 17 states that the Act's exemption of nonprofit organizations from the registration requirements does not apply to the antifraud provisions.

The antifraud provisions of federal and state securities laws are very broad. They have been construed to prohibit a wide variety of activities, including the following:

- making false or misleading statements about church securities

- failing to disclose material risks associated with securities

- manipulating the church's financial records in order to facilitate the sale of securities

- failing to establish a debt service or sinking fund reserve out of which church securities will be retired

- making false predictions

- recommending the sale of securities to investors without regard to their financial condition

- inducing transactions that are excessive in view of an investor's financial resources

- borrowing money from an investor

- commingling investors' funds with the personal funds of another, such as a salesman

- deliberately failing to follow an investor's instructions; making unfounded guarantees

- misrepresenting to investors the true status of their funds

- representing that funds of investors are insured or "secure" when in fact they are not

- representing that investments are as safe as if they had been made in a bank, when this is not the case

- representing that securities have been approved of or recommended by the state securities commission or that the commission has passed in any way on the merits or qualifications of the securities or of any agent or salesman

Key point. *There are two additional considerations that churches should consider before offering securities. First, some securities may be regulated under state and federal banking law. For example, it is possible that the issuance of "demand notes" (notes redeemable by investors "on demand") would violate state and federal banking laws. Demand notes are basically deposit arrangements which may trigger banking regulation. Second, complex accounting principles apply to some securities programs. It is essential for churches to work with a CPA firm with experience in representing nonprofit organizations that issue securities.*

In a leading case, the federal Securities and Exchange Commission brought an action in federal court seeking to enjoin a church and its leader from violating the antifraud provisions of the Securities Act of 1933.[76] The church had solicited funds through investment plans consisting essentially of the sale of interest-bearing notes to the general public. The notes were promoted through advertising literature extolling the security of the investment. For example, one advertisement stated in part:

> You may be a Christian who has committed his life into the hands of God, but left his funds in the hands of a floundering world economy. Financial experts everywhere are predicting a disaster in the economy. They say it is only a matter of time. . . . God's economy does not sink when the world's economy hits a reef and submerges! Wouldn't it be wise to invest in His economy?

The Securities and Exchange Commission argued that the church had defrauded investors by such representations when in fact it had a substantially increasing operating deficit that had jumped from $42,349 to $203,776 in the preceding three years. This fact was not disclosed to investors.

The church argued that religious organizations are protected by the First Amendment from the reach of securities laws. In rejecting this contention, the court observed: "Defendants constantly emphasize that they are engaged in 'God's work.' No court has ever found that conduct, by being so described, is automatically immunized from all regulation in the public interest."[77] The court quoted with approval the United States Supreme Court's earlier observation that "[n]othing we have said is intended even remotely to imply that, under the cloak of religion, persons may, with impunity, commit frauds upon the public."[78] The court found it irrelevant that investors had a "religious" motivation, that most investors were "believers," and that the church did not intend to defraud or deceive anyone.

A number of churches and other religious organizations have been

---

[76] Securities and Exchange Commission v. World Radio Mission, Inc., 544 F.2d 535 (1st Cir. 1976).

[77] *Id.* at 539 n.7.

[78] *Id.* at 537 n.3, quoting Cantwell v. Connecticut, 310 U.S. 296, 306 (1940). The court was "surprised . . . by defendants' recitation of the parable of the servants entrusted with their master's talents. We do not question the parable, but insofar as it indicates a duty to make loans, it is to make profitable ones. A servant contemplating lending to a possibly shaky enterprise would do well to note the final verse." *Id.* at 538 n.6.

investigated by the federal Securities and Exchange Commission and by state securities commissions. In most cases, the investigation was prompted by the complaint of an investor.[79]

Churches that violate state securities laws face a variety of potential consequences under state and federal securities laws. These include investigations, hearings, subpoenas, injunctions, criminal actions, cancellation of sales, suits for monetary damages by aggrieved investors, monetary fines, and revocation of an exemption, or registration, of securities.

Key point. *It is important to recognize that "good faith" (a lack of an intention to deceive, or lack of knowledge that a particular transaction is either fraudulent or otherwise in violation of securities law) does not necessarily protect against liability. To illustrate, some courts have ruled that the sale of unregistered securities in violation of state securities law is punishable despite the innocent intentions of the seller.[80] However, civil lawsuits by investors alleging fraud in the sale of securities must demonstrate an actual intent to deceive or defraud.[81]*

Case Studies

• *A church issues $200,000 in 10-year promissory notes to its members and spends all of the proceeds on a new education building. The failure to establish a "sinking fund" out of part of the proceeds received from the sale of these securities, and out of which the securities will be repaid at maturity, constitutes securities fraud. This is a good example of how churches can unwittingly engage in securities fraud.*

• *A church issues 10-year, 10 percent promissory notes to several of its members. No prospectus, offering circular, or other literature is filed with the state securities commission or made available to investors. The failure to provide prospective investors with a prospectus (also called an "offering circular") constitutes securities fraud. Once again, this illustrates how churches can innocently commit securities fraud.*

• *A church plans to issue $300,000 in promissory notes. It composes a prospectus describing much of the financial background of the church. The prospectus also contains the following four statements: (1) "The membership of the church has*

---

[79] *See, e.g.*, In the Matter of Keep the Faith, Inc., Ariz. Corp. Com., Dec. 54503 (April 25, 1985) (issuer incorrectly stated that its securities program did not involve a donation and did not disclose material information to investors, including the interest rate and term of the securities, and the background and financial condition of the issuer); In the Matter of Johnson Financial Services, Inc., Ga. Securities Div., No. 50-84-9500 (August 6, 1984) (salesperson falsely represented that he was working with a Presbyterian church to help sell its bonds, that he was a licensed salesperson, and that the church bonds he was offering earned 18 percent "tax free" for years); In the Matter of Tri-County Baptist Church, Mich. Corp. and Secs. Bureau, No. 84-32-S (June 11, 1984) (church failed to maintain an escrow account for proceeds of bond sales and did not apply proceeds as described in prospectus).

[80] Moerman v. Zipco, Inc., 302 F. Supp. 439 (E.D.N.Y. 1969), *aff'd*, 422 F.2d 871 (2nd Cir. 1970); Trump v. Badet, 327 P.2d 1001 (Ariz. 1958).

[81] The United States Supreme Court so held in Ernst & Ernst v. Hochfelder, 425 U.S. 185 (1976). While the Ernst decision dealt only with proof of an intent to deceive under the antifraud provisions of federal securities law, the decision has been held to apply by implication to private actions under the antifraud provisions of state securities laws. *See, e.g.*, Greenfield v. Cheek, 593 P.2d 293 (Ariz. 1978).

increased during each of the past ten years, so it can be expected that membership growth will continue to occur." (2) "These securities have been exempted from registration by the state securities commission and thus you are assured that they have been carefully studied and approved by the state." (3) "A copy of this prospectus shall at all times be maintained in the church office for the benefit of any prospective investor." (4) "Interest on these obligations is guaranteed." Each of these statements may constitute securities fraud.

• Same facts as the previous question. The church decides not to include the following information in its prospectus out of a concern that this information might make the church's securities less attractive: (1) A lawsuit is pending against the church alleging malpractice on the part of the pastor. (2) The total dollar value of securities to be offered. (3) A statement that no sinking fund reserve exists. (4) A statement that for two of the past five years the church's expenses exceeded revenues. Omitting any of this information from the church's prospectus may constitute securities fraud.

• A church finance company failed to comply with the provisions of the Indiana Securities Act regarding the registration of securities prior to the offering and sale of certain securities to Indiana residents. As a result, the company and state securities commission entered into a settlement agreement which required the company to pay a fine and make rescission offers to all Indiana residents who purchased unregistered, non-exempt securities.[82]

• In 1992, the Michigan Corporations and Securities Bureau revoked the exemptions of a denominational church loan fund, and ordered it to discontinue the sale of any securities, because of the offer and sale of unregistered, nonexempt securities from 1987 though 1991 in violation of state securities law. In 1993, the loan fund registered $10 million in securities. Following the expiration of this registration in 1994, the loan fund sold more than $1.3 million in unregistered, nonexempt securities to 95 Michigan residents. Because of this second violation of state securities law, the Bureau took the following steps: (1) It revoked and denied the availability of any exemption for the loan fund's securities for a period of five years. All securities issued during that five-year period would have to be registered under state law. (2) The Bureau ordered the loan fund to give written notice to its investors that they may have certain rights to have their money refunded because of the loan fund's violations of state securities law. (3) The Bureau ordered the loan fund to "retain an experienced securities attorney" before any future attempt to register its securities.[83]

• The Virginia Division of Securities investigated a church's securities program, and concluded that the church violated state securities law by selling unregistered securities in the form of bonds called "Certificates of Faith," and using unregistered agents in the sale of the securities. The church entered into a settlement offer with the Division, which required it to make a rescission offer to all bondholders including an explanation for the reason for the rescission offer. The church also agreed to offer only securities that are registered under the Virginia Securities Act or are exempted from

---

[82] In the Matter of Church Extension Plan (Lifeline Extension Pool), 1997 WL 2449 (Ind. Div. Sec. 1997).

[83] In the Matter of the Missions and Church Extension Trust Fund, 1996 WL 173463 (Mich. Corp. Sec. Bureau 1996). *See also* In re Lutheran Association for Church Extension, Inc., 1993 WL 304762 (Fla. Dept. Banking and Finance 1993).

registration, and to offer and sell such securities only through agents who are registered under the Virginia Securities Act or who are exempted from registration.[84]

• A state corporation commission launched an investigation into a church's bond program as a result of the following allegations: (1) the church's prospectus omitted disclosure of defaults by the church on bonds it issued in 1984 and 1987; (2) the financial statements included with the church's prospectus failed to properly reflect the total accrued interest on outstanding bonds; and (3) the prospectus issued to investors falsely represented that the church was current in its sinking fund payments for prior bond offerings. The commission entered into a settlement with the church which contained a number of terms, including the following: (1) payment of a fine; (2) an assurance that the church would not engage in any further practices in violation of state securities law; (3) an audit of the church's financial records; (4) the formulation of a financial plan by which all holders of outstanding bonds will be paid full principal and interest in accordance with the terms of their bond agreements; and (5) distribute to all bondholders a disclosure document, approved by the commission, disclosing all previous omissions, the church's current financial status, and its plan for the full repayment of all outstanding bonds.[85]

• A church began selling to investors what it called "certificates of deposit." The pastor allegedly told potential purchasers that the certificates of deposit would be used to finance the improvement or expansion of the church and to build a retirement complex. He represented or caused others to represent that the church would pay certificate holders between 12 and 16 percent interest on a quarterly basis and that interest payments would continue until the maturity of the certificate (5 years after the date of issuance). He further promised that, when the certificate matured, the investor would be entitled to repayment of the principal plus the balance of any outstanding interest. The pastor further informed investors that they would not have to pay income taxes on the interest payments they received from the church and that the investment was safe because it was backed by the assets of the church. The church raised over $1.6 million dollars from the sale of the certificates to 90 investors, 27 of whom were church members. The pastor took a significant portion of the certificate proceeds for his personal use. Among other things, he purchased 4 airplanes, a house for his mother, sports cars and passenger trucks, and made a down payment on his daughter's house. The pastor resigned when his actions were uncovered, and the church filed for bankruptcy protection.

The pastor was later prosecuted for 12 counts of securities fraud under federal law, including the following: (1) He "converted approximately $900,000 of certificate funds to the personal benefit of himself and family members." (2) He represented or caused others to represent that the church would pay certificate holders between 12 and 16 percent interest on a quarterly basis and that interest payments would continue until the maturity of the certificate (5 years after the date of issuance). (3) He promised that when the certificate matured, the investor would be entitled to repayment of the principal plus the balance of any outstanding interest. (4) He told investors that they would not have to pay income taxes on the interest payments they received from the church. (5) He told investors that their investments were safe

---

[84] Commonwealth of Virginia v. Unity Christ Church, 1996 WL 392586 (Va. Corp. Com. 1996).

[85] Commonwealth of Virginia v. Zion Apostolic Christian Memorial Church, 1998 WL 514271 (Va. Corp. Com. 1998).

because they were backed by the assets of the church. (6) At no time did the pastor tell investors that the money from the sale of certificates was to be used for the personal expenses of the pastor and his family. The pastor was convicted on all counts and sentenced to prison.

A federal appeals court affirmed the pastor's conviction, and an increase in his sentence to the "aggravating" circumstance that he breached a position of trust. The court concluded, "Because [the pastor] was the church's financial decisionmaker, church-member investors and church personnel trusted him to be the sole, unsupervised manager of the church's finances. This position of trust allowed the pastor to control the church's bank accounts and misapply the certificate funds clandestinely. Because he was the church's pastor and spiritual leader, his congregation undoubtedly trusted him to further the church's religious mission. His position of trust allowed him to use his authority to mislead church-member investors into believing that the church needed the certificate funds for building projects and to persuade them to invest their money for the good of the church and its endeavors. The trial court therefore correctly determined that the pastor occupied and abused a position of trust."[86]

• *A man (Walt) spent six months each year in Massachusetts and the other six months in Florida. While living in Florida, Walt met Pastor Jim, the pastor of a local church. Pastor Jim told Walt about the plans to build a new sanctuary, and he suggested that Walt purchase mortgage-backed bonds to help finance the building. The church had issued bonds valued at $1.7 million. A prospectus given to prospective investors stated that the property owned by the church was more than sufficient to cover the value of the bonds. A securities salesman later met with Walt, and informed him that the bonds were a good investment in that they had a high interest rate, that Pastor Jim was a good, young pastor who planned to get his Ph.D. and that the bonds were secure because of the value of the church property. The salesman also told Walt that if he invested $300,000 in the bonds, he would be repaid within six months. A few weeks later Walt purchased the bonds. Over the next several months, when Walt was back in Massachusetts, Pastor Jim called him several times asking him to purchase additional bonds. The pastor assured Walt that the value of the church property exceeded the value of the bonds, and that Walt would be repaid in a few months. Pastor Jim and two other church officers traveled to Massachusetts to meet personally with Walt. However, Walt refused to purchase any more bonds. The church paid Walt interest on the bonds for the next two years, until Pastor Jim informed him that the church was no longer able to meets its obligations. Walt sued the church for securities fraud.[87]*

• *In 2002 the United States Securities and Exchange Commission (SEC) filed a civil enforcement action alleging that from at least 1996 though at least 2002 a "loan fund" operated by a religious denomination (the "church") fraudulently raised $85 million from the sale of investment notes to thousands of investors nationwide. The loan fund was formed by the church in 1921 for the primary purpose of raising funds to loan to churches for the construction of new churches and to fund renovations of existing churches of the denomination.*

The SEC claimed that, in connection with the offer and sale of the investment notes, the loan fund repeatedly made material misrepresentations and omitted to state

---

[86] United States v. Lilly, 37 F.3d 1222 (7th Cir. 1994).

[87] Bearse v. Main Street Investments, 170 F.Supp.2d 107 (D. Mass. 2001).

material facts in its "solicitation materials" and offering circulars concerning the financial condition of the loan fund, and the primary use of investment note proceeds and the safety and risks associated with the investment notes. Each of the loan fund's offering circulars included an unqualified, independent auditor's report and a consolidated statement of financial condition.

Specifically, the SEC lawsuit alleged that the loan fund embarked upon a fraudulent scheme to conceal from investors the severe financial difficulties it had suffered. For example, the loan fund improperly used a provision of the tax code as a vehicle to generate non-existent income. This income was recognized by the loan fund on its consolidated statement of financial condition and was used to offset its losses. As a result, for several years the loan fund improperly recognized nearly $25 million in non-existent income that was used to offset other losses and thereby avoided recording at least $26 million in losses.

The SEC lawsuit further alleged that instead of using investment proceeds primarily to fund church loans (as promised in its advertising literature and offering circulars) the loan fund used the proceeds to fund speculative real estate transactions; fund losses at these failing properties; and make interest and principal payments to prior investors. The SEC lawsuit also claimed that as a result of the loan fund's deteriorating financial condition, it was unable to maintain the promised cash reserves stated in its offering circulars, which were distributed to investors nationwide.

In 2003 a federal judge in Indiana approved a plan for repayment of investors. The plan had been developed by the SEC, investors representatives, and loan fund, and submitted to the court for approval. The plan called for the liquidation of all loan fund assets for the benefit of the investors (most of whom were unsecured noteholders). This plan is still being implemented, but church officials are advising thousands of noteholders nationwide that they should not expect to receive more than "35% to 60%" of their investments.

• A church engaged in a chain distributor scheme of marketing ministerial credentials was found guilty of a fraudulent practice.[88] The church, whose archbishop was an attorney who had been disbarred for tax fraud in connection with the activities of the church, encouraged persons to become members by purchasing ministerial credentials for $3,500. Once the fee was paid, the new minister would name and establish his own church chartered by the parent church. He could then either make donations to his "church" or take a vow of poverty placing all his property in the name of his church and then pay all personal and family expenses through the church's account, thereby avoiding all taxes. Each minister was given the right to act as a "missionary representative" and was entitled to a ten percent commission for each new member he recruited into the church. After recruiting two fully paid members in one month, the missionary representative was granted advancement to the "missionary supervisor" level and thereby became eligible to receive a special bonus of $500 for each new fully paid minister recruited. After the missionary supervisor level, one could become a "director" and receive a 40 percent commission. Ministers were enticed through a demonstration of number doubling. Two became four, eight became sixteen, thirty-two became sixty-four, and commissions mounted from $350 to a total of $1,023,500 when 2,047 new recruits were added. A chart was prepared to give dramatic visual impact on how to become a millionaire. A court summarily concluded that such a scheme was fraudulent, and that application of state securities law to the church did not violate the First Amendment.

---

[88]   People v. Life Science Church, 450 N.Y.S.2d 664 (1982).

3. The Sarbanes-Oxley Act

The Sarbanes-Oxley Act amends federal law to permit private lawsuits for securities fraud violations to be brought not later than two years after its discovery, or five years after the date of the violation, whichever is earlier.

Case Studies

• *A small church does not have a CPA audit its financial statements each year. Does the Sarbanes-Oxley Act apply to it? No, except for the following: (1) It is a crime to knowingly alter, destroy, mutilate, conceal, cover up, falsify, or make a false entry in any document with the intent to impede, obstruct, or influence the investigation or proper administration of any matter within the jurisdiction of any federal department or agency; (2) private lawsuits for securities fraud violations may now be brought no later than two years after discovery, or five years after the date of the violation, whichever is earlier; (3) makes it a federal crime to retaliate against an employee (or anyone else) for providing truthful information to a law enforcement officer relating to the commission of a federal offense.*

• *To raise funds for a new building, a church sells bonds through its minister and board to church members. The church board assumes that the church is exempt from any legal restrictions, and so does not comply with the provisions of the state securities law. No "offering circular" (prospectus) is provided to prospective investors describing the securities and various risks, no one who sells the securities complies with agent registration requirements mandated by state law, and the church fails to create a "sinking fund" with a portion of the proceeds received from the sale of the securities. Within one year the church sells $400,000 of its promissory notes, but eventually defaults on all of them. Four years after the notes were sold, several investors sued the church in federal court alleging various counts of securities fraud under federal law. The church is not a public company and therefore is not subject to most of the provisions of the Sarbanes-Oxley Act. However, the Act extends the statute of limitations for securities fraud claims under federal law to not later than two years after discovering the fraud, or five years after the date of the violation, whichever is earlier. This extended statute of limitations for federal securities fraud claim applies to lawsuits brought against churches.*

• *A church issues $1,000,000 in promissory notes for the construction of a new educational facility. It prepares a prospectus describing the securities, the history of the church, and the church's financial condition. However, the prospectus fails to mention that the church has run budget deficits for each of the past 3 years, and that attendance has declined by 25 percent over that same period. The church board decided that this information was too negative to be put in the prospectus and would make the church's notes too unattractive to investors. Several years later, the church defaults on the notes, and some investors sue the church for securities fraud under federal law on the basis of the church's decision to omit information in the prospectus regarding deficits and attendance declines. The church is not a public company and therefore is not subject to most of the provisions of the Sarbanes-Oxley Act. However, the Act extends the statute of limitations for securities fraud claims under federal law to not later than two years after discovering the fraud, or five years after the date of the* *violation, whichever is earlier. This extended statute of limitations for federal securities fraud claim applies to lawsuits brought against churches.*

4. Protecting Churches and Church Members from Investment Fraud

Many churches, and church members, have been victimized by investment fraud. This section will assist church leaders in protecting church assets, and the assets of church members, from such scams.

Case Study

• *A church raises $250,000 for its building fund but is still years away from reaching the goal specified by the congregation before construction can begin. This year the pastor meets Jon, an "investment expert," who seems very knowledgeable about investment opportunities. Jon claims that he can turn the 1 percent return the church is earning on its building fund in a local bank to 30 percent or even 50 percent. The pastor is skeptical at first, but begins to see Jon as an answer to prayer. "Within just a few years, we will be able to begin construction on our new sanctuary," he muses. The pastor is also impressed by Jon's description of a "high yield investment program" involving international banks. The pastor invites Jon to make a presentation to the church board. Jon assures the board that the investment program only involves the "top ten world banks." The board is impressed, and votes to turn over the investment of the church's building fund to Jon. Within a few months, Jon suggests that the pastor promote the investment program to members of the congregation. With the pastor's encouragement, many church members invest their own funds in Jon's program. After several months, the pastor, board, and individual investors begin to wonder when they will receive their 50 percent return on their investments. Jon assures them that it is only a matter of time. A year passes, and still no earnings have been reported. Federal investigators contact the pastor and explain that Jon was engaged in a multi-million dollar securities scam, and that there is little chance that the church, or the individual investors, will ever receive back their invested funds much less any earnings. The pastor is devastated, as is the church board. Some church members invested their life savings in what they believed was a blessing from God. Several members begin blaming the pastor and board.*

Sound unbelievable? It shouldn't. Investment scams have victimized many churches and church members, and no church is immune. This section will explain the most common forms of securities fraud, provide several examples from real life, address the fiduciary duty of church leaders to invest church funds prudently, and provide practical steps that church leaders can take to minimize if not eliminate this risk.

Investment fraud is a risk not only to churches, but also to church members. Church leaders who familiarize themselves with the information in this section not only will be protecting their church, but they also will be protecting members from scams. As a result, we recommend that every church leader be asked to review this information.

Let's begin with a simple principle that will protect churches and church members against most investment scams—"if it sounds too good to be true, it is."

In the pages that follow you will be introduced to several tragic cases of securities fraud involving churches and church members. In every one of these cases, the tragedy could have been avoided through heeding this simple principle.

This section addresses the following topics:

- common investment scams

- illustrative cases

- SEC enforcement actions

- liability of church leaders

- reducing the risk of investment fraud

Common investment scams

The kinds of investment scams that have victimized churches and church members are too numerous to mention. Here are some common and recurring ones.

(1) pyramid schemes

In the classic "pyramid" scheme, participants attempt to make money solely by recruiting new participants into the program. The hallmark of these schemes is the promise of sky-high returns in a short period of time for doing nothing other than handing over your money and getting others to do the same.

The promoters behind a pyramid scheme may go to great lengths to make the program look like a legitimate multi-level marketing program. But despite their claims to have legitimate products or services to sell, the promoters simply use money coming in from new recruits to pay off early stage investors. But eventually the pyramid will collapse. At some point the schemes get too big, the promoter cannot raise enough money from new investors to pay earlier investors, and many people lose their money.

The Federal Trade Commission offers the following advice about pyramid schemes:

Steer clear of multilevel marketing plans that pay commissions for recruiting new distributors. They're actually illegal pyramid schemes. Why is pyramiding dangerous? Because plans that pay commissions for recruiting new distributors inevitably collapse when no new distributors can be recruited. And when a plan collapses, most people (except perhaps those at the very top of the pyramid) end up empty-handed.

If you're thinking about joining what appears to be a legitimate multilevel marketing plan, take time to learn about the plan before signing on.

What's the company's track record? What products does it sell? How does it back up claims it makes about its product? Is the product competitively priced? Is it likely to appeal to a large customer base?

What up-front investment do you have to make to join the plan? Are you committed to making a minimum level of sales each month? Will you be required to recruit new distributors to be successful in the plan?

Use caution if a distributor tells you that for the price of a "start-up kit" of inventory and sales literature—and sometimes a commitment to sell a specific amount of the product or service each month—you'll be on the road to riches. No matter how good a product and how solid a multilevel marketing plan may be, expect to invest sweat equity as well as dollars for your investment to pay off.

(2) Ponzi schemes

Ponzi schemes are a type of illegal pyramid scheme named for Charles Ponzi, who duped thousands of New England residents into investing in a postage stamp speculation scheme back in the 1920s. Ponzi thought he could take advantage of differences between U.S. and foreign currencies used to buy and sell international mail coupons. Ponzi told investors that he could provide a 40 percent return in just 90 days compared with five percent for bank savings accounts. Ponzi was deluged with funds from investors, taking in $1 million during one three-hour period. Though a few early investors were paid off to make the scheme look legitimate, an investigation found that Ponzi had only purchased about $30 worth of the international mail coupons.

A Ponzi scheme is closely related to a pyramid because it revolves around continuous recruiting, but in a Ponzi scheme the promoter generally has no product to sell and pays no commission to investors who recruit new "members." Instead, the promoter collects payments from a stream of people, promising them all the same high rate of return on a short-term investment. In the typical Ponzi scheme there is no real investment opportunity, and the promoter just uses the money from new recruits to pay obligations owed to longer-standing members of the program. This is often called "stealing from Peter to pay Paul." In fact some law enforcement officers call Ponzi schemes "Peter-Paul" scams.

Both Ponzi schemes and pyramids are quite seductive because they may be able to deliver a high rate of return to a few early investors for a short period of time. Yet, both pyramid and Ponzi schemes are illegal because they inevitably must fall apart. No program can recruit new members forever. Every pyramid or Ponzi scheme collapses because it cannot expand long enough to satisfy current and new investors. When the scheme collapses, most investors find themselves at the bottom, unable to recoup their losses.

Ponzi schemes continue to work on the "rob-Peter-to-pay-Paul" principle, as money from new investors is used to pay off earlier investors until the whole scheme collapses. Many churches and church members have been defrauded out of funds by investing in such schemes.

Key point. *Here's a good common sense rule to follow when evaluating investment options, "If it looks too good to be true, don't touch it."*

Another definition of a Ponzi scheme is "a fraudulent investment scheme in which money contributed by later investors generates artificially high dividends for the original investors, whose example attracts even larger investments."[89]

(3) Nigerian investment scams

Nigerian advance-fee fraud has been around for decades, but now seems to have reached epidemic proportions. According to the Federal Trade Commission (FTC) some citizens are receiving dozens of offers a day from supposed Nigerians politely promising big profits in exchange for help moving large sums of money out of their country. And apparently, many compassionate consumers are continuing to fall for the convincing sob stories, the unfailingly polite language, and the unequivocal promises of money. These advance-fee solicitations are scams, according to the FTC.

Here is a typical scenario. Claiming to be Nigerian officials, businesspeople or the surviving spouses of former government officials, con artists offer to transfer millions of dollars into your bank account in exchange for a small fee. If you respond to the initial offer, you may receive "official looking" documents. Typically, you're then asked to provide blank letterhead and your bank account numbers, as well as some money to cover transaction and transfer costs and attorney's fees. You may even be encouraged to travel to Nigeria or a border country to complete the transaction. Sometimes, the scam promoters will produce trunks of dyed or stamped money to verify their claims. Inevitably, though, emergencies come up, requiring more of your money and delaying the "transfer" of funds to your account; in the end, there aren't any profits for you to share, and the promoter has vanished with your money.

Incredibly, many church members, and some churches, have fallen victim to Nigerian investment scams. If you're tempted to respond to an offer, the FTC suggests you stop and ask yourself two important questions:

> • *Why would a perfect stranger pick you, also a perfect stranger, to share a fortune with?*

> • *Why would you share your personal or business information, including your bank account numbers or your company letterhead, with someone you don't know?*

The U.S. State Department cautions against traveling to the destination mentioned in the letters. According to State Department reports, people who have responded to these "advance-fee" solicitations have been beaten, subjected to threats and extortion, and in some cases, murdered.

Key point. *If you receive an offer via email from someone claiming to need your help getting money out of Nigeria (or any other country, for that matter) forward it to the FTC at uce@ftc.gov. If you have lost money to one of these schemes, call your local Secret Service field office. You also can call 202-406-5572 for information.*

---

[89] BLACK'S LAW DICTIONARY 1180 (7th ed.1999).

(4) prime bank scams

Prime bank scams are yet another investment scam that has been perpetrated against churches and church members. Here is how the SEC describes these scams:

Lured by the promise of astronomical profits and the chance to be part of an exclusive, international investing program, many investors have fallen prey to bogus "prime bank" scams. These fraudulent schemes involve the use of so-called "prime" bank, "prime" European bank or "prime" world bank financial instruments, or other "high yield investment programs" ("HYIP"s). Persons who promote these schemes often use the word "prime" (or a synonymous phrase, such as "top fifty world banks") to cloak their programs with an air of legitimacy. They seek to mislead investors by suggesting that well regarded and financially sound institutions participate in these bogus programs. But prime bank and other related schemes have no connection whatsoever to the world's leading financial institutions or to banks with the word "prime" in their names.

How do prime bank scams work? Here is the SEC explanation:

Prime bank programs often claim investors' funds will be used to purchase and trade "prime bank" financial instruments on clandestine overseas markets in order to generate huge returns in which the investor will share. However, neither these instruments, nor the markets on which they allegedly trade, exist. To give the scheme an air of legitimacy, the promoters distribute documents that appear complex, sophisticated and official. The sellers frequently tell potential investors that they have special access to programs that otherwise would be reserved for top financiers on Wall Street, or in London, Geneva or other world financial centers. Investors are also told that profits of 100% or more are possible with little risk.

The SEC warns that nonprofit organizations are often targeted by the promoters of these scams, and that promoters have demonstrated "remarkable audacity, advertising in national newspapers, such as *USA Today* and the *Wall Street Journal*." Some promoters avoid using the term "Prime Bank note," and tell prospective investors that their programs do not involve prime bank instruments in an effort to demonstrate that their programs are not fraudulent. Regardless of the terminology, the basic pitch, that the program involves trading in international financial instruments, remains the same, and investors should continue to be vigilant against such fraud.

The SEC has provided the following warning signs of prime bank or other fraudulent bank-related investment schemes.

- **Excessive guaranteed returns.** These schemes typically offer or guarantee spectacular returns of 20 to 200 percent monthly, absolutely risk free! Promises of unrealistic returns at no risk "are hallmarks of prime bank fraud."

• **Fictitious financial instrument.** Despite having credible-sounding names, the supposed "financial instruments" at the heart of any prime bank scheme simply do not exist. Exercise caution if you've been asked to invest in a debt obligation of the top 100 world banks, Medium Term Bank Notes or Debentures, Standby Letters of Credit, Bank Guarantees, an offshore trading program, a roll program, bank-issued debentures, a high yield investment program, or some variation on these descriptions. Promoters frequently claim that the offered financial instrument is issued, traded, guaranteed, or endorsed by the World Bank or an international central bank.

• **Extreme secrecy.** Promoters claim that transactions must be kept strictly confidential by all parties, making client references unavailable. They may characterize the transactions as the best-kept secret in the banking industry, and assert that, if asked, bank and regulatory officials would deny knowledge of such instruments. Investors may be asked to sign nondisclosure agreements.

• **Exclusive opportunity.** Promoters frequently claim that investment opportunities of this type are by invitation only, available to only a handful of special customers, and historically reserved for the wealthy elite.

• **Claims of inordinate complexity.** Investment pitches frequently are vague about who is involved in the transaction or where the money is going. Promoters may try to explain away this lack of specificity by stating that the financial instruments are too technical or complex for "non-experts" to understand.

You should be especially watchful for prime-bank related schemes promoted over the Internet.

Illustrative cases

Summarized below are several actual cases of investment scams that have victimized churches and church members. Many involve variations of Ponzi or pyramid schemes.

Case Studies

• *A promoter (Jerry) of a "Ponzi" style investment scheme pled guilty to 17 counts of securities fraud and mail fraud in connection with the fraudulent sale of securities to several church members. Jerry's leadership position in the church caused some victims to trust him. A number of his victims commented that he manipulated their faith to gain access to their money. For example, one victim testified that "the church out there where we went, where Jerry went, endorsed him highly, the pastor did. I trusted the pastor, and thus, we trusted Jerry." Another victim described how Jerry prayed with her just before he showed her fraudulent layouts for his purported developments. A letter from a former church member contained the following description of Jerry's activities:*

> *Jerry was constantly being praised from the pulpit as an "anointed Christian businessman," with visiting prophets prophesying about his future successes*

and blessings from God. His later legal problems were called demonic attacks by these same people. . . . Normally I could spot someone like Jerry a mile away, but believing the church's active promotion of him, I turned off my internal alarms. . . . Jerry skillfully manipulated my faith in God to his advantage, looking me in the eye while praying to God to bless the investment, all the while stealing my life savings. . . . To summarize, Jerry is an expert at using people's faith in God as a means of getting to their savings, reaching through their souls to pick their pockets, taking not only their savings but also their faith.

Jerry used his victims' faith to target investors. A brochure printed by the church invited parishioners to invest with Jerry, announcing that *"in almost every case, our plan will be able to at least match or out perform your current yields, and at the same time earn dividends for our church and its future. These funds will become the backbone of our plan to build the church campus and retire all debt within five years."* In soliciting parishioners' investments, Jerry announced:

We can take . . . individuals who have $200 dollars in a savings account or $200,000 in mutual funds, and we can allow you to retain the principal, but you use that interest . . . to help build God's kingdom, and also receive the same rate that you're receiving currently from the bank. . . . I consider it a real honor and a privilege to be able to be an elder of this church and to be able to take part . . . in a vision that . . . will allow us to quadruple in size and when we finally get this facility, we're going to be able to minister to so many more people.

A federal appeals court affirmed Jerry's guilt, but ordered a trial court to reconsider the length of his prison sentence.[90]

• *A church hired a treasurer (Steve) as a compensated employee. Steve was responsible for the church's bookkeeping, payment of bills, and a general responsibility for the church's financial accounting. At the time he became treasurer, he was employed as a loan officer by a local bank. Steve invested a large amount of the church's funds with an investment firm. He later testified that he wanted to become a "hero" by investing the church's money in stocks and securities and thereby increasing the church's funds. Steve urged the investment firm to invest the church's funds in speculative stock. Over the next few years, the value of the church's portfolio plummeted, creating a financial crisis for the church. Steve confessed that he had invested the church's funds in speculative investments, and that most of the investments had "failed." Church board members occasionally signed "authorization" forms giving Steve the authority to invest the church's funds. But the board exercised insufficient oversight over Steve's activities to ascertain the true status of church funds. The church later sued the investment firm for malpractice and securities fraud.*[91]

• *An investment advisor (Jerry) derived his income through various social contacts, including his church. He lured several church members into investing in commodities and a gold mine. Jerry received 5% of each person's investment to cover "personal expenses," plus 25% of all profits. As an inducement to investing with him, Jerry*

---

[90] United States v. Luca, 183 F.3d 1018 (9th Cir. 1999).

[91] Yellowstone Conference of the United Methodist Church v. Davidson, 741 P.2d 794 (Mont. 1987).

"personally guaranteed" a 25% return over the first year. If an account failed to perform sufficiently, he would pay the guaranteed return from his personal assets. No risks were explained to the investors, who were generally unsophisticated. Rather than receive any return after the first year, the investors were informed that Jerry's practices had caused the loss of "a substantial portion of their investment." No guarantee was forthcoming from Jerry at that time but he assured investors that he was withdrawing their funds and transferring them to another commodities broker who would "recover" their original investment plus the guaranteed amount within a "relatively short period of time." Other than a partial return of funds to a select few, the investors received nothing, but were convinced by Jerry to leave their remaining funds in his control with the promise that he would recover their original investment plus much more by investing their funds in a gold mine in Arizona. Jerry informed all the investors there was "the possibility of becoming as financially independent as you want" and that he "had spent years and thousands of dollars acquiring financial information." In fact, the investors lost virtually all of their investments.[92]

• A religious ministry operated and marketed a "double-your-money" scheme called the "Faith Promises Program." The ministry used a bank as a major depository and source of financial services while operating the Ponzi scheme. Eventually, the Ponzi scheme swindled more than fifteen thousand victims out of an estimated five hundred million dollars. Many of the founders of the scheme were convicted for a variety of federal offenses. The ministry filed for bankruptcy protection. Several investors later sued the ministry's bank, claiming that it was responsible for the ministry's fraud on the basis of negligence and breach of fiduciary duty. A court ruled that the relationship of the ministry to the bank was a fiduciary one, but not the relationship between individual investors and the bank and therefore the bank was not liable to the investors for the ministry's fraud. The court concluded, "To hold the bank liable in this situation, essentially, would be to instill on banking institutions the power to regulate what their customers do with their money, a power this court cannot and will not establish. As such, the bank had no duty to disclose any material facts to the investors, even if it had knowledge of such facts."[93]

• A business representing itself as a nondenominational, non-sectarian international Christian ministry (formed in the Dutch Antilles Island of Aruba) placed the following advertisement in an entrepreneur magazine with a nationwide circulation: "Need extra income? [We] would like to show Christian families how working together they can become debt free. Call [a toll-free telephone number] and request the Christian program." Persons who responded to the ad were mailed literature that offered financial assistance through participation in a monthly fund-raising project. By providing others with "love gifts" in the amount of $30, $60, or $100 per month, a participant became eligible to receive monetary "gifts of love" from a "3-wide x 7-level deep network." Of the monthly payments, 30 percent went to the ministry and 70 percent was for "love gifts" to be forwarded to earlier participants in the program. New participants recruited and sponsored other participants, creating an upline of up to seven levels. A participant received a portion of the monthly "love gift" payments made by those in one's upline. A participant became eligible to receive "love gifts" from others by making monthly payments and by sponsoring others to join the program. The literature represented that it was possible

---

92   Stokes v. Henson, 265 Cal. Rptr. 836 (Cal. App. 1990).

93   O'Halloran v. First Union National Bank, 205 F.Supp.2d 1296 (M.D. Fla. 2002).

for a participant to receive $10,800 per month from this program. The program was also promoted through radio ads to Kansas residents who needed extra income through a "Christian program." In response to these advertisements, approximately 30 Kansas residents sent for information about the program. The Kansas securities commission concluded that the program was a security, and that it violated securities law in the following ways: (1) neither the securities nor those selling them had been registered; and (2) investors were not informed that the ministry had been issued a cease and desist order by the state securities commission a few years earlier. The commissioner ordered the ministry to discontinue any further offers or sales of its program to residents of Kansas unless the securities are registered in advance.[94]

• A securities dealer offered for sale and sold securities in a local church's mortgage bond investment program. The offering materials for such securities contained a letter which indicated that the bonds were "A" rated when, in fact, they had not received any independent rating. The Texas securities commission determined that this representation was misleading, and it ordered the dealer to discontinue any further references to "ratings" unless it obtained an independent rating from a recognized securities rating agency. It also ordered the dealer to pay a fine, and make "rescission offers" to all persons who invested in any securities accompanied by materials containing the misleading representation. A rescission offer is an offer by an issuer of securities to an investor, offering to buy back the investor's securities.[95]

• In 2001 the SEC Securities and Exchange Commission filed charges against two companies relating to a fraudulent trading scheme that raised approximately $22 million from at least 50 investors, many of whom were members of the same religious denomination. According to the SEC, the defendants fraudulently offered and sold unregistered securities in an "international bank-related financial instrument trading program" that was completely fictitious. The defendants promoted their trading program under various names, including Swiss Asset Management, Wall Street South, and Resource F. The SEC claimed that the companies' agents solicited investors using misrepresentations that the investment involved high-quality debt instruments of very large international banks, that the investors' principal was never at risk and could be returned after one year, and that investors would receive profits of approximately four to five percent every month (or 48 to 60 percent annually).

During the initial stages of the fraud, investors received monthly payments that the defendants represented were "profits" on their investment. However, monthly payments to investors eventually stopped. Despite numerous requests, no investors received the return of their investment. Further, since the cessation of monthly payments, promoters regularly sent letters to investors making excuses for the cessation of payments, and making the false statements that trading and monthly payments would resume soon. These letters included a request that investors contribute money to purported "legal efforts" to obtain the return of investors' funds.

A federal court entered an order barring certain officers of the defendants from engaging in further fraudulent activity and freezing their assets to ensure that assets were preserved to pay investors their lost principal.

---

[94] In the Matter of Agape International Ministries, 1995 WL 582034 (Kan. Sec. Com. 1995).

[95] In the Matter of California Plan of Church Finance, Inc., 1997 WL 403287 (Tex. State Securities Board 1998).

• The SEC filed a lawsuit in federal court seeking to halt an ongoing nationwide affinity fraud, primarily targeting African-American churches, conducted by an individual (the defendant) through a bogus company. The SEC alleged that the defendant engaged in a deliberate scheme to defraud investors by making false and misleading statements in connection with the unregistered offer and sale of securities in the form of investment contracts in a "church funding project." The defendant raised at least $3 million from over 1000 investing churches located throughout the United States. The SEC claimed that through various promotional means, including a website, the defendant's presentations at group meetings and religious conferences, telephone solicitations, mailings and a commissioned sales force, the defendant solicited churches to invest in the church funding project by falsely promising huge financial returns. Specifically, for each investment of $3,000, the defendant promised to pay a return of $500,000! He told investors that his company would fund the promised returns from a pool of money it received for this purpose from four sources—profit-making corporations; federal government grants; other Christian institutions; and profits from a series of world-wide Christian-based resorts to be built and run by a "sister corporation." In fact, the defendant did not have any commitments from profit-making corporations or other institutions to fund this project, and he built no resorts. As a result of this scam, the defendant has outstanding commitments to investors of at least $500 million. The SEC asked the court to permanently enjoin the defendant from selling securities, and also sought an asset frieze, disgorgement of profits, civil penalties, and an order preventing the destruction of documents.

• In 2001 the SEC sued an individual (the defendant) alleging that he defrauded a church out of $900,000. The SEC claimed that the defendant used his investment advisory firm to misappropriate hundreds of thousands of dollars in "soft dollar credits" generated by securities transactions made on the church's behalf in an account that the defendant created with a broker-dealer. Soft dollar credits are created when an investment adviser and a broker-dealer enter into an arrangement in which a percentage of commissions are used to pay for products and services, such as research, that help the adviser in making investment decisions. Because soft dollar credits are generated by commissions paid by the advisory client, they are assets of the client. Soft dollar arrangements are permissible under the securities laws if there is appropriate disclosure to the client about the products and services for which the soft dollars will be used, as well as disclosure that the client may pay higher commission rates as a result of the soft dollar arrangement.

The SEC alleged that as part of the scheme to misappropriate soft dollar credits, the defendant submitted over a hundred invoices to the broker-dealer for payments with soft dollars that had been generated by trading in the church's account. Many of the invoices were in the name of a "shell entity" the defendant controlled, and falsely indicated that it had provided services that were payable with soft dollars. The broker-dealer paid hundreds of thousands of dollars to this shell company based on these false invoices. The defendant personally picked up these payments from the broker-dealer and deposited them into bank accounts that he controlled. He then withdrew the majority of the funds for his personal use.

The SEC claimed that the church was not informed that its soft dollars were being used for the defendant's personal benefit, and that the defendant violated his fiduciary duty of "best execution" for his client's securities trades by fraudulently setting the commissions paid by the church at a rate that was approximately five times higher than the average rate charged for soft dollar transactions at the time. The SEC also charged that the defendant "churned" the church's endowment account, frequently causing the church to accumulate large positions of stock in a company only to sell the entire position weeks later at a similar price. These actions were taken to generate additional soft dollar credits, which the defendant then misappropriated.

The SEC asked a federal court to grant injunctive relief, disgorgement of improperly-obtained benefits, plus civil penalties. This case was settled by the parties, with the defendant agreeing to pay back $1.2 million (all but $300,000 was waived based on his financial inability to pay).

• In 2001 the SEC Securities and Exchange Commission filed charges against two companies relating to a fraudulent trading scheme that raised approximately $22 million from at least 50 investors, many of whom were members of the same religious denomination. According to the SEC, the defendants fraudulently offered and sold unregistered securities in an "international bank-related financial instrument trading program" that was completely fictitious. The defendants promoted their trading program under various names, including Swiss Asset Management, Wall Street South, and Resource F. The SEC claimed that the companies' agents solicited investors using misrepresentations that the investment involved high-quality debt instruments of very large international banks, that the investors' principal was never at risk and could be returned after one year, and that investors would receive profits of approximately 4-5% every month (or 48-60% annually).

During the initial stages of the fraud, investors received monthly payments that the defendants represented were "profits" on their investment. However, monthly payments to investors eventually stopped. Despite numerous requests, no investors received the return of their investment. Further, since the cessation of monthly payments, promoters regularly sent letters to investors making excuses for the cessation of payments, and making the false statements that trading and monthly payments would resume soon. These letters included a request that investors contribute money to purported "legal efforts" to obtain the return of investors' funds.

A federal court entered an order barring certain officers of the defendants from engaging in further fraudulent activity and freezing their assets to ensure that assets were preserved to pay investors their lost principal.

• In 2001 the SEC sued an individual (the defendant) alleging that he defrauded a church out of $900,000. The SEC claimed that the defendant used his investment advisory firm to misappropriate hundreds of thousands of dollars in "soft dollar credits" generated by securities transactions made on the church's behalf in an account that the defendant created with a broker-dealer. Soft dollar credits are created when an investment adviser and a broker-dealer enter into an arrangement in which a percentage of commissions are used to pay for products and services, such as research, that help the adviser in making investment decisions. Because soft dollar credits are generated by commissions paid by the advisory client, they are assets of the client. Soft dollar arrangements are permissible under the securities laws if there is appropriate disclosure to the client about the products and services for which the soft dollars will be used, as well as disclosure that the client may pay higher commission rates as a result of the soft dollar arrangement.

The SEC alleged that as part of the scheme to misappropriate soft dollar credits, the defendant submitted over a hundred invoices to the broker-dealer for payments with soft dollars that had been generated by trading in the church's account. Many of the invoices were in the name of a "shell entity" the defendant controlled, and falsely indicated that it had provided services that were payable with soft dollars. The broker-dealer paid hundreds of thousands of dollars to this shell company based on these *false invoices. The defendant personally picked up these payments from the broker-dealer and deposited them into bank accounts that he controlled. He then withdrew the majority of the funds for his personal use.*

The SEC claimed that the church was not informed that its soft dollars were being used for the defendant's personal benefit, and that the defendant violated his fiduciary duty of "best execution" for his client's securities trades by fraudulently setting the commissions paid by the church at a rate that was approximately five times higher than the average rate charged for soft dollar transactions at the time. The SEC also charged that the defendant "churned" the church's endowment account, frequently causing the church to accumulate large positions of stock in a company only to sell the entire position weeks later at a similar price. These actions were taken to generate additional soft dollar credits, which the defendant then misappropriated.

The SEC asked a federal court to grant injunctive relief, disgorgement of improperly-obtained benefits, plus civil penalties. This case was settled by the parties, with the defendant agreeing to pay back $1.2 million (all but $300,000 was waived based on his financial inability to pay).

Reducing the Risk of Investment Fraud—SEC Recommendations

As you read through the cases summarized above, you may be amazed that anyone could have fallen for these scams. But the truth is that in each case church members and leaders found the investment scheme to be legitimate, and did not realize that they were being victimized. Are there specific steps that church members and leaders can take to reduce the risk of financial fraud? Fortunately, the answer is yes. A first step is to be familiar with the four specific kinds of investment fraud described above (pyramid schemes, Ponzi schemes, Nigerian investments, and prime bank investments). A second step is to review the actual cases summarized above. Third, review the following recommendations from the United States Securities and Exchange Commission.

(1) if it sounds too good to be true, it is

High-yield investments tend to involve extremely high risk. Never invest in an opportunity that promises "guaranteed" or "risk-free" returns. Words like "guarantee," "high return," "limited offer," or "as safe as a C.D." may be a red flag. No financial investment is "risk free" and a high rate of return means greater risk. Watch out for claims of astronomical yields in a short period of time. Be skeptical of "off-shore" or foreign investments. And beware of exotic or unusual sounding investments, especially those involving so-called "prime bank" securities. Compare promised yields with current returns on well-known stock indexes. Any investment opportunity that claims you'll get substantially more could be highly risky. And that means you might lose money.

> "Are there specific steps that church members and leaders can take to reduce the risk of financial fraud? Fortunately, the answer is yes."

(2) "guaranteed returns" aren't

Every investment carries some degree of risk, and the level of risk typically correlates with the return you can expect to receive. Low risk generally means low yields, and high yields typically involve high risk. If your money is perfectly safe, you'll most likely get a low return. High returns represent potential rewards for folks who are willing to take big risks. Most fraudsters spend a lot of time trying to convince investors that extremely high returns are "guaranteed" or "can't miss." Don't believe it.

(3) check out the company before you invest

If you've never heard of a company, broker, or adviser, spend some time checking them out before you invest. Most public companies make electronic filings with the SEC that can be inspected on the SEC website. Some smaller companies don't have to register their securities offerings with the SEC, so always check with your state securities regulator. You'll find that telephone number in the government section of your phone book. Or call the North American Securities Administrators Association (NASAA) at (202) 737-0900. Many online investment scams involve unregistered securities. One simple phone call can make the difference between investing in a legitimate business or squandering your money on a scam.

Your state securities department can tell you whether the person pushing the investment opportunity has a disciplinary history by checking the Central Registration Depository (CRD). You can also obtain a partial disciplinary history by contacting NASD's toll-free public disclosure hot-line at (800) 289-9999 or visiting their website at http://www.nasd.com.

If a promoter only lists a P.O. box, you'll want to do a *lot* of work before investing your money.

(4) if it is that good, it will wait

Scam artists usually try to create a sense of urgency, implying that if you don't act *now* you'll miss out on a fabulous opportunity. But savvy investors take time to do their homework before investing. If you're being pressured to invest, especially if it is a once-in-a-lifetime, too-good-to-be-true opportunity that "just can't miss," just say "no." Your wallet will thank you.

(5) understand your investments

Scam artists frequently use a lot of big words and technical-sounding phrases to impress you. But have faith in yourself! If you don't understand an investment, don't buy it. If a salesman isn't able to explain a concept clearly enough for you to understand, it isn't your fault. Don't make it your problem by buying!

(6) beauty isn't everything

Don't be fooled by a pretty website—they are remarkably easy to create.

(7) is the person offering the securities licensed?

Find out if the person or firm selling the investment needs to be licensed. Call your state securities regulator and ask whether the person or firm is licensed to do business in your state and whether they have a record of complaints or fraud. You can also get this information by calling NASD's public disclosure hotline at (800) 289-9999.

(8) be especially skeptical of investing via the Internet

You should be skeptical of investment opportunities you learn about through the Internet. When you see an offering on the Internet (whether it's on a company's website, in an online newsletter, on a message board, or in a chat room) you should assume it's a scam until you've done your homework and proven otherwise. Get the facts *before* you invest, and only invest money you can afford to lose.

(9) be skeptical of offshore investment opportunities

Watch out for offshore scams and investment opportunities in other countries. When you send your money abroad, and something goes wrong, it's more difficult to find out what happened and to locate your money.

(10) call the SEC

If you have any doubts about an investment opportunity, call the SEC or your state securities department. You can get the telephone numbers by visiting their websites.

---

10 Questions to Ask Before You Invest

The SEC suggests that prospective investors ask the following 10 questions before investing funds:

1. Is the investment registered with the SEC and the state where I live?

2. Is the person recommending this investment licensed with my state securities agency? Is there a record of any complaints about this person or the firm he or she works for?

3. How does this investment match my investment objectives?

4. Will the sales representative send me the latest reports that have been filed on this company?

5. What are the costs to buy, hold, and sell this investment? How easily can I sell?

6. Who is managing the investment? What experience do they have? Have they made money for investors before?

7. What is the risk that I could lose the money I invest?

8. What return can I expect on my money? When?

9. How long has the company been in business? Is it making money, and if so, how? What is their product or service? What other companies are in this business?

10. How can I get more information about this investment, such as audited financial statements, annual and quarterly reports, a prospectus?

Copyright Law

Resource. *The application of copyright law to churches is discussed fully in R. Hammar's,* The Church Guide to Copyright Law *(by the publisher of this text).*

The United States Constitution gives Congress the power to enact laws that "promote the progress of . . . [the] useful arts, by securing for limited times to authors . . . the exclusive right to their respective writings." In 1790, under the power granted by the new Constitution, Congress enacted the first copyright law. Congress enacted several other copyright laws in the ensuing years, and in 1870 enacted the first comprehensive copyright statute. This law was substantially revised in 1909. In 1976, Congress enacted the current copyright act, which became effective on January 1, 1978. It is known as the Copyright Act of 1976.

In commenting on the purpose of the original constitutional provision, the United States Supreme Court has observed:

> [The Constitution] describes both the objective which Congress may seek and the means to achieve it. The objective is to promote the progress of . . . the arts. . . . To accomplish its purpose, Congress may grant to authors the exclusive right to the fruits of their respective works. An author who possesses an unlimited copyright may preclude others from copying his creation for commercial purposes without permission. In other words, to encourage people to devote themselves to intellectual and artistic creation, Congress may guarantee to authors . . . a reward in the form of control over the sale or commercial use of copies of their works.[96]

Compensation of authors is thus a secondary purpose of the copyright law.

Securing Copyright Protection

Key point 9-05.01. *Authors and composers receive initial copyright protection as soon as they create an original work in a tangible form.*

1. Initial Copyright Protection

The objective of copyright law is to promote the progress of the useful arts by granting authors certain exclusive rights in their works. Under the Copyright Act of 1976, authors and composers receive initial copyright protection as soon as they create an original work of authorship that is "fixed" in a "tangible medium

---

[96] Goldstein v. California, 412 U.S. 546, 555 (1973).

of expression."[97] There are then three prerequisites to initial copyright protection in a work: (1) the work must be original, (2) it must be a work of authorship, and (3) it must be fixed in a tangible medium of expression.

A work is *original* if an author created it by his or her own skill, labor, and judgment, and not by directly copying or evasively imitating the work of another. One court has stated that "originality means that the work owes its creation to the author and thus in turn means that the work must not consist of actual copying."[98] In summary, originality connotes independent creation.

Originality does *not* necessarily mean novelty or creativity. One court observed that "there must be independent creation, but it need not be invention in the sense of striking uniqueness, ingeniousness, or novelty," and that the test of originality "is concededly one with a low threshold in that 'all that is needed . . . is that the author contributed something more than a merely trivial variation, something recognizably his own.'"[99]

For a work to be entitled to initial copyright protection, it must constitute a *work of authorship* as defined by the Copyright Act. Section 102 of the Act provides that works of authorship include

1. literary works, such as books, periodicals, and manuscripts

2. musical works, including any accompanying words

3. dramatic works, including any accompanying music

4. pantomimes and choreographic works

5. pictorial, graphic, and sculptural works

6. motion pictures and other audiovisual works

7. sound recordings

Names and titles are not subject to copyright protection. They may be entitled to protection under federal trademark law if they are affixed to or associated with products or services and serve to identify the source of the products or services in a unique way.

Section 103 stipulates that compilations and derivative works also are entitled to copyright protection. A *compilation* is defined as "a work formed by the collection and assembling of pre-existing materials . . . that are selected, coordinated, or arranged in such a way that the resulting work as a whole constitutes an original work of authorship." A *derivative work* is defined as "a work based upon one or more pre-existing works, such as a translation, musical arrangement, dramatization, fictionalization, abridgement, condensation, or any

---

[97] 17 U.S.C. § 102(a).

[98] L. Batlin & Son, Inc. v. Snyder, 536 F.2d 486, 490 (2nd Cir. 1976), *cert. denied,* 429 U.S. 857 (1976).

[99] *Id.*

other form in which a work may be recast, transformed, or adapted."

For a work to be entitled to initial copyright protection, it must be fixed in some *tangible medium of expression*. Ideas, concepts, and discoveries therefore are not eligible for copyright protection until they are reduced to a tangible form.

2. Post-Publication Copyright Protection—Works First Published Before March 1, 1989

The initial copyright protection that an author receives under the Copyright Act persists until the author publishes his work. The Act defines *publication* as "the distribution of copies . . . of a work to the public by sale or other transfer of ownership, or by rental, lease, or lending."[100] Once an author publishes a work, he or she may have to comply with certain other requirements to perpetuate the initial copyright protection.

For works published prior to March 1, 1989, section 401(a) of the Copyright Act specified:

> Whenever a work . . . is published in the United States or elsewhere by authority of the copyright owner, a notice of copyright as provided by this section shall be placed on all publicly distributed copies from which the work can be visually perceived, either directly or with the aid of a machine or device.

This requirement is known as the "notice" requirement, and compliance with it is essential to the continuation of copyright protection following the publication of a work first published prior to March 1, 1989. No registration was necessary to perfect copyright protection in a work first published before March 1, 1989.

3. Post-Publication Copyright Protection—Works First Published on or after March 1, 1989

On March 1, 1989, the United States became a party to the "Berne Convention"—an international copyright convention established in the 19th Century and endorsed by nearly 80 nations. Participation by the United States in this significant convention generally will increase the international protections available to American authors. To become a party to the convention, Congress had to make various changes in our copyright law (unwillingness to make the required changes was one of the major reasons that it took the United States a century to join the convention). Perhaps the most important change related to copyright notice. Mandatory notice of copyright has been abolished for works published for the first time on or after March 1, 1989. Failure to place a copyright notice on copies of works that are publicly distributed can no longer result in the loss of copyright. Obviously, this is a significant change in our copyright law, since prior to March 1, 1989, the failure to affix a valid copyright notice to a publicly distributed work could have resulted in loss of copyright protection. While copyright notices are no longer required to obtain copyright protection in

---

[100] 17 U.S.C. § 101.

works first published on or after March 1, 1989, the Copyright Office "strongly recommends" that publishers place a notice of copyright on such works. One of the benefits of such notices is that an infringer will not be able to claim that he or she "innocently infringed" a work. In summary, while in some cases a copyright notice may no longer be a technical requirement, it should nevertheless always be used.

The Berne Convention is not retroactive. As a result, the notice requirements for works first published prior to March 1, 1989, remain unchanged. To illustrate, works first published between January 1, 1978 and February 28, 1989 without a valid copyright notice (as defined below) generally lost their copyright protection unless they were registered with the Copyright Office within five years of first publication (and a valid notice added to all copies distributed after discovery of the omission). Works first published before January 1, 1978 without a valid copyright notice generally lost all copyright protection immediately (with some exceptions). Obviously, the change in the notice requirement will result in considerable confusion among churches regarding the copyright status of literary or musical works. For example, suppose that a church would like to make copies of a piece of sheet music. The fact that the music does not bear a copyright notice does *not* mean that the work is not copyrighted. Clearly, it will now be more difficult for churches to determine whether or not they are free to make copies of some works. Churches cannot safely assume that a work is "in the public domain" merely because it does not contain a valid copyright notice.

In summary, while copyright notices are no longer technically required for most works first published on or after March 1, 1989, they should still be used.

copyright notices

What, then, is a valid copyright notice? The contents and placement of a valid copyright notice are described in sections 401(b) and (c) of the Copyright Act. A valid notice consists of three elements: (1) the symbol ©, the word "Copyright," or the abbreviation "Copr."; *and* (2) the year of first publication of the work (in the case of compilations and derivative works incorporating previously published material, the year of first publication of the compilation or derivative work is sufficient); *and* (3) the name of the owner of copyright in the work, or an abbreviation by which the name can be recognized, or a generally known alternative designation of the owner.

Section 401(c) provides that the notice shall be affixed to copies of the work "in such manner and location as to give reasonable notice of the claim of copyright." To illustrate, Copyright Office regulations specify that a copyright notice for a work published in book form may be affixed on the title page, the page immediately following the title page, either side of the front or back cover, the first page of the main body of the work, the last page of the main body of the work, or any page between the front page and first page of the main body of the work if there are no more than 10 pages between the front page and the first page of the main body of the work and the notice is prominently displayed and set apart. Similar rules apply to musical works. Other rules apply to single-leaf works, audiovisual works, machine-readable works, and pictorial works. The Copyright

Office regulations themselves provide that they merely illustrate acceptable notice placements. They are not exhaustive, and acceptable alternatives probably exist. Of course, it is prudent to follow the Copyright Office guidelines since compliance with them is conclusive evidence that you have affixed your copyright notice in an appropriate position.

What is the effect of a work that is published with a defective or omitted notice? Works first published on or after March 1, 1989, require no copyright notice, so an omitted or defective notice has no legal effect. However, note that section 401(d) of the Copyright Act specifies that if a work first published on or after March 1, 1989 contains a valid copyright notice, "then no weight shall be given" to an "innocent infringement" defense. That is, no infringer can argue that he or she "innocently" infringed on another's work if that work contained a valid copyright notice. If the notice does not satisfy the requirements of sections 401(b) and 401(c), the implication is that an infringer can assert an innocent infringement defense. The same concept applies to phonorecords under section 402(d). What about works first published prior to March 1, 1989? Section 405(a) of the Copyright Act specifies:

> With respect to copies and phonorecords publicly distributed by authority of the copyright owner before [March 1, 1989], the omission of the copyright notice described in sections 401 through 403 from copies or phonorecords publicly distributed by authority of the copyright owner does not invalidate the copyright in a work if
>
> (1) the notice has been omitted from no more than a relatively small number of copies . . . distributed to the public; or
>
> (2) registration for the work has been made before or is made within five years after the publication without notice, and a reasonable effort is made to add notice to all copies . . . that are distributed to the public in the United States after the omission has been discovered; or
>
> (3) the notice has been omitted in violation of an express requirement in writing that, as a condition of the copyright owner's authorization of the public distribution of copies . . . they bear the prescribed notice.

Also, note that if someone distributes copies of a copyrighted work without authorization from the copyright owner, and no copyright notice appears on such copies, the copyright in the work is not affected since the copies were made and distributed without authorization.

effect of omitting the copyright notice

Can one be guilty of copyright infringement for innocently infringing on a copyrighted work from which the copyright notice had been omitted? For works first published on or after March 1, 1989, the answer is yes—since copyright notices are no longer required to ensure copyright protection. However, the Copyright Act indicates that an infringer can assert the defense of "innocent infringement" to avoid or reduce damages if the infringed work either had no copyright notice or had a defective notice (not meeting the requirements of sections 401(b) and 401(c)).

What if the work was first published prior to March 1, 1989? Assuming that the omission of the copyright notice did not invalidate the copyright (i.e., one of the three exceptions referred to above applies), the innocent infringer incurs no liability for any infringing acts "committed before receiving actual notice that registration for the work has been made . . . if such person proves that he or she was misled by the omission of notice."[101] Omission of copyright notice ordinarily will result in loss of copyright protection (in works first published before March 1, 1989) if none of the three exceptions described above applies.

copyright notices containing an error

A related question is the effect of an error in the copyright notice. For example, what if a notice has an error in the name of the copyright owner, or in the date of first publication, or either the name or date is omitted? The copyright law specifies that if the name listed in a copyright notice is not the name of the copyright owner, the copyright in the work is not affected. In some cases, innocent infringers are protected if they were misled by the recital of the wrong person in the copyright notice.[102] A copyright notice that recites a year of first publication that is more than one year later than the year in which publication in fact first occurred, the work is considered to have been published without any notice. If the notice recites a year of first publication that is earlier than the actual year of first publication, the copyright in the work is not affected, but any period of time computed from the year of publication for purposes of any provision in the copyright law is computed from the erroneous date.[103] If a copyright notice contains either no name or no date, the work is considered to have been published without any notice.[104]

The Deposit Requirement   § 9-05.02

Key point 9-05.2. *Copyright owners must "deposit" two copies of their work with the Copyright Office within three months of publication. Failure to do so may result in fines or penalties, but it will not affect the copyright in a work.*

Although copyright registration is not required, the Copyright Act establishes a mandatory deposit requirement for works published with notice of copyright in the United States. In general, the copyright owner, or the owner of the exclusive right of publication in a work, has a legal obligation to deposit in the Copyright

---

[101] *Id.* at § 405(b).

[102] *Id.* at § 406(a).

[103] *Id.* at § 406(b).

[104] *Id.* at § 406(c).

Office, within three months of publication, two copies (or in the case of sound recordings, two phonorecords) for the use of the Library of Congress. Failure to make the deposit can result in fines and penalties, but does not affect copyright protection.

Section 408(b) of the Act specifies that a single deposit can satisfy both the deposit and registration requirements. This provision requires that the single copy must be accompanied by the prescribed application and registration fee. The Copyright Office regulations exempt various kinds of works from the deposit requirements, including sermons and speeches (when published individually and not as a collection of the works of one or more authors), literary or musical works published only as embodied in phonorecords, computer programs published only in the form of machine-readable copies, and works first published as individual contributions to collective works.

Copyright Ownership §9-05.03

Key point 9-05.03. *Copyright ownership vests initially in the author of a work.*

Who owns the copyright in a work, and what difference does it make? Section 201(a) of the Copyright Act states simply that "copyright in a work . . . vests initially in the author or authors of the work." The Act goes on to state that "the authors of a joint work are coowners of copyright in the work." Again, this is straightforward and needs no explanation. There is one aspect of copyright ownership that is more difficult to understand, namely, a "work made for hire." Works made for hire are addressed in the following section.

Works Made for Hire §9-05.04

Key point 9-05.04. *Works created by employees within the scope of their employment are "works made for hire." The employer is deemed to be the "author" of such a work, and owns the copyright in it unless it executes a signed writing assigning the copyright back to the employee.*

1. In General

It is common for church employees to compose music or write books or articles in their church office during office hours. What often is not understood is that such persons do not necessarily own the copyright in the works they create. While the one who creates a work generally is its author and the initial owner of the copyright in the work, section 201(b) of the Copyright Act specifies that "in the case of a work made for hire, the employer or other person for whom the work was prepared is considered the author . . . and, unless the parties have expressly agreed otherwise in a written instrument signed by them, owns all of the rights comprised in the copyright."

The copyright law defines "work made for hire" as "a work prepared by an employee within the scope of his or her employment." There are two requirements that must be met: (1) the person creating the work is an employee, and (2) the employee created the work within the scope of his or her employment. Whether or not one is an employee will depend on the same factors used in determining whether one is an employee or self-employed for federal income tax reporting purposes.[105] However, the courts have been very liberal in finding employee status in this context, so it is possible that a court would conclude that a work is a work made for hire even though the author reports his or her federal income taxes as a self-employed person.

The second requirement is that the work must have been created within the scope of employment. This requirement generally means that the work was created during regular working hours, on the employer's premises, using the employer's staff and equipment. This is often a difficult standard to apply. As a result, it is desirable for church employees to discuss this issue with the church leadership to avoid any potential misunderstandings.

Examples

• Pastor B is senior minister of his church. He is in the process of writing a devotional book. Most of the writing is done during regular church office hours, in his office in the church, using church equipment and a church secretary. Pastor B's contract of employment does not address the issue of copyright ownership in the book, and no written agreement has ever been executed by the church that addresses the matter. Under these facts, it is likely that the book is a work made for hire. The result is that the church is the author of the book, it is the copyright owner, and it has the sole legal right to assign or transfer the copyright in the book.

• Pastor T is minister of music at her church. She has composed several songs and choruses, all of which were written during regular office hours at the church, using church equipment (piano, paper, etc.). The church has never addressed the issue of copyright ownership in a signed writing. It is likely that the songs and choruses are works made for hire. The result is that the church is the author of these materials, it is the copyright owner, and it has the sole legal right to assign or transfer the copyright in these works.

• Same facts as the preceding example, except that Pastor T composes the music in the evening and on weekends in her home. While she is an employee, she did not compose the music "within the scope of her employment," and therefore the music cannot be characterized as works made for hire. The legal effect of this conclusion is that Pastor W owns the copyright in the music, and is free to sell or transfer such works in any manner she chooses without church approval.

• Same facts as the previous example, except that Pastor T composes many of her works both at home and at the church office. Whether or not a particular work is a work made for hire is a difficult question under these circumstances. The answer will

---

[105] *See* R. HAMMAR, CHURCH AND CLERGY TAX GUIDE chapter 2 (published annually by the publisher of this text).

depend upon the following factors: (1) the portion of the work that is composed at the church office, compared to the portion composed at home; (2) the portion of the work created with church equipment, compared to the portion created with Pastor T's personal equipment; (3) the portion of the work created during regular office hours, compared to the portion created after hours; and (4) the adequacy of Pastor T's personal records to document each of these factors. Unfortunately, a staff member's records may be inadequate. In such a case, work made for hire status will depend upon the staff member's own testimony, and the testimony of other witnesses (such as other staff members).

2. The Parties "Expressly Agree Otherwise"

Section 201(b) of the Copyright Act, quoted above, specifies that "in the case of a work made for hire, the employer or other person for whom the work was prepared is considered the author . . . and, *unless the parties have expressly agreed otherwise in a written instrument signed by them,* owns all of the rights comprised in the copyright." This provision permits an employer and employee to execute a written, signed agreement that recognizes the employee as the owner of "all of the rights comprised in the copyright." To illustrate, a church and its senior pastor could agree, in a signed writing, that the pastor owns all of the rights comprised in the copyright to his or her creative works.

A question that often arises is whether the church's tax-exempt status is jeopardized by such an agreement. One of the conditions for exemption from federal income taxation is that none of a church's assets inure to the private benefit of any individual (other than as reasonable compensation for services rendered). Is this condition violated when a church agrees that an employee retains the rights to works that he or she creates? In answering this question, there are two points that must be considered:

First, neither the IRS, nor any court, has ever revoked the tax-exempt status of a religious organization on the ground that it allowed employees to retain the rights to works made for hire and that this arrangement constituted prohibited inurement of the church's assets to private benefit.

Second, it is helpful to consider the example of private universities. Private universities are exempt under section 501(c)(3) of the Internal Revenue Code, as are churches and other religious organizations. Many if not most private universities have adopted copyright policies that allow professors to retain the rights to the material they create in the scope of their employment (i.e., lectures, notes, audiovisual presentations), consistent with long-standing academic tradition. This means that professors are free to use their lectures, notes, and related materials if they accept a position at another academic institution. Some of these policies create exceptions in the case of material specifically commissioned by the university. A typical university policy states, in relevant part:

COPYRIGHT OWNERSHIP; ASSERTION OF RIGHTS

A. Traditional Faculty Authorship Rights - In keeping with longstanding academic custom, the University recognizes faculty ownership of copyright in traditional works of authorship created by faculty such as textbooks, other works of nonfiction and novels, articles, or other creative works, such as poems, musical compositions and visual works of art, whether such works are disseminated in print or electronically.

B. **Assertion of Rights by the University** - The University asserts copyright ownership in any work of authorship that is: (i) created with substantial use of University resources, financial support or non-faculty University personnel beyond the level of common resources provided to faculty; (ii) created or commissioned for use by the University; or (iii) created under the terms of a sponsored project where the terms of the sponsored project require that copyright be in the name of the University. . . .

This policy represents a written agreement by the university and its faculty that recognizes "traditional faculty authorship rights" in lectures, notes, articles, and related materials. Note that this is not a formal assignment or transfer of rights by the university to faculty members. Rather, it is a mutual acknowledgment of the traditional rights of faculty to the works they create in the course of their employment, and thereby satisfies section 201(b) of the Copyright Act, quoted above, which permits employers and employees to expressly agree in a written instrument signed by them that the employer does not own all of the rights comprised in the copyright to a work made for hire. It is less likely that such an agreement will result in prohibited inurement of the university's assets than if the university assigned its rights in a work made for hire to the employee after the work's creation. It is perhaps for this reason that the IRS has never revoked the tax-exempt status of a private college or university for adopting a similar copyright policy.

The point, of course, is that churches and other religious organizations should be treated in the same manner. Most clergy would be shocked to learn that their sermons are works made for hire that are owned by their employing church, and that their sermons cannot be used in any other churches with which they are later employed without the permission of the church with which they were employed when the sermons were created. This can become a contentious issue in the case of clergy whose sermons are recorded and sold publicly by the church. Should a pastor leave a church, and accept a position with another church, who has the legal authority to fulfill requests for recorded sermons that were created while employed by the former church? Such confusion can be eliminated through an appropriate copyright policy. Such a policy should be drafted by an attorney with experience in handling intellectual property issues.

If a church fails to adopt an appropriate copyright policy, then the issue of inurement is more clearly implicated should a church formally assign its rights in a work made for hire to the employee who created it.

DID YOU KNOW?
Doing Outside Work at Home

Do you have a writer or composer on staff at your church? If so, it is possible that this person is doing some writing or composing on church premises, using church equipment, during office hours. One way to avoid the problems associated with work made for hire status is to encourage staff members to do all their writing and composing at home. Tell staff members that (1) if they do any writing or composing at church during office hours, their works may be works made for hire; and (2) the church owns the copyright in such works. By urging staff members to do all their personal writing and composing at home, the church also will avoid the difficult question of whether works that are written partly at home and partly at the office are works made for hire.

However, it is likely that pastors' sermons will be considered works made for hire, whenever and wherever they are composed, since sermons are the most important function that a pastor performs.

Prior to the enactment of the Copyright Act of 1976, it was generally assumed that professors' lectures were an exception to the work for hire doctrine.[106] Perhaps the best example of this view is a decision by a California appeals court in 1969.[107] The court addressed directly the question of whether a professor or his employing university owned the copyright in the professor's lectures. In ruling that the professor owned the copyright, the court observed:

Indeed the undesirable consequences which would follow from a holding that a university owns the copyright to the lectures of its professors are such as to compel a holding that it does not. Professors are a peripatetic lot, moving from campus to campus. The courses they teach begin to take shape at one institution and are developed and embellished at other. That, as a matter of fact, was the case here. [The professor] testified that the notes on which his lectures were based were derived from a similar course which he had given at another university. If [this] is correct, there must be some rights of that school which were infringed at [the professor's current university]. Further, should [he] leave [his current university] and give a substantially similar course at his next post, [the university] would be able to enjoin him from using the material, which according to [the university], it owns.

---

[106] *See, e.g.,* R. Dreyfuss, *The Creative Employee and the Copyright Act of 1976,* 54 Univ. Chi. L. Rev. 590 (1987).

[107] Williams v. Weisser, 78 Cal. Rptr. 542 (Cal. App. 1969).

The court referred to a federal appeals court decision addressing the copyright ownership in Admiral Rickover's speeches.[108] The speeches in question were prepared by the admiral after normal working hours or while traveling. The California court noted that

> a person in Admiral Rickover's position . . . has no normal working hours any more than a university professor. Whatever distinctions between "on" and "off-duty" hours might be appropriate in the case of an hourly employee who punches a clock, they are quite out of place in cases such as Rickover and the one at bar. . . . It is thus apparent that no authority supports the argument that the copyright to [professor's] notes is in the university. The indications from the authorities are the other way and so is common sense.

It is important to note that any special exemption professors' notes enjoyed from the work made for hire doctrine was undermined if not abolished by the Copyright Act of 1976. As noted above, the section 201(b) of the Act specifies that "in the case of a work made for hire, the employer . . . is considered the author . . . and, unless the parties have expressly agreed otherwise in a written instrument signed by them, owns all of the rights comprised in the copyright." As a result, cases decided before 1978 (when the Act took effect) are of limited relevance, since prior copyright law contained no provision comparable to section 201. Copyright ownership in a minister's sermons likely will be determined by focusing on whether or not the minister created the sermons within the scope of his or her employment, and the terms of any copyright policy adopted by the church.

Key point. *The pre-1978 view that professors owned the copyright in the works they created in the course of their employment remains relevant for two reasons. First, it corroborates the "traditional view," frequently cited in university copyright policies, that professors own the results of their labor. Second, neither the IRS nor any court, prior to 1978, ruled that this traditional position jeopardized the tax-exempt status of any college or university as a result of the "inurement" of school assets to the private benefit of individuals. This is strong, though not conclusive, evidence that such policies (before of after 1978) do not constitute prohibited inurement.*

Case Study

A federal appeals court ruled that books written by a religious leader were not works made for hire and therefore the leader himself, rather than the organization for which he worked, was the owner of the copyright in the books. The court noted that the books in question were written prior to the enactment of the Copyright Act of 1976, and so it applied the works made for hire provision under prior copyright law (the Copyright Act of 1909).[109]

---

[108] Public Affairs Associates, Inc. v. Rickover, 284 F.2d 262 (D.C. Cir. 1960).

[109] Self-Realization Fellowship Church v. Ananda Church of Self-Realization, 206 F.3d 1322 (9th Cir. 2000).

Duration of Copyright Protection

§ 9-05.05

Key point 9-05.05. *The copyright term for most works created after 1977 is the life of the author plus 70 years. The term for works published prior to 1978, and in their initial or renewal copyright term as of October 27, 1998, is 95 years from the date of the original copyright.*

A copyright does not last for an indefinite or unlimited time. The provision in the United States Constitution giving Congress authority to create copyright protection specifies that such protection shall be only "for limited times." The "limited times" vary depending upon the circumstances. Under the copyright law that was in effect before 1978, copyright was secured either on the date a work was published (with an appropriate copyright notice), or on the date of registration if the work was registered in unpublished form. In either case, the copyright lasted for a first term of 28 years from the date it was secured. During the last (28th) year of the first term, the copyright was eligible for renewal. If renewed, the copyright was extended for a second term of 28 years. If not renewed, the copyright expired at the end of the first 28-year term.

Congress enacted legislation in 1992 and 1998 amending the duration of copyrights.[110] The current duration rules are as follows:

(1) Works originally copyrighted before 1950 and renewed before 1978

These works have automatically been given a longer copyright term. Copyrights that had already been renewed and were in their second term at any time between December 31, 1976, and December 31, 1977, do not need to be renewed again. They have been automatically extended to last for a total term of 95 years (a first term of 28 years plus a renewal term of 67 years) from the end of the year in which they were originally secured. Note two important points:

• This extension applies not only to copyrights less than 56 years old but also to older copyrights that had previously been extended in duration under a series of Congressional enactments beginning in 1962. As in the case of all other copyrights subsisting in their second term between December 31, 1976, and December 31, 1977, inclusive, these copyrights will expire at the end of the calendar year in which the 95th anniversary of the original date of copyright occurs.

• A special transitional situation arose with respect to first-term copyrights that were originally secured in 1950 and that became eligible for renewal during the calendar year 1977. If renewal registration was made before January 1, 1978, the duration of the copyright was extended to the full period of 75 years without the need for further renewal. However, even if renewal registration was not made before

---

[110] The Sonny Bono Copyright Term Extension Act, signed into law on October 27, 1998, amends section 302 of the Copyright Act.

January 1, 1978, renewal for the second 47-year term could be made under the 1976 law at any time between January 1, 1978, and December 31, 1978.

(2) Works originally copyrighted between January 1, 1950, and December 31, 1963

Copyrights in their first 28-year term on January 1, 1978, still had to be renewed in order to be protected for the second term. If a valid renewal registration was made at the proper time, the second term will last for 67 years. However, if renewal registration for these works was not made within the statutory time limits, a copyright originally secured between 1950 and 1963 expired on December 31st of its 28th year, and protection was lost permanently.

(3) Works originally copyrighted between January 1, 1964, and December 31, 1977

A 1992 amendment to the copyright law makes renewal registration optional. The copyright is still divided between a 28-year original term and a 67-year renewal term, but a renewal registration is not required to secure the renewal copyright. The renewal vests on behalf of the appropriate renewal claimant upon registration or, if there is no renewal registration, on December 31 of the 28th year.

Key point. *The 1998 legislation extending copyright terms does not restore protection to works that are in the public domain.*

(4) Works originally copyrighted after 1977

For works created and fixed in a tangible medium of expression for the first time on or after January 1, 1978, the Copyright Act of 1976 as amended in 1998 establishes a single copyright term and different methods for computing the duration of a copyright. Works of this sort fall into two categories:

• **Works created on or after January 1, 1978.** For works created after its effective date, the U.S. copyright law adopts the basic "life-plus-seventy" system already in effect in most other countries. A work that is created (fixed in tangible form for the first time) on or after January 1, 1978, is automatically protected from the moment of its creation and is given a term lasting for the author's life, plus an additional 70 years after the author's death.

In the case of "a joint work prepared by two or more authors who did not work for hire," the term lasts for 70 years after the last surviving author's death. For works made for hire, and for anonymous and pseudonymous works (unless the author's identity is revealed in Copyright Office records), the duration of copyright will be 95 years from first publication or 120 years from creation, whichever is shorter.

• **Works in existence but not published or copyrighted on January 1, 1978.**
Works that had been created before the current law came into effect but had neither been published nor registered for copyright before January 1, 1978, automatically are given federal copyright protection. The duration of copyright in these works will generally be computed in the same way as for new works: the life-plus-70 or 95/120-year terms will apply to them as well. However, all works

in this category are guaranteed at least 25 years of statutory protection. The law specifies that in no case will copyright in a work of this sort expire before December 31, 2002, and if the work is published before that date the term will extend another 45 years, through the end of 2047.

Registration

Key point 9-05.06. *Copyright owners may register their works with the Copyright Office. While this is not a legal requirement, it does provide copyright owners with valuable benefits.*

The owner of a copyright in a work may register the copyright claim by delivering two complete copies of the best edition of a published work or one complete copy of an unpublished work, along with an application form and a nominal application fee to the Copyright Office. Deposits made to fulfill the deposit requirements of Section 407 may be used to satisfy the deposit requirements for registration if they are accompanied by the appropriate application form and the prescribed fee.

Section 408(a) unequivocally states that "registration is not a condition of copyright protection." While registration is not necessary to secure copyright protection, it is advisable in some cases for a variety of reasons, including the following:

1. It is an inexpensive and simple procedure.

2. It establishes a public record or a copyright claim.

3. Section 411 of the Copyright Act provides that "no action for infringement of the copyright in any work shall be instituted until registration of the copyright claim has been made . . . ." This is a significant advantage of registration. If the copyright claim has not been registered, the copyright owner cannot seek redress in the civil courts for acts of infringement. A number of courts have held, however, that a copyright owner of an unregistered work can sue an infringer by simply registering the claim of copyright even though the infringement occurred prior to registration. This rule would not apply if the infringement suit were brought after the limitations period (generally 3 years) following the initial act of infringement.

4. Section 504(c) of the Copyright Act allows a copyright owner to collect "statutory damages" from an infringer in lieu of proving actual damages. Statutory damages often comprise the only meaningful measure of damages since actual damages are difficult to prove. However, section 412 specifies that "no award of statutory damages . . . shall be made for (1) any infringement of copyright in an unpublished work commenced before the effective date of its registration, or (2) any infringement of copyright commenced after first publication of the work and before the

effective date of its registration, unless such registration is made within three months after the first publication of the work."

5. Section 410(c) provides that "in any judicial proceedings the certificate of a registration made before or within five years after first publication of the work shall constitute prima facie evidence of the validity of the copyright and of the facts stated in the certificate." What is the significance of this rule? Simply this—a copyright claimant who has registered a claim of copyright in a work within five years before or after first publication does not have the burden of proving the validity of the copyright claim in an infringement suit.

6. Section 205(c) of the Copyright Act provides that "recordation of a document in the Copyright Office gives all persons constructive notice of the facts stated in the recorded document, but only if . . . registration has been made for the work." This provision means that the public is "on notice" of any transfers, licenses, mortgages, and other documents pertaining to copyrights if such documents are recorded in the Copyright Office and the underlying works are registered.

7. Generally, omission of a valid copyright notice from a work first published before March 1, 1989 invalidates the copyright in the work. However, section 405(a)(2) of the Copyright Act provides that omission of the notice on such a work will not invalidate the copyright if "registration for the work has been made before or is made within five years after the publication without notice, and a reasonable effort is made to add notice to all copies or phonorecords that are distributed to the public in the United States after the omission has been discovered."

8. The Copyright Office reviews every application for registration to ensure that the legal formalities needed to ensure protection are satisfied. Often, the Copyright Office will call to the attention of a copyright owner an error in the registration application or in the copyright notice that can ensure that copyright protection is preserved. This review, however, is limited to the applicant's compliance with technical requirements. The merits of a particular claim of copyright ordinarily are not evaluated.

9. Registration of a copyright in some cases may enhance the marketability of an author's or composer's work. For example, a person checking Copyright Office records on a particular subject may inadvertently find a work, and contact the copyright owner regarding a publishing opportunity.

10. Registration of a musical work may entitle the copyright owner to "compulsory royalty payments" in the event that someone else makes a recording of the work. This provision has special relevance in the context of audio recording of church worship services in which copyrighted music is performed.

11. Registration allows the owner of the copyright to record the registration with the U. S. Customs Service for protection against the importation of infringing copies.

Registration may be made at any time within the life of the copyright. Unlike the law before 1978, when a work has been registered in unpublished form, it is not necessary to make another registration when the work becomes published, although the copyright owner may register the published edition, if desired.

Copyright registration is a fairly simple procedure in many cases. To register a work, send the following three items in the same envelope or package to the Register of Copyrights, Copyright Office, Library of Congress, Washington, D.C. 20559:

(a) *A properly completed application form.* Complete the application using black ink or a typewriter, and either an original Copyright Office form or a clear photocopy made on a good grade of white paper. Applications not meeting these requirements will be returned. There are several registration forms. The more commonly used forms include: (a) Form TX for non-dramatic literary works (e.g., compilations, computer programs, contributions to periodicals, dissertations, fiction, lectures, letters, nonfiction, poetry, sermons, song lyrics without music), (b) Form PA for published and unpublished works of the performing arts (musical and dramatic works, choreographic works, motion pictures and other audiovisual works), and (c) Form SR for published and unpublished sound recordings (e.g., music, sermons).

(b) *A nonrefundable filing fee per application.*

(c) *A nonrefundable deposit of the work being registered.* The deposit requirements vary in particular situations. Generally, two copies of the work must be filed along with the registration application. Section 408(b) of the Copyright Act specifies that the deposit and registration requirements can be satisfied simultaneously.

The Copyright Owner's Exclusive Rights

§ 9-05.07

Key point 9-05.07. *The Copyright Act gives copyright owners the following exclusive rights—reproduction, adaptation, distribution, performance, and display. Anyone who violates one or more of these exclusive rights commits copyright infringement.*

Section 106 of the Copyright Act gives a copyright owner the following five "exclusive rights":

(a) to reproduce the copyrighted work in copies or phonorecords;

(b) to prepare derivative works based upon the copyrighted work;

(c) to distribute copies or phonorecords of the copyrighted work to the public by sale or other transfer of ownership, or by rental, lease, or lending;

(d) in the case of literary, musical, dramatic, and choreographic works, pantomimes, and motion pictures and other audiovisual works, to perform the copyrighted work publicly; and

(e) in the case of literary, musical, dramatic, and choreographic works, pantomimes, and pictorial, graphic, or sculptural works, including the individual images of a motion picture or other audiovisual work, to display the copyrighted work publicly.

These five exclusive rights are sometimes referred to as the rights of reproduction, adaptation, publication, performance, and display. They comprise the "bundle of rights" that constitute or define copyright. It is unlawful for anyone to violate any of the exclusive rights of a copyright owner. These rights, however, are not unlimited in scope. The approach of the Copyright Act is to set forth the copyright owner's exclusive rights in broad terms in section 106, and then to provide various limitations, qualifications, or exemptions in sections 107 through 118 of the Act.

Infringement

§ 9-05.08

Key point 9-05.08. *Copyright infringement occurs when one violates any one or more of the exclusive rights of a copyright owner.*

Section 501 of the Copyright Act states that "anyone who violates any of the exclusive rights of the copyright owner . . . is an infringer of the copyright." Of the five exclusive rights, the one causing the most difficulties for churches is the copyright owner's exclusive right to reproduce the work (i.e., make copies). Obviously, an infringement occurs when someone makes a verbatim copy of copyrighted material. But what if someone produces a work that is similar but not identical to another's copyrighted work? Can this constitute infringement on the copyright owner's exclusive right of reproduction?

The courts generally have resolved this question by applying the following presumption—access by the alleged infringer to the copyrighted material, plus substantial similarity between the allegedly infringing material and the copyrighted work, creates a presumption of infringement. The alleged infringer of course can claim that his work was an independent creation. However, the closer the similarity between the two works, the less likely it is that such a claim will prevail. Other relevant factors to consider in such a case would be the experience and training of the alleged infringer, his previous publishing record, the likelihood that he was capable of independently producing the work, and prior instances of infringement on his part. Some copyright owners intentionally insert errors in their works. The alleged infringer's claim of independent creation will seldom succeed if such errors are duplicated.

The House Report to the Copyright Act of 1976 specifies that "wide departures or variations from the copyrighted work would still be an infringement as long as the author's 'expression' rather than merely the author's 'ideas' are taken."[111]

Such precedent leaves little doubt that most reproductions of copyrighted materials by churches will constitute an infringement of the exclusive right of copyright owners to reproduce their works. To cite just a few examples—the copying of copyrighted chorus or hymn lyrics onto a transparency or bulletin insert ordinarily will amount to an infringement, since a substantial quantity of the original work is reproduced, the amount reproduced is significant in terms of quality, and the copy serves the same function as the original work. To illustrate, in one case a publisher reproduced the chorus lyrics of two famous copyrighted songs in songsheet pamphlets, maintaining that the reproduction of only chorus lyrics of copyrighted songs was so trivial in nature and amount as to constitute noninfringing fair use. The court found such reproductions to be an infringement, and rejected the publisher's claim that its reproductions constituted fair use. Though only the chorus lyrics were reproduced (and not the regular verse lines or music), the court found that "the chorus of a musical composition may constitute a material and substantial part of the work and it is frequently the very part that makes it popular and valuable."[112]

Similarly, another court found the reproduction of chorus lyrics in a song sheet magazine to be an infringement rather than fair use, since the reproduction "met the same demand on the same market" as the original.[113] The courts in each of these two cases gave a narrow interpretation of fair use because the function served by the infringing use directly satisfied a function that was served by the copyright owner's sheet music.

Obviously, verbatim copying of the lyrics and melody of a copyrighted musical work (for use by the choir, a soloist, an accompanist, or an instrumental group) would constitute infringement.

Often overlooked is the fact that both the musical score and lyrics of a hymn or chorus are eligible for copyright protection. Section 102(a) of the Copyright Act states that copyright protection subsists in original "musical works, including any accompanying words," that are reduced to a tangible form. Persons who compose both the music and lyrics of an original hymn are entitled to copyright protection for both. This has important consequences. It means, primarily, that no one can make copies of either the music or lyrics without authorization. To illustrate, a church will infringe upon this copyright protection if it inserts only the words of a particular song in a booklet or on a songsheet, or types them on a piece of paper and projects them onto a screen.

---

[111] House Report on the Copyright Act of 1976, p. 61.

[112] Johns & Johns Printing Co. v. Paull-Pioneer Music Corp., 102 F.2d 282 (8th Cir. 1939).

[113] Leo Feist, Inc. v. Song Parodies, Inc., 146 F.2d 400 (2nd Cir. 1944).

It is also important to recognize that one of the copyright owner's exclusive rights is the right to prepare derivative works based upon the copyrighted work. Derivative works include musical arrangements. Therefore, it is not permissible for anyone other than the copyright owner or one whom the copyright owner has authorized to create an arrangement of a copyrighted musical work. To illustrate, one church choir director who made a choral arrangement of a copyrighted hymn without authorization was found to be guilty of copyright infringement.[114] The director's arrangement consisted of the entire score of the copyrighted hymn plus the insertion of a four-measure introduction. The director made several copies of his arrangement on the church's duplicating machine. Each copy contained the director's name and identified him as the arranger. The copyright owner brought a lawsuit against the director and his church, alleging copyright infringement. A federal appeals court found the director and his employing church jointly liable for copyright infringement. The court found the director's lack of intent to infringe to be irrelevant, and concluded that the copying of all or substantially all of a copyrighted musical work could not be considered "fair use."

It is permissible to make arrangements of preexisting musical works if the preexisting work is in the public domain or if the copyright owner of the preexisting work grants permission. Section 103 of the Act states that lawfully made derivative works are entitled to copyright protection if they otherwise qualify. Section 103 also stipulates that copyright protection in a derivative work extends only to the material contributed by the author of such work as distinguished from the preexisting material employed in the work. Thus, although a musical arrangement of a public domain song is subject to copyright protection, the copyright protection extends only to the new musical score and not to the lyrics of the preexisting work. As a result, churches can copy the lyrics of such arrangements without infringing the arranger's copyright.

A federal court has rejected the claim that the First Amendment right to freely exercise one's religion immunized from liability for copyright infringement a group of priests who toured the country giving unauthorized performances of the rock opera *Jesus Christ Superstar*.[115]

Case Studies

• *A religious radio station that broadcast copyrighted religious music without permission was found guilty of "willful infringement" and was assessed statutory damages of $52,500. The station manager admitted that he played copyrighted songs on the radio, and that he had no license or permission to do so. He defended his actions by noting that "the artists have publicly stated their intent to minister through their Christian music" and that "their intent to minister is further accomplished by radio stations broadcasting their music to a listening audience." The court rejected this reasoning and assessed statutory damages of $52,500 against the station for willful copyright infringement. The court based this result on 15 proven infringements at*

---

[114] Wihtol v. Crow, 309 F.2d 777 (8th Cir. 1962).

[115] Robert Stigwood Group Limited v. O'Reilly, 346 F. Supp. 376 (D. Conn. 1972), *rev'd on other grounds,* 530 F.2d 1096 (2nd Cir. 1976), *cert. denied,* 429 U.S. 848 (1976).

$3,500 each. The court also ordered the station to pay the attorneys fees the copyright owners incurred in maintaining their infringement lawsuit. This case serves as a useful reminder of the consequences associated with the willful infringement of another's copyright. It is common for church leaders to assume that they can infringe upon religious music or literature at will since the writers and composers of such material obviously had a religious motivation and in effect have "donated" their work to the church. Not only is this assumption inappropriate, but as this case demonstrates, it can lead to statutory damages for willful infringement.[116]

• A federal court in Massachusetts ruled that a trade show organizer was liable for copyright infringement occurring because of the unauthorized performance of copyrighted music by 6 of 2,000 exhibitors at a national trade show. This was so despite the fact that the organizer's contract with exhibitors contained a statement instructing exhibitors to comply with copyright law. This did not shift liability. The court concluded that the organizer retained sufficient control over the exhibitors to make it responsible for their copyright infringement. Control was demonstrated by (1) the rules and regulations that the organizer had established for exhibitors; (2) agents of the organizer circulated among the exhibitors to "ensure compliance" with the rules and regulations; (3) agents of the organizer were available during the convention to address exhibitor needs and respond to complaints; and (4) the organizer had the authority to restrict exhibits that were objectionable. The court stressed that the organizer could have prohibited exhibitors from playing or performing copyrighted music, but did not. The fact that exhibitors' contracts required them to comply with the copyright law did not prevent the organizer from liability for the exhibitors' copyright infringements, since the organizer "must shoulder responsibility when the instruction is not followed." The court awarded damages of $1,000 for each violation (a total of $6,000).[117]

• A federal appeals court ruled that copyright infringement had occurred even though only lyrics were copied. The court observed: "Song lyrics enjoy independent copyright protection as literary works . . . and the right to print a song's lyrics is exclusively that of the copyright holder. . . . A time-honored method of facilitating singing along with music has been to furnish the singer with a printed copy of the lyrics. Copyright holders have always enjoyed exclusive rights over such copies. While projecting lyrics on a screen and producing printed copies of the lyrics, of course, have their differences, there is no reason to treat them differently for purposes of the Copyright Act." Many churches make unauthorized copies of song lyrics. Sometimes the lyrics are printed in a church bulletin. In other cases they are duplicated onto a transparency. In either case, or in any other case when lyrics are copied without authorization, copyright infringement has occurred. Church leaders need to understand that lyrics are entitled to copyright protection independently from the musical score.[118]

• A federal appeals court ruled that a church violates the copyright law when it publicly distributes an unauthorized copy of copyrighted materials. The Church of Jesus Christ of Latter-Day Saints (the "Church") acquired a single copy of a copyrighted genealogical text and made several unauthorized copies which were distributed to the

---

[116] Meadowgreen Music Company v. Voice in the Wilderness Broadcasting, Inc., 789 F. Supp. 823 (E.D. Tex. 1992).

[117] Polygram International Publishing, Inc. v. NEVADA/TIG, Inc., 855 F. Supp. 1314 (D. Mass. 1994).

[118] ABKCO v. Stellar Records, 96 F.3d 60 (2nd Cir. 1996).

Church's "branch libraries." When the copyright owner learned of the Church's actions, it demanded that further distribution be stopped immediately. The Church recalled and destroyed many of the copies that it had made. It was concerned that nine libraries continued to possess unauthorized copies, and it wrote them each a letter asking them to locate and return any offending copies. The copyright owner visited a number of libraries, and found unauthorized copies at two locations. The owner sued the Church for copyright infringement. A federal appeals court ruled that the Church might be liable for copyright infringement. It observed: "A copyright infringement is a violation of any of the exclusive rights of the copyright owner. One of those exclusive rights is the right to distribute copies . . . of the copyrighted work to the public by sale or other transfer of ownership, or by rental, lease, or lending. Generally, as permitted by what is known as the first-sale doctrine, the copyright owner's right to distribute a copyrighted work does not prevent the owner of a lawful copy of the work from selling, renting, lending, or otherwise disposing of the lawful copy. For example, a library may lend an authorized copy of a book that it lawfully owns without violating the copyright laws. However, distributing unlawful copies of a copyrighted work does violate the copyright owner's distribution right and, as a result, constitutes copyright infringement. In order to establish distribution of a copyrighted work, a party must show that an unlawful copy was disseminated to the public." The court agreed with the copyright owner in this case that when a library "adds a work to its collection, lists the work in its index or catalog system, and makes the work available to the borrowing or browsing public, it has completed all the steps necessary for distribution to the public."[119]

• A federal appeals court ruled that Andrew Lloyd Webber may have engaged in copyright infringement of a religious song composed by Ray Repp, a composer of liturgical music. Ray Repp has written religious music for more than thirty years, and is a leading composer and performer of liturgical folk music. His music is included in many hymnals and songbooks, and has been published by the Lutheran, Episcopal, Presbyterian, and Catholic churches as well as by the Church of the Brethren. In 1978 he wrote the song "Till You." The song is liturgical in nature, and is based on passages from the Book of Luke commonly known as the "Magnificat." It has been distributed on albums and cassettes, as well as 25,000 copies of sheet music. Repp claimed that Andrew Lloyd Webber had access to this song and unlawfully copied it in writing the "Phantom Song" in his musical "The Phantom of the Opera." A federal district court dismissed the lawsuit largely on the basis of Webber's own testimony that he never heard the song, that he disliked "pop church music," and that his interest in church music was limited to the "English choral tradition." Repp appealed, and a federal appeals court reversed the district court's ruling and ordered the case to proceed to trial. The court noted that "if the two works are so strikingly similar as to preclude the possibility of independent creation, copying may be proved without a showing of access." The court continued: "While there was little, if any, evidence demonstrating access, there was considerable evidence that Phantom Song is so strikingly similar to Till You as to preclude the possibility of independent creation and to allow access to be inferred without direct proof." In support of its conclusion the court referred to two expert musicologists who had testified that there was "no doubt" that Webber's "Phantom Song" was strikingly similar to and based upon "Till You."[120]

---

[119] Hotaling v. Church of Jesus Christ of Latter-Day Saints, 118 F.3d 199 (4th Cir. 1997).

[120] Repp v. Webber, 132 F.3d 862 (2nd Cir. 1997).

The "Religious Service" Exemption to Copyright Infringement

§ 9-05.09

Key point 9-05.09. *A copyrighted musical or dramatico-musical work of a religious nature may be performed or displayed in the course or services at a place of religious worship or other religious assembly. This is an exception to the copyright owner's exclusive right to publicly perform the work.*

Section 110(3) of the Copyright Act specifies that the "performance of a nondramatic literary or musical work or of a dramatico-musical work of a religious nature, or display of a work, in the course of services at a place of worship or other religious assembly" is not an infringement of copyright. *Performance of a nondramatic literary work* means reading from a book or periodical in a nondramatic manner. Thus, for example, a copyrighted translation of the Bible can be quoted publicly in the course of religious services, as can any book or periodical of a religious nature.

Without the exception contained in section 110, such readings might constitute copyright infringement since one of a copyright owner's exclusive rights is the right to perform his work publicly. Similarly, a copyrighted musical work of a religious nature can be performed in the course of services at a place of worship or other religious assembly. Therefore copyrighted hymns, solo materials, orchestrations, and choral arrangements of a religious nature may be performed in religious services. Without the exception contained in section 110, such performances might constitute copyright infringements.

Dramatico-musical works of a religious nature may also be performed in the course of religious services. Such works include certain performances of sacred music that may be regarded as dramatic, such as oratorios and cantatas. Also exempted from copyright infringement are displays of works of all kinds in the course of religious services. The exemption is not intended to cover performances of secular operas, musical plays, motion pictures, and the like, even if they have an underlying religious or philosophical theme and take place in the course of religious services.

To be exempted under section 110, a performance or display must be "in the course of services," and thus activities at a place of worship that are for social, educational, fundraising, or entertainment purposes are excluded. Some performances of these kinds may be exempted under section 110(4). This section exempts from copyright infringement certain performances of nondramatic literary or musical works that are performed without admissions charge or that are performed with an admissions charge if the proceeds are used exclusively for educational, religious, or charitable purposes and not for private financial gain, unless the copyright owner has served notice of objection to the performance at least seven days before the performance.

Since the performance or display must also occur "at a place of worship or other religious assembly," the exemption would not extend to religious broadcasts or other transmissions to the public at large, even if the transmissions were sent from a place of worship. Nor would the exemption apply to the public distribution of tape recordings of religious services containing any copyrighted materials. Thus, while a copyrighted religious musical work may be performed at a religious service, publicly distributed tape recordings of the service that reproduce the copyrighted work do not constitute a performance of the work in the course of services at a place of worship and, accordingly, such recordings are not exempt under section 110. On the other hand, as long as services are being conducted before a religious assembly, the exemption would apply even if they were conducted in such places as auditoriums and outdoor theaters.

The exemption provided by section 110 exempts only religious performances in the course of religious services from copyright infringement. The Act states that to *perform* a work means to recite or render it. Performance of a copyrighted hymn or choral arrangement thus means to sing it, and performance of a copyrighted cantata means to present it. There is therefore no license to copy a copyrighted work, such as by duplicating a single piece of music for all of the members of a choir, since duplication does not constitute a performance even though the duplicated copies may eventually be used in a performance. Only the copyright owner has the right to reproduce a copyrighted work by making copies. Similarly, a church may not assemble a booklet of copyrighted hymns or choruses (lyrics or music) for use by its members in the course of religious services since this would necessitate copying the protected works. Of course, a church can duplicate a musical work or lyrics whose copyright term has expired or that never was subject to copyright protection since such works are considered to be in the public domain.

In 1976, a publisher of religious music sued the Catholic Bishop of Chicago as representative of various churches in the archdiocese of Chicago that allegedly were infringing upon the publisher's copyrights by unauthorized duplication and use of its songs in "homemade or pirated hymnals" prepared for use in worship services. As a result of an agreement between the parties, over 80,000 "homemade" hymnals and song collections containing the allegedly infringing materials were collected from parishes in Chicago and impounded by the court. Thereafter, the publisher investigated other large dioceses and archdioceses in the United States to determine if unauthorized copying was occurring elsewhere. The publisher, claiming to have found copyright violations nationwide, notified the bishop in each area that local parishes were violating the copyright law by reproducing the publisher's copyrighted music without permission in the "pirated" songbooks. The publisher requested the bishops' assistance in determining the extent of the violations, and in voluntarily compensating it for the violations. When no assistance or compensation was offered, the publisher sought a court injunction restraining the National Conference of Catholic Bishops (NCCB) and the United States Catholic Conference (USCC) from further violations of the copyright law.[121] Specifically, the publisher alleged that the NCCB and USCC violated the law by

---

[121] F.E.L. Publications v. National Conference of Catholic Bishops, 466 F. Supp. 1034 (N.D. Ill. 1978), *aff'd,* 754 F.2d 216 (7th Cir. 1985).

failing to provide adequate direction to the dioceses and parishes concerning the proper use of [the publisher's] copyrighted materials and thereby caused, permitted and materially contributed to the publication, distribution and/or sale in many of the archdioceses and dioceses . . . of songbooks including songs which were copies largely from [the publisher's] aforementioned copyrighted work.[122]

The court, while refusing to grant an injunction, did recognize that the publisher had stated a claim for which relief could be granted.

Case Study

• A federal district court in Alabama ruled that the religious services exemption to copyright infringement, which permits the performance of copyrighted religious music in the course of religious services, did not apply to broadcasts of those services. A radio station owner claimed that the religious services exemption allowed him to broadcast copyrighted compositions that were performed during church services. Section 110 of the Copyright Act creates an exemption to copyright infringement for the "performance of a nondramatic literary or musical work or of a dramatico-musical work of a religious nature, or display of a work, in the course of services at a place of worship or other religious assembly." The court observed:

> The critical language here is "at a place of worship or other religious assembly"; the exception says nothing about broadcasts in general and, more specifically, broadcasts from a place of worship. True, it could be argued the exemption should apply where, although the songs are being broadcast, there is an audience at the place of worship; in short, the exemption, it could be argued, should apply because the conditions to the exemption have been satisfied. Thus, it could be argued, the exemption should apply to all simultaneous performances as long as one of the performances falls within the exemption.

> However, the law is clear that radio broadcasting is itself a separate public performance which can constitute an infringement. Thus, the mere fact that a radio broadcast of a song is simultaneous with the playing of the song at a place of worship does not mean that broadcast falls within the religious exemption; playing to the audience at the place of worship and playing to a broadcast audience are separate public performances. . . . A singer is performing when he or she sings a song; a broadcasting network is performing when it transmits his or her performance; . . . a local broadcaster is performing when it transmits the network broadcast; a cable television system is performing when it retransmits the broadcast to its subscribers.

> This understanding of the religious exemption is supported by its legislative history, which provides that the exemption does "not extend to religious broadcasts or other transmissions to the public at large, even where the transmissions were sent from the place of worship." H. Rep. No. 94-1476.

---

[122] *Id.* at 1039.

As a result, the court concluded that the religious exemption did not allow the radio station owner "to broadcast copyrighted songs, performed during church services, without authorization, since such broadcasts are not 'at a place of worship.'"[123]

Other Exceptions to Copyright Infringement

§ 9-05.10

Key point 9-05.10. *There are several exceptions to copyright infringement, including fair use, religious displays, nonprofit performances, and authorization from a copyright owner to use his or her work.*

1. Fair Use

Section 107 of the Copyright Act specifies that

the fair use of a copyrighted work, including such use by reproduction in copies or phonorecords or by any other means specified [in section 106], for purposes such as criticism, comment, news reporting, teaching (including multiple copies for classroom use), scholarship, or research, is not an infringement of copyright. In determining whether the use made of a work in any particular case is a fair use the factors to be considered shall include—(1) the purpose and character of the use, including whether such use is of a commercial nature or is for nonprofit educational purposes; (2) the nature of the copyrighted work; (3) the amount and substantiality of the portion used in relation to the copyrighted work as a whole; and (4) the effect of the use upon the potential market for or value of the copyrighted work.

Fair use is one of the most common defenses invoked by persons charged with copyright infringement. Unfortunately, it is very difficult to define. Even section 107 does not define the term but rather recites "factors to be considered" in determining if a particular use is a fair use.

There is little doubt that many reproductions of copyrighted materials by churches will fail to constitute noninfringing fair use.

copying

Certainly any verbatim copying of an entire work will almost never constitute fair use. Examples of this type of copying include the duplication of a musical work for members of the choir, a bulletin insert, a soloist, accompanist, instrumental group, or for use as a transparency or slide. Even copying of a significant portion (in terms of either quantity or quality) of a copyrighted work ordinarily will fail to constitute noninfringing fair use. An example would be the copying of only the lyrics (and not the melody) of a copyrighted chorus or hymn. In all of these cases,

---

[123] Simpleville Music v. Mizell, 451 F.Supp.2d 1293 (M.D. Ala. 2006).

a finding of fair use will be unlikely because (1) such acts of copying constitute mere reproductions of a work in order to use it for its intrinsic purpose; (2) the nature of the work involved does not suggest a broad definition of fair use; (3) the amount of copyrighted material that is copied is significant in terms of both quantity and quality; (4) similar acts of copying by other churches would "adversely affect the market for or value of the copyrighted work." In other words, none of the four fair use factors ordinarily will support a finding of fair use.[124]

Another difficult question is the verbatim copying of only small portions of copyrighted material. When does such use constitute infringement on the copyright owner's exclusive right of reproduction? There is no easy answer to this question. Courts generally evaluate both the quantity of copyrighted material that is copied verbatim, and its quality. That is, what percentage of the copyrighted work was copied, and how much of the allegedly infringing work consisted of the copied material? Further, how significant was the "quality" of the copied material? Was it the essence of the work as a whole, or was it incidental or insignificant?

A federal appeals court, in a case involving a religious organization's unauthorized use of copyrighted materials, observed:

> The extent of copying must be assessed with respect to both the quantitative and the qualitative significance of the amount copied to the copyrighted work as a whole. In the first place, even if the borrowed expression from the book does not exceed one percent of defendants' course materials (itself a questionable calculation in light of defendants' overly narrow view of the book's protected expression), that argument is not really on point, because it is the relative portion of the copyrighted work—not the relative portion of the infringing work—that is the relevant comparison. Taken to its extreme, such a view would potentially permit the wholesale copying of a brief work merely by inserting it into a much longer work. Moreover, though the amount of expression copied may be quantitatively small with respect to the length of the book (constituting approximately 180 prose pages), the qualitative importance of the portion copied . . . is significant enough to preclude the grant of summary judgment for defendants on this ground. . . .

---

[124] *But cf.* New Era Publications International v. Carol Publishing Group, 904 F.2d 152 (2nd Cir. 1990). A federal appeals court ruled that the use of several extended quotations of a religious leader reproduced without permission in an uncomplimentary biography constituted fair use. The court evaluated each of the 4 "fair use factors" and concluded that all of them supported the finding of fair use. With regard to the first factor, the court concluded that biographies, and particularly critical biographies, generally constitute fair use. The proposed book used quotations from the religious leader's published writings "for the entirely legitimate purpose of making his point that [the leader] was a charlatan and his church a dangerous cult." While the author no doubt expected to make a profit, this was a secondary purpose. As to the second factor, the court again emphasized that the proposed book was a biography, and that biographies generally constitute fair use. The court observed that "biographies, of course, are fundamentally personal histories and it is both reasonable and customary for biographers to refer to and utilize earlier works dealing with the subject of the work and occasionally to quote directly from such works." The third fair use factor asks how much of the copyrighted work is quoted—both in terms of quantity and quality. The court concluded that only small portions of several works were quoted, rather than larger selections of any one work. Further, the portions quoted were not "key portions" of any of the books. Finally, the court concluded that the fourth factor led to a finding of fair use, since the biography would have little if any impact on the sale of the copyrighted works.

Two points bear particular emphasis. First, "the amount and substantiality of the portion used" is measured with respect to the "copyrighted work as a whole," not to the putatively infringing work. Defendants therefore go astray in focusing on the argument that the copyrighted expression taken from [its copyrighted material] amounts to a small fraction of the [allegedly infringing work]. A taking may not be excused merely because it is insubstantial with respect to the infringing work. No plagiarist can excuse the wrong by showing how much of his work he did not pirate.

Second, in analyzing the amount and substantiality of the portion used, a court considers not only the quantity of the materials used, but their quality and importance, too. Quantitatively, the amount of verbatim copying or paraphrasing appears to be a small portion of [the copyrighted material]. But the amount taken may be substantial from a qualitative perspective if the defendant has copied the "heart of the book." That may very well be the case here; as the district court observed, "the inherent value of [the copyrighted material] comes not just from the sales techniques and concepts, but particularly from the way they were selected, coordinated, or arranged . . . . Nonetheless, we might have found the bare-bones copying of chapter headings and subheadings . . . to be insubstantial, if defendants had stopped there. In such a scenario, the amount taken might have been deemed negligible because one could hardly imagine that the headings and subheadings, divorced from context and any explanation, could have a substitution effect on the market for [the copyrighted materials]. But the incorporation of [substantive materials] adds flesh to the organizational bones and renders the whole of defendants' copying substantial enough that demand for the book or derivative works might be reduced.[125]

The courts have found copying of the following amounts of copyrighted material to constitute copyright infringement:

- two identical bars of a musical work;[126]

- four notes and two words, which comprised the "heart of the composition;"[127]

- three sentences (that were used for advertising purposes);[128]

- three sentences;[129]

---

[125] Peter Letterese And Associates, Inc. v. World Institute Of Scientology Enterprises, 2008 WL 2652291 (11th Cir. 2008) quoting the United States Supreme Court's ruling in Harper & Row, 471 U.S. 539 (1985).

[126] Robertson v. Batten, Barton, Durstine and Osborn, Inc., 146 F. Supp. 795 (S.D. Cal. 1956).

[127] Elsmere Music, Inc. v. National Broadcasting Co., 482 F. Supp. 741 (S.D.N.Y. 1980), aff'd, 623 F.2d 252 (2nd Cir. 1980).

[128] Henry Holt & Co. v. Liggett & Myers Tobacco Co., 23 F. Supp. 302 (E.D. Pa. 1938).

[129] Amana Refrigeration, Inc. v. Consumers Union of the United States, Inc., 431 F. Supp. 324 (N.D. Iowa 1977).

- eight sentences;[130]

- less than one percent of the copyrighted work;[131]

- the phrase "put on a happy face;"[132]

- at least one-third of 17 letters and at least ten percent of 42 letters; letters were paraphrased on at least 40 percent of a book's 192 pages, and the copied material comprised an important part of the whole;[133]

- the fair use defense was not necessarily unavailable to a religious organization that copied an entire magazine article mocking a prominent minister;[134]

- copying of single words and short phrases from copyrighted material constituted noninfringing fair use.[135]

However, copying of the following portions of copyrighted material was held not to constitute infringement upon the copyright owner's exclusive right of reproduction:

- a sentence and a half;[136]

- 16 words;[137]

- two sentences.[138]

What about paraphrasing? For example, does infringement occur if a reproduction does not contain any "word-for-word" copying of original material but merely paraphrases it? Probably so, since a number of courts have held that "paraphrasing is tantamount to copying in copyright law."[139] Another court has observed that copying "cannot be limited literally to the text, else a plagiarist would escape by immaterial variations."[140]

---

[130] Martin Luther King, Jr. Center for Social Change, Inc. v. American Heritage Products, Inc., 508 F. Supp. 854 (N.D. Ga. 1981).

[131] Hedeman Products Copr. v. Tap-Rite Products Corp., 228 F. Supp. 630 (D.N.J. 1964).

[132] American Greetings Corp. v. Kleinfab Corp., 400 F. Supp. 228 (S.D.N.Y. 1975).

[133] Salinger v. Random House, Inc., 811 F.2d 90 (2nd Cir. 1987).

[134] Hustler Magazine Inc. v. Moral Majority Inc., 796 F.2d 1148 (9th Cir. 1986).

[135] Arica Institute, Inc. v. Palmer, 970 F.2d 1067 (2nd Cir. 1992).

[136] Toulmin v. The Rike-Kumler Co., 316 F.2d 232 (6th Cir. 1963).

[137] Suid v. Newsweek Magazine, 503 F. Supp. 146 (D.D.C. 1980).

[138] Jackson v. Washington Monthly Co., 481 F. Supp. 647 (D.D.C. 1979).

[139] *See, e.g.*, Davis v. E.I. duPont de Nemours & Co., 240 F. Supp. 612 (S.D.N.Y. 1965). *See also* Donald v. Zack Meyer's T. V. Sales and Service, 426 F.2d 1027 (5th Cir. 1970) (in copyright law, paraphrasing is equivalent to outright copying).

[140] Nichols v. Universal Pictures Co., 45 F.2d 119 (2nd Cir. 1930).

the fair use guidelines

One of the most common fair use issues concerns the reproduction of copyrighted materials for educational purposes. In 1975, negotiating teams representing authors, publishers, and the "Ad Hoc Committee of Educational Institutions and Organizations on Copyright Law Revision" met informally in an attempt to reach a "meeting of the minds" as to permissible educational uses of copyrighted material. The parties reached an agreement, known as the Agreement on Guidelines for Classroom Copying in Not-For-Profit Educational Institutions with Respect to Books and Periodicals. The House Report on the Copyright Act of 1976 reprinted the Agreement in full, and further noted that the guidelines set forth in the Agreement "are a reasonable interpretation of the minimum standards of fair use."[141]

The educational guidelines are very restrictive, and rarely will apply to churches. They apply primarily to copying by teachers in not-for-profit educational institutions for their own research or class preparation, and also to limited copying for classroom use. There are strict requirements as to the amount of material that can be copied under the guidelines for classroom use. For example, in the case of literary works ("prose"), teachers are limited to (a) either a complete article, story or essay of less than 2,500 words, or (b) an excerpt from any prose work of not more than 1,000 words or 10 percent of the work, whichever is less, but in any event a minimum of 500 words. Other requirements apply. The guidelines also warn that "copying shall not substitute for the purchase of books, publishers' reprints or periodicals."

Shortly after the guidelines for books and periodicals were formulated, representatives of music publishers and music educators met to draft guidelines relative to music. It must be emphasized that the stated purpose of the guidelines, as with the guidelines for books and periodicals, was "to state the minimum and not the maximum standards of educational fair use." The parties acknowledged that "there may be instances in which copying which does not fall within the guidelines . . . may nonetheless be permitted under the criteria of fair use." Nevertheless, the House Report on the Copyright Act of 1976 reprinted the guidelines in full,[142] and further noted that the guidelines "are a reasonable interpretation of the minimum standards of fair use." Like the guidelines for books and periodicals, the music guidelines are very restrictive and rarely will apply to churches. Perhaps most importantly, these guidelines permit "emergency photocopying to replace purchased copies which for any reason are not available for an imminent performance provided purchased replacement copies shall be substituted in due course." Clearly, this provision will be of little use to churches, since it requires that (1) copies of music have been purchased, (2) they are unavailable for an imminent performance because they are suddenly destroyed or lost, and (3) the church purchases replacement copies in due course.

---

[141] House Report on the Copyright Act of 1976, pp. 68-70. Representatives of the American Association of University Professors and of the Association of American Law Schools strongly criticized the guidelines on the ground that they were too restrictive with respect to classroom situations at the college and graduate level.

[142] *Id.* at pp. 70-71.

The application of the fair use defense to religious organizations is illustrated by the following cases.

Case Studies

• *A federal appeals court ruled that the use of several extended quotations of a religious leader reproduced without permission in an uncomplimentary biography constituted fair use. The court evaluated each of the 4 "fair use factors" and concluded that all of them supported the finding of fair use. With regard to the first factor, the court concluded that biographies, and particularly critical biographies, generally constitute fair use. The proposed book used quotations from the religious leader's published writings "for the entirely legitimate purpose of making his point that [the leader] was a charlatan and his church a dangerous cult." While the author no doubt expected to make a profit, this was a secondary purpose. As to the second factor, the court again emphasized that the proposed book was a biography, and that biographies generally constitute fair use. The court observed that "biographies, of course, are fundamentally personal histories and it is both reasonable and customary for biographers to refer to and utilize earlier works dealing with the subject of the work and occasionally to quote directly from such works." The third fair use factor asks how much of the copyrighted work is quoted—both in terms of quantity and quality. The court concluded that only small portions of several works were quoted, rather than larger selections of any one work. Further, the portions quoted were not "key portions" of any of the books. The court concluded that the fourth factor led to a finding of fair use, since the biography would have little if any impact on the sale of the copyrighted works.*[143]

• *A federal appeals court ruled that a religious chorus did not infringe upon the copyright of an allegedly similar song composed by another songwriter a few years earlier. The court noted: "Even a casual comparison of the two compositions compels the conclusion that the two compositions are practically identical. Given the limited number of musical notes (as opposed to words in a language), the combination of those notes and their phrasing, it is not surprising that a simple composition of a short length might well be susceptible to original creation by more than one composer. This is particularly true in certain genres of music where familiar phrasing is present. Here the genre is church music. We are only dealing with a basic melody—not lyrics or harmonic background or accompaniment—here, only a short melody is at issue. However, in the realm of copyright, identical expression does not necessarily constitute infringement. Just as two paintings of the same subject in nature may appear identical, the two paintings' origins may be of independent creation. We have cautioned trial courts "not to be swayed by the fact that two works embody similar or even identical ideas." The court noted that composer of the allegedly infringing music could "fully negate any claim of infringement if he can prove that he independently created [his work]." It concluded that there was substantial evidence that the allegedly infringing work was independently created, including affidavits of several witnesses who corroborated the independent creation of the allegedly infringing work.*[144]

---

[143] New Era Publications International v. Carol Publishing Group, 904 F.2d 152 (2nd Cir. 1990).
[144] Calhoun v. Lillenas Publishing, 298 F.3d 1228 (11th Cir. 2002).

• *A federal court in California ruled that an instructor who made copies of copyrighted religious books and tapes for instructional purposes was guilty of copyright infringement. The court rejected the instructor's defense of "fair use." It concluded that she failed all four fair use factors. The purpose of the copying was commercial (the copied materials were sold to students); the nature of the copyrighted works were creative and thus entitled to a higher degree of protection; the amount copied (the entire copyrighted works) was substantial; and, the impact of the copying on the copyright owner's rights was significant since the instructor's act of unauthorized copying "fulfilled the demand for the original works and [will] diminish or prejudice their potential sale." Finally, the court rejected the instructor's claim that her copying met the standards for "fair use" as set forth in the so-called "fair use guidelines" for classroom copying of educational materials. In 1975, groups of authors and publishers adopted guidelines for classroom copying in nonprofit educational institutions. The House Report on the Copyright Act of 1976 reprinted these guidelines in full, and further noted that they "are a reasonable interpretation of the minimum standards of fair use." The guidelines apply only to educational copying of literary works (books, articles, poetry, charts, etc.). Among other things, the guidelines specify that a teacher may make a single copy of a chapter from a book or an article from a periodical for use in teaching or in preparing to teach. The court observed that the instructor's copying in this case "was not restricted to one copy for her own use in teaching" and therefore was not eligible for a fair use exemption. The guidelines also permit teachers to make multiple copies of a copyrighted work for classroom use, but several restrictions apply. For example, a teacher may make multiple copies of an entire article of less than 2,500 words or an excerpt from a longer work so long as the excerpt is not more than the lesser of 1,000 words or 10 percent of the entire work. Further, the decision to use the work must be "spontaneous" in the sense that it is so close in time to the date the work is to be used that it would be unreasonable to expect a timely reply to a request for permission to reproduce it. There also are strict limitations on the number of times this exception can be used. The court concluded that this exemption did not apply: "[T]he undisputed evidence shows [that the instructor's] copying was not limited and spontaneous, but was extensive and methodical, and consisted of copying from the same author, time after time. This is clearly not within the letter or spirit of the congressional guidelines."*[145]

• *A Michigan court ruled that a church had to pay $1.6 million in damages for recording a soloist's performance during a religious service without her permission and then selling CDs of the service to church members and the general public. The court concluded that the church's failure to obtain the soloist's permission to record and distribute her solo was a negligent act. Note that this case was not a copyright infringement case. Rather, the plaintiff sued the church for the unauthorized recording and sale of a solo she performed during a worship service. This theory of liability is completely separate from copyright infringement.*[146]

2. Religious Displays

Section 109(c) provides that "the owner of a particular copy lawfully made . . . is entitled, without the authority of the copyright owner, to display that copy

---

[145] Bridge Publications, Inc. v. Vien, 827 F. Supp. 629 (S.D. Cal. 1993).

[146] Edwards v. Church of God in Christ, 2002 WL 393577 (Mich. App. 2002).

publicly, either directly or by the projection of no more than one image at a time, to viewers present at the place where the copy is located." Section 109(d) provides further that the privilege granted under section 109(c) does not, unless authorized by the copyright owner, "extend to any person who has acquired possession of the copy or phonorecord from the copyright owner, by rental, lease, loan, or otherwise, without acquiring ownership of it."

This section is of considerable relevance to many churches, and particularly to those that use transparencies and slides of copyrighted music in the course of worship services. Recall that one of the exclusive rights of a copyright owner is the right to display a copyrighted work publicly. Section 109(c) limits this exclusive right by adopting the general principle that the *lawful owner* of a copy of a copyrighted work should be able to put the copy on public display without the consent of the copyright owner. The House Report to the Copyright Act of 1976 provides that a copyright owner's exclusive right of public display

> would not apply where the owner of a copy wishes to show it directly to the public, as in a gallery or display case, or indirectly as through an opaque projector. Where the copy itself is intended for projection, as in the case of a photographic slide, negative, or transparency, the public projection of a single image would be permitted as long as the viewers are "present at the place where the copy is located" . . . . [T]he public display of an image of a copyrighted work would not be exempted from copyright control if the copy from which the image was derived were outside the presence of the viewers. . . . Moreover, the exemption would extend only to public displays that are made "either directly or by the projection of no more than one image at a time."[147]

Perhaps most significantly, the House Report specifies that section 109(d) qualifies the privilege granted in section 109(b) "by making it clear that [it does] not apply to someone who merely possesses a copy or phonorecord without having acquired ownership of it. Acquisition of an object embodying a copyrighted work . . . carries with it no privilege to . . . display it publicly under section 109(b)."[148]

Section 109(c) would authorize the use of an opaque projector to display a copy of a musical work in the course of choir rehearsals or church services since the opaque projector displays an image of a lawfully made copy consisting ordinarily of either sheet music or a page in a hymnal. But if a church makes a transparency of an existing copyrighted musical work without authorization, such a transparency would not be a lawfully made copy and thus could not be displayed without infringing the owner's copyright. Section 109(b) would authorize the display of a transparency in the course of choir rehearsals or church services if the transparency constituted a lawfully made copy. This could occur in three ways. First, a transparency purchased from an authorized vendor would be a lawful copy and could be displayed publicly. Second, a transparency of a public

---

[147] *Id.* at pp. 79-80.

[148] *Id.* at p. 80.

domain work could be fabricated and displayed. Third, a transparency made with the express permission of the copyright owner would be a lawful copy.

Congress has stated that the purpose of section 109 is not only to preserve the traditional privilege of the owner of a copy to display it directly, but also to place reasonable restrictions on the ability of others to display it indirectly in such a way that the copyright owner's market for reproduction and distribution of copies would be affected.[149] Accordingly, it is likely that continued public display of a copyrighted work by a church would tend to result in a loss of the protection afforded by section 109(b). For example, if a church choir director projected a copyrighted musical arrangement on a screen for several weeks in succession in an effort to have his choir memorize the work, the repetitive display of the work might not be eligible for protection under section 109(b).

3. The Nonprofit Performance Exception

Section 110(4) contains a general exception to the exclusive right of a copyright owner to publicly perform his or her copyrighted work. It provides:

> [P]erformance of a nondramatic literary or musical work otherwise than in a transmission to the public, without any purpose of direct or indirect commercial advantage and without payment of any fee or other compensation for the performance to any of its performers, promoters, or organizers, [does not constitute copyright infringement] if—(A) there is no direct or indirect admission charge; or (B) the proceeds, after deducting the reasonable costs of producing the performance, are used exclusively for educational, religious, or charitable purposes and not for private financial gain, except where the copyright owner has served notice of objection to the performance under the following conditions; (i) the notice shall be in writing and signed by the copyright owner or such owner's duly authorized agent; and (ii) the notice shall be served on the person responsible for the performance at least seven days before the date of the performance, and shall state the reasons for the objection; and (iii) the notice shall comply, in form, content, and manner of service, with requirements that the Register of Copyrights shall prescribe by regulation.

Let's consider a number of important aspects of this important exemption.

(1) The performance must not have a profit motive.

(2) No fee or compensation can be paid to the performers (or promoters or organizers) for the performance. This condition does not prevent performers from receiving a salary for duties that include a particular performance. For example, performances by a school band do not lose the benefit of this exemption merely because the band conductor is a music teacher who receives an annual salary for

---

[149] *Id.*

performing his duties, so long as he receives no fee or payment for any particular performance.

(3) There must either be no direct or indirect admissions charge, or alternatively, if an admissions charge is assessed, then any amounts left after deducting the reasonable costs of producing the performance must be used solely for educational, religious, or charitable purposes. If there is an admissions charge, then the copyright owner is given the authority to "veto" the performance by serving upon the person responsible for the performance a notice objecting to the performance. Such a notice must be in a writing that is signed by the copyright owner; it must be served upon the person responsible for the performance at least seven days before the date of the performance; and, it must state the reasons for the objection. The impact of this provision is limited severely by the fact that section 110(4) does not require that the copyright owner be notified that his or her work is going to be performed at a nonprofit event with an admissions charge.

4. Authorization from Copyright Owner

Even if none of the exceptions to copyright infringement discussed above is clearly applicable, a particular use of copyrighted material may be authorized by the copyright owner. For example, assume that a church choir director wishes to perform a particular song during a worship service, that he has a single octavo, and that he cannot obtain additional copies locally and it is too late to order copies by mail. While this "emergency need" to make unauthorized copies is not a recognized exception to copyright infringement, the director is free to contact the copyright owner directly and request permission to make copies. If permission is granted, then the making of copies will not constitute infringement.

Many music publishers have very liberal policies with respect to church music. Some music publishers grant "blanket licenses" to churches, authorizing them to make copies of any song in the publisher's repertory for an annual fee. Occasionally, several publishers and composers will assign the right to license the use of their works to a single company in return for the payment of a royalty. The company acts as a clearinghouse on behalf of the publishers and composers, granting blanket licenses to churches in exchange for a fee that is apportioned among the various publishers and composers. Perhaps the first such arrangement involving religious music was implemented by F.E.L. Publications, Ltd., in the 1970s. F.E.L. obtained the rights to 1400 songs, and offered annual licenses to churches for a fee of $100. The annual license authorized a church to copy any of the listed songs. Further, the purchaser was granted the right to perform the music and text at not-for-profit performances for purposes of worship or classroom use. A church that wanted to use one of F.E.L.'s listed songs could not deal directly with any of the authors or composers whose musical works or copyrights had been exclusively assigned to F.E.L.

F.E.L.'s annual license differed from traditional marketing of music in that it did not distinguish between songs, but charged a lump sum for which the licensee received the use rights to all of F.E.L.'s 1400 available compositions, even though the purchaser desired to use only a few of the more popular songs. It also differed from usual marketing practices in that it relied heavily on the licensee to patrol its own use. On the anniversary date of the license, the customer had to destroy all copies made of the virtually unlimited number allowed, unless it elected to pay F.E.L another $100 for an additional annual license.[150]

A federal district court found the F.E.L. blanket licensing scheme to be a "tying contract" that was illegal under the Sherman Antitrust Act. Specifically, the court observed that

> by obtaining assignments of the songs with the right, on behalf of the composers, to license their use for an annual fee, and by obtaining assignment of copyrights for the same purpose, F.E.L. either absolutely controls or has ownership power over copyrights to hymnals, songbooks, and the 1400 religious songs listed in its master title index. A Catholic church or parish that wants to purchase the right to copy and use a song either in one of F.E.L.'s hymnals, songbooks, or those listed in its master title index, cannot deal directly with owners of the copyrighted works listed by F.E.L. In most instances, a church or parish does not desire permission to use all of F.E.L.'s listed songs; there is no interest in all of the songs in F.E.L.'s hymnals, songbooks, and listed in the master index. The most desired are about 25 or 30 of the more popular or "blockbuster" songs. Yet, F.E.L.'s policy has always been "all or nothing"; the church or parish desiring to purchase the right to copy and use some of the listed songs has to pay for permission to use all of them. The songs are different; in many instances, the composers are different, yet purchase of the right to use the more popular has been tied by F.E.L. to the purchase of all, including the less popular. It is now well known that a tying arrangement whereby a party agrees to sell one product but only on condition that the buyer also agrees to purchase a different or tied product is prohibited by the Sherman Act, and by the Clayton Act.

The F.E.L. license was an exclusive license, meaning that a composer gave F.E.L. the sole right to market his or her song. While an in-depth discussion of the legality of such licenses is beyond the scope of this book, it should be noted that a few courts have upheld the legal validity of nonexclusive licenses. For example, ASCAP and BMI operate in much the same manner as F.E.L. in the sense that members give ASCAP and BMI the right to license the performance or broadcast of members' copyrighted works. ASCAP and BMI in turn grant blanket licenses authorizing licensees, for a flat fee, to use any work in the ASCAP or BMI repertory. ASCAP and BMI have been the target of several lawsuits alleging violation of federal antitrust laws (because of "tying arrangements"). So far, ASCAP and BMI blanket

---

[150] F.E.L. Publications v. Catholic Bishop of Chicago, 506 F. Supp. 1127 (N.D. Ill. 1981).

licenses have been upheld on the ground that they are nonexclusive. This means that ASCAP and BMI members retain the right to directly license their works to third parties. Churches that obtained a license from F.E.L. were not afforded this right (they granted F.E.L. the exclusive right to license the performance and reproduction of their works).

the CCLI license

A similar approach is offered by Christian Copyright Licensing, Inc. (CCLI) of Portland, Oregon. CCLI has attempted to avoid the antitrust issue by having publishers and composers enter into nonexclusive assignments of their musical works with CCLI. While CCLI acts as a clearinghouse for several publishers and composers, the publishers and composers remain free to directly market and license their works to individual churches. Churches that purchase a blanket license from CCLI are authorized to make copies of any song in the CCLI repertory (which includes the works of several publishers and composers) for congregational use, for the duration of the license period (ordinarily one year). This means, for example, that churches are free to make bulletin inserts and transparencies. Churches also are authorized to make audio and video recordings of services that contain copyrighted music (in the CCLI repertory), provided that copies of the recording are distributed for less than a specified cost, and do not exceed a specified number. The making of certain musical arrangements is also permitted.

Churches must make a record of what songs they sing or perform in the course of a year, and file reports with CCLI. These reports help CCLI allocate royalties to the various publishers and composers. The fee that a church pays is based on a number of variables, including the size of the church and the kind of copying involved. In principle, the CCLI approach has the advantage of making compliance with copyright law much easier.

Church leaders can learn more about the CCLI license by visiting the CCLI website (www.ccli.com) or by calling 1-800-234-2446. Further, note that CCLI licenses only apply to limited cases of reproduction and performance of religious musical works. They do not convey any authorization to duplicate literary works (books and articles), and they do not apply in all cases to reproduction or performance of music. As a result, a CCLI license is should not be viewed as a solution to all of a church's copyright concerns.

Key point. *CCLI also offers licenses that authorize (subject to certain limitations) the use of videos at church activities, and the use of television and movie clips as sermon illustrations.*

What a CCLI License Does and Does Not Permit

A CCLI license DOES authorize a church to do the following:

☐ Print songs and hymns in bulletins, programs, liturgies, and songsheets.

☐ Create your own customized songbooks or hymnals.

☐ Create overhead transparencies, slides, or use any other format whereby songs are visually projected, such as computer graphics and projection.

☐ Arrange, print and copy your own arrangements, vocal and instrumental, of songs where no published version is available.

☐ Record your worship services by audio or video means, provided you only record "live" music (instrumental and vocal). Accompaniment "tracks" cannot be reproduced. You may also charge up to a specified amount for audio and video recordings.

A CCLI license DOES NOT authorize a church to do the following:

☐ Photocopy or duplicate octavos, cantatas, musicals, handbell music, keyboard arrangements, vocal scores, orchestrations, or other instrumental works.

☐ Translate songs from English into another language. This can only be done with the approval of the respective publisher.

☐ Rent, sell, or lend copies made under the license to groups outside the church or to other churches. (It is permissible to distribute tapes to shut-ins, missionaries, or others outside the church.)

☐ Assign or transfer the license to another church or group without CCLI's approval.

Electronic Media

§ 9-05.11

Key point § 9-05.11. *Publishers cannot place the contents of magazines and other periodicals in online electronic databases and on CD-ROMs without obtaining the permission of writers whose articles were included in those periodicals.*

Many religious organizations have published periodicals for many years, and would like to reprint those periodicals on a website or on a CD-ROM. If they required the authors of each article ever published in their periodical to assign all rights (including copyright) to the publisher, then there is no need to obtain consent. However, in most cases there is no such history. Either no agreements were ever used, or they were used for only some years, or they did not clearly assign copyright to the publisher. In any of these cases, the authors retain copyright in their articles. But, according to section 201(c) of the Copyright Act, the publisher has the right without the authors' consent of "reproducing and distributing the contributions as part of that particular collective work, any revision of that collective work, and any later collective work in the same series." This issue was addressed by the United States Supreme Court in an important ruling.[151] The case involved writers who contributed articles to several prominent periodicals, including the *New York Times*, *Newsday*, and *Sports Illustrated*. The publishers sold the contents of their periodicals (including all of the individual articles) to "LEXIS/NEXIS" for inclusion in online electronic databases and on CD-ROMs. Each article was retrievable by users in isolation, clear of the original print publication's content. Six authors sued the publishers, claiming that the inclusion of their articles in the online electronic databases and on CD-ROMs violated their copyright interests. The publishers disagreed, claiming that the writers had authorized the publication of their articles in an online electronic format, and that the republication of articles in "collective works" is permitted by the Copyright Act. These two defenses will be considered separately below.

Did the writers transfer to the publishers the right to republish their articles in an electronic format? The publishers claimed that they did. Some publishers relied solely on "oral agreements" with writers. One publisher pointed to a written contract that all writers signed which transferred to the publisher "the right to first publish" the article in the same periodical. Another publisher relied on a special endorsement printed above the signature line on checks issued to writers in payment for their articles. The endorsement read: "Signature required. Check void if this endorsement altered. This check accepted as full payment for first-time publication rights to material described on face of check in all editions published by [the publisher] and for the right to include such material in electronic library archives." The Court concluded that none of the writers had legally transferred any rights to their publishers to republish the articles in an electronic format.

Section 201(c) of the Copyright Act specifies that "copyright in each separate contribution to a collective work is distinct from copyright in the collective work as a whole, and vests initially in the author of the contribution. In the absence of an express transfer of the copyright or of any rights under it, the owner of copyright in the collective work is presumed to have acquired only the privilege of reproducing and distributing the contributions as part of that particular collective work, any revision of that collective work, and any later collective work in the same series." Magazines, journals, and other periodicals containing articles written by several authors are "collective works." According to section 201(c), persons who contribute articles to collective works retain the copyright in their articles unless they have assigned them to the publisher. If they have not assigned the copyright in their articles to the publisher, then the publisher has the limited privilege of "reproducing and distributing the contributions as part of that particular collective work, any revision of that collective work, and any later collective work in the same series."

Since the writers had not assigned any rights to the publishers other than the right to "first publish" their articles, the remaining question was whether the republication of the collective works in an electronic format was a "reproduction" or "revision" of the collective work. If so, then it was permissible according to

---

[151] Tasini v. New York Times Co., 121 S.Ct. 2381 (2001).

section 201(c). The Court concluded that the republication of the collective works (magazines and journals) on CD-ROMs and in online electronic databases was not a reproduction or revision, and so the inclusion of the articles in these media violated the copyright interests of the authors. It observed,

> A newspaper or magazine publisher is thus privileged to reproduce or distribute an article contributed by a freelance author, absent a contract otherwise providing, only "as part of" any (or all) of three categories of collective works: (a) "that collective work" to which the author contributed her work, (b) "any revision of that collective work," or (c) "any later collective work in the same series." In accord with Congress' prescription, a "publishing company could reprint a contribution from one issue in a later issue of its magazine, and could reprint an article from a 1980 edition of an encyclopedia in a 1990 revision of it; the publisher could not revise the contribution itself or include it in a new anthology or an entirely different magazine or other collective work."
>
> Essentially, section 201(c) adjusts a publisher's copyright in its collective work to accommodate a freelancer's copyright in her contribution. If there is demand for a freelance article standing alone or in a new collection, the Copyright Act allows the freelancer to benefit from that demand; after authorizing initial publication, the freelancer may also sell the article to others. . . . When an author produces a work which later commands a higher price in the market than the original bargain provided, the copyright statute is designed to provide the author the power to negotiate for the realized value of the work. It would scarcely "preserve the author's copyright in a contribution" as contemplated by Congress if a newspaper or magazine publisher were permitted to reproduce or distribute copies of the author's contribution in isolation or within new collective works.

The Court noted that collective works were not republished intact by LEXIS/ NEXIS. Rather, individual articles were available to users, completely detached from the collective work in which they originally appeared. As such, the Court concluded that the articles no longer were part of a collective work and so the section 201(c) exception could not apply. It observed,

> In determining whether the articles have been reproduced and distributed "as part of" a "revision" of the collective works in issue, we focus on the articles as presented to, and perceptible by, the user of the databases. In this case, the databases present articles to users clear of the context provided either by the original periodical editions or by any revision of those editions. The databases first prompt users to search the universe of their contents: thousands or millions of files containing individual articles from thousands of collective works (*i.e.*, editions), either in one series or in scores of series. When the user conducts a search, each article appears as a separate item within the search result. [In some databases] an article

appears to a user without the graphics, formatting, or other articles with which the article was initially published. In [other databases] the article appears with the other materials published on the same page or pages, but without any material published on other pages of the original periodical. In either circumstance, we cannot see how the database perceptibly reproduces and distributes the article "as part of" either the original edition or a "revision" of that edition. . . . The databases offer users individual articles, not intact periodicals. In this case, media neutrality should protect the authors' rights in the individual articles to the extent those articles are now presented individually, outside the collective work context, within the databases' new media.

Let's review the key points of this important ruling:

(1) Authors who contribute an article to a magazine or journal, and who do not sign a document assigning any rights to the publisher, retain the copyright in their article and the publisher has only the minimal right to publish the article in its collective work and in any reproduction or revision of that collective work or any later collective work in the same series. Such articles may be republished in an online electronic database or on a CD-ROM so long as they are presented along with the entire collective work in which they first appeared. However, the publisher does not have the right to republish articles in isolation and detached from the collective work in which they appeared.

(2) Authors can assign some or all of their rights to a publisher in a written agreement. Copyright is divisible, so authors can assign any portion of their legal interests to a publisher. For example, authors can assign all of their copyright, in which case the publisher can republish the article in any format at any time in the future without having to obtain the authors' consent. Further, the publisher (and not the authors) would respond to any requests from other publishers to reprint the article. Authors can assign partial rights to a publisher, such as the rights to republish the article in any format or medium at any time in the future. The Supreme Court noted that "it bears reminding that these publishers and all others can protect their interests by private contractual arrangement."

(3) Many religious organizations have published periodicals for many years, and would like to reprint those periodicals on a website or on a CD-ROM. According to section 201(c) of the Copyright Act, the publisher has the right without the authors' consent of "reproducing and distributing the contributions as part of that particular collective work, any revision of that collective work, and any later collective work in the same series." As the Supreme Court noted, this provision gives publishers the right to republish articles

in electronic or digital media so long as the entire collective work in which they appeared is published. If the articles are accessible individually and detached from the collective works in which they first appeared, then section 201(c) does not apply and the republication violates the authors' copyright interests.

(4) In some cases, a religious organization that publishes a periodical will own the copyright in the articles as a result of the "work made for hire" doctrine. The Copyright Act specifies that the copyright in any work created by an employee in the course of his or her employment belongs to the employer rather than the employee unless the employer has assigned the copyright back to the employee in a signed writing. For example, if a religious organization publishes a periodical that contains articles submitted by employees, the copyright in those articles belongs to the organization so long as (1) they were written by employees in the course of their employment, and (2) the employer did not assign the copyright back to the employees in a signed writing. If an article is a work made for hire, the copyright in that article belongs to the employer and so there is no need to obtain the author's consent for any future publication of that article, in any medium or format including websites and CD-ROMs.

(5) There is another category of work made for hire that should be considered. The Copyright Act specifies that "works made for hire" include "a work specially ordered or commissioned for use as a contribution to a collective work . . . if the parties expressly agree in a written instrument signed by them that the work shall be considered a work made for hire." To illustrate, a religious organization can commission the writing of an article by an author, and the article will be a work made for hire (and the copyright will belong to the publisher) if the parties execute a written agreement confirming that article is a work for hire.

(6) If authors retain the copyright in their articles, a publisher's limited authority to republish the collective work (including the articles) in the future does not include the right to revise the text of the articles. That right belongs exclusively to the authors, unless they have assigned it to the publisher.

Government Investigations

§ 9-06

As has been noted elsewhere,[152] the IRS possesses broad authority to inspect church records. This authority has been upheld on numerous occasions. Government investigations may be initiated by other federal agencies as well. To illustrate:

- The Postal Service can investigate "any scheme or artifice to defraud, or . . . obtaining money or property by means of false or fraudulent pretenses, representations, or promises" in connection with the use of the mail.[153]

- The Federal Communications Commission can investigate complaints regarding a broadcast licensee's performance/

- The Equal Employment Opportunity Commission can investigate the compliance of religious organizations with the Civil Rights Act of 1964.

- The Securities and Exchange Commission can investigate instances of fraudulent activities in the offer and sale of securities.

- The Occupational Safety and Health Administration can investigate alleged violations of the Occupational Safety and Health Act.

- The United States Citizenship and Immigrations Services Department can investigate the immigration status of persons who perform services for compensation, including those employed by religious organizations.

- The Department of Labor, Wage and Hour Division, can investigate compliance with the federal minimum wage and overtime pay requirements.

- The Department of Justice can investigate alleged violations of federal law.

- The Environmental Protection Agency can investigate alleged violations of federal environmental laws.

- The Federal Department of Transportation can investigate violations of bus regulations.

State and municipal agencies are authorized to investigate a range of activities that may violate applicable law.

It is common for the investigatory authority of federal, state, and local agencies to extend to religious organizations. In some cases, this authority may be limited.

---

[152] *See* § 6-03, *supra.*

[153] 18 U.S.C. § 1341.

Judicial Resolution
of Church Disputes

§ 9-07

Key point 9-07. *The First Amendment allows civil courts to resolve internal church disputes so long as they can do so without interpreting doctrine or polity.*

1. Decisions of the United States Supreme Court

In *Watson v. Jones*,[154] the United States Supreme Court developed a framework for the judicial review of ecclesiastical disputes that has persisted essentially unchanged until today, more than a century later. The Court began its landmark opinion by acknowledging that "religious organizations come before us in the same attitude as other voluntary associations for benevolent or charitable purposes, and their rights of property, or of contract, are equally under the protection of the law, and the actions of their members subject to its restraints." Though recognizing in principle the authority of civil courts to address the "rights of property, or of contract" of ecclesiastical organizations or officers, the Court proceeded to severely limit this authority. Most importantly, the Court held that "whenever the *questions of discipline, or of faith, of ecclesiastical rule, custom, or law* have been decided by the highest church judicatory to which the matter has been carried, the legal tribunals must accept such decisions as final, and as binding on them . . . ." The Court explained this fundamental limitation on the authority of the courts to review ecclesiastical controversies pertaining to faith or discipline as follows:

> All who unite themselves to such a body do so with an implied consent to its government, and are bound to submit to it. But it would be a vain consent and would lead to the total subversion of such religious bodies, if anyone aggrieved by one of their decisions could appeal to the secular courts and have them reversed. It is of the essence of these religious unions, and of their right to establish tribunals for the decision of questions arising among themselves, that those decisions should be binding in all cases of ecclesiastical cognizance subject only to such appeals as the organism itself provides for.
>
> Nor do we see that justice would be likely to be promoted by submitting those decisions to review in the ordinary judicial tribunals. Each of these large influential bodies . . . has a body of constitutional and ecclesiastical law of its own, to be found in their written organic laws, their books of discipline, in their collections of precedents, in their usage

---

[154] 80 U.S. 679, 722 (1871) [hereinafter cited as Watson]. *See also* Bernard, *Churches, Members, and the Role of the Courts: Toward a Contractual Analysis*, 51 Notre Dame Lawyer 545 (1976); Dusenberg, *Jurisdiction of Civil Courts over Religious Issues*, 20 Ohio St. L.J. 508 (1959); Ellman, *Driven from the Tribunal: Judicial Resolution of Internal Church Disputes*, 69 Cal. L. Rev. 1380 (1981); C. Esbeck, *Tort Claims Against Churches and Ecclesiastical Officers: The First Amendment Considerations*, 89 W. Va. L. Rev. 22-23 (1986); Gilkey, *The Judicial Role in Intra-Church Disputes Under the Constitutional Guarantees Relating to Religion*, 75 W. Va. L. Rev. 105 (1972); Patton, *The Civil Courts and the Churches*, 54 U. Pa. L. Rev. 391 (1906); Young and Tigges, *Into the Religious Thicket—Constitutional Limits on Civil Court Jurisdiction over Ecclesiastical Disputes*, 47 Ohio St. L.J. 475 (1986).

and customs, which to each constitute a system of ecclesiastical law and religious faith that tasks the ablest minds to become familiar with. It is not to be supposed that the judges of the civil courts can be as competent in the ecclesiastical law and religious faith of all these bodies as the ablest men in each are in reference to their own. It would therefore be an appeal from the more learned tribunal in the law which should decide the case, to one which is less so.[155]

Similarly, the Court observed:

The decisions of ecclesiastical courts, like every other judicial tribunal, are final, as *they are the best judges of what constitutes an offense against the word of God and the discipline of the church.* Any other than those courts must be incompetent judges of matters of faith, discipline, and doctrine; and civil courts, if they should be so unwise as to attempt to supervise their judgments on matters which come within their jurisdiction would only involve themselves in a sea of uncertainty and doubt which would do anything but improve either religion or good morals.[156]

The Court based this fundamental limitation on civil court review of ecclesiastical controversies involving faith or discipline upon jurisdictional grounds:

But it is a very different thing where a subject matter of dispute, strictly and purely ecclesiastical in its character—a matter over which the civil courts exercise no jurisdiction, *a matter which concerns theological controversy, church discipline, ecclesiastical government, or the conformity of the members of the church to the standards of morals required of them*—becomes the subject of its action. It may be said here, also, that *no jurisdiction has been conferred upon the tribunal* to try the particular case before it, or that, in its judgment, it exceeds the powers conferred upon it, or that the laws of the church do not authorize the particular form of proceeding adopted; and, in a sense often used in the courts, all of those may be said to be questions of jurisdiction. But it is easy to see that if the civil courts are to inquire into all these matters, the whole subject of doctrinal theology, the usages and customs, the written laws, and fundamental organization of every religious denomination may, and must, be examined into with minuteness and care, for they would become, in almost every case, the criteria by which the validity of the ecclesiastical decree would be determined in the civil court. This principle would deprive these bodies of the right of construing their own church laws . . . and would, in effect, transfer to the civil courts where property rights were concerned the decision of all ecclesiastical questions.[157]

---

[155] *Id.* at 729.

[156] *Id.* at 732.

[157] *Id.* at 733 (emphasis added).

The *Watson* ruling may be summarized as follows:

(1) the civil courts may *never* intervene in ecclesiastical disputes involving questions of ecclesiastical doctrine, polity, discipline, practice, or administration;

(2) civil courts may in some cases adjudicate the "rights of property, or contracts" of ecclesiastical organizations and officers; and

(3) civil courts have no jurisdiction to adjudicate the "rights of property, or of contracts" if matters of ecclesiastical faith, discipline, or practice are implicated in the controversies and an ecclesiastical body has authority to determine the issue.

The third consideration was based on three additional factors: (a) civil judges are incompetent to resolve questions of religious doctrine; (b) church members have voluntarily joined the church and have given their implied consent to its internal governance; and (c) the structure of our political system requires a severe limit on involvement by the civil courts in the affairs of religious bodies so as to secure religious liberty.

The *Watson* case remains uncompromised today. Indeed, in 1952 the Supreme Court elevated it to the level of First Amendment jurisprudence.[158]

One year after the *Watson* ruling, the Supreme Court again emphasized that it had *"no power to revise or question ordinary acts of church discipline*, or of excision from membership," nor to "decide who ought to be members of the church, nor whether the excommunicated have been regularly or irregularly cut off."[159]

In 1928, the Supreme Court observed, in a case involving the authority of an ecclesiastical organization to discipline a minister:

Because the appointment is a canonical act, it is the function of the church authorities to determine what the essential qualifications of a [clergyman] are and whether the candidate possesses them. In the absence of fraud, collusion, or arbitrariness, the decisions of the proper church tribunals on matters purely ecclesiastical, although affecting civil rights, are accepted in litigation before the secular courts as conclusive, because the parties . . . made them so by contract or otherwise.[160]

The Court's ruling in *Gonzalez* is significant, for it is a specific prohibition of civil court interference in the determinations of ecclesiastical bodies regarding the qualifications of clergy—*even if "civil rights" are involved*—absent fraud, collusion, or arbitrariness. As will be noted later, the Supreme Court subsequently eliminated arbitrariness and severely limited fraud and collusion as available grounds for civil court review.

---

[158] Kedroff v. St. Nicholas Cathedral, 344 U.S. 94 (1952) [hereinafter cited as *Kedroff*].

[159] Bouldin v. Alexander, 82 U.S. (15 Wall.) 131, 139-40 (1872) (emphasis added).

[160] Gonzalez v. Roman Catholic Archbishop, 280 U.S. 1, 16-17 (1928) (Justice Brandeis) (emphasis added) [hereinafter cited as *Gonzalez*].

In 1952, the Supreme Court in the *Kedroff* ruling[161] reaffirmed its pronouncement in *Watson* that civil courts have no authority to resolve *"questions of discipline, or of faith, or of ecclesiastical rule, custom, or law."* The Court, referring to the *Watson* case, observed that "the opinion radiates, however, a spirit of freedom for religious organizations, and independence from secular control or manipulation, in short, *power to decide for themselves, free from state interference, matters of church government as well as those of faith and doctrine.* Freedom to select the clergy . . . we think must now be said to have federal constitutional protection as a part of the free exercise of religion against state interference." Significantly, the Court also observed:

> There are occasions when civil courts must draw lines between the responsibilities of church and state for the disposition or use of property. *Even in those cases when the property right follows as an incident from decisions of the church custom or law on ecclesiastical issues, the church rule controls.* This under our Constitution necessarily follows in order that there may be free exercise of religion.[162]

The *Kedroff* decision is important since it specifically holds that alleged deprivations or interference with "property rights" cannot serve as a basis for civil court review of ecclesiastical determinations regarding the qualifications or dismissal of clergy where "the property right follows as an incident from decisions of the church . . . on ecclesiastical issues." This important language should be read together with the Court's statement in the *Gonzalez* case that "the decisions of the proper church tribunals [on matters regarding the qualifications of clergy], *although affecting civil rights*, are accepted in litigation before the secular courts as conclusive," except under extraordinary circumstances described below. These two rulings indicate that dismissed clergy will not be able to have their dismissals reviewed by the civil courts merely because they claim that their civil or property rights have been violated.

In 1969, the Supreme Court reaffirmed the principle of judicial nonintervention in church disputes involving ecclesiastical discipline, faith, or practice, citing with approval *Watson*, *Gonzalez*, and *Kedroff*.[163] The Court did acknowledge, however, that there is room for "marginal civil court review" of ecclesiastical controversies involving the disposition of *church real estate* following a church schism. Nevertheless, even this narrow review is "severely circumscribed" by the First Amendment, since the civil courts have "*no* role in determining ecclesiastical questions in the process of resolving church property disputes." The Court added:

> First Amendment values are plainly jeopardized when church property litigation is made to turn on the resolution by civil courts of controversies

---

[161] 344 U.S. 94 (1952).

[162] *Id.* at 120 (emphasis added).

[163] Presbyterian Church v. Mary Elizabeth Blue Hull Memorial Presbyterian Church, 393 U.S. 440 (1969) [hereinafter cited as *Presbyterian Church*].

over religious doctrine and practice. If civil courts undertake to resolve such controversies in order to adjudicate the property dispute, the hazards are ever present of inhibiting the free development of religious doctrine and implicating secular interests in matters of purely ecclesiastical concern. Because of these hazards, the First Amendment enjoins the employment of organs of government for essentially religious purposes; the amendment therefore commands civil courts to decide church property disputes without resolving underlying controversies over religious doctrine.[164]

In 1976, the Supreme Court again addressed an ecclesiastical controversy.[165] In *Serbian*, however, this issue was not control of church property, but rather the legal right of a defrocked bishop to challenge his expulsion in civil court. The Illinois Supreme Court, citing *Gonzalez*,[166] had reversed the decision of the Serbian Eastern Orthodox Diocese expelling the bishop. The court reasoned that the Diocese had not followed its own bylaws and accordingly its decision to expel was "arbitrary" and, on the basis of *Gonzalez*, subject to civil court review. In reversing the Illinois Supreme Court's ruling, the United States Supreme Court observed:

> The conclusion of the Illinois Supreme Court that the decisions of the [Diocese] were "arbitrary" was grounded upon an inquiry that persuaded the Illinois Supreme Court that the [Diocese] had not followed its own laws and procedures in arriving at those decisions. We have concluded that whether or not there is room for "marginal civil court review" under the narrow rubrics of "fraud" or "collusion" when church tribunals act in bad faith for secular purposes, no "arbitrariness" exception—in the sense of an inquiry whether the decisions of the highest ecclesiastical tribunal of a hierarchical church complied with church laws and regulations—is consistent with the constitutional mandate that civil courts are bound to accept the decisions of the highest judicatories of a religious organization of hierarchical polity on matters of discipline, faith, internal organization, or ecclesiastical rule, custom or law. For civil courts to analyze whether the ecclesiastical actions of a church judicatory are in that sense "arbitrary" must inherently entail inquiry into the procedures that canon or ecclesiastical law supposedly require the church adjudicatory to follow, or else into the substantive criteria by which they are supposedly to decide the ecclesiastical question. But this is exactly the inquiry that the First Amendment prohibits . . . .[167]

The Court rejected an attempt by a defrocked bishop to force civil court review on the basis of an alleged deprivation of a "property right," since the alleged

---

[164] *Id.* at 449.

[165] Serbian Eastern Orthodox Diocese v. Milivojevich, 423 U.S. 696 (1976) [hereinafter cited as *Serbian*].

[166] *See* note 160, *supra*, and accompanying text.

[167] *Id.* at 712-713.

property right was incidental to the underlying issue of ecclesiastical discipline and "the civil courts must accept that consequence as the incidental effect of an ecclesiastical determination that is not subject to judicial abrogation, having been reached by the final church judicatory in which authority to make that decision resides."

Serbian is significant for the following reasons: (a) it reaffirmed the rule of judicial nonintervention in cases of ecclesiastical discipline over which an ecclesiastical organization has jurisdiction; (b) it rejected the claim that civil courts can justify intervention in cases of ecclesiastical discipline on the basis of alleged deprivation of "property rights," if the alleged deprivation is a mere incidental effect of the underlying disciplinary process; and (c) it categorically rejected civil court review of ecclesiastical disciplinary proceedings on the basis of "arbitrariness," and *defined arbitrariness as a failure by a church to follow its own rules and procedures*. The Court based these conclusions on the following grounds: (a) civil courts are forbidden by the First Amendment from engaging in "searching inquiry" into the organizational documents of religious organizations; (b) civil judges have no training, experience, or expertise in matters of ecclesiastical law or governance; and (c) "constitutional concepts of due process, involving secular notions of fundamental fairness or impermissible objectives," are not relevant to matters of ecclesiastical cognizance which typically "are reached and are to be accepted as matters of faith whether or not rational or measurable by objective criteria."

The most recent decision of the Supreme Court came in 1979.[168] Like *Presbyterian Church*, *Jones* involved a dispute over control of church real estate following a schism. The Court reaffirmed the long-established principle that "the First Amendment prohibits civil courts from resolving church property disputes on the basis of religious doctrine and practice," and that "the amendment requires that civil courts defer to the resolution of issues of religious doctrine or polity by the highest court of a hierarchical church organization." The Court then specifically held that *questions of church membership and ecclesiastical discipline are matters of ecclesiastical doctrine and accordingly are beyond the reach of the civil courts*:

> Issues of church doctrine and polity pervade the provisions of the [Presbyterian] Book of Church Order dealing with the identity of a local congregation. The local church corporation consists of "all the communing members on the active role" of the church. The "active role," in turn, is composed "of those admitted to the Lord's table who are active in the church's life and work." The session is given the power "to suspend or exclude from the Lord's Supper those found delinquent, according to the Rules of Discipline." The session is subject to "the review and control" of the Presbytery's general authority to "order whatever pertains to the spiritual welfare of the churches under its care."[169]

---

[168] Jones v. Wolf, 443 U.S. 595 (1979) [hereinafter cited as *Jones*].

[169] *Id.* at 609 n.7.

Clearly, on the basis of this language, any determination by a church or denomination agency regarding the qualifications or lack of qualifications of a minister goes to the very essence of religious doctrine, and is not reviewable by a civil court. This result is not affected by a dismissed minister's claim that his or her civil, contract, or property rights were abridged as a result of the disciplinary process. To hold otherwise would be to ignore a century of Supreme Court precedent. The Court in *Jones* did acknowledge that in the context of disputes over *church property*, a civil court may engage in limited review so long as there is "no consideration of doctrinal matters, whether the ritual and liturgy or worship or the tenets of faith." For example, civil courts can resolve church property disputes on the basis of "neutral principles of law" involving no inquiries into religious doctrine, polity, or practice. One authority has aptly summarized *Jones* and its antecedents as follows:

> In short, civil authorities must always forego questions which are essentially religious as a matter of noninterference in the affairs of religious associations. Included in such matters are doctrine, discipline, appointment and removal of religious personnel, church polity, internal administration, and religious practice. In disputes principally over control of real estate, however, states may adopt a neutral principles of law approach so long as civil judges do not become entangled in questions essentially religious in the course of the rule's application.[170]

"The United States Supreme Court over the past century has consistently held that the civil courts are prohibited from interfering in ecclesiastical controversies involving issues of ecclesiastical doctrine, polity, practice, or administration."

In summary, the United States Supreme Court over the past century has consistently held that the civil courts are prohibited from interfering in ecclesiastical controversies involving issues of ecclesiastical doctrine, polity, practice, or administration. Determinations of ecclesiastical organizations regarding the standards of church membership or the qualifications of clergy indisputably involve such intrinsically ecclesiastical concerns and accordingly are not reviewable by the civil courts. This is so even if an ecclesiastical determination results in an alleged deprivation of property, contract, or civil rights, and even if the ecclesiastical process was arbitrary in the sense that it was not in accordance with the church organization's own internal rules and procedures.

While the Supreme Court has repudiated its 1928 ruling in *Gonzalez* to the extent that "arbitrariness" is no longer an available basis for civil court review of ecclesiastical determinations, it has left open "fraud" and "collusion" as possible

---

[170] C. Esbeck, *Tort Claims Against Churches and Ecclesiastical Officers: The First Amendment Considerations*, 89 W. VA. L. REV. 22-23 (1986).

grounds for review. However, the Court in *Serbian* severely limited the availability of "fraud and collusion" as grounds for civil court review by limiting their use to those occasions "when church tribunals act in bad faith for secular purposes." The mere assertion of fraud or collusion thus cannot invoke civil court review of ecclesiastical determinations regarding church discipline. A plaintiff also must establish that the alleged fraud or collusion was motivated by "bad faith for secular purposes." It would be extraordinary indeed to ever find a religious organization guilty of such conduct, and, understandably, none has ever been found to be so. The Supreme Court in *United States v. Ballard*,[171] anticipating the *Serbian* limitation, specifically held that frauds perpetrated by religious organizations are not redressable by the civil courts when matters of "religious faith or experience" are involved or implicated. The Court observed:

> Men may believe what they cannot prove. They may not be put to the proof
> of their religious doctrines or beliefs. Religious experiences which are as
> real as life to some may be incomprehensible to others. Yet the fact that they
> may be beyond the ken of mortals does not mean that they can be made
> suspect before the law. Many take their gospel from the New Testament.
> But it would hardly be supposed that they could be tried before a jury
> charged with the duty of determining whether those teachings contained
> false representations. The miracles of the New Testament, the Divinity
> of Christ, life after death, the power of prayer, are deep in the religious
> convictions of many. If one could be sent to jail because a jury in a hostile
> environment found those teachings false, little indeed would be left of
> religious freedom.[172]

Similarly, no court has ever found an ecclesiastical organization guilty of the *Serbian* definition of "collusion."

2. Decisions of State and Lower Federal Courts

State and lower federal courts have been asked to intervene in a wide variety of internal church disputes. Generally, such courts have followed the analysis developed by the United States Supreme Court in the cases summarized above. To be sure, some state and lower federal court decisions have deviated from the Supreme Court's analysis, but such cases ordinarily can be explained on the ground that they preceded some of the key Supreme Court decisions. Many state and lower courts have deviated from the Supreme Court's analysis because of unfamiliarity or ignorance.

The response by state and lower federal courts to many of the more common forms of internal church dispute are discussed fully in other sections of this text. Examples include:

---

[171] 322 U.S. 78 (1944).

[172] *Id.* at 86-87.

- church property disputes following a schism within a local church;[173]

- clergy dismissals;[174]

- discipline and dismissal of church members;[175]

- personal injuries resulting from the negligence or misconduct of church workers;[176]

- sexual seduction of counselees by clergy;[177]

- removal of officers and directors;[178]

- procedural irregularities in church business meetings;[179]

- access by members to church records;[180]

- dismissal of church employees;[181]

- clergy malpractice;[182] and

- personal liability of officers and directors.[183]

Political Activities by Churches and Other Religious Organizations § 9-08

In order to maintain their exemption from federal income taxes, churches and other religious organizations must comply with several requirements specified in section 501(c)(3) of the tax code. One of these requirements is that the organization not participate or intervene in any political campaign on behalf of (or in opposition to) any candidate for public office. Another requirement is that the organization not engage in substantial efforts to influence legislation.

---

[173] *See* chapter 7, *supra.*
[174] *See* § 2-04, *supra.*
[175] *See* § 6-10, *supra.*
[176] *See* chapter 10, *infra.*
[177] *See* § 4-11, *supra.*
[178] *See* § 6-06.4, *supra.*
[179] *See* § 6-12.4, *supra.*
[180] *See* § 6-03.1, *supra.*
[181] *See* § 8-22, *supra.*
[182] *See* § 4-05, *supra.*
[183] *See* § 6-07, *supra.*

Resource. *The prohibition of lobbying and campaign activities by churches is addressed fully in* R. Hammar, The Church and Clergy Tax Guide *(published annually by the publisher of this text).*

Bankruptcy Law

Key point 9-09. *Bankruptcy trustees are prohibited by the federal Religious Liberty and Charitable Donation Protection Act from recovering contributions made by bankrupt debtors to a church or other charity prior to declaring bankruptcy, unless the contributions were made with an intent to defraud creditors. This protection extends to any contribution amounting to less than 15 percent of a debtor's gross annual income, or more if the debtor can establish a regular pattern of giving more. In addition, the Act bars bankruptcy courts from rejecting a bankruptcy plan because it allows the debtor to continue making contributions to a church or charity. Again, this protection applies to debtors whose bankruptcy plan calls for making charitable contributions of less than 15 percent of their gross annual income, or more if they can prove a pattern of giving more.*

In the past, churches were adversely affected by federal bankruptcy law in two ways. First, many courts ruled that bankruptcy trustees could recover contributions made to a church by a bankrupt donor within a year of filing a bankruptcy petition. Second, church members who declared bankruptcy were not allowed by some bankruptcy courts to continue making contributions to their church. These harmful restrictions were eliminated last year when Congress enacted the Religious Liberty and Charitable Donation Protection Act. The Act, which is actually an amendment to the bankruptcy code, provides significant protection to churches as well as to church members who file for bankruptcy. This section will review the background of the Act, explain its key provisions, and demonstrate its application with practical examples.

1. Authority of Bankruptcy Trustees to Recover Charitable Contributions

background

Section 548(a) of the bankruptcy code authorizes a bankruptcy trustee to "avoid" or recover two kinds of "fraudulent transfers" made by bankrupt debtors within a year of filing for bankruptcy:

(1) **Intent to defraud.** Section 548(a)(1) gives a bankruptcy trustee the legal authority to recover "any transfer of an interest of the debtor in property . . . that was made or incurred on or within one year before the date of the filing of the petition, if the debtor voluntarily or involuntarily made such transfer or incurred such obligation with actual intent to hinder, delay, or defraud any entity to which the debtor was or became, on or after the date that such transfer was made or such obligation was incurred, indebted."

(2) **Transfers of cash or property for less than "reasonably equivalent value."**
Section 548(a)(2) gives a bankruptcy trustee the legal authority to recover "any transfer of an interest of the debtor in property . . . that was made or incurred on or within one year before the date of the filing of the petition, if the debtor voluntarily or involuntarily . . . received less than a reasonably equivalent value in exchange for such transfer or obligation and was insolvent on the date that such transfer was made or such obligation was incurred, or became insolvent as a result of such transfer or obligation . . . or intended to incur, or believed that the debtor would incur, debts that would be beyond the debtor's ability to pay as such debts matured."

In the past, many bankruptcy trustees contacted churches, demanding that they return donations made by bankrupt debtors within a year of filing for bankruptcy. They argued that charitable contributions made by bankrupt debtors to a church are for less than "reasonably equivalent value," and therefore can be recovered by bankruptcy trustees under the second type of "fraudulent transfer" mentioned above. Donors and churches protested such efforts. They insisted that donors *do* receive valuable benefits in exchange for their contributions, such as preaching, teaching, sacraments, and counseling. Not so, countered bankruptcy trustees. These benefits would be available whether or not a donor gives anything, and so it cannot be said that a donor is receiving "reasonably equivalent value" in exchange for a contribution. Many courts agreed with this logic, and ordered churches to turn over contributions made by bankrupt debtors. This created a hardship for many churches. After all, most churches had already spent the debtor's contributions before being contacted by the bankruptcy trustee, and so "returning" them (especially if they were substantial) was often difficult.

These arguments were conclusively resolved by Congress in 1998 with the enactment, by unanimous vote, of the Religious Freedom and Charitable Donation Protection Act. In introducing the House bill, Congressman Packard observed:

Mr. Speaker, how much of the work done by your church or favorite charity depends on the generous donations of parishioners and contributors like yourself? Did you know that creditors can take already donated money from them because current bankruptcy law allows them to do so? It's unbelievable, but it's true. In a recent case, a United States Federal Bankruptcy Trustee brought an action against the Crystal Evangelical Free Church of New Hope, Minnesota. In doing so, this unprecedented case reinterpreted the Bankruptcy Code to mean that if an individual gives money to a non-profit group within one year of declaring bankruptcy, creditors can come after the group to re-claim this money. Why? Because an individual must receive something of "reasonable equivalent value" in return for a monetary donation. Mr. Speaker, current law essentially says that if an individual has filed for bankruptcy, he cannot simply donate money to a charitable organization or to the church. However, because the

Bankruptcy Code allows for certain "entertainment exemptions," taking a luxury vacation, purchasing liquor, buying a new car, or making 1-900 calls to psychics, are all reasonable expenditures. This case outraged me and I decided to do something about it. I introduced legislation in early October to protect certain charitable contributions. Known as the *Religious Liberty and Charitable Donation Protection Act*, this legislation will amend U.S. Code to protect our nation's churches and charities from the hands of creditors. Mr. Speaker, H.R. 2604, the *Religious Liberty and Charitable Donation Protection Act,* will allow your church or favorite charity to continue to thrive and prosper. Donations received in good faith from individuals will not be taken from their pockets by creditors. I encourage all of my colleagues to co-sponsor this important legislation. As the holidays quickly approach, we must work to address the needs of our churches, charities and the less fortunate who rely on their vital services. H.R. 2604 will do just that.

The key to the Act was the following provision, which is an amendment to section 548(a)(2) of the bankruptcy code:

A transfer of a charitable contribution to a qualified religious or charitable entity or organization shall not be considered to be a transfer [subject to recovery by a bankruptcy trustee] in any case in which—(A) the amount of that contribution does not exceed 15 percent of the gross annual income of the debtor for the year in which the transfer of the contribution is made; or (B) the contribution made by a debtor exceeded the percentage amount of gross annual income specified in subparagraph (A), if the transfer was consistent with the practices of the debtor in making charitable contributions.

Key point. Note that there are two separate protections here: (1) bankruptcy trustees cannot recover contributions made by a bankrupt debtor for less than reasonably equivalent value within a year prior to filing for bankruptcy if the contributions amount to 15 percent or less of the debtor's gross annual income; and, (2) bankruptcy trustees cannot recover contributions made by a bankrupt debtor for less than reasonably equivalent value within a year prior to filing for bankruptcy if the contributions exceed 15 percent of the debtor's gross annual income, and the amount of the contributions are consistent with the debtor's giving practices.

Key point. It is critical to note that this provision only amends the second type of "fraudulent transfer" described at the beginning of this section—transfers of cash or property made for less than "reasonably equivalent value" within a year of filing a bankruptcy petition. The Act does not amend the first kind of fraudulent transfer— those made with an actual intent to defraud.

The meaning of the above-quoted section was addressed in a committee report accompanying the Act. The report reads, in part:

[The Act] protects certain charitable contributions made by an individual debtor to qualified religious or charitable entities within one year preceding the filing date of the debtor's bankruptcy petition from being avoided by a bankruptcy trustee under section 548 of the Bankruptcy Code. The bill protects donations to qualified religious organizations as well as to charities . . . [The Act] is not intended to diminish any of the protections against prepetition fraudulent transfers available under section 548 of the Bankruptcy Code. If a debtor, on the eve of filing for bankruptcy relief, suddenly donates 15 percent of his or her gross income to a religious organization, the debtor's fraudulent intent, if any, would be subject to scrutiny under . . . the Bankruptcy Code. This fifteen percent "safe harbor" merely shifts the burden of proof and limits litigation to where there is evidence of a change in pattern large enough to establish fraudulent intent. As Professor Laycock explained during the subcommittee hearing on this bill: "If I have been going along for years putting $5 a week in the collection plate and all of a sudden, before I file for bankruptcy, I clean out my last account and give 15 percent of my last year's income to my church, the trustee and the bankruptcy judge will look at the timing, the amount, the circumstances, the change in pattern, and they will say those are all badges of fraud. They will say I had the actual intent to hinder or defraud my creditors, and that is recoverable under section 548(a)(1). The fraud scenario is not going to happen."

Likewise, Senator Grassley . . . stated: "[T]he bill does not amend section 548(a)(1) of the Bankruptcy Code. This section lets bankruptcy courts recover any transfer of assets on the eve of bankruptcy if the transfer was made to delay or hinder a creditor. Therefore, if the bill is enacted, we don't have to worry about a sudden rash of charitable giving in anticipation of bankruptcy. Such transfers would obviously be for the purpose of hindering creditors and would still be subject to the bankruptcy judge's powers. In other words, there really isn't much room for abuse as a result of [this] legislation."

In addition, [the Act] protects the rights of certain debtors to tithe or make charitable contributions after filing for bankruptcy relief. Some courts have dismissed a debtor's chapter 7 case (a form of bankruptcy relief that discharges an individual debtor of most of his or her personal liability without any requirement for repayment) for substantial abuse under section 707(b) of the Bankruptcy Code based on the debtor's charitable contributions. . . .

The Religious Freedom and Charitable Donation Protection Act Checklist

Here is a checklist that will be a helpful resource in applying the new law:

Step #1: Did the bankruptcy debtor make one or more contributions of cash or property to a church within a year preceding the filing of a bankruptcy petition?

☐ If not, stop here. A bankruptcy trustee cannot recover the debtor's contributions from the church.

☐ If yes, go to step #2

Step #2: In making contributions to the church, did the debtor have an actual intent to hinder, delay, or defraud his or her creditors? In deciding if an intent to defraud exists, consider the timing, amount, and circumstances surrounding the contributions, as well as any change in the debtor's normal pattern or practice.

☐ If yes, a bankruptcy trustee can recover from the church contributions made by the debtor within a year prior to the filing of the bankruptcy petition.

☐ If not, go to step #3.

Step #3: Did the debtor receive "reasonably equivalent value" for the contributions made to the church? Note that reasonably equivalent value will not include such "intangible" religious services as preaching, teaching, sacraments, or counseling.

☐ If yes, stop here. A bankruptcy trustee cannot recover the debtor's contributions from the church.

☐ If no, go to step #5.

Step #4: Is the value of the debtor's contributions 15 percent or less of his or her gross annual income?

☐ If yes, stop here. A bankruptcy trustee cannot recover the debtor's contributions from the church.

☐ If no, go to step #5.

Step #5: Is the value of the debtor's contributions consistent with the practices of the debtor in making charitable contributions?

☐ If yes, stop here. A bankruptcy trustee cannot recover the debtor's contributions from the church.

☐ If no, a bankruptcy trustee can recover from the church contributions made by the debtor within a year prior to the filing of the bankruptcy petition.

Let's illustrate the impact of this provision with some practical examples.

Examples

• *Bob has attended his church for many years. For the past two years, his contributions to his church have averaged $50 per week, or about $2,500 per year. Bob's gross annual income for the current year is about $40,000. On May 15 Bob files for bankruptcy. A bankruptcy trustee contacts the church treasurer, and demands that the church turn over all contributions made by Bob during the year prior to the date he filed for bankruptcy. The Religious Freedom and Charitable Donation Protection Act applies directly to this scenario, and protects the church from the reach of the trustee, since: (1) the amount of Bob's annual contributions in the two previous years in which the contributions were made did not exceed 15 percent of his gross annual income (15 percent of $40,000 = $6,000); and (2) the timing, amount, and circumstances surrounding the contributions, as well as the lack of any change in the debtor's normal pattern or practice, suggest that Bob did not commit intentional fraud, and so the trustee cannot recover contributions on this basis.*

• *Same facts as the previous example, except that in addition to his weekly giving Bob made a one-time gift to the church building fund in the amount of $5,000. Bob's total giving for the year preceding the filing of his bankruptcy petition now totals $7,500, or nearly 19 percent of his gross annual income. As a result, he is not eligible for the 15 percent "safe harbor" rule. The trustee will be able to recover the $7,500 in contributions made by Bob to the church within a year of filing the bankruptcy petition, unless Bob can demonstrate that giving 19 percent of his gross annual income is consistent with his normal practices in making charitable contributions. It is unlikely that Bob or the church will be able to satisfy this condition, since the gift to the building fund was a "one time" extraordinary gift for Bob that was unlike his giving pattern in any prior year.*

• *Barb believes strongly in giving to her church, and for each of the past several years has given 20 percent of her income. On June 1 of the current year she files for bankruptcy. A bankruptcy trustee contacts the church treasurer, and demands that the church turn over all contributions made by Barb for the year prior to the date she filed for bankruptcy. The Religious Freedom and Charitable Donation Protection Act applies directly to this scenario, and protects the church from the reach of the trustee, since: (1) the amount of Barb's annual contributions for the years in which the contributions were made exceeded 15 percent of her gross annual income, but she had a consistent practice in prior years of giving this amount; and (2) the timing, amount, and circumstances surrounding the contributions, as well as the lack of any change in the debtor's normal pattern or practice, suggest that Barb did not commit intentional fraud, and so the trustee cannot recover contributions on this basis.*

• *Bill has attended his church sporadically for the past several years. For the past few years, his contributions to his church have averaged less than $1,000 per year. Bill's gross annual income for the current and previous year is about $80,000. Bill is facing a staggering debt load due to mismanagement and unrestrained credit card charges. He wants to declare bankruptcy, but he has a $15,000 bank account that he wants to protect. He decides to give the entire amount to his church in order to keep it from the bankruptcy court and his creditors. He gives the entire balance to his church on June 1. On July 1, Bill files for bankruptcy. A bankruptcy trustee contacts the church treasurer, demanding that the church turn over the $15,000 contribution.*

The Religious Freedom and Charitable Donation Protection Act does not protect Bill or the church. The timing, amount, and circumstances surrounding the contribution of $15,000 strongly indicate that Bill had an actual intent to hinder, delay, or defraud his creditors. This conclusion is reinforced by the fact that the gift was contrary to Bill's normal pattern or practice of giving. As a result, the trustee probably will be able to force the church to return the $15,000.

• A federal court in New Jersey ordered a church to return a $20,000 contribution to a bankruptcy court that had been made by a church member within a year before he filed for bankruptcy. The contribution amounted to 74 percent of the member's total annual income. The court acknowledged that section 548(a)(2) of the Bankruptcy Code allows debtors to give up to 15 percent of their income to charity in the year prior to filing for bankruptcy, or a larger amount that is "consistent with the practices of the debtor in making charitable contributions." The court noted that the Bankruptcy Code provides no guidance as to interpretation of the phrase "consistent with the practices of the debtor in making charitable contributions." However, it concluded that "in this case it is beyond reasonable dispute that the debtor's $20,000 donation to the church was not consistent with his prior practices in making charitable contributions. The next largest donation made by the debtor during the prior two years was $2,000. The $20,000 donation also exceeds his total annual donations for each of [the previous three years]. It would be a gross distortion of the concept of consistency to hold that this donation was consistent with the debtor's prior practices in making charitable contributions." The court rejected the church's argument that an uncharacteristically large donation can be disregarded in an evaluation of "consistency" on the ground that it came from an unexpected "windfall," such as an inheritance.[184]

Key point. *Whenever a donor makes a large gift of cash or property to a church, church leaders should be alert to the fact that a bankruptcy trustee may be able to recover the contribution at a later date if the donor files for bankruptcy within a year after making the gift and none of the exceptions described in this section applies.*

2. Making Charitable Contributions after Filing for Bankruptcy

The bankruptcy code states that a court may not approve a bankruptcy plan unless it provides that all of a debtor's "projected disposable income to be received in the three-year period beginning on the date that the first payment is due under the plan will be applied to make payments under the plan." In addition, a court can dismiss a bankruptcy case to avoid "substantial abuse" of the bankruptcy law. Many courts have dismissed bankruptcy cases on the ground that a debtor's plan called for a continuation of charitable contributions.

The Religious Freedom and Charitable Donation Protection Act of 1998 clarifies that bankruptcy courts no longer can dismiss bankruptcy cases on the ground that a debtor proposes to continue making charitable contributions. This assumes that the debtor's contributions will not exceed 15 percent of his or her gross annual income for the year in which the contributions are made (or a higher percentage if consistent with the debtor's regular practice in making charitable contributions).

---

[184] Jackson v. The Church of Manalapan, 249 B.R. 373 (D.N.J. 2000).

The committee report accompanying the Act states:

In addition [the bill] protects the rights of certain debtors to tithe or make charitable contributions after filing for bankruptcy relief. Some courts have dismissed a debtor's chapter 7 case . . . for substantial abuse under section 707(b) of the bankruptcy code based on the debtor's charitable contributions. The bill also protects the rights of debtors who file for chapter 13 to tithe or make charitable contributions. Some courts have held that tithing is not a reasonably necessary expense or have attempted to fix a specific percentage as the maximum that the debtor may include in his or her budget.

Let's illustrate the impact of this provision with a few practical examples.

Examples

• *A bankruptcy court in Arkansas ruled that a bankruptcy trustee could not object to a couple's bankruptcy plan on the ground that they proposed to continue making contributions of approximately ten percent to their church.*[185]

• *Brad files a chapter 7 bankruptcy petition. Brad's plan states that he will use all available "disposable income" to pay his creditors during the three year period following the approval of his plan. But the plan permits Brad to continue making contributions to his church, which in the past have averaged 10 percent of his income. Some creditors object to the plan, and demand that the court reject it, since Brad will be making contributions to his church rather than using these funds to pay off his lawful debts. The Religious Liberty and Charitable Donation Protection Act of 1998 specifies that the court cannot reject Brad's bankruptcy plan because of the charitable contributions—since the contributions are less than 15 percent of his gross annual income.*

• *Same facts as the previous example, except that Brad's plan proposes to pay contributions to his church in the amount of 25 percent of his gross annual income. Brad would rather that his church receive all available income than his creditors. Several creditors object to this plan. The court probably will deny Brad's request for bankruptcy protection, since the substantial contributions proposed in his plan exceed 15 percent of his gross annual income, and are not consistent with his prior practice of making charitable contributions.*

• *A bankruptcy court in Montana ruled that a bankruptcy trustee could not object to a couple's bankruptcy plan on the ground that they proposed to continue making contributions to their church in the amount of seven percent of their gross income.*[186]

---

[185] In re Petty, 338 B.R. 805 (E.D. Ark. 2006).

[186] In re Cavanagh, 242 B.R. 707 (D. Mont. 2000).

Instructional Aids to Chapter 9

Key Terms

charitable solicitation

copyright

copyright notice

derivative work

infringement

publication

securities fraud

security

testamentary gift

Uniform Securities Act

Learning Objectives

- Recognize that churches are not immune from all forms of government regulation.

- Understand the application of various financial regulations to churches, including regulation of charitable solicitations, limitations on charitable giving, and securities law.

- Understand the basic elements of copyright law, and their application to church practices.

- Understand the application of the Charitable Contribution and Charitable Donation Act to churches.

Short-Answer Questions

1. Are churches immune from all forms of government regulation? Explain.

2. Under what circumstances may a state regulate a person's religious beliefs?

3. Laws regulating religious organizations may be upheld by the courts if they meet what four requirements?

4. A church operates a preschool. The preschool is subject to health and safety standards under a state law that is designed to protect children. A state agency learns that the preschool is in violation of a number of safety standards, including the fact that exit doors open inward rather than outward. The agency orders the church to comply with these standards, but the pastor refuses. He insists that the church is subject to the "lordship" of Jesus Christ, and not the state. Is he correct? How would a civil court evaluate the pastor's position?

5. A church is considering the use of a professional fund-raiser to assist in raising funds for a new building. What two kinds of state regulation may apply?

6. A state law requires all religious organizations that solicit over half of their financial support from non-members to register with the state. Is this law constitutional? Explain.

7. M, a widow, executes a will on July 1st of this year, leaving $500,000 to her church. She dies on September 15th of this year, and her children contest the gift to the church. The minister of the church asks for your opinion concerning the legal validity of this gift. What would you say?

8. Same facts as the previous question except that M had no surviving children or grandchildren. Would this change your opinion?

9. Summarize the United States Supreme Court's ruling in Larsen v. Valente.

10. Summarize the United States Supreme Court's ruling in the Village of Schaumburg case.

11. Define mortmain law.

12. How many states have mortmain laws?

13. What was the purpose of mortmain laws? Do you believe this purpose is legitimate?

14. An elderly man dies, leaving a will that was executed 25 days prior to his death, that leaves half of his estate to his church. Is this will valid? Explain.

15. To raise funds for a new building, a church sells bonds through its minister and board members to church members. The church assumes that it is exempt from any legal restrictions. Is this a prudent assumption? Explain.

16. How many states have enacted securities laws?

17. Identify two common forms of security that are issued by churches for fund-raising purposes.

18. Are churches automatically exempt from registering their securities under state law? Are they required to "register" those persons who will be promoting and selling church securities?

19. Under what circumstances will a church be exempt from the prohibition of fraudulent activities in the sale of securities?

20. A church wants to raise $500,000 for a new building by issuing promissory notes. The pastor learns that churches are exempt from registering their securities under state law, and so he assumes that the church can proceed to issue the notes. Is this a prudent assumption? Explain.

21. A church wants to raise $500,000 for a new building by issuing promissory notes. The securities are not exempt from registration under state law, and so the church retains an attorney who registers the securities. The pastor actively encourages church members to purchase securities. On one occasion, he met with G, an elderly widow of modest means, and persuades her to purchase a $10,000 note. Evaluate the propriety of this transaction.

22. A church issues $1 million in 10-year promissory notes to its members and spends all of the proceeds on a new education building. Has the church committed securities fraud? Explain.

23. A church issues 10-year, 10 percent promissory notes to several of its members. No prospectus, offering circular, or other literature is filed with the state securities commission or made available to investors. Has the church committed securities fraud? Explain.

24. To help promote the sale of church notes, a minister assures his congregation during a sermon that the notes are as safe "as the Rock of Gibraltar" since they were issued on behalf of the church. Is this statement legally appropriate? Explain.

25. A local church plans to issue $1 million in promissory notes. It prepares a prospectus describing the securities, the history of the church, and the church's financial condition. The prospectus also contains the following five statements. Indicate whether each statement is legally permissible.

   a. "The membership of the church has increased during each of the past ten years, so it can be expected that membership growth will continue to occur."

   b. "These securities have been exempted from registration by the state securities commission and thus you are assured that they have been carefully studied and approved by the state."

   c. "A copy of this prospectus shall at all times be maintained in the church office for the benefit of any prospective investor."

   d. "Interest on these obligations is guaranteed."

   e. "The church was established in 1935."

26. Same facts as the previous question. The church decides not to include the following information in its prospectus. Indicate after each statement whether its omission is legally permissible.

   a. A lawsuit is pending against the church alleging that the church is liable on the basis of negligence for the injuries suffered by two minors who were sexually molested by a volunteer church worker. The lawsuit is asking for $5 million.

   b. The total dollar value of securities to be offered.

   c. A statement that no sinking fund reserve exists.

   d. A statement that for three of the past five years the church's expenses exceeded revenues.

   e. A statement that for two of the past three years the church's attendance has declined.

   f. A statement that the pastor was installed one year ago.

27. Can a church be liable for securities fraud if it in good faith did not know that its activities were fraudulent? Explain.

28. To raise funds for a remodeling project, a church solicits three-year pledge commitments from church members. Is this practice subject to state securities law?

29. Are churches subject to the federal Securities Act of 1933? Explain.

30. Define pyramid scheme.

31. Define Ponzi scheme.

32. What is the Berne Convention? How did it affect copyright law in the United States?

33. A church choir director sees a piece of sheet music that she would like to duplicate for members of the choir. The sheet music contains no copyright notice. Does this necessarily mean that it is in the public domain? Explain.

34. Which of the following is a requirement of current copyright law: (a) affixation of a copyright notice to publicly distributed copies of a copyrighted work first published since March of 1989; (2) registration; (3) deposit of 2 copies with the Copyright Office.

35. Pastor L is minister of music at his church. He composes a religious work during office hours at the church, using church equipment and supplies. Answer the following questions:

a. Who owns the copyright in this work? Explain.

b. What is the name used by the Copyright Act for this kind of work?

c. How could the copyright ownership have been vested in another party?

d. What is the term of copyright protection for this work?

e. Define inurement, and explain the relevance of this term to a church's tax-exempt status.

f. Does the transaction in this example constitute inurement? Why or why not? If it does, how can this conclusion be avoided?

36. D composes a religious song this year. How long will the copyright last in the work? Are any renewals necessary?

37. List the five exclusive rights of a copyright owner.

38. What is copyright infringement?

39. During morning worship services at a church the following activities occur. Explain whether or not each activity constitutes copyright infringement:

a. The church congregation sings two copyrighted hymns in the church hymnal.

b. The church choir sings a copyrighted song.

c. The choir director purchased only one copy of the song the choir performed, and made copies for every member of the choir on church duplicating equipment.

d. A vocalist sings a copyrighted song as a solo, making a copy of the music for an accompanist.

e. The church prints the lyrics (not the music) of a religious song in the bulletin.

f. The church makes an audio recording of the worship service

g. The church makes a video recording of the worship service.

h. The lyrics of a copyrighted religious song are displayed on a screen using an overhead projector (a church employee typed the lyrics on a transparency).

i. A minister reads a chapter from a copyrighted translation of the Bible.

40. Would the so-called "fair use guidelines" excuse any of the activities described in the previous question?

41. The music minister of a local church displays chorus lyrics on a wall during worship services by means of an opaque projector. Is this practice legally permissible? Explain.

42. The music minister of a local church composed a new arrangement of a copyrighted hymn and had the choir perform it during worship services. Has the minister, or the church, violated the copyright law? Explain.

43. A church prints the lyrics of a copyrighted song on a bulletin insert and on an overhead transparency. Does either practice constitute "fair use"? Explain.

44. A church conducts a Saturday evening concert featuring a musical group. The church does not charge an admissions fee, but it does pay a fee to the musical group. Does the "nonprofit performance" exemption to copyright infringement apply? The religious services exemption?

45. A church shows videos to its youth group. Some of the tapes were purchased by the church, and others were rented at a local video store. Does the showing of these videos to the youth group constitute copyright infringement? What if no admissions fee is charged?

46. A church purchases the current version of a popular word processing program for use on the church computer. A staff member enjoys the program so much that she takes it home and copies it onto her personal computer. Is this permissible?

47. A church secretary is assembling the church bulletin for next week. She comes across a poem that she would like to include. Since the poem does not contain a notice of copyright, she assumes that it is in the public domain. Is this a safe assumption?

48. Using university copyright policies as a guide, how might a church ensure that its pastor owns the rights in his own sermons without jeopardizing the church's tax-exempt status?

49. A pastor writes a book. What is the duration of the copyright in this work?

50. Must copyright owners register their works with the United States Copyright Office? Explain.

51. Is it legally permissible to paraphrase another's copyrighted work, so long as verbatim copying is avoided?

52. What are three common church practices that a CCLI copyright license will permit? What are three practices that a CCLI copyright license will not permit?

53. Evaluate the likelihood that a civil court would intervene in each of the following church disputes:

a. A minister claims that her dismissal violated the church bylaws.

b. A minister claims that his dismissal was based on fraud and collusion.

c. A church dismisses a member on the basis of doctrinal deviation. The member challenges the dismissal in court.

d. A church splits, and both factions claim title to the church's properties.

e. A church member sues a minister on the basis of malpractice.

f. A church is sued for copyright infringement.

g. A minister challenges a congregational vote to dismiss him, arguing that the meeting was not called in accordance with church bylaws.

54. J has attended a church for many years. For the past three years, her contributions to the church have averaged $100 per week, or about $5,000 per year. J's gross annual income for the current year is about $50,000. On July 15 J files for bankruptcy. A bankruptcy trustee demands that the church turn over all contributions made by J during the year prior to the date he filed for bankruptcy. How should the church respond?

55. Same facts as the previous example, except that in addition to his weekly giving J made a one-time gift to the church's missions fund of $10,000. Does this change your answer? Explain.

56. T believes strongly in giving to her church, and for each of the past several years has given 20 percent of her income. On July 1 of the current year she files for bankruptcy. A bankruptcy trustee demands that the church turn over all contributions made by T for the year prior to the date she filed for bankruptcy. How should the church respond?

57. D has attended church occasionally over the past several years. For the past few years, his contributions to his church have averaged less than $2,000 per year. D's gross annual income for the current and previous year is about $50,000. D wants to declare bankruptcy, but he has a $20,000 bank account that he wants to protect. He decides to give the entire amount to his church in order to keep it from the bankruptcy court and his creditors. He gives the entire balance to his church on June 1. On July 1, D files for bankruptcy. A bankruptcy trustee demands that the church turn over the $20,000 contribution. How should the church respond?

58. B files a chapter 7 bankruptcy petition. B's plan states that he will use all available "disposable income" to pay his creditors during the three year period following the approval of his plan. But the plan permits B to continue making contributions to his church, which in the past have averaged 10 percent of his income. Some creditors object to the plan, and demand that the court reject it, since B will be making contributions to his church rather than using these funds to pay off his lawful debts. What is the likely outcome of this case? Will the court accept B's bankruptcy plan?

59. Same facts as the previous example, except that B's plan proposes to pay contributions to his church in the amount of 25 percent of his gross annual income. B would rather that his church receive all available income than his creditors. Several creditors object to this plan. What is the likely outcome of this case? Will the court accept B's bankruptcy plan?

Essay Questions

1. Persons often uncritically jump to the conclusion that churches should never be subject to government regulation, under any circumstances. Do you agree? If not, what arguments could you make to oppose such an absolutist view? Construct a rule that in your opinion strikes an appropriate balance between legitimate government regulation and a church's right to be free of undue governmental interference.

2. Many churches are offended when they learn that a publisher of religious music has prosecuted a church for copyright infringement. Should Congress amend the Copyright Act to exempt churches from the prohibition against copyright infringement? Explain.

3. The Bankruptcy Code permits debtors to obtain bankruptcy relief even though they make payments of up to 15 percent of their annual income to their church. Some believe that such a rule facilitates stealing from creditors, or, as one court concluded, "makes Jesus Christ a priority creditor." Can this rule be justified ethically or scripturally? Explain.

CHAPTER TEN

Church Legal Liability

Legal Briefs

Churches are exposed to legal liability as a result of a number of acts and omissions, many of which have been addressed in previous chapters. This chapter addresses church liability based on four types of negligence—vicarious liability for the negligence of employees; negligent selection; negligent retention; and negligent supervision, plus liability based on counseling, breach of fiduciary duty, ratification, and defamation.

> "Negligence refers to conduct that creates an unreasonable and foreseeable risk of harm to another's person or property, and that in fact results in the foreseeable harm. "

Negligence refers to conduct that creates an unreasonable and foreseeable risk of harm to another's person or property, and that in fact results in the foreseeable harm. Churches can be liable on the basis of negligence in a variety of ways, four of which are addressed in this chapter. To illustrate, churches can be vicariously liable for the negligence of employees committed within the course of their employment under the legal principle of respondeat superior. Churches also may be liable on the basis of negligence in the selection, retention, or supervision of employees and volunteer workers.

In recent years, some courts have found churches liable on the basis of a breach of a fiduciary duty for injuries occurring on their premises or in the course of their activities. This chapter also addresses church liability for defamation, and surveys a number of defenses available to churches that are sued on the basis of these theories of liability.

Thankfully, for each of the liabilities examined in this chapter, "risk management" is emphasized, and churches are provided with several suggestions to reduce their risk of legal liability.

The chapter concludes with an analysis of the liability of denominational agencies for the activities of affiliated churches and clergy. This is a question of increasing concern to many denominations.

This chapter is written with two purposes in mind: (1) to explain several common and significant theories of church liability; and (2) to assist church leaders in adopting strategies to manage or reduce these risks. The good news is that by implementing relatively simple precautions, church leaders can significantly reduce the risk of church liability.

Table 10-1

Churches can be sued for a variety of acts and omissions. Table 10-1 lists the ten most common sources of individual church liability for the years 2001 through 2007.[1] Table 10-2 lists the five most common categories of church liability over the same period of time. Categories are broader than individual sources of liability, since they combine similar theories of liability. Both tables will provide church leaders with an excellent understanding of the most common sources of liability facing churches.

Table 10-1
The Top Ten Sources of Church Liability from 2000-2007

rank	2000	2001	2002	2003	2004	2005	2006	2007
1	personal injury	zoning	zoning	zoning	zoning	sex with child	sex with child	property disputes
2	zoning	personal injury	personal injury	personal injury	sex with child	zoning	zoning	sex with child
3	property disputes	property disputes	sex with child	property disputes	property disputes	property disputes	personal injury	zoning
4	contract disputes	clergy privilege	clergy removal	sex with child	personal injury	personal injury	property disputes	personal injury
5	clergy removal	property taxes	contract disputes	contract disputes	property taxes	insurance coverage	insurance coverage	insurance coverage
6	sex with child	employee termination	property disputes	estates	insurance coverage	religious freedom	clergy removal	contract disputes
7	estates	sex with child	estates	sex with adult	sex discrimination	sex discrimination	religious freedom	property taxes
8	sex with adult	contract disputes	insurance coverage	insurance coverage	clergy privilege	property taxes	sex discrimination	estates
9	insurance coverage	workers compensation	sex with adult	clergy removal	estates	clergy removal	sex with adult	clergy removal
10	property taxes	defamation	property taxes	property taxes	construction disputes	securities	property taxes	clergy privilege

---

[1] Tables 1 and 2 are based on the author's review of every reported court decision in all 50 state courts and all federal courts. State trial court rulings are not reflected, nor are claims or settlements not involving a reported court decision.

Table 10-2
The Top Five Categories of Church Liability from 2000-2007

rank	2000	2001	2002	2003	2004	2005	2006	2007
1	employ-ment disputes	employ-ment disputes	employ-ment disputes	property disputes	employ-ment disputes	sexual acts	sexual acts	property disputes
2	personal injury	personal injury	zoning	employ-ment disputes	property disputes	employ-ment disputes	employ-ment disputes	sexual acts
3	property disputes	property disputes	per-sonal injury	personal injury	zoning	property disputes	zoning disputes	employ-ment disputes
4	zoning	sexual acts	sexual acts	sexual acts	sexual acts	zoning	property disputes	zoning
5	sexual acts	zoning	prop-erty disputes	zoning	personal injury	personal injury	personal injury	personal injury

All of the theories of church liability listed in Tables 10-1 and 10-2 are addressed in *Pastor, Church & Law*, plus several more. The following theories of church liability are addressed in other chapters:

- discipline and removal of ministers;[2]
- undue influence;[3]
- invasion of privacy;[4]
- clergy malpractice;[5]
- breach of contract;[6]
- refusal to permit inspection of church records;[7]
- church names;[8]
- removal of officers and directors;[9]
- discipline and removal of members;[10]
- procedural irregularities in church business meetings;[11]

[2] Section 2-04, *supra.*

[3] Section 4-03, *supra.*

[4] Section 4-04, *supra.*

[5] Section 4-05, *supra.*

[6] Section 4-06, *supra.*

[7] Section 6-03.1, *supra.*

[8] Section 6-05, *supra.*

[9] Section 6-06.4, *supra.*

[10] Section 6-10, *supra.*

[11] Section 6-12, *supra.*

Table 10-2

- church property disputes;[12]

- zoning law;[13]

- violation of municipal building codes;[14]

- violation of local landmarking ordinances;[15]

- eminent domain;[16]

- violation of restrictive covenants;[17]

- materialman's liens;[18]

- adverse possession;[19]

- premises liability;[20]

- workers compensation;[21]

- violations of the Fair Labor Standards Act;[22]

- several kinds of employment discrimination;[23]

- termination of employees;[24]

- reference letters;[25]

- securities law violations;[26]

- copyright law violations;[27]

This chapter addresses the following additional theories of church liability:

- vicarious liability for the negligence of employees

- negligent selection

- negligent retention

- negligent supervision

---

[12] Sections 7-01 through 7-04.

[13] Section 7-06, *supra.*

[14] Section 7-08, *supra.*

[15] Section 7-10, *supra.*

[16] Section 7-11, *supra.*

[17] Section 7-13, *supra.*

[18] Section 7-15, *supra.*

[19] Section 7-18, *supra.*

[20] Section 7-20, *supra.*

[21] Section 8-07, *supra*

[22] Section 8-08, *supra.*

[23] Sections 8-09 through 8-21, *supra.*

[24] Section 8-22, *supra.*

[25] Section 8-24, *supra.*

[26] Section 9-04, *supra.*

[27] Section 9-05, *supra.*

- counseling
- breach of fiduciary duty
- ratification
- defamation
- denominational liability
- church vans
- inspection of computers
- prayer lists
- defibrillators
- Sarbanes-Oxley

Key point. *This chapter has two purposes: (1) to explain several common and significant theories of church liability; and (2) to assist church leaders in adopting strategies to manage or reduce these risks. The good news is that by implementing relatively simple precautions, church leaders can significantly reduce the risk of church liability.*

Negligence as a Basis for Liability—In General

§ 10-01

Negligence is conduct that creates an unreasonable risk of foreseeable harm to the person or property of another, and which results in the foreseeable harm. The important point to recognize is that negligence need not be intentional. For example, negligence may include conduct that is simply careless, heedless, or inadvertent.

Churches can be liable on the basis of negligence in a number of ways. First, they can be liable for their own negligence. Examples here include the negligent selection or negligent retention of church workers, or the negligent supervision of church activities. To illustrate, a church may be guilty of negligent selection if it hires a convicted child molester or uses a driver with numerous traffic violations. A church may be guilty of negligent supervision if it uses an inadequate number of qualified adults to supervise a church youth activity.

Churches also can be liable for the negligence of employees and volunteers occurring within the scope of their work. Employers generally are responsible for the negligence of an employee (or volunteer) occurring within the scope or course of employment. This vicarious or imputed liability of an employer for the negligence of an employee is known as *respondeat superior* (the "employer responds"). All of these forms of negligence are addressed in the following sections of this chapter.

Respondeat superior= the "employer responds"

Vicarious Liability (Respondeat Superior)

§ 10-02

Key point 10-02. *The doctrine of respondeat superior imposes vicarious liability on employers for the negligent acts of their employees committed within the scope of their employment.*

Churches are often sued on the basis of respondeat superior for the negligence of church workers. Often, the negligence of church workers is associated with the use of a car, and includes such conduct as excessive speed, disregarding a stop sign or stop light, driving a vehicle with defective brakes, driving a vehicle at night without lights, failing to yield the right of way, or making a turn from an improper lane. While these actions may be intentional, they often are attributable to momentary carelessness or thoughtlessness. Churches also have been sued on the basis of respondeat superior for incidents of sexual molestation committed by a church worker during a church activity.

Why should a church be legally responsible for the negligence of a church worker? After all, the church certainly did not authorize such conduct and ordinarily did not even anticipate that it would occur. Perhaps the most commonly quoted justification for this theory is the following:

> What has emerged as the modern justification for vicarious liability is a rule of policy, a deliberate allocation of risk. The losses caused by the torts of employees, which as a practical matter are sure to occur in the conduct of the employer's enterprise, are placed upon the enterprise itself, as a required cost of doing business. They are placed upon the employer because, having engaged in an enterprise which will, on the basis of all past experience, involve harm to others through torts of employees, and sought to profit by it, it is just that he, rather than the innocent injured plaintiff, should bear them; and because he is better able to absorb them, and to distribute them, through prices, rates or liability insurance, to the public, and so to shift them to society, to the community at large. Added to this is the makeweight argument that an employer who is held strictly liable is under the greatest incentive to be careful in the selection, instruction and supervision of his servants, and to take every precaution to see that the enterprise is conducted safely.[28]

Makeweight = counterweight; counterbalance

---

[28] *See generally* W. PROSSER, THE LAW OF TORTS § 69 (4th ed. 1971). Quoted in Stevens v. Roman Catholic Bishop of Fresno, 123 Cal. Rptr. 171 (Cal. App. 1975).

As we will see later in this chapter, some courts have recognized that this logic has little if any application to churches and other nonprofit organizations.

Under the doctrine of respondeat superior, an employer is responsible for the injuries caused by its employees only if (1) an employer-employee relationship existed at the time of the injury, (2) the injury was caused by an employee's negligence, and (3) the employee was acting in the course of his or her employment at the time of the injury. These three elements will be considered individually.

Key point. *A church worker whose negligence or misconduct results in injury to another person is not insulated from personal liability by the respondeat superior doctrine. Church workers whose conduct injures other persons in the course of their church duties can be sued directly by injured victims. Often, both the worker and the church are sued.*

"Church workers whose conduct injures other persons in the course of their church duties can be sued directly by injured victims. Often, both the worker and the church are sued."

The Requirement of Employee Status § 10-02.1

Key point 10-02.1. *Employers may be liable on the basis of respondeat superior only for the acts of employees.*

Churches can be liable on the basis of respondeat superior for the negligent acts of employees committed within the course or scope of their employment. A number of courts have addressed the question of whether clergy are "employees" for purposes of imposing liability on an employing church. One of the first such cases was a decision by the Supreme Court of California.[29] The case involved a 12-year-old boy who lost a leg and suffered serious injuries to his other leg because of an accident caused by the reckless driving of the pastor of a Presbyterian "missions" church. At the time of the accident, the boy was standing on the "running board" of a car driven by the church's pastor at an excessive rate of speed (he was "racing" a car driven by a seminary student). The boy's family sued the pastor individually, as well as the presbytery of San Francisco (the presbytery overseeing the local

---

[29] Malloy v. Fong, 232 P.2d 241 (Cal. 1951).

missions church). The court was asked to determine whether an ecclesiastical body could be sued on account of the negligence of one of its ministers acting in the course of his employment.

Noting that there was "no compelling reason" why a religious organization should not be liable for the negligence of its employees, the court proceeded to determine whether a minister could be characterized as an employee. In reaching its decision that a minister could be deemed an employee, the court relied on well-established criteria employed by the courts in determining the status of other workers:

> Whether a person performing work for another is an employee or self-employed depends primarily upon whether the one for whom the work is done has the legal right to control the activities of the alleged employee. The power of the employer to terminate the services of the employee gives him the means of controlling the employee's activities. "The right to immediately discharge involves the right of control." It is not essential that the right of control be exercised or that there be active supervision of the work of the employee. The existence of the right of control and supervision establishes the existence of an employment relationship.[30]

The court also found that a minister could be deemed a church employee under the criteria set forth in the *Restatement of Agency* (an authoritative legal treatise):

(1) An employee is a person employed to perform service for another in his affairs and who, with respect to his physical conduct in the performance of the service, is subject to the other's control or right to control.

(2) In determining whether one acting for another is an employee or self-employed, the following matters of fact, among others, are considered:

(a) the extent of control which, by the agreement, the employer may exercise over the details of the work;

(b) whether or not the one employed is engaged in a distinct occupation or business;

(c) the kind of occupation, with reference to whether, in the locality, the work is usually done under the direction of the employer or by a specialist without supervision;

(d) the skill required in the particular occupation;

(e) whether the employer or the workman supplies the instrumentalities, tools, and the place of work for the person doing the work;

---

[30] 232 P.2d at 249 (citations omitted). The terms *employer* and *employee* have been used instead of *principal* and *agent*.

(f) the length of time for which the person is employed;

(g) the method of payment, whether by the time or by the job;

(h) whether or not the work is a part of the regular business of the employer; and

(i) whether or not the parties believe they are creating the relationship of employer and employee.[31]

In concluding that the negligent pastor was an agent of the presbytery (and not an independent contractor), the court noted the following two additional considerations. First, the presbytery exercised significant control over "missions" churches (it held title to all church property, assisted with the churches' finance, and paid a portion of clergy salaries). Second, the presbytery had the authority to approve or disapprove a missions church's selection of its pastor. Following the installation of such a pastor, "he was not responsible to the local church but only to the presbytery. The presbytery, not the church, had the power to remove him. Furthermore, he could not transfer to another pastorate without permission of the presbytery, and in fact he was a member of the presbytery rather than of the local church."

The court concluded: "The existence of the right of control and supervision establishes the existence of an agency relationship [making the employer legally responsible for the acts of an employee committed within the scope of his or her employment]. The evidence clearly supports the conclusion of the jury that such control existed in the present case. The right of the presbytery to install and remove its ministers, to approve or disapprove their transfer to other jurisdictions, and to supervise and control the activities of the local churches, particularly those in the mission stage, is inconsistent with a contrary conclusion." The court emphasized that "we are not here called upon to determine the liability of the presbytery for negligence in the activities of a fully established and independently incorporated Presbyterian church which has passed from the mission stage." Clearly, the Malloy case would not support liability of the presbytery for the activities of clergy serving such churches, since there would be none of the control by the presbytery over the activities of the local church that in Malloy was deemed sufficient to establish an agency relationship between the presbytery and a pastor of a missions church.

Key point. *Cases addressing the correct reporting status (employee or self-employed) of ministers for income tax reporting purposes are relevant, though not controlling, in deciding whether or not a minister is an employee whose negligence is imputed to his or her employing church under the doctrine of respondeat superior.*[32]

---

[31] RESTATEMENT OF AGENCY § 220 (1933). The terms *employer* and *employee* have been used instead of the terms *principal* and *agent*. Compare the current RESTATEMENT (SECOND) OF AGENCY § 220 (1958) which is identical to the quoted provision except that it adds a further factor: "(j) whether the [employer] is or is not in business."

[32] For a complete discussion of the reporting status of ministers for income tax reporting purposes, see R. HAMMAR, CHURCH AND CLERGY TAX GUIDE, chapter 2 (published annually by the publisher of this text).

The principle of respondeat superior imposes liability upon churches for injuries caused by the negligence of employees. Some courts have extended this doctrine to cover injuries caused by the negligence of uncompensated volunteers. However, a church generally is not responsible for the misconduct of independent contractors. Independent contractors are persons who offer their services to the public and are generally engaged to do some particular project, usually for a specified sum, and who perform the task with little or no supervision or control. They are not considered to be employees.[33]

In summary, under the doctrine of respondeat superior a church can be liable for the negligent acts of employees committed within the scope or course of their employment. Are clergy "employees" of their church for purposes of this doctrine? If so, their negligent acts committed within the scope of their employment may be imputed to their employing church. What about nonminister church workers? Cases addressing the employee status of both clergy and nonminister workers are summarized in the following examples.

Case Studies

clergy

> • The Alabama Supreme Court ruled that a Catholic order was not legally responsible for the actions of a priest who had entered an abortion clinic and injured a woman while destroying several pieces of equipment with a sledge hammer.[34] The priest, a member of the Benedictine Society, had been appointed pastor of a local parish and "pro-life coordinator" for the local diocese by the bishop. The injured woman sued the Benedictine Society and the priest's immediate superior (an abbot), claiming that the priest was an "agent" of the society and accordingly that the society was legally responsible for his conduct. In particular, she argued that the priest "was a member of the society and, as such, was subject to [his abbot's] orders as it related to his 24-hour life as a monk, including the authority to recall him to the abbey." The supreme court concluded that the woman had produced no evidence demonstrating an agency relationship between the society and the priest: "The Benedictine Order is a clerical order. [The priest] is a monk in that society and [the abbot] is his superior. However, the relationship between [the priest] and the society was ecclesiastical and did not necessarily create a . . . principal/agent relationship. Furthermore, the fact that [the priest] is a monk 24 hours a day does not necessarily mean that his membership in the society makes the society liable for all of his actions." The court further observed

---

[33] *See generally* R. HAMMAR. CHURCH AND CLERGY TAX GUIDE, chapter 2 (published annually by the publisher of this text).

[34] Wood v. Benedictine Society of Alabama, Inc., 530 So.2d 801 (Ala. 1988). This case is significant for the following reasons. First, it recognizes that the mere existence of ecclesiastical authority by a denominational agency over a minister does not, by itself, make the minister an "agent" of the denomination. Second, the court used an interesting analogy to support its conclusion—that of a seminary's relationship with its graduates. The seminary confers a degree upon each graduate, but that action, standing alone, does not make the seminary liable for the subsequent actions of its graduates. Similarly, many denominations confer ecclesiastical credentials upon clergy, but this procedure, by itself, should never authorize persons injured by the actions of a minister to sue the denomination. Third, the state supreme court affirmed a "directed verdict" by the trial court. A directed verdict is a decision by the trial judge, before the case is submitted to the jury, that the plaintiff's case is not supported by any evidence and accordingly that the case need not be submitted to a jury. This is an extraordinary action for a trial court to take, and it is reserved for only the most meritless claims. The fact that such a verdict was involved in this case, and was upheld by the state supreme court, reinforces the position taken by the court.

that "the law with regard to ecclesiastical orders and religious societies [is] that the relationship is essentially ecclesiastical in nature. I would analogize this to situations where a young man may be in a seminary and the seminary is asked to supply a preacher or a minister for a congregation. The fact that the young minister may have some alma mater does not make the seminary responsible for his behavior in the event he elects to commit a burglary or some other act which he might consider to be ordained by divine aegis or providence. It would not in and of itself make the seminary responsible for his behavior." The court further noted that there was no evidence "that the Benedictine Society was acting in a principal-agency capacity with the [priest]. Further, the court finds there was no employment as that term implies or no employment in the sense required for negligent employment."

• A church was sued for injuries and damages caused by the reckless driving of its pastor. The injured victim alleged that the pastor was an employee of his church, and thus the employer-church was vicariously liable for the consequences of the pastor's negligence committed in the course of employment. The church denied liability on the ground that its pastor was self-employed and not an employee, and accordingly his negligence could not be imputed to the church. The California Supreme Court concluded that the pastor was an employee of his church and that his negligence was imputable to the church.[35]

• The Colorado Supreme Court concluded that a pastor was an "agent" of his denomination, and as a result the denomination could be liable on the basis of negligent hiring for his sexual relationship with a woman in the course of marital counseling. The court acknowledged that "a prerequisite to establishing negligent hiring is an employment or agency relationship." Did such a relationship exist between the diocese and the assistant pastor? The court said "yes." It defined an agency relationship as one in which one person (the "agent") acts on behalf of another (the "principal") subject to the other's control. The court continued, "At trial, sufficient evidence was presented to establish that the structure of the Episcopal Church was such that the diocese and [the bishop] had and exercised the right of control over the manner of work performed by a priest as well as the hiring, compensation, counseling performed by the priest and discipline of the priest. The evidence was sufficient, in this case, to support the finding of an agency relation between the diocese and [the pastor]." The court noted that in addition to controlling certain aspects of hiring, compensation, and discipline, the diocese also controls and supervises the duties of pastors in their role as counselors. It observed that the bishop had "given talks" about counseling issues to pastors in the diocese. In addition, the diocese "had specific printed regulations on pastoral counseling and that these regulations describe the form counseling should take. The regulations include such details as how appointments are to be kept, what attire is to be worn, where in the room the prayer book and desk should be, and even how the pastor should sit." The court concluded, "All of these facts indicate that a priest is not independent of the diocese but is controlled by the diocese and the bishop. The priest's education is monitored by the bishop, he is put through a screening for hire by the diocese which includes psychological evaluation. The priest's compensation is affected by the bishop, the priest's discipline is controlled by the bishop, and every part of the form of the priest's counseling is regulated by the diocese. The evidence at trial created a factual issue regarding whether an agency relationship existed. The trial court properly submitted this issue to the jury for

---

[35] Vind v. Asamblea Apostolica De La Feen Christo Jesus, 307 P.2d 85 (Cal. 1957). In reaching this decision, the court employed the same criteria used by the California Supreme Court in the *Malloy* case. *See* note 29, *supra*, and accompanying text.

determination and the jury found that there was an agency relationship between [the assistant pastor] and the diocese."[36]

• The Kansas Supreme Court concluded that injuries caused by a Catholic priest's negligent driving were not imputable to his diocese since the priest was self-employed rather than an employee.[37] In reaching this conclusion, the court applied the "right to control test" under which a worker is considered to be an employee if the employer either controls or has the right to control the person's work. In concluding that the priest was not an employee, the court relied on the following factors: (1) the priest's "day-to-day activities are within his own discretion and control"; (2) the priest is authorized under canon law to do whatever he feels necessary to carry out his duties; (3) he sets his own hours and vacation; (4) he makes out his own paycheck, and hires and fires non-clergy workers; (5) he has complete discretion in purchasing church supplies and paying bills out of parish funds; (6) his work requires a high level of skill and experience and is generally done without supervision; and (7) he was driving his own car at the time of the accident and had obtained his own insurance on the vehicle. Under these facts, the court concluded that the priest was not an employee of the church. Since self-employed persons are not subject to an employer's control with respect to the manner and methods of performing their duties, the diocese was not responsible for the priest's negligence. The court acknowledged that the priest was clearly subject to the "ecclesiastical control" of his bishop, the diocese, and the Catholic Church, but such control was not relevant in determining the issue of legal control for purposes of imputing liability to the diocese on the basis of respondeat superior. The court also noted that the diocese "followed the majority of dioceses in issuing a W-2 form to each priest," but did this practice inconsistent with its conclusion that the priest was self-employed for purposes of respondeat superior. This decision is significant because it recognizes that (1) a church or religious denomination will not necessarily be legally accountable for the negligence of a minister merely because the minister is subject to the "ecclesiastical control" of the church or denomination, and (2) ministers who are treated as employees for federal income tax purposes (and are issued W-2 forms) will not necessarily be considered employees for purposes of holding their church or denomination legally responsible for their actions under the principle of respondeat superior.

• In a case of enormous importance to denominational agencies, a Minnesota appeals court applied the "bar association analogy" in concluding that a regional church and national church (the "church defendants") were not liable for the sexual misconduct of a pastor since the relationship between them and credentialed clergy (which resembled the relationship between state bar associations and licensed attorneys) was too attenuated to justify the imposition of liability for clergy misconduct. The court noted that under the respondeat superior doctrine, "an employer is vicariously liable for the acts of an employee committed within the course and scope of employment." The victim argued that an employment relationship existed between the pastor and church

---

[36]   Moses v. Diocese of Colorado, 863 P.2d 310 (Colo. 1993).

[37]   Brillhart v. Scheier, 758 P.2d 219 (Kan. 1988). A dissenting judge felt that the priest was an employee, and that his negligence should have been imputed to the diocese. The dissenter pointed to the following factors: (1) the diocese issued the priest W-2 forms each year; (2) the priest was on call 24 hours a day; (3) the priest's term of employment was indefinite; (4) the priest's work clearly furthered the regular business of the diocese; (5) the priest "was not engaged in an independent occupation in the sense that he contracts with different churches to perform pastoral services on a job-by-job basis; rather, he is engaged solely in his parish and can accept no other assignments without the consent of the bishop."

defendants because he was an ordained minister in good standing and his name was on the "clergy roster." Further, she claimed that the church defendants exercised enough control over a pastor's ministry to give rise to an employment relationship. In particular, she noted that the church defendants (1) determine who is qualified to be a minister; (2) demand that ministers agree and abide by their constitutions and bylaws; and (3) retain the authority to discipline ministers, including the authority to remove them from their pastoral ministry. The court concluded that these facts "did not automatically mean a true employment relationship exists" that would support the imposition of liability on the church defendants for the misconduct of ministers on the basis of respondeat superior. The court drew an analogy to the relationship between attorneys and the state supreme court. In Minnesota, the supreme court "through the Rules of Professional Conduct, sets forth the rules and standards by which lawyers must adhere. If these rules are violated, the court may discipline the responsible attorney. But this relationship between the supreme court and the disciplined attorney is not an employment relationship. There has to be something more." Similarly, the regional and national churches in this case had "limited control over the pastor." But, "the congregation, not the umbrella entity, has the responsibility for hiring and firing the pastor, setting forth the terms and conditions of employment, supplying the pastor with parsonage, vacation and supplies, and paying the pastor. [It] is the congregation, not the [regional or national churches], which employs the minister." The court concluded that the church defendants were not liable on the basis of respondeat superior for the pastor's acts of molestation because an employment relationship did not exist. In addition, his wrongful acts were not committed in the course of his employment, as required by the respondeat superior doctrine.[38]

• An Ohio appeals court ruled that churches cannot be responsible for a pastor's defamatory comments unless they are made in the course of employment and in furtherance of the mission and functions of the church. A pastor allegedly made a defamatory statement to a government official, suggesting that a church member had embezzled church funds. The members sued the church, claiming that it was legally responsible for the pastor's defamatory statement on the basis of respondeat superior. The court concluded that the church could not be liable, since the pastor was not an employee. The court observed, "[A] church may now be held liable for its own torts as well as for the tortious acts of its employees or agents imputed to it by the respondeat superior doctrine. . . . [W]hile plaintiff alleged an employment or agency relationship between the [pastor] and the church in his complaint, obviously to invoke the respondeat superior doctrine, he never developed the precise nature of that relationship from an evidentiary standpoint at trial." In other words, it was not clear that the pastor was a church employee, or that he was acting in the course of his employment when he made the allegedly defamatory remarks, and as a result the church could not be liable on the basis of respondeat superior.[39]

nonminister church workers

• A Louisiana appeals court ruled that a church was responsible for injuries sustained in an automobile accident caused by the negligent driving of a deacon while on church business.[40] The deacon was driving his vehicle to pick up supplies for use

---

[38] C.B. ex rel. L.B. v. Evangelical Lutheran Church in America, 726 N.W.2d 127 (Minn. App. 2007).

[39] Cooper v. Grace Baptist Church, 612 N.E.2d 357 (Ohio App. 1992).

[40] Whetstone v. Dixon, 616 So.2d 764 (La. App. 1993).

in a church remodeling project. A bee entered his vehicle through an open window and landed on his arm. He began slapping at the bee, momentarily took his eyes off the road, and ran into two vehicles. The driver of one of the vehicles was killed, and her daughter was severely injured. A lawsuit was filed by the deceased woman's husband and surviving children against the deacon and the church. A state appeals court concluded that the church was responsible for the deacon's negligent driving. It noted that a church will be responsible for the actions of its "servants," and defined a servant as one "employed to perform the services and affairs of another and who is subject to the other's control or right to control with respect to the physical conduct in the performance of the services." The court continued, "In [this] case, the issue involves a religious organization's liability for the negligence of one of its deacons, who is not compensated for his services. An individual who volunteers services without an agreement for or expectation of reward may be deemed the servant of the one accepting those services. Whether the volunteer is to be considered a servant generally depends on the religious organization's right to control the activities of the volunteer." The court concluded that the church had sufficient control over the deacon to make him the church's servant: "[The deacon] was more than a casual volunteer and indeed was a non-employee leader of [the church]. Both the church membership and the board of deacons had the right to exercise and did, in fact, exercise control over him. The membership had the right to discharge him from his position as a deacon if he failed to perform his duties. The deacon board was responsible for the planning and execution of the church remodeling project and [the chairman of the deacon board] had the authority to assign specific tasks to the members of the deacon board. Moreover, regarding the specific task at issue, members of the deacon board directed [the negligent deacon] concerning the materials to purchase, designated the approved places to obtain the specified materials and designated the general time by which delivery was expected. Although the specific time and route for travel were not dictated . . . this [deacon] held one of the highest levels of authority and responsibility within the hierarchy of the church such that precise details were unnecessary."

• A Louisiana appeals court ruled that a church could not be liable on the basis of respondeat superior for sexual assaults committed by a volunteer worker.[41] A volunteer youth worker in a Catholic church provided tutoring services to a teenage girl who was experiencing difficulty with algebra. The volunteer engaged in repeated and unwelcome sexual assaults. The girl's parents later filed a lawsuit on behalf of their minor daughter against the tutor, the local church, the archdiocese, and the youth organization. The church defendants argued that they could not be legally responsible for the volunteer tutor's conduct since a "master-servant" relationship did not exist between the tutor and the church defendants. A state appeals court agreed. It observed, "Louisiana's law on vicarious liability based on the respondeat superior doctrine is clear. Under the express provisions of [the Louisiana Civil Code] masters and employers are answerable for the damage occasioned by their servants and overseers, in the exercise of the functions in which they are employed. Under the jurisprudence interpreting this provision, the determination of whether a party may be held vicariously liable for the torts of another depends on whether the [one committing the misconduct] is characterized as a servant. . . . [This] case involves a religious or charitable organization's liability for the torts of a volunteer. Generally, one who volunteers services without an agreement for or expectation of reward may be a

---

[41] Doe v. Roman Catholic Church, 602 A.2d 129 (La. App.1992).

servant of one accepting such services. Determination of whether a given volunteer is in fact a servant generally depends on the charitable organization's right to control the activities of the volunteer. Determination of the right to control is a question of fact, based on consideration of the following factors: (1) degree to which the charity orders the volunteer to perform specific actions; (2) degree of contact between the charity and the volunteer; and (3) structural hierarchy of the charity. . . ." This test was not met in this case, the court concluded.

• The Supreme Court of New Hampshire ruled that a church was not responsible for injuries caused by the negligent driving of a volunteer church worker.[42] A man operating a motorcycle sustained permanent injuries when he was struck by a car driven by a church volunteer. The volunteer was a certified public accountant and elected member of the church finance committee, and at the time of the accident was in the process of delivering church financial records to the church treasurer. The motorcycle operator sued the church, arguing that it was responsible for the volunteer's negligence on the basis of the respondeat superior doctrine. The trial court dismissed the lawsuit, ruling that the volunteer "was performing services for the church as an independent contractor. She was not an employee of the church and the church had no control over her actions on the day of the accident, or any other day. . . . Therefore, the [church] is not vicariously liable for the alleged negligence of [the volunteer]." The motorcycle operator appealed, and the state supreme court ruled in favor of the church. The supreme court began its opinion by noting that the question in this case was whether or not to extend the respondeat superior doctrine to volunteer workers. The court did not see any reason why the respondeat superior doctrine should not be applied to volunteer workers, but it insisted that this could occur only if "the community would consider the person an employee." The court concluded that the volunteer in this case would not be considered an employee by the community: "[A] lthough the church may have had control over the tasks assigned to [the volunteer], it had no right to control the physical performance or the details of the accounting services she performed." As a result, the court concluded that the respondeat superior doctrine did not apply, and accordingly the church was not legally responsible for the injuries caused by the volunteer's negligent driving.

• An Ohio court ruled that a denominational agency was not responsible for a local church elder's actions even though it exercised ecclesiastical control over him.[43] The elder, while driving his car, struck another vehicle. The impact killed the driver of the other vehicle and injured a passenger. The elder served as an elected but uncompensated official of a subdivision ("district") of a state denominational agency, and at the time of the accident was involved in distributing fliers for a district event. A lawsuit was brought by the injured passenger and the family of the deceased driver (the "victims") against national and state denominational agencies on the ground that they were legally responsible for the elder's actions. A trial court dismissed the lawsuit, and the case was appealed. The victims argued that the ecclesiastical control maintained by the church agencies was sufficient to make them liable for the elder's actions on the basis of the legal doctrine of respondeat superior. The court observed that "respondeat superior liability attaches only where the work performed is that of a master, and the servant is subject to the control of the master in performing the work." The victims claimed that the church agencies had sufficient "control" over the elder to make them

---

[42] Boissonnault v. Bristol Federated Church, 642 A.2d 328 (N.H. 1994).

[43] Nye v. Kemp, 646 N.E.2d 262 (Ohio App. 1994).

liable for his actions since they could revoke his license as an ordained minister if they found that he was not living up to the moral standards required by the denomination. Further, the victims pointed out that the elder was an official with a subdivision of the state denominational agency, and as such he was subject to control by the national and state agencies. The court concluded that these aspects of ecclesiastical control did not make the national or state church agencies liable for the elder's actions. It noted that the elder received no compensation from either the national or state agency, and that he had been elected rather than appointed to his office. It then observed, "[The elder] was not an employee of [the national, state, or district agencies]. [The national and state agencies] had no control over [the district]. [The national and state agencies] had no right to control where the [district] meetings were held, when they were held, who held them, topics that were covered, advertising of the meeting, or any other aspect of these meetings. [The national and state agencies] further had nothing to do with the fliers that [the elder] was distributing at the time of the accident. [The elder] controlled the distribution of the fliers. [He] made the initial decision to deliver the fliers in the first place. [He] also selected who would receive them and when he would deliver them. [He] had no salary, no set hours, no vacation or sick leave, and no bosses or supervisors in his role as chairman of [the district]. Furthermore, [he] supplied his own vehicle and was not reimbursed for gas or mileage. . . . In the instant action, it is clear that [the elder] was not receiving any compensation as an employee. Furthermore, it is also clear that [the state agency] did not supply [him] with the car or the fliers or any of the tools necessary to complete the promotion of this fellowship meeting. [The state agency] did not control the details and quality of [the elder's] work, the hours that [he] worked, the route that he was traveling, or his length of employment. Accordingly . . . this court agrees that reasonable minds could only conclude that [the elder] was not the agent of either [the national or state agency]. Accordingly, the trial court properly found that [these agencies] were not liable for the acts of [the elder]."

In summary, the determination of a minister's status for purposes of imputing liability to an employing church on the basis of respondeat superior is a complex inquiry that requires an analysis of all of the facts of each case. More recent court decisions are less likely to jump to the conclusion that clergy are employees. Some courts have drawn the helpful distinction between ecclesiastical and temporal control. The fact that a church exercises ecclesiastical control over a minister should not be controlling in determining whether or not the minister is an employee for purposes of assigning legal liability to his or her employing church. Courts should focus on aspects of temporal control in determining whether or not a minister is an employee for such purposes.

Negligent Conduct § 10-02.2

The doctrine of respondeat superior imputes an employee's negligence to his or her employer. The term *negligence* was defined at the beginning of this chapter. Some courts have expanded respondeat superior to make employers liable for an employee's intentional or even criminal misconduct, if the employee was attempting to serve the employer's interests.[44]

---

[44] These cases are addressed in the next subsection.

Course of Employment

§ 10-02.3

Key point 10-02.3. *Churches can be legally responsible on the basis of the respondeat superior doctrine for the actions of their employees only if those actions are committed within the course of employment and further the mission and functions of the church. Intentional and self-serving acts of church employees often will not satisfy this standard.*

The doctrine of respondeat superior imputes an employee's negligence to his or her employer only if the negligence occurred in the course of employment. It often is difficult to ascertain whether employees are acting in the course of their employment at the time of a negligent act. Generally, conduct of an employee is in the course of employment if (1) it is of the kind the employee is employed to perform, (2) it occurs during the hours and within the geographical area authorized by the employment relationship, and (3) it is motivated, at least in part, by a desire to serve the employer. An employer generally will not be responsible for the misconduct of an employee that occurs before or after working hours, that occurs an unreasonable distance from an authorized work area, or that occurs while the employee is engaged in personal business.

> **Example.** *A federal appeals court concluded that a Methodist church was legally responsible for the copyright infringement of a minister of music since "the only inference that reasonably can be drawn from the evidence is that in selecting and arranging the song . . . for use by the church choir [the minister] was engaged in the course and scope of his employment by the church."*[45]

The courts have generally ruled that deciding whether a church employee was acting within the scope of his or her employment at the time of a wrongful act is permissible so long as no interpretation of church doctrine is involved.[46]

Many persons who have been sexually assaulted by church workers have attempted to sue their church or a denominational agency on the basis of respondeat superior. Most courts have rejected such efforts, on the ground that the offender was not acting within the scope of his or her employment while engaging in such acts. A few courts have interpreted the concept of "scope of employment" more broadly, and have found churches liable on the basis of respondeat superior. Examples of both kinds of cases are presented below.

1. Cases Refusing to Apply Respondeat Superior to Intentional or Criminal Acts

Most courts have refused to hold churches liable on the basis of respondeat superior for the sexual misconduct of employees or volunteers.

---

[45] Wihtol v. Crow, 309 F.2d 777 (8th Cir. 1962).

[46] *See, e.g.,* Olson v. First Church of Nazarene, 661 N.W.2d 254 (Minn. App. 2003). The plaintiffs' claims did not involve "an inquiry into what the cleric's role is within the church or his duties generally. The court need only determine whether the pastor, when he sexually penetrated [the victim] was providing ongoing, private spiritual advice, aid, or comfort to her in his capacity as a cleric and the court does not need to examine the content of the advice, aid, or comfort given."

Case Studies

• *A California appeals court ruled that a Catholic archdiocese was not responsible on the basis of respondeat superior for the seduction of a 16-year-old girl by several priests. The girl claimed that she had become pregnant through the priests' misconduct, that the priests used their influence to persuade her to remain silent, and that the priests sent her to the Philippine Islands to give birth. The court concluded that for the archdiocese to be liable under the theory of respondeat superior for the priests' conduct, their conduct had to be characteristic of the activities of the church or otherwise reasonably foreseeable. The court observed, "It would defy every notion of logic and fairness to say that sexual activity between a priest and a parishioner is characteristic of the Archbishop of the Roman Catholic Church. . . . Similarly, [the girl] has not pointed out any fact which could lead this court to the conclusion that the Archbishop ratified the concupiscent acts of the priests."[47]*

• *A California court, in ruling that a church was not legally responsible for a Sunday school teacher's repeated rape of a young boy, observed, "Certainly [the teacher] was not employed to molest young boys. There is no evidence the acts occurred during Sunday school. . . . There is no evidence to suggest that [the teacher's] conduct was actuated by a purpose to serve [the church]. Rather, the acts were independent, self-serving pursuits unrelated to church activities. Finally, [the teacher's] acts of sexual molestation were not foreseeable in light of the duties he was hired to perform. There is no aspect of a Sunday school teacher's or member's duties that would make sexual abuse anything other than highly unusual and very startling. We conclude [the teacher's] acts against [the boy] were neither required, incidental to his duties, nor foreseeable. They were, therefore, not within the scope of his employment.[48]*

• *A Connecticut court ruled that a church and diocese were not liable on the basis of respondeat superior for a priest's sexual molestation of a minor. The church defendants claimed that they could not be liable on the basis of respondeat superior for intentional misconduct committed by an employee for personal purposes and outside of the scope of employment. The court agreed. It noted that an employer is liable for the acts of an employee "only when that conduct is actuated, at least in part, by a purpose to serve the employer." The critical question "is whether the employee was engaged in the employer's business or had abandoned that business while harming the plaintiff." The court concluded that because the plaintiff made no claim that the priest's acts of sexual abuse were done "in any way to advance*

> "Our survey of national jurisprudence reveals that the majority of jurisdictions considering the issue of sexual contact between an ecclesiastic officer and a parishioner have held that the act is outside the scope of employment as a matter of law. N.H. v. Presbyterian Church (U.S.A.), 1999 WL 1013547 (Okla. 1999)."

---

[47] Milla v. Roman Catholic Archbishop of Los Angeles, 232 Cal. Rptr. 685 (1986).

[48] Scott v. Central Baptist Church, 243 Cal. Rptr. 128 (4th Dist. App. 1988).

or further the business of the church or diocese, even in some misguided manner, these counts fail to set forth a cause of action imposing vicarious liability upon these defendants."[49]

• *A District of Columbia appeals court affirmed a trial court's summary judgment in favor of a church in a case alleging that the church was responsible for the sexual misconduct of a church custodian.*[50] *The court ruled that the sexual misconduct did not grow out of and was not generated by the employment and therefore the acts did not occur while the employee was acting within the scope of his employment. The court relied on the definition of "scope of employment" contained in section 228 of the Restatement of Agency: "(1) Conduct of a servant is within the scope of employment if, but only if: (a) it is of the kind he is employed to perform; (b) it occurs substantially within the authorized time and space limits; (c) it is actuated, at least in part, by a purpose to serve the master; and; (d) if force is intentionally used by the servant against another, the use of force is not unexpectable by the master. (2) Conduct of a servant is not within the scope of employment if it is different in kind from that authorized, far beyond the authorized time and space limits, or too little actuated by a purpose to serve the master."*

• *A Florida court ruled that a denominational agency, and a local church (the "church defendants") were not liable on the basis of respondeat superior for the sexual misconduct of a pastor. The court concluded that "there is no respondeat superior liability for the alleged sexual misconduct by [the pastor]. As a matter of common sense, having sexual relations with a counselee is not part of the job responsibilities of a minister. Plainly the sexual conduct alleged by [the victim] was for the personal motives of the pastor, and not designed to further the interests of the church."*[51]

• *An Illinois court ruled that a church and a parent denomination were not legally responsible for a pastor's sexual assault of three boys.*[52] *The court emphasized that the pastor's assault constituted a deviation from the pastor's "scope of employment." Since the assault did not occur within the scope or course of the pastor's employment, it could not be imputed to the church or parent denomination.*

• *The Kentucky Supreme Court ruled that a diocese was not liable for a priest's sexual misconduct on the basis of respondeat superior. The court observed: "To accept such a theory would in effect require the diocese to become an absolute insurer for the behavior of anyone who was in the priesthood and would result in strict liability on the*

49 Dumais v. Hartford Roman Catholic Diocese, 2002 WL 31015708 (Conn. Super. 2002). *But see* Doe v. Norwich Roman Catholic Diocesan Corporation, 309 F.Supp.2d 247 (D. Conn. 2004). The court conceded that "in many cases of alleged sexual abuse by priests, the courts have held that respondeat superior is not applicable to hold a church or diocese liable, because such acts by the priests are not in furtherance of the church's business." However, it concluded that "the priest allegedly assaulted plaintiff during counseling sessions in attempt to bring her closer to the church and her religious faith, thereby increasing financial donations to the church and volunteer time spent by plaintiff and her family in furtherance of the church's business. Accordingly, the court finds that the acts as alleged, however misguided, are not so clearly outside the priest's scope of employment that the question is one of law. Therefore, the court denies the church defendants' motions to dismiss this count."

50 Mosely v. The Second New St. Paul's Baptist Church, 534 A.2d 346 (D.C. App. 1987).

51 Elders v. The United Methodist Church, 2001 WL 804567 (Fla. App. 2001).

52 Mt. Zion State Bank v. Central Illinois Conference of the United Methodist Church, 556 N.E.2d 1270 (Ill. App. 1990).

part of the diocese for any actionable wrong involving a parishioner. We must conclude that such an argument is absurd. Certainly, the scope of employment of a priest could include marriage counseling, but it clearly does not include adultery."[53]

• A Minnesota court ruled that a regional and national church were not liable on the basis of respondeat superior for the sexual misconduct of a pastor since those acts were not committed in the course of his employment. Rather, they occurred at the pastor's residence. The victim never alleged that she went to visit the pastor "for any type of religious counseling or any other reason connected to his status as a retired minister." In fact, she testified that she never attended any religious service conducted by the pastor, and knew him only as a family friend.[54]

• A federal appeals court, applying Missouri law, ruled that "a priest does not act in the furtherance of the business or interests of his employer when he engages in sexual misconduct with parishioners."[55]

• A New York court ruled that a Catholic church and diocese could not be liable on the basis of respondeat superior for the sexual molestation of an 11-year-old boy by a Catholic priest. The court noted that "no New York case has been cited in which an employer has been held vicariously liable for intentional sexual misconduct by an employee," and that sexual misconduct by a priest "on its face scarcely seems to fall within the scope of employment of a priest" as would be necessary for the church and diocese to be liable.[56]

• The Ohio Supreme Court ruled that state and national denominational offices could not be sued on the basis of respondeat superior as a result of the sexual misconduct of clergy.[57] The court noted that this doctrine generally does not apply to the intentional misconduct of employees if the misconduct is not designed to further the interests of the employer. The court observed, "It is well-established that in order for an employer to be liable under the doctrine of respondeat superior, the tort of the employee must be committed within the scope of employment. [However] . . . where the tort is intentional . . . the behavior giving rise to the tort must be calculated to facilitate or promote the business for which the [employee] was employed. . . . [The] employer would not be liable if an employee physically assaulted a patron without provocation. . . . [A]n intentional and willful attack committed by an agent or employee, to vent his own spleen or malevolence against the injured person, is a clear departure from his employment and his principal or employer is not responsible therefor. In other words, an employer is not liable for independent self-serving acts of his employees which in no way facilitate or promote his business." The court concluded, "[The denomination]

---

[53] Osborne v. Payne, 31 S.W.3d 911 (Ky. 2000).

[54] C.B. ex rel. L.B. v. Evangelical Lutheran Church in America, 726 N.W.2d 127 (Minn. App. 2007).

[55] Newyear v. Church Ins. Co., 155 F.3d 1041 (8th Cir. 1998). *See also* Gibson v. Brewer, 952 S.W.2d 239, 246 (Mo. 1997), in which the Missouri Supreme Court rejected an attempt by parents of a minor who was sexually abused by a priest to hold a diocese liable under the theory that the priest was acting with the scope of employment. The court held that "intentional sexual misconduct by a priest and intentional infliction of emotional distress are not within the scope of employment of a priest and are in fact forbidden." *Accord* Gray v. Ward, 950 S.W.2d 232 (Mo. 1997) (intentional sexual activity by a priest does not "fall within the scope of employment of a priest, and the diocese cannot be held liable under an agency theory").

[56] Jones by Jones v. Trane, 591 N.Y.S.2d 927 (Sup. 1992).

[57] Byrd v. Faber, 565 N.E.2d 584 (Ohio 1991).

in no way promotes or advocates nonconsensual sexual conduct between pastors and parishioners. The [state and national denominational offices] did not hire [the pastor] to rape, seduce, or otherwise physically assault members of his congregation. Furthermore, the [plaintiffs] have alleged no fact indicating that the [denominational offices] should reasonably have foreseen that [the pastor] would behave in this manner toward his parishioners. Consequently, [plaintiffs] have failed to state a claim of respondeat superior or liability on the part of the church, and the trial court was correct in dismissing that portion of their complaint."

• *An Ohio court ruled that a church and denominational agency were not liable for a pastor's sexual relationship with a female member of his congregation. The court noted that "in order for an employer to be liable under the doctrine of respondeat superior, the act of the employee must be committed within the scope of employment." Further, if the employee's act is intentional, the act must be "calculated to facilitate or promote the business for which the employee was employed. Thus, an employer is not liable for independent self-serving acts of his employees which in no way facilitate or promote his business." The court concluded that it was "difficult to conceive of pastoral fornication with a parishioner as a legitimate religious belief or practice." In other words, "intentional sexual activity is not related to a cleric's duties, nor does it further church interests. Therefore, that conduct does not fall within the scope of a cleric's employment."*[58]

• *The Oklahoma Supreme Court ruled that a denomination (the "national church") was not legally responsible for a pastor's acts of child molestation. The court noted that respondeat superior "is a legal doctrine holding an employer liable for the willful torts of an employee acting within the scope of employment in furtherance of assigned duties." It conceded that sexual assaults generally are not within the scope of employment, unless "(1) the act is fairly and naturally incident to the employer's business; (2) the act occurs while the employee is engaged in an act for the employer; or (3) the assault arises from a natural impulse growing out of or incident to the attempt to complete the master's business." The court further observed: "Our survey of national jurisprudence reveals that the majority of jurisdictions considering the issue of sexual contact between an ecclesiastic officer and a parishioner have held that the act is outside the scope of employment as a matter of law. We agree. Ministers should not molest children. When they do, it is not a part of the minister's duty nor customary within the business of the congregation. Rather than increasing membership, the conduct would assuredly result in persons spurning rather than accepting a faith condoning the abhorrent behavior. No reasonable person would conclude that the pastor's sexual misconduct was within the scope of employment or in furtherance of the national organization's business."*[59]

• *A federal court in Vermont ruled that a church was not liable for its pastor's acts of child molestation on the basis of respondeat superior. The church insisted that it could not be liable on this basis since the pastor's acts were outside the scope of his duties. The court agreed. It noted that conduct is within the scope of employment when it is of the kind the employee is employed to perform; it occurs substantially within the authorized "time and space limits" of the employment relationship; it is motivated, at*

---

[58]   DePietro, 825 N.E.2d 630 (Ohio App. 2005).

[59]   N.H. v. Presbyterian Church (U.S.A.), 1999 WL 1013547 (Okla. 1999).

least in part, by an intent to serve the employer; and, in cases of intentional or criminal acts, is foreseeable by the employer. The court concluded that the victim could point to no evidence that the pastor's actions were within the scope of his employment with the church. It observed: "Although some of the assaults took place on church grounds, no reasonable jury could find that his actions were either within the scope of his duties or in furtherance of the church's business."[60]

Several other courts have concluded that churches cannot be sued on the basis of respondeat superior if church workers were not engaged in the course of their employment at the time their conduct resulted in injuries to others. To illustrate, the following kinds of conduct were deemed not to have occurred within the course of employment: a minister sexually seduced a woman during marital counseling;[61] seven Catholic priests allegedly engaged in a sexual relationship with a female parishioner;[62] a teacher at a church-operated school engaged in sexual relations with a minor;[63] a Catholic nun was driving a car on personal rather than church business.[64]

2. Cases Applying Respondeat Superior to Intentional or Criminal Acts

A small minority of courts have found churches liable on the basis of respondeat superior for the sexual misconduct of employees and volunteers. In reaching such a conclusion, these courts have interpreted the concept of "course of employment" very broadly.

Case Studies

• *The Alaska Supreme Court ruled that a pastoral counseling center could be sued on the basis of respondeat superior by a woman who was sexually seduced by a counselor.*[65] *The woman claimed that she had visited the counselor on several occasions, and that the pastoral counselor "negligently handled the transference phenomenon" by taking advantage of her sexually. She allegedly suffered severe emotional injuries, and as a result sued the center and two of its directors for damages. She claimed that the center was legally responsible for the counselor's misconduct on the basis of respondeat superior. In explaining the "transference phenomenon," the director of the center explained that "transference is a phenomenon that occurs*

---

[60]   Doe v. Newbury Bible Church, 2005 WL 1862118 (D. Vt. 2005).

[61]   *See, e.g.,* Destefano v. Grabian, 763 P.2d 275 (Colo. 1988) (the court ruled that the church and a parent denomination might be liable on the basis of negligent hiring or negligent supervision); Schmidt v. Bishop, 779 F. Supp. 321 (S.D.N.Y. 1991); Bladen v. First Presbyterian Church, 857 P.2d 789 (Okla. 1993); Erickson v. Christenson, 781 P.2d 383 (Or. App. 1989) (the court ruled that the church and a parent denomination might be liable on the basis of negligent hiring or negligent supervision); J. v. Victory Baptist Church, 372 S.E.2d 391 (Va. 1988) (the court ruled that the church was not liable on the basis of respondeat superior, but might be liable on the basis of negligent retention or supervision if it were aware of previous incidents of misconduct but did nothing to monitor the employee's behavior); Lund v. Capel, 675 P.2d 226 (Wash. 1984).

[62]   Milla v. Tamayo, 232 Cal. Rptr. 685 (1986).

[63]   Scott v. Blanchet High School, 747 P.2d 1124 (Wash. App. 1987).

[64]   Mattingly v. State Department of Health, 509 So.2d 82 (La. App. 1987). *See also* Ambrosio v. Price, 495 F. Supp. 381 (D. Nebr. 1979).

[65]   Doe v. Samaritan Counseling Center, 791 P.2d 344 (Alaska 1990).

that is similar to a state of dependency in which the client begins to project the roles and relationships and the images and experiences that they have had with other people previously in their life, especially other significant people such as mother, father, brothers, sisters, early teachers and adult models, upon the therapist." The director acknowledged that the transference relationship is very "delicate" and "fragile," and that a counselor has "a professional and ethical responsibility to manage that relationship so that the client is not damaged in any way." A trial court summarily dismissed the lawsuit, concluding that the center was not responsible for the intentional and unauthorized misconduct of a counselor. The case was appealed directly to the state supreme court, which reversed the trial court's decision and ordered the case to proceed to trial. The court announced a very broad interpretation of the respondeat superior doctrine. The court concluded that an employer could be responsible for an employee's sexual misconduct that "arises out of and is reasonably incidental to the employee's legitimate work activities"—even if the misconduct was intentional and unauthorized by the employer. This ruling ignores the vast majority of court rulings that have rejected an employer's legal responsibility for the intentional misconduct of an employee.

• A Louisiana appeals court found a church-affiliated hospital liable for the sexual misconduct of an employee who had been thoroughly screened and supervised.[66] The hospital hired a male nursing assistant for a psychiatric ward after conducting a thorough background check that showed no criminal record and no unfavorable references from former employers. After working for six months, this employee raped a 16-year-old girl. The victim sued the hospital. The appeals court concluded that the hospital could not be liable for the assault on the basis of negligent hiring, because of the thorough nature of its pre-employment investigation. However, the court concluded that the hospital was legally responsible for the assault on the basis of "vicarious liability." The court noted that when determining whether an employer is responsible for an employee's actions, the following factors must be considered: (1) was the employee's act "primarily employment rooted"; (2) was the employee's act "reasonably incidental to the performance of the employee's duties"; (3) did the employee's act occur on the employer's premises; and (4) did the act occur during normal working hours. Not all of these factors must be present for an employer to be responsible for an employee's actions. The court concluded that the hospital was responsible for the assault in this case because the assault occurred on the employer's premises while the employee was on duty, and the assault was "reasonably incidental to the performance of his duties as a nurse's assistant although totally unauthorized by the employer and motivated by the employee's personal interest." Further, the court observed that the assault was "closely connected to his employment duties so that the risk of harm faced by the young female victim was fairly attributable to his employer."

• The Oregon Supreme Court ruled that a church can be liable for the sexual misconduct of an employee on the basis of respondeat superior, so long as the misconduct was a direct outgrowth of actions by the employee that were within the scope of his or her employment. The court noted that under the doctrine of respondeat superior, "an employer is liable for an employee's torts, including intentional torts, if the employee was acting within the scope of employment." In order for an employee's acts to be within the scope of employment, the following factors must be present: (1)

---

[66]   Samuels v. Southern Baptist Hospital 594 So.2d 571 (La. App. 1992).

the conduct occurred within the time and space limits authorized by the employment; (2) the employee was motivated, at least partially, by a purpose to serve the employer; and (3) the act must have been of a kind that the employee was hired to perform. The court conceded that a pastor's alleged sexual assaults on a victim clearly were outside the scope of his employment, but it concluded that his employing church could still be liable on the basis of respondeat superior if "acts that were within [the pastor's] scope of employment resulted in the acts which led to injury to plaintiff." The court noted that it would be extraordinary to find an act of intentional misconduct, such as sexual molestation, to be within the scope of an employee's employment. But, it insisted that this is not necessary. Rather, the question is whether the pastor was performing any acts that were within the scope of his employment that ultimately caused the victim's injuries. The court concluded that this test was met: "The complaint alleges that [the pastor] used his position as youth pastor, spiritual guide, and confessor to [the victim] and his family to gain their trust and confidence, and thereby to gain the permission of [the victim's] family to spend large periods of time alone with [him]. By virtue of that relationship, [the pastor] gained the opportunity to be alone with [the victim], to touch him physically, and then to assault him sexually. The complaint further alleges that those activities were committed in connection with [the pastor's] employment as youth pastor, that they were committed within the time and space limitations of [his] employment, that they were committed out of a desire, at least partially and initially, to fulfill [his] employment duties as youth pastor, and that they generally were of a kind and nature that he was required to perform as youth pastor."[67]

• A Washington state appellate court concluded that a Catholic diocese could be sued on the basis of respondeat superior for damages resulting from the alleged sexual molestation of minors by a Catholic priest.[68] A Catholic diocese in Louisiana suspended a priest from performing his "priestly duties" after he admitted to sexual misconduct with minors. The priest was asked to leave the diocese, and he eventually was admitted (with the approval of the diocese) to a rehabilitation program in another state. Just prior to the priest's discharge from this program, the diocese informed him that his "options in the ministry were severely limited if not nil," and that "because of the possibility of legal action and the responsibility on the part of any institution that might hire you, I think realistically that for church employment you are a very poor risk." The diocese further advised the priest that he would not be permitted to perform priestly duties upon his release, and that he was not to return to the diocese. Following his release from the rehabilitation program, the priest accepted a job as a counselor of adolescents in an alcohol and drug rehabilitation center in a private hospital. He was terminated from this job because of complaints of sexual abuse by former patients. Eight adolescents and one adult sued the hospital, the priest, as well as his diocese and bishop. The plaintiffs alleged that the diocese had negligently supervised the priest, and that it should have warned the private hospital of his pedophilia. The appeals court agreed that "an employer may be held liable for acts beyond the scope of employment because of its prior knowledge of the dangerous tendencies of its employee." The diocese argued that it could not be liable for the misconduct of the priest, since his actions did not arise out of his priestly duties and accordingly were not within the scope of his employment relationship with the diocese. In rejecting this claim, the court observed that "the duty of obedience which [the priest] owed the

---

[67] Fearing v. Bucher, 977 P.2d 1163 (Ore. 1999).
[68] Does 1-9 v. Compcare, Inc., 763 P.2d 1237 (Wash. App. 1988).

diocese encompassed all phases of his life and correspondingly the diocese's authority over its cleric went beyond the customary employer/employee relationship. . . . Despite his employment with [the hospital], the employment relationship between [the priest] and the diocese continued."

Inapplicability to Nonprofit Organizations § 10-02.4

Key point 10-02.4. *The fundamental policy supporting the doctrine of respondeat superior is "risk allocation." That is, an employer can allocate or shift the risk of injuries caused by the operation of its business to the consumers of its products and services by increasing the cost of those products and services to reflect the cost of personal injury claims. This policy has no application to churches and other charities that are incapable of exacting higher "contributions" from their members to cover personal injury claims. Some courts have recognized the impropriety of applying the respondeat superior doctrine to religious organizations.*

The policy considerations supporting vicarious liability rest upon the fundamental principle of risk allocation. That is, an employer has the unique ability to allocate the risks of inevitable injuries suffered by the consumers of its products and services through price adjustments.[69] By increasing its prices, the employer allocates the risk of injuries to the consumers of its products and services. As reasonable as this policy may be in the context of "for-profit" employers, it has no application to most nonprofit employers who have no ability to allocate risk to consumers through price increases. Certainly this is true of religious organizations, which would find it difficult if not impossible to compel members to donate larger amounts to "allocate risks" to the "consumers" of its services. For this reason, the rule of vicarious liability should be used sparingly, if at all, in the context of nonprofit employers. Some courts have recognized that the concept of vicarious liability has little if any relevance in the context of nonprofit religious organizations. To illustrate, one judge made the following observation in a case involving the alleged liability of a religious employer for the sexual misconduct of an employee:

> Spreading the cost of therapist-patient sex to the consumers of mental health services is unfair. Therapist-patient sex, although not uncommon, is not an inevitable cost of mental health care. It is a cost imposed by therapists who intentionally disregard the standards of conduct of mental health professionals for personal sexual gratification.[70]

The same judge also rejected the contention that a religious employer can "allocate risk" by purchasing liability insurance:

---

[69] *See* note 28, *supra*, and accompanying text.

[70] Doe v. Samaritan Counseling Center, 791 P.2d 344, 354 (Alaska 1990) (dissenting opinion).

Imposing vicarious liability would tend to make malpractice insurance, already a scarce and expensive resource, even harder to obtain. It is also unclear whether malpractice insurance would even cover sexual misconduct. Whether or not mental health employers could insure against this risk, they would have to raise the cost of their services dramatically. Mental health services would be denied to those who are least able to pay. While victims of therapist sexual misconduct may enjoy a greater chance of being compensated, the cost of creating that benefit in reduced access to mental health services is unacceptable.[71]

The California Supreme Court ruled that a public school district was not legally responsible, on the basis of respondeat superior, for the injuries suffered by a 15-year-old boy who was sexually assaulted by his high school math teacher.[72] This case is significant for a couple of reasons. First, the court rejected the application of the respondeat superior doctrine not on the basis of the facts of the case, but rather on the basis of the doctrine's own theoretical justifications. The court observed that

> although the facts of this case can be made to fit a version of the respondeat superior doctrine, we are unpersuaded that they should be or that the doctrine is appropriately invoked here. We draw our decision not from the various factual scenarios in which vicarious liability has or has not been imposed on employers for the torts of their employees, but instead from the underlying rationale for the respondeat superior doctrine.[73]

The court stated the rationale for the respondeat superior doctrine as follows:

> Three reasons have been suggested for imposing liability on an enterprise for the risks incident to the enterprise: (1) [I]t tends to provide a spur toward accident prevention; (2) it tends to provide greater assurance of compensation for accident victims; and (3) at the same time it tends to provide reasonable assurance that, like other costs, accident losses will be broadly and equitably distributed among the beneficiaries of the enterprises that entail them.[74]

The court rejected all three reasons as a basis for imposing liability on the school district in this case. The court observed:

> The first of these three considerations just noted plays little role in the

---

[71] *Id.* at 353-354.

[72] John R. v. Oakland Unified School District, 256 Cal. Rptr. 766 (Cal. 1989).

[73] *Id.* at 773 (emphasis added).

[74] *Id.* at 773-74, quoting the California Supreme Court's decision in Perez v. Van Groningen & Sons, Inc., 227 Cal. Rptr. 106, 108 (Cal. 1986), which was quoting 5 Harper, James & Gray, The Law of Torts (2nd ed. 1986) § 26.5 n. 21 (citations omitted).

allocation of responsibility for the sexual misconduct of employees generally, and with respect to the unique situation of teachers, indicates that untoward consequences could flow from imposing vicarious liability on school districts. Although it is unquestionably important to encourage both the careful selection of these employees and the close monitoring of their conduct, such concerns are, we think, better addressed by holding school districts to the exercise of due care in such matters and subjecting them to liability only for their own direct negligence in that regard. Applying the doctrine of respondeat superior to impose, in effect, strict liability in this context would be far too likely to deter districts from encouraging, or even authorizing, extracurricular and/or one-on-one contacts between teachers and students or to induce districts to impose such rigorous controls on activities of this nature that the educational process would be negatively affected. . . .

Nor is the second consideration—the assurance of compensation for accident victims—appropriately invoked here. The acts here differ from the normal range of risks for which costs can be spread and insurance sought. The imposition of vicarious liability on school districts for the sexual torts of their employees would tend to make insurance, already a scarce resource, even harder to obtain, and could lead to the diversion of needed funds from the classroom to cover claims.

The only element of the analysis that might point in favor of vicarious liability here is the propriety of spreading the risk of loss among the beneficiaries of the enterprise. School districts and the community at large benefit from the authority placed in teachers to carry out the educational mission, and it can be argued that the consequences of an abuse of that authority should be shared on an equally broad basis. But the connection between the authority conferred on teachers to carry out their instructional duties and the abuse of that authority to indulge in personal, sexual misconduct is simply too attenuated to deem a sexual assault as falling within the range of risks allocable to a teacher's employer. It is not a cost this particular enterprise should bear, and the consequences of imposing liability are unacceptable.[75]

It is very significant that the California Supreme Court rejected so decisively the application of the respondeat superior doctrine in the context of sexual misconduct of teachers. Surely the same considerations apply to religious organizations.

The court's rejection of the availability of insurance coverage as a justification for extending the respondeat superior principle to charities is important. Insurance coverage is not an effective means for churches to allocate risk, for a few very significant reasons. First, insurance is expensive, sometimes prohibitively so for smaller churches. Second, insurance coverage is becoming increasingly difficult for religious organizations to obtain. Third, insurance policies contain numerous exclusions—in some cases excluding one or more of a church's greatest risks.

---

[75] *Id.* at 774.

Fourth, covered risks are subject to the dollar limits of the policy. In some cases, higher risks have reduced coverage. Churches are uninsured for damages claimed in excess of the policy limits.

In a case upholding the validity of a state law limiting the liability of charities, the New Jersey Supreme Court made the following significant observation:

> The principle of charitable immunity was deeply rooted in the common law of New Jersey. The principle is premised on the fact that charitable associations are created to pursue philanthropic goals and the accomplishment of those goals would be hampered if they were to pay tort judgments in cases similar to this matter. . . . [A] person who makes a charitable contribution expects his donation to further the goals of the organization, and not to be used to satisfy lawsuits which bear no direct relationship to those goals.[76]

The court also noted that the state limitation on charity liability reflected the inapplicability of the respondeat superior doctrine to charitable organizations.

Negligent Selection of Church Workers—In General   § 10-03

One of the most significant legal risks facing churches today is negligent selection. The term *negligence* means carelessness or a failure to exercise reasonable care. *Negligent selection*, then, means carelessness or a failure to exercise reasonable care in the selection of a worker. Consider the following examples:

Examples

• *A church employs a pastor without any investigation into his background. The pastor seduces a counselee during marriage counseling. The victim sues the church, claiming that it is responsible for her injuries on the basis of negligent selection. It is later learned that the pastor committed adultery with a member of his prior congregation. No one in his present church asked for any information or references from the former congregation.*

• *A church board hires a youth pastor despite its knowledge that the youth pastor engaged in inappropriate sexual relations with an adolescent member of his youth group in a prior church. The board wants to give the youth pastor a "second chance." Six months after being hired, a parent alleges that her adolescent daughter was molested by the youth pastor. The church is later sued by the victim and her mother, who allege that the church is responsible for the youth pastor's misconduct on the basis of negligent selection.*

---

[76] Rupp v. Brookdale Baptist Church, 577 A.2d 188, 190 (N.J. Super. 1990), quoting in part from Bottari, The Charitable Immunity Act, 5 Seton Hall Legis. J. 61, 63-64 (1980).

• A church leader asks a church member if he would drive several members of the church youth group to an activity. The member agrees to do so. While driving to the activity, the member is involved in an accident while driving at an excessive rate of speed. Some of the children are injured. Parents later learn that the driver had a suspended driver's license as a result of numerous traffic violations. No one at the church was aware of the member's driving history, and no one ever attempted to find out. The church is later sued by two of the families, who allege that the church is responsible for the driver's actions on the basis of negligent selection.

• D is a computer technician who feels a "calling" to a counseling ministry. While D is a college graduate, she is not a minister and has never studied psychology or counseling. She is not a licensed counselor. D's church uses D as a part-time volunteer counselor. D counsels with G, a 25-year-old woman with severe emotional problems. D persuades G that her problems are a result of the fact that she was sexually molested by her father when she was a child. G has no recollection of any inappropriate conduct by her father, and at first is repelled by this suggestion. Over the course of several meetings, G comes to believe that D is correct. This results in a complete estrangement from her father. G's father sues the church, claiming that it is responsible for the harm to his family as a result of its negligent selection of D as a counselor.

• A church takes a group of 25 young children to a local lake for an afternoon of swimming. There are three adults who accompany the group. No lifeguards are on duty. One of the children drowns, and no one is able to resuscitate her because none of the adult chaperones is qualified to perform resuscitation techniques. The victim's parents sue the church, claiming that their child's death was caused by the church's negligent selection of the adult chaperones. They assert that the church should have selected at least one adult worker who was qualified to perform resuscitation techniques.

• A church has difficulty recruiting adults to work in the infant nursery during church services, and so it often uses adolescents. On one occasion, two 13-year-old girls were overseeing several infants. One of the infants broke a leg when she fell off a diaper changing table while one of the 13-year-old girls was changing her diaper. The infant's parents threaten to sue the church on the basis of negligent selection for their child's injuries.

Negligent Selection of Church Workers— Sexual Misconduct Cases Involving Minor Victims

§ 10-04

Resource. **For comprehensive training for church leaders, staff, and volunteers, see R. Hammar, Reducing the Risk, 3rd edition: Keeping Your Ministry Safe from Child Sexual Abuse (by the publisher of this text). Online training is available at ReducingTheRisk.com.**

Key point 10-04. *A church may be liable on the basis of negligent selection for a worker's molestation of a minor if the church was negligent in the selection of the worker. Negligence means a failure to exercise reasonable care, and so negligent selection refers to a failure to exercise reasonable care in the selection of the worker. Liability based on negligent selection may be imposed upon a church for the acts of employees and volunteers.*

In recent years, several churches have been sued as a result of the sexual molestation of minors by church workers on church property or during church activities. Common examples include the molestation of children and adolescents by youth pastors, camp counselors, Sunday school teachers, church custodians, volunteer youth workers, and others. In many of these cases, the victim alleges either or both of the following two theories: (1) the church was negligent in hiring the offender without adequate screening or evaluation, or (2) the church was negligent in its supervision of the offender. The second of these theories (negligent supervision) is discussed later in this chapter.

As noted above, the term negligence refers to conduct that creates an unreasonable risk of foreseeable harm to others. It connotes carelessness, heedlessness, inattention, or inadvertence. It is important to recognize that churches are not "guarantors" of the safety and well-being of children. They are not absolutely liable for every injury that occurs on their premises or in the course of their activities. Generally, they are responsible only for those injuries that result from their negligence.

Negligent selection simply means that the church failed to act responsibly and with due care in the selection of workers (both volunteer and compensated) for positions involving the supervision or custody of minors. Victims of molestation who have sued a church often allege that the church was negligent in not adequately screening applicants. The typical church hires just about anyone who expresses an interest in working in a volunteer capacity with the youth in the church. Even applicants for compensated positions are not screened by many churches.

DID YOU KNOW?

Often, when an incident of molestation occurs the senior minister is later asked to testify in court regarding steps that the church took to prevent the incident. The victim's lawyer asks, "What did you or your staff do to prevent this incident from occurring—what procedures did you utilize to check the molester's background and suitability for work with children?" All too often, the minister's answer is "nothing." The jury's reaction to such a response is predictable.

A single incident of abuse or molestation can devastate a church. Parents often become enraged, the viability of the church's youth and children's programs is jeopardized, and church leaders may be blamed for allowing the incident to happen. But far more tragic is the emotional trauma to the victim and the victim's family, and the enormous potential legal liability the church faces.

There is good news, however. Church leaders can take relatively simple yet effective steps to significantly reduce the likelihood of such an incident occurring. This chapter will review some of the more significant reported court rulings, and then suggest a number of preventive measures that any church can implement in order to reduce the risk of such incidents.

▶ *No one understands or appreciates risk better than insurance companies. Risk evaluation is their business. As a result, it is very important to observe that a number of church insurance companies have reduced the insurance coverage they provide for sexual misconduct, and in some cases they have excluded it entirely. Some companies are suggesting that these incidents are excluded under the provision in most policies excluding damages based on intentional, criminal conduct (most acts of sexual molestation involve criminal activity). Church leaders should review their church liability insurance policy to determine whether the church has any coverage for acts of sexual misconduct, and if so, whether such coverage has been limited in any way. If you fit within either category, the risk management recommendations in this chapter are of even greater relevance.*

Table 10-3
Why Sexual Misconduct Is One of the Greatest Legal Risks Facing Churches Today
Church liability for the sexual misconduct of employees and volunteers is one of the most significant legal risks facing churches today for a number of reasons, including the following:
(1) **Many opportunities.** There ordinarily are many opportunities within the church for persons to engage in sexual misconduct with adults or children. Churches have many children involved in a variety of programs, and many pastors engage in extensive counseling.
(2) **Trust.** Churches are institutions of trust, and many members and leaders cannot conceive of acts of sexual misconduct occurring on their premises. As a result, they do not see a need to institute procedures and policies that will reduce the risk of such behavior.
(3) **Money damages.** The amount of money damages that courts award in such cases can be substantial.
(4) **Limited insurance coverage.** Most church insurance policies either exclude sexual misconduct claims, or significantly reduce the amount of coverage. This means that many churches face a potentially large and underinsured risk.

Table 10-3

Why Sexual Misconduct Is One of the Greatest Legal Risks Facing Churches Today

(5) **Other damages.** The damage that such claims cause to victims, victims' families, offenders, congregations, and church leaders is considerable.

(6) **Board liability.** Board members face personal liability in such cases if they refused to take steps to address this risk or ignored danger signals, and their conduct amounts to "gross negligence."[77]

(7) **Punitive damages.** Churches face the possibility of being assessed punitive damages if church leaders willfully refused to address this risk or ignored danger signals. Punitive damages are designed to "punish" wrongdoers for reckless or grossly negligent conduct. They are not covered by church insurance policies.

(8) **Polarization.** Congregations often are polarized in the aftermath of an incident of sexual misconduct. Some members insist that the offender be forgiven, while others focus on issues of justice, accountability, and protection.

Court Decisions Recognizing Negligent Selection Claims

§ 10-04.1

Key point 10-04.1. *Some courts have found churches liable on the basis of negligent selection for the molestation of a minor by a church worker if the church failed to exercise reasonable care in the selection of the worker.*

This section reviews court decisions in which a church or other religious organization was found liable on the basis of negligent selection for a worker's acts of child molestation. Several of the leading cases are summarized below.

Case Studies

• *The Alaska Supreme Court ruled that a church could be legally responsible for the alleged sexual abuse of a 3-year-old child that occurred in a church nursery.[78] The court concluded that the church could be responsible on the basis of "negligent hiring" since it did not exercise a sufficiently high degree of care in selecting the volunteer worker who allegedly committed the abuse. In particular, the court emphasized that the church had not interviewed the volunteer regarding her own history of child abuse,*

---

[77] See § 6-08, *supra.*

[78] Broderick v. King's Way Church, 808 P.2d 1211 (Alaska 1991).

and did not conduct any "background check." The court observed: "The employer, in selecting an employee, must exercise a degree of care commensurate with the nature and danger of the business in which he is engaged and the nature and grade of services for which the employee is intended. In the present case, [the church] was in the business of providing a safe place for the care of young children whose parents were attending church services. It engaged [the attendant] to make sure that those children were properly cared for. We consider it self-evident that the selection of individuals to whom the care and safety of young children will be entrusted requires a relatively high level of care before it may be considered reasonable. [The church] did not interview [the attendant] or conduct a background check, nor has it offered any evidence that [the attendant's] past sexual abuse did not affect her competency." The court rejected the church's claim that it was not required to conduct an interview of background check on the nursery attendant since she was a mere volunteer rather than an employee. It noted simply that a volunteer "may be subject to the same interview and background checks" as any other worker, so long as the volunteer is subject to the control of the employer. The court emphasized that adults who experienced sexual abuse as children are much more likely to be child abusers than the general population. It quoted from an article on child abuse: "One of the predisposing conditions [to child sexual abuse] that has been of considerable interest to clinicians and researchers is an experience of sexual abuse in childhood. Being sexually victimized as a child is a common experience for adult sex offenders and mothers of victims of sexual mistreatment. Moreover, childhood experiences of sexual abuse have been found at higher rates among those who victimize or are mothers of victims than in comparison groups." In summary, the court concluded that a church can be legally responsible on the basis of negligent selection for acts of sexual molestation inflicted by a nursery attendant if the church (1) failed to interview the attendant to determine whether or not the attendant had been a victim of sexual abuse as a minor, and (2) did not conduct any background investigation into the attendant's suitability and fitness as a child care worker.

• *A California court ruled that a church was responsible on the basis of "negligent hiring" for the sexual molestation of a 13-year-old boy by his pastor.*[79] *However, the court concluded that the church was not responsible for the victim's molestation of his 6-year-old sister. The pastor was hired after being suspended from the ministry for a number of years because of allegations that he had molested a child. He later molested a 13-year-old boy who attended the church. The court noted that "in California, an employer can be held liable for negligent hiring if he knows the employee is unfit, or has reason to believe the employee is unfit or fails to use reasonable care to discover the employee's unfitness before hiring him." The court noted that the local church's pastoral search committee was aware that the pastor previously had "stepped down" from the ministry for some reason. Yet, the church did not "investigate or make any inquiry" regarding the pastor's fitness to serve. The court observed that the local church's pastoral selection committee was aware of "some difficulty with [the pastor's] reappointment to the active ministry and understood he had been on a sabbatical of some kind. . . . Nevertheless, [the church] did not investigate or make any inquiry regarding [the pastor's] fitness to serve as pastor." The court rejected the sister's claim that the church was liable for her brother's acts of molestation. At the trial, a child psychiatrist testified that the 13-year-old brother had molested his sister because of his experience with the pastor. The psychiatrist explained that abused*

---

[79] Evan F. v. Hughson United Methodist Church, 10 Cal. Rptr.2d 748 (Cal. App. 3 Dist. 1992).

and molested children often abuse and molest others. She noted that the brother had not previously engaged in any incidents of child molestation, and that the pastor's assaults had triggered a premature sexual stimulation and "awakening" of the boy (who was then an early adolescent entering puberty). The psychiatrist concluded that the boy, in molesting his sister, was "re-enacting" or "acting out" his own molestation experience of a larger person overpowering a smaller one. The court, in rejecting the sister's claim, observed, "[T]he theory of negligent hiring here encompasses the particular risk of molestation by an employee with a history of this specific conduct. It does not encompass acts done by non-employees, such as the 13-year-old brother, or consequences involving less particular, even speculative, hazards. To conclude otherwise would impose liability on the person who hired the person who molested the person who molested the person in the sister's position. This convoluted syntax alone argues against imposing liability in this situation."

• A Colorado court dismissed a lawsuit brought by a woman alleging that her church acted improperly and unlawfully when it dismissed her after she made complaints of sexual harassment and child molestation against another minister.[80] The woman alleged that between 1968 and 1975, when she was a minor, her stepfather committed various acts of sexual assault against her when they resided together. Her stepfather was a minister at the time, and later became president of his denomination. The woman pursued ministerial studies and was licensed as a minister. After serving as a minister in the State of Washington she moved to the Denver area to start a new church. She later learned that her stepfather, with whom she had severed all ties, was also pastoring a church in the Denver area. She learned that her stepfather was allegedly sexually harassing women church employees and a woman parishioner in his Denver church. She reported this alleged harassment, as well as the sexual abuse she had suffered from her stepfather as a minor, to denominational officers. In response, the stepfather filed charges with the denomination against the woman, claiming that her allegations were false and demanding a full investigation. After an investigation, denominational officers revoked the woman's license and denied her the opportunity to open a new church. The woman responded by filing a lawsuit against her stepfather and her denomination alleging several theories of liability including illegal retaliation by denominational officials in response to her charges of sexual harassment, and negligent hiring of her stepfather by denominational officials. The court acknowledged that "[a]n employer may be liable for harm to others for negligently employing an improper person for a task that may involve risk to others." The woman claimed that her stepfather had been involved in an extramarital affair with a parishioner at another church prior to his present assignment and that denominational officials failed to investigate this allegation. The court concluded that "the extramarital affair was sufficiently different from [the woman's] allegations against [her stepfather] and, thus, did not create a duty on the part of the church to foresee [his] conduct." Further, the court noted that during the time the woman was allegedly abused as a child, her stepfather was not a minister, and that she did not allege that denominational officials knew or should have known of the stepfather's alleged sexual abuse of his stepdaughter when they hired him."

• A Florida court ruled that a 27-year-old man who had been molested by a priest when he was a minor was barred by the statute of limitations from suing his church.[81]

---

[80] Van Osdol v. Vogt, 892 P.2d 402 (Colo. App. 1994). *Accord* Bear Valley Church of Christ v. DeBose, 928 P.2d 1315 (Colo. 1996).

[81] Doe v. Dorsey, 683 So.2d 614 (Fl. App. 1996).

As a result, the court was not required to decide whether or not the First Amendment prevents the civil courts from resolving negligence claims brought against churches for the sexual misconduct of clergy. However, the court did make the following observation: "In any event, we are persuaded that just as the state may prevent a church from offering human sacrifices, it may protect its children against injuries caused by pedophiles by authorizing civil damages against a church that knowingly (including should know) creates a situation in which such injuries are likely to occur. We recognize that the state's interest must be compelling indeed in order to interfere in the church's selection, training and assignment of its clerics. We would draw the line at criminal conduct."

• A Florida court ruled that the First Amendment religion clauses did not prevent it from resolving a lawsuit claiming that a church and denominational agency were legally responsible on the basis of negligent hiring for a minister's acts of child molestation. The court noted that "most of the courts which have rejected these types of claims have done so based on the belief that to determine liability they would be required to interpret church doctrine." On the other hand, those courts that have accepted these claims "see their role as simply applying neutral principles of law to nonreligious conduct." The court concluded: "In their complaint, the plaintiffs alleged that they were both employees and parishioners of the defendant church, that they were sexually assaulted and battered by [the priest] while working at the defendant church, and that, despite knowing that [the priest] had committed several sexual assaults and batteries, he was retained by the defendants as a priest and given the task of supervising the plaintiffs. The issue to be determined by the court, therefore, is whether the defendants had reason to know of [the priest's] misconduct and did nothing to prevent reasonably foreseeable harm from being inflicted upon the plaintiffs. This determination is one governed by tort law and does not require inquiry into the religious doctrines and practices of the Catholic church."[82]

• A New York court ruled that a Catholic church and diocese could be sued on the basis of negligent hiring as a result of the sexual molestation of an 11-year-old boy by a Catholic priest.[83] The victim and his sister were both enrolled in a parochial school operated by the church. An associate pastor at the church (who also served as director of religious education for the school) obtained permission from the victim's mother to take him to an athletic facility at a local college to play racquetball and basketball and go swimming. While in the shower room prior to entering the pool, the pastor allegedly removed all his clothing and made the victim do the same. He then molested the victim. The boy's mother later sued the pastor, church, and diocese, claiming that her son had suffered substantial emotional injuries. She alleged that the church and diocese were liable on the basis of negligent hiring. Specifically, she asserted that the church and diocese were liable for the misconduct of the pastor on the basis of their own negligence in hiring and placing him in contact with boys with inadequate investigation of his background and with actual or "constructive" knowledge of his propensities. The court rejected the argument of the church and diocese that permitting the civil courts to find religious organizations liable on the basis of negligent hiring of clergy would constitute excessive governmental interference with church autonomy in violation of the First Amendment guaranty of religious freedom. The court observed, "[If the mother is] successful in establishing that, with knowledge

---

[82] Doe v. Malicki, 771 So.2d 545 (Fla. App. 2000).

[83] Jones by Jones v. Trane. 591 N.Y.S.2d 927 (Sup. 1992).

that the priest was likely to commit sexual abuse on youths with whom he was put in contact, his employers placed or continued him in a setting in which such abuse occurred, the fact that the placement occurred in the course of internal administration of the religious units does not preclude holding the institutions accountable to the victim of their neglect in administration. Indeed, a contrary holding—that a religious body must be held free from any responsibility for wholly predictable and foreseeable injurious consequences of personnel decisions, although such decisions incorporate no theological or dogmatic tenets—would go beyond First Amendment protection and cloak such bodies with an exclusive immunity greater than that required for the preservation of the principles constitutionally safeguarded."

• *A federal court in Rhode Island ruled that the First Amendment did not prevent it from resolving a lawsuit brought by victims of clergy sexual misconduct against church officials.[84] Three adult males sued diocesan officials for injuries they allegedly sustained when they were molested by two priests several years before. The victims claimed that prior to the acts of molestation, the diocese knew that the priests were pedophiles and not only failed to take appropriate preventative action, but also actively concealed the priests' sexual misconduct. The court rejected the diocese's argument that the First Amendment guaranty of religious freedom prevents the civil courts from imposing liability on religious organizations for failing to properly screen or supervise clergy: "[T]here is no indication that the reasonably prudent person standard established by tort law and the requirements of Roman Catholic doctrine are incompatible. The [diocese does] not claim that the Roman Catholic Church either condones or tolerates sexual abuse of children. On the contrary, they have made it clear that the Catholic Church considers such conduct to be opprobrious. . . . Briefly stated, there is no indication that, by taking the kind of preventative action required by tort law, the [diocese] would have violated any 'doctrine, practice or law' of the Roman Catholic Church. In the absence of such a conflict, subjecting the [diocese] to potential tort liability does not violate [its] right to the free exercise of religion."*

• *A federal court in Vermont ruled that an adult who claimed to have been sexually abused by a nun some 40 years earlier could sue a Catholic diocese for his alleged injuries.[85] The lawsuit claimed that the diocese was liable for the priest's acts on the basis of negligence. The court rejected the argument of the diocese that the lawsuit was barred by the First Amendment guaranty of religious freedom. Specifically, it argued that by permitting the victim to sue the diocese, the court would be forced to determine what is acceptable behavior by a minister or other religious practitioner in a religious institution such as a church-run orphanage. The court agreed in part with this argument: "The plaintiff's allegations of intentional and negligent conduct on the part of [the diocese] in hiring and supervising [the nun] and in fostering an environment in which sexual and physical abuse could occur give rise to serious constitutional concerns. Inquiry by a court or jury into the policies and practices of a religious organization in supervising and hiring clergy and other religious officials may foster excessive entanglement with religion. On the other hand, if hiring was done with knowledge that a prospective employee had perverted sexual proclivities, the institution might well be held accountable even though the hiring was part of the administration of a religious facility."*

---

[84] Smith v. O'Connell, 986 F. Supp. 73 (D.R.I. 1997).

[85] Barquin v. Roman Catholic Diocese, 839 F. Supp. 275 (D. Vt. 1993).

• *The Virginia Supreme Court ruled that a church and its pastor could be sued by a mother whose child was sexually assaulted by a church employee.[86] A mother sued a church and its pastor, alleging that her 10-year-old daughter had been repeatedly raped and assaulted by a church employee. She asserted that the church and minister were legally responsible on the basis of several grounds, including "negligent hiring" (referred to as negligent selection in this chapter). Specifically, she alleged that when the employee was hired, the church and minister either knew or should have known that he had recently been convicted of aggravated sexual assault on a young girl, that he was on probation for the offense, and that a condition of his probation was that he not be involved or associated with children. Despite these circumstances, the individual was hired and entrusted with duties that encouraged him to come freely into contact with children, and in addition was given keys to all of the church's doors. The mother alleged that the employee in fact came into contact with her daughter on the church's premises, and had sexual intercourse with her on numerous occasions. The court ruled that the church could be sued on the basis of negligent selection. It rejected the church's contentions that the theory of negligent selection either was not recognized under Virginia law, or was not recognized in the context of church employers. The court also rejected the church's contention that it could not be responsible for criminal acts of employees: "To say that a negligently hired employee who acts willfully or criminally thus relieves his employer of liability for negligent selection when willful or criminal conduct is precisely what the employer should have foreseen would rob the tort of vitality . . . ." The court also rejected the church's contention that it could not be liable for the employee's acts of molestation since they had not occurred within the scope of employment. It acknowledged that church liability based on respondeat superior required that the employee's acts be committed within the scope of employment. However, "negligent hiring is a doctrine of primary liability; the employer is principally liable for negligently placing an unfit person in an employment situation involving an unreasonable risk of harm to others. Negligent hiring, therefore, enables plaintiffs to recover in situations where respondeat superior's scope of employment limitation previously protected employers from liability.*

Court Decisions Rejecting Negligent Selection Claims

§ 10-04.2

Key point 10-04.2. *Some courts have found churches not liable on the basis of negligent selection for the molestation of a minor by a church worker since the church exercised reasonable care in the selection of the worker.*

This section reviews court decisions in which a church or other religious organization was found not liable on the basis of negligent selection for a worker's acts of child molestation. Note that several courts have concluded that the First Amendment's "nonestablishment of religion" and "free exercise of religion" clauses prevent the civil courts from resolving negligent selection claims involving clergy misconduct.

---

[86] J. v. Victory Baptist Church, 372 S.E.2d 391 (Va. 1988).

Case Studies

• A federal appeals court ruled that an archdiocese was not responsible for the alleged molestation of a minor by a priest.[87] The victim claimed that the archdiocese should have known that the priest had a history of sexual improprieties and that he would continue to pursue those activities when under its employ. He insisted that a minimal background check would have revealed the priest's pattern of sexual activity with minors. The court, in rejecting this argument, observed, "The record, however, permits of no conclusion that the [archdiocese] suspected that [the priest] had engaged in sexual improprieties or might do so in the future. It is doubtful that the archdiocese . . . knew anything about [his] darker side. [He] was diligent in guarding his secrets. He did not disclose his extracurricular activities to anyone at anytime in the course of his employment and, from his perspective, with good reason. No tangible evidence in the form of a criminal history or discipline exists that would have been uncovered in a background check."

• The Alabama Supreme Court concluded that a church-operated preschool was not responsible for the kidnapping of a three-month-old infant by three adolescent sisters employed by the preschool.[88] At the time of the kidnapping, there was no qualified adult teacher, other than the administrator herself, directly supervising the sisters. The administrator later testified that the other teachers had "gone for the day" and that she thought one of the sisters had intentionally distracted her while the other two slipped the baby out the front door undetected. The local police and the Federal Bureau of Investigation investigated the incident, eventually found the baby, and reunited her with her parents. The parents experienced severe shock as a result of the kidnapping, and later sued the preschool. They claimed that the preschool was legally responsible for the kidnapping on the basis of negligent hiring of the three sisters. They pointed out that the preschool used girls who were only 12, 14, and 17 years of age to care for infants. And, there was evidence that the two older sisters had been physically (and perhaps sexually) abused by members of their family, and that the oldest sister lied to the center's administrator by telling her that she was pregnant. The court rejected the parents' claim that this evidence demonstrated that the preschool had been guilty of negligent hiring.

• A California court ruled that a Catholic church was not responsible on the basis of negligent hiring for a priest's acts of child molestation, since it had not been aware of any similar incidents of misconduct at the time the priest was employed.[89] The court acknowledged that "an employer may be liable to a third person for the employer's negligence in hiring or retaining an employee who is incompetent or unfit." However, the court qualified this rule by noting that "one who employs another to act for him is not liable . . . merely because the one employed is incompetent, vicious, or careless. If liability results it is because, under the circumstances, the employer has not taken the care which a prudent man would take in selecting the person for the business in hand. . . . Liability results . . . not because of the relation of the parties, but because the employer . . . had reason to believe that an undue risk of harm would exist because of the employment." The court noted that the harm the victim suffered was criminal sexual abuse of a minor by her priest. It observed, "There is nothing in the record to

---

[87] Tichenor v. Roman Catholic Church, 32 F.3d 953 (5th Cir. 1994).

[88] Hargrove v. Tree of Life Christian Day Care Center, 699 So.2d 1242 (Ala. 1997).

[89] Roman Catholic Bishop v. Superior Court, 50 Cal. Rptr.2d 399 (Cal. App. 1996).

indicate [the priest] had a criminal history or had been previously implicated in sexual abuse of a minor. Thus the church could not have had antecedent knowledge of [his] purported criminal dangerousness." That is, evidence that the priest had engaged in sexual misconduct with adults did not necessarily make him a risk to children. The court observed that the victim failed to prove any facts "showing an undue risk of harm that [the priest] would commit criminal child sexual abuse if he were employed by the church." But even if evidence of sexual misconduct with adults would be relevant in evaluating a priest's risk of committing similar acts upon children, the church "had no actual knowledge of [his] sexual activity with [her] or anyone else until it heard [her] mother's report and [the priest's] admissions." In other words, the church could not be responsible for the priest's molestation of the victim on the basis of negligent hiring if it had no knowledge of any prior misconduct by the priest at the time he was hired or ordained. The court noted further noted that "the legal duty of inquiry [the victim] seeks to impose on the church as an employer would violate the employee's privacy rights. Privacy is a fundamental liberty implicitly guaranteed by the federal Constitution and is explicitly guaranteed under the California Constitution as an inalienable right. The right encompasses privacy in one's sexual matters and is not limited to the marital relationship. Although the right to privacy is not absolute, it yields only to a compelling state interest. Here there was no compelling state interest to require the employer to investigate the sexual practices of its employee. Moreover, the employer who queries employees on sexual behavior is subject to claims for invasion of privacy and sexual harassment. Similarly [the victim's] contention that the church should have required [the priest] to undergo a psychological evaluation before hiring him is unavailing. An individual's right to privacy also encompasses mental privacy. We conclude the church did not fail to use due care in hiring [the priest]."

• *An Illinois court ruled that a church and a parent denomination were not legally responsible for a pastor's sexual assault of three boys.*[90] *The boys' parents sued the pastor, his church, and a denominational agency, claiming that the boys had suffered severe emotional damage. The parents claimed that the denominational agency negligently assigned the pastor to the church, knowing of a prior assault on another boy several years earlier. A jury returned a verdict against the agency in the amount of $450,000 ($150,000 per boy) on the basis of its alleged negligence. However, a state appeals court reversed the verdict and dismissed the negligence verdict against the agency. It is significant to note that the court observed that "the jury could well have determined that the [agency] took adequate precaution in having [the pastor] counseled and should not have been held to have reasonably foreseen that [he] would be likely to commit the acts of sexual assault." This case suggests that churches and denominations may be legally responsible on the basis of negligent hiring if they hire or retain a minister after learning that he or she was guilty of sexual misconduct in the past. However, the court emphasized that mere knowledge of previous incidents of sexual misconduct does not automatically create legal liability. Liability for negligent hiring or retention requires that the actions of the church or denomination created a foreseeable and unreasonable risk of harm to others.*

• *A federal court in Kentucky ruled that a national church was not liable on the basis of negligent selection for a missionary's sexual molestation of a minor. The court noted that "an employer can be held liable when its failure to exercise ordinary care in*

---

[90] Mt. Zion State Bank v. Central Illinois Conference of the United Methodist Church, 556 N.E.2d 1270 (Ill. App. 1990).

hiring or retaining an employee creates a foreseeable risk of harm to a third person." It concluded that the national church was not negligent since the missionary's wrongful acts were not foreseeable: "The evidence of record of this matter demonstrates that the church required candidates for its missionary program to complete an involved application process and undergo multiple levels of screening by various church officers. The evidence further reveals that missionaries, once selected, continued to meet regularly for interviews with church officers during their tenure in the missionary program. Finally, the unrefuted evidence shows that the church did not receive information at any time during the application or training process or prior to [the missionary's] alleged encounter with [the victim] that would lead [church leaders] to believe that he had ever or would ever commit a sexual act with a child. Plaintiff has marshaled no evidence to suggest that the national church knew or should reasonably have known that he was somehow unfit to serve as a missionary or that his placement or retention of a missionary created an unreasonable risk of harm to [the victim] or that any such information came to light prior to the national church learning of the [molestation] at which time the church terminated his service as a missionary."[91]

• A Louisiana appeals court ruled that a church-affiliated hospital was not liable on the basis of negligent selection for the sexual misconduct of an employee who had been thoroughly screened and supervised. The hospital hired a male nursing assistant for a psychiatric ward after conducting a thorough background check that showed no criminal record and no unfavorable references from former employers. After working for six months, this employee raped a 16-year-old girl. The victim sued the hospital. The appeals court concluded that the hospital could not be liable for the assault on the basis of negligent hiring, because of the thorough nature of its pre-employment investigation.[92]

• A federal district court in Michigan ruled that a church school and various church agencies were not liable on the basis of negligent hiring, supervision, or retention, for the sexual molestation of a minor student by a priest.[93] In rejecting the victim's claim that the school and church agencies had been guilty of "negligent hiring," the court observed, "Questions of hiring and retention of clergy necessarily will require interpretation of church canons, and internal church policies and practices. It is well-settled that when a court is required to interpret canon law or internal church policies and practices, the First Amendment is violated because such judicial inquiry would constitute excessive government entanglement with religion. . . . [An] inquiry into the decision of who should be permitted to become or remain a priest necessarily would involve prohibited excessive entanglement with religion. Therefore [the victim's] claims of negligence predicated upon a negligent hiring theory will be dismissed." The court further observed that even if there was not a constitutional bar to recognizing a negligent hiring claim in this case, this claim would still have to be dismissed since "there was absolutely not a shred of evidence in the record that either the [school or any church agency] had any notice of the abuse proclivities of [the offending priests] prior to their 'hiring' of them as priests or teachers . . . ."

---

91 Olinger v. Corporation of the President, 521 F.Supp.2d 577 (E.D. Ky. 2007).

92 Samuels v. Southern Baptist Hospital 594 So.2d 571 (La. App. 1992).

93 Isely v. Capuchin Province, 880 F. Supp. 1138 (E.D. Mich. 1995).

• *A Minnesota court ruled that a church and denominational organization were not legally responsible on the basis of negligent hiring for a pastor's acts of child molestation.[94] The molester served as pastor of a church and was accused of sexually abusing numerous young boys during his tenure. He admitted abusing some of the children, including a 10-year-old boy (the "victim"). The victim later sued the pastor and his former church. The court defined "negligent hiring" as "the negligence of an employer in placing a person with known propensities, or propensities which should have been discovered by reasonable investigation, in an employment position in which, because of the circumstances of employment, it should have been foreseeable that the hired individual posed a threat of injury to others." In ruling that the church had not been negligent in hiring the pastor, the court observed, "There is no evidence [the church] had actual knowledge of [the pastor's] propensities to commit sexual abuse before he was hired. Moreover, it would have been contrary to the evidence for the jury to have concluded that [the church] should have learned of [his] propensities through reasonable investigation. The regional church body had direct knowledge that [the pastor] had sexually abused a child two years before he was hired by [the church]. But it is undisputed that the regional church did not tell [the church] about this incident and took no action against [the pastor] that might have been discovered by [the church]. The record does not permit an inference that [the church] could have learned about [the pastor's] propensities from the regional church, which was unwilling to disclose this information voluntarily. . . . [T]he trial court suggested that if [the church] had simply called [the pastor's] previous employer it might have learned that [he] had been accused of sexual abuse at that church. If this search is reasonably seen as a part of the hiring process in this church organization in 1964, a proposition we do not review, we find no evidence in the record to show that [the pastor's] previous employer was aware of any accusations of sexual abuse against him. [The victim] has not presented any evidence of another source that [the church] might reasonably have investigated to discover [the pastor's] dangerous propensities, so the jury could not have determined that [it] negligently hired [him]."*

• *The Missouri Supreme Court ruled that a diocese could not be liable for the sexual misconduct of a priest.[95] A Catholic priest served as associate pastor of a church. He invited a young boy and one of the boy's friends to spend the night and watch movies in the church parsonage. One of the boys later alleged that the priest sexually molested him. When the boy's parents learned of the allegations, they immediately notified the diocese. Officials of the diocese allegedly told them that "this happens to young men all the time" and that their son "would get over it." Diocese employees urged the parents to meet with the priest to resolve the situation. After hearing of similar incidents between the priest and other young boys, the parents "expressed their concerns to the diocese." They were told that the incident with their son was "an innocent pat on the butt" and that they should "forgive and forget" and get on with their lives. According to the parents, the diocese continued to ignore them until the priest eventually was removed from the diocese. The parents sued the diocese. Among other things, they claimed that the diocese was negligent in "hiring or ordaining" and then retaining the priest. The court noted that "religious organizations are not immune from civil liability for the acts of their clergy," and that "if neutral principles of law can*

---

[94] M.L. v. Magnuson, 531 N.W.2d 831 (Minn. App. 1995).

[95] Gibson v. Brewer, 952 S.W.2d 239 (Mo. 1997), citing the United States Supreme Court decision in Kedroff v. St. Nicholas Cathedral of Russian Orthodox Church, 344 U.S. 94 (1952).

be applied without determining questions of religious doctrine, polity, and practice, then a court may impose liability." However, the court cautioned that "questions of hiring, ordaining, and retaining clergy . . . necessarily involve interpretation of religious doctrine, policy, and administration. Such excessive entanglement between church and state has the effect of inhibiting religion, in violation of the First Amendment. By the same token, judicial inquiry into hiring, ordaining, and retaining clergy would result in an endorsement of religion, by approving one model for church hiring, ordination, and retention of clergy. A church's freedom to select clergy is protected 'as a part of the free exercise of religion against state interference.' Ordination of a priest is a 'quintessentially religious' matter, whose resolution the First Amendment commits exclusively to the highest ecclesiastical tribunals of this hierarchical church."

• An Ohio court ruled that a church was not liable on the basis of negligent selection for the molestation of several young children by two adolescent boys who served as volunteer teachers. The parents claimed that if the church had checked with the boys' school guidance counselor it would have learned that one of the boys was unfit to work with minors. The court rejected this argument. It concluded that the parents "have not shown that the school could have divulged the information to the church prior to the regrettable incident with the children." As a result, the church could not be liable on the basis of negligent selection.[96]

• A Pennsylvania court ruled that a church was not liable for its pastor's molestation of a young girl since it exercised reasonable care in screening him. Although conceding that the church required the pastor to complete an extensive questionnaire, interviewed him at length and discussed his suitability with all 14 references that he provided, the victim's parents insisted that the church "should have investigated further." They claimed that the church should have questioned the 14 references "more closely" and should have asked additional questions of the pastor himself concerning his prior sexual behavior. If the church had done so, the parents argued, it would have discovered that he had a homosexual affair while in high school, had made a subtle advance on his wife's younger brother more than ten years prior to his employment by the church, had exposed himself from the window of his previous home, and may have abused his own son. The court conceded that employers have a duty "to exercise reasonable care in selecting, supervising and controlling employees." However, it insisted that employers cannot be liable unless "it is shown that the employer knew or, in the exercise of ordinary care, should have known of the necessity for exercising control of his employee." The court reviewed the facts cited by the parents as proof of the church's alleged failure to exercise reasonable care in the selection, supervision, and retention of the pastor, and concluded: "We find that [the church's screening process] was reasonably thorough under the circumstances present at the time. We do not agree that the church had a duty specifically to inquire about all of [the pastor's] prior sexual conduct in an attempt to ascertain if, for example, he had ever had a homosexual liaison or abused a child. [He] was apparently a happily married man with a stable family. He fully cooperated in the application and interview process. He had no criminal record and had never been arrested or investigated for any crime, sexual or otherwise. In addition . . . the church contacted every reference [he] provided, which included people who had knowledge of his in his previous ministerial positions and throughout his military service. Not a single person contacted provided information

[96] Doe v. First Presbyterian Church (USA), 710 N.E.2d 367 (Ohio App. 1998).

that would have given a reasonable person any hint that his sexual propensities needed to be investigated further. All of the references expressed very positive sentiments regarding [the pastor] personally as well as his suitability for the senior minister position. Lastly, even if the church members who were engaged in the hiring process had inquired further of [the pastor] himself regarding his past personal behavior, he testified that he might well not have revealed anything negative since he was both anxious to get the job and in a state of denial."[97]

• *A Washington state appeals court ruled that a church-operated school was not legally responsible for damages resulting from an alleged sexual relationship between a teacher and a student.*[98] *The student's parents had sued the school and church for "negligent hiring" and "negligent supervision." The court rejected both allegations. With regard to the school's alleged negligent hiring, the court observed that "the hiring process employed by the school suggests it took reasonable care in hiring [the teacher]. . . . The process appears sufficient as a matter of law to discover whether an individual is fit to teach at [the school]."*

• *The Wisconsin Supreme Court ruled that the statute of limitations prevented a woman from suing a Catholic archdiocese for the alleged acts of molestation by a priest nearly 40 years before.*[99] *The woman claimed that the priest entered into a sexual relationship with her in the late 1950s when she was a high school student, and that as a result of the priest's behavior she "has suffered and continues to suffer from severe emotional distress, causing and contributing to the break-up of her marriage, separation from her children, loss of jobs and other difficulties." The woman's lawsuit claimed that the archdiocese was responsible for her injuries on the basis of negligent hiring. In particular, she claimed that the archdiocese knew or should have known that the priest had engaged in similar acts of misconduct with other parishioners, and yet negligently failed to remove him as a priest. In rejecting this claim, the court noted, "To establish a claim for negligent hiring or retention [the woman] would have to establish that the archdiocese was negligent in hiring or retaining [the priest] because he was incompetent or otherwise unfit. But, we conclude that the First Amendment to the United States Constitution prevents the courts of this state from determining what makes one competent to serve as a Catholic priest since such a determination would require interpretation of church canons and internal church policies and practices. Therefore [the suit] against the archdiocese is not capable of enforcement by the courts. . . . Examining the ministerial selection policy, which is 'infused with the religious tenets of the particular sect,' entangles the court in qualitative evaluation of religious norms. Negligence requires the court to create a 'reasonable bishop' norm. Beliefs in penance, admonition and reconciliation as a sacramental response to sin may be the point of attack by a challenger who wants a court to probe the tort law reasonableness of the church's mercy toward the offender. . . . The tort of negligent selection of unsuitable teachers has been recognized in civil courts. If negligent selection of a potential pedophile for the religious office of priest, minister or rabbi is a tort as to future child victims, will civil courts also hear Title VII challenges by the non-selected seminarian against the theological seminary that declines to ordain a plaintiff into ministry because of his psychological profile? How far shall the courts' qualitative*

---

[97] R.A. v. First Church of Christ, 2000 WL 232599 (Pa. Super. 2000).

[98] Scott v. Blanchet High School, 747 P.2d 1124 (Wash. App. 1987).

[99] Pritzlaff v. Archdiocese of Milwaukee, 533 N.W.2d 780 (Wis. 1995).

entanglement with religious selectivity extend?" The court concluded by observing that "the tort of negligent hiring and retention may not be maintained against a religious governing body due to concerns of excessive entanglement" between church and state.

Table 10-4 Ten Risks Associated with Sexual Misconduct		
risk	**increase risk**	**decrease risk**
#1 negligent selection— inadequate screening	• no screening • inadequate screening (e.g., no contacts with references)	• adequate screening process for all volunteers and employees • reference checks • 6 month rule • criminal checks when indicated
#2 negligent supervision	• inadequate number of trained and screened adults present during youth activities	• develop minimum staffing rules (call other charities for assistance, such as Red Cross or Boy Scouts) • 2 adult rule
#3 negligent retention	• fail to investigate allegations of prior misconduct by a current volunteer or employee	• prompt investigation of any allegation regarding prior misconduct by a current volunteer or employee
#4 inadequate response	• deny allegations of misconduct • minimize the severity • blame the victim and family	• prompt investigation of charges • compliance with state child abuse reporting law • refer to denominational agency if applicable • communication with victim and family • contact legal counsel • contact insurance agent
#5 ratification	• church leaders ignore allegations of sexual misconduct	• church leaders respond immediately to allegations of sexual misconduct • see #4 above

Table 10-4
Ten Risks Associated with Sexual Misconduct

risk	increase risk	decrease risk
#6 inadequate boundaries in counseling	• no restrictions or limitations on adults who counsel with other adults or minors	• no opposite sex counseling without third person present • opposite sex counseling only when other staff are visible • limit number of sessions • limit length of sessions • women counsel women • video feed to other location • telephone counseling • counseling brochure
#7 inadequate insurance coverage	• coverage for sexual misconduct not addressed during insurance review • church leaders have no idea how much coverage exists • unfamiliarity with exclusions and limitations • failure to notify • no directors and officers coverage	• familiarity with policy and its terms, conditions, and exclusions • prompt notification of any potential claim • directors and officers insurance
#8 inadequate education	• staff and membership not informed why screening and supervisory procedures are followed	• inform staff and membership of magnitude of risk • periodic emphasis • use state child abuse personnel

Table 10-4
Ten Risks Associated with Sexual Misconduct

risk	increase risk	decrease risk
#9 failure to comply with child abuse reporting laws	• church leaders are unfamiliar with the state child abuse reporting law • church leaders handle child abuse allegations "in house"	• church leaders are familiar with state child abuse reporting law (definition of abuse, who are mandatory reporters, clergy privilege) • get updated copy of statute at least annually • become acquainted with someone in state child abuse reporting office
#10 inadequate counsel	• use of legal counsel with no experience in handling such claims	• use of legal counsel with experience in working with churches and with sexual misconduct claims

Risk Management

§ 10-04.3

Key point 10-04.3. *Churches can reduce the risk of liability based on negligent selection for the sexual molestation of minors by adopting risk management policies and procedures.*

Risk Management Resources

Churches must exercise reasonable care in the selection of ministers, nonminister employees, and volunteers in order to avoid potential liability based on negligent selection. The publisher of this text has produced several resources to assist church leaders in satisfying the standard of reasonable care in the selection of workers. These resources include:

(1) *Reducing the Risk: Keeping Your Ministry Safe from Child Sexual Abuse* (kit includes one training DVD, one leader's guide, ten trainee workbooks, and ten Screening and Selection Forms for Volunteers); and Reducing the Risk online training. Both are available at www.ReducingTheRisk.com.

(2) *The 4-Hour Legal Training Kit for Church Boards* (eight 30-minute presentations by Richard Hammar orient church board members to the critical legal and tax issues that face them and their church).

(3) *Pastor, Church & Law* (4th ed. 2007-2008) (four-volume series that addresses dozens of legal risks, and provides helpful risk management strategies.

(4) plus several other newsletters, recordings, books, and an online legal library, all of which are available on the publisher's website, www. ChurchLawToday.com.

Incidents of sexual misconduct involving minor victims can be devastating to the victim, the victim's family, the offender, the church leadership, and the church itself. The good news is that churches can significantly reduce the risk of such incidents by taking a few simple precautions. These precautions are addressed more fully in the resources noted above. Here is a summary of eight risk management strategies:

1. A Written Application Form

Churches can significantly reduce their risk of legal liability for negligent selection (and the likelihood that an incident of abuse or molestation will occur) by having every applicant for youth work (volunteer or compensated) complete a "screening application." At a minimum, the application should ask for the applicant's name and address, the names of other youth-serving organizations in which the applicant has worked as an employee or volunteer, a full explanation of any prior criminal convictions, and the names of two or more references. The application should be completed by every applicant for any position involving the custody or supervision of minors. The application should also be completed by current employees or volunteers having custody or supervision over minors.

There is some confusion regarding the need to ask applicants (who will be working with minors) if they were sexually molested when they were a minor. The confusion stems from a 1991 decision by the Alaska Supreme Court.[100] The court concluded that adults who experienced sexual abuse as children are much more likely to become child abusers than the general population. It quoted from an article on child abuse: "One of the predisposing conditions [to child sexual abuse] that has been of considerable interest to clinicians and researchers is an experience of sexual abuse in childhood. Being sexually victimized as a child is a common experience for adult sex offenders and mothers of victims of sexual mistreatment. Moreover, childhood experiences of sexual abuse have been found at higher rates among those who victimize or are mothers of victims than in comparison groups."

No other court has followed this decision, and so only in Alaska should churches ask applicants for youth or children's work if they were abused as minors. Churches in other states should consult with an attorney regarding the use of such a question on their application forms.

2. Contact References

Having current or prospective employees and volunteers complete an application form does not significantly reduce a church's risk of negligent selection. Significant risk reduction occurs if the church takes the following additional steps:

- If an applicant is unknown to you, confirm his or her identity by requiring photographic identification (such as a state driver's license). Child molesters often use pseudonyms.

---

[100] Broderick v. King's Way Church, 808 P.2d 1211 (Alaska 1991).

• Contact each person and organization listed as a reference in the application, and request a written reference. If you do not receive back the written reference forms, then contact the references by telephone and prepare a written memorandum noting the questions asked and the reference's responses. Sample reference forms (for use by mail or telephone) are contained in the resources mentioned above. Show the date and method of the contact, the person making the contact as well as the person contacted, and a summary of the reference's remarks. Such forms, when completed, should be kept with an applicant's original application. They should be kept permanently.

There are two basic kinds of references: personal and institutional. Personal references are persons that an applicant lists on his or her application. Usually, church leaders are not familiar with such references, and so they are of limited value. Further, the FBI profile on preferential child molesters states that one of the characteristics of pedophiles is that there only adult friends tend to be other pedophiles. This further diminishes the value of personal references. The best reference is an institutional reference. This is a reference from another institution with which the applicant has worked with minors either as a paid employee or an unpaid volunteer. Obviously, obtaining a positive reference from one or more other institutions that have actually observed the applicant interact with minors is the gold standard in terms of references. Some applicants have not worked with other youth-serving institutions in the past, and so no institutional reference is available. In such cases, a church's only option is to obtain personal references. However, risk can be reduced by limiting personal references to members of the church.

For pastoral applicants, the best reference will be from a denominational office with which the church is affiliated. If the church is not affiliated with a denomination, then the best reference will be from board members in other churches in which the applicant has served. Sample reference forms are contained in the Reducing the Risk resource kit available from the publisher of this text (www.ReducingTheRisk.com).

For nonminister employees and volunteers, the best references will be from other churches or charities in which the applicant has worked with minors. Examples include Boy Scouts, Girl Scouts, Big Brothers/Big Sisters, YMCA, public or private schools, youth sports, or other churches or religious organizations. Seek a reference from every such organization in which the applicant has served. Your application form should ask applicants to list all such organizations, including contact information.

• Be sure you are aware of any additional legal requirements that apply in your state. For example, a number of states have passed laws requiring church-operated child-care facilities to check with the state before hiring any applicant for employment to ensure that each applicant does not have a criminal record involving certain types of crimes. You will need to check with an attorney for guidance.

- The church must treat as strictly confidential all applications and records of contacts with churches or other references. Such information should be marked "confidential," and access should be restricted to those few persons with a legitimate interest in the information.

Churches should keep the following additional considerations in mind when preparing a screening procedure:

The screening procedure should apply to all workers—both compensated and volunteer. Acts of molestation have been committed by both kinds of workers.

> "The highest risks involve male workers in programs that involve overnight activities or unsupervised activities. Persons in this category should be carefully screened."

- The screening procedure should apply to new applicants as well as current workers. Obviously, churches need to use some common sense here. For example, if your 4th grade Sunday school teacher is a 60-year-old woman with 25 years teaching experience in your church, you may decide that reference checks are unnecessary. The highest risks involve male workers in programs that involve overnight activities or unsupervised activities. Persons in this category should be carefully screened.

- If the screening application and reference forms seem overly burdensome, consider the following:

(1) Your church liability insurance policy may exclude or limit coverage for acts of child molestation. If so, you have a potentially enormous uninsured risk. Reducing this risk is worth whatever inconvenience might be generated in implementing a screening procedure. Just ask any member of a church in which such an incident has occurred.

(2) The screening procedure is designed primarily to provide a safe and secure environment for the youth of your church. Unfortunately, churches have become targets of child molesters because they provide immediate and direct access to children in a trusting and often unsupervised environment. In order to provide some protection for the youth of your church against such persons, a screening procedure is imperative.

(3) The relatively minor inconvenience involved in establishing a screening procedure is a small price to pay for protecting the church from the devastation that often accompanies an incident of molestation.

(4) The resistance to screening will diminish as more charities screen volunteer workers.

(5) Think of the screening procedure in terms of risk reduction. A church is free to hire workers without any screening or evaluation whatever, but such a practice involves the highest degree of legal risk. On the other hand, a church that develops a responsible screening procedure has a much lower risk.

(6) The services of a local attorney should be solicited in drafting an appropriate screening form to ensure compliance with state law. It is also advisable that such forms be shared with a church's insurance company for its comments. You also should consider sharing your form with the state agency that investigates reports of child abuse.

(7) Obtain copies of the application forms used by the Boy Scouts, Big Brothers, and similar organizations. As a result of numerous lawsuits, these organizations have developed effective application forms. Review these forms, and use them as resources when preparing your own forms. The state agency responsible for investigating reports of child abuse may have application forms for you to review, and they often are willing to review the application forms that churches prepare.

3. Interviews

The final candidates for a church position should be interviewed. This will provide the church with an opportunity to inquire into each applicant's background and make a determination as to each person's suitability for the position under consideration. The "selection and screening kits" described at the beginning of this section contain sample interview questions.

Higher risk individuals (e.g., single males) and persons applying for higher risk positions (e.g., boys groups, scouting groups, camps, overnight or largely unsupervised activities involving either male or female children or adolescents) should be interviewed by a staff member who has been trained to identify child molesters. Law enforcement personnel and local offices of state agencies responsible for investigating reports of child abuse often have materials that can be used to train the staff member who will conduct interviews. These resources should be utilized.

4. Six Month Rule

Churches can reduce the risk of incidents of sexual molestation by adopting a policy restricting eligibility for any volunteer position involving the custody or supervision of minors to those persons who have been members in good standing of the church for a minimum period of time, such as six months. Such a policy gives the church an additional opportunity to evaluate applicants, and will help to repel persons seeking immediate access to potential victims.

5. Screening Minor Workers

Using children's workers who are under 18 years of age is a common church practice. However, note the following considerations:

1. The younger the worker's age, the greater the risk to the church. A church must exercise reasonable care, some courts have said a "high" degree of care, in the selection and supervision of children's workers. Obviously, using workers who are 10 years of age in a church nursery will expose the church to greater risk than using someone who is 17.

2. It is imperative that at least one adult be present at all times if minors are used as volunteer workers in any program or activity involving minors. Ideally, two adults should be present, so that if one of them must be absent temporarily, the other will be there.

3. If a minor is injured, the church may be legally responsible on the basis of negligence if the injury resulted from the church's failure to exercise a reasonable degree of care in the selection or supervision of its workers. Courts often look to the practices of local charities, and sometimes national charities, in establishing a reasonable standard of care. As a result, it is often helpful for church leaders to contact other youth-serving charities in the area to ascertain their practices and policies on specific issues. Using local affiliates of national charities is the best practice. If you would like to use minors to work with younger children, ask some of these other charities about their response to this question. Do they use minors as volunteer workers in programs involving younger children? If so, what limits to they impose, and what policies have they enacted? By aligning your church's practices to that of several charities, you will go a long way in demonstrating that your church exercised a sufficient degree of care and therefore was not negligent.

4. Every church should carefully screen children's workers. But, how is this done? You obviously cannot perform criminal records checks on persons under 18 years of age, and even for persons who are 18 or 19 a criminal records check will have limited significance. You really need to approach the screening of adolescents in a different manner. Let me suggest two options.

   First, obtain two to three reference letters from persons who have seen the applicant interact with other minors (this would include church workers, coaches, school teachers, scout leaders, etc.). You want an opinion from such persons about the applicant's suitability for working with minors. Obviously, if you receive two to three references from such persons, you have very compelling evidence that you exercised reasonable care in the selection process, and in the final analysis, this is the standard by which you will be judged if your church is sued for the molestation of a child by an adolescent worker. The bottom line is that you cannot conduct criminal records checks on such persons, but you must take other steps to demonstrate reasonable care.

Second, contact local youth-serving charities such as the public school district, Boy/Girl Scouts, YMCA, Boys/Girls Clubs, etc. and ask them what screening they use for adolescent workers. Be sure to make a record of each contact. By basing your screening policy on "community practice" you will be reducing your risk of liability based on negligent screening.

5. One final point. If you compensate minors who work with children in your church, then you need to be aware that you may need to pay them the minimum wage (under state of federal law, whichever is greater), and that state or federal child labor laws may apply. Both of these issues need to be carefully addressed to ensure compliance with the law.

6. Criminal Records Checks

In this section, we will review the various kinds of criminal records checks that are available to church leaders when screening employees and volunteer workers.

Different Kinds of Criminal Records Checks

(1) county criminal records checks

Every county maintains records of criminal convictions. In fact, most experts believe that county criminal records databases are by far the most accurate because they contain the records of all court convictions and orders that may or may not get transmitted to state or federal repositories. While county criminal records may be the most accurate, they only cover a very limited geographical area. A person may live in a one county and have been convicted of a crime in a neighboring county. A criminal records check of county records in the county of residence would disclose a "clean" record. Further, many persons have lived in different counties, and so conducting a criminal records check of only the current county of residence may fail to disclose a criminal record.

There are two ways for your church to conduct county criminal records checks:

(1) Contact the appropriate county agency (often the sheriff's department) and request a criminal records check.

(2) Use a fee-based criminal records check service that will conduct a check for you.

These two options for conducting county criminal records checks are discussed more fully later in this section.

The effectiveness of county checks can be increased by performing checks in multiple counties. For example, if an applicant for youth work discloses his counties of residence for the last several years, and a church conducts criminal records checks in each of those counties, the effectiveness of this type of screening increases (as does the cost).

(2) state criminal records checks

The sex offender registries required by state Megan's Laws are a form of state criminal records check. But, in most states church leaders also can access general criminal records information that is not limited to sexual offenses.

State-level criminal history records are collected, maintained, and disseminated by "state central repositories," which are agencies or bureaus within state governments. These repositories are often housed within the state police or a cabinet-level agency with public safety and criminal justice responsibilities, such as the Department of Law Enforcement or the Department of Public Safety. All 50 states and the District of Columbia have established central repositories for criminal history records.

Criminal history information includes information about any arrests, along with available "disposition data." Disposition data often include information about "final" dispositions, including police decisions to drop all charges, prosecutor decisions to not prosecute the cases, and trial court dispositions. Where court action results in a conviction, the criminal history record should show the sentence imposed and information about correctional reception and release.

> "According to U.S. Department of Justice statistics, more than 59 million individual offenders were in the criminal history files of the state central repositories in 2000. In comparison, the repositories held only 30.3 million subjects in their criminal history files in 1984, and 42.4 million in 1989."

Some repositories include information about pretrial release or confinement and "nonfinal" or "interim" dispositions, such as prosecutor decisions to file, modify, or drop charges referred by the police.

While some state repositories collect comprehensive arrest and disposition information about misdemeanor offenses, most repositories collect information only about the most serious classes of misdemeanor offenses. This lack of comprehensive misdemeanor arrest and disposition data has been identified as one of the major deficiencies in state criminal history record systems.

There is enormous variation in the extent to which state central repositories have automated their criminal history records. State repositories have been making rapid progress in the last decade in automating their criminal history files. Eighteen state repositories in 1995 reported that 100 percent of their criminal history records were automated. By 1999, 40 states reported that more than 75 percent of their criminal history records were automated, compared to 26 states in 1992. By 1999, only five jurisdictions had automated less than 50 percent of their files and only two states lacked any automated criminal history records. Overall, about 53 million of the estimated 59 million criminal history records maintained by the state repositories nationwide were automated as of 2000. In addition, the states have made a significant investment in the automation of criminal fingerprint files. Every state now operates or has access to automated fingerprint technology.

The accuracy and completeness of criminal history records is the single most serious problem in criminal record information systems. A recent government survey found that in 32 states representing 64 percent of the nation's population, only 60 percent of arrests within the past five years had final dispositions recorded. In addition, about one-half of the state-reported criminal history records maintained by the FBI do not have final dispositions. The inaccuracy of arrest and disposition data also is a problem. Of the few in-depth audits or reviews of the accuracy of the information maintained by state and federal criminal record repositories, most found unacceptable levels of inaccuracies.

Although the FBI has proposed model criminal history record formats over the years, adoption of a uniform criminal history record format has never occurred. State and federal repositories have been left to adopt their own record formats and approaches concerning the types of offenses that should be included on criminal history records and the types of information about these offenses that should be included. Not surprisingly, this has resulted in considerable diversity in the formats of the criminal history records presently generated by the state repositories, as well as in the content of these records. For example, while virtually all repositories attempt to obtain and record information about all felony offenses, there is diversity concerning the types of misdemeanor offenses, if any, included on criminal history records. Moreover, there are considerable differences in the way state penal codes designate particular offenses as felonies or misdemeanors. There is also diversity concerning the types of case processing information obtained and recorded by the repositories. While some repositories attempt to obtain little more than arrest charges and final dispositions, other repositories record other information, including bail and pretrial release data, pretrial detention data, prosecutor charge modifications, and correctional admission and release data.

Key point. *The U.S. Department of Justice has stated that "formats in use vary so greatly that it is probably true that no two state criminal history record formats are identical and many of them are not even similar."*

States place few or no restrictions on the dissemination of conviction records, and a number of states do not restrict the dissemination of arrest records less than 1 year old. Nonconviction records, however, including records of cases with no disposition recorded after the passage of a year or longer, are restricted in most states and in some states may not be disseminated at all for noncriminal justice purposes or may be disseminated only for limited and specifically defined purposes.

There are two ways for your church to conduct state criminal records checks:

(1) Contact the appropriate state agency and request a criminal records check. In most states, you have the choice of obtaining a "name" or "fingerprint" check. The information required to obtain a check using a person's name (and not fingerprints) varies from state to state. Some states charge a fee, while others do not. Some states allow you to submit a request for a criminal records check on an official website, while others do not. Some states require the signature of the person whose criminal record is being searched, while others do not. Also, the criminal record that is searched (arrests, convictions, incarceration, release) varies from state to state. A check using a person's name is usually faster than a fingerprint check, but it is also more prone to error and misidentification. For a listing of state offices you can contact to conduct a criminal records check, visit the website of the National Foundation to Prevent Child Sexual Abuse (www.fbifingerprintchecks.com/news.html). Click on the "State Public Records Agency Contact" tab and you will be taken to a listing of contact information for all 50 states. Or, you can simply call your local police or sheriff's department.

(2) Use a fee-based criminal records check service that will conduct a check for you. There are thousands of such services available on the Internet, and their services and fees vary. Many of these companies are reputable. A good way to select a company is to find the companies that are used by national youth-serving charities. Using a company that has been selected by reputable national charities to conduct criminal records checks for youth workers is evidence that your church exercised reasonable care in the selection of workers.

Keep in mind that a state check only covers criminal records maintained by one state. It is common for churches to have applicants for children's or youth ministry positions who have lived in more than one state in recent years. In such a case, you should consider conducting a criminal records check in each state of residence, or a national check.

Key point. *In a 2003 ruling upholding the constitutionality of state "Megan's Laws," the United States Supreme Court noted that not only is it common for sex offenders to engage in repeat offenses, but such offenses often are committed in different states. The Court referred to one study that found that 38 percent of all repeat sex offenses "took place in jurisdictions other than where the previous offense was committed." This is an important observation, since it shows that county or even state criminal records checks may not detect a criminal past.[101]*

"....not only is it common for sex offenders to engage in repeat offenses, but such offenses often are committed in different states."

---

[101] Smith v. Doe, 538 U.S. 84 (2003).

(3) Megan's Laws

In 2003, the United States Supreme Court issued two decisions upholding the constitutionality of state "Megan's Laws" requiring sex offenders to register with the state and making these registries accessible by the public.[102] These registries are now a viable option in a church's screening procedures. What's more, in most states these checks can be done for free online without the knowledge or consent of the person you are checking. As a result, an increasing number of churches are checking their state sex offender registry for anyone who will have unsupervised access to minors. But church leaders should be aware of four limitations associated with these checks:

(1) Sex offender registries only include convictions for specified sex crimes. Other crimes (kidnapping, murder, assault, etc.) are also relevant in making a decision regarding the suitability of a person to have access to minors.

(2) Sex offender registries only contain criminal convictions after a specified date (which in many states is fairly recent).

(3) Sex offender registries only include criminal records in one state.

(4) Sex offender registries are not easily accessible by the public in some states. For example, in some states the sex offender registry is maintained by law enforcement agencies, and the public can review the registry only by contacting such an agency.

As a result, church leaders should never view a sex offender registry check as the only screening procedure that is necessary. At best, it is one component in an overall screening strategy that includes an application, interview, reference checks, and possibly other criminal records checks.

In most states, accessing the sex offender registry is simple and easy. You simply go to a state-sponsored website, type the name of a person, and click "search."

> "Church leaders should never view a sex offender registry check as the only screening procedure that is necessary."

Key point. *If you do a sex offender registry search, be sure that you retain a copy of the results even if a person's name is not listed on the registry. This will document that you performed a search, which will be relevant evidence in the event that your church is later sued on the basis of "negligent selection" for the molestation of a child by that person.*

---

[102] Connecticut Department of Public Safety v. Doe, 538 U.S. 1 (2003); Smith v. Doe, 538 U.S. 84 (2003).

Key point. *What do you do if you discover that your state sex offender registry contains the name of an applicant for youth ministry? First, you need to be absolutely sure that the registry identified the same person as the one you were investigating. In some cases, the registry will contain other personal identifying information (address, phone number, photo, etc.) that will confirm a person's identity. If not, then call the telephone number listed on the registry website, and ask for additional information.*

You can quickly find links to the Megan's Law sex offender registries of all 50 states on the following website: http://www.klaaskids.org/pg-legmeg.htm. Just click on your state and you will be directed to information that is specific to your state, including the name and telephone number of a contact person you can call with any questions; a summary of the kinds of sex offenders who are required to register; and, a link to search the registry via the internet (if available).

(4) "national" criminal records checks

In a highly mobile society such as ours, with persons moving frequently between states, it is clear that county or even state criminal records checks are of limited value. Many see "national" criminal records checks as the ideal form of screening. It is important to distinguish between three very different kinds of "national" criminal records checks:

(1) Some private companies that offer "national" criminal records checks do nothing more than search the sex offender registries maintained by every state pursuant to "Megan's Laws." Such checks are of very limited value, because they only determine if a person is a registered sex offender (in one or more states). As noted previously, sex offender registries only include convictions for specified sex crimes; they only contain criminal convictions after a specified date (which in many states is fairly recent); and are not easily accessible in all states, meaning that a "national" search of sex offender registries may not cover all 50 states.

(2) Some private companies that offer "national" criminal records checks review the criminal records repositories maintained by states. Some of these companies only review records that are available online (which omits some states). These checks are more effective than searches of state sex offender registries because they provide more complete coverage of criminal records and are not limited to recent convictions. However, some states do not permit access to their criminal records database by private, non-governmental entities such as churches or private screening companies. In a case upholding the constitutionality of state "Megan's Laws," the Supreme Court referred to one study that found that 38% of all repeat sex offenses "took place in jurisdictions other than where the previous offense was committed." This is an important observation, for two reasons. First, it shows that county or even state criminal records checks may not detect a criminal past; and second, it suggests that churches should consider performing multi-state or national criminal records checks.

(3) The FBI maintains a national criminal records database, but it is accessible only by designated state agencies. Private companies cannot perform these checks, although church leaders often do not understand this. These checks are addressed in the next section.

(5) FBI criminal records checks

Prior to 1971, the means of obtaining access to a national search was by application to the FBI, which, under congressional authorization dating back to 1924, maintained criminal record files containing fingerprints and arrest and disposition information pertaining to federal and state offenders. Most search applications were handled by mail and required manual processing by FBI personnel. In 1971, the FBI's National Crime Information Center (NCIC) implemented an online interstate computerized system called the Computerized Criminal History (CCH) Program. Like the FBI manual system, CCH was a "national repository" system; that is, full criminal history records for federal and state offenders from participating states were maintained in the FBI's centralized database. The system was used for both criminal justice and noncriminal justice purposes. Applications for searches for authorized noncriminal justice purposes required the submission of fingerprint cards by mail to the FBI.

The CCH system continued to operate throughout the 1970s even though state participation was poor, due primarily to objections to the cost and difficulty of maintaining duplicate files on state offenders at both the state and federal levels. The FBI's centralized files were continued during this period, and the agency began automating them in 1974. Most state officials preferred the development of a "decentralized" national criminal history record system; that is, a system that would not require the continuance of a duplicative national repository of state offender records, but that instead would undertake to strengthen the state repositories and provide the means of tying them together into a viable interstate system relying on state-maintained records.

Prior to the 1970s, it was generally conceded that most of the existing state repositories lacked the technology to participate in such a program. By the end of that decade, however, substantial progress had been made in improving existing state repositories. Recognizing this progress, the U.S. Department of Justice and state officials approved the Interstate Identification Index concept in 1978. This database is an interstate computer network that allows national criminal history record searches to determine if a person has a record anywhere in the country. The Index is designed to tie automated criminal history record databases of state central repositories and the FBI together into a national system by means of an "index-pointer" approach. Under this approach, the FBI maintains an automated master name index, referred to as the National Identification Index (NII), which includes names and identifying data concerning all persons whose automated criminal history records are available by means of the Interstate Identification Index. If a search of this index indicates that an individual has a criminal record, the index will "point" the inquiring agency to the FBI or to one or more of the state repositories from which the record or records may be obtained. The inquiring agency may then obtain the records directly from the indicated sources.

The FBI also maintains the National Fingerprint File (NFF), a database of fingerprints relating to an arrested or charged individual maintained by the FBI to provide positive identification of persons listed in the Interstate Identification Index. The major advantage of the Index approach is the shift from reliance on FBI-maintained state offender records for national search purposes to reliance on state-maintained records for such purposes. The two main advantages are: (1) criminal history records maintained by the state repositories are more accurate and complete than state offender records maintained by the FBI, and (2) if state repositories provide record responses for national search purposes, the FBI can discontinue the maintenance of its files of state offender records.

In summary, the role of the FBI as a provider of national criminal records checks is changing. The current approach is for states to send only "first arrest" information to the FBI, which will use the data to keep current the Interstate Identification Index. States will collect any subsequent criminal history information on the offenders, and will make offenders' entire criminal histories and related information available for queries from other states or from authorized federal entities. This process will spare state repositories and the FBI from maintaining costly duplicate records, and will provide greater access to state-level criminal history information, which is generally more accurate than that maintained at the federal level. Under this approach, the FBI will maintain these systems:

- The Interstate Identification Index, which will permit authorized organizations to determine whether any state or federal repository maintains a criminal history record about a particular individual.

- The National Fingerprint File, which will provide positive identification of all offenders indexed in the national system.

FBI criminal records have historically been available only to law enforcement agencies. In recent years, private employers have argued that they should be entitled to obtain criminal history record information for background checks on prospective employees who will be placed in sensitive positions handling substantial amounts of money or other valuable assets or, even more importantly, caring for vulnerable populations, such as children or elderly persons. In response, Congress passed legislation in the 1980s permitting federally held criminal history record information to be released for employment background checks for positions at certain kinds of banking institutions and securities organizations. Congress later mandated FBI criminal records checks of persons wanting to purchase handguns (the "Brady Bill"), and made these records accessible to public housing agencies in screening applicants for public housing. In 1993, Congress enacted the National Child Protection Act, which authorized certain youth-serving charities to conduct national criminal records checks using FBI records. This important legislation is summarized later in this section. It is this legislation that enables churches to have access to FBI records in screening persons who will work with minors.

Key point. *More than half of the 13 million fingerprint cards submitted to the FBI in a recent year were for noncriminal justice background checks. The increased background check duties strained the capacity of many repositories to meet their responsibilities. Agencies mailing fingerprint cards to the FBI in 1998, for example, waited an average of 72 days for a response. Meanwhile, a growing backlog of unprocessed prints surpassed 750,000.*

Fingerprint Technology

The FBI only performs criminal records checks upon receipt of "10-print" fingerprints. Many states will also perform criminal records checks using fingerprint identification. In many cases, fingerprints are taken manually with ink and cards. But increasingly fingerprints are being taken electronically because the process is more convenient and accurate.

Law enforcement agencies first explored the potential of "digitized" fingerprint images in the 1960s, and the first automated fingerprint reading machines based on digitized images began to appear in the early 1970s. Subsequent advances and refinements improved fingerprint technology to such a degree that many state-level criminal history repositories and some law enforcement agencies in larger cities began to implement automated fingerprint identification systems (AFIS) in the 1980s. Today, nearly every state has access to AFIS technology.

AFIS has the capacity to use an optical scanner, or a "livescan" as they are called in the criminal justice community. A person's fingers are placed one at a time on a glass plate and scanned. The device transforms the fingerprint images into unique bit maps consisting of rows and columns of dots, each with stored bits of data. The digitized images can then be attached to an email for electronic transmission through a network to a criminal history repository. The repository's AFIS quickly searches its stored digitized images for a match. Responses can be returned on-line in a matter of hours or less. AFIS eliminates the need to take multiple sets of prints, as the images can be easily copied. Technicians can also determine fingerprint quality on site and retake inferior quality prints before sending them to the repository.

While virtually all state criminal history repositories have implemented automated fingerprint systems, there are significant variations as to how they use the technology. Some states have been electronically transmitting fingerprint images and accompanying personal and criminal history data to the FBI for several years. But, most state repositories are not yet capable of electronically transmitting data to the FBI, even though they have implemented AFIS internally. Some states are installing livescan devices in every county for transmitting data to the state criminal history repository. Others plan to install livescan devices in larger metropolitan areas, but law enforcement agencies in rural areas will continue to mail fingerprint cards to state repositories.

Table 10-5
Criminal Records Checks— A Summary of the Options

criminal records check	advantages	disadvantages	comments
county records	the most accurate criminal records check	• limited geographical coverage • requires consent of applicant	• more effective for persons who have lived and worked in the same county for several years • doing multiple county checks increases their effectiveness, but at a higher cost
sex offender registry of one state	• in most states these checks can be done online • no cost • consent of applicant not required • fast	of limited value because only convictions for certain sex crimes committed after a specified date are listed	limited value, but easy and cheap, so many churches use these checks as one component of a screening program (often in conjunction with other kinds of criminal records checks)
state criminal records check	• coverage of an entire state • not limited to sex crimes	• not as accurate as county checks • errors are common (especially if fingerprints are not checked) • not accessible by churches in all states • may require fingerprints • limited geographical coverage • requires consent of applicant • may take weeks or months to receive results	• more effective for persons who have lived and worked in the same state for several years • doing multiple state checks increases their effectiveness, but at a higher cost

Table 10-5
Criminal Records Checks— A Summary of the Options

criminal records check	advantages	disadvantages	comments
"national" check of all or most state sex offender registries	• most state registries are available online and can be checked quickly and for free • provides greater protection than checking one state's registry	• of limited value because only convictions for certain sex crimes committed after a specified date are listed • most churches do not have the time to conduct these searches (a private company must be used on a fee basis)	• limited value, but easy and cheap • checking dozens of state registries for several persons is time-consuming
"national" check of all or most state criminal records	• greater geographical coverage • not limited to sex crimes	• not as accurate as county checks • errors are common (especially if fingerprints are not checked) • not accessible by churches in all states • may require fingerprints • most churches do not have the time to conduct these searches (a private company must be used on a fee basis) • requires consent of applicant • may take weeks or months to receive results	many experts view this as the most effective criminal records check currently available

Table 10-5
Criminal Records Checks— A Summary of the Options

criminal records check	advantages	disadvantages	comments
"national" check of FBI database	• greater geographical coverage • not limited to sex crimes	• not as accurate as county checks • errors are common (because states often do not transmit complete information) • not directly accessible by churches • requires fingerprints • requires consent of applicant • may take weeks or months to receive results	many experts view this as a very effective criminal records check

The National Child Protection Act (1993)

In 1993, Congress passed the National Child Protection Act[103] as a bold new attack against the molestation of children in "youth serving" organizations. The most important provision in the Act specifies:

A state may have in effect procedures (established by state statute or regulation) that require qualified entities designated by the state to contact an authorized agency of the state to request a nationwide [FBI] background check for the purpose of determining whether a provider has been convicted of a crime that bears upon the provider's fitness to have responsibility for the safety and well-being of children, the elderly, or individuals with disabilities.

qualified entities and providers

The Act permits "qualified entities" that are designated by the states to obtain nationwide criminal records checks. The Act defines a qualified entity as "a business or organization, whether public, private, for-profit, not-for-profit, or voluntary, that provides child care or child care placement services . . . ." There is little doubt that this definition includes churches that operate child care or preschool facilities. But does it also include churches that do not operate a school or preschool, but that offer Sunday School, nursery services, and other youth

---

[103] 42 U.S.C. § 5119a.

activities and programs involving supervision or instruction of minors? The Act does not address this question directly, but it does define the term "child care" to include "the provision of care, treatment, education, training, instruction, supervision, or recreation to children by persons having unsupervised access to a child."

It is likely that the operation of a Sunday School, nursery, and many if not most kinds of youth and children's programs would constitute "the provision of education, training, instruction, supervision, or recreation to children." As a result, it is likely that a church is a "qualified entity" even if it does not operate a school or a formal child care or preschool program. This interpretation is reasonable, and furthers the purposes of the legislation.

It is also important to review the Act's definition of the term provider, since a qualified entity may request an FBI criminal background check to determine if a provider has been convicted of a crime that bears upon that person's fitness to have responsibility for the safety and well-being of children. The Act defines the term provider as a person who

(1) is employed by or volunteers with a qualified entity; owns or operates a qualified entity; or has or may have unsupervised access to a child to whom the qualified entity provides child care; and

(2) seeks to be employed by or volunteer with a qualified entity; seeks to own or operate a qualified entity; or seeks to have or may have unsupervised access to a child to whom the qualified entity provides child care

There is no question that this definition will include the vast majority of persons who work with minors in a church. Note also that the law defines a provider as someone who "has or may have unsupervised access to a child to whom the qualified entity provides child care." This definition is so broad that it undoubtedly includes a much longer list of individuals, including custodians and spouses or friends of child care workers. Indeed, it is so broad that it could be interpreted to include any person who enters church property or attends any church activity. Clearly, this was not the intention of Congress, and it will be up to the courts to clarify the meaning of the term provider.

The Act makes it clear that the states specify which types of child care positions require criminal history checks. As noted above the Act contains a very broad definition of a child care "provider," but the committee report explaining the Act emphasizes that

[not] all occupations and volunteer positions within that broad definition merit the time and expense of criminal history records checks. There are other means available to protect children from abuse, including the checking of prior employment history and character references and proper training and supervision of employees and volunteers. The committee expects that the states, in deciding which types or categories of positions require criminal history background checks, will consider the degree to

which a particular position or child care activity offers opportunities to those who would abuse children. The committee expects that the states will find, for example, that positions involving long-term or ongoing contact with children in one-on-one situations merit criminal history record checks and that positions that involve infrequent direct contact or contact only in group settings do not merit such checks. The bill as amended leaves that decision to the respective states.

This language is critical, for it can be interpreted as establishing two levels of scrutiny in screening youth workers:

level 1—criminal records check

This level is required of those child care workers (providers) designated by state law. The committee report suggests that this level of screening be performed for "positions involving long-term or ongoing contact with children in one-on-one situations."

level 2—other screening methods

This level, according to the committee report, includes one or more of the following kinds of activities:

- check prior employment history

- check references

- training

- supervision

The committee report suggests that this level of screening be performed for "positions that involve infrequent direct contact or contact only in group settings."

procedure for checking criminal records

The Act establishes minimum requirements for state procedures for background checks. It clarifies that:

- Such checks must be based on fingerprints.

- A qualified entity may not request a background check of a provider unless the provider first provides a set of fingerprints and completes and signs a statement that (1) contains the name, address, and date of birth of the provider; (2) represents that the provider has not been convicted of a crime or, if the provider has been convicted of a crime, contains a description of the crime and the particulars of the conviction; (3) notifies the provider that the qualified entity may request a background check; (4) notifies the provider of the provider's "due process" rights (described below); and (5) notifies the provider that prior to the completion of the background check the qualified entity may choose to deny the provider unsupervised access to a child to whom the qualified entity provides child care.

• Providers must be informed by qualified entities that they have the right: (1) to obtain a copy of any background check report; and (2) to challenge the accuracy and completeness of any information contained in any such report and obtain a prompt determination as to the validity of such challenge before a final determination is made by the state agency regarding the provider's suitability for working with children.

• The designated state agency, upon receipt of a background check report lacking final disposition data (that is, no indication of how a criminal charge was resolved) shall conduct research in whatever state and local recordkeeping systems are available in order to obtain complete data.

• The designated state agency shall make a determination whether the provider has been convicted of a crime that bears upon his or her fitness to have responsibility for the safety and well-being of children and shall convey that determination to the qualified entity.

• The actual criminal record on a provider will not be conveyed to the qualified entity, but only an indication from the designated state agency whether the individual has been convicted of or is under pending indictment for a crime that bears upon his or her fitness to have responsibility for the safety and well-being of children.

Volunteers for Children Act (1998)

The National Child Protection Act had two flaws that prevented it from accomplishing its noble objective. First, it required states to enact implementing legislation giving nonprofit youth-serving organizations access to FBI criminal records checks. Second, it did not require the states to enact such legislation. Unfortunately, only a few states did so. As a result, churches and other youth-serving organizations (Red Cross, Boy/Girl Scouts, Boys/Girls Clubs, Big Brothers/Sisters, Little League, Salvation Army, etc.) were unable to obtain FBI criminal records checks. They were left with the options of (1) doing no criminal records checks, (2) doing criminal records checks using county courthouse records, or, in some states (3) doing criminal records checks using state criminal records.

The benefits of doing a national criminal records check were unavailable. This is the reason that the Volunteers for Children Act was enacted—to enable youth-serving organizations in all states to conduct FBI criminal records checks.

The Volunteers for Children Act remedied the flaws in the National Child Protection Act by amending it to read:

In the absence of state [implementing legislation] a qualified entity [designated by the state] may contact an authorized agency of the state to request nationwide criminal fingerprint background checks.

DID YOU KNOW?

A 1997 General Accounting Office (GAO) report concluded that "national fingerprint-based background checks may be the only effective way to readily identify the potentially worst abusers of children, that is the pedophiles who change their names and move from state to state to continue their sexually perverse patterns of behavior."

In summary, the Volunteers for Children Act allows churches to obtain FBI criminal records checks if they meet the definition of a "qualified entity" under state law. However, churches may not contact the FBI directly to obtain criminal records checks. They must proceed through a designated state agency (usually the state police).

The Volunteers for Children Act did not help significantly because it did not address three key limitations on the use of national criminal records checks by churches: (1) checks are available only through a designated state agency; (2) high cost; and (3) lengthy response times. Clearly, there was a need for additional legislation in order for the National Child Protection Act to fulfill its lofty objectives.

The National Child Protection Improvement Act was introduced in the United States Senate in 2001. It would have allowed churches and other youth-serving charities to conduct FBI criminal records searches directly, without going through a state agency. In addition, the legislation mandated that such checks be at no cost (for volunteer workers), and that a records search be conducted within 15 days. This legislation only attracted minimal support, and died in committee.

How to Interpret Criminal Records

Churches that conduct criminal records checks often are at a loss to know how to interpret the results they receive. To illustrate, assume that a church conducts a criminal records check on John, who has applied to work as a volunteer in the church's youth program. Assume that the check results in one or more of the following records:

- a conviction for child molestation that occurred 20 years ago

- an arrest and prosecution for child molestation, with probation

- an arrest and prosecution for child molestation, with no conviction

- an arrest for child molestation, with a plea bargain (John pled guilty to disorderly conduct)

- a conviction for driving while intoxicated

- a conviction for burglary

- a conviction for armed robbery

- a conviction for assault and battery

- a conviction for embezzlement

How should the church respond? Which, if any, of these results would disqualify John from working in the church's youth program? This is a very difficult question. Consider some options:

(1) At a minimum, church leaders should contact the prosecutor's office or the police and ask about the case. Mention that you are considering using the individual in a position in the church that will involve contact with minors. Often, a representative of the prosecutor's office, or a detective or other investigating officer, will respond to inquiries from the church concerning the facts of the case. Such input will be very significant in evaluating an applicant's suitability for working with minors. Remember, there are many reasons why a person may not be convicted of the crime of child abuse or molestation. Often, prosecuting attorneys are consumed with "major" crimes, and do not have the resources to devote to every case of child abuse. In other words, you cannot assume that a person who is charged but not convicted of child abuse poses no risk to your church. Further investigation is imperative in such cases.

(2) Find out if the person is on parole. If so, speak with the person's parole officer. In some cases, persons are released from prison prior to the end of their sentence and placed on parole for a period of time. In order to qualify for parole, a felon ordinarily must agree to a number of conditions. In cases involving sexual offenses with minors, these conditions may include prohibitions on working in any capacity with minors, attending church, or coming within a specified distance from minors.

(3) Most states have enacted laws requiring criminal records checks on any applicant for employment in a public school or state-licensed preschool. State law generally specifies the crimes that disqualify a person from working in these facilities. Some churches use these same lists to determine which crimes will disqualify a person from working with children. These lists generally include more than sexually motivated crimes. For example, many crimes involving assaults or personal injury often are included. Many crimes are not automatic disqualifiers, because they do not necessarily suggest a risk of child abuse or molestation. These often include property offenses.

(4) The federal Volunteers for Children Act (summarized earlier in this section) permits churches and other charities that are designated as "qualified entities" by state law to obtain FBI criminal records checks on persons who will be working with minors. Ten sets of fingerprints must be obtained for each applicant. These are delivered to the designated state agency, which will in turn send them to the FBI. Criminal records checks under the Volunteers for Children Act are not mandatory. Rather, they simply offer another option to screen youth workers.

One of the best features of the Volunteers for Children Act is that it relieves churches and other charities of the need to evaluate inconclusive criminal records. The designated state agency reviews the results of the FBI check, and then informs the church or charity whether or not to use the applicant. If an applicant was charged with child molestation but not convicted, or pled guilty to a lesser offense, it is the state's responsibility to determine whether or not the individual should be used. The state does not disclose to the church or charity the nature of the criminal background. Rather, it simply informs the church or charity whether or not it should use the applicant in question. It remains to be seen how many churches will obtain FBI criminal records checks. Obviously, many churches will not want to obtain ten sets of fingerprints on every applicant or worker. However, FBI checks should be viewed as an option that can be used, at a minimum, when an applicant's criminal record is inconclusive.

(5) In some states it is unlawful for employers to make employment decisions about employees or applicants for employment on the basis of "expunged" or "sealed" criminal records.

(6) In some states it is unlawful for employers to make employment decisions about employees or applicants for employment on the basis of arrests.

What the Courts Have Said about Criminal Records Checks

No court, in any reported decision, has found a church liable on the basis of negligent selection for the molestation of a child on the ground that the church failed to conduct a criminal records check on the molester before using him to work with children.

A few courts have ruled that a church was not liable on the basis of negligent selection for the molestation of a child by a volunteer worker on the ground that the church conducted a criminal records check on the offender before allowing him to work with children. To illustrate, a Georgia court concluded that a private school was not responsible for the alleged sexual molestation of a 13-year-old girl by a male staff member, because it conducted a criminal records check prior to hiring the staff member that revealed no criminal history.[104]

In addition, a Texas court ruled that a church had a "self-imposed duty" to conduct criminal records checks on youth workers, because of a policy the church had

---

[104] Doe v. Village of St. Joseph, Inc., 415 S.E.2d 56 (Ga. App. 1992).

adopted years before. Because the church violated its own policy in selecting a youth worker without performing a criminal records check, it violated this self-imposed duty. However, the court concluded that the church was not legally responsible for the worker's acts of child molestation because even if the church had conducted a criminal records check it would not have discovered any information suggesting that the worker posed a threat to children.[105]

Criminal records checks tend to prove that a church was not negligent in selecting a youth worker. However, churches should not assume that such checks are the only method of screening to be employed. Application and reference checks (especially from other organizations in which an applicant has worked with minors) are essential.

Set forth below are summaries of several court decisions addressing criminal records checks by non-religious organizations. These cases reflect three principles. First, the few courts that have addressed the issue have concluded that employers generally do not have a duty to conduct criminal records checks. Second, a duty to conduct criminal records checks may arise when an employer knows of a person's propensity to engage in conduct that may injure others. Third, criminal records checks that reveal a criminal record cannot be used as proof of negligent hiring if the previous crimes do not suggest that a person is a risk of the specific kind of harm that he later causes.

Case Studies

• *A Georgia court ruled that a church and denominational agency were not responsible on the basis of negligent hiring for an associate pastor's sexual relationship with a female member of his congregation. The court acknowledged that "a jury may find that employers who fill positions in more sensitive businesses without performing an affirmative background or criminal search on job applicants failed to exercise ordinary care in hiring suitable employees." But, it concluded that even if the local church and regional church had performed a background check which included interviews of the pastor's former employers, "the evidence does not show [that his] background information would have placed [the local church or regional church] on notice that it was reasonably foreseeable from his tendencies or propensities that he could cause the type of harm . . . which arose from his alleged betrayal of his counseling relationship . . . ."[106]*

• *In holding that an employer was not liable for an employee's assault, a New York court concluded: "An employer is under no duty to inquire as to whether an employee has been convicted of crimes in the past. Liability will attach on such a claim only when the employer knew or should have known of the employee's violent propensities. Here, there is no evidence that the employer knew of its employee's violent propensities, nor is there any indication that anything transpired that would have alerted it to the possibility that an assault would take place."[107]*

[105] Frith v. Fairview Baptist Church, 2002 WL 1565664 (Tex. App.-Dallas 2002).

[106] Poole v. North Georgia Conference, 615 S.E.2d 604 (Ga. App. 2005).

[107] Yeboah v. Snapple, Inc., 729 N.Y.S.2d 32 (Sup. Ct. 2001).

• A New York court refused to find a school liable on the basis of negligent hiring for the molestation of a minor by a volunteer art teacher. In rejecting the victim's claim that the school failed to conduct an adequate criminal records check at the time it started using the volunteer teacher, the court observed, "Whether or not the school could have been more thorough in checking the teacher's background, his actions do not support a claim of negligent hiring because a routine background check would not have revealed his propensity to molest minors. Plaintiff points to nothing which would have been revealed by checking his criminal history. Having interviewed the teacher and having obtained a reference the school had no duty to investigate further, in the absence of facts which would lead a reasonably prudent person to suspect the prospective volunteer of dangerous propensities."[108]

• A New York court concluded that "the fact that the employee may have used drugs in the past is irrelevant to any propensity to commit an act of sexual aggression. Similarly, the fact that he was HIV positive and a homosexual in no way equates with propensity to commit a sexual assault. That the employee may have made inappropriate expenditures or hired ex-convicts to perform community service at the shelter similarly cannot be equated with a claim that the church negligently supervised or retained him with respect to an alleged sexual assault."[109]

• An Ohio court ruled that an employer cannot be liable on the basis of negligent hiring for an employee's sexual harassment of another employee on the ground that it failed to conduct a criminal records check at the time of hire. The court concluded, "The victim implies that the employer was negligent in its hiring of the offender because it failed to investigate his criminal background, which she alleges would have revealed a prior conviction for assault. However, the evidence presented demonstrated that the offender denied that he had any felony convictions in his job application and he denied that he had been convicted of any offense other than a minor traffic violation in his application for a fidelity bond. The employer was under no duty to conduct a criminal background check.[110]

• An Ohio court refused to find a charity liable on the basis of negligent selection for the sexual molestation of a minor by an instructor. In rejecting the victim's claim that the charity should have conducted a criminal records check, the court observed, "A claim of negligent hiring exists if a plaintiff establishes, at a minimum, that the employer knew or should have known of the employee's criminal propensity. The victim has failed to cite authority to support his proposition of law that the charity had a duty to institute a prehiring investigation of the instructor's criminal background. The victim also has not presented evidence demonstrating that, even if a prehiring investigation was completed, the charity would have known of the instructor's propensity. Here, the instructor did not have a criminal background regarding this type of act or any other illegal activity."[111]

• A bakery employee was attacked and severely injured by a temporary worker who had been supplied by an employment agency to perform unskilled manual labor. The victim sued the employment agency, claiming that it was liable for the assailant's behavior on the basis of negligent hiring because it conducted a criminal records check on the assailant

---

[108] Koran I v. New York City Board of Education, 683 N.Y.S.2d 228 (Sup. Ct. 1998).

[109] Osvaldo D. v. Rector Church Wardens and Vestrymen of the Parish of Trinity Church of New York, 834 N.Y.S.2d 94 (N.Y.A.D. 2007).

[110] Steppe v. Kmart Stores, 737 N.E.2d 58 (Ohio App. 1999).

[111] Kuhn v. Youlten, 692 N.E.2d 226 (Ohio App. 1997).

only in one county (where he had lived for the previous four years) and failed to discover criminal convictions in a neighboring county in the same area. A Texas court dismissed the case, but a state appeals court reversed this decision and ordered the case to proceed to trial. It concluded that the victim should be allowed to prove that the employment agency was negligent in conducting a criminal records check in only one county.[112]

• *While driving a delivery truck, a driver stopped to "stretch his legs," wandered to an apartment complex, and sexually assaulted a woman. The victim sued the trucking company for the negligent hiring of the driver. She argued that the company had a duty to check the driver's criminal background and that such an investigation would have revealed a history of sexually predatory behavior, thereby making his assault foreseeable. A Texas court ruled that the trucking company had no such duty. It held that while the company had a duty to the driving public to employ competent drivers, the duty did not require the company to conduct independent investigations into its employees' nonvehicular criminal backgrounds.[113]*

• *A Texas court rejected the argument that an employer was liable on the basis of negligent hiring for a sexual assault on a customer by one of its employees because it failed to conduct a criminal records check. The court observed, "In the present case, the victim claims the employer had a duty to investigate its employee's criminal background. Such an investigation would have revealed that the employee had three forgery convictions. Whether the employer would have fired the employee had he discovered the forgery convictions is irrelevant. The question is whether the employee's criminal conduct and the type of harm that befell the victim were foreseeable and presented a risk that the employer was required to guard against by investigating the employee's criminal background. Under these facts, we hold the conduct and harm were not foreseeable and therefore the employer did not owe the victim a legal duty. . . . Nor does this case impose on the employer a duty to diligently investigate the employee's background because of potential contact with particularly vulnerable individuals." However, the court suggested that an employer has a higher duty of care in selecting persons who will have access to minors, although it did not specify whether or not this would require a criminal records check (and if so, what kind). The court noted that requiring small employers to check "criminal and military records and other sources of such data on all current and prospective employees, would impose a great administrative burden and cost on a small business."[114]*

• *The Supreme Court of Virginia ruled that an apartment building owner was not responsible on the basis of negligent hiring for the sexual assault of a female tenant by a male maintenance supervisor. In rejecting the victim's claim that the building owner's failure to conduct a criminal records check when it hired the assailant was proof of negligent hiring, the court observed, "The owner did not investigate the assailant's prior criminal record, if any; under these facts, he was not obligated to do so in the exercise of reasonable care. In the employment application, the assailant represented that he had 'absolutely never engaged' in 34 types of criminal behavior, except traffic violations. Additionally, in the application he also denied conviction 'in the past seven years' of 28 listed felonies. The victim dwells on a part of the opening statement of the owner's attorney. He said that a criminal records check would have disclosed that he wrote a bad*

---

[112] Wise v. Complete Staffing Services, 56 S.W.2d 900 (Tex. App. 2001).

[113] Guidry v. National Freight, Inc., 944 S.W.2d 807 (Tex. App. 1997).

[114] Houser v. Smith, 968 S.W.2d 542 (Tex. App. 1998).

check for $1.29 and another for $9 when he was 20 years of age. Even if this can be considered part of the evidence in the case, it is the only indication in the entire record that the assailant had been convicted of non-traffic offenses. Even if the owner had learned of these petty offenses, it would not have been alerted to the fact that he would engage in criminal sexual activity."[115]

Should Your Church Conduct Criminal Records Checks?

There are several factors for church leaders to consider in deciding whether or not to conduct criminal records checks on persons who potentially could have unsupervised access to minors on church property, in church vehicles, or in the course of church activities. These factors include the following:

(1) No court has found a church liable for a youth worker's sexual misconduct on the ground that it failed to conduct a criminal records check.

(2) Churches are not legally required to conduct criminal records checks unless specifically required by law. To illustrate, in many states church-operated schools and preschools must conduct criminal records checks on employees.

(3) Criminal records checks will reduce a church's risk of being found liable for the negligent selection of youth workers.

(4) The minimum acceptable standard of care in the selection of youth workers appears to be changing. It is possible, if not likely, that the courts someday will find churches liable on the basis of negligent selection for the sexual misconduct of a volunteer or employee having unsupervised access to minors if no criminal records check was performed before the individual was hired. This conclusion is based on several considerations, including the following:

• Over the past few years many national youth-serving charities have begun mandating criminal records checks for volunteers who work with minors. This list includes the Boy Scouts, Little League, and Youth Soccer. As more and more youth-serving charities conduct criminal records checks on volunteers, it is only a matter of time before a court concludes that such checks are a necessary component of "reasonable care" in the selection of youth workers. Such a finding would make it negligent for a church not to conduct such checks.

• The 106th Congress, 2nd session, stated during discussions of the Volunteer Organization Safety Act of 2000 (HR 4424) that: "It is the sense of Congress that to be effective, a background check must be fast, accurate, cost-effective and performed on everyone having regular contact with young people in a youth service organization."

---

[115] Southeast Apartments Management, Inc. v. Jackman, 513 S.E.2d 395 (Va. 1999).

Should Your Church Conduct Criminal Records Checks?

- The federal General Accounting Office noted in a recent study that "national fingerprint-based background checks may be the only effective way to readily identify the potentially worst abusers of children, that is the pedophiles who change their names and move from state to state to continue their sexually perverse patterns of behavior." equired by state law), and return it to the appropriate government office.

- A number of courts have suggested that a charity's duty of care in selecting workers is higher when those workers will be working with children. Some of these cases are summarized earlier in this section. While the courts have clearly defined what this "higher" duty of care means in practical terms, it is certainly predictable that one day it will mean the use of criminal records checks in selecting such workers.

- Criminal records checks are relatively inexpensive, and fast.

(5) There is little justification for a church not conducting a sex offender registry search at a minimum, especially in states where these checks are available online, and for free. However, as noted in the table accompanying this section, such checks have serious limitations and should never be regarded as the only screening procedure.

(6) There are different kinds of criminal records checks available. See the table accompanying this section for a summary of the options and the advantages and disadvantages of each option. The best options are an FBI fingerprint check (obtained through your designated state agency which often will be the state police), or a search of multiple state databases using a reputable private company. There are hundreds if not thousands of private companies that will perform criminal records checks for a fee. But, be careful when selecting one. Remember, private companies cannot access the FBI database, and so be wary of companies that offer "national" checks. Ask what they mean by "national." In particular, what criminal records are searched, and in which states. If in doubt, go with a private company that has been selected by national youth-serving charities to conduct their criminal records checks on volunteers. Companies such as Safe Hiring Solutions and Choicepoint have been selected by a number of national and local charities on the basis of their review of the many options. You can find more information on selecting a background check provider at www.ScreenChurchStaff.com.

Remember, not only is it common for sex offenders to engage in repeat offenses, but such offenses often are committed in different states. In a 2003 case upholding the constitutionality of state "Megan's Laws," the United States Supreme Court referred to one study that found that 38% of all repeat sex offenses "took place in jurisdictions other than where the previous offense was committed." This is an important observation, for two reasons. First, it shows that county or even state criminal records checks may not detect a criminal past; and second, it suggests that churches should consider performing multi-state or national criminal records checks.

Should Your Church Conduct Criminal Records Checks?

(7) While it is certainly desirable for churches to adopt policies on certain matters, any deviation from such policies can result in automatic liability. It is common for churches to adopt policies at the urging of an "advocate" within the congregation. But, if the advocate leaves the church, there may be no one with the same commitment to ensuring that the policies are followed. This is especially true of policies relating to the screening and supervision of youth workers. The lesson is clear. If your church has implemented policies for the screening of youth workers, it is imperative that those policies be followed. Any deviation may result in liability based on a breach of your self-imposed duty. It is a good practice for church leaders to periodically review church policies. Are they being enforced? Do we need them? Are changes needed? Should we abandon some policies? If screening policies are not being consistently followed, then steps should be taken immediately to insure that they are consistently followed, or, appropriate modifications must be made.

(8) If your church decides to conduct criminal records checks, be sure that you conduct checks on any person who may have unsupervised access to children. This will include persons who work with minors of any age, but it also will include persons who sometimes are overlooked such as custodians and any church employee.

(9) This section has addressed criminal records checks in the context of the protection of minors. There are other reasons why a church might want to conduct criminal records checks, including for persons who will drive vehicles for the church or who will handle money. Many churches also conduct background checks on the credit history of some job applicants, or confirm their educational background and professional certifications.

(10) Church leaders sometimes are unsure how to interpret a criminal record. For example, does a prior conviction for theft disqualify someone from working with minors? Be sure you review the section in this section entitled "How to Interpret Criminal Records" for helpful information in this regard.

(11) Criminal records checks are not the only step a church should take in screening workers. They are one link in a chain. Keep in mind that most child molesters have no criminal record. Effective protection comes with a multi-faceted approach that includes a suitable application form, reference checks, an interview, criminal records checks, and a six-month rule (volunteers are not allowed to work with children until they have been members of the church for at least six months).

DID YOU KNOW?

Census Bureau statistics released in 2003 show that (1) 120 million (46 percent) of the nation's population in 2000 lived in a different home than they did in 1995; (2) 25 percent moved within the same county, 10 percent between counties in the same state and 8 percent between states (3 percent moved from abroad); (3) Nevada led all states in the mobility of its population, followed by Colorado, Arizona, and California; (4) in 2000, about 60 percent of the U.S. population lived in the state where they were born (Louisiana, Pennsylvania and Michigan had the highest proportion of residents who lived in the state where they were born).

Key point. *If you conduct a criminal records check on an applicant, and discover a previous crime, be sure that the crime is listed on the person's application form (assuming that you ask for a description of all prior criminal convictions). If it is not mentioned, then this may indicate fraud. Such a person is an even greater risk than if the crime were disclosed.*

Executive Summary: Criminal Records Checks

No court has found a church liable for a youth worker's sexual misconduct on the ground that it failed to conduct a criminal records check.

Criminal records checks will reduce a church's risk of being found liable for the negligent selection of youth workers.

It is possible, if not likely, that the courts one day will find churches liable on the basis of negligent selection for the sexual misconduct of a volunteer or employee having unsupervised access to minors if no criminal records check was performed before the individual was hired. This conclusion is based on several considerations, including the fact that a growing number of youth-serving charities have begun requiring criminal records checks for volunteers who work with minors.

There are several different kinds of criminal records checks. A table in this section summarizes the main options.

Churches that decide to conduct criminal records checks often don't know how to begin. A good approach is to follow the practice of other youth-serving charities. Contact the local school district, Boy/Girl Scouts, Big Brothers/Sisters and see what kinds of checks they are performing. Tying your church's policy to the practices of other reputable charities helps to reduce your risk of negligent selection.

Executive Summary: Criminal Records Checks

Not only is it common for sex offenders to engage in repeat offenses, but such offenses often are committed in different states. Local criminal records checks may not detect a criminal past.

If your church decides to conduct criminal records checks, be sure that you conduct checks on any person who may have unsupervised access to children. This will include persons who work with minors of any age, but it also will include persons who sometimes are overlooked such as custodians and any church employee.

Criminal records checks are not the only step a church should take in screening workers. They are one link in a chain. Keep in mind that most child molesters have no criminal record. Effective protection comes with a multi-faceted approach that includes a suitable application form, reference checks, an interview, criminal records checks, and a 6-month rule (volunteers are not allowed to work with children until they have been members of the church for at least 6 months).

6. Other Background Checks

There are other aspects of an applicant's background that can be checked. These include:

- educational background (one of the most common misrepresentations that is made on employment application forms);

- employment (confirming that the applicant worked for prior employers listed on the application form);

- motor vehicle records;

- social security number check (confirms identity and residential history);

- credit history; and

- professional licenses and certifications.

The types of searches selected for any particular applicant will vary depending upon the risks and responsibilities associated with the position.

7. Limit "Second Chances"

Church leaders often "err on the side of mercy" when making employment decisions. This attitude can contribute to a negligent selection claim—if a church gives an applicant a "second chance" despite knowledge of prior sexual misconduct, and the conduct is repeated. What the church views as mercy may be viewed as negligence by a jury.

Should a church hire an applicant for youth work who has been guilty of child molestation in the past? Occasionally, such persons freely admit to a prior incident, but insist that they no longer are a threat because of the passage of time or a conversion experience. There are two options:

• The church could refuse to use the person in any compensated or volunteer position in the church (including, but not limited to, working with minors). This approach eliminates the risk of negligent selection, and it would be appropriate in the case of a pedophile. Pedophiles are persons who are sexually attracted to pre-adolescent children. The FBI "profile" on pedophiles indicates that such persons are "incurable" and predatory. They are always seeking new victims. Obviously, such persons create a significant risk to children and churches.

• The church could encourage such an individual to work in the church, but in a position not involving access to children. This is a reasonable accommodation of the individual's desire to serve the church. A church that permits such an individual to work with children will have a virtually indefensible position should another incident of molestation occur. Some churches have given convicted child molesters a "second chance" by allowing them to work with children—often on the basis that the person has had a religious conversion and no longer is a threat to children. The courts have not been sympathetic to such a defense. To illustrate, one court cited with approval the following testimony of a psychiatrist:

In the years that I have been doing this work, I probably have treated people from every religious denomination. We have seen priests, ministers, rabbis who have engaged in pedophilic [i.e., child molestation] behavior, so attendance at a church or being high up in a religious hierarchy doesn't contraindicate that a person is a [pedophile]. . . . They tell us that they have repented, that they have found the Lord and no longer have the problem they were accused of having. So we don't see religiosity as solving the problem."[116]

Churches that place a known child molester in a position involving access to children are taking an enormous risk.

8. Arbitration Policy

Consider the adoption of a church "arbitration policy." Such a policy, if adopted by the church membership at a congregational meeting as an amendment to the church's bylaws, may force church members to resolve their disputes (with the church, pastor, board, or other members)

> "Churches that place a known child molester in a position involving access to children are taking an enormous risk."

within the church consistently with the pattern suggested in 1 Corinthians 6:1-8. While a discussion of arbitration policies is beyond the scope of this section,

---

[116] Dutchess County Department of Social Services v. G., 534 N.Y.S.2d 64 (N.Y. 1988).

churches should recognize that arbitration is an increasingly popular means of resolving disputes in the secular world since it often avoids the excessive costs and delays associated with civil litigation and the uncertainty of jury verdicts. Of course, any arbitration policy should be reviewed by a church's liability insurer before being implemented. Such an approach, at a minimum, merits serious consideration by any church.

Using Homosexuals as Youth or Children's Workers § 10-04.4

Key point 10-04.4. *The courts have generally ruled, in recent years, that homosexuals are no more likely than heterosexuals to molest children. Churches may be liable for the sexual misconduct of any employee or volunteer, regardless of sexual orientation, on the basis of negligence in the selection, retention, or supervision of that person.*

Does the use of homosexual adults as volunteers in a church's youth or children's program expose the church to an increased risk of liability? A number of courts have ruled, in recent years, that homosexuality does not disqualify someone from working with minors. Consider the following illustrative cases:

(1) Doe v. British Universities N.A. Club, 788 F. Supp. 1286 (D. Conn. 1992)
    A federal district court in Connecticut rejected the argument that child molestation was a "foreseeable consequence of sexual orientation," noting that there was not "one scintilla of credible evidence to suggest that homosexuals pose a greater risk of committing sexual molestation, assault, or criminal conduct than heterosexuals" and that "to find otherwise would be to hold that homosexuals are predisposed towards molesting or sexually assaulting minor males simply by virtue of their sexual orientation. The court cannot and will not adopt such a position absent sufficient evidentiary support."

(2) Kendrick v. East Delavan Baptist Church, 886 F. Supp. 1465 (E.D. Wis. 1995)
    A church hired a full-time teacher at its private school. The teacher removed a young boy (the victim) from class and disciplined him on at least ten occasions. On four of these occasions, the teacher engaged in sexual contact with the victim. The victim never informed either his parents or any church or school officials about the teacher's behavior. Two months before the end of the teacher's tenure at the school, the school administrator received complaints from the parents of another boy regarding inappropriate behavior by the same teacher. The administrator immediately launched an investigation of these charges under the direction of the church board. He interviewed the teacher and the boy whose parents made the accusations, held a number of meetings with the parents and the church board, and ultimately concluded that the allegations involving the teacher could not be "proved or disproved."

The boy's parents were not satisfied with this result, and they continued to demand the teacher's removal. It was at this time that the administrator heard a rumor that the teacher had "had some problem with homosexuality" prior to his employment by the church. In response to this rumor, the administrator contacted the church-affiliated college the teacher had attended, and was informed that the teacher had been temporarily dismissed from the college for a brief period after confessing that he had engaged in homosexual activity on a weekend retreat. Another round of meetings occurred involving the teacher, the administrator, and the president of the college. The three agreed that, even though no wrongdoing by the teacher had been proven, the best way to resolve the controversy was for the teacher to resign. He immediately did so—both as a teacher and as a member of the church.

When the victim was twenty years old, he sued the church claiming that it was legally responsible for the teacher's misconduct. The victim claimed that the church was responsible for his injuries on the following grounds, including negligent selection. The victim insisted that the administrator's failure to more adequately screen the teacher prior to hiring him was the cause of his injuries since the administrator would not have hired the teacher had he more thoroughly checked his academic and work history and discovered that he had been temporarily suspended from college for "homosexual activity." The court disagreed:

> [T]here is a complete lack of evidence in the record regarding any
> connection between engaging in homosexual activity (whether or not one
> identifies himself as a homosexual) and pedophilic behavior. There is no
> evidence in the record to indicate that the incident at [college] involved
> children. Based on this, it seems clear that, had [the administrator] learned
> of this information prior to [the time he hired the teacher] he would not
> have breached a duty of care to protect students had he hired [the teacher].
> And if hiring [the teacher] under such circumstances would not have
> constituted a breach of duty, then hiring him without the benefit of such
> information cannot . . . be considered a cause in fact of the [victim's] harm.
> Even assuming, then, that a more thorough background check would
> have uncovered this information, a [jury] would have no logical basis
> for concluding that, based on issues relating to sexual orientation, [the
> administrator] would have found [the teacher] to be unfit to teach, or an
> increased risk to children.

(3) *Porter v. Harshfield, 948 S.W.2d 83 (Ark. 1997)*

The Arkansas Supreme Court ruled that homosexuality "in no way" indicates that a person is a higher risk of committing a sexual assault. While this case involved an employee of a medical clinic, the court's ruling is relevant to all employers including churches and other religious organizations. A radiologist hired a male medical technician to work in his clinic. The technician sexually assaulted a male patient while performing an ultrasound examination for possible gallbladder problems. The patient sued the doctor, claiming that he was responsible for the technician's actions on the basis of negligent hiring since he

(1) failed to contact the hospital where the technician previously had worked to find out why he left; and (2) was aware that the technician was a homosexual. The court repeatedly rejected the victim's assertion that homosexual orientation renders a person a higher risk of committing sexual assaults. It concluded that evidence of the technician's homosexuality was not enough to make the doctor guilty of negligent hiring. It noted that "we know of no" connection "between sexual orientation and a predisposition to commit sexual assault."

(4) Dale v. Boy Scouts of America, 734 A.2d 1196 (N.J. 1999)

The New Jersey Supreme Court ruled that the Boy Scouts of America violated a state public accommodations law by barring homosexuals from serving as scout leaders. This ruling was later reversed by the United States Supreme Court (see next case). However, the case is relevant because it represents a unanimous decision by a state supreme court that homosexuals pose no greater risk of molestation or harm to minors than heterosexuals. To illustrate, one of the court's justices, in a concurring opinion, observed:

> [A] lesbian or gay person, merely because he or she is a homosexual, is no more or less likely to be moral than a person who is a heterosexual. Accordingly . . . there is no reason to view a gay scoutmaster, solely because he is a homosexual, as lacking the strength of character necessary to properly care for and impart BSA humanitarian ideals to the young boys in his charge. . . . Another particularly pernicious stereotype about homosexuals is implicit in Boy Scouts' arguments: the sinister and unspoken fear that gay scout leaders will somehow cause physical or emotional injury to scouts. The myth that a homosexual male is more likely than a heterosexual male to molest children has been demolished.

The concurring justice cited the following articles in support of his conclusion:

- Carole Jenny et al., *Are Children at Risk for Sexual Abuse by Homosexuals?*, 94 PEDIATRICS 41 (1994) (concluding that most child abuse appears to be committed by situational child abusers who present themselves as heterosexuals)

- Nicholas Groth & H. Jean Birnbaum, *Adult Sexual Orientation and Attraction to Underage Persons,* 7 ARCHIVES SEXUAL BEHAV. 175 (1978) (concluding that "homosexuality and homosexual pedophilia are not synonymous [and] that the adult heterosexual male constitutes a greater sexual risk to underage children than does the adult homosexual male")

- Gregory M. Herek, *Myths About Sexual Orientation: A Lawyer's Guide to Social Science Research,* 1 L. & SEXUALITY 133 (1991) (citing studies and concluding that "it appears from these studies that gay men are no more likely than heterosexual men to molest children")

- David Newton, *Homosexual Behavior and Child Molestation: A Review of the Evidence*, 13 ADOLESCENCE 29 (1978) (surveying data concerning male homosexuality and child molestation and concluding that "there is no reason to believe that anything other than a random connection exists between homosexual behavior and child molestation").

The concurring justice concluded: "In light of this evidence, the belief that a gay scoutmaster poses a risk to young boys because of his sexual orientation is patently false, and cannot in any way bolster Boy Scouts' First Amendment defense. Accordingly, it must be rejected as an unfounded stereotype."

(5) *Boy Scouts of America v. Dale*, 530 U.S. 640 (2000)

The United States Supreme Court ruled, by a vote of 5-4, that a New Jersey civil rights law requiring the Boy Scouts to use a gay activist as a scout leader violated the Boy Scouts' First Amendment right of association. When scouting officials learned from a newspaper article that one of their scoutmasters was a homosexual activist, they terminated his services, explaining that the Boy Scouts "specifically forbid membership to homosexuals." The former scoutmaster sued the Boy Scouts claiming that it had violated a New Jersey "public accommodations" law by dismissing him. The New Jersey law prohibits, among other things, discrimination on the basis of sexual orientation in places of public accommodation.

The Supreme Court conceded that the public perception of homosexuality in this country has changed, and that homosexuality "has gained greater societal acceptance." However, "this is scarcely an argument for denying First Amendment protection to those who refuse to accept these views. The First Amendment protects expression, be it of the popular variety or not. . . . [T]he fact that an idea may be embraced and advocated by increasing numbers of people is all the more reason to protect the First Amendment rights of those who wish to voice a different view."

This case is significant because four of the Court's nine justices saw no reason why homosexual men should not be allowed to oversee adolescent males in scouting programs, and the other five justices did not specifically address the issue.

(6) *Doe v. Liberatore*, 478 F.Supp.2d 742 (M.D. Pa. 2007)

A federal court in Pennsylvania, in a case involving the molestation of an altar boy by a priest, stressed that "it does not follow that a homosexual is more likely than a heterosexual to prey on minors of the same sex. As such, standing alone [the priest's] homosexual behavior with adults would be irrelevant as to the issue of whether the church defendants had notice that he had a propensity to sexually abuse a minor male." While the court concluded that Allen's homosexuality did not make the church defendants liable on the basis of negligent selection, it did conclude that his "grooming" behavior with an adult homosexual was relevant in assessing the church defendants' response to similar behavior involving a minor, since such behavior (which included gifts, overnight trips, and spending the night at the church rectory) indicated the likelihood of sexual contact.

> If the church and its elders contradict the complaint and aver that their
> religious beliefs and doctrine are "homophobic," plaintiff will publicly
> denounce his former ecclesiastical employers as a bunch of ignorant bible-
> thumping knuckle-dragging pitch-fork toting rednecks, masquerading as
> a tolerant church. Or, if they take the bait and "admit" that their doctrine
> is not "homophobic," the plaintiff will be able to rake them over the
> scriptural coals by forcing them to distance themselves from various texts
> in Leviticus, or Romans or whatever, and force them to defend the merits
> of the fine nuances of their theology as he presses the point that, yes,
> they really are "homophobic." If the latter happens, further proceedings
> will turn this case into a theological circus that will make the Scopes Trial
> look like a boring treatise on insurance law. *[From a dissenting opinion
> in a case involving defamation and invasion of privacy claims brought
> against a church by a minister who was dismissed on account of his
> homosexuality. Gunn v. Mariners Church, Inc., 2005 WL 1253953 (Cal. App.
> 2005, unpublished).]*

Aver= to allege as a fact

Key point. *These cases do not suggest that churches are legally required to employ homosexuals as volunteer or compensated youth workers. Rather, they suggest that churches that choose to utilize homosexuals as children's and youth workers are not exposing minors or themselves to an elevated risk so long as they do a proper background check that discloses no information suggesting that the person poses a risk of harm to minors.*

In conclusion, few if any courts in recent years that have ruled concluded that homosexuality makes someone unfit to work with minors. The current state of the law seems to be that churches can treat homosexuals the same way they treat heterosexuals. That is, you can allow them to work with minors so long as you exercise reasonable care in selecting and supervising them, and respond promptly to any allegations or incidents of misconduct. Regardless of someone's sexual orientation, this means that a church should adopt the same precautions that are mentioned in this chapter.

Also, note that unpaid volunteers are not protected by any state or federal employment discrimination law. So, if a church decides that it simply does not want to allow homosexuals to work with minors, then it is free to do so. No court has ever found a church liable for doing so. Several states prohibit employers from discriminating against employees on the basis of sexual orientation, but so far each of these laws contains a broad exemption for religious organizations.[117]

---

[117] *See generally* § 8-21.2, *supra.*

Negligent Selection of Church Workers—Sexual Misconduct Cases Involving Adult Victims § 10-05

Key point 10-05. *A church may be liable on the basis of negligent selection for a worker's molestation of an adult if the church was negligent in the selection of the worker. Negligence means a failure to exercise reasonable care, and so negligent selection refers to a failure to exercise reasonable care in the selection of the worker. Liability based on negligent selection may be imposed upon a church for the acts of employees and volunteers.*

In recent years, several churches have been sued as a result of sexual contact by clergy with adults. Most of these cases have involved sexual contact with church employees or with counselees. Nearly all of the cases have involved sexual contact between male clergy and adult female employees or counselees. The personal liability of ministers for engaging in such acts is addressed in a previous chapter.[118] This section will address the question of whether the minister's employing church can be legally responsible for the minister's acts on the basis of its negligent selection of the minister.

As noted earlier in this chapter, the term *negligence* refers to conduct that creates an unreasonable risk of foreseeable harm to others. It connotes carelessness, heedlessness, inattention, or inadvertence. Negligent selection of a minister means that the church failed to act responsibly and with due care in the selection of a minister who later engages in some form of foreseeable misconduct. To illustrate, assume that a church hires a minister without any background check, and fails to discover that the minister had been dismissed by another church because of committing adultery with two women. A year later, it is discovered that the minister has engaged in adultery with a married woman in the course of marital counseling. The woman sues the church, claiming that the minister's conduct caused her emotional and psychological harm, and that her church is legally responsible for the minister's acts on the basis of negligent selection. She insists that had church leaders contacted the other church they would have discovered the minister's background and would not have hired him.

Church leaders can take relatively simple yet effective steps to significantly reduce the likelihood of such incidents occurring. This section will review some of the more significant reported court rulings, and then suggest a number of preventive measures that any church can implement in order to reduce the risk of such incidents.

▶ *No one understands or appreciates risk better than insurance companies. Risk evaluation is their business. As a result, it is very important to observe that a number of church insurance companies have reduced the insurance coverage they provide for sexual misconduct, and in some cases they have excluded it entirely. Some companies*

---

[118] *See* § 4-11, *supra.*

are suggesting that these incidents are excluded under the provision in most policies excluding damages based on intentional, criminal conduct (most acts of sexual molestation involve criminal activity). Church leaders should immediately review their church liability insurance policy to determine whether the church has any coverage for acts of sexual misconduct, and if so, whether such coverage has been limited in any way. If you fit within either category, the risk management recommendations in this chapter are of even greater relevance.

Key point. *Be sure to review Table 10-3 and Table 10-4.*

Court Decisions Recognizing Negligent Selection Claims § 10-05.1

Key point 10-05.1. *Some courts have found churches liable on the basis of negligent selection for the sexual misconduct of a church worker involving another adult if the church failed to exercise reasonable care in the selection of the worker.*

This section reviews court decisions in which a church or other religious organization was found liable on the basis of negligent selection for a minister's sexual contacts with an adult.

Case Studies

• *The Colorado Supreme Court ruled that a denominational agency was responsible, on the basis of negligent hiring and supervision, for a pastor's sexual misconduct. A local church board employed a new pastor, who later engaged in a sexual relationship with a woman in the course of marital counseling. At the time the new pastor was hired, the denominational agency failed to provide the church board with any of the information about the pastor contained in its personnel files. Included in the pastor's personnel file were reports of psychological examinations that were conducted as a result of his seeking ordination. These reports indicated that he had problems with depression, low self-esteem, and possessed a "sexual identification ambiguity." The woman claimed that the denominational agency's failure to disclose this information, and its consent to the employment of the pastor by the congregation, amounted to negligent hiring. The state supreme court agreed. It concluded, "[The pastor's] duties included counseling and close association with parishioners at the church. The diocese was in possession of a psychological report which concluded that [the assistant pastor] has a "sexual identification ambiguity." Another psychological report indicated that [the pastor] had a problem with depression and suffered from low self-esteem. An expert testified that a large number of clergy who have sexual relationships with their parishioners do so partially as a result of suffering from depression and low self-esteem. [The pastor's] struggle with his sexual identity and his problems with depression and low self-esteem put the diocese on notice to inquire further whether [the assistant pastor] was capable of counseling parishioners. These reports gave the diocese a reason to believe [the pastor] should not be put in a position to counsel vulnerable individuals and that he might be unable to handle the transference phenomenon. The failure to communicate this knowledge to the vestry and subsequent placement of [the pastor] in the role of counselor breached the diocese's duty of care to [the victim]."*[119]

• *A Colorado court ruled that a minister and a denominational agency could be sued by a woman with whom the minister had sexual contacts.*[120] *A woman (the victim) attended a church for a few years, and began to volunteer her services for a variety of activities including the remodeling of a classroom. She engaged in these volunteer services on the recommendation of a therapist who suggested that she work in a "safe environment" to overcome her fears of the workplace. The victim's volunteer work caused her to come in contact with her minister after normal working hours. On one occasion the minister approached her while she was remodeling a classroom, began caressing her back, and told her, "I love you Dianne, you mean so much to me." A few days later, the minister called the victim into his office where the two of them sat next to each other on a small couch. The minister again caressed her and expressed his love for her. Following a third incident, the victim informed two other women in the church about the minister's behavior, and one responded, "Oh my God, not you too." A few months later a denominational agency with which the church was affiliated held a meeting in response to a formal complaint it had received regarding the minister's conduct. Six women attended this meeting, and all described similar incidents of unwelcome verbal comments and physical contact involving the minister. As a result of this meeting, the minister was suspended. The victim later sued her church and a denominational agency on the basis of several theories of liability, including negligent hiring of the minister. She alleged that the agency had been made aware of at least one prior act of sexual misconduct involving the minister, and was aware that he had a problem with alcohol abuse. The court ruled that the agency could be liable on the basis of negligent hiring, despite the agency's argument that the ordination and discipline of ministers is an ecclesiastical matter involving theological concerns over which the civil courts cannot exercise jurisdiction. The court noted simply that neither the minister nor the agency claimed that the minister's "method of communicating with parishioners by touching, hugging, and expressing affection was based on any religious tenet or belief."*

Court Decisions Rejecting Negligent Selection Claims § 10-05.2

Key point 10-05.2. *Some courts have found churches not liable on the basis of negligent selection for the sexual misconduct of a minister or other church worker involving another adult since the church exercised reasonable care in the selection of the worker.*

This section reviews court decisions in which a church or other religious organization was found not liable on the basis of negligent selection for inappropriate sexual contact with an adult by a minister or other church worker. Note that

---

[119] Moses v. Diocese of Colorado, 863 P.2d 310 (Colo. 1993).

[120] Winkler v. Rocky Mouton Conference, 923 P.2d 152 (Colo. App. 1995).

several courts have concluded that the First Amendment's "nonestablishment of religion" and "free exercise of religion" clauses prevent the civil courts from resolving negligent selection claims involving clergy misconduct.

Case Studies

• *A Florida court ruled that it was barred by the First Amendment from resolving a woman's lawsuit claiming that she had been the victim of a priest's sexual misconduct.[121] A woman sought out a priest for marital counseling, and alleged that the priest engaged in sexual contacts with her. The woman sued her church and diocese, claiming that they were aware of prior incidents involving sexual misconduct during counseling by the same priest. Despite this knowledge, nothing was done to address the problem. The church and diocese asked the court to dismiss the lawsuit against them on the ground that a resolution of the woman's claims would result in an "excessive entanglement" of the court with religious beliefs in violation of the First Amendment. The court agreed. It began its opinion by noting that the First Amendment prohibits any governmental practice (including judicial resolution of internal church disputes) that would lead to an "excessive entanglement" between church and state. The court noted that excessive entanglement occurs "when the courts begin to review and interpret a church's constitution, laws, and regulations." The court concluded that the resolution of a negligent hiring, supervision, or retention claim against a church or diocese would amount to an excessive entanglement in violation of the First Amendment: "Our examination of case law presenting both sides of this question leads us to conclude the reasoning of those courts holding the First Amendment bars a claim for negligent hiring, retention, and supervision is the more compelling. In a church defendant's determination to hire or retain a minister, or in its capacity as supervisor of that minister, a church defendant's conduct is guided by religious doctrine and/or practice. Thus, a court's determination regarding whether the church defendant's conduct was 'reasonable' would necessarily entangle the court in issues of the church's religious law, practices, and policies. 'Hiring' in a traditional sense does not occur in some religions, where a person is ordained into a particular position in the church, and assigned to one parish or another. A court faced with the task of determining a claim of negligent hiring, retention, and supervision would measure the church defendants' conduct against that of a reasonable employer; a proscribed comparison."*

• *A Georgia court dismissed a lawsuit brought by a woman against her church and a denominational agency as a result of injuries she allegedly sustained during a sexual relationship with her pastor.[122] The woman had received counseling from the pastor on a number of occasions, despite the fact that the pastor had informed her that she should discontinue the counseling sessions with him and find another counselor because he was sexually attracted to her. Despite this request, the woman did not discontinue the counseling sessions, and the two began having "phone sex" conversations. The woman claimed that the pastor initiated the first such conversation but that at times she would call him. She insisted that while she led him to believe she was participating in the "phone sex," she was, in reality, only pretending. The woman alleged that toward the end of their counseling relationship the pastor called*

---

[121] Doe v. Evans, 718 So.2d 286 (Fla. App. 1998).

[122] Alpharetta First United Methodist Church v. Stewart, 473 S.E.2d 532 (Ga. App. 1996).

her at home and asked her to come to his office so they could have sex. She drove to his office and the two engaged in intercourse. The woman quit seeing the pastor when she learned that he was engaged to be married to another woman. The woman and her husband sued their church and a denominational agency on the basis of negligent hiring of the pastor. Specifically, they claimed that both the church and denominational agency failed to exercise reasonable care in the selection of the pastor. In rejecting this claim, the court observed, "An employer may not be held liable for negligent hiring or retention unless the [victim] shows the employer knew or should have known of the employee's violent and criminal propensities. Specifically, the [couple] must show that the church and the [denominational agency] knew or should have known of [the associate pastor's] propensity for sexual misconduct. . . . . There is nothing in the record before us to show the church or [denominational agency] should have been on notice prior to ordaining [the associate pastor] that he had a propensity for sexual misconduct." As proof that the church and denominational agency had been negligent in ordaining or hiring the associate pastor, the couple noted that he had been suspended for a year while in seminary for cheating on a Hebrew examination, and that his psychological evaluation indicated certain problems, such as difficulty controlling his impulses, a tendency to use poor judgment, a tendency to disregard the rights of others, and a likelihood to express aggression in a physical manner. The court disagreed that these facts proved that either the church or denominational agency was guilty of negligent selection: "These types of generalized findings, without more, are not sufficient to put the church and [denominational agency] on notice of a propensity for sexual misconduct." The court pointed out that the psychological evaluation (which consisted of the Minnesota Multiphasic Personality Inventory, the Interpersonal Behavior Survey, the Strong-Campbell Interest Inventory, and the Sentence Completion Test) also showed several positive characteristics such as, "He is very social and interested in leadership in service to other people. . . . He shows a pattern of interest moderately like those of successful ministers or social workers." The court also summarized the many precautions that were taken prior to the time the pastor was ordained, including a two-year internship, letters of recommendation, psychological testing, and extensive interviews by an ordination committee.

• *A Georgia court ruled that a church and denominational agency were not responsible on the basis of negligent hiring for damages caused by a pastor's sexual relationship with a female member of his congregation. The court observed:*

> *With regard to the claim of negligent hiring, evidence shows [that the defendant] was interviewed by the District Committee of Ordained Ministry and then by the Conference Board of Ordained Ministry, and [the plaintiff] does not show that during this process either body was informed of misconduct by the pastor during his previous employment. As a prospective minister [the defendant] was also required to undergo a psychological evaluation. A psychologist with [a University] School of Medicine evaluated the pastor. The doctor's report did not show that he was unfit to serve as a pastor and was generally positive. [The plaintiff] points to nothing in the record showing that during the hiring process either [the local church or regional church] became aware of anything in [the defendant's] background indicating he was unsuited for employment as a minister or which put them on notice that further investigation was warranted.*
> *[The plaintiff] contends that if church officials had interviewed some of [the defendant's] former employers they would have discovered information indicating that he was not adequately trained as a counselor and had misused his*

position to take advantage of parishioners and counseled persons. [The plaintiff] submitted affidavits from two . . . former employers. The affidavit of one pastor disclosed that, while employed as a youth and music minister, [the defendant] allegedly sexually assaulted a young man. The defendant, who was married at the time, also reportedly tried to date a "young lady at the church." The pastor of a second church where the defendant had been employed as the minister of music, stated that a young parishioner accused him of touching her on the breast. The pastor also claimed that after the personnel committee declined to increase the compensation of the church pianist, [the defendant] increased the pay of the church pianist out of his budget and in violation of church policy.

The court acknowledged that *"a jury may find that employers who fill positions in more sensitive businesses without performing an affirmative background or criminal search on job applicants failed to exercise ordinary care in hiring suitable employees."* But, it concluded that even if the local church and regional church had performed a background check which included interviews of the defendant's former employers, *"the evidence does not show this background information would have placed [the local church or regional church] on notice that it was reasonably foreseeable from [the defendant's] tendencies or propensities that he could cause the type of harm sustained by [the plaintiff], which arose from [the defendant's] alleged betrayal of his counseling relationship with him. Accordingly, we conclude that [the church defendants] have demonstrated that no genuine issue of fact remains as to the negligent hiring claim."*[123]

• *An Indiana court ruled that neither a church nor a denominational agency could be sued on the basis of negligent hiring for injuries suffered by a woman who was molested by her pastor when she was a minor.*[124] *The woman claimed that the pastor began molesting her when she was seven years old, and that the molestation continued until she was 20. The court concluded that neither the church nor the denominational agency could be liable on the basis of negligent selection of the pastor. The court observed that the pastor was hired by the church in 1954, and that there was no evidence whatsoever that the church or either denominational agency was aware of any misconduct on his part at that time.*

• *A Kentucky court ruled that a church could not be liable for a pastor's sexual misconduct since there was "no evidence in the record that [he] had any history of sexual misconduct involving parishioners, or that the church had any knowledge that [he] might engage in such misconduct."*[125]

• *A Louisiana court ruled that an Episcopal diocese was not legally responsible for the suicide of a woman allegedly caused by a sexual relationship with an Episcopal priest.*[126] *The husband of a woman who committed suicide sued a priest and diocese, claiming that his wife's suicide had been caused by the sexual misconduct of the priest. The lawsuit alleged that the priest was guilty of malpractice by taking advantage of an emotionally dependent woman and then abusing his position of trust to engage in sexual intercourse with her on numerous occasions. The husband claimed that*

---

[123] Poole v. North Georgia Conference, 615 S.E.2d 604 (Ga. App. 2005).

[124] Konkle v. Henson, 672 N.E.2d 450 (Ind. App. 1996).

[125] Payne v. Osborne, 1999 WL 354495 (Ky. App. 1999).

[126] Roppolo v. Moore, 644 So.2d 206 (La. App. 4 Cir. 1994).

the priest's behavior violated the teachings of the Episcopal Church as well as the ninth commandment ("thou shalt not covet they neighbor's wife") and the sixth commandment ("thou shalt not commit adultery"). The husband claimed that the diocese was responsible for his wife's suicide on the basis of several grounds, including a failure to adequately investigate the priest as to his emotional, psychological, and moral fitness to be a minister of the Episcopal Church. In dismissing the husband's allegation of "negligent selection" of the priest by the diocese, the court observed, "[A] ny inquiry into the policies and practices of [churches] in hiring or supervising their clergy raises . . . First Amendment problems of entanglement . . . which might involve the court in making sensitive judgments about the propriety of [churches'] supervision in light of their religious beliefs."

• A Maryland court ruled that a church and denominational agency were not liable on the basis of clergy malpractice for injuries sustained by a woman who was seduced by a pastor while working at a church camp. And, since the court refused to find the pastor legally responsible for the victim's injuries on the basis of malpractice, the church could not be liable on the basis of negligent hiring.[127]

• A Minnesota court ruled that a church and denominational agency could not be liable on the basis of negligent hiring for the sexual misconduct of a pastor. The court concluded that a resolution of the negligent hiring claim against the church defendants would "entangle" church and state in violation of the First Amendment's nonestablishment of religion clause. It observed: "The church defendants argue that [the plaintiff's] hiring-related claims implicate core, fundamental church doctrines governing identification of individuals called to the ministry. We agree. A determination of whether the statutorily required inquiries were made of a pastor-candidate's former employers does not involve church doctrine, but a determination of how that information should be used in a hiring decision would force the court into an examination of church doctrine governing who is qualified to be a pastor. When claims involve core questions of church discipline and internal governance, the Supreme Court has acknowledged that the inevitable danger of governmental entanglement precludes judicial review."[128]

• An Ohio court ruled that a church and denominational agency were not liable on the basis of negligent hiring for a pastor's sexual relationship with a female member of his congregation. The court noted that negligent hiring and retention requires (1) the existence of an employment relationship; (2) the employee's incompetence; (3) the employer's knowledge of such incompetence; (4) the employee's act or omission causing the plaintiff's injuries; and (5) the employer's negligence in hiring or retaining the employee as the proximate cause of plaintiff's injuries." The victim claimed that the church defendants had prior knowledge of the pastor's sexual proclivities. She testified in her deposition that the pastor told her that an associate pastor at the church had confronted him about a previous "sexual" and "inappropriate situation" with a woman, and so she and the pastor had to "be careful." The court rejected this evidence of proof that the church defendants had prior knowledge of the pastor's propensity to engage in sexual contact with church members, for two reasons. First, the associate pastor denied ever having had prior knowledge of improper sexual conduct

---

[127] Borchers v. Hrychuk, 727 A.2d 388 (Md. App. 1999).

[128] J.M.v. Minnesota District Council, 658 N.W.2d 589 (Minn. App. 2003).

on the part of the pastor. Second, even if the associate pastor had such knowledge, "it cannot be imputed to the church defendants because there is no evidence to suggest that [the associate pastor] acquired that knowledge while acting within the scope of his employment. An employee's knowledge is imputed to his employer only if the employee obtained the knowledge while acting within the scope of his employment."[129]

• The Nebraska Supreme Court ruled that a Catholic diocese could not be liable on the basis of negligent hiring for the sexual misconduct of a priest.[130] The priest had engaged in sexual contact with a woman during marital counseling. The woman sued the priest, claiming that he had been negligent and that his negligence contributed to the sexual relationship and her injuries. Specifically, she claimed that the priest was negligent (1) by failing to properly counsel her concerning her marital and family relationships when he knew or should have known she was having domestic difficulties; (2) by failing to remove himself as parish priest when he knew or should have known that a continuing relationship with her would cause her emotional harm; and (3) by violating his oath of celibacy. The court rejected this theory of liability, noting simply that "so far as we have been able to determine, no jurisdiction to date has recognized a claim for clergy malpractice." The woman also sued her diocese, claiming that it had been negligent in failing to properly investigate the priest's background by inquiring into his relations with other women while he was acting as a parish priest in other parishes when it knew, or should have known, that he had been actively involved in relationships with women in violation of his vows of celibacy on more than one occasion in the past. In rejecting each of these claims of liability against the diocese, the court observed simply that "if there is no tort liability to the [woman] against [the priest] individually, it follows that the diocese cannot be held liable for his conduct."

• A federal court in New York refused to find a church or denomination agency liable on the basis of "negligent placement, retention, or supervision" for a pastor's sexual contacts with a woman during marital counseling.[131] The court made the following statement in rejecting the woman's claim that the church and denomination had been guilty of negligence: "[A]ny inquiry into the policies and practices of the church defendants in hiring or supervising their clergy raises . . . First Amendment problems of entanglement . . . which might involve the court in making sensitive judgments about the propriety of the church defendants' supervision in light of their religious beliefs."

• The Ohio Supreme Court ruled that state and national denominational offices could not be sued on the basis of negligent hiring as a result of the sexual misconduct of clergy.[132] A woman who had engaged in a sexual relationship with her pastor in the course of marital counseling sued the denominational offices, claiming that they were responsible for her injuries on the basis of negligent hiring. The lawsuit alleged that the state and national denominational offices "knew, or should have known of the inclination of [the pastor] to commit such actions and were reckless or negligent in allowing said [pastor] to assume the position of pastor . . . ." The court acknowledged

---

[129] DePietro, 825 N.E.2d 630 (Ohio App. 2005).

[130] Schieffer v. Catholic Archdiocese, 508 N.W.2d 907 (Neb. 1993).

[131] Schmidt v. Bishop, 779 F. Supp. 321 (S.D.N.Y. 1991).

[132] Byrd v. Faber, 565 N.E.2d 584 (Ohio 1991). *Accord* Doe v. Turner, 1994 WL 369956 (Ohio App. 1994), Mirick v. McClellan, 1994 WL 156303 (Ohio App. 1994); Gebhart v. College of Mount St. Joseph, 665 N.E.2d 223 (Ohio App. 1995).

that "if a church hires an individual despite knowledge of prior improper behavior in his former church-related employment, the church may be liable in tort for negligent hiring." However, the court insisted that a lawsuit that merely alleges that a religious organization is guilty of "negligent hiring," but that recites no facts supporting such an allegation, must be dismissed. Since the woman's lawsuit contained no reference whatsoever to any facts to support a claim of negligent hiring, it had to be dismissed. The court observed, "We hold today that . . . greater specificity in pleading is required when a claim is brought against a religious institution for negligent hiring due to the myriad of First Amendment problems which accompany such a claim. In order to survive a . . . motion to dismiss, a plaintiff bringing a negligent hiring claim against a religious institution must plead facts with particularity. Specifically, the plaintiff must plead facts which indicate that the individual hired had a past history of criminal conduct, tortious, or otherwise dangerous conduct about which the religious institution knew or could have discovered through reasonable investigation. The mere incantation of the elements of a negligent hiring claim, i.e., the abstract statement that the religious institution knew or should have known about the employee's criminal or tortious propensities, without more, is not enough to enable a plaintiff to survive a motion to dismiss for failure to state a claim [upon which relief can be granted]. . . . While even the most liberal construction of the First Amendment will not protect a religious organization's decision to hire someone who it knows is likely to commit criminal or tortious acts, the mere incantation of an abstract legal standard should not subject a religious organization's employment policies to state scrutiny. Consequently, in order to survive a motion to dismiss, a plaintiff bringing a negligent hiring claim must allege some fact indicating that the religious institution knew or should have known of the employee's criminal or tortious propensities." The court ruled that the woman's lawsuit had to be dismissed, since it "alleged no fact indicating that [the pastor] had a past history of criminal or tortious conduct about which the [denominational offices] knew or should have known."

• The Oklahoma Supreme Court ruled that a married couple could not sue their church and former pastor for damages they allegedly incurred as a result of an adulterous affair between the former pastor and the wife.[133] The husband and wife sued the church and former pastor as a result of the pastor's conduct. The lawsuit alleged that the church was negligent in the selection of the pastor since it knew or should have known about the wife's affair and a previous affair in Texas. The church insisted that it did not know of the affair or of the alleged incident in Texas, and that it did not condone such behavior. The court concluded that the church was not responsible for injuries resulting from the minister's conduct. It observed that the First Amendment guaranty of religious freedom did not shield churches from liability for personal injuries arising "from acts unrelated to religious practices protected by the First Amendment." However, it insisted that all of the couple's claims against the church had to be dismissed. It observed, "Neither the claims by the husband nor the wife against the minister are cognizable in Oklahoma. . . . Because their claims against the minister also serve as the basis for the claims against the church for its negligent hiring and supervision of the minister, that claim is also not cognizable."

• A Texas court summarily dismissed a lawsuit alleging that a church was responsible on the basis of negligence for its pastor's sexual relationship with a counselee. The

---

[133] Bladen v. First Presbyterian Church, 857 P.2d 789 (Okla. 1993).

victim claimed that the church was negligent in hiring, training and supervising the pastor. The court observed: "As a general rule, courts will not attempt to right wrongs related to the hiring, firing, discipline, or administration of clergy. The training and supervision of clergy are part of the administration of clergy. To recover for negligent hiring, retention, or administration in a case such as this, a plaintiff must show that the church employed an incompetent servant and that the church knew, or by the exercise of reasonable care should have known, that the minister was incompetent or unfit. It must be shown that the church knew or should have known that the minister's conduct as a counselor presented an unreasonable risk of harm to others. In the present case, [the church] established as a matter of law that it exercised reasonable care and yet did not know of any incompetence or sexual misconduct by [the pastor] either before his hiring or during his employment, until the church was notified [of the affair with the woman]. When the church was notified, it terminated him as pastor the very next day. . . . [T]here was no evidence that [the church] should have known that [the pastor] was likely to engage in misconduct during counseling. In light of the uncontroverted evidence of [the church's] diligence and lack of notice, the trial court properly [dismissed the case]."[134]

Risk Management § 10-05.3

Key point 10-05.3. *Churches can reduce the risk of liability based on negligent supervision for sexual misconduct involving adult victims by adopting risk management policies and procedures.*

Resources. **Churches must exercise reasonable care in the selection of ministers, nonminister employees, and volunteers in order to avoid potential liability based on negligent selection. The publisher of this text has produced several resources to assist church leaders in satisfying the standard of reasonable care in the selection of workers. These resources are available on the publisher's website, www.churchlawtoday.com or by calling 1-800-222-1840.**

This section has addressed church liability on the basis of negligent selection for sexual misconduct by ministers and other church workers with adult victims. Churches can reduce the risk of liability based on negligent selection by adopting some or all of the strategies described in section 10-04.3.

Key point. *Many cases of sexual misconduct with adult victims arise out of a counseling relationship. There are a number of steps that churches can take to reduce the risk of such behavior occurring in the course of a counseling relationship, and many of these are addressed later in this chapter.[135]*

---

[134] Hodges v. Kleinwood Church of Christ, 2000 WL 994337 (Tex. App. 2000).

[135] *See* § 10-12, *infra.*

Negligent Selection of Church Workers—Other Cases

§ 10-06

Key point 10-06. *A church may be legally responsible on the basis of negligent selection for injuries resulting from the acts of a minister or other worker not involving sexual misconduct.*

Negligent selection claims are not limited to cases involving sexual misconduct. They can arise anytime that a church's failure to exercise reasonable care in the selection of an employee or volunteer leads to a foreseeable injury. Here are some examples:

- Using adolescents as attendants in the church nursery.

- Selecting adult workers without any training in CPR or other resuscitation techniques to accompany a youth group to any event involving swimming or boating.

- Selecting lay counselors with inadequate professional training.

- Selecting drivers for any church-sponsored activity without checking their driving record.

For example, if a church uses a driver with a suspended drivers license, or with a history of traffic offenses, then it may be responsible on the basis of negligent selection for injuries caused by the driver's negligence. To reduce the risk of liability in this context, churches should refrain from using any driver without taking the following steps:

(1) Have each prospective driver complete an application form that asks for the person's drivers license number, type of drivers license and expiration date, a description of any driving restrictions, and a history of traffic accidents and moving violations.

(2) Ask the church's liability insurance carrier to check on the individual's driving record. Often, insurance companies will perform this task if requested, at no charge. The insurance company should be requested to update its research on all drivers of church vehicles periodically, to screen out persons with a recent history of unsafe driving.

(3) Discontinue using any driver if reports are received that he or she is operating a church vehicle in a negligent manner. Fully investigate such reports, and do not use the individual again unless the investigation clearly demonstrates that the complaints were without merit.

(4) If the prospective driver is a new member, then ask for the names and addresses of other churches in which he or she has worked as a driver.

Contact those other churches and ask if they are aware of facts that would indicate that the individual should not be used as a driver. Make a written record of such contacts.

(5) Periodically invite a local law enforcement officer to speak to all drivers concerning safety issues.

(6) Require all drivers to immediately inform the church of any traffic convictions.

Key point. *The risk management strategies addressed in section 10-04.3 can be used to manage the risk of these other kinds of negligent selection.*

Case Study

• A Georgia court ruled that a member of an unincorporated church could sue his church for injuries he sustained while participating in a construction project, and that the church could be liable for the member's injuries on the basis of its negligent hiring of an incompetent construction foreman. The court noted that the church made no attempt to investigate the qualifications of the construction foreman. When he volunteered for the job, the church merely accepted his offer without further inquiry. And, although there was some evidence that he had some experience with residential construction, this did not necessarily make him qualified to serve as foreman of the church project. The court noted that he had testified that he had "no background, experience, education, or training in commercial construction." Further, a builder testified that "a contractor with limited residential experience is not necessarily competent to complete a commercial construction project such as a church addition." In addition, an engineer reviewed the structure of the platform designed by the foreman and concluded that it was "wholly insufficient for its intended purpose." This evidence persuaded the court that the victim could sue the church for negligent hiring.[136]

Negligent Retention of Church Workers—In General
§ 10-07

Key point 10-07. *A church may exercise reasonable care in selecting ministers or other church workers but still be responsible for their misconduct if it "retained" them after receiving information indicating that they posed a risk of harm to others.*

A church may use reasonable care in selecting ministers or other church workers but still be responsible for their misconduct if it "retained" them after receiving information indicating that they posed a risk of harm to others.

---

[136] Piney Grove Baptist Church v. Goss, 565 S.E.2d 569 (Ga. App. 2002).

> "An employer has a duty to refrain from retaining employees with known dangerous proclivities" and may be liable on the basis of negligent retention when "during the course of employment, it becomes aware or should have become aware of problems with an employee that indicated his unfitness, and fails to take further action such as investigating, discharge or reassignment." Olson v. First Church of Nazarene, 661 N.W.2d 254 (Minn. App. 2003).

Example. *A visitor attends a church service and recognizes the church's associate pastor as a convicted child molester. No one else in the church is aware of the associate pastor's background. The visitor discloses this fact in a letter to the senior pastor, who shares it with the church board. The board decides not to take any action. It bases its decision on the fact that the associate pastor is well-liked by the congregation, and that the incident of child molestation occurred ten years ago. Several months later, the board learns that the associate pastor molested a child on church premises. The victim and her family sue the church. They claim that the church is responsible for the victim's injuries on the basis of negligent retention. That is, the church retained the pastor after receiving information suggesting that he represented a risk to others.*

Court Decisions Recognizing Negligent Retention Claims § 10-07.1

Key point 10-07.1. *Some courts have found churches liable on the basis of negligent retention for the sexual misconduct of ministers and other church workers on the ground that the church was negligent in retaining the offender after receiving credible information indicating that he or she posed a risk of harm to others.*

Some courts have concluded that churches can be sued on the basis of negligent retention for the sexual misconduct of ministers and other church staff.

Case Studies

• *A federal appeals court concluded that two female church employees could sue the minister who had seduced them since he had "held himself out" as a qualified marital counselor.[137] However, the court dismissed all of the employees' claims against the*

---

[137] Sanders v. Casa View Baptist Church, 134 F.3d 331 (5th Cir. 1998).

church, including negligent retention. The court acknowledged that "an employer that negligently retains in his employ an individual who is incompetent or unfit for the job may be liable to a third party whose injury was proximately caused by the employer's negligence." However, to prove negligent retention, the two women had to show that the church "knew or should have known that [the former minister's] conduct as a supervisor or counselor presented an unreasonable risk of harm to others." The court concluded that there was no evidence that the church "know or should have known" that the former minister was engaging in marital counseling or that he was likely to engage in sexual misconduct or disclose confidences as a marriage counselor.

• An Indiana court ruled that the First Amendment does not prevent a woman from suing her church and a denominational agency on account of injuries she suffered as a result of being molested by her pastor when she was a minor.[138] The woman claimed that the pastor began molesting her when she was seven years old, and that the molestation continued until she was 20. The woman sued her church and the regional and national denominational agencies with which her church was affiliated. The court concluded that the national church was not liable on the basis of negligent retention for the actions of the pastor. It observed, "The [national church], which is only affiliated with the local church and [regional agency] through its constitution and judicial procedures, was not informed. The evidence . . . does not indicate that [the woman] invoked the judicial procedures, which is the only mechanism by which the [national church] could have taken action against [the pastor]. According to the judicial procedures, the [regional agency] forms a committee to investigate alleged misconduct upon the submission of a complaint signed by two or more persons. Only after this investigation is completed and the [regional agency] determines that the evidence warrants a trial does the [national church] become involved. [The woman] has not alleged . . . that she or anyone else ever filed a complaint against [the pastor] with the [regional agency]. Therefore, the [national church] could not have disciplined [the pastor]. Accordingly, we conclude that because the evidence does not show that the [national church] was aware of [the pastor's] actions, summary judgment in favor of the [national church] is proper on [the woman's] claims for negligent . . . retention."

• A North Carolina court ruled that the First Amendment did not prevent it from resolving a sexual harassment lawsuit brought by three female church employees against their church and denominational agencies.[139] Three female church employees (the "plaintiffs") sued their church and various church agencies as a result of the sexual misconduct of a pastor. The lawsuit alleged that the pastor "committed inappropriate, unwelcome, offensive and nonconsensual acts of a sexual nature against the plaintiffs, variously hugging, kissing and touching them, and made inappropriate, unwelcome, offensive and nonconsensual statements of a sexually suggestive nature to them." The lawsuit further alleged that the local church and church agencies "knew or should have known" of the pastor's propensity for sexual misconduct but failed to take any actions to warn or protect the plaintiffs from his wrongful activity. The court began its opinion by noting that the key issue was whether the First Amendment prevents "the filing of a negligent retention and supervision claim against a religious organization, when that claim is based on the conduct of a cleric of that organization." The court concluded that if a resolution of the plaintiffs' legal claims did not require an interpretation of church doctrine, then "the First Amendment is not implicated and

---

[138] Konkle v. Henson, 672 N.E.2d 450 (Ind. App. 1996).
[139] Smith v. Privette, 495 S.E.2d 395 (N.C. App. 1998).

neutral principles of law are properly applied to adjudicate the claim." The court then noted that North Carolina recognizes negligent supervision and retention as separate bases of legal liability. To support a claim of negligent retention and supervision against an employer, a plaintiff must prove that "the incompetent employee committed a tortious act resulting in injury to plaintiff and that prior to the act, the employer knew or had reason to know of the employee's incompetency." The court concluded, "We acknowledge that the decision to hire or discharge a minister is inextricable from religious doctrine and protected by the First Amendment from judicial inquiry. We do not accept, however, that resolution of the plaintiffs' negligent retention and supervision claim requires the trial court to inquire into the church defendants' reasons for choosing [the pastor] to serve as a minister. The plaintiffs' claim, construed in the light most favorable to them, instead presents the issue of whether the church defendants knew or had reason to know of [the pastor's] propensity to engage in sexual misconduct, conduct that the church defendants do not claim is part of the tenets or practices of [their religion]. Thus, there is no necessity for the court to interpret or weigh church doctrine in its adjudication of the plaintiffs' claim for negligent retention and supervision. It follows that the First Amendment is not implicated and does not bar the plaintiffs' claim against the church defendants."

• A Minnesota court ruled that the First Amendment nonestablishment of religion clause did not prevent it from resolving a negligent retention claim against a church as a result of a pastor's sexual relationship with a female church member. The court acknowledged that "an employer has the duty to refrain from retaining employees with known dangerous proclivities," and that an employer may be liable for negligent retention when "during the course of employment, it becomes aware or should have become aware of problems with an employee that indicated his unfitness, and the employer fails to take further action such as investigating, discharge or reassignment." The court concluded that the First Amendment did not bar resolution of this claim: "A court need evaluate only what the church knew or should have known about the pastor's propensity to engage in sexual penetration with persons who sought spiritual or religious advice from him, and, if there was such knowledge, whether it acted reasonably to prevent such conduct. The issue is not negligent retention as it relates to the pastor's provision of spiritual advice. The issue . . . is whether the church acted reasonably after it became aware or should have become aware of any problems with the pastor sexually penetrating persons being privately given spiritual advice, aid, or comfort. This inquiry does not pose any risk of entanglement with religious doctrine or procedure and no burdening of religious practice."[140]

• An Ohio court ruled that a church and denominational agency could be sued on the basis of negligent retention for the sexual misconduct of a minister. The court noted that an employer may be liable on the basis of negligent retention for injuries caused by an employee if the employer knew or should have know that the employee might engage in such conduct. The victim insisted that this standard was established by the fact that he was in the priest's room in the church rectory "hundreds of times until 11:00 PM, and, on dozens of occasions, until 2:00 AM." The court agreed, noting that the church defendants' "failure to intervene in the priest's actions, despite their alleged constructive knowledge of them, allegedly permitted the abuse to continue and is the cause of the injuries."[141]

---

[140] Olson v. First Church of Nazarene, 661 N.W.2d 254 (Minn. App. 2003). *Accord* Doe v. Redeemer Lutheran Church, 531 N.W.2d 897 (Minn. App. 1995).

[141] Mills v. Deehr, 2004 WL 1047720 (Ohio App. 2004).

• *The Pennsylvania Supreme Court ruled that a church and diocese could be legally responsible on the basis of negligent retention for a priest's repeated acts of child molestation occurring off of church premises. The court concluded: "Here [the diocese] knew for certain that [the priest] had a propensity for pedophilic behavior and was aware of several specific instances of such conduct. [It] knew that placing him in a position in which he would have contact with children would afford [him] ample opportunity to commit further acts of abuse, which would likely result in extreme harm to the children under his supervision. Knowing all of this [the diocese] had a duty to take appropriate precautions to prevent him from molesting any more children, e.g., by assigning him to a position in which he would not have any contact with children, by ensuring that he sought treatment for his disorder, or by terminating his employment altogether. [The diocese], however, did not attempt to prevent the foreseeable harm, and instead undertook a course of conduct that increased the risk that [the priest] would abuse . . . children. [Its] inaction in the face of such a menace is not only negligent, it is reckless and abhorrent."[142]*

• *A federal court in Pennsylvania ruled that there was sufficient evidence to find a church liable for a priest's acts of child molestation on the basis of negligent retention and negligent supervision, but not on the basis of negligent hiring. The court noted that there was evidence that an adolescent boy (the "victim") was sleeping in the priest's home, and that the priest had taken the victim on several overnight trips and provided him with several gifts. The court concluded that "a reasonable jury could conclude that there was adequate warning to the church defendants that [the priest] was grooming the plaintiff for a homosexual relationship, and that it may well have already begun. The notice of the plaintiff's sleepovers in the rectory, the gifts given to him and the overnight trips is sufficient to allow a reasonable jury to conclude that the church defendants were negligent or reckless in retaining him as a priest." A reasonable jury also could conclude that the church defendants "were negligent or reckless in permitting, or failing to prevent [the priest's] conduct upon church premises, given the plaintiff's statement that he routinely sexually abused him while they slept in his bedroom in the church rectory."[143]*

Court Decisions Rejecting Negligent Retention Claims   § 10-07.2

Key point 10-07.2. Many courts have ruled that the First Amendment prevents churches from being legally responsible on the basis of negligent retention for the misconduct of ministers.

Some courts have concluded that the First Amendment prevents churches from being sued on the basis of negligent retention for the sexual misconduct of ministers.

---

[142] Hutchinson v. Luddy, 1999 WL 1062862 (Pa. 1999).

[143] *Doe v. Liberatore*, 478 F.Supp.2d 742 (M.D. Pa. 2007).

Case Studies

• A federal appeals court ruled that a school was not liable on the basis of negligent retention for the molestation of two young girls by a teacher despite the fact that it was aware of a prior, similar complaint by another girl because the school thoroughly investigated the prior complaint, concluded that it was unsubstantiated, and took appropriate steps to monitor and restrict the employee.[144]

• A Colorado court threw out a lawsuit brought by a woman alleging that her church acted improperly and unlawfully when it dismissed her after she made complaints of sexual harassment and child molestation against another minister.[145] The woman alleged that when she was a minor, her stepfather committed various acts of sexual assault against her when they resided together. Her stepfather was a minister at the time, and later became president of his denomination. The woman pursued ministerial studies and was licensed as a minister. After serving as a minister in the State of Washington, she moved to the Denver area to start a new church. She later learned that her stepfather, with whom she had severed all ties, was also pastoring a church in the Denver area. She learned that her stepfather was allegedly sexually harassing women church employees and a woman parishioner in his Denver church. She reported this alleged harassment, as well as the sexual abuse she had suffered from her stepfather as a minor, to denominational officers. In response, the stepfather filed charges with the denomination against the woman, claiming that her allegations were false and demanding a full investigation. After an investigation, denominational officers revoked the woman's license and denied her the opportunity to open a new church. The woman responded by filing a lawsuit against her stepfather and her denomination, alleging several theories of liability including negligent retention of her stepfather. In rejecting the woman's claim of negligent retention, the court noted that "[a]n employer may be subject to liability for negligent supervision and retention if the employer knows or should have known that an employee's conduct would subject third parties to an unreasonable risk of harm." The court concluded that any resolution of these theories of liability would involve the civil courts in a church's decision-making processes contrary to the First Amendment guaranty of religious freedom.

• A federal court in Connecticut dismissed a lawsuit brought by two adult brothers against their church and diocese for injuries they allegedly sustained when they were sexually molested while minors by a priest.[146] The brothers alleged that the church and diocese were legally responsible for the priest's acts on the basis of negligent retention because they were aware that the priest had received treatment sessions for sexual abuse of minors over a 15-year period at Catholic treatment centers in New Mexico and Maryland. The court accepted affidavits from church officials claiming that they had no knowledge (or reason to suspect) that the priest had ever participated in any retreat or treatment for sexual abuse of any kind. The court concluded, based on these affidavits, that the church and diocese had no prior knowledge of any sexual misconduct on the part of the offending priest, and so the negligence claim had to be dismissed.

---

[144] Davis v. DeKalb County School District, 233 F.3d 1367 (11th Cir. 2000). *Accord* Ehrens v. Lutheran Church, 385 F.3d 232 (2nd Cir. 2004).

[145] Van Osdol v. Vogt, 892 P.2d 402 (Colo. App. 1994).

[146] Nutt v. Norwich Roman Catholic Diocese, 921 F. Supp. 66 (D. Conn. 1995). *See also* Martinelli v. Bridgeport Roman Catholic Diocese, 989 F. Supp. 110 (D. Conn. 1997); Doe v. Norwich Roman Catholic Diocesan Corporation, 268 F.Supp.2d 139 (D. Conn. 2003).

• A Georgia court dismissed a lawsuit brought by a woman against her church and a denominational agency as a result of injuries she allegedly sustained during a sexual relationship with her pastor.[147] The woman and her husband claimed that the church defendants were liable for the pastor's conduct on the basis of negligent retention. Specifically, they argued that the church defendants left the pastor in his position despite knowledge that he posed a risk of harm to women. This knowledge consisted of the following three facts: (1) There were rumors at the church about the pastor's relationship with another woman who was a church employee. (2) A letter to the senior pastor from a prospective church member put the church and denominational agency on notice of the associate pastor's propensity for sexual misconduct. In the letter, a woman claimed that the associate pastor came to her house in an intoxicated condition, made inappropriate comments, and touched her on the knee. (3) The woman informed the church's new associate pastor of her relationship with his predecessor. The court concluded that this evidence did not render the church defendants negligent for retaining the associate minister. With regard to the rumors of an improper relationship with the female church employee, the court noted that the associate pastor later married this woman; the associate pastor denied any inappropriate conduct with this woman when confronted about it by the senior pastor; the senior pastor recommended that the associate pastor be transferred to another church on the basis of these rumors; and the associate pastor's "personal, consensual relationship with [the employee] is totally unrelated to the type of conduct complained of by [the woman in this lawsuit]." With regard to the letter, the court noted that the senior pastor immediately called the woman and met with her to discuss the letter; the senior pastor also discussed it with the associate pastor who denied the events in the letter; the senior pastor conducted a thorough investigation and determined the woman was not telling the truth; the senior pastor testified that at no time did any woman come to him and say she was having a sexual relationship with the associate pastor; the senior pastor testified that he was never, at any time, led to believe that the associate pastor was a threat to women parishioners; and the senior pastor stated, in an affidavit, that "in fact, I believe that [the associate pastor] possibly had an excellent future in the ministry." With regard to the woman's disclosure to the church's new associate pastor of her relationship with his predecessor, the court noted that she also told him she was not ready to come forward and tell anyone else about the relationship. Therefore she "cannot now complain of [his] failure to act when she told him she was not ready to disclose her relationship with [the associate pastor]. The court also noted that the woman's communications to the new associate pastor were privileged and could not be disclosed without her permission. The court concluded, "The record is also devoid of any probative evidence tending to show the [church defendants] were or should have been on notice of a propensity for sexual misconduct after [the associate pastor] became a minister at the church. The [couple] make numerous allegations as to [the associate pastor's] conduct with different women but have submitted no admissible evidence in support of this contention."

• A Georgia appeals court dismissed a daughter's lawsuit against a priest and Catholic diocese claiming that her father murdered her mother and then killed himself as a

---

[147] Alpharetta First United Methodist Church v. Stewart, 473 S.E.2d 532 (Ga. App. 1996).

result of an adulterous affair between the mother and a priest.[148] The daughter claimed that her mother had been seduced by the priest, and that her father shot and killed her mother and then shot himself after finding out about it. The daughter claimed that the diocese was responsible for her parent's deaths on the basis of negligent hiring and retention of the priest. She insisted that if the diocese had adequately investigated the matter and "defrocked" the priest, the deaths would not have occurred. The court concluded that the diocese did not have sufficient proof that the priest had acted improperly. It observed, "To the contrary, all signs point to the unreliability of [the mother's] declarations. She told a friend that she did not have an affair with [the priest] and in an official church investigation by the church she denied any involvement with the priest. She wrote a letter to [her] archbishop in which she stated that she had fantasized an affair with [the priest] because her husband was away on business and she was lonely. She asked the archbishop for forgiveness and stated that she was seeking professional help." The court concluded that the priest and diocese "produced evidence demonstrating that [the priest] did not have a sexual relationship with [the mother]. [The daughter] has failed to come up with evidence to the contrary."

• A federal district court in Michigan ruled that a church school and various church agencies were not liable on the basis of negligent hiring, supervision, or retention for the sexual molestation of a minor student by a priest.[149] The court, in summarily rejecting the victim's claim that the school and church agencies had been guilty of "negligent hiring," observed, "Questions of hiring and retention of clergy necessarily will require interpretation of church canons, and internal church policies and practices. It is well-settled that when a court is required to interpret canon law or internal church policies and practices, the First Amendment is violated because such judicial inquiry would constitute excessive government entanglement with religion. . . . [An] inquiry into the decision of who should be permitted to become or remain a priest necessarily would involve prohibited excessive entanglement with religion. Therefore [the victim's] claims of negligence predicated upon a negligent hiring theory will be dismissed."

• A Minnesota court ruled that a church and denominational organization were not legally responsible on the basis of negligent retention for a pastor's acts of child molestation.[150] The molester had served as pastor of a church for nearly 25 years, and was accused of molesting numerous young boys during his tenure. The court defined "negligent retention" as "occurring when, during the course of employment, the employer becomes aware or should have become aware of problems with an employee that indicated his unfitness, and the employer fails to take further action such as investigating, discharge, or reassignment." The victim pointed to the following facts in supporting his claim that the church had been guilty of negligent retention: (1) some church members knew the pastor had an interest in children and youth ministry; (2)

---

[148] Boehm v. Abi-Sarkis, 438 S.E.2d 410 (Ga. App. 1993). *See also* Poole v. North Georgia Conference, 615 S.E.2d 604 (Ga. App. 2005). The court acknowledged that a church member claimed that an associate pastor had given a woman hugs of "inappropriately long duration," and the church's youth pastor stated that he had observed an inappropriate relationship between the associate pastor and the woman. However, the court concluded that neither allegation supported a claim of negligent retention against the church since neither allegation was ever brought to the attention of church leaders, or involved conduct showing that the associate pastor had a tendency to engage in sexual contact with female counselees.

[149] Isely v. Capuchin Province, 880 F. Supp. 1138 (E.D. Mich. 1995).

[150] M.L. v. Magnuson, 531 N.W.2d 831 (Minn. App. 1995). *Accord* Mulinix v. Mulinix, 1997 WL 585775 (Minn. App. 1997).

some church members knew the pastor was counseling children in private, including discussions of sexual and relationship issues; (3) some church members knew that, as part of his confirmation curriculum, the pastor discussed sexuality with children during the final interview; (4) some church members knew the pastor taught the boys about circumcision in confirmation classes, though a parent was always present during these lectures; (5) other incidents of sexual abuse occurred at the church at a time when other people would normally be around and the pastor took no special precautions to hide the abuse. The court concluded that the church was not guilty of negligent retention, since "[t]here is no evidence [it] had actual knowledge of [the pastor's] propensities to commit sexual abuse prior to the time [the victim] was abused." It observed, "There is no evidence that members in 1973 should have foreseen abuse because their clergyperson was interested in youth ministry or counseled children in private. We are mindful that most personal counseling occurs in private. And by itself, evidence of a youth ministry interest and counseling activity does not show that the congregation should suspect the pastor is engaging in sexual abuse. Nor is it reasonable to infer, at least without other evidence, knowledge in 1973 that a pastor will engage in sexual abuse merely because he or she counsels children on sexual issues. There is no evidence that counseling on sexual issues was outside a pastor's purview or so unusual that it should have raised suspicions of sexual abuse. We agree that the details of some of [the pastor's] discussions on sexuality were highly unusual and perhaps would have alerted [the church] to a problem. But there is no evidence that anyone reported the contents of these discussions to [the church's] decisionmakers nor has [the victim] explained how these [church] members could otherwise have learned the details of these conversations. . . . Finally, the jury could not conclude that [the church] should have known about other incidents of abuse simply because they occurred at the church when other people were probably in the building. The incidents all occurred in private, and there is no evidence that people who may have been in the building knew anything more than the fact that counseling sessions occurred. . . . If this evidence alone is sufficient to support a negligent retention verdict, it would appear impossible for a church to avoid liability without prohibiting pastors from counseling children in private or prohibiting discussion of sexual issues. We are not prepared to hold that every church must take these measures to avoid liability for negligent retention, much less that this standard can govern church practices retroactive to a time more than two decades past."

• The Missouri Supreme Court ruled that the First Amendment barred it from resolving a lawsuit in which a Catholic diocese was sued as a result of a priest's acts of sexual molestation.[151] An adult male alleged that when he was about 14 years old he went to a Catholic priest for confession and counseling about various concerns, some of a sexual nature. The priest initiated a sexual relationship with the victim that lasted about 10 years. The victim alleged that when the priest was "hired or ordained" the diocese "knew or reasonably should have known of prior sexual misconduct or a propensity to such conduct" by him. The victim sued the diocese on the basis of several theories of liability including negligent retention. The court concluded that a resolution of the victim's claims against the diocese would violate the First Amendment.

• A New York court ruled that a Catholic diocese could not be sued on the basis of negligent hiring for a priest's acts of child molestation, but it could be sued for

---

[151] Gray v. Ward, 950 S.W.2d 232 (Mo. 1997). *Accord* Gibson v. Brewer, 952 S.W.2d 239 (Mo. 1997).

negligent supervision and negligent retention.[152] The offending priest was ordained in Venezuela and moved to the United States with a letter of reference from his archbishop. He later molested at least one minor (the "victim"). The victim sued the local diocese, claiming that it was legally responsible for the priest's conduct on the basis of negligent hiring, negligent supervision, and negligent retention. He alleged that the diocese became aware of the danger the priest posed to minors after hiring him as a result of comments both he and the priest made to other priests regarding inappropriate behavior. The court noted that if the victim or the priest made such statements to other priests, then the diocese might be legally responsible for the priest's actions on the basis of negligent retention and negligent supervision. The court insisted that imposing liability on the diocese under such circumstances "would not violate constitutional and statutory guarantees of free exercise of religion and separation of church and state" since "there is no indication that requiring increased supervision of [the priest] or the termination of his employment by the [diocese] based upon [his] conduct would violate any religious doctrine or inhibit any religious practice." The court concluded that there was evidence that the retention of the priest by the diocese was dictated by religious doctrine. It insisted that "religious entities have some duty to prevent injuries incurred by persons in their employ whom they have reason to believe will engage in injurious conduct."

• A New York court ruled that a church could not be liable on the basis of negligent supervision or negligent retention for the sexual misconduct of a minister, since imposing liability on these grounds would violate the First Amendment. The court noted: "Any attempt by the court to define standards and rules under which a priest is retained or supervised necessarily and impermissibly involves the court in church doctrine."[153]

• A federal court in New York refused to find a church or denomination agency liable, on the basis of "negligent placement, retention, or supervision," for a pastor's sexual contacts with a woman during marital counseling.[154] The court made the following statement in rejecting the woman's claim that the church and denomination had been guilty of negligence: "[A]ny inquiry into the policies and practices of the church defendants in hiring or supervising their clergy raises . . . First Amendment problems of entanglement . . . which might involve the court in making sensitive judgments about the propriety of the church defendants' supervision in light of their religious beliefs. Insofar as concerns retention or supervision, the pastor of a Presbyterian church is not analogous to a common law employee. He may not demit his charge nor be removed by the session, without the consent of the presbytery, functioning essentially as an ecclesiastical court. The traditional denominations each have their own intricate principles of governance, as to which the state has no rights of visitation. Church governance is founded in scripture, modified by reformers over almost two millennia. As the Supreme Court stated [long ago]: 'It is not to be supposed that the judges of the civil courts can be as competent in the ecclesiastical law and religious faith of all these bodies as the ablest men in each are in reference to their own. It would therefore be an

---

[152] Kenneth R. v. Roman Catholic Diocese, 654 N.Y.S.2d 791 (N.Y.A.D. 1997). *See also* Ehrens v. The Lutheran Church-Missouri Synod, 269 F.Supp.2d 328 (S.D.N.Y. 2003), holding that a local church was not liable for the negligent retention of a pastor since it had no authority to remove him.

[153] Mars v. Diocese of Rochester, 763 N.Y.S.2d 885 (Sup. Ct. 2003).

[154] Schmidt v. Bishop, 779 F. Supp. 321 (S.D.N.Y. 1991).

appeal from the more learned tribunal in the law which should decide the case, to the one which is less so.'[155] It would therefore also be inappropriate and unconstitutional for this court to determine after the fact that the ecclesiastical authorities negligently supervised or retained the [pastor]. Any award of damages would have a chilling effect leading indirectly to state control over the future conduct of affairs of a religious denomination, a result violative of the text and history of the [First Amendment]."

• *An Ohio court ruled that a denominational agency was not liable on the basis of negligent retention for a pastor's sexual misconduct involving a member of his congregation since it had no prior notice that he presented a risk of such behavior. The plaintiff contended that the denomination was negligent in retaining the pastor after learning that he was receiving psychological counseling and taking psychiatric drugs for clinical depression. The court noted that to prove negligent retention one must show "(1) the existence of an employment relationship; (2) the employee's incompetence; (3) the employer's actual or constructive knowledge of such incompetence; (4) the employee's act or omission causing the plaintiff's injuries; and (5) the employer's negligence in hiring or retaining the employee as the proximate cause of plaintiff's injuries." The court concluded that the plaintiff failed to satisfy most of these requirements; "[The plaintiff] has failed to present evidence of the existence of any employment relationship between the pastor and the denomination. It has further failed to present evidence that the pastor's admission of depression interfered with or affected his ministry duties at [his church]. [A denominational officer] stated that depression does not call for action by the [denomination] unless it was perceived by the congregation or the pastor to be a major interference with the ministry of the congregation. Furthermore, the estate failed to set forth any evidence that the denomination had knowledge of the pastor's incompetence. As such, [the negligent retention claim] lacks merit."[156]*

• *An Ohio court ruled that a church could be liable on the basis of negligent retention for the molestation of several young children by two adolescent boys who served as volunteer teachers. The court noted that after one of the boys had worked with children at the church for some time, the church "became aware of problems with his performance." It mentioned the following: (1) A complaint by one parent that one of the boys had played roughly with children. (2) A complaint that one of the boys let a child sit on his lap. (3) A report that one of the boys was seen speaking with another teenager when he should have been attending to the children. (4) The church had a policy of requiring that an adult be present with the teenage caregivers, but it is clear that the two perpetrators "managed to circumvent this policy on numerous occasions, with appalling and disastrous results."[157]*

• *The Oklahoma Supreme Court ruled that a denomination (the "national church") was not legally responsible on the basis of negligent retention for a pastor's acts of child molestation. The court acknowledged that employers may be liable for negligence in hiring, supervising or retaining an employee. But it pointed out that "the critical element for recovery is the employer's prior knowledge of the employee's propensities*

---

[155] Watson v. Jones, 80 U.S. 679 (1872).

[156] Stewart v. West Ohio Conference of the United Methodist Church, (Ohio App. 2003). *Accord* DePietro, 825 N.E.2d 630 (Ohio App. 2005).

[157] Doe v. First Presbyterian Church (USA), 710 N.E.2d 367 (Ohio App. 1998).

to create the specific danger resulting in damage." As a result, in order for the national church to be responsible for the pastor's acts, the victims would have to prove that "the national organization had notice of [his] deviant sexual tendencies" before his transfer to the church where the molestation occurred. The court concluded that the national church "lacked knowledge sufficient to impose liability."[158]

• A Texas court ruled that a church and regional denominational agency were not liable on the basis of negligent retention for the sexual assault of a church secretary by a pastor because they had no knowledge of prior acts of sexual misconduct by the pastor. The court noted that an employer is liable for negligent retention only if it retains in its employ an incompetent worker "whom the employer knows was incompetent or unfit, thereby creating an unreasonable risk of harm to others." A plaintiff's injury "must be the result of the employer's continued employment of a knowingly unfit employee." The court noted that neither the local church nor the parent denomination had any prior knowledge of sexual misconduct by the pastor. The court conceded that several complaints had been made against him in the past, but none involved sexual misconduct.[159]

• A federal court in Vermont ruled that a church was not liable for its pastor's acts of child molestation on the basis of negligent retention. It noted that negligence requires foreseeability of the harm that was suffered, and concluded that "there is no evidence that the church knew or should have known of the pastor's propensity to molest young boys. An employer is under a duty to control his employees from intentionally harming another only when he knows or should know of the necessity and opportunity for exercising such control. Because the church did not know of the pastor's propensities, it was under no duty to protect the victim from his volitional, criminal acts."[160]

• The Wisconsin Supreme Court ruled that the statute of limitations prevented a woman from suing a Catholic archdiocese for the alleged acts of molestation by a priest nearly 40 years before.[161] The woman claimed that the priest entered into a sexual relationship with her in the late 1950s when she was a high school student, and that as a result of the priest's behavior she "has suffered and continues to suffer from severe emotional distress, causing and contributing to the break-up of her marriage, separation from her children, loss of jobs and other difficulties." The woman's lawsuit claimed that the archdiocese was responsible for her injuries on the basis of several factors, including negligent retention. Specifically, she alleged that the archdiocese knew or should have known that the priest had a sexual problem and acted "willfully, intentionally and in wanton and reckless disregard of the rights and safety of plaintiff by failing to remove [him] from serving as a priest." In rejecting the woman's claim, the court observed, "To establish a claim for negligent hiring or retention [the woman] would have to establish that the archdiocese was negligent in hiring or retaining [the priest] because he was incompetent or otherwise unfit. But, we conclude that the First Amendment to the United States Constitution prevents the courts of this state from determining what makes one competent to serve as a Catholic priest since such

---

[158] N.H. v. Presbyterian Church (U.S.A.), 1999 WL 1013547 (Okla. 1999).

[159] Doe v. South Central Spanish District of the Church of God, 2002 WL 31296620 (Tex. App. 2002).

[160] Doe v. Newbury Bible Church, 2005 WL 1862118 (D. Vt. 2005).

[161] Pritzlaff v. Archdiocese of Milwaukee, 533 N.W.2d 780 (Wis. 1995).

a determination would require interpretation of church canons and internal church policies and practices. Therefore [the suit] against the archdiocese is not capable of enforcement by the courts." The court concluded, "Assuming they exist at all, the torts of negligent hiring and retention may not be maintained against a religious governing body due to concerns of excessive entanglement, and that the tort of negligent training or supervision cannot be successfully asserted in this case because it would require an inquiry into church laws, practices and policies."

Risk Management   § 10-07.3

Key point 10-07.3. *Churches can reduce the risk of liability based on negligent retention for sexual misconduct involving adult or minor victims by adopting risk management policies and procedures.*

How can churches reduce the risk of liability based on negligent retention of a minister or lay worker who engages in inappropriate conduct with an adult or child? While churches cannot eliminate this risk, they can take steps to reduce it. Consider the following:

1. Investigate

Whenever a church leader receives credible information suggesting that a church employee or volunteer may represent a risk of harm to others, an immediate and thorough investigation should be initiated. Remember this— once such information is received, the church is "put on notice" of the risk and may be legally responsible on the basis of negligent retention for future acts of misconduct by the church worker if it does nothing to investigate or respond to the information. The investigation should include a thorough review of the accusation. This ordinarily will include some or all of the following procedures:

- Interviews with the victim (and the victim's family, if the victim is a minor).

- Interviews with the alleged perpetrator (and the perpetrator's family, if the perpetrator is a minor).

- Collection of corroborating evidence, such as (1) witnesses; (2) other victims; or (3) documentary evidence including letters and photos.

- Consultation with the church's insurance agent.

- Consultation with the church's attorney.

- Consultation with the denominational officers.

- Consultation with other churches or charities in which the alleged perpetrator has worked, to identify whether any similar acts of misconduct have occurred. If so, this tends to prove a pattern, and supports the inference that the victim's account is correct.

• If the alleged misconduct constitutes a crime, conduct a criminal records check to determine if the worker has a history of such acts. If so, this tends to prove a pattern, and supports the inference that the victim's account is correct.

• If the alleged misconduct constitutes child abuse under state law, then church leaders must comply immediately with applicable reporting requirements. By reporting the alleged abuse to the state, the church ordinarily is relieved of any obligation to launch its own investigation. State social services agencies generally prefer that churches refrain from conducting their own independent investigation of child abuse allegations since such preemptive and unprofessional investigations often compromise the integrity and effectiveness of the state's own investigation. A church may suspend an employee or volunteer who is accused of child abuse, pending the outcome of the state's investigation.

Key point. *Many churches are associated with denominations that are empowered to investigate allegations of pastoral misconduct. If this is the case, the accusations should be turned over immediately to denominational officials.*

Key point. *Churches that ignore allegations of wrongdoing by a pastor or lay worker face a number of risks in addition to negligent retention. These include (1) liability based on "ratification" of the minister's actions; (2) punitive damages; and (3) possible personal liability for members of the church board.*

2. Restrictions

If the church's investigation results in credible evidence to support the victim's allegations, then the church can reduce its risk of negligent retention by imposing appropriate restrictions on the alleged wrongdoer. The nature and extent of such restrictions will vary depending on a number of circumstances, including the nature and severity of the alleged wrongs and the strength of the evidence. If a church ignores credible evidence of wrongdoing and imposes no restrictions on the alleged wrongdoer, it is exposed to liability based on negligent retention from the time it learned of the allegations.

Key point. *Here is an excellent question to ask when evaluating a church's risk of negligence (in hiring, retention, or supervision): How would a jury view our actions? Would it conclude that our actions were reasonable? If such a conclusion is not certain, then the risk of negligence exists.*

> "How would a jury view our actions? Would it conclude that our actions were reasonable? If such a conclusion is not certain, then the risk of negligence exists."

Negligent Supervision of Church Workers—In General

§ 10-08

▶ *A number of courts, in addressing the question of whether clergy are employees or self-employed for federal income tax reporting purposes, have observed that churches generally exercise relatively little supervision or control over clergy.[162] Such cases can be used by churches in defending against negligent supervision claims involving clergy misconduct.*

Churches can use reasonable care in selecting workers, but still be liable for injuries sustained during church activities on the basis of negligent supervision. The term *negligence* means carelessness or a failure to exercise reasonable care. *Negligent supervision*, then, refers to a failure to exercise reasonable care in the supervision of church workers and church activities. Churches have been sued on the basis of negligent supervision in a variety of contexts. Consider the following examples:

Examples

• *A minor is sexually molested by a volunteer church youth worker on church premises. The minor's parents sue the church, claiming that it is responsible for their child's injuries on the basis of negligent supervision. They claim that the molestation never would have occurred had the church exercised proper supervision over its workers and activities.*

• *A male youth pastor has sexual contact with a 16-year-old female in the church youth group. The incident occurred on a church-sponsored trip. The minor's parents sue the church, claiming that it is responsible for their child's injuries on the basis of negligent supervision. They claim that the incident never would have occurred had the church exercised proper supervision over its youth pastor.*

• *A male pastor has sexual contact with an adult female in the course of a counseling relationship. The woman later sues the church, claiming that it is responsible for her injuries on the basis of negligent supervision. She claims that the incident would not have occurred had the church exercised proper supervision over its pastor.*

• *An adolescent boy is injured while playing in a church-sponsored basketball game. The minor's parents sue the church, claiming that it is responsible for their child's injuries on the basis of negligent supervision. They claim that the molestation never would have occurred had the church exercised proper supervision over its workers and activities.*

• *A 5-year-old girl drowns while participating in a church-sponsored trip to a local lake. The minor's parents sue the church, claiming that it is responsible for their child's death on the basis of negligent supervision. They claim that the death never would have occurred had the church exercised proper supervision over its workers and activities.*

---

[162] *See, e.g.,* Weber v. Commissioner, 60 F.3d 1104 (4th Cir. 1995).

• A 10-year-old boy is injured when he falls off a cliff while participating in a church-sponsored camping trip. The minor's mother sues the church, claiming that it is responsible for her child's injuries on the basis of negligent supervision. She claims that the accident never would have occurred had the church exercised proper supervision over its workers and activities.

• A 6-month-old infant breaks her leg while in the church nursery. There were two attendants on duty in the nursery, both of whom were 15-year-old girls. The accident occurred when the attendant who was changing the infant's diaper temporarily left the infant unattended. The infant's parents sue the church, claiming that the accident never would have occurred had the church exercised proper supervision over its workers and activities.

Key point. Churches are not "guarantors" of the safety and well-being of those persons who participate in their programs and activities. Generally, they are responsible only for those injuries that result from their negligence.

Negligent Supervision of Church Workers—Sexual Misconduct Cases Involving Minor Victims

§ 10-09

Many of the cases in which churches have been sued for negligent supervision involve incidents of child molestation. A child is molested on church premises, or during a church activity, and the child's parents sue the church. While the parents may allege that the church was negligent in selecting or retaining the offender, they also may assert that the church was negligent in supervising the offender and its premises and activities. One court defined negligent supervision of children as follows:

> The measure of duty of a person undertaking control and supervision of a child to exercise reasonable care for the safety of the child is to be gauged by the standard of the average responsible parent; such person is not an insurer of the safety of the child and has no duty to foresee and guard against every possible hazard. The measure of precaution which must be taken by one having a child in his care, who stands in no relation to the child except that he has undertaken to care for it is that care which a prudent person would exercise under like circumstances. As a general rule, a person who undertakes the control and supervision of a child, even without compensation, has the duty to use reasonable care to protect the child from injury. Such person is not an insurer of the safety of the child. He

is required only to use reasonable care commensurate with the reasonably foreseeable risk of harm.[163]

Court Decisions Recognizing Negligent Supervision Claims § 10-09.1

Key point 10-09.1. *Some courts have found churches liable on the basis of negligent supervision for a worker's acts of child molestation on the ground that the church failed to exercise reasonable care in the supervision of the victim or of its own programs and activities.*

> The court concluded that the church knew of the risk the pastor was to children, and yet "instead of keeping him away from children altogether, they disregarded [his] misconduct and allowed him to have unsupervised contact with children. Instead of responding to [his] pedophilic behavior, they concealed and ignored it. [The church] knew [his] history and was in a position to prevent him from repeating it, yet for years it willfully allowed him to go on molesting children with impunity. [Its] inaction in the face of such a menace is not only negligent, it is reckless and abhorrent."[164]

This section reviews court decisions in which a church or other religious organization was found liable on the basis of negligent supervision for a worker's acts of child molestation.

Case Studies

• *The Colorado Supreme Court ruled that a church whose pastor molested a young boy could be sued on the basis of negligent supervision of the pastor.[165] A 7-year-old boy (the "victim"), who was experiencing emotional trauma, was encouraged by his pastor to enter into a counseling relationship with him. The boy's mother approved, and the counseling sessions lasted for a number of years. From the very first counseling session the victim claimed that the pastor engaged in sexual contact with him, including having him sit on the pastor's lap while the pastor massaged his thighs and genitals. While these "massages" were occurring the pastor would tell the victim that "your father loves you, your mother loves you, God loves you, and I love you." Two other adult males claimed that the pastor had engaged in similar behavior with them when they were minors, including a physical inspection of their genitals to see if they had been "properly circumcised." The parents of two other boys complained to the church board about the pastor's counseling methods, and in particular his practice of inspecting genitals to check for proper circumcision. Nearly a year later the board responded by directing the pastor to discontinue his counseling of minors. A few*

---

[163] Wallace v. Boys Club of Albany, Georgia, Inc., 439 S.E.2d 746 (Ga. App. 1993).

[164] The Supreme Court or Pennsylvania in Hutchinson v. Luddy, 1999 WL 1062862 (Pa. 1999).

[165] Bear Valley Church of Christ v. DeBose, 928 P.2d 1315 (Colo. 1996).

months later the pastor was dismissed. The victim and his mother sued the church, claiming that it was responsible for the pastor's acts on the basis of several grounds including negligent supervision. A jury returned a verdict in favor of the victim, and this verdict was affirmed by the state supreme court. The court rejected the church's claim that allowing civil judgments against pastoral counselors and their churches based upon conduct occurring during counseling sessions could so "entangle" the government with religious practices as to violate the First Amendment. It acknowledged that "the decision to hire or discharge a minister is itself inextricable from religious doctrine." However, a court must "distinguish internal hiring disputes within religious organizations from general negligence claims filed by injured third parties."

• In a decision that will be of direct relevance to churches, a Georgia court ruled that a local Boys Club could be sued by the parents of a five-year-old boy who was abducted and molested when he wandered off the Boys Club premises without adult supervision.[166] The victim was enrolled in a summer day camp conducted by the Boys Club in his community. Boys in the program ranged from 6 to 11 (an exception was made in the case of the victim), and the boys were to be under the direct supervision of an adult worker at all times. An adult was stationed at a desk by the front door of the facility, and no child was allowed to leave the premised unattended. Nevertheless, the victim was able to walk out the front door and go around the building to look at the swimming pool without adult supervision. While outside, the boy was abducted and sexually molested. No adult staff member was aware of the victim's absence until his big brother brought it to the staff's attention. A search proved fruitless. The boy was later found in a nearby forest by police. The parents later sued the Boys Club and a state appeals court ruled that the parents could sue the Boys Club on the basis of negligent supervision. The appeals court began its opinion by explaining the "duty of care" that is imposed on institutions that care for or work with children: "As a general rule, a person who undertakes the control and supervision of a child, even without compensation, has the duty to use reasonable care to protect the child from injury. Such person is not an insurer of the safety of the child. He is required only to use reasonable care commensurate with the reasonably foreseeable risk of harm." Applying this standard to the facts of this case, the court concluded that the question was "whether a prudent person caring for a five or six-year-old child under similar circumstances would have allowed the child to leave the building without an older person, and thus whether [the Boys Club] breached its duty of care." The Boys Club insisted that it could not be liable since no similar incidents had ever occurred on its premises. The court rejected this argument, noting that in the case of negligent supervision "what is reasonably foreseeable is not exclusively dependent upon what is known about a specific place." The proper question is "what may happen to any child at any place." Based on this standard the court concluded that the risk of abduction was foreseeable.

• An Indiana court ruled that the First Amendment does not prevent a woman from suing her church and a denominational agency on account of injuries she suffered as a result of being molested by her pastor when she was a minor.[167] The woman claimed that the pastor began molesting her when she was seven years old, and that the molestation continued until she was 20. The woman sued her church and regional

---

[166] Wallace v. Boys Club of Albany, Georgia, Inc., 439 S.E.2d 746 (Ga. App. 1993).

[167] Konkle v. Henson, 672 N.E.2d 450 (Ind. App. 1996).

and national denominational agencies. The court concluded that the national church was not liable on the basis of negligent supervision or retention for the actions of the pastor. It observed, "The [national church], which is only affiliated with the local church and [regional agency] through its constitution and judicial procedures, was not informed. The evidence . . . does not indicate that [the woman] invoked the judicial procedures, which is the only mechanism by which the [national church] could have taken action against [the pastor]. According to the judicial procedures, the [regional agency] forms a committee to investigate alleged misconduct upon the submission of a complaint signed by two or more persons. Only after this investigation is completed and the [regional agency] determines that the evidence warrants a trial does the [national church] become involved. [The woman] has not alleged . . . that she or anyone else ever filed a complaint against [the pastor] with the [regional agency]. Therefore, the [national church] could not have disciplined [the pastor]. Accordingly, we conclude that because the evidence does not show that the [national church] was aware of [the pastor's] actions, summary judgment in favor of the [national church] is proper on [the woman's] claims for negligent hiring, supervision, and retention." The court concluded that there was evidence that the local church and regional agency were aware of the pastor's actions, and therefore they could be sued for negligent supervision and retention. The court sent the case back to the trial court for trial.

• The Maine Supreme Court ruled that a Catholic diocese could be sued on the basis of negligent supervision and breach of a fiduciary duty for a priest's molestation of an adolescent male who served as an altar boy and attended a church school, and whose parents were partially incapacitated and unable to fully oversee his upbringing. The victim claimed that the diocese was responsible for his injuries on the basis of its negligent supervision of the priest after learning of his propensity to sexually abuse boys and its failure to report him to the police and notify members of the parish. The court stressed that "the constitutional guarantee of religious freedom mandates that we carefully balance the relevant societal interests and the potential interference with religious freedom when assessing claims against religious organizations based on allegations of abusive conduct by members of the clergy." It concluded that a "special relationship" between a church and a victim of clergy sexual abuse "may give rise to a duty on the part of the church to prevent harm caused by the intentional acts of its clergy."[168]

• A Minnesota court ruled that a church could be sued on the basis of negligent supervision as a result of a pastor's acts of child molestation.[169] *The pastor served as both pastor and youth program teacher at the church. He lived in a third floor apartment at the church's youth center. The victim attended confirmation classes at the church, and the pastor was his instructor. The victim so admired the pastor that he wanted to become a pastor himself. The victim often went with the pastor to make*

---

[168] Fortin v. Roman Catholic Bishop of Portland, 871 A.2d 1208 (Me. 2005).

[169] Doe v. Redeemer Lutheran Church, 531 N.W.2d 897 (Minn. App. 1995). *Accord* C.B. ex rel. L.B. v. Evangelical Lutheran Church in America 726 N.W.2d 127 (Minn. App. 2007). A Minnesota court, in rejecting the argument that a church was liable on the basis of negligent supervision for the molestation of minor, noted that "to make out a successful claim for negligent supervision, the plaintiff must prove (1) the employee's conduct was foreseeable; and (2) the employer failed to exercise ordinary care when supervising the employee. In negligence cases, foreseeability means a level of probability that would lead a prudent person to take effective precautions. If the abusive behavior was objectively foreseeable, then the inquiry must focus on whether the employer took reasonable precautions, beforehand, to prevent the abuse."

calls or visit other churches. He also attended church camp during the summer and at times stayed overnight at the pastor's apartment. When the victim was 13 to 16 years old, he was molested by the pastor. Prior to his abuse, the victim was a good student and athlete. After the abuse, his grades dropped and he quit playing team sports. During his late teens, he was hospitalized as a result of an attempted suicide. He later suffered from alcohol abuse and social phobia including panic attacks. A jury returned a verdict in favor of the victim, and a state appeals court affirmed this judgment. The appeals court concluded that the church had been negligent in permitting the sexual abuse to occur. This conclusion was based in part on the following facts: (1) During the time the victim was being molested, a church trustee saw the pastor kissing another adolescent boy on the mouth. The pastor, upon seeing the trustee, blushed and ran back to his apartment. The trustee informed another trustee of this incident, along with two members of the church council. No action was taken. (2) During the time the victim was being molested, another church trustee was approached by a local teacher and asked if the pastor was a child molester. This same trustee's uncle told him that he heard something went on at a cabin at church camp and asked if the pastor was "straight." (3) During the time the victim was being molested, a church trustee's son had to make up some work for confirmation classes at the pastor's home. When he returned home, he told his father that the pastor wanted him "to get under the sheets" with him. (4) During the time the victim was being molested, a student in the confirmation class testified that during a confirmation class at the church she thought she saw the pastor engage in an act of child abuse. She told her parents and the church's "intern pastor" what she saw. The girl and her parents quit attending the church after this incident. (5) During the time the victim was being molested, another confirmation student told the church's intern pastor that the pastor had "put his arm around him all of the time" and showered with the boys.

• *A New York court ruled that a school was liable on the basis of negligent supervision for the rape of a 12-year-old girl that occurred when she left a school outing without permission.*[170] *The victim and her class of 30 students were attending a school outing at a public park. She left the group to have lunch at a nearby pizza restaurant. Upon returning to the park, she discovered that her class had left. Instead of returning to school, she walked home. While walking home, she was abducted and raped by two adolescent males. The victim sued the school, claiming that her injuries were caused by its negligent supervision of the class outing. A jury found the school negligent, and awarded the victim $3 million in damages. The verdict was based in part on the testimony of an expert in school safety that the school had departed from "safe and common practices." In particular, he noted the following: (1) there should have been at least one more adult supervising the group of 30 elementary-age children (only two adults were present during the outing); (2) students were not "paired off" as buddies; (3) arrangements were not made to have the class meet together at least once each hour while at the park; (4) students were not told that they could not leave the park alone; and (5) students were not told that they would only be dismissed from the outing after they returned to school. The safety expert also testified that the teacher in charge of the outing should have taken several steps immediately upon discovering that a child was missing. These included (1) notifying the school immediately to seek guidance from his superiors; (2) notifying the park police; (3) asking another teacher to take the children back to school so he could continue the search for the missing child;*

---

[170] Bell v. Board of Education, 687 N.Y.S.2d 1325 (A.D. 1997).

(4) remaining in the park until shortly before dismissal time to give the victim more time to return; and (5) notifying school officials upon his return that the victim was still missing. The case was appealed, and the state's highest court affirmed the trial court's judgment in favor of the victim. The court concluded, "[W]e cannot say that the intervening act of rape was unforeseeable as a matter of law. A rational jury hearing the trial testimony could have determined, as the jury did in this case, that the foreseeable result of the danger created by [the school's] alleged lack of supervision was injury such as occurred here. A [jury] could have reasonably concluded that the very purpose of the school supervision was to shield vulnerable schoolchildren from such acts of violence. As we have previously recognized, when the intervening, intentional act of another is itself the foreseeable harm that shapes the duty imposed, the defendant who fails to guard against such conduct will not be relieved of liability when that act occurs."

• *A New York appeals court ruled that a Catholic church and diocese could be sued as a result of the sexual molestation of an 11-year-old boy by a Catholic priest.[171] The victim and his sister were both enrolled in a parochial school operated by the church. An associate pastor at the church (who also served as director of religious education for the school) obtained permission from the victim's mother to take him to an athletic facility at a local college to play racquetball and basketball and go swimming. While in the shower room prior to entering the pool, the pastor allegedly removed all his clothing and made the victim do the same. He then kissed and fondled the victim against his will. The boy's mother later filed a lawsuit on behalf of her son naming the church and diocese as defendants. She alleged that her son had suffered substantial emotional, mental, and physical injuries, and that she had incurred substantial expenses in providing therapy for him. Specifically, she alleged that the church and diocese were liable for the misconduct of the pastor on the basis of their own negligence in hiring and placing the pastor in contact with boys with inadequate investigation of his background and with actual or "constructive" knowledge of his propensities, and in failing periodically to evaluate his activities. The court rejected the argument of the church and diocese that permitting the civil courts to find religious organizations liable on the basis of negligent hiring or supervision of clergy would constitute excessive governmental interference with church autonomy in violation of the First Amendment guaranty of religious freedom. The court observed, "[If the mother is] successful in establishing that, with knowledge that the priest was likely to commit sexual abuse on youths with whom he was put in contact, his employers placed or continued him in a setting in which such abuse occurred, the fact that the placement occurred in the course of internal administration of the religious units does not preclude holding the institutions accountable to the victim of their neglect in administration. Indeed, a contrary holding—that a religious body must be held free from any responsibility for wholly predictable and foreseeable injurious consequences of personnel decisions, although such decisions incorporate no theological or dogmatic tenets—would go beyond First Amendment protection and cloak such bodies with an exclusive immunity greater than that required for the preservation of the principles constitutionally safeguarded."*

• *A New York court found a school liable on the basis of negligence for the molestation of a kindergarten student in a school restroom.[172] The court's ruling is of direct*

---

[171] Jones by Jones v. Trane, 591 N.Y.S.2d 927 (Sup. 1992).

[172] Garcia v. City of New York, 646 N.Y.S.2d 508 (A.D. 1996).

relevance to churches and church-operated schools. The student was permitted to go to the bathroom alone, where he was molested by an older student. The child's parents sued the school, and a jury found that the child's kindergarten teacher had been negligent in allowing the child to go to the bathroom unaccompanied. The child was awarded $500,000 in damages. The school appealed, and a state appeals court upheld the finding of negligence. The court began its opinion by noting that "while we recognize the general rule that educational institutions are not the insurers of the safety of their students and cannot be held liable for every instance in which one pupil injures another, schools are, however, under a duty to adequately supervise their students and are liable for foreseeable injuries which are [directly] caused by the absence of such supervision." The court noted that this duty "derives from the fact that the school, once it takes over physical custody and control of the children, effectively takes the place of their parents and guardians." The court noted that in this case the child was sent from his classroom (while class was in session) to the school bathroom, alone and unsupervised, where the assault occurred. Further, "[t]his was done despite two separate school memoranda, circulated amongst the school's staff, which explicitly provided security procedures to the contrary." The first memoranda stated that "teachers are instructed to send all pupils under third grade to the bathroom with a partner." The second memorandum stated that "to further insure security any child leaving your room or corridor area must have a pass. Young children should go in pairs." A school principal testified that the reason for these rules is to make young children more secure from attack by older students. She also stated that she considered the bathroom to be a place where young children "are particularly vulnerable." The court concluded that the school "did not act with ordinary prudence in allowing the five-year old plaintiff to proceed to the bathroom alone." The school insisted that it could not have been negligent since it was not aware of any previous acts of molestation occurring in its bathroom. The court disagreed. It acknowledged that schools generally must have notice of prior similar misconduct to be liable for assaults upon older students, since school personnel "cannot reasonably be expected to guard against all of the sudden, spontaneous acts that take place among students daily." However, in the case of a young child who is sent by his teacher to a public bathroom unescorted, the potential danger to the child "can be reasonably foreseen and could have been prevented by adequate supervision of the school." As a result, "while it would be reasonable to allow high school students to go to a public bathroom unaccompanied, the same practice surely does not apply to a five-year old child, who is unable to resist, is defenseless against attack, and poses an easy target for sexual molestation or other assaults. Stated another way, even the most prudent parent will not guard his or her teen at every moment in the absence of some foreseeable danger of which he or she has notice; but a five-year-old child in a public bathroom should be supervised or, at the very least, be accompanied by another child."

• A New York court ruled that a Catholic diocese could be sued on the basis of negligent supervision for a priest's acts of child molestation.[173] The offending priest was ordained in Venezuela and moved to the United States with a letter of reference from his archbishop. He later molested a minor (the "victim"). The victim later sued the diocese, claiming that it was legally responsible for the priest's conduct on the basis of negligent hiring, negligent supervision, and negligent retention. A trial court dismissed all of the victim's claims against the diocese, and the victim appealed. A

---

[173] Kenneth R. v. Roman Catholic Diocese, 654 N.Y.S.2d 791 (N.Y.A.D. 1997).

state appeals court concluded that the diocese could be sued for negligent supervision and negligent retention. The victim alleged that the diocese became aware of the danger the priest posed to minors after hiring him as a result of comments both he and the priest made to other priests regarding inappropriate behavior. The court noted that if the victim or the priest made such statements to other priests, then the diocese might be legally responsible for the priest's actions on the basis of negligent retention and negligent supervision. The court insisted that imposing liability on the diocese under such circumstances "would not violate constitutional and statutory guarantees of free exercise of religion and separation of church and state." The court conceded that other courts have concluded that the First Amendment may bar victims from suing churches or clergy on the basis of conduct "finding its basis in religious beliefs and practices." This was not the case here, however, since "there is no indication that requiring increased supervision of [the priest] or the termination of his employment by the [diocese] based upon [his] conduct would violate any religious doctrine or inhibit any religious practice."

• A federal court in Pennsylvania ruled that there was sufficient evidence to find a church liable for a priest's acts of child molestation on the basis of negligent retention and negligent supervision, but not on the basis of negligent hiring. The court noted that there was evidence that an adolescent boy (the "victim") was sleeping in the priest's home, and that the priest had taken the victim on several overnight trips and provided him with several gifts. The court concluded that "a reasonable jury could conclude that there was adequate warning to the church defendants that [the priest] was grooming the plaintiff for a homosexual relationship, and that it may well have already begun. The notice of the plaintiff's sleepovers in the rectory, the gifts given to him and the overnight trips is sufficient to allow a reasonable jury to conclude that the church defendants were negligent or reckless in retaining him as a priest." A reasonable jury also could conclude that the church defendants "were negligent or reckless in permitting, or failing to prevent [the priest's] conduct upon church premises, given the plaintiff's statement that he routinely sexually abused him while they slept in his bedroom in the church rectory."[174]

Court Decisions Rejecting Negligent Supervision Claims § 10-09.2

Key point 10-09.2. *Some courts have found churches not liable on the basis of negligent supervision for a worker's acts of child molestation on the ground that the church exercised reasonable care in the supervision of the victim and of its own programs and activities.*

This section reviews court decisions in which a church or other religious organization was found not liable on the basis of negligent supervision for a worker's acts of child molestation.

---

[174] *Doe v. Liberatore, 478 F.Supp.2d 742 (M.D. Pa. 2007).*

Case Studies

• A federal appeals court ruled that an archdiocese was not responsible for the alleged molestation of a minor by a priest.[175] An adult male sued a priest, a local Catholic church, and an archdiocese claiming that while he was a minor the priest performed illicit sexual acts upon him. The plaintiff alleged that the archdiocese and church were liable because they knew or should have known that illicit acts were being performed on their premises and at the priest's home. He charged that they failed to protect him or take appropriate measures to ascertain or correct the situation. Moreover, he alleged that they knew or should have known that they were fostering the priest's illicit activities and providing him with the means with which to conduct such activities. In rejecting the plaintiff's claim that the archdiocese was responsible for his injuries on the basis of negligent supervision, the court observed: "Employers do not have a duty to supervise their employees when the employees are off-duty or not working. Employers also are not liable for failure to supervise when the employee engages in independent criminal conduct which results in the plaintiff's injuries. Moreover, an employer's duty to supervise does not include a duty to uncover his employees' concealed, clandestine, personal activities. . . . It is unfortunate, to say the least, that the frequency with which these cases have surfaced suggests that the clergy at [the local church] were naive. There is, however, nothing to indicate that the archdiocese or [church] knew or should have known of what was taking place in [the priest's] private world."

• The Alabama Supreme Court ruled that a church was not legally responsible for the sexual molestation of a 10-year-old girl.[176] A 10-year-old girl lived near a church that operated a kindergarten at which her aunt was the head teacher. The girl's mother instructed her to walk to the church following school, and then have her aunt escort her home when she quit work at 5:30 p.m. One day, while waiting on the church property for her aunt, the girl was raped by an adolescent male. The girl was raped a second time by the same adolescent several days later. The girl did not disclose the rapes to anyone until, during a routine medical examination, the family physician found evidence of sexual relations. The girl at first denied that she had ever engaged in sexual relations, but later acknowledged that the adolescent male (who was known to her) had raped her on two occasions. The girl's mother later filed a lawsuit against the church, claiming that it had failed to use "due care" in watching and supervising the girl "thereby allowing" the rape to occur. A trial court ruled in favor of the church, and the mother appealed. The state supreme court agreed that the church could not be legally responsible for the girl's injuries. The court acknowledged that there may have been an oral agreement between the mother and the aunt to care for the girl after school. However, the court insisted that "there was no evidence that [the victim] was, in fact, under the care of the church." The court continued, "[T]he mere fact that an injury has occurred is not evidence of negligence and . . . in negligent supervision cases negligence will not be found by inference. Assuming, without deciding, that there was an agreement that [the victim] was to be supervised and cared for by the church, [the victim] failed to produce any evidence demonstrating that the church negligently supervised her on the days she says she was assaulted and raped. Thus, a finding that [the girl] was negligently supervised on the days in question could be had only

---

[175] Tichenor v. Roman Catholic Church, 32 F.3d 953 (5th Cir. 1994).

[176] N.J. v. Greater Emanuel Temple Holiness Church, 611 So.2d 1036 (Ala. 1992).

by inference [and] we may not draw that inference here." The court also emphasized that churches ordinarily cannot be found guilty of negligent supervision without some special relationship or special circumstances that were not present in this case: "[T]he general rule is that absent special relationships or circumstances, a person has no duty to protect another from criminal acts of a third person. . . . [A defendant cannot] be held liable for the criminal act of a third party unless the defendant knew or had reason to know that the criminal act was about to occur on the defendant's premises."

• A California court ruled that a Catholic church was not responsible on the basis of negligent supervision for a priest's acts of child molestation, since "nearly all" of the acts of molestation occurred when the priest "took the victim from her home to various public places and hotels."[177]

• A federal court in Connecticut dismissed a lawsuit brought against a church and diocese by two adults who had been sexually molested by a priest when they were minors.[178] The court ruled that the church and diocese were not responsible for the victims' injuries on the basis of respondeat superior or negligence. The court cautioned that churches and denominational agencies are potentially liable on the basis of negligence for injuries sustained by victims of sexual molestation if they have knowledge of prior sexual misconduct by the molester. However, since the victims could not prove that church officials either knew or should have known of any previous sexual misconduct by the offending priest, the negligence claims had to be dismissed. The court ruled that the First Amendment guaranty of religious freedom does not necessarily protect a church or denominational agency from liability in a lawsuit based on negligent hiring, retention, or supervision if the victim's claims do not implicate issues of ecclesiastical concern.

• A federal district court in Michigan ruled that a church school and various church agencies were not liable on the basis of negligent hiring, supervision, or retention, for the sexual molestation of a minor student by a priest.[179] The court found that there was no constitutional prohibition to the recognition of a negligent supervision claim against a church school or agency, since such claims "can be decided without determining questions of church law and policies." However, the court refused to find the school or church agencies liable on this basis since "only a few jurisdictions" recognize "negligent supervision" as a basis of liability, and no court in Wisconsin (where the molestation occurred) had ever recognized negligent supervision as a basis of liability. The court made the following additional observation: "The precise issue, as this court sees it . . . is not whether now—20 years after the occurrences upon which plaintiff's claims are predicated—the Wisconsin Supreme Court would adopt the tort of negligent supervision, but rather whether, had the claim been presented to the Wisconsin Court in 1974-78 [when the acts of molestation occurred] would the court have recognized it then? This is consistent with the generally accepted principle that a tort action is to be determined by application of the law which existed at the time of the occurrence of the events upon which the action is predicated. . . . This reflects this court's concern . . . that it would be unfair to juxtapose contemporary mores and contemporary causes of action upon parties

---

[177] Roman Catholic Bishop v. Superior Court, 50 Cal. Rptr.2d 399 (Cal. App. 1996).

[178] Nutt v. Norwich Roman Catholic Diocese, 921 F. Supp. 66 (D. Conn. 1995). *See also* Doe v. Norwich Roman Catholic Diocesan Corporation, 268 F.Supp.2d 139 (D. Conn. 2003).

[179] Isely v. Capuchin Province, 880 F. Supp. 1138 (E.D. Mich. 1995).

for events which occurred in a different era with a different level of social awareness of problems."

• The Minnesota Supreme Court ruled that a school was not liable on the basis of negligent supervision for the sexual seduction of a high school student by a female teacher.[180] The teacher used a counseling relationship with a male student as the basis for a sexual relationship that continued for several months. Most of the sexual encounters occurred during regular school hours on school premises. The victim later sued the school, claiming that it was responsible for his injuries on the basis of negligent supervision. In rejecting the victim's claim that the school was guilty of negligent supervision, the court observed: "[The school] performed standard teacher evaluations of [the teacher]. In addition to the evaluations [school officials] made several unannounced visits to [the teacher's] classrooms. Because the school had no public address system, all messages were hand-delivered by staff and students to classrooms throughout the course of the school day. Even with all of this interaction during the school day, the [secret] relationship between teacher and student was never observed. A school cannot be held liable for actions that are not foreseeable when reasonable measures of supervision are employed to insure adequate educational duties are being performed by the teachers, and there is adequate consideration being given for the safety and welfare of all students in the school. The safety and welfare of the students in a school setting is paramount. However, in this case, closer vigilance would not have uncovered the relationship because both participants worked hard to conceal it."

• A Minnesota appeals court ruled that a church and denominational organization were not legally responsible on the basis of negligent supervision for a pastor's acts of child molestation.[181] The molester was accused of sexually abusing numerous young boys during his tenure as senior pastor at a church. He admitted abusing some of the children, including a 10-year-old boy (the "victim"). The victim sued the pastor, his former church, and national and regional church bodies. The trial court concluded that the church had been negligent in supervising the pastor, but a state appeals court reversed this judgment. The court defined "negligent supervision" as "the failure of the employer to exercise ordinary care in supervising the employment relationship, so as to prevent the foreseeable misconduct of an employee from causing harm to other employees or third persons." The court added that negligent supervision "derives from the doctrine of respondeat superior" so the victim "must prove that the employee's actions occurred within the scope of employment in order to succeed on this claim." It is important to note that the court stressed the difficulty inherent in supervising clergy: "Even assuming that [the pastor's] abuse of [the victim] occurred within his scope of employment, there was insufficient evidence for the jury to conclude that [the church] failed to exercise ordinary care in supervising [him]. By the nature of the position, a clergyperson has considerable freedom in religious and administrative leadership in a church. The clergy also require privacy and confidentiality in order to protect the privacy of parishioners. There was no evidence that the supervision provided by [the church] differed from the supervision a reasonable church would provide. Nor was there any evidence of further reasonable supervision that could have prevented [the pastor]

---

[180] P.L. v. Aubert, 545 N.W.2d 666 (Minn. 1996).

[181] M.L. v. Magnuson, 531 N.W.2d 831 (Minn. App. 1995).

from abusing [the victim]. There was not enough evidence from which a reasonable jury could conclude that [the church] negligently supervised [the pastor]."

• The Missouri Supreme Court ruled that a diocese could not be liable for the sexual misconduct of a priest.[182] A Catholic priest served as associate pastor of a church. He invited a young boy and one of the boy's friends to spend the night and watch movies in the church parsonage. One of the boys later alleged that the priest sexually molested him. The parents sued the diocese, claiming that it was responsible for the priest's acts on the basis of several grounds, including negligent supervision. The parents asserted that after the priest was ordained the diocese had a duty to supervise his activities, which it failed to do. The parents claimed that the diocese "knew or reasonably should have known of prior sexual misconduct and a propensity to such conduct" by the priest. Once again, the court disagreed: "Adjudicating the reasonableness of a church's supervision of a cleric—what the church 'should know'—requires inquiry into religious doctrine. . . . [T]his would create an excessive entanglement, inhibit religion, and result in the endorsement of one model of supervision. Not recognizing the cause of negligent failure to supervise clergy is not an establishment of religion because it is a 'nondiscriminatory religious-practice exemption.'[183] It achieves 'a benevolent neutrality which will permit religious exercise to exist without sponsorship and without interference.'[184] Nonrecognition of this negligence tort preserves 'the autonomy and freedom of religious bodies while avoiding any semblance of established religion.'"

• A New York Court ruled that a church was not liable on the basis of negligent supervision for the sexual misconduct of an employee. It concluded: "As to theories concerning supervision or retention, we note the employee had worked as a coordinator at the church for at least five years prior to the alleged incident. During that period, the church did not receive any complaints about the employee, and did not know of anyone else who had received complaints about him. Plaintiff himself had never heard of any complaints, and the employee had never been convicted of any crime."[185]

• An Ohio court ruled that a church was not responsible for the rape of a six-year-old boy occurring on church property during Sunday school.[186] The boy attended a Sunday school class of about 45 first and second graders. One adult female teacher was present on the day of the rape along with two teenage volunteers (one male and one female). During "story time," the victim became disruptive, and the teacher allowed the male volunteer to "take him back and color" in an unused room. The adult teacher did not check on the boy for the remainder of the Sunday school session. The boy's mother alleged that the male volunteer took her son to an unused room, raped him, and threatened to kill him if he "told anyone." The boy and his mother later sued the church, claiming that the boy's injuries were a result of the church's "negligent supervision" of its agents. The court noted that "negligence does not consist of failing to take extraordinary measures which hindsight demonstrates would have been helpful." The court further observed that a church is "not an insurer of the safety" of

---

[182] Gibson v. Brewer, 952 S.W.2d 239 (Mo. 1997).

[183] Employment Division v. Smith, 494 U.S. 872, 879 (1990).

[184] Walz v. Tax Commission, 393 U.S. 664 (1970).

[185] Osvaldo D. v. Rector Church Wardens and Vestrymen of the Parish of Trinity Church of New York, 834 N.Y.S.2d 94 (N.Y.A.D. 2007).

[186] Bender v. First Church of the Nazarene 571 N.E.2d 475 (Ohio App. 1989).

persons on its premises, but rather has only a *"duty of ordinary care to avoid injury consistent with [existing] facts and circumstances."* The court emphasized that the victim and his mother *"have presented no evidence that [the church] knew, or in the exercise of reasonable diligence should have known of or anticipated a criminal sexual assault by [the alleged rapist] upon another."* The victim and his mother placed great significance upon evidence that *"a similar incident had occurred several years earlier."* In rejecting the relevance of this evidence the court observed simply that *"there is no evidence that the church or its agents knew, or in the exercise of diligence, should have known of such prior activity."*

• An Ohio court ruled that a hospital was not liable on the basis of negligent supervision for a chaplain's acts of child molestation.[187] A Catholic priest was assigned by his religious order to serve both as a hospital chaplain and as a campus minister. On several occasions he sexually molested a minor male. The court emphasized that the acts of molestation occurred in the chaplain's home and were unrelated to any hospital or campus activity. It concluded, *"[L]iability under a theory of negligent supervision is premised on the employment relationship. In the case at hand, the alleged attacks did not occur while [the chaplain] was working at the hospital or the college; the alleged assaults occurred in [his] private residence at night. The [victim] failed to come forward with any evidence that the hospital or college had any right or duty to supervise [the chaplain] outside the employment context. Although the employment relationship of a priest is not conducive to an 'office hours' definition, even if one accepts the broader definition of employment as a certain role or capacity, [the chaplain] was acting outside these as well at the time that the alleged assaults occurred. [The victim] was staying with [the chaplain] at the times of the alleged attacks because of the [victim's] family's friendship with their former parish priest. [The chaplain's] interaction with [the victim] was completely unrelated to [his] role as either hospital chaplain or campus minister. Thus, the [victim] failed to establish a duty on the part of the hospital or the college to supervise [the chaplain] at the time of the alleged assaults."*

• A Pennsylvania court ruled that a church and diocese could not be legally responsible for a priest's repeated acts of child molestation occurring off of church premises.[188] A Catholic priest repeatedly molested a number of boys. His pattern was to befriend young boys, lure them into a sense of trust, and then molest them. He often would take boys out to meals, do special favors for them, and take them shopping or on trips. One victim, who had been molested more than fifty times by the priest, sued the church and diocese on the basis of negligent supervision. The court ruled that the church and diocese could not be guilty of negligent supervision since all of the priest's acts of molestation occurred off of church premises. The court noted that the Restatement of Torts (an authoritative legal text) imposes liability for negligent supervision upon employers only for misconduct occurring on their premises. It pointed out that all of the priest's acts of molestation occurred in motel rooms while on trips, and not on church premises.

• A Tennessee court ruled that a church-operated preschool was not legally responsible for a sexual assault committed by a four-year-old boy on another 4-year-old boy, since

---

[187] Gebhart v. College of Mount St. Joseph, 665 N.E.2d 223 (Ohio App. 1995).

[188] Hutchinson v. Luddy, 683 A.2d 1254 (Pa. Super. 1996).

the assault was not foreseeable.[189] A four-year-old boy (the "victim") was enrolled in a church-operated preschool program. One day he asked for permission to use the restroom which was located 40 feet down the hall. The teacher informed the victim that he would have to wait until another four-year-old boy returned from the restroom. When the other boy returned to the classroom the teacher gave the victim permission to go to the restroom. While the victim was in the restroom, the boy who had just returned asked for permission to "get a drink." The teacher allowed him to do so, but cautioned him not to enter the restroom. The teacher stood in the doorway of the classroom so she could monitor the boy and the classroom at the same time. A few moments later the teacher had to leave the doorway to attend to a crying child. Upon returning to the doorway some two or three minutes later, she saw the victim and the other boy running together down the hallway toward the classroom. While the teacher was attending the crying child, the boy who had gone to get a drink entered the restroom and sexually assaulted the victim. Neither child was being supervised by an adult while absent from the classroom. The victim's parents sued the church, claiming that it was responsible for their son's injuries on the basis of negligent supervision. A trial court ruled in favor of the church, and the parents appealed. The school conceded that it had a duty to exercise reasonable care in the supervision of children under its control. However, it insisted that a sexual assault between two four-year-old boys was so unforeseeable that there was no duty to guard against it. The school's director testified that the school had never received a complaint or report about sexual assaults or misconduct among its preschoolers, and that it had never received a complaint concerning the behavior of the boy who committed the molestation. A state appeals court ruled that the school was not guilty of negligent supervision because the sexual assault was not reasonably foreseeable. The court noted that there can be liability for negligence unless a victim's injuries were a reasonably foreseeable result of the negligent behavior. This test was simply not met. The court observed, "[T]he acts alleged in the complaint are unforeseeable as a matter of law. The alleged acts would be considered vile and reprehensible between two adults, but between two four-year-old boys, the alleged acts are even more shocking and appalling. We do not believe that a reasonable person would ever foresee this type of behavior between boys of that age. The possibility of an accident of this general character could not have been foreseen by [the church or school]. [The school] presented affidavits showing that a sexual assault had never occurred in the school, and that the school had no reason to suspect this behavior from [the assailant]. Moreover, we should consider the fact that the teacher could not reasonably foresee that a child that had just used the restroom facilities would return to the restroom instead of the classroom after getting a drink of water in the school hall."

• A Texas court rejected a parent's claim that a church was responsible on the basis of negligent supervision for the molestation of her daughter by a youth pastor.[190] A mother enrolled her daughter in a private school operated by a local church. A few months later, the mother discovered three sexually explicit letters which she believed were correspondence between her daughter and the youth pastor (who also taught at the school). These letters, along with explicit entries in the daughter's diary, led the mother to believe that her daughter and the youth pastor were engaging in sexual activities. She took the evidence to the senior minister of the church, asking for his

---

[189] Roe v. Catholic Diocese of Memphis, 950 S.W.2d 27 (Tenn. App. 1996).

[190] Eckler v. The General Council of the Assemblies of God, 784 S.W.2d 935 (Tex. App. 1990).

assistance. Unsatisfied with the investigation, the mother sued the church and a national denominational agency. She claimed that the national church was responsible for the youth pastor's acts on the basis of negligent supervision. In rejecting this claim, the court noted that negligence requires proof that someone's conduct actually caused injuries to another, and it concluded that the national church's act of ordaining or licensing clergy in no way was the cause of the girl's injuries. Further, in rejecting the plaintiff's claim that the national church used "less than ordinary care" in discharging its "continuing duty" to monitor and supervise its clergy, the court observed that the national church "exercises no supervisory powers over the local ministers" and "is not responsible for the day-to-day oversight of the ministers." Since the national church had no duty to supervise clergy, "it is impossible that lack of supervision . . . was a substantial factor in causing plaintiff's injuries."

• *A Washington state court ruled that a church school was not legally responsible for damages resulting from an alleged sexual relationship between a teacher and student.[191] In rejecting the claim of the victim's parents that the school had been guilty of negligent supervision, the court agreed that "schools have a duty to supervise their students," and to take precautions to protect students from dangers that may reasonably be anticipated. However, "at some point the event is so distant in time and place that the responsibility for adequate supervision is with the parents rather than the school." Such was the case here, concluded the court, since the alleged misconduct occurred off school property during noninstructional hours.*

• *A federal district court in Wisconsin ruled that a church was not legally responsible for the molestation of a young boy by a teacher at the church's school.[192] A church hired a full-time teacher at its private school. While the teacher was employed by the school he removed a young boy (the victim) from class and disciplined him on at least ten occasions. On four of these occasions, the teacher engaged in sexual contact with the victim. At the time of these incidents, the school had a written policy that permitted corporal punishment of students to be inflicted only by a parent with a teacher present. The school also had an "unwritten policy" that allowed teachers to administer corporal punishment outside the presence of a student's parents if another adult were present and the parents were later notified. The victim alleged that the church was negligent in failing to properly supervise the teacher, and that this negligence contributed to his injuries. Specifically, the victim argued that the school should have limited the number of times the teacher could have disciplined students, since this would have minimized the risk of molestation. In other words, the victim insisted that a church school has a continuing duty to supervise teachers. The court disagreed that churches or schools have so pervasive a duty of supervision. It based this conclusion on the following considerations: (1) It noted that the right of teachers to discipline students is "unquestionably reasonable and done in nearly every educational setting." (2) It "is not unusual for some students to be reprimanded . . . numerous times over the course of a school year." (3) The administrator received no complaints regarding the improper removal of the victim or any other student from class. Accordingly "from the perspective of [church] officials [the teacher] was administering discipline in the same manner as other instructors. While [he] could have been abusing his trust during the process, there is absolutely no indication*

---

[191] Scott v. Blanchet High School, 747 P.2d 1124 (Wash. App. 1987).

[192] Kendrick v. East Delavan Baptist Church, 886 F. Supp. 1465 (E.D. Wis. 1995).

that [the administrator] or other school officials were notified or should have been aware that child abuse or any violation of the [church's] corporal punishment policies was occurring." The court concluded that "in order to pursue a claim of negligent supervision in this case, the [victim] must show that [church] officials had notice of [the teacher's] improper conduct with [the victim] or other students. What from the outside appeared to be a normal and common exercise of authority in this case may very well have been something quite different; [church] officials, however, had no reason to suspect [the teacher] of wrongdoing at any time prior to the [accusations made by the parents of the other boy]." However, the court ruled that the church was "placed on notice" of the teacher's potential wrongdoing when the parents of the other student communicated their accusations to school officials. The school had a duty to supervise the teacher's actions from this time forward, and as a result any molestation occurring during this period of time could be attributable to the church's negligent supervision. The court concluded, however, that the victim failed to prove that any of the incidents of molestation occurred after the school was made aware of the teacher's alleged violation of policy.

Risk Management
§ 10-09.3

Key point 10-09.3. *Churches can reduce the risk of liability based on negligent supervision for the sexual molestation of minors by adopting risk management policies and procedures.*

▶ *A number of courts, in addressing the question of whether clergy are employees or self-employed for federal income tax reporting purposes, have observed that churches generally exercise relatively little supervision or control over clergy.[193] Such cases can be used by churches in defending against negligent supervision claims involving clergy misconduct.*

Churches can reduce the risk of liability, based on negligent supervision, for the sexual molestation of minors by adopting risk management policies and procedures. Here is a listing of policies and procedures that some churches have adopted:

1. Two-Adult Policy
Consider adopting a "two-adult" policy. Such a policy simply says that no minor is ever allowed to be alone with an adult during any church activity. This rule reduces the risk of child molestation, and also reduces the risk of false accusations of molestation.

Examples

• *A church has a policy requiring two adults to work in the nursery. However, the policy does not prohibit children from being in the custody of less than two adults. On a Sunday morning during worship services, one adult temporarily leaves the nursery for ten minutes to speak with another church member. A few days later the parents of one*

---

[193] *See, e.g.,* Weber v. Commissioner, 60 F.3d 1104 (4th Cir. 1995).

of the infants in the nursery suspect that their child has been molested. Suspicion is focused on the church nursery. Since the two nursery workers cannot prove that they both were present with the child throughout the entire worship service, they cannot "prove their innocence." The worker who was present in the nursery while the other worker was temporarily absent is suspected of wrongdoing, even though she is completely innocent.

• A church sponsors a campout for young boys. Some of the boys are accompanied by their fathers, but several are not. One tent is occupied by an adult volunteer worker and one boy. This arrangement violates the two-adult rule.

• A youth pastor takes home a group of five teenagers following an activity at church. After taking four of the teenagers to their homes, he is left in his car with a 15-year-old female. This arrangement violates the two-adult rule.

2. No Early Releases of Minors

Only release minors from church activities to the parent or legal guardian who brought them, or to a third person that the parent or guardian has authorized in writing to receive custody of the child. Churches are legally responsible for the safety of a minor from the time they receive custody until the time they return custody of the minor to his or her parent or legal guardian. As a result, a church may be liable for injuries occurring to a child who is released prematurely.

3. Claim Check Procedure

Consider adopting a "claim-check" policy for children in the church nursery. As a parent drops a child off at the church nursery, pin a plastic number on the child's clothes and give the parent an identical number. Inform parents that only those persons presenting the corresponding number will be given custody of children. This policy is designed to prevent the kidnapping of children by noncustodial parents, or by child molesters. Numbers should be assigned on a random basis for each service. Unfortunately, in many churches the nursery is staffed by minors who are inclined to transfer custody to anyone who asks for a child. Sets of plastic numbers can be obtained from a variety of manufacturers. Ask a local restaurant that has a "coat check" booth. The concept is the same.

4. Greater Scrutiny if Knowledge of Prior Incidents

If an incident of child molestation occurs on church premises, or in the course of a church activity off of church premises, the church's duty of supervision increases. The church will be held to a higher standard of supervision because of such knowledge. It is important for church leaders to be aware of this, and to be diligent in implementing some or all of the risk management procedures mentioned in this section.

5. Video Technology

The installation of video cameras in strategic locations can serve as a powerful deterrent to child molesters, and can reduce a church's risk of negligent supervision. Consider the following uses:

• **Nursery areas.** Video cameras are helpful in a church's nurseries, since infants and very young children are present who are incapable of explaining symptoms of molestation. In such cases, innocent nursery workers may be suspected who lack the ability to conclusively prove their innocence. Video cameras can be helpful in documenting how symptoms of molestation may have occurred, and in proving the innocence or guilt of nursery workers.

Example. *Shortly after returning home from church on a Sunday morning, a father notices evidence that his infant daughter was molested. He becomes very angry and distraught, and immediately calls his pastor to report the incident. He even mentions a particular nursery worker as the likely offender. The pastor meets with the father at church later that afternoon. The church installed a video camera in the nursery a few years ago, and the pastor replays the tape that was made that morning. The tape reveals no acts of molestation. The father is satisfied that the molestation did not occur at church. He takes his daughter to a doctor the next day, and learns that the child was not molested. The "symptoms" of molestation in fact were caused by a skin disorder. The case is resolved to everyone's satisfaction, because of the video evidence. But consider what might have happened if the church did not have a video camera in the nursery. The father may have been convinced that his daughter was a victim of molestation, and an innocent nursery worker may have been wrongfully accused.*

• **Restrooms.** Church restrooms present a unique risk of molestation for both infants and older children. After all, they are frequented by children, they are easily accessible, and they often are in remote locations or are not adequately supervised. A video camera in a hallway outside a restroom that is frequented by minors can be a powerful deterrent to child molesters. It also will provide church leaders and local authorities with evidence in the event that a minor is molested in a church restroom.

6. An Adequate Number of Qualified Adults

Any activity involving minors should be staffed with an adequate number of qualified adults. This will help to demonstrate that the church exercised reasonable care in the supervision of minors, and reduce the risk of liability based on negligent supervision in the event that a minor is molested.

▶ *It is often helpful to contact other institutions for assistance with staffing ratios. For example, some churches base their adult to child ratio in the nursery to what the state requires of licensed day care facilities. You may also contact the Red Cross, Salvation Army, or similar organizations. The point is this: if you can demonstrate that you based your adult to child ratio on the established practices of other similar organizations in your community, then this will be a strong defense in the event you are accused of liability (for an injury to a child) on the basis of negligent supervision.*

7. Off-site activities

Be especially careful of off-site activities such as field trips and camping. These outings can be difficult to control. It is essential that an adequate number of adults are present. While on the trip, precautionary measures must be implemented to assure adequate supervision of the group. For example, some churches group children in pairs, always keep the entire group together, and have frequent "roll calls." Once again, you can call other community-based organizations for guidance.

8. Restrooms

As noted above, church restrooms present a unique risk of molestation. They are frequented by children, they are easily accessible, and they often are in remote locations that are not adequately supervised. Church leaders can take steps to reduce this risk. Consider the following:

- **Video technology.** Using video cameras outside of church restrooms is a powerful deterrent to molesters, and provides the church with helpful evidence in the event of an allegation of molestation. This precaution is described above.

- **Designated restrooms.** Restrict young children's restroom breaks to restrooms that have limited access to adults, if this is possible.

- **Two-adult rule.** Have two adults accompany children in groups to the restroom, whenever possible. Do not allow one adult to take one or more children to the restroom.

- **"Half doors."** Consider installation of "half doors" that will permit adults to have partial vision into restrooms used by young children.

- **Architecture.** Unauthorized access to nursery areas by outsiders should be discouraged or prevented by the physical layout. Many churches accomplish this with counters staffed by an adult worker or attendant.

- **State regulations.** State regulations that apply to licensed child care facilities ordinarily do not apply to church nurseries, but they will contain a wealth of information that may be useful in adopting policies to reduce the risk of molestation and other injuries. Further, compliance with selected regulations can be cited as evidence that your church should not be legally responsible on the basis of negligent supervision for such incidents.

- **Parental notification.** Churches should discourage parents from allowing their children to wander around unaccompanied on church property. This notification can take place in parents' meetings, in church bulletins or newsletters, or through direct appeals prior to or during worship services. Children who wander unaccompanied on church property often were sitting with a parent during a worship service and were permitted to leave (usually to go to the restroom). In other words, unaccompanied children wandering around on church premises often do so with their parents' permission. Parents should be encouraged to accompany their children to the restroom or any other destination, and not let them leave the service unattended.

• **Restricting access.** The risk of liability can be reduced by restricting access to unsupervised restrooms where molestation may occur. If possible, lock doors to cut off access to remote and unused areas of the church.

• **Ushers.** A church can exercise supervision over its restrooms by having ushers observe access to them during services. For example, if a young child leaves a service to use a restroom, ushers should be alert to others entering the restroom while the minor is present. If an older child or adult enters the same restroom while the unaccompanied minor is present, this is a potential risk that must be addressed. If the minor does not exit the restroom within a brief period of time, an usher may wish to enter the restroom until the minor leaves. Some churches have restrooms that can only accommodate one person, and that can be locked from the inside. Such facilities can reduce the risk of molestation so long as an usher ensures that a minor enters a vacant restroom alone, the door is locked behind him or her, and no one is permitted access to the room until the minor exits. By following such precautions, it soon will be apparent that the church is monitoring access to restrooms, and this will reduce the risk of molestation.

In addition, ushers should be instructed to be alert for minors leaving services or wandering around unaccompanied on church property. Ushers should be informed of the risks associated with such behavior, and should be prepared to confront the minor and direct him or her back to a parent or supervised children's activity.

9. Encouraging Parents to Accompany Their Children

Churches can reduce the risk of liability based on negligent supervision by encouraging parents of younger children to accompany their child to youth programs and activities.

10. Prevent Access to Remote Areas

Acts of child molestation on church premises often occur in remote, unsupervised rooms or areas. A church can reduce its risk of liability based on incidents of molestation occurring in such locations by restricting access to them. If possible, lock vacant rooms that are not being used, or exercise supervision over them. For example, the church could designate a board member or other responsible adult to roam throughout the church during worship services. Such a policy will deter potential molesters, and will help to demonstrate that the church is exercising reasonable care in the supervision of its premises.

11. Windows

Install windows in all doors to classrooms and other areas that are frequented by minors. This will reduce isolation and make it easier to supervise activities.

12. Supervision of Known Molesters

What should church leaders do when they learn that a known child molester is attending their church? This is a complex question. The presence of such a person on church premises creates a substantial risk to the church. If the person molests a child on church premises, or during an off-site church activity, the church will be faced with a very difficult case to defend. The church will need to demonstrate that it exercised a high degree of care and vigilance in the supervision of the individual. Here are some points that may help in making an informed decision:

1. According to the FBI profile on "preferential molesters," pedophiles who molest pre-adolescent children (generally, under the age of 13) should be considered "incurable" and highly promiscuous. The profile indicates that pedophiles often molest well over one hundred children over the course of their lives, and engage in predatory behavior. Such persons present churches, and young children in a congregation, with one of the highest known risks.

   In the case of a sex offender who committed one or more offenses many years ago, and who has had an impeccable reputation ever since, some church leaders are inclined to "err on the side of mercy" and allow the person to attend the church with little if any supervision. The same is true for offenses that church leaders deem "superficial." In either event, remember that if the person is a pedophile, the passage of time will have little relevance to his propensity to molest minors today.

2. Conduct a criminal records check. Church leaders must be fully informed regarding the person's criminal background. If the person has lived in one state for his entire adult life, then a state check may suffice. But, if he has lived in more than one state, then a national check or multiple state checks must be pursued.

3. If the individual is on probation, track down his probation officer and ask about the conditions that have been imposed on him. In some cases, such persons are not even allowed to attend church. If the probation officer says that the person is free to attend church, ask the officer if he or she would recommend that you allow him to attend your church, and if so, under what conditions. Obtain this information in writing, or, if that is not possible, make a detailed written account of what the officer tells you.

4. When a church allows a convicted child molester to resume normal activities within a church, this exposes the church and church board members to potentially astronomical legal liability. If the person should ever have sexual contact with a minor on church premises, or in the course of church activities, the church could face a staggering degree of liability at the hands of a jury that would be incredulous that such a person was allowed to return to the church. This would be especially true if the person was allowed to have any involvement with children in the church, but it could apply even if the person was not officially involved in children's programs. The bottom line is that the public will no longer tolerate such behavior. What's more, they are outraged by it, and they will express that outrage in the judgments (including punitive damages) they award.

5. A church would face possible punitive damages if a convicted child molester was allowed to resume normal activities within a church and then molested another child. Such damages are not covered by the church's insurance policy, and so the assets of the church (building, vehicles, general fund, etc.) would all be exposed.

6. Churches have three options in dealing with a registered sex offender.

First, they can do nothing. This option is common, but not advisable.

Second, a church can condition the sex offender's church attendance on signing a "conditional attendance agreement" that imposes the following conditions:

- The offender will not work with minors in any capacity in the church.

- The offender will not transport minors to or from church, or any church activity.

- The offender will not attend any youth or children's functions while on church property, except for those involving his or her own child or children, and only if in the presence of a chaperone.

- The offender will always be in the presence of a designated chaperone while on church property. This includes religious services, educational classes, activities, and restroom breaks. The chaperone will meet the offender at the entrance of the church, and accompany the offender on church premises until returned to his or her vehicle.

- A single violation of these conditions will result in an immediate termination of the offender's privilege to attend the church.

- The conditional attendance agreement option will not be available unless the church's insurer is informed and confirms that coverage will not be affected.

- The conditional attendance option will not be available unless the offender's probation officer (if any) approves it.

Key point. *A conditional attendance agreement reduces risk, but does not eliminate it.*

Third, a church can adopt a policy of total exclusion, meaning that the offender is not permitted to attend church services or activities. This option is advisable if for any reason the conditional attendance option is not feasible or enforceable, or if the offender's crimes are so serious that exclusion is the only appropriate option. This will be a judgment call made by the pastor and board.

The selection of one of these three options will depend on the circumstances of each case. It is advisable to have an attorney assist in choosing the most appropriate option.

7. Members of a church board can be personally liable if a jury concludes that they acted with gross negligence. It takes very little imagination to foresee a jury concluding that church board members who allow a convicted sex offender to have unrestricted access to church property have acted with gross negligence.

8. Churches that choose an option other than total exclusion should check with the church's insurance company to determine if this decision will affect coverage for future claims.

9. A question that often arises is whether church leaders should inform the congregation that a registered sex offender is attending services. This will not be an issue if a church elects the "exclusion" option, since the offender will not be allowed on church premises. If the chaperone or "conditional attendance" options are selected, or if a church chooses to impose no restrictions on such persons, then the issue of congregational notification should be considered. There are various approaches that a church can take, including the following:

   a. Have the membership (in an annual business meeting) approve a policy on handling registered sex offenders. The policy should describe the restrictions that will be imposed on such persons, and address the issue of disclosure to the congregation. The important point here is that the purpose of congregational notification is to increase scrutiny of sex offenders and thereby reduce the risk of sexual assaults on church property or during church activities. But, if the church membership approves the total exclusion option (mentioned above), then there would be no need for congregational notification. The same would be true for a chaperone policy in many cases. However, if the membership opts for the conditional attendance agreement, or prefers not to impose any restrictions on registered sex offenders, then the need for congregational notification is greatly increased.

   b. One psychiatrist who has worked extensively with pedophiles has recommended that a pedophile never be allowed to attend a church unless he first discloses his orientation (and criminal record, if applicable) to the entire church congregation. In so doing, he places everyone on notice of the potential risk, and ensures that he will be closely monitored.

10. Some church leaders believe that if they obtain a written opinion from a licensed psychotherapist that the individual does not pose a risk of sexually molesting minors (or adults) in the church, then the church can go ahead and allow the person to attend church without limitation other

than a ban on any youth or children's ministry. This approach should not be used without the approval of the church's attorney.

11. Draft a policy addressing the church's response to registered sex offenders attending the church, and have it adopted by the congregation during an annual or special business meeting. This would allow the membership to discuss this issue in a rational manner.

In making a final decision, there will always be those in church leadership who will urge mercy and restoration. That's fine. These are biblical principles. But the Bible also speaks to issues of accountability and protection of the innocent. Jesus' harshest words were directed at those who would "cause one of these little ones who believes in me to stumble." He also said that the "second great commandment" is to love one's neighbor as oneself. How can church leaders even begin to think they are taking this commandment seriously when they allow a convicted sex offender to have unrestricted access to the church?

13. Small Groups

The fact that a church promotes small group meetings exposes it to potential liability for injuries that occur to children who are being supervised. Those injuries may arise in a number of ways, and could include child molestation by a volunteer worker, parent, or an older child; personal injuries occurring during games, "horseplay," or fighting; choking; or poisoning. All of these risks can be greatly reduced if a church adopts certain safeguards, including the following:

- Use at least two volunteer workers to oversee the children. One worker is unacceptable. If only one worker shows up for a particular meeting, then a member of the small group will have to assist in the supervision of children, or the meeting must be canceled.

- Segregate the children into different groups based on age, if possible, with two volunteer workers in each group (risks increase dramatically if "power inequity" exists, such as older children being grouped together with preschoolers).

- Volunteer workers should be adults. The risk of injury and molestation increases moderately if one adult and one adolescent worker are used together; and the risk increases dramatically if only minors are used to supervise children. One obvious solution is to have parents themselves take turns serving as supervisors for the children.

- Volunteer workers must be screened (application, reference checks, criminal records check).

- If young children (preschoolers) are present, the area where they will be supervised should be thoroughly inspected prior to each meeting to remove any toxic or dangerous substances or devices.

- Individual members of the small group should make unannounced and periodic visits to the area where children are being supervised.

- Older children should be encouraged to report any inappropriate behavior that occurs during these meetings.

- Restroom breaks present a significant risk. Appropriate safeguards will depend on the layout of the home and the age of the children. Children must not be allowed to wander off to a restroom alone, or with one or more older children. The best practice would be to contact parents and have them escort their child to the restroom. Most other responses will create unacceptable risks. Some cases of child molestation occurring in private homes during small group meetings have involved children wandering off to unsupervised areas of the home.

There have been cases of children being sexually molested, or injured, during small group meetings in members' homes, so this is a risk that churches must take seriously. Safeguards must not be viewed as "nuisances" to be ignored, but rather as essential measures to ensure the safety and well-being of vulnerable children. If meaningful and effective precautions cannot be implemented, then the church has no alternative but to discontinue child care at these meetings.

14. Follow Policies

It is absolutely essential to familiarize youth workers with the church's policies and to be sure that these policies are followed. At a minimum, this should be part of an orientation process for all new workers (both paid and volunteer). Periodic training sessions are also desirable to reinforce nursery policies.

15. Review of Policies

It is a good practice to have your risk management procedures reviewed periodically by a local attorney and by your church insurance agent. Such a review will help to ensure that your policies are current and effective.

Negligent Supervision of Church Workers—Sexual Misconduct Cases Involving Adult Victims §10-10

Many of the cases in which churches have been sued for negligent supervision involve incidents of sexual contact with adults. The most common example includes sexual contact between a male pastor and a female counselee in the course of a counseling relationship. While the counselee may allege that the church was negligent in selecting or retaining the pastor, she also may assert that the church was negligent in supervising the pastor.

Court Decisions Recognizing
Negligent Supervision Claims §10-10.1

Key point 10-10.1. *Some courts have found churches liable on the basis of negligent supervision for a minister's acts of sexual misconduct involving adult church members on the ground that the church failed to exercise reasonable care in the supervision of the minister.*

This section reviews court decisions in which a church or other religious organization was found liable on the basis of negligent supervision for a minister's acts of sexual misconduct.

Case Studies

• *The Colorado Supreme Court found an Episcopal diocese and bishop legally responsible for a pastor's sexual misconduct with a female parishioner on the basis of a number of grounds, including negligent supervision.[194] The court observed, "An employer may therefore be subject to liability for negligent supervision if he knows or should have known that an employee's conduct would subject third parties to an unreasonable risk of harm. . . . Both the diocese and [the bishop] had previous exposure to the problem of sexual relationships developing between priests and parishioners because the problem had arisen seven times before. The psychological reports gave notice that further supervision may be required. The reports indicate problems of sexual identification ambiguity, depression and low self-esteem. [The pastor's] file also indicated he had problems with authority. [He] had an inability to respond to superior authority. A reasonable person would have inquired further into [his] known difficulty in dealing with superior authority, and would have assumed a greater degree of care in monitoring his conduct. In light of its knowledge, it was reasonable for the jury to determine the [bishop and diocese] should have been alert to the possibility of problems with [the pastor] and taken adequate steps to insure [he] was not in a position where he could abuse the trust he enjoys as a priest conducting counseling."*

• *An Illinois court ruled that a church could be sued by a woman who was sexually seduced by her pastor during marriage counseling.[195] The woman and her husband claimed that during the course of marital counseling the pastor initiated and continued a sexual relationship with the woman, thereby aggravating the problems in her marriage, alienating them from their church and church community, and causing them emotional and psychological damage. The couple sued the church for negligence. Specifically, they claimed that the church was negligent in failing to supervise the pastor despite the fact that it knew or should have known that his previous attractions to female congregation members created an unreasonable risk that his religious and marital counseling would be ineffective and potentially detrimental to those being counseled. The couple insisted that the church had a duty to all members of the*

---

[194] Moses v. Diocese of Colorado, 863 P.2d 310 (Colo. 1993).
[195] Bivin v. Wright, 656 N.E.2d 1121 (Ill. App. 1995).

congregation to use reasonable care in supervising its pastor with respect to providing religious and counseling services. The couple claimed that the pastor's actions had damaged them in a number of ways, including the wife's contraction of two venereal diseases, medical bills incurred in treating these venereal diseases, psychological damages, counseling expenses, and irreparable deterioration in their marriage. A trial court dismissed the lawsuit on the ground that it was barred by the First Amendment guaranty of religious freedom. The couple appealed. A state appeals court reversed the trial court's dismissal of the case and ordered the case to proceed to trial. The court acknowledged that "Illinois courts have generally refused to decide cases that require a judicial interpretation of religious doctrine or church law." However, "where doctrinal controversy is not involved in a church dispute, mandatory deference to religious authority is not required by the First Amendment, and the court may choose from a variety of approaches in resolving the dispute." It noted that the courts can resolve disputes over control of church property so long as they can do so on the basis of "neutral principles of law" requiring no examination of religious doctrine. The court applied the same "neutral principles of law" approach in this case involving alleged church liability for the sexual misconduct of its pastor. It observed, "Although the neutral principles of law approach is usually applied to disputes over church property, we cannot conclude from plaintiffs' complaint that the instant cause cannot be decided using neutral principles of negligence law, developed for use in all negligence disputes, without interpretation of religious doctrine or church law, just as would be a secular dispute in a negligence case. . . . We cannot conclude from plaintiffs' complaint that their cause of action against [the church] will infringe upon, or place a burden upon, the church's freedom to exercise its religion. Inquiring into whether the church was negligent in its failure to protect plaintiffs from the sexual misconduct of its minister may not call into question the church's religious beliefs or practices or subject them to analysis or scrutiny. As we have pointed out, the minister's sexual misconduct was not rooted in the church's religious beliefs and was outside the boundaries of the church's ecclesiastical beliefs and practices. Thus, resolving this dispute may not require any interpretation of church doctrine or any regulation of ecclesiastical activity."

• A New York court ruled that a woman stated a valid claim for negligent retention and supervision against a church based on the sexual misconduct of the pastor in the course of marriage counseling. The court noted that a church officer allegedly was informed that the pastor was having an affair with the woman, that the affair had lasted for more than two years, and that the church allowed the marital counseling to continue while at the same time urging the woman's husband not to file a grievance with a denominational agency that would have led to an investigation. According to the woman and her husband, the church knew, or should have known, of the pastor's propensity to engage in harmful conduct, but decided to look the other way.[196]

• A North Carolina court ruled that the First Amendment did not prevent it from resolving a sexual harassment lawsuit brought by three female church employees against their church and denominational agencies.[197] Three female church employees (the "plaintiffs") sued their church and various denominational agencies as a result of the sexual misconduct of a pastor. The lawsuit alleged that the pastor "committed

---

[196] *Vione v. Tewell, 820 N.Y.S.2d 682 (N.Y. Sup. 2006).*

[197] Smith v. Privette, 495 S.E.2d 395 (N.C. App. 1998).

inappropriate, unwelcome, offensive and nonconsensual acts of a sexual nature against the plaintiffs, variously hugging, kissing and touching them, and made inappropriate, unwelcome, offensive and nonconsensual statements of a sexually suggestive nature to them." The plaintiffs further alleged that the pastor's actions amounted to sexual harassment. The lawsuit further alleged that the local church and denominational agencies "knew or should have known" of the pastor's propensity for sexual harassment, but failed to take any actions to warn or protect the plaintiffs from his wrongful activity. A state appeals court noted that the key issue was whether the First Amendment prevents "the filing of a negligent retention and supervision claim against a religious organization, when that claim is based on the conduct of a cleric of that organization." The court noted that the local church and denominational agencies asserted that the civil courts were without jurisdiction to resolve plaintiffs' claims against them because the courts' resolution of these claims requires inquiry into religious doctrine. The court disagreed. It noted that the First Amendment "does not grant religious organizations absolute immunity from liability. For example, claims against religious organizations have long been recognized for premises liability, breach of a fiduciary duty, and negligent use of motor vehicles." The court concluded that if a resolution of the plaintiffs' legal claims did not require the interpretation of church doctrine, then "the First Amendment is not implicated and neutral principles of law are properly applied to adjudicate the claim."

• An Oregon court ruled that a woman who was sexually seduced by her minister in the course of a counseling relationship could sue her church on the basis of negligent supervision.[198] The woman alleged that the church "knew or should have known that [the minister] was not adequately trained as a counselor and that it knew or should have known that he had misused his position in the past to take advantage or parishioners and counseled persons . . . [and] failed to investigate claims of his sexual misconduct [or] warn parishioners of his misuse of his position . . . ." The court stressed that it was not finding the church responsible. Rather, it simply was rejecting the trial court's conclusion that the lawsuit failed to state facts for which the law provides a remedy.

• A federal court in Rhode Island ruled that the First Amendment did not prevent it from resolving a lawsuit brought by victims of clergy sexual misconduct against church officials.[199] Three adult males sued diocesan officials for injuries they allegedly sustained as minors when they were molested by two priests. The victims claimed that prior to the acts of molestation, the diocese knew that the priests were pedophiles and not only failed to take appropriate preventative action, but also actively concealed the priests' sexual misconduct. The diocese claimed that the First Amendment prevented the civil courts from resolving these claims. The court conceded that an internal church dispute cannot be resolved by a civil court if resolution of the dispute would require the court to interpret religious doctrine or ecclesiastical law. But the court rejected the proposition that a secular court lacks jurisdiction over a case simply because it "calls into question the conduct of someone who is a church official." The court rejected the diocese's argument that the First Amendment prevents the civil courts from imposing liability on religious organizations for failing to properly screen or supervise clergy: "[T] here is no indication that the reasonably prudent person standard established by tort

---

[198] Erickson v. Christenson, 781 P.2d 383 (Or. App. 1989).

[199] Smith v. O'Connell, 986 F. Supp. 73 (D.R.I. 1997).

law and the requirements of Roman Catholic doctrine are incompatible. The [diocese does] not claim that the Roman Catholic Church either condones or tolerates sexual abuse of children. On the contrary, they have made it clear that the Catholic Church considers such conduct to be opprobrious. . . . Briefly stated, there is no indication that, by taking the kind of preventative action required by tort law, the [diocese] would have violated any 'doctrine, practice or law' of the Roman Catholic Church. In the absence of such a conflict, subjecting the [diocese] to potential tort liability does not violate [its] right to the free exercise of religion."

• A Washington state court ruled that a Catholic Archdiocese was liable for the negligent supervision of a supervisor who sexually harassed a female employee.[200] A female housekeeper at a conference center owned by the archdiocese claimed that a maintenance director began sexually harassing her shortly after he began his job. The harassment consisted of numerous sexually explicit and offensive statements. The maintenance director eventually was fired. The female employee later sued the archdiocese, claiming that it was legally responsible for his acts on the basis of negligent supervision. A jury ruled in favor of the female employee, and this ruling was affirmed by a state appeals court.

Court Decisions Rejecting Negligent Supervision Claims § 10-10.2

Key point 10-10.2. *Many courts have ruled that the First Amendment prevents churches from being legally responsible on the basis of negligent supervision for the sexual misconduct of ministers.*

This section reviews court decisions in which a church or other religious organization was found not liable on the basis of negligent supervision for a minister's sexual contact with an adult. Many courts have concluded that the First Amendment's "nonestablishment of religion" and "free exercise of religion" clauses prevent the civil courts from resolving negligent supervision claims involving clergy misconduct. To illustrate, the United States Supreme Court observed in a landmark case more than a century ago: "It would therefore also be inappropriate and unconstitutional for this court to determine after the fact that the ecclesiastical authorities negligently supervised or retained the defendant Bishop. Any award of damages would have a chilling effect leading indirectly to state control over the future conduct of affairs of a religious denomination, a result violative of the text and history of the establishment clause."[201]

Some courts have noted the inherent difficulty of supervising ministers in the performance of their duties, and in particular their counseling activities. As one court observed:

---

[200] Wheeler v. Catholic Archdiocese of Seattle, 829 P.2d 196 (Wash. App. 1992).

[201] Watson v. Jones, 80 U.S. 679 (1871).

By the nature of the position, a clergyperson has considerable freedom in religious and administrative leadership in a church. The clergy also require privacy and confidentiality in order to protect the privacy of parishioners. There was no evidence that the supervision provided by [the church] differed from the supervision a reasonable church would provide. Nor was there any evidence of further reasonable supervision that could have prevented [the pastor] from abusing [the victim]. There was not enough evidence from which a reasonable jury could conclude that [the church] negligently supervised [the pastor].[202]

▶ *A number of courts, in addressing the question of whether clergy are employees or self-employed for federal income tax reporting purposes, have observed that churches generally exercise relatively little supervision or control over clergy.[203] Such cases can be used by churches in defending against negligent supervision claims involving clergy misconduct.*

Case Studies

• *A federal appeals court ruled that a religious order was not responsible for the alleged seduction of a female parishioner by a Catholic priest.[204] The woman sued the religious order claiming that it was responsible for her injuries on the basis of several grounds, including negligent supervision. The court concluded that the order was not responsible for the priest's misconduct on the basis of negligent supervision, since it had no duty to supervise him. While it was true that the order had received a complaint about the priest's behavior with another woman some eight years before, the priest performed his duties under the direction and control of the archbishop and was accountable to the archbishop. Accordingly, the order had no duty to supervise the priest's actions.*

• *The Colorado Supreme Court ruled that a diocese was not responsible for a priest's sexual contacts with a woman during counseling.[205] The woman sued the diocese on the basis of a number of grounds, including negligent supervision. Specifically, she alleged that the diocese had knowledge of previous indiscretions by the same priest, which had the effect of imposing upon the diocese a duty to supervise him. The court observed that a religious organization may be liable for negligent supervision if it has reason to know that a minister is likely to harm others. Liability results "because the employer antecedently had reason to believe that an undue risk of harm would exist because of the employment." The court concluded that "a person who knows or should have known that an employee's conduct would subject third parties to an unreasonable risk of harm may be directly liable to third parties for harm proximately caused by his conduct."*

• *A Florida court ruled that it was barred by the First Amendment from resolving a woman's lawsuit claiming that she had been the victim of a priest's sexual*

---

[202] M.L. v. Magnuson, 531 N.W.2d 831 (Minn. App. 1995).

[203] *See, e.g.,* Weber v. Commissioner, 60 F.3d 1104 (4th Cir. 1995).

[204] Doe v. Cunningham, 30 F.3d 879 (7th Cir. 1994).

[205] Destefano v. Grabian, 763 P.2d 275 (Colo. 1988).

misconduct.[206] A woman sought out a priest for marital counseling, and alleged that the priest engaged in sexual contact with her. The woman sued her church and diocese, claiming that they were aware of prior incidents involving sexual misconduct during counseling by the same priest. Despite this knowledge, nothing was done to address the problem. She claimed that the church and diocese engaged in negligent hiring, supervision, and retention of the priest. The church and diocese asked the court to dismiss the lawsuit against them on the ground that a resolution of the woman's claims would result in an "excessive entanglement" of the court with religious beliefs in violation of the First Amendment. The court agreed with the church and diocese, and dismissed the lawsuit against them. It noted that the First Amendment prohibits any governmental practice (including judicial resolution of internal church disputes) that would lead to an "excessive entanglement" between church and state. It continued, "Our examination of case law presenting both sides of this question leads us to conclude the reasoning of those courts holding the First Amendment bars a claim for negligent hiring, retention, and supervision is the more compelling. In a church defendant's determination to hire or retain a minister, or in its capacity as supervisor of that minister, a church defendant's conduct is guided by religious doctrine and/ or practice. Thus, a court's determination regarding whether the church defendant's conduct was 'reasonable' would necessarily entangle the court in issues of the church's religious law, practices, and policies. 'Hiring' in a traditional sense does not occur in some religions, where a person is ordained into a particular position in the church, and assigned to one parish or another. A court faced with the task of determining a claim of negligent hiring, retention, and supervision would measure the church defendants' conduct against that of a reasonable employer; a proscribed comparison."

• A Georgia court ruled that a church and denominational agency were not responsible on the basis of negligent supervision for an associate pastor's sexual relationship with a female member of his congregation. In rejecting the negligent supervision claim, the court pointed out that (1) the associate pastor had been formally evaluated by his senior pastor on an annual basis; (2) a parish committee evaluated him annually; and (3) he was required to complete a yearly self-evaluation which was submitted to the senior pastor who conducted a personal interview. According to the senior pastor, the associate pastor received "high marks" on objective and subjective criteria, and the evaluation process raised no "negative issues."[207]

• A Louisiana court ruled that an Episcopal diocese was not legally responsible for the suicide of a woman allegedly caused by a sexual relationship with an Episcopal priest.[208] The woman's husband claimed that the diocese was responsible for his wife's suicide on the basis of several grounds, including negligent supervision. In rejecting this basis of liability, the court observed, "[A]ny inquiry into the policies and practices of the church defendants in hiring or supervising their clergy raises . . . First Amendment problems of entanglement . . . which might involve the court in making sensitive judgments about the propriety of the church defendants' supervision in light of their religious beliefs. . . . The traditional denominations each have their own intricate principles of governance, as to which the state has no rights of visitation. Church governance is founded in scripture, modified by reformers over almost two millennia. As the Supreme Court stated

---

[206] Doe v. Evans, 718 So.2d 286 (Fla. App. 1998).

[207] Poole v. North Georgia Conference, 615 S.E.2d 604 (Ga. App. 2005).

[208] Roppolo v. Moore, 644 So.2d 206 (La. App. 1994).

long [ago]: 'It is not to be supposed that the judgment of the civil courts can be as competent in the ecclesiastical law and religious faith of all these bodies as the ablest men in each are in reference to their own. It would therefore be an appeal from the more learned tribunal in the law which should decide the case, to one which is less so.'"[209]

• *The Maine Supreme Court ruled that the First Amendment prevented a couple from suing their church as a result of a priest's sexual relationship with the wife.*[210] *The couple insisted that their claim for negligent supervision against the church could be resolved on the basis of neutral principles of law without violating the First Amendment. They claimed that a review of the church's knowledge of any risk presented by the priest and the reasonableness of its supervisory acts would involve "nothing beyond the application of secular legal standards to secular conduct." The court observed that it had never recognized "negligent supervision" as a basis for liability, and that even if it did, the First Amendment barred its application to the church in this case. The court observed, "The tort of negligent supervision is based upon the concept that principals have certain duties to supervise those under their control. When a civil court undertakes to compare the relationship between a religious institution and its clergy with the agency relationship of the business world, secular duties are necessarily introduced into the ecclesiastical relationship and the risk of constitutional violation is evident. The exploration of the ecclesiastical relationship is itself problematic. To determine the existence of an agency relationship based on actual authority, the trial court will most likely have to examine church doctrine governing the church's authority over [the offending priest]." The court acknowledged that a few courts in other states have allowed churches to be sued on the basis of the negligent supervision of clergy. It also noted that other courts have recognized negligent supervision claims against churches "when the plaintiff alleges that the defending church knew that the individual clergyman was potentially dangerous." The court rejected all of these cases. It observed, "[T]hese few courts have failed to maintain the appropriate degree of neutrality required by the United States and Maine Constitutions. . . . We conclude that, on the facts of this case, imposing a secular duty of supervision on the church and enforcing that duty through civil liability would restrict its freedom to interact with its clergy in the manner deemed proper by ecclesiastical authorities and would not serve a societal interest sufficient to overcome the religious freedoms inhibited."*

• *The Nebraska Supreme Court ruled that a Catholic Archdiocese was not legally responsible for damages suffered by a woman who engaged in sexual relations with a priest.*[211] *The woman began counseling with her priest concerning family matters. At the time she claimed to be "vulnerable" because of prior emotional problems. While she was in this vulnerable state and during the course of pastoral counseling, she alleged that the priest engaged in sexual contacts with her over the course of nine years. The woman later sued the priest and archdiocese on the basis of a number of grounds. Among other things, the woman claimed that the archdiocese had been negligent in failing to supervise the priest in his relations with female parishioners*

---

[209] Watson v. Jones, 80 U.S. 679 (1871).

[210] Swanson v. Roman Catholic Bishop, 692 A.2d 441 (Maine 1997). *See also* Napieralski v. Unity Church, 802 A.2d 391 (Me. 2002).

[211] Schieffer v. Catholic Archdiocese, 508 N.W.2d 907 (Neb. 1993).

when it knew, or should have known, that he had sexual affairs in the past. The court concluded that the woman had no legal claim against the priest, and as a result the claims against the archdiocese had to be dismissed. It observed simply that "[i]f there is no tort liability to the [woman] against [the priest] individually, it follows that the archdiocese cannot be held liable for his conduct."

• *A federal court in New York refused to find a pastor guilty of malpractice on the basis of his sexual seduction of a church member he had counseled for several years.[212] The woman sued the church and a denominational agency on the basis of several grounds, including negligent supervision. In rejecting this basis of liability, the court observed, "[A]ny inquiry into the policies and practices of the church defendants in hiring or supervising their clergy raises . . . First Amendment problems of entanglement . . . which might involve the court in making sensitive judgments about the propriety of the church defendants' supervision in light of their religious beliefs. Insofar as concerns retention or supervision, the pastor of a Presbyterian church is not analogous to a common law employee. He may not demit his charge nor be removed by the session, without the consent of the presbytery, functioning essentially as an ecclesiastical court. The traditional denominations each have their own intricate principles of governance, as to which the state has no rights of visitation. Church governance is founded in scripture, modified by reformers over almost two millennia. As the Supreme Court stated [long ago]: 'It is not to be supposed that the judges of the civil courts can be as competent in the ecclesiastical law and religious faith of all these bodies as the ablest men in each are in reference to their own. It would therefore be an appeal from the more learned tribunal in the law which should decide the case, to the one which is less so.'[213] It would therefore also be inappropriate and unconstitutional for this court to determine after the fact that the ecclesiastical authorities negligently supervised or retained the [pastor]. Any award of damages would have a chilling effect leading indirectly to state control over the future conduct of affairs of a religious denomination, a result violative of the text and history of the [First Amendment]."*

• *The Ohio Supreme Court ruled that a church was not liable on the basis of negligent supervision for a pastor's sexual contact with a woman during counseling.[214] The church had been sued by the former husband of the woman, who claimed that the pastor's conduct resulted in the breakdown of their marriage. The supreme court concluded that the First Amendment guaranty of religious freedom did not prevent churches from being sued on the basis of a minister's sexual misconduct since "we find it difficult to conceive of pastoral fornication with a parishioner or communicant as a legitimate religious belief or practice in any faith." The court concluded, however, that the minister could not be liable for any injury suffered by the former husband, since any liability based on "alienation of affections" had been abolished by the legislature several years before. The court concluded that the church could not be liable if the pastor was not: "[A]n underlying requirement in actions for negligent supervision and negligent training is that the employee is individually . . . guilty of a claimed wrong against the employer. Because no action can be maintained against [the minister] in the instant case, it is obvious that any imputed actions against the church are also untenable." The court emphasized that it found the alleged conduct on the*

---

[212] Schmidt v. Bishop, 779 F. Supp. 321 (S.D.N.Y. 1991).

[213] Watson v. Jones, 80 U.S. 679 (1872).

[214] Stock v. Pressnell, 527 N.E.2d 1235 (Ohio 1988).

part of the minister to be "reprehensible," but concluded that there was no basis for relief available to the husband.

• An Ohio court ruled that a church was not liable on the basis of negligent supervision for the sexual relations its pastor had with a woman in the course of a counseling relationship. The woman claimed that the church was aware of the pastor's behavior, but did nothing to intervene and stop it, and as a result was liable for her alleged injuries on the basis of negligent supervision. The court noted that "an underlying requirement in actions for negligent supervision and negligent training is that the employee is individually liable for a tort or guilty of a claimed wrong against a third person, who then seeks recovery against the employer. In this case, it is undisputed that the lone sexual encounter between [the pastor and the woman] was consensual. In that regard, it is a fundamental principle of the common law that volenti non fit injuria—to one who is willing, no wrong is done."[215]

• The Oklahoma Supreme Court ruled that a married couple could not sue their church and former pastor for damages they allegedly incurred as a result of an adulterous affair between the former pastor and the wife.[216] The couple claimed that the church was liable for the pastor's acts on the basis of several grounds, including negligent supervision. The court concluded that the church was not responsible for injuries resulting from the minister's conduct, since none of the couple's claims against the pastor were viable. It observed, "Neither the claims by the husband nor the wife against the minister are cognizable in Oklahoma. . . . Because their claims against the minister also serve as the basis for the claims against the church for its negligent hiring and supervision of the minister, that claim is also not cognizable."

• A Texas court ruled that a church and regional denominational agency were not liable for the sexual assault of a church secretary by a pastor because they had no knowledge of prior acts of sexual misconduct by the pastor. The court noted that "an employer has a duty to adequately hire, train, and supervise employees, and the negligent performance of those duties may impose liability on an employer if injuries result from the employer's failure to take reasonable precautions to protect others from the misconduct of its employees." However, the court stressed that "absent a showing of foreseeability, a defendant cannot be liable as a matter of law for negligent hiring, supervision, or retention." The church defendants established that they "could not have known of the sexual assault of [the victim] or any sexual misconduct" prior to the time of the assault. The victim failed to produce evidence of such knowledge, and since "there was no evidence that the church defendants failed to take reasonable precautions to protect her from the pastor's misconduct" the case had to be dismissed.[217]

• A Washington court ruled that it was barred by the First Amendment guaranty of religious freedom from resolving a woman's claim that her Buddhist temple was liable on the basis of negligent supervision for a religious leader's sexual assaults. The court noted that the temple congregation regarded their leader with reverence and devotion,

---

[215] DiPietro v. Lighthouse Ministries, 825 N.E.2d 630 (Ohio App. 2005) citing Prosser and Keeton, The Law of Torts (5th Ed.1984) 112, Section 18.

[216] Bladen v. First Presbyterian Church, 857 P.2d 789 (Okla. 1993).

[217] Doe v. South Central Spanish District of the Church of God, 2002 WL 31296620 (Tex. App. 2002).

and were constrained by Buddhist teachings to not criticize him. The court concluded that if it were "to review the conduct of the temple to determine whether it should have exercised more or better supervision of [of the leader] it would necessarily entangle itself in the religious precepts and beliefs [of the temple]. The truth of the above beliefs is not open to question by civil courts. Should the temple have been other than obedient to [its leader] under the circumstances of this case? Should the temple have seen faults in or criticized him? Should the temple have slandered him by calling into question the activities of which it had knowledge? We can see no way that a civil court could avoid interpreting the above religious doctrine in determining whether the temple was liable for negligent supervision and retention. In short, there are no neutral principles of law governing this case that would permit a civil court to resolve the question of liability against the temple."[218]

• *The Wisconsin Supreme Court ruled that a Catholic Diocese could not be sued as a result of an alleged sexual relationship that began when a woman initiated a counseling relationship with a priest who served as a hospital chaplain and counselor.[219] The chaplain met with and counseled with a woman (the "victim") with respect to medical and emotional problems she was experiencing after the death of her baby. After her release from the hospital, the victim continued to meet with the chaplain. They dined together, visited art museums, attended pro-life rallies, exchanged gifts, and discussed politics, personal problems, and life in general. The victim viewed the priest as her pastoral counselor during these meetings because he gave her advice to help her cope with stress and depression. On one occasion the priest invited the victim to his family's cabin, where they engaged sexual intercourse. Sexual relations continued for another year, until the victim informed a bishop of the affair. The victim later sued the chaplain and diocese. She claimed that the diocese was legally responsible for the chaplain's misconduct on the basis of negligent supervision. The victim conceded that the diocese was not aware of her affair with the chaplain until she disclosed it to the bishop. The court concluded that the First Amendment prohibited it from resolving the victim's negligent supervision claim: "The reconciliation and counseling of the errant clergy person involves more than a civil employer's reprimand of three day suspension without pay for misconduct. Mercy and forgiveness of sin may be concepts familiar to bankers, but they have no place in the discipline of bank tellers. For clergy, they are interwoven in the institution's norms and practices. Therefore, due to the strong belief in redemption, a bishop may determine that a wayward priest can be sufficiently reprimanded through counseling and prayer. If a court was asked to review such conduct to determine whether the bishop should have taken some other action, the court would directly entangle itself in the religious doctrines of faith, responsibility, and obedience. Likewise . . . negligent supervision claims would require a court to formulate a 'reasonable cleric' standard, which would vary depending on the cleric involved, i.e., reasonable Presbyterian pastor standard, reasonable Catholic archbishop standard, and so on. Such individualized standards would be required because . . . church doctrines and practices are intertwined with the supervision and discipline of clergy. . . . This further explains why this court has held that negligent supervision claims are prohibited by the First Amendment under most if not all circumstances."*

---

[218] S.H.C. v. Lu, 54 P.3d 174 (Wash. App. 2002).

[219] L.L.N. v. Clauder, 563 N.W.2d 434 (Wis. 1997).

Risk Management

Key point 10-10.3. *Churches can reduce the risk of liability based on negligent supervision for sexual misconduct involving adult victims by adopting risk management policies and procedures.*

This section has addressed church liability on the basis of negligent supervision for sexual misconduct by ministers and other church workers with adult victims. Churches can reduce the risk of liability, based on negligent supervision, by adopting some of the strategies described in section 10-09.3.

Key point. *Many cases of sexual misconduct with adult victims arise out of a counseling relationship. There are a number of steps that churches can take to reduce the risk of such behavior occurring in the course of a counseling relationship, and many of these are addressed later in this chapter.[220]*

▶ *A number of courts, in addressing the question of whether clergy are employees or self-employed for federal income tax reporting purposes, have observed that churches generally exercise relatively little supervision or control over clergy.[221] Such cases can be used by churches in defending against negligent supervision claims involving clergy misconduct.*

Negligent Supervision of Church Workers—Other Cases

Key point 10-11. *A church may be legally responsible on the basis of negligent supervision for injuries resulting from a failure to exercise adequate supervision of its programs and activities.*

Other circumstances in which courts have found churches guilty of negligent supervision include a youth activity in which a 9-year-old boy was killed when a utility pole crushed him;[222] a church picnic during which a 15-year-old boy was rendered a quadriplegic when he fell out of a tree;[223] a church picnic at which a child drowned;[224] allowing a dangerous condition to continue in a crowded church service, which resulted in injury to a member;[225] permitting a snowmobile party

---

[220] *See* § 10-12, *infra.*

[221] *See, e.g.,* Weber v. Commissioner, 60 F.3d 1104 (4th Cir. 1995).

[222] Glorioso v. YMCA of Jackson, 540 So.2d 638 (Miss. 1989).

[223] Logan v. Old Enterprise Farms, Ltd., 544 N.E.2d 998 (Ill. App. 1989).

[224] Herring v. R.L. Mathis Certified Dairy Co., 162 S.E.2d 863 (Ga. 1968), *aff'd in part and rev'd in part,* Bourn v. Herring, 166 S.E.2d 89 (Ga. 1969). *See also* L.M. Jeffords v. Atlanta Presbytery, Inc., 231 S.E.2d 355 (Ga. 1976); Brown v. Church of Holy Name of Jesus, 252 A.2d 176 (R.I. 1969).

[225] Bass v. Aetna Insurance Co., 370 So.2d 511 (La. 1979).

on farmland without making an adequate inspection for dangerous conditions;[226] and failing to adequately supervise the activities of a church-sponsored scout troop.[227]

Case Studies

• *An Arizona court ruled that a church was not responsible for injuries suffered by a 4-year-old child at the church's child care facility.*[228] *A 4-year-old child broke his leg while in a child care center operated by a church. The injury occurred when the child fell while running, although no employee of the child care center actually saw the boy fall. The boy's parents later sued the church, claiming that their son's injuries were a direct result of the church's negligence in failing to adequately supervise children. Specifically, they alleged that the church has a legal duty to watch and supervise children within its care, and that this duty was breached "as no one saw [the boy] as he fell." A trial court dismissed the lawsuit, and a state appeals court affirmed this decision. The appeals court relied on the following statement by the state supreme court in a previous case: "To hold that [a teacher] had to anticipate [a student's] act and somehow circumvent it is to say that it is the responsibility of a school teacher to anticipate the myriad of unexpected acts which occur daily in and about schools and school premises, the penalty for failure of which would be financial responsibility in negligence. We do not think that either the teacher or the district should be subject to such harassment nor is there an invocable legal doctrine or principle which can lead to such an absurd result."[229] The court noted, "While supervisors of a day nursery are charged with the highest degree of care toward the children placed in their custody, they are nevertheless not the absolute insurers of their safety and cannot be expected or required to prevent children from falling or striking each other during the course of normal childhood play." The court insisted that "a short absence from supervision of a child is not the proximate cause of the child's injury if the supervisor's presence and attention would not have prevented the injury." The court concluded, "[The boy] slipped out of view of the caregiver for a few seconds at most. No evidence has been presented that he would not have been injured had he been in the caregiver's sight." Accordingly, the parents "have failed to present any evidence to support an inference that the caregiver's supervision, whether negligent or not, proximately caused [the boy's] broken leg."*

• *A California court ruled that a church was not responsible on the basis of negligent supervision for injuries suffered by a volunteer worker who fell while on a ladder repainting the church. The victim alleged that the church was liable for his injuries on the basis of negligent supervision because it knew or should have known that the volunteers who held the ladder had poor judgment and would act with reckless disregard for his safety, and failed to sufficiently investigate the volunteers before assigning them to the work. The court rejected this basis of liability, noting that "holding a ladder is unskilled work" and that the victim produced no evidence showing*

---

[226] Sullivan v. Birmingham Fire Insurance Co., 185 So.2d 336 (La. 1966), *cert. denied*, 186 So.2d 632 (La. 1966).

[227] Kearney v. Roman Catholic Church, 295 N.Y.S.2d 186 (N.Y. 1968).

[228] Ward v. Mount Calvary Lutheran Church, 873 P.2d 688 (Ariz. App. 1994).

[229] Morris v. Ortiz, 437 P.2d 652 (1968).

that the volunteers "were somehow incapable of properly holding the ladder." Further, the victim admitted that the volunteers had held the ladder correctly for a significant length of time prior to the accident. The mere fact that the victim fell "is not sufficient to show that the volunteers let go of the ladder because they were somehow incapable of the job and the church should have known it."[230]

• *A Louisiana court ruled that a church was liable for injuries sustained by a youth group member who was struck by a vehicle while crossing a busy street.[231] A church's youth minister took a group of 37 teenagers and four adult chaperones to an out-of-town youth evangelism conference. Most attendees were high school age. After checking into their motel, the group went to a McDonald's restaurant, which was located on a heavily traveled four-lane road. By then it was getting dark, although the area was well lighted. The arrival of the youth group immediately crowded the McDonald's, filling all serving lines. Some of the boys noticed a small pizza parlor in a strip mall across the street with apparently no waiting. Several of the boys in the group decided they would prefer to eat pizza without the wait. Three of the boys asked the youth minister if they could leave, cross the street, and get pizza. The minister said "yes," and walked them to the street to make sure they crossed safely. He did not lead the boys to a nearby traffic light because he considered that more dangerous. Meanwhile, three younger boys decided they wanted pizza. They assumed it was okay for them to cross the street since they saw the other three older boys doing so. The younger boys exited the McDonald's and ran across the street, passing the first group in the middle of the street in an effort to be first in line for pizza. One of the boys was "buzzed" by a speeding minivan when he was in the middle of the street. One of the members of the youth group was a 12-year-old boy with cerebral palsy (the "victim"). When he saw the other boys going to get pizza, he decided he was too hungry to wait at McDonald's. He did not ask the youth minister or any of the chaperones for permission to leave; he just left the restaurant and started across the street, without stopping or looking. In the middle of the street, he saw headlights. He lifted his arm defensively and was knocked to the ground, sustaining serious injuries. The victim and his parents sued their church. They asserted that the accident had been caused by the negligent supervision of the event by the youth minister and church. Specifically, they claimed that the youth minister and the chaperones did not prevent the 12-year-old victim from leaving the group; they did not notice him going out the door, crossing the parking lot and proceeding across the street; and they did not escort the boys to the street to assure safe crossing or lead them to the traffic light where the crossing would be safer. They also claimed that the youth minister and the adult chaperones made no plans for the boys to return safely to McDonald's after they finished their pizza. In essence, they "abandoned" the boys across the street. The court ruled that the church was guilty of negligent supervision. It observed, "Temporary custodians of children, such as school personnel and day care workers, are charged with the highest degree of care towards the children left in their custody, but are not insurers of the children's safety; supervisors must follow a standard of care commensurate with the age of the children under the attendant circumstances. The duty does not require individual supervision of each child at all times and places. However, fairly close supervision is required when students take a walking trip across a major thoroughfare." The court noted simply that "it is negligent for the adult leader to abandon the children."*

---

[230] Amarra v. International Church of the Foursquare Gospel, 2003 WL 254023 (Cal. App. 2003).

[231] Bell v. USAA Casualty Insurance Company, 707 So.2d 102 (La. App. 1998).

• A Michigan court ruled that a church was liable on the basis of negligent supervision for injuries sustained by a small boy who slipped and fell off of a piece of exercise equipment on the church's property. The court observed: "A teacher owes a duty to exercise reasonable care over students in his or her charge. . . . The evidence showed that three teachers were on the playground. The victim wandered away from the group unnoticed by the assistant assigned to his class, climbed on the monkey bars, fell and was injured. There was no evidence that the other teachers were supervising him. Such evidence was sufficient to create a question as to the issue of negligent supervision. It is plausible that the victim would not have wandered off from the group or at least not gone on the monkey bars unsupervised had there been proper supervision."[232]

• A New York court ruled that a religious organization that owned a camp was not legally responsible for injuries sustained by a 12-year-old camper who fell while climbing a tower without permission. The court concluded that the camping organization provided the victim with proper supervision: "The standard of care for persons having children entrusted to their care in this summer camp setting is that of a reasonably prudent parent. In such a setting, constant supervision is neither feasible nor desirable because "one of the benefits of such an institution is to inculcate self-reliance in the campers which an overly protective supervision would destroy." Although [the camping organization] had supervisors at the campfire, [the victim] told them that she was leaving to look for sticks in the woods; she did not tell them that she was going to climb the tower. Nor is [the campground owner] liable for negligent supervision; it had no control over the day-to-day activities of the children attending the camp."[233]

• A New York court ruled that a church was not liable for injuries suffered by a child who fell from a piece of playground equipment on church property during an organized "after school" program. The court concluded that no reasonable person could conclude that the victim's injuries were due to the church's negligence: "The victim was not engaged in any rough or inappropriate play prior to the accident and the church was not on notice of any horseplay or defective condition so as to warrant closer supervision or intervention. Accordingly, the degree of supervision afforded by the church was reasonable and adequate under the circumstances, and the child's injury was not caused by a lack of supervision."[234]

• A New York court ruled that a volunteer who was injured while trimming a tree on church property could sue the church.[235] In response to requests by the pastor (both from the pulpit and in the church bulletin) for volunteers to trim trees on the church

---

[232] Daniels v. New St. Paul Tabernacle Church, 2003 WL 1984453 (Mich. App. 2003). One judge dissented from the court's ruling. Calling the case a "frivolous action," he observed: "Here, three adults were supervising fifteen children at the time of the accident. The ratio required by the state Department of Consumer and Industry Services is one caregiver present for every ten children. . . . The child's sudden and unexpected action of losing his grasp of the monkey bars was a true accident. The child fell off the playground equipment owned by the church. There's no allegation of any defect in the equipment. This is an accident. The incident did not occur as a result of any negligence of any individual." The dissenting judge also noted that the church was not guilty of negligence since "greater supervision would not have prevented the victim from losing his grasp of the monkey bars."

[233] Gustin v. Association of Camps Farthest Out, Inc., 2000 WL 1686 (N.Y.A.D. 1999).

[234] Berdecia v. City of New York, 735 N.Y.S.2d 554 (N.Y.A.D. 2001).

[235] Lichtenthal v. St. Mary's Church, 561 N.Y.S.2d 134 (N.Y. Sup. 1990).

property, some 75 men gathered on a Saturday morning. At one point, one of the men was on a ladder cutting off a 30-foot limb with a chain saw. When the limb was cut through, it whipped around and struck the ladder, knocking the man to the ground and injuring him seriously. He sued several of the other volunteers and the church, claiming that they had been negligent in failing to stabilize the limb adequately, in failing to warn him of the need for safety equipment, and in failing to provide him with adequate safety equipment and supervision. The court ruled that the injured volunteer could sue the church for his injuries. It concluded, "As a landowner, [the church] owed a duty of reasonable care under the circumstances to prevent foreseeable injury to [the victim]. . . . No safety devices were provided, nor was professional supervision provided. An accident of the kind herein could be found to be foreseeable under such circumstances." Under these facts, the court concluded that the victim had presented enough evidence as to the church's alleged negligence to submit the case to a jury.

• A North Carolina court refused to dismiss a church from a lawsuit brought by a 13-year-old girl who was locked in a walk-in freezer in the church kitchen.[236] An equipment company sold a walk-in freezer to a church. The freezer was "field assembled" by the seller on the church's premises, and it was tested to be sure that it operated properly. The inside of the freezer door contained a label stating, "You are not locked in! The manufacturer of this unit has equipped it with a . . . latch assembly. You cannot be locked in, even if the door closes behind you and the cylinder is locked. By pushing the inside release on the inside of this unit, you many operate the latch and open the door." One evening, some eight months later, a 13-year-old girl (the "victim") was working as a volunteer at the registration desk in the church's "family life center" (a gymnasium). While on duty, the victim went to the church's kitchen to get some ice for a soft drink. She was wearing shorts and a t-shirt, but no shoes. Once inside the kitchen, the victim heard a noise that she thought came from the freezer. She opened the freezer door and stepped inside. When she did, the freezer door closed behind her. She immediately pushed the red release button on the inside of the door, but the door would not open. She repeatedly attempted to open the door, but her efforts were unsuccessful. She began banging on the door with her hands and feet, pushing on the door with her shoulder, and screaming. After an hour of futile attempts to open the door or attract someone's attention, she became tired and sat down. She had lost all feeling in her feet which were completely white. Despite being tired, she continued to kick the door feebly. Later that evening, someone discovered the victim in the freezer. By that time, she had suffered severe frostbite to her feet and legs. Paramedics took her to a local hospital where she remained for nearly two months and where she had five operations. During the first operation, all ten of her toes were amputated. During later operations, she received several skin grafts. The victim and her mother filed a lawsuit against the manufacturer, seller, and church. Among other things, the lawsuit alleged that the church had been negligent in the supervision of the freezer. The court rejected the church's motion to be dismissed from the case.

• A Pennsylvania court ruled that a seminary was responsible for the drowning death of a 12-year-old boy.[237] The victim was swimming with a group of altar boys from a Catholic church at a seminary-owned pool. The victim's mother sued the seminary,

---

[236] Crews v. W. A. Brown & Son, Inc., 416 S.E.2d 924 (N.C. App. 1992).

[237] Rivera v. Philadelphia Theological Seminary, 580 A.2d 1341 (Pa. Super. 1990).

alleging that it had been negligent in allowing the boys to use the pool without a qualified lifeguard on duty. At the time of the drowning, the pool was under the supervision of a priest. The jury concluded that both the seminary and church were negligent, and it awarded more than $1 million in damages. A state appeals court affirmed this judgment. The court observed that "it is clear that [the evidence] was sufficient to support the jury's finding that the seminary had breached a duty owed to the minor decedent. The seminary, as owner of the pool, had a duty to exercise those precautions which a reasonably prudent owner would have taken to prevent injury to those persons whom it knew or should have known were using the pool. . . . A jury could have found, in view of the evidence, that the seminary knew or should have known that its pool was being used by children and that it failed to exercise reasonable care to prevent injury to them." The court further observed that "it was for the jury to determine whether the seminary had been negligent in failing to take reasonable precautions to prevent access to its pool when a competent lifeguard was not present and whether the seminary could reasonably rely upon [the priest] to supervise the activities of the boys while they were using the pool."

• A Texas court ruled that a church was not liable, on the basis of negligent supervision, for injuries suffered by a teenager who broke his neck during a youth activity. A church's youth pastor (Pastor Kevin) organized a back-to-school activity for the church's teenagers, which included a game of "capture the flag." During this game, played in a church member's hay pasture, a 15-year-old boy (the victim) broke his neck while trying to take the flag from two other teenage boys who were holding onto the flag and carrying it toward their team's base. The victim's parents sued the church, claiming that it had been negligent in supervising Pastor Kevin and that its negligence caused the injury. A state appeals court concluded that the church was not negligent. It referred to the senior pastor's testimony, in which he recounted how he had carefully checked the references for Pastor Kevin and the training he had received in preparation to be a church youth minister. Pastor Kevin had been instructed on providing recreational activities for teenagers during his seminary education. Part of this training focused on providing a safe environment for church youth activities. During the three years while Pastor Kevin was youth minister for the church, he continued his training to improve his performance as a youth minister. The senior pastor asserted that Pastor Kevin had done an outstanding job as youth minister for the church, and explained that he regularly supervised games and other recreational activities for the church's teenagers. Even the victim's parents conceded during their testimony that Pastor Kevin had been a good youth minister for the church. All of the other witnesses at trial testified to the good job that Pastor Kevin did in handling all of his responsibilities as a youth minister. No one offered an opposing view, or suggested that the church was negligent in its supervision of Pastor Kevin." The court concluded that there was no evidence suggesting that the church had negligently supervised Pastor Kevin, and therefore the lawsuit had to be dismissed.[238]

---

[238] Lynch v. Pruitt Baptist Church, 2005 WL 736998 (Tex. App. 2005).

Risk Management

§ 10-11.1

Key point 10-11.1. *Churches can reduce the risk of liability based on negligent supervision for injuries not involving sexual misconduct by adopting risk management policies and procedures.*

Churches can reduce the risk of liability based on negligent supervision for injuries not involving sexual misconduct by adopting risk management policies and procedures. Several risk management strategies addressed in section 10-09.3 are relevant in this context as well, and should be reviewed carefully. Here are some additional risk management strategies:

1. Adequate Number of Qualified Adults

Use an adequate number of adults to supervise all church activities, especially those involving minors. Also, be sure that the adult supervisors are adequately trained to respond to emergencies.

2. Checking the Policies of Other Charities

Check with the Red Cross, YMCA, Boy Scouts, and similar organizations to obtain guidelines on the number of adults to use, the training of adult workers (based on the type of activity involved), and other safety procedures. Reliance on such standards makes it much less likely that a church will be guilty of negligent supervision. Be sure that you document your research.

3. Swimming and Other Water Sports—Off of Church Premises

If your church sends minors on a trip that will involve swimming (or the possibility of swimming), there are a number of steps that you can take that will reduce the risk of drowning, and the church's risk of liability. They include the following:

> • Encourage parents to accompany their children. The court in this case concluded that the charity's duty of care was greater because the victim's mother was not present.

> • Have both parents sign a permission form that authorizes their child to participate in the event, and that discloses whether or not the child can swim. In some cases, it is not feasible or possible to have both parents sign (due to divorce, separation, or death). But church leaders should recognize that the best protection comes for having both parents sign.

> • If the parental permission form indicates that the child cannot swim, then church leaders must recognize that they are assuming a greater risk by allowing the child to participate. This risk can be avoided by not allowing the child to participate. As one court noted in a case involving the drowning of a 12-year-

old girl who could not swim, "the accident could have been prevented by not allowing her into the pool."[239] If parents consent to their child's participation despite his or her inability to swim, then under no circumstances should the child be allowed to attend the event without appropriate restrictions. The nature of these restrictions will depend on a number of factors, including the age of the child, the degree of supervision provided by adults, the availability of trained lifeguards, and the relative risk of the location. For example, lakes generally pose more danger than pools, because (1) the water is not clear, making it more difficult to monitor the activities of children or to quickly locate a missing child; (2) concealed hazards may exist below the surface; (3) emergency medical services often are more distant; and (4) the area is more likely to be unsupervised, with no lifeguards present. Selecting appropriate restrictions is often a very difficult task for the persons in charge of an event. One recommendation that may help is to ask other local charities (Red Cross, YMCA, Boy Scouts, Girl Scouts) what their policy would be under the same circumstances. Be sure to make a record of the person you spoke with, and the suggestion that this person made.

• Go to locations that have certified lifeguards on duty.

• Check with your church insurance agent for additional recommendations.

• Check with your denominational offices for additional recommendations.

4. Swimming and Other Water Sports—On Church Premises

Some churches have a swimming pool on their property, as do many denominational agencies and parachurch ministries. A pool creates a number of risks, including drowning, slips and falls, and spinal cord injuries as a result of diving accidents. These risks can be reduced in several ways. Churches have used some or all of the following procedures to reduce these risks:

• Most communities have enacted zoning regulations that govern the construction and maintenance of swimming pools. These regulations often address fencing, locks, signs, and depth markings. Be sure the pool complies with all zoning requirements since a failure to do so can result in automatic legal liability for a death or injury.

• Most communities have laws governing the operation of a pool as a place of public accommodation. Check with city health or safety officials, or with a city council member, for details. Again, be sure the pool is in full compliance, since a violation can lead to automatic liability. These requirements often address the number and training of life guards, maximum pool capacity, and hygienic measures. If there are no such laws in your community that apply to your pool, then consider adopting the rules that apply to other kinds of public swimming pools, if any. This will provide a defense to a charge of negligent supervision.

---

[239] Turner v. Parish of Jefferson, 721 So.2d 64 (La. App. 1998).

If your community has no laws governing public swimming pools, then contact other local charities with pools (such as the YMCA) and consider following their rules.

• Place a water alarm in the pool when it is not in use. Such an alarm is triggered by splashing, and it can alert adults to the unauthorized presence of a child in the pool.

• Place a video camera in the pool area so that the pool can be monitored for unauthorized access when not in use.

• Use certified lifeguards. Local laws may specify the minimum number, based on the number of persons present. If not, check with the YMCA for recommendations.

• Do not install a diving board. Many swimming pool accidents are associated with the use of diving boards.

• Be sure the water is clean and of excellent visibility at all times.

• Install a safety rope separating the shallow from the deep end of the pool.

• Check with your church insurance agent for additional recommendations.

5. Avoid Hazardous Activities

Avoid high-risk activities. Some activities, such as rope-repelling, explosives, and the use of firearms, are so hazardous that a church may be deemed "strictly liable" if an accident occurs, no matter how much care was exercised in supervising the event.

6. Hayrides

Hayrides are inherently risky activities that have resulted in injuries and deaths to many persons. Many courts have found the sponsors of these events, including churches, liable for any deaths or injuries that may occur, usually on the basis of negligent selection of the driver of the truck or tractor that pulls the wagon, or negligent supervision of the event itself. Churches should not authorize or schedule such events (for minors or adults) without stringent safeguards to protect against injury and death. Here are 15 precautions to consider:

1. If minors are among the passengers, be sure that an adequate number of adult supervisors are present. Appropriate background checks should be performed on each one. Remember, hayrides sometimes occur partly or entirely at night, when darkness may conceal the conduct of child molesters on board a hay wagon. A similar risk occurs whenever movies are shown at church events with the lights dimmed or turned off. Check with other local charities, and the public school district, for their input regarding the appropriate number of adult supervisors when minors are present on hayrides.

2. Ideally, hayrides should be conducted during daylight so that hazards can be perceived and avoided both on and off the wagon. These may include bumps and holes in the road ahead, a lose hitch, or children dangling their legs over the side of the wagon.

3. No smoking, candles, lanterns, or other sources of flame should be allowed on hay wagons.

4. The wagon should never go faster than an adult can walk.

5. The wagon should be thoroughly inspected prior to use. Be alert to safety defects involving the hitch and wheels. If inherently dangerous conditions exist, the trip should be cancelled.

6. Check with other local charities that conduct hayrides, and see what risk management precautions they employ. The practices of other charities will constitute the standard of care by which your church will be judged. So, by aligning your practices to those of other charities, including the public schools, you will be managing risk.

7. If only adults are participating on a hayride, consider having them sign assumption of risk forms. Such forms are not a substitute for appropriate risk management.

8. Passengers should remain seated at all times while the hay wagon is moving. Adult supervisors must ensure that this policy is strictly followed, for both minors and adult passengers.

9. If minors are among the passengers, be sure that their parents have signed a form that (i) consents to their child's participation on the hayride; (ii) provides their contact information; (iii) designates one or more persons to make emergency medical decisions on behalf of their child if for any reason they cannot be reached; and (iv) lists any medical conditions or allergies that may be relevant in the event of a medical emergency.

10. If the wagon will be pulled by a truck or tractor, it is imperative for the church to exercise reasonable care in the selection of this person. Find out who the driver will be, and check the person's qualifications well before your hayride. Use an experienced driver who is familiar with the road. Find out how many times the driver has participated in hayrides; obtain references; check the person's driving record; find out how many accidents, if any, the person has been involved in while participating in hayrides. Do not use persons whose background suggests that they may pose a risk of harm to participants.

11. Never hitch more than one wagon to the tractor or truck.

12. Stay off pubic roads. This is especially true of roads with heavy traffic traveling at high rates of speed.

13. Ask local law enforcement for their recommendations on a road to use. In some cases, your local law enforcement agencies may offer to escort the hayride. At a minimum, they may offer safety recommendations.

14. Have adults drive a vehicle in front of and behind the wagon.

15. Do not let minors ride on a tractor, or in the back of a truck, that is pulling the wagon.

Counseling—In General

§ 10-12

Key point 10-12. *Churches face a number of legal risks when they offer counseling services by ministers or laypersons. These include negligent selection, retention, or supervision of a counselor who engages in sexual misconduct or negligent counseling. A church also may be vicariously liable for a counselor's failure to report child abuse, breach of confidentiality, and breach of a fiduciary relationship.*

Most churches offer some form of counseling services. The most common example would be counseling of church members by a minister. Many churches also offer lay counseling services. Some limit these services to members of the congregation, while others target the general public and promote their counseling ministry in the local media and telephone directory. Some churches use counselors or psychologists who are licensed by the state, while others use unlicensed laypersons with little if any professional training. Counseling ministries can provide an excellent and needed service, and represent a "point of contact" with the community. However, there are a number of important legal concerns that should be considered by any church that offers such services, or that is considering doing so in the future. The more important concerns are summarized in this section.

1. Pastoral Counselors

The legal risks associated with pastoral counseling include malpractice and sexual misconduct. Both risks have been addressed in other sections of this text.[240] Section 10-12.1 reviews several risk management strategies that are designed to reduce the risk of church liability for the acts of pastoral and lay counselors.

2. Lay Counselors

There are several legal concerns for church leaders to consider before offering lay counseling services. The more important concerns are addressed below.

(1) negligent counseling

"Negligent counseling" is a legal risk associated with lay counseling programs. It can arise in a number of ways. Some persons may claim that their emotional problems were aggravated rather than helped by lay counseling. Others may

---

[240] *See* §§ 4-05, 4-11, 10-05, and 10-10.

claim that lay counselors have a legal duty to refer suicidal persons to medical professionals having the authority to involuntarily commit such persons, and that they are responsible for the suicide of a counselee who is not referred.

In 1988, the California Supreme Court ruled that "nontherapist clergy" do not have a duty to refer suicidal persons to medical professionals.[241] However, the court emphasized that its ruling applied only to clergy who are not therapists. This ruling has been followed by courts in many other states. The key point is this: there is no assurance that lay counselors working on behalf of a church share the virtual immunity from liability enjoyed by nontherapist clergy counselors. This is so whether or not the lay counselors are licensed counselors or psychologists under state law.

(2) child abuse reporting

Counselors often receive allegations of child abuse from counselees. It is imperative for church leaders to be familiar with their state's child abuse reporting statute and ensure that all counselors are aware of their reporting obligations, if any, under state law. Keep in mind that these statutes are amended frequently, so updated copies should be obtained at least annually. Lay counselors are mandatory child abuse reporters in most states.

Several states have enacted laws authorizing victims of child abuse to sue mandatory reporters who were aware of the abuse but who chose not to report it. For example, a minor who is being abused by a step-parent learns that a church counselor was aware of the abuse but did not report it. The minor may sue the counselor (and the church) arguing that the failure to report the abuse aggravated the injury. The statute of limitations on such claims does not even begin to run until the minor reaches the age of majority, meaning that contingent liability for such claims can persist for many years. Further, many states have enacted laws suspending the statute of limitations until an adult survivor of child abuse "discovers" that he or she was injured by the abuse. This can extend the statute of limitations for a significant amount of time.

It is essential that any church counselor be apprised of his or her legal obligations under state law with respect to this important issue.[242]

(3) seduction of counselees

There have been a number of lawsuits over the past few years brought by women who were seduced or sexually assaulted by male clergy and mental health professionals. Often the misconduct occurred or started in the course of counseling sessions. As much as we would like to deny it, private counseling sessions involving dependent or emotionally vulnerable persons can present unique and sometimes formidable temptations. If inappropriate sexual contacts are initiated, there can be substantial damage to the victim and the victim's family. But this is not all. The costs of such behavior often devastate the counselor as well, and lead to criminal charges, loss of professional credentials, future unemployability, and

---

[241] Nally v. Grace Community Church, 253 Cal. Rptr. 97 (1988).

[242] See generally § 4-08, supra.

unavailability of any insurance coverage for either a legal defense or payment of damages. Clearly, steps must be taken to reduce or eliminate this risk.

But there is another risk associated with counseling—the risk of false accusations of inappropriate behavior. Unfortunately, in some cases false accusations are brought against counselors by persons seeking a legal settlement or pursuing some other ulterior motive. It is imperative for counselors to recognize that a false accusation can be as devastating as a true one.

Because of the unique temptations that counseling can present, and the possibility of false accusations, "defensive measures" should be taken by pastors and others who engage in counseling. There are two highly effective ways to deal with these risks. Some of these are addressed in section 10-12.1.

(4) confidentiality

Another very important consideration in church counseling is the concept of confidentiality. Counselors (and the church) can be sued if they intentionally or inadvertently disclose confidential information to third parties. Obviously, this can occur in several ways—for example, the counselor directly communicates the information, or the counselor's counseling notes are accessible to church staff. Counselors need to be strictly admonished to maintain the confidences shared with them. The one exception relates to child abuse reporting. A legal duty to report known or reasonably suspected cases of child abuse generally overrides the duty to maintain confidences (at least for persons who are required to report under state law).

(5) negligent hiring

The church should carefully screen any candidate for a lay counseling position to ensure, as much as possible, the suitability of the person for a counseling ministry. The screening process should include contacts with former churches with which the member has been affiliated or in which the counselor has worked in a counseling capacity, an appropriate screening form, and communication with a number of references. Of course, all of these contacts must be noted in writing and placed in a confidential file. In some cases, a criminal records check should be considered—for example, if an individual being considered for a counseling position has "no background," or there are unsubstantiated allegations involving prior misconduct. The important consideration is this: the church can be sued for injuries inflicted by a lay counselee if the church either knew or should have known of a dangerous propensity of the counselor.

Churches have been sued by victims of clergy sexual misconduct on the ground that they failed to do an adequate job of screening the minister at the time he or she was hired. Churches wanting to lower this risk will develop screening procedures for clergy applicants.

(6) negligent supervision

The church should consider adopting mechanisms to ensure that unlicensed lay counselors are supervised by appropriately trained and licensed mental health professionals.

The church should also develop a counseling policy setting forth standards on such issues as suicidal counselees, counselees threatening harm to others, counselees who confess to criminal activities, and counselees who are child abusers. Unlicensed lay counselors should understand clearly their responsibilities with regard to these kinds of crises. In most cases they should be advised to refer crisis cases immediately to a designated licensed mental health professional. Of course, this does not mean that the church counselor must sever all ties with the individual. Quite to the contrary, the spiritual counseling offered by the church counselor may continue simultaneously with the counseling provided by the licensed professional.

It is also important for the counseling policy to prohibit lay counselors from engaging in controversial therapies such as "repressed memories" and diagnosis and treatment of multiple personality disorders.

(7) fees

Some churches charge a prescribed fee for counseling services. Are such fees deductible as charitable contributions to the church? The answer is no. The Supreme Court has ruled that prescribed payments for prescribed services are never deductible as charitable contributions.[243] If the counseling is provided free of charge as a ministry of the church, voluntary payments made by counselees to the church probably could be deducted as charitable contributions. However, if the church establishes or even "recommends" a prescribed fee, the IRS would not recognize such payments as tax deductible. To be deductible, the payments must in fact be voluntary, the counseling services must be available to all without a fixed or suggested charge, and those unable to pay must receive the same consideration as those who are able to pay for the counseling services.

Key point. These are some of the legal considerations that should be addressed before any counseling program is initiated. If conducted on a professional basis, with due regard to the legal environment in which we live, counseling ministries can serve a significant nurturing function.

Risk Management § 10-12.1

Key point 10-12.1. Churches can reduce the risk of liability associated with pastoral or lay counseling by adopting risk management policies and procedures.

Churches can implement a number of risk management strategies to reduce the risk of liability associated with pastoral or lay counseling. These include the following:

1. Reducing the Risk of Sexual Misconduct and False Accusations

Churches have adopted a number of precautions to reduce the risk of sexual

---

[243] Hernandez v. Commissioner, 109 S. Ct. 2136 (1989).

misconduct by pastoral and lay counselors. These precautions also reduce the risk associated with false accusations. Consider the following:

(1) the "third person" rule

One effective way to deal with these risks is to adopt a policy prohibiting any male minister or counselor on staff from counseling privately with an unaccompanied female (*i.e.,* opposite sex counseling) unless a third person is present. The third person may be the minister's or counselor's spouse, another minister on staff, or a mature and trusted church employee (preferably female).

Key point. *Does the presence of a third person negate the "clergy-penitent" privilege for clergy counselors, meaning that either the pastor or counselee can be compelled to answer questions in a court of law regarding the communications? Not necessarily. In some states, the privilege applies so long as no one other than persons "in furtherance of the communication" are present. It is possible that a court would conclude that a third person who is present during a pastoral counseling session as a matter of church policy is present "in furtherance of the communication." As a result, the privilege may be preserved. Further, some courts have ruled that the clergy-penitent privilege is not negated by the presence of a guard during pastoral counseling with prison inmates if the guard's presence is required by law or prison policy. A court may reach the same conclusion in the context of a church policy mandating the presence of a third person during "opposite sex" pastoral counseling sessions.*

Key point. *Even if the privilege is negated by the presence of a third person, this risk must be weighed against the reduced risk that will occur.*

Key point. *Some churches that have a ministry to the deaf use a deaf member to serve as the third person. Such a person is ideal, for he or she can observe the entire session but does not apprehend what is said.*

Key point. *There have been no reported cases involving a claim of sexual seduction of a male counselee by a female counselor. As a result, churches using female counselors are reducing their risks significantly. Of course, there remains the possibility of a male counselee making unfounded accusations against a female counselor, and as a result churches using female counselees may want to consider adopting the same precautions that apply to male counselors.*

(2) women counsel women

Since the vast majority of cases of inappropriate sexual behavior involve male counselors and female counselees, churches can significantly reduce their risk by using women to counsel women.

(3) other measures

Churches have implemented a number of other measures to reduce the risk of sexual misconduct, or false claims of sexual misconduct, during pastoral or lay counseling sessions. These include one or more of the following:

- **Windows.** Installing a window in the pastor's office making all counseling sessions clearly visible to office staff. Of course, such a precaution is effective only if other staff are present and visible throughout the counseling session. This means that the church should implement a policy limiting counseling sessions to office hours when other staff are present and visible.

• **Open doors.** Some counselors conduct counseling sessions in a room with an open door, so that office staff can clearly see the counselor or counselee. Of course, such a precaution is effective only if other staff are present and visible throughout the counseling session. This means that the church should implement a policy limiting counseling sessions to office hours when other staff are present and visible.

• **Telephone counseling.** Many smaller churches have no "staff" that is present and visible in the church office during counseling sessions. Some of these churches limit opposite sex counseling sessions to those involving a third person or those that are conducted by telephone.

• **Video cameras.** Some churches have installed a video camera (without audio) in the office where counseling occurs. The video can be transmitted to a monitor in another location in the church where it is observed by a church employee. Or, the camera can simply record the entire session. If sessions are recorded, tapes should be retained indefinitely, or until they are reviewed by two designated church members who prepare a written summary stating whether or not they observed any inappropriate acts. This review can be performed in "fast forward" mode, and should not take long.

• **Boundaries.** Many courts have recognized the psychological principle of "transference." To illustrate, one court defined transference as "a phenomenon that occurs that is similar to a state of dependency in which the client begins to project the roles and relationships and the images and experiences that they have had with other people previously in their life, especially other significant people such as mother, father, brothers, sisters, early teachers and adult models, upon the therapist."[244] Another court defined transference as "a process whereby a patient undergoing psychotherapy for a mental or emotional disturbance (particularly a female patient being treated by a male psychotherapist) develops such overwhelming feelings of warmth, trust, and dependency towards the therapist that she is deprived of the will to resist any sexual overtures he might make."[245] Similarly, another court observed, "Transference is the term used by psychiatrists and psychologists to denote a patient's emotional reaction to a therapist and is generally applied to the projection of feelings, thoughts and wishes onto the analyst, who has come to represent some person from the patient's past . . . . Transference is crucial to the therapeutic process because the patient unconsciously attributes to the psychiatrist or analyst those feelings which he may have repressed towards his own parents.... [I]t is through the creation, experiencing and resolution of these

[244] Doe v. Samaritan Counseling Center, 791 P.2d 344 (Alaska 1990).

[245] Alpharetta First United Methodist Church v. Stewart, 473 S.E.2d 532 (Ga. App. 1996).

feelings that [the patient] becomes well. . . . Understanding of transference forms a basic part of the psychoanalytic technique."[246]

Pastoral and lay counselors often are tempted to engage in inappropriate sexual contact with a counselee because of unfamiliarity with this phenomenon. They misinterpret transference as affection, and fail to engage in anti-transference precautions that reduce the risk of inappropriate physical or emotional bonding. These precautions can include one or more of the following: (1) require a third person to be present for any counseling occurring off of church premises; (2) allow one-on-one counseling on church premises only during office hours if other staff members are present and visible; (3) limit counseling sessions to 45 minutes; and (4) permit no more than five counseling sessions with the same person during a calendar year.

Key point. *Churches that adopt any of these other measures must recognize that they are not reducing risk as much as if they applied the "third person rule" or required women to counsel women. It is imperative that churches adopting these lesser measures incorporate them into official church policy and strictly monitor them to prevent any deviations. Remember, windows or open doors are of no value if a counseling session extends beyond normal office hours and the church staff leaves.*

2. Other Risks

Another significant risk of lay counseling, when unlicensed counselors are used, is negligence in selecting and using a counselor with little if any formal training. Churches can reduce this risk by adopting a number of risk management strategies. Consider the following:

(1) counseling policy

Churches that use unlicensed lay counselors should prepare a suitable brochure or statement clearly communicating to each counselee that the church considers counseling to be an essential aspect of its ministry, and that it is important for persons seeking counseling to recognize certain legal considerations that apply in the context of counseling. These may include many considerations, including the fact that the counselee understands and agrees that counseling is provided on the basis of the following conditions:

- The counselors are engaged solely in spiritual counseling based on their understanding of the Bible, and they are not engaged in the practice of psychology, professional counseling, or psychotherapy.

- State law may require a counselor to report allegations of child abuse to civil authorities.

- Statements made in confidence to a pastor in the course of counseling ordinarily are "privileged," meaning that neither the counselee nor the pastor can be compelled to disclose in a court of law any statements made in the

---

[246] Bladen v. First Presbyterian Church, 857 P.2d 789 (Okla. 1993).

course of the counseling. However, the presence of a third party during a counseling session may jeopardize the privilege, since the counseling may no longer be considered "confidential." To illustrate, statements made in the course of pastoral counseling may not be privileged if a counselee brings a friend along to the counseling session.

• Any statements made in confidence in the course of counseling will be kept in strict confidence by the counselor. As noted above, the duty to maintain confidences may not apply in the context of child abuse. Further, the counselor may reserve the right to disclose confidential information in specified situations (such as threats of suicide, or an intent to harm another person).

(2) avoid controversial therapies

Counselors should be instructed to avoid any controversial counseling techniques that have been associated in recent years with staggering levels of liability (such as age regression therapy or multiple personality disorders).

(3) referrals

Counselors should have a clear understanding of those cases that need to be referred to a professional counselor.

▶ *When referring counselees to a professional counselor, it is important to avoid endorsing the person. Simply inform the counselee that the counselor is state licensed (as a counselor, psychologist, or psychiatrist), and has satisfactorily served a number of other members of the congregation.*

(4) insurance

Does the counselor have counseling insurance? If so, what are the coverage amounts? What exclusions exist? These are questions that should be addressed prior to the time the counselor begins counseling. Also check to see if the church's liability insurance policy covers the counseling activities.

(5) legal agreement

Consider executing a legal agreement with the counselor that expresses the conditions of the arrangement.

(6) disclaimer

Have every counselee sign a form acknowledging that the counselor is not acting as an agent or representative of the church, and that the counselor is not acting under the control or supervision of the church.

(7) use of the term "counselor"

It is unlawful in most states for unlicensed persons to use the term *counselor* or *counseling* in connection with their services. Pastors who engage in counseling of church members in the course of performing their pastoral duties are exempted from this limitation, but lay counselors generally are not even though they are working in a church.

Breach of a Fiduciary Duty   § 10-13

In recent years, some courts have ruled that certain "special relationships" are "fiduciary" in nature and impose "fiduciary duties." A few courts have concluded that the following relationships are fiduciary in nature: a pastor and a counselee, a lay church counselor and a counselee, and volunteer youth workers and minors. Persons having a fiduciary duty toward another may be legally responsible for injuries they cause to the other person. In some cases, churches themselves are sued for breaching a fiduciary duty. Cases recognizing and rejecting fiduciary duty claims against churches are summarized below.

Court Decisions Recognizing Fiduciary Duty Claims   § 10-13.1

Key point 10-13.1. *A few courts have found churches and denominational agencies liable on the basis of a breach of a fiduciary duty for the sexual misconduct of a minister. In some cases, the church or agency is found to be vicariously liable for the minister's breach of a fiduciary duty, but in others the church or agency is found to have breached a fiduciary duty that it had with the victim.*

This section reviews court decisions in which a church or other religious organization was found liable on the basis of breaching a fiduciary duty.

> "Courts in other jurisdictions are divided on whether it is constitutionally permissible to subject a member of the clergy to tort liability for the breach of a fiduciary duty to a parishioner. Some have adopted the view that the claim a clergyman violated a fiduciary duty is simply another way of saying that he committed malpractice, and is barred by the First Amendment for the same reasons. . . . Other courts reject this view, however, and allow claims by parishioners that clergymen breached a fiduciary duty as a result of sexually inappropriate conduct in the course of pastoral counseling, believing such claims can be adjudicated without reference to religious doctrine or practice where the conduct at issue is not part of the beliefs and practices of the defendant's religion. In the view of these courts, an action for breach of fiduciary duty does not require establishing a standard of care and its breach but merely proof that a vulnerable parishioner trusted and sought counseling from the pastor and a violation of that trust, which constitutes a breach of fiduciary duty."[247]

---

[247] Richelle v. Roman Catholic Archbishop, 2003 WL 329036 (Cal. App. 2003).

Case Studies

• *A California court ruled that a pastor and his employing church could be liable on the basis of his sexual seduction of a female member of his congregation, but only if the member was vulnerable on the basis of age, mental capacity, illness, or a counseling relationship. The victim claimed that her relationship with the pastor was a "fiduciary relationship" that the pastor breached by engaging in sexual relations with her. The court noted that the concept of "fiduciary relationship" was a murky one, and that "a range of the relationships could potentially be characterized as fiduciary." In general, however, a fiduciary relationship is based on the "vulnerability" of one party based on advanced age, youth, lack of education, mental incapacity, grief, sickness, or some other incapacity. The court concluded that "a pastor may be subject to tort liability for sexually inappropriate and injurious conduct that breaches a fiduciary duty arising out of a confidential relation with a parishioner, provided the alleged injurious conduct was not dictated by a sincerely held religious belief or carried out in accordance with established beliefs and practices of the religion to which the pastor belongs, and there is no other reason the issues cannot be framed for the [jury] in secular rather than sectarian terms."[248]*

• *The Colorado Supreme Court ruled that an Episcopal diocese and bishop were responsible for a pastor's sexual misconduct with a female member of the congregation who had sought him out for counseling. The court concluded that the bishop and diocese breached their "fiduciary duty" to the victim. The court noted that a fiduciary relationship exists when there is a special relationship of trust, confidence, and reliance between two persons, and when one of them assumes a duty to act in the other's best interests. The court acknowledged that the clergy-parishioner relationship "is not necessarily a fiduciary relationship." However, the clergy-parishioner relationship often involves "the type of interaction that creates trust and reliance" and in some cases will constitute a fiduciary relationship. The court concluded that a fiduciary relationship existed between the bishop and the victim on the basis of the following factors: (1) The bishop was in a superior position and was able to exert substantial influence over the victim. An unequal relationship between two parties can be evidence of a fiduciary relationship, since the party with the greater influence and authority often assumes a duty to act in the dependent party's best interests. (2) The bishop, in his meeting with the victim, served as a counselor to the victim and not as a representative of the diocese. If he was acting only as a representative of the diocese, he failed to convey that fact to the victim and led her to believe that he was acting in her interest. The court concluded that the bishop and diocese had breached their fiduciary duty to the victim by not acting in her "utmost good faith" (by taking no action to help her, not assisting her in understanding that she was not solely responsible for the sexual relationship, and not recommending counseling for her).[249]*

• *A Colorado court ruled that a denominational agency could be sued by a woman with whom a minister had sexual contacts.[250] The court noted that the following facts supported the existence of a fiduciary relationship between the victim and the*

---

[248] *Id.*

[249] Moses v. Diocese of Colorado, 863 P.2d 310 (Colo. 1993). *Accord* DeBose v. Bear Valley Church of Christ, 890 P.2d 214 (Colo. App. 1994), *aff'd*, 928 P.2d 1315 (Colo. 1996).

[250] Winkler v. Rocky Mouton Conference, 923 P.2d 152 (Colo. App. 1995).

denominational agency: the agency conducted a meeting with six women regarding the minister's inappropriate behavior with them; the agency provided a therapist to help the women; the agency sent a letter to the church's membership stating in part that "we are equally concerned for the healing of any persons who have been hurt. They will continue to receive appropriate help for their healing and restoration." The victim claimed that the denominational agency breached its fiduciary duty by failing to provide adequate counseling to the six women with whom the minister had engaged in inappropriate sexual conduct; undermining the credibility of the women by informing their congregation that there was nothing in the minister's personnel file indicating he had problems; failing to protect the women who brought complaints against the minister from verbal attacks; and not informing the congregation that it found the women's complaints credible. The court concluded that sufficient evidence existed for the jury to conclude that the agency breached its fiduciary duty.

• A federal court in Connecticut ruled that a woman who had been molested by a priest when she was a minor could sue her church and other church agencies on the basis of a breach of fiduciary duty. The court defined a fiduciary relationship as one "characterized by a unique degree of trust and confidence between the parties, one of whom has a superior knowledge, skill or expertise and is under a duty to represent the interests of the other." In concluding that such a relationship existed between the victim and church defendants, the court observed: "Plaintiff was a member of the church or diocesan sponsored activities . . . and the church choir, and consulted with the priest for spiritual and religious counseling, as encouraged by defendants. Additionally, the priest attended dinners at the plaintiff's family home and vacationed with them. Furthermore, plaintiff alleges that defendants knew or should have known that the priest engaged in a sexual relationship with another woman prior to his [current] assignment."[251]

• The Florida Supreme Court ruled that it was not barred by the First Amendment from resolving a woman's lawsuit claiming that she had been the victim of a priest's sexual misconduct. The court ruled that the church and diocese could be liable for the priest's acts on the basis of a breach of a fiduciary duty: "The counselor-counselee relationship has been characterized as a fiduciary one. As the Colorado Supreme Court has explained, a clergy member who undertakes a counseling relationship creates a fiduciary duty 'to engage in conduct designed to improve the [plaintiffs'] marital relationship. As a fiduciary, [the clergy member] was obligated not to engage in conduct which might harm [the plaintiffs' marital] relationship.' Accordingly, we hold that when a church, through its clergy, holds itself out as qualified to engage in marital counseling and a counseling relationship arises, that relationship between the church and the counselee is one that may be characterized as fiduciary in nature. We thus stress that the liability in this case rests on the assertion of an abuse of a marital counseling relationship through an inappropriate sexual relationship."[252]

• The Maine Supreme Court ruled that a Catholic diocese could be sued on the basis of a breach of a fiduciary duty for a priest's molestation of an adolescent male who served as an altar boy and attended a church school, and whose parents were partially incapacitated and unable to fully oversee his upbringing. The court reasoned that the

---

[251] Doe v. Norwich Roman Catholic Diocesan Corporation, 309 F.Supp.2d 247 (D. Conn. 2004).

[252] Doe v. Evans, 814 So.2d 370 (Fla. 2002).

victim's special involvement in the activities of the church as both a parochial school student and an altar boy "distinguished his status from that of a general member of the church." For example, his involvement required "that he be physically present at the church more often than a general member and that he have substantially greater day-to-day contact with members of the clergy and faculty than would a general member." The court concluded that a special relationship did exist between the victim and his church and diocese that supported claims of both negligent supervision and breach of a fiduciary duty: "[The victim] has asserted the existence of a special relationship that ineluctably involved the actual placement of trust, as well as a substantial disparity of power and influence between him and the diocese. By its very nature, such a special relationship renders a child vulnerable to the possibility of abuse at the hands of a miscreant employee. An established and close connection between a child and an organization, whether religious, academic, or otherwise, is a reasonable basis, informed by both common sense and common experience, to impose a duty on the organization to prevent harm to the child. [The victim's] allegations establish a special relationship between him and the diocese as his fiduciary. Such a relationship gave rise to a duty to protect on the part of the diocese if the diocese had reason to believe that a priest posed a substantial risk of harm to a child in Michael's circumstances. The duty does not exist simply because of [the victim's] status as a student and altar boy, but because of the added assertion that the diocese knew or should have known of the risk of harm posed by the priest who abused him."[253]

• An Ohio court ruled that a church and denominational agency could be sued on the basis of a breach of a fiduciary duty for the sexual misconduct of a minister. The court noted that the church defendants allowed the priest to supervise and coach youth activities. And, "because it is reasonable to claim the church had a duty to protect the participants in its youth program from its agents, the lawsuit . . . is sufficient to state a claim" for breach of fiduciary duty. The church defendants argued that they could not be liable for breaching a fiduciary duty since they were not legally required to report child abuse ("mandatory reporters") under state law. The court acknowledged that the church defendants were not mandatory reporters, but concluded that this was irrelevant to the question of liability. It pointed out that the lawsuit alleged that "despite numerous opportunities to discover the abuse, the church ignored the hundreds of acts of abuse which occurred not only in its rectory, but even in its [sanctuary]. The plaintiff has stated a cause of action for breach of fiduciary duty when the church had constructive notice of the abuse."[254]

• A federal court in Pennsylvania ruled that a church and diocese could be liable on the basis of a breach of a fiduciary duty for a priest's sexual misconduct. The court noted that under Pennsylvania law "a fiduciary relationship will be found to exist when the circumstances make it certain the parties do not deal on equal terms, but, on the one side there is an overmastering influence, or, on the other, weakness, dependence, or trust, justifiably reposed; in both an unfair advantage is possible." The court concluded: "This definition fits the relationship of a priest and a parishioner once the priest accepts the parishioner's trust and accepts the role of counselor. In such a case, the parishioner has justifiably placed his trust in the priest. In order to receive and make use of a priest's advice and counsel, a parishioner must necessarily depend upon

---

[253] Fortin v. Roman Catholic Bishop of Portland, 871 A.2d 1208 (Me. 2005).

[254] Mills v. Deehr, 2004 WL 1047720 (Ohio App. 2004).

the priest's knowledge and expertise, resulting in the priest's superiority and influence over the parishioner. Thus, once a counseling relationship has commenced, the parishioner and priest no longer deal on equal terms. This unequal relationship affords the priest opportunity to abuse the trust and confidence reposed in him or prey on a weak and dependent parishioner to his own benefit. The relationship therefore becomes fiduciary in nature and the recognition of a breach of fiduciary duty claim is necessary to protect a beholden parishioner from a self-serving priest."

The court also concluded that a fiduciary relationship existed between the church defendants and the plaintiff: "As to a diocese and its officials, a diocese exerts an overmastering influence over a plaintiff, or a plaintiff exhibits weakness, dependence on or justifiable trust in the diocese and its officials when, as here, the plaintiff is a minor and is involved in the church beyond that of a mere parishioner, whether by virtue of his serving the church, participating in church-sponsored activities, or receiving counseling from a priest. When the plaintiff is a minor, the power differential between the plaintiff and priest is magnified. This power differential makes it difficult for a minor who is involved in the church to refuse the unwelcome sexual advances of a priest or report such an advance to his parents or the authorities. Minors participating in church activities are therefore dependent on the diocese for protection, and the diocese is responsible to provide it. This vulnerability requires the diocese to be vigilant so that minors who are serving the church, participating in church activities, or receiving counseling from a diocesan priest are doing so in an environment free from the threat of sexual abuse.[255]

Court Decisions Rejecting Fiduciary Duty Claims § 10-13.2

Key point 10-13.2. *Several courts have refused to hold churches and denominational agencies liable on the basis of a breach of a fiduciary duty for the sexual misconduct of a minister. In some cases, this result is based on First Amendment considerations.*

This section reviews court decisions in which a church or other religious organization was found not liable on the basis of breaching a fiduciary duty. Many courts have concluded that the First Amendment's "nonestablishment of religion" and "free exercise of religion" clauses prevent the civil courts from resolving such claims involving clergy misconduct.

---

[255] Doe v. Liberatore, 478 F.Supp.2d 742 (M.D. Pa. 2007). The court stressed that recognition of the plaintiff's breach of fiduciary duty claim against the priest and church defendants did not offend the First Amendment since the claim "only raises the issues of whether the parties did not deal on equal terms, but, rather, on the one side there was an overmastering influence, or, on the other, weakness, dependence, or trust, justifiably reposed; in both an unfair advantage is possible, whether that unfair advantage was exploited by Allen, and whether the church defendants failed to provide and maintain a safe environment for the plaintiff to participate in church activities. No inquiry need be made into church doctrine or other ecclesiastical matters. No professional standard of care need be set for clergy. There is no risk of excessive governmental entanglement with religion."

Case Studies

• *A federal appeals court, applying Illinois law, ruled that a church and denominational agency were not legally responsible for a pastoral counselor's sexual contacts with a female counselee.[256] In rejecting the woman's claim that the church and denominational agency were legally responsible for her injuries on the basis of a breach of a fiduciary duty they owed her, the court observed, "At the outset [we] note that [the woman] cited no Illinois authority establishing that Illinois recognizes such a fiduciary duty. . . . Moreover, given the constitutional difficulties that would be encountered if a cause of action for breach of fiduciary duty were permitted under these circumstances, we ought to be particularly cautious in assuming that Illinois has taken such a step. If the court were to recognize such a breach of fiduciary duty, it would be required to define a reasonable duty standard and to evaluate [the pastor's] conduct against that standard, an inquiry identical to that which Illinois has declined to undertake in the context of a clergy malpractice claim and one that is of doubtful validity under the free exercise [of religion] clause [of the First Amendment]. It is clear that Illinois would not entertain a claim for breach of fiduciary obligation under the circumstances alleged here."*

• *A Florida court ruled that it was barred by the First Amendment from resolving a woman's claim that her priest and church were responsible on the basis of a breach of a fiduciary duty for the priest's acts of sexual misconduct.[257] The woman had sought out a priest for marital counseling, and alleged that the priest engaged in sexual contacts with her. The woman sued her church and diocese, claiming that they were aware of prior incidents involving sexual misconduct during counseling by the same priest. Despite this knowledge, nothing was done to address the problem. She claimed that the priest breached a fiduciary duty by becoming romantically involved with her, and that the church and diocese had a fiduciary relationship with her (because she reported the priest's misconduct to them) that was breached. A state appeals court concluded that resolving the woman's breach of fiduciary duty claims (against the priest, church, and diocese) would constitute excessive entanglement between church and state in violation of the First Amendment: "Taking the allegations of [her] complaint as true, [she] alleged the church defendants owed her a fiduciary duty, yet definition of that duty necessarily involves the secular court in church practices, doctrines, and belief. To establish a breach of the fiduciary duty allegedly owed to [her] by the church defendants, [she] would need to establish the church remained inactive in the face of her allegations against [the priest]. However, the church's policies undoubtedly differ from the rules of another employer, and may require the nonsecular employer to respond differently when faced with such allegations. When a secular court interprets church law, policies, and practices it becomes excessively entangled in religion. We align ourselves with those courts finding a First Amendment bar to a breach of fiduciary duty claim as against church defendants, concluding resolution of such a claim would necessarily require the secular court to review and interpret church law, policies, and practices."*

---

[256] Dausch v. Rykse, 52 F.3d 1425 (7th Cir. 1994).

[257] Doe v. Evans, 718 So.2d 286 (Fla. App. 1998).

• The Missouri Supreme Court ruled that a diocese could not be liable on the basis of a breach of a fiduciary duty for the sexual misconduct of a priest.[258] A Catholic priest served as associate pastor of a church. He invited a young boy and one of the boy's friends to spend the night and watch movies in the church parsonage. One of the boys later alleged that the priest sexually molested him. The boy's parents sued the diocese. They alleged that the diocese "stood in a fiduciary relationship" with them and their son because they were the recipients of services that were directed and monitored by the diocese. Further, the diocese "held a fiduciary relationship of trust and confidence" with the family. The court concluded that these "general conclusions" were not sufficient to support the parents' claim of a breach of a fiduciary duty.

• The North Dakota Supreme Court ruled that a denominational agency could not be liable for a pastor's sexual misconduct on the basis of a breach of a fiduciary duty.[259] A police officer was killed in the line of duty. His widow sought out her pastor for counseling. Within a few months, the pastor initiated a sexual relationship with the widow. The affair lasted for nearly a year, at which time the pastor was assigned to a position in another state. The couple continued their relationship for seven years, meeting four or five times each year at "workshops" around the country. Eventually, the widow informed a denominational official about the pastor's relationship with her. The pastor was promptly removed from his position within the church. The widow later sued the denominational agency, claiming that it owed her a fiduciary duty after it learned of the affair, and that it breached this duty by failing to intervene or respond appropriately. The court concluded that the widow had failed to prove that the denominational agency owed her a fiduciary duty. It observed that a fiduciary duty is based on the existence of a fiduciary relationship, and it concluded that such a relationship exists "when one is under a duty to act or give advice for the benefit of another upon matters within the scope of the relationship." It further noted that a fiduciary relationship "generally arises when there is an unequal relationship between the parties." Did the widow have a fiduciary relationship with her denominational agency on the basis of its alleged knowledge of the affair? No, concluded the court. It observed, "Although there was evidence [the agency and one of its officials] were informed about the intimacy between the [pastor and widow], we are not persuaded that knowledge, by itself and without some other action to assume control of the matter, raises an inference that the [agency] assumed a fiduciary duty to [the widow]."

• The Ohio Supreme Court rejected a woman's attempt to sue her church and pastor for injuries she allegedly suffered because of a sexual relationship with her pastor.[260] A husband and wife who had been experiencing marital problems went to a Lutheran minister for counseling. They selected him because "he held himself out to the public . . . as a minister and counselor trained and able to provide counseling for marital difficulties." During the final three or four weeks of counseling, the minister allegedly engaged in consensual sexual relations with the wife. These relations, and the counseling, ended when the husband learned of the affair. The husband, who was later divorced from his wife, sued both the minister and his church. The suit against the minister alleged a breach of fiduciary duty, among other things. The state supreme court dismissed all of the husband's claims. It noted that the breach of fiduciary claim, like the husband's other claims, had to be dismissed since they all sought damages

---

[258] Gibson v. Brewer, 952 S.W.2d 239 (Mo. 1997).

[259] L.C. v. R.P. 563 N.W.2d 799 (N.D. 1997).

[260] Stock v. Pressnell, 527 N.E.2d 1235 (Ohio 1988).

based on the minister's seduction of the wife, and as such were barred by the state law prohibiting lawsuits based on "alienation of affections."

• A South Carolina court ruled that a denominational agency and one of its officials were not liable on the basis of a breach of a fiduciary duty for a pastor's acts of sexual harassment of three female church members.[261] The court concluded that no fiduciary relationship existed between the women and either the denominational agency or its superintendent. It noted that the women had no contact with the agency and their only direct contact with the superintendent was a single meeting involving one of the women. The court stressed that while the superintendent received the women's initial accusations, "his mere occupation of the position of superintendent did not create a fiduciary relationship with these [women]." Further, the women's personal expectation that the agency or superintendent would "take action" on their complaints did not create a fiduciary relationship: "The steps taken unilaterally by the [women] do not constitute an attempt on their part to establish the relationship alleged, and there is no evidence that [the agency or superintendent] accepted or induced any special, fiduciary bond with any of [the women] under these facts in any event." The court also concluded that even if a fiduciary relationship did exist, it was not violated since "there is no evidence of a breach of that duty. There is no evidence that [the agency or superintendent] acted other than in good faith and with due regard to [the women's] interests."

Risk Management §10-13.3

Key point 10-13.3. *Churches can reduce the risk of liability based on breach of fiduciary duty by adopting risk management policies and procedures.*

"Breach of fiduciary claims" against churches and other religious organizations are rarely successful. The few exceptions generally have involved claims of sexual misconduct by clergy in the course of a counseling relationship. The risk of such claims can be reduced by implementing the same strategies mentioned in section 10-12.1 in the context of counseling activities.

Ratification §10-14

Key point 10-14. *Churches may be liable on the basis of "ratification" for the unauthorized act of a minister or other church worker if it is aware of the act and voluntarily affirms it.*

A few courts have found churches liable on the basis of "ratification" for the acts of clergy and lay workers. Ratification is "the affirmance by a person of a prior act which did not bind him but which was done or professedly done on his account, whereby the act, as to some or all persons, is given effect as

---

[261] Brown v. Pearson, 483 S.E.2d 477 (S.C. App. 1997).

if originally authorized by him."[262] Stated differently, a church can be liable for the unauthorized acts of an employee or volunteer if it ratifies those acts either expressly or by implication. In order to be liable for unauthorized acts on the basis of ratification, a church must have knowledge of all material facts surrounding the acts and voluntarily affirm them. A church may ratify contracts, promissory notes, deeds, and other legal documents that are signed without authorization, and it may ratify acts causing personal injuries. In many cases, a church ratifies an unauthorized act by accepting or retaining the benefits of the transaction. To illustrate, if a church treasurer without authorization signs a contract to purchase a vehicle on behalf of the church, the church will be liable on the contract on the basis of ratification if it retains and uses the vehicle without objection.

Case Studies

• *A federal appeals court ruled that an archdiocese was not responsible on the basis of "ratification" for the alleged molestation of a minor by a priest.[263] The court also rejected the victim's claim that the archdiocese "ratified" the priest's actions by not addressing them despite suspicious circumstances. According to the victim, suspicion translates into "constructive knowledge" which is tantamount to a "passive ratification" of the priest's activities. The court noted that "[t]his is a novel proposition to be sure," and it refused to recognize it.*

• *A Colorado court ruled that a church could be sued on the basis of "ratification" for the molestation of a child by a pastor.[264] A 7-year-old boy (the "victim"), who was experiencing emotional trauma, was encouraged by his pastor to enter into a counseling relationship with him. The boy's mother approved, and the counseling sessions lasted for a number of years. From the very first counseling session the victim claimed that the pastor sexually molested him. A jury found the church liable for the pastor's misconduct on the ground that it "ratified" his actions. On appeal, the church insisted that (1) intentional misconduct by a pastor cannot be ratified; (2) it could not ratify actions of the pastor that were outside the scope of his employment; and (3) there was insufficient evidence that it ratified the pastor's actions. The court disagreed with all three objections. In rejecting the church's first objection, the court observed that "[a]n employer can assume liability for the tortious conduct of its employee by approving and ratifying such conduct, irrespective whether that conduct is intentional or negligent." Similarly, in rejecting the church's second objection the court observed that "[a]n employer may ratify the unauthorized act of its employee, i.e., an act not within the scope of the employment, and thereby become obligated to the same extent as if the principal had originally authorized the act." As a result, "it is no defense for the church here that [the pastor's] alleged conduct with the minor fell outside the scope of his defined job responsibilities." Finally, in responding to the church's third objection that there was insufficient evidence that it ratified the pastor's*

---

[262] RESTATEMENT, AGENCY 2d § 82.

[263] Tichenor v. Roman Catholic Church, 32 F.3d 953 (5th Cir. 1994).

[264] DeBose v. Bear Valley Church of Christ, 890 P.2d 214 (Colo. App. 1994), *aff'd*, 928 P.2d 1315 (Colo. 1996).

misconduct, the court observed: "In order for an employer to be liable by ratification for the unauthorized act of its employee, the evidence must establish the employer's adoption and confirmation of that act. And, an employer must have full knowledge of the character of the employee's act before it may be said to have ratified that act. The fact that an employer retains an employee after gaining knowledge of the employee's tortious conduct is evidence that may prove ratification of the employee's acts. However, retention of an employee, without more, is not conclusive evidence of such ratification. Further, numerous acts of an employee committed over a period of time can constitute evidence of an implied ratification of that conduct by the employer. . . . Here, the evidence was sufficient to allow the finding that the church elders were aware of [the pastor's] alleged inappropriate counseling behavior as early as 1986. It began receiving complaints from various parishioners with respect to his conduct, starting in 1986 and continuing through 1987 and 1988. Indeed, the minutes of several church elders' meetings during 1986 and 1987 reflect that the elders were concerned with respect to the church's "liability and responsibility" for [the pastor's] counseling; that [he] might be involved in "medical," rather than religious counseling; and that "many parents are complaining" about [him]. Further, there was evidence, as noted, of specific complaints against [the pastor] made by various parishioners, and there was other evidence that the church failed effectively to respond to such allegations."

Defamation §10-15

Key point 10-15. *The First Amendment limits, but does not eliminate, a church's liability for defamation.*

Defamation consists of the following elements:

(1) oral or written statements about another person

(2) that are false

(3) that are "published" (that is, communicated to other persons), and

(4) that injure the other person's reputation

If the words are oral, the defamation is sometimes called slander. If the words are written, the defamation may be referred to as libel. Although this terminology is still widely used, there is a tendency to refer to both slander and libel as defamation.

The courts have been reluctant to subject churches to civil liability on the basis of defamation. In many cases, this reluctance is rooted in the fact that allegedly defamatory statements made by church officials orally or in church publications involve pervasively religious concerns such as the discipline of members or clergy. The courts have responded to defamation claims against churches in the following five ways:

1. No Civil Court Jurisdiction

Some courts have concluded that the First Amendment deprives them of jurisdiction to resolve defamation claims against churches, at least if doctrinal or other pervasively religious issues are involved.

Case Studies

• *A federal appeals court ruled that civil courts lack authority to resolve disputes between dismissed clergy and their former church or denomination.[265] A minister was dismissed by his denomination. He later sued the denomination, claiming that his dismissal violated established procedures set forth in the denomination's bylaws. He alleged that his dismissal violated various "contract and property rights," and was defamatory. The court concluded that the First Amendment guaranty of religious freedom prevents the civil courts from resolving lawsuits brought by dismissed ministers against former churches or denominations "however a lawsuit may be labeled." In other words, the fact that a dismissed minister alleges breach of contract, defamation, emotional distress, or similar "secular" theories of liability will not enable the civil courts to resolve what in essence is a dispute between a minister and his or her church or denomination. The court observed, "However a suit may be labeled, once a court is called upon to probe into a religious body's selection and retention of clergymen, the First Amendment [guaranty of religious freedom] is implicated . . . . The relationship between an organized church and its ministers is its lifeblood. The minister is the chief instrument by which the church seeks to fulfill its purpose. Matters touching this relationship must necessarily be recognized as of prime ecclesiastical concern."*

• *A federal appeals court ruled that it was barred by the First Amendment from resolving a lawsuit brought against a denomination by a dismissed minister. The court noted that the allegedly defamatory statements occurred in the course of a church disciplinary proceeding that led to the minister's dismissal. The court concluded: "It is clear that regardless of how the claims set forth in the plaintiffs' complaint may be labeled, resolving the claims would require this court to enter into areas implicating the First Amendment. The claims of breach of contract, interference with business relationships, conspiracy, invasion of privacy, and defamation, as well as his request for a declaratory judgment that the charging body within the [national church] lacked the legal or other proper authority to bring charges against him, all implicate the [national church's] internal disciplinary proceedings. As a result, this court cannot have jurisdiction over them."[266]*

• *A federal appeals court refused to allow a "disfellowshiped" Jehovah's Witness to sue her former church for defamation, invasion of privacy, fraud, and outrageous conduct.[267] The disfellowshiped member claimed that she had been aggrieved by the Jehovah's Witness practice of "shunning," which requires members to avoid all social contacts with disfellowshiped members. The court, acknowledging that the harm suffered by disfellowshiped members is "real and not insubstantial," nevertheless*

---

[265] Natal v. Christian and Missionary Alliance, 878 F.2d 1575 (1st Cir. 1989). *Accord* Pierce v. Iowa-Missouri Conference of Seventh-Day Adventists, 534 N.W.2d 425 (Iowa 1995).

[266] Church of God, 153 Fed.Appx. 371 (6th Cir. 2005).

[267] Paul v. Watchtower Bible and Tract Society of New York, 819 F. 2d 875 (9th Cir. 1987).

concluded that permitting disfellowshiped members to sue their church for emotional injuries "would unconstitutionally restrict the Jehovah's Witness free exercise of religion." The constitutional guaranty of freedom of religion, observed the court, "requires that society tolerate the type of harm suffered by [disfellowshiped members] as a price well worth paying to safeguard the right of religious difference that all citizens enjoy."

• A Florida court ruled that it was barred by the First Amendment from resolving a woman's defamation claim against her church. However, the court did not dismiss the woman's defamation claim against her pastor.[268]

• A Missouri court ruled that it was barred by the First Amendment from resolving a former church school principal's claim that she had been defamed by statements made by her former employer prior to her termination, but it did allow her to sue on the basis of a defamatory statement allegedly made when she was no longer an employee. The court concluded: "To allow the defamation claims to be litigated would be to allow civil court jurisdiction to enter the back door of the religious entity in question and allow judicial probing of procedure and church polity, with [a jury] sitting in judgment on whether the viewpoint, values, politics, and educational practices of the diocese. . . . The allegedly defamatory statements in question in this case were generally made in connection with the decisions of the church officials as to the non-renewal of the plaintiff's contract, and were made by, to, and about people who were part of the religious organization in question. . . . This case involves the ability of this church and diocese to operate within its own sphere according to its own methods, without judicial interference. . . . As a practical matter, it is impossible to separate the defamation from the non-renewal . . . . To allow a defamation suit to be litigated in connection with the termination of a church officer would tend to have a chilling effect on the management of the religious entity and the "communication of important ideas and candid opinions."

    While most of the allegedly defamatory statements were made prior to the non-renewal of the plaintiff's contract, one was made afterwards. The court concluded that this communication "was not connected to the non-renewal issue, but instead came a substantial period of time after the personnel issues were resolved." As a result, the court allowed the plaintiff to sue the church defendants on the basis of this communication. However, it cautioned that the trial court "must consider First Amendment protections related generally to the governance of the diocese . . . and also the defense of common law conditional privilege, as well as any other defenses."[269]

• A Louisiana court ruled that a minister could not sue state and national church officials for defamation.[270] A pastor disciplined certain members of his congregation, who thereafter were accepted as members in a neighboring church of the same denomination. The pastor protested the action of the neighboring church to both national and state denominational officials. These officials declined to assist the pastor, whose congregation thereafter "protested" this result by withholding financial support to the national organization. This prompted the national church to remove the pastor from both state and national offices that he held. The pastor later resigned

---

[268] The House of God Church v. White, 792 So.2d 491 (Fla. App. 2001).

[269] Gaydos v. Blaeuer, 81 S.W.3d 186 (Mo. App. 2002).

[270] McManus v. Taylor, 521 So.2d 449 (La. App. 1988).

from the denomination, and sued the state and national offices for defamation. The court, in concluding that it lacked jurisdiction to resolve the dispute, relied upon a 1976 decision of the United States Supreme Court, which held that the United States Constitution "permits hierarchical religious organizations to establish their own rules and regulations for internal discipline and government, and to create tribunals for adjudicating disputes over these matters. When this choice is exercised and ecclesiastical tribunals are created to decide disputes over the government and direction of subordinate bodies, the Constitution requires that civil courts accept their decisions as binding upon them."[271] The Louisiana court concluded that "[i]t would be ludicrous to believe that the constitutional principles upheld by the United States Supreme Court . . . could be satisfied by allowing this intrusion into the disciplinary proceedings of an ecclesiastical board. To allow defamation suits to be litigated to the fullest extent against members of a religious board who are merely discharging the duty which has been entrusted to them by their church could have a potentially chilling effect on the performance of those duties."

• A Maryland court ruled that a former candidate for the priesthood could not sue his diocese or church officials for defamation.[272] The candidate entered seminary and pursued training in preparation for ordination as a priest. Less than a year before he was to be ordained, he was informed by a church official that he was being "released" from the diocese and as a result would never be considered for the priesthood. The candidate sued the archbishop on behalf of the diocese and various church officials, claiming that the decision to "release" him was based on defamatory information shared with the diocese. Specifically, the candidate claimed that a priest provided a reference to church officials in which he asserted that the candidate had engaged in "sexually motivated conduct" with certain staff members in a former parish. The candidate claimed that church officials repeated this information with knowledge that it was false and with an intent to harm his chances for ordination to the priesthood. He sought more than $2 million in damages. A Maryland appeals court ruled that the case had to be dismissed. It summed up pertinent decisions of the United States Supreme Court by noting that "the withdrawal of ecclesiastical controversies from civil jurisdiction has been a broad one." The court was not prepared to say that the civil courts can never resolve disputes between a church and its ministers. However, "When the conduct complained of occurs in the context of, or is germane to, a dispute over the plaintiff's fitness or suitability to enter into or remain a part of the clergy . . . . it is difficult to see how the forbidden inquiry could be avoided. Questions of truth, falsity, malice, and the various privileges that exist often take on a different hue when examined in the light of religious precepts and procedures that generally permeate controversies over who is fit to represent and speak for the church. . . . It is apparent from these allegations . . . that the very heart of the [lawsuit] is a decision by [the candidate's] clerical supervisors to prevent him from becoming a priest. The allegedly defamatory statements were made by them with that intent, thereby evidencing a determination on their part—whether valid and fair or invalid and unfair—that [the candidate] was not a suitable candidate for the priesthood. That the offensive conduct was so directed is what brings this case squarely within the protective ambit of the First Amendment."

---

[271] Serbian Eastern Orthodox Diocese v. Milivojevich, 426 U.S. 696 (1976).

[272] Downs v. Roman Catholic Archbishop, 683 A.2d 808 (Md. App. 1996).

• A Minnesota court ruled that a female associate pastor could sue her senior pastor for sexual harassment on account of his repeated sexual advances toward her and the "hostile work environment" that he created, but the woman's allegations of breach of contract, defamation, and wrongful dismissal were barred by the First Amendment.[273] The court concluded that the woman's defamation claim "is based on the church's stated reason for her discharge as 'inability to conduct her ministry efficiently.' This claim would require a . . . review of the church's reasons for discharging her, an essentially ecclesiastical concern. . . . The impermissible entanglement of doctrinal and disciplinary issues is sufficient to support the dismissal of this claim." The court concluded that "the prohibition against litigating matters at the core of a church's religious practice requires dismissal of [the woman's] discharge-related claims."

• A Minnesota court ruled that a church member could not challenge his dismissal in court.[274] The pastor of a church asked two church members (a husband and wife) to sign a document guarantying payment of certain church debts. The pastor represented to them that if the church ever defaulted on its debts the church would sell its property and use the proceeds to pay back any funds the couple advanced pursuant to the guaranty. The couple signed the guaranty agreement. A few months later, they were notified that the church had been late in making several payments on its bank loans. The couple retained an attorney and discontinued their contact with the church. They did not notify the church of any intent to terminate their membership. Their attorney wrote the pastor and requested that the couple be released from their guaranty commitment. The pastor responded by sending the couple a letter dismissing them from membership in the church. The pastor cited the following reasons for terminating their membership: (1) a lack of financial stewardship; (2) a desire to create division and strife in the fellowship; and (3) the dissemination of lies with the intent to hurt the reputation of the church. The pastor's letter was read to the entire congregation. Several months later the pastor met with the couple, and admitted that no proceeds from the sale of church property would be shared with them. The couple then filed a lawsuit against the pastor and church, alleging fraud, defamation, and breach of contract. A state appeals court dismissed the lawsuit. It began its opinion by observing that the First Amendment "precludes judicial review of claims involving core questions of church discipline and internal governance." The court concluded that the couple's claims all involved core questions of church discipline that it was not able to resolve. With regard to the couple's defamation claim, the court pointed out that a defamatory statement must be false and that "since an examination of the truth of [the pastor's] statements would require an impermissible inquiry into church doctrine and discipline, the [trial court] did not err in concluding that the defamation claim is precluded by the First Amendment." The court added that "the fact that the letter was disseminated only to other members of the church strengthens the conclusion that [the pastor's] statements involved and were limited to church doctrine."

• A federal district court in Minnesota dismissed a minister's lawsuit alleging that church officials had defamed him.[275] A denomination decided not to elevate a congregation to mission status, thereby cutting off all subsidies and in effect terminating the minister who served the congregation. The minister sued his

---

[273] Black v. Snyder, 471 N.W.2d 715 (Minn. App. 1991).

[274] Schoenhalls v. Main, 504 N.W.2d 233 (Minn. App. 1993).

[275] Farley v. Wisconsin Evangelical Lutheran Synod, 821 F. Supp. 1286 (D. Minn. 1993).

denomination for defamation, alleging that denominational officials published both oral and written defamatory statements about him that damaged his reputation and professional status. The denomination claimed that the civil courts lacked jurisdiction to resolve religious disputes such as this. The court agreed with the denomination and dismissed the lawsuit. It noted that "the United States Supreme Court has determined that civil courts generally may not inquire into a religious organization's activities on matters of religious doctrine or authority and that courts lack subject matter jurisdiction over most disputes stemming from a religious organization's actions." The court rejected the minister's claim that resolving a defamation claim would be permissible: "Although factual scenarios might exist where resolution of a defamation action against a religious organization would not require the court to undertake an inquiry in violation of the First Amendment, this case does not present such a situation. [The minister's] defamation claim challenges [the denomination's] authority . . . to comment on [the minister's] actions and abilities as a . . . minister. Resolution of . . . the defamation claim would require the court to review the [denomination's] bases for terminating him, an ecclesiastical concern, and the veracity of the [denomination's] statements. The court determines that such an inquiry would implicate the concerns expressed in the First Amendment. Based on that determination, the court concludes that it has no jurisdiction over this matter."

• The Montana Supreme Court ruled that a husband and wife who had been "disfellowshipped" from a Jehovah's Witness congregation could not sue the church for defamation.[276] The couple had been disfellowshipped for marrying contrary to church doctrine. In announcing the decision to the congregation, the overseer remarked that the couple had been living in adultery according to church teachings and had been disfellowshipped for "conduct unbecoming Christians." The overseer added that "we got the filth cleaned out of the congregation, now we have God's spirit." The court concluded that such comments were not defamatory since they were privileged and protected by the constitutional guaranty of religious freedom. As to the defense of privilege, the court remarked that "it is firmly established that statements of church members made in the course of disciplinary or expulsion proceedings, in the absence of malice, are protected by a qualified privilege." The remarks of the overseer were privileged, concluded the court, and did not involve malice since "malice is defined as reckless disregard for the truth [and] does not include hatred, personal spite, ill-will, or a desire to injure." The court added that it "would be violating the [church's] right to free exercise of religion if [it] were to find [the church's] statements actionable under state defamation law."

• An Ohio court dismissed a lawsuit brought by two former ministers against their church and denomination.[277] A church hired a husband and wife as "co-pastors." A few years later, the couple were dismissed. They sued their former church on the basis of several theories of liability, including defamation. In particular, they asserted that the church defamed them by publishing negative comments regarding their ministry and alleged financial misconduct. In rejecting the claim of defamation, the court concluded, "One who falsely and without a privilege to do so publishes a slander which ascribes to another conduct, characteristics, or a condition incompatible with the proper conduct of his lawful business, trade, or profession is liable to the other.

---

[276] Rasmussen v. Bennett, 741 P.2d 755 (Mont. 1987).

[277] Salzgaber v. First Christian Church, 583 N.E.2d 1361 (Ohio App. 1991).

However, inquiry by a civil court into the truth or falsity of the statements by [church officials] would require review of subjective judgments made by religious officers and bodies concerning [the co-pastors'] conduct of the pastorate and financial misdealings. Inquiry would be ecclesiastical in nature and constitutionally prohibited."

• *An Ohio court ruled that it could not review a dismissed member's lawsuit claiming that his church had defamed him.*[278] *The church member sought access to his church's financial records. When church leaders denied this request, the member filed a lawsuit in which he asked a court to order the church to turn over the records. Following the filing of this lawsuit, church leaders attempted to dismiss the member from church membership. The member filed another lawsuit against his church, claiming that the attempt to dismiss him was in violation of the church's bylaws; caused severe emotional distress; and was defamatory. A state appeals court rejected the ousted member's claim that the civil courts could resolve his defamation against the church and its trustees. The ousted member asserted that the church trustees had defamed him by stating that he had lied, that he was "in league with Satan," that he had been "overtaken by a fall," that he was a "defiler of the temple" and an enemy of the church, and that he was "sleeping around," and that a court could resolve the defamation issue without any interpretation of religious doctrine or beliefs. The court disagreed, "In this case, all of the statements alleged . . . to be defamatory arose out of the underlying dispute between him and the church regarding the propriety of his conduct in suing the church to obtain its records and the church's subsequent decision to remove [him] from church membership. [His lawsuit] makes clear that the dispute between the parties regarding [his] lawsuit against the church was based on biblical interpretation. The move to disfellowship [him] therefore arose from a dispute regarding his conformity . . . to the standard of morals required of him by his church. The allegedly defamatory statements made by church members, trustees or agents in terminating [his] membership in the church are therefore inextricably intertwined with ecclesiastical or religious issues over which secular courts have no jurisdiction."*

• *The Oklahoma Supreme Court ruled that a church could not be sued for defamation by two church members who had been disciplined because of sexual misconduct.*[279] *A church convened a disciplinary hearing to determine the membership status of two sisters accused of fornication. Neither sister attended, and neither sister withdrew her membership in the church. Following the hearing, both sisters received letters from the church informing them that their membership had been terminated. The sisters sued the church and its leaders, claiming that the church's actions in delivering the termination letters and disclosing their contents "to the public" constituted defamation, intentional infliction of emotional distress, and invasion of privacy. A trial court dismissed the lawsuit, and the sisters appealed directly to the state supreme court which upheld the dismissal of the case. The court began its opinion by rejecting the sisters' claim that the contents of the termination letters had been disclosed improperly to the public. This allegation was based entirely on a conversation between a church board member and another member of the church. The member asked the board member why the board was "going after" the sisters, and the board member replied that it was on account of "fornication." The court concluded that this comment*

---

[278] Howard v. Covenant Apostolic Church, Inc., 705 N.E.2d 385 (Ohio App. 1997).

[279] Hadnot v. Shaw, 826 P.2d 978 (Okla. 1992). *See also* Trice v. Burress, 137 P.3d 1253 (Okla. App. 2006).

did not constitute a disclosure of the contents of the letters "to the public," and accordingly there had been no defamation or invasion of privacy. The court recognized an absolute constitutional protection for the membership determinations of religious organizations (assuming that the disciplined member has not effectively withdrawn his or her membership): "[The relationship between a church and its members] may be severed freely by a member's positive act at any time. Until it is so terminated, the church has authority to prescribe and follow disciplinary ordinances without fear of interference by the state. The First Amendment will protect and shield the religious body from liability for the activities carried on pursuant to the exercise of church discipline. Within the context of church discipline, churches enjoy an absolute privilege from scrutiny by the secular authority."

• A Texas court ruled that a bishop and diocese could not be liable on the basis of defamation for statements made about a priest's status within the church.[280] A priest had a history of conflict with his diocese culminating in his association with a dissident Catholic sect. A parishioner asked the priest's bishop about the priest's standing in the Catholic Church, and was informed that "he is not in good standing with his diocese and does not enjoy the [authority] to function as a priest in [this] or any other diocese." The bishop advised another person that the priest was excommunicated, and not in good standing, and "says mass to a small number of people, including elderly women who have been deceived by him." The bishop later sent a memorandum to "all pastors" advising them to refrain from advertising or encouraging a mass being offered by the priest who was described as an "excommunicated priest who has left the Catholic Church." The priest sued the bishop and diocese, claiming that these communications were defamatory. A state appeals court disagreed. The court observed that the First Amendment "forbids the government from interfering with the right of hierarchical religious bodies to establish their own internal rules and regulations." As a result the civil courts cannot "intrude into the church's governance or religious or ecclesiastical matters, such as theological controversy, church discipline, ecclesiastical government, or the conformity of members to standards of morality." Furthermore, the court noted, "[C]ourts will not attempt to right wrongs related to the hiring, firing, discipline or administration of clergy. Although such wrongs may exist and may be severe, and although the administration of the church may be inadequate to provide a remedy, the preservation of the free exercise of religion is deemed so important a principle it overshadows the inequities which may result from its liberal application." The court rejected the priest's claim that the dispute did not involve ecclesiastical considerations: "[The priest's] claims arise from his divestiture of priestly authority; thus, his [legal] claims are inseparable from the privileged aura of ecclesiastical exemption. [The bishop's] administrative duties include informing members of the Catholic Church of the status of its clergy. We believe that statements made by a bishop in carrying out his administrative duties concerning an excommunication made before, during or after an excommunication, are all part of an ecclesiastical transaction—the divestiture of priestly authority." The court acknowledged that "there may be circumstances where a bishop or other church authority makes statements which overstep the bounds of [his or her] administrative duties." For example, "when statements are made by a church authority which are clearly intended to defame or inflict emotional distress, the authority has overstepped the bounds of his administrative duties and the statements may fall outside ecclesiastical protection."

---

[280] Tran v. Fiorenza, 934 S.W.2d 740 (Tex. App. 1996).

This was not true in this case, however, since the bishop's statements all related to the priest's standing in the Catholic Church.

2. Common Interest Privilege

Many courts have concluded that the law should encourage churches to communicate matters of "common interest" to members without fear of being sued for defamation. These courts have ruled that churches are protected by a *qualified privilege* when communicating with church members about matters of mutual concern or common interest. This means that such communications cannot be defamatory unless made with malice. Malice in this context means that the person who made the allegedly defamatory remark knew that it was false, or made it with a reckless disregard as to its truth or falsity. This is a difficult standard to prove, which means that communications between churches and church members will be defamatory only in exceptional cases.

▶ *The common interest privilege is addressed in section 4-02.3 in the context of clergy who are sued for defamation.*

Case Studies

• *A California court ruled that a national church could not be sued for allegedly defamatory statements made in the course of a doctrinal explanation in one of its publications.*[281] *A minister of the Worldwide Church of God wrote an article in a church publication that addressed the Church's newly developed and misunderstood doctrine on divorce and remarriage. The article contained statements that allegedly defamed the former spouse of a prominent Church official. The court concluded that "our accommodation of the competing interests of our society—one protecting reputation, the other, the free exercise of religion—requires that we hold that in order for a plaintiff to recover damages for defamatory remarks made during the course of a doctrinal explanation by a duly authorized minister, he or she must show, by clear and convincing evidence, that the defamation was made with 'constitutional malice,' that is with knowledge that it was false or with reckless disregard of whether it was false or not." Such a rule, observed the court, "strikes an appropriate balance between our citizens' reputational interests and our society's interest in protecting the right to free exercise of religion." The court rejected the Church's claim that the constitutional guaranty of religious freedom prevents ministers from ever being sued for defamatory statements made in the course of doctrinal explanations. Such suits are constitutionally permissible, concluded the court, but a plaintiff has the difficult burden of proving "malice" by "clear and convincing evidence."*

• *A Louisiana court ruled that a church did not commit defamation when it published derogatory statements in a church newsletter.*[282] *A Catholic priest became upset when he suspected that a monument company that did work at a church cemetery was guilty of using church utilities without paying for them. He wrote a letter to the owner of the monument company which stated, in part: "Stated simply, your workers*

---

[281] McNair v. Worldwide Church of God, 242 Cal. Rptr. 823 (2d App. Dist. 1987).

[282] Redmond v. McCool, 582 So.2d 262 (La. App. 1991).

entered our property, and used [church] utilities without permission, and that is theft. I could have them arrested and charged, for your information." A copy of the letter was sent to the diocese. A week later, the priest published the following statement in a church newsletter (that was mailed to 362 families): "For your information, I have been obliged [to inform the monument company] that it is forbidden . . . to perform work of any kind in [the cemetery]. The company has persisted in ignoring my cemetery policies, and has a 'come as you please, go as you please' attitude and uses our electrical utilities without permission. The utilities come out of cemetery funds (e.g., your pocket)." The monument company sued the priest, the local church, and the diocese when it learned of the statement in the newsletter. The court rejected the company's claim of defamation. It observed, "The elements of a defamation action are: (1) a defamatory statement, (2) publication, (3) falsity, (4) actual or implied malice, and (5) resulting injury. A statement which imputes the commission of a crime to another is defamatory per se and as a result, falsity and malice are presumed, but not eliminated as requirements." The court concluded that the statements by the priest in the letter and church newsletter were false, but that they were not defamatory since the priest made them with a reasonable belief that they were true and accordingly they were not made with "malice."

• *A Minnesota court ruled that the First Amendment's "nonestablishment of religion" clause prevented it from resolving a dismissed minister's lawsuit against his former church.*[283] *A church installed a new pastor. From the beginning, the pastor's relationship with the congregation was strained. When the church council reduced the pastor's salary to less than $4,000, the pastor sued the church and a denominational agency. He alleged several theories of liability, including defamation. Specifically, he claimed that members of the church defamed him by making the following statements about him in public meetings that harmed his reputation and his ability to obtain another call: he did not attend a wedding rehearsal; he made a false statement regarding a church member's attendance at a retirement party; he insisted that his salary should be paid before the church's mortgage; he failed to visit in the hospital a woman with cancer; he failed to respond to a member's telephone call regarding an infant's death; he breached his duty of confidentiality by telling others of a member's abusive father and by stating that the member had a problem with authority; he charged $500 for conducting a wedding; he received eleven weeks of vacation; he had jeopardized the church's insurance policy by taking the church bus to camp; and while out of town, he returned only for the funerals of friends. The court concluded that these statements did not defame the pastor, since they were protected by a "conditional privilege." The court explained that "a communication is conditionally privileged . . . if it is made upon a proper occasion, from a proper motive, and . . . based upon reasonable or probable cause." This principle rests upon the courts' determination that "statements made in particular contexts or on certain occasions should be encouraged despite the risk that the statements might be defamatory." The court concluded that the members' alleged statements about the pastor qualified for this privilege since they all were communicated "at task force meetings or church council meetings and dealt with [the pastor's] actions as a pastor." Further, there was no evidence that the members were acting "out of the kind of malice or ill will that defeats the privilege." The pastor also claimed that he was defamed when a bishop's assistant told a church official that he was "paranoid." This statement was made during a phone conversation in which the church official and the bishop's*

---

[283] Singleton v. Christ the Servant Evangelical Lutheran Church, 541 N.W.2d 606 (Minn. App. 1996).

assistant discussed conflicts in the church, the pastor's position at the church, and the pastor's compensation. The court found these comments to be "within the conditional privilege." Further, there was no evidence that the bishop's assistant made the statement out of malice or ill will.

• An Ohio court ruled that a letter addressed by a church official to "members and friends" of the church, in which he explained why the church board dismissed a church secretary, might have been defamatory.[284] A woman was employed as an office secretary for her church for approximately eight years. She was informed by church officials that her employment was being terminated. The woman claimed that church officials did not express any dissatisfaction with her work performance. She later received a letter confirming the termination of her employment. The letter did not state any reasons for the termination. A church official later circulated a letter in which he stated that the woman had been "fired" as church secretary. The letter was directed to the "Fellow Members and Friends" of the church. In the letter, the official stated that the church board of trustees had cited "insubordination, some incompetency, and inability to maintain confidentiality" as some of the reasons for the termination. A few months later, the woman sued her church for defamation. A state appeals court threw out the case on the basis of a "qualified privilege." It defined the concept of qualified privilege as follows: "In order to qualify for this privilege, a defendant must establish that (1) he acted in good faith; (2) there was an interest to be upheld; (3) the statement was limited in its scope to the purpose of upholding that interest; (4) the occasion was proper; and (5) the publication was made in a proper manner and only to the proper parties. Once the defendant establishes the defense of qualified privilege, the plaintiff may not recover for defamation unless he can present clear and convincing evidence that the defamatory statement was made with actual malice." Was the letter sent by the church official to "members and friends" of the church protected against defamation by this qualified privilege? The court began its opinion by observing that members of the church would "logically be interested in, and proper parties to, the subject letter. Obviously, the letter concerned a church interest; i.e., [the woman's] ability to perform her duties as secretary for the church. It was written by a church [official], and was limited in scope to informing the members of the reasons for [the woman's] termination." However, the court ordered the case to proceed to trial, because it was not convinced that the letter had been distributed "only to the proper parties, i.e., the church membership." While the church official insisted that the letter had been sent only to members of the church, the woman claimed that "of the approximately 150 persons or households to whom the letter was mailed, seventeen were not members of the church," and that one of the recipients was another church. The court pointed out that the church failed to "indicate that the other church was in any way affiliated with it, and did not provide any evidence to show that the other church had a valid interest in the subject matter of the letter. Therefore, we conclude that a question of fact exists, with regard to the one church on the mailing list, as to whether the publication was limited to proper parties."

• An Oklahoma court ruled that the First Amendment guaranty of religious liberty, as well as the concept of qualified privilege, protected a church from being sued for defamation as a result of the senior pastor's statement to a church member that

---

[284] Baker v. Spinning Road Baptist Church, 1998 WL 598094 (unpublished decision, Ohio App. 1998).

a former youth pastor had been dismissed because he had been "questioning his sexuality." The court defined a qualified privilege as follows: "A church or other religious organization ordinarily bears no tort liability for statements by or between church officers or members concerning the conduct of other officers or members, because communications between members of a religious organization concerning the conduct of other members or officers in their capacity as such are qualifiedly privileged as matters affecting a common interest or purpose. This is especially so where the publication is made in response to a request rather than volunteered by the publisher. So, where the alleged defamatory statements are exchanged by or between members of the congregation during or as result of either a church's decision to employ, retain or terminate a clergyman or lay employee, or a church's review of the performance of a clergyman or lay employee, the conditional privilege shields the church from liability for defamation."

A qualified privilege is "qualified" in the sense that it will not apply if the person making an allegedly defamatory statement does so with "malice." In this context, malice means either a knowledge that the statement was false, or a reckless disregard as to its truthfulness.

The court noted that a church member had asked the senior pastor why Pastor Eric had been terminated, which amounted to a request for information "concerning [his] conduct or qualifications for office." The allegedly defamatory statement occurred in the course of the pastor's response to this inquiry, that is, "during an exchange between one member of the congregation and another member of the congregation concerning the acts of a third member of the congregation." The court concluded that "the uncontroverted evidence thus demonstrates publication of the complained-of statement occurred on a conditionally privileged occasion, and the record contains no evidence even remotely suggesting the destruction of the conditional or qualified privilege by abuse or malice."[285]

3. Statements Made at Ecclesiastical Disciplinary Hearings

Some courts have ruled that statements made at church disciplinary hearings are protected by a *qualified privilege*. This means that such communications cannot be defamatory unless made with malice. Malice in this context means that the person who made the allegedly defamatory remark knew that it was false, or made it with a reckless disregard as to its truth or falsity. This is a difficult standard to prove, which means that communications made in the course of church disciplinary hearings will be defamatory only in exceptional cases.

4. Defamation Claims Not Involving Doctrinal Inquiries

A few courts have concluded that the First Amendment does not prevent them from resolving defamation claims by ministers against churches and denominational agencies to the extent such claims can be resolved without any inquiry into religious doctrine or polity.

---

[285] *Trice v. Burress*, 137 P.3d 1253 (Okla. App. 2006).

Case Studies

• *A federal appeals court ruled that a minister could not sue his denomination for allegedly failing to follow its bylaws in suspending him, but he could sue the denomination for defamation.[286] As one of its services for member churches, a denomination prepares and circulates personal information files on its ministers to churches interested in hiring pastors and advises them on the background and suitability of individual ministers. The denomination placed a document in a minister's file stating that his spouse had previously been married. The minister claimed that the denomination took this action without consulting him or verifying the accuracy of the information, and that the information in fact was untrue. The minister alleged that because churches within the denomination automatically disqualify a minister if his personal file shows that his spouse has been divorced, the denomination effectively excluded him from consideration for employment as a pastor by circulating this false information. At the time the denomination was circulating the erroneous statement about his spouse, the minister was actively, and unsuccessfully, seeking employment in a local church. Even though he was established in his profession and over three hundred churches were in need of a pastor, the minister did not obtain a position with any church. He sued the denomination, seeking monetary damages for his loss of income during the time that it circulated the false information about his spouse. The court concluded that the First Amendment did not bar the minister's defamation claim: "The First Amendment proscribes intervention by secular courts into many employment decisions made by religious organizations based on religious doctrine or beliefs. Personnel decisions are protected from civil court interference where review by civil courts would require the courts to interpret and apply religious doctrine or ecclesiastical law. The First Amendment does not shield employment decisions made by religious organizations from civil court review, however, where the employment decisions do not implicate religious beliefs, procedures, or law. At the present stage of this litigation we are unable to predict that the evidence offered at trial will definitely involve the district court in an impermissible inquiry into the [denomination's] bylaws or religious beliefs. [The minister] has alleged that although over three hundred congregations were in need of a pastor he did not receive an offer of employment from any congregation while the [denomination] was circulating false information about his spouse. [His] fitness as a minister is not in dispute because his name was on the [denomination's] roster of eligible ministers during the relevant period. . . . The [denomination] has not offered any religious explanation for its actions which might entangle the court in a religious controversy in violation of the First Amendment. [The minister] is entitled to an opportunity to prove his secular allegations at trial."*

• *The Alaska Supreme Court ruled that a denominational official could be sued on the basis of defamation and interference with contract for making disparaging comments about another minister who recently had been hired by a local church.[287] A minister left a pastoral position in Alaska and accepted a call as minister of a church in Tennessee. When he presented himself to the church to begin his duties, he was informed by church officials that because of derogatory information the church had received from a denominational official in Alaska, the church would not hire him. The presbyter had informed church leaders that the minister was divorced, dishonest, unable to*

[286] Drevlow v. Lutheran Church, Missouri Synod, 991 F.2d 468 (8th Cir. 1993).

[287] Marshall v. Munro, 845 P.2d 424 (Alaska 1993).

perform pastoral duties because of throat surgery, and that he had made an improper sexual advance to a church member in Alaska. The minister sued the presbyter for defamation, interference with contract, and breach of contract. A trial court dismissed the lawsuit on the ground that it was without jurisdiction to decide matters of internal church discipline. The minister appealed to the state supreme court. The supreme court ruled that while the civil courts lacked jurisdiction to resolve the breach of contract claim, they could resolve the defamation and interference with contract claims. With regard to the defamation claim the court observed, "The questions raised by the defamation claim concern only the statements made by [the presbyter]. There is no need for the court to involve itself in [the pastor's] qualifications. The court needs to determine only if [the presbyter] actually said: (1) [the pastor] was divorced; (2) [the pastor] was dishonest; (3) [the pastor] had throat surgery disabling him as a pastor; and (4) [the pastor] made improper advances to a member of the congregation. If [the presbyter] raises the defenses of truth and of privilege, the court need only determine if the facts stated were true and if [the presbyter] made the statements with malice (a reckless disregard for the truth or falsity). There is no need to determine if [the pastor] was qualified to be a pastor or what those qualifications may be." The court rejected the presbyter's claim that this dispute is ecclesiastical in nature because his comments were made in the course of his official duties. The court did acknowledge, however, that "civil common law has long protected this exact type of communication by granting a conditional privilege." The court quoted the general rule as follows, "The common interest of members of religious . . . associations . . . is recognized as sufficient to support a privilege for communications among themselves concerning the qualifications of the officers and members and their participation in the activities of the society. This is true whether the defamatory matter related to alleged misconduct of some other member that makes him undesirable for continued membership, or the conduct of a prospective member. So too, the rule is applicable to communications between members and officers of the organization concerning the legitimate conduct of the activities for which it was organized." That is, the presbyter's statements concerning the fitness of the pastor for the Tennessee church relate to a matter of common interest among members of the church. Accordingly, the presbyter's statements were protected by a qualified or conditional privilege. This means that such statements cannot be defamatory unless they are made with legal malice. In this context, legal malice means either a knowledge that the statements were false, or a reckless disregard as to their truth or falsity. The court noted that "determining whether [the presbyter] acted with actual malice will not require the court to delve into ecclesiastical concerns. Rather, the issue is whether [he] had reasonable grounds for believing the defamatory statements and whether they were motivated by actual malice. This question can be resolved without considering [the pastor's] church related duties and is within the court's jurisdiction."

• *A New Jersey court allowed a woman to sue her church on the basis of defamation as a result of an associate pastor's disclosure to the congregation that the woman had engaged in a sexual relationship with the senior pastor.*[288]

---

[288] F.G. v. MacDonell, 677 A.2d 258 (N.J. Super. 1996).

5. Defenses to Defamation

There are several defenses available to churches that are sued for defamation. These are reviewed in section 4-02.3 in the context of clergy who are sued for defamation.

Case Studies

• *A Georgia court ruled that it could not resolve a lawsuit brought by church members against their church as a result of defamatory statements made by other church members.*[289] *A church and several of its members were sued by other members who claimed that they had been defamed by several statements made about them. The lawsuit alleged that in the course of a New Year's Eve church service, certain members intentionally and maliciously announced to the congregation that each of the plaintiffs "was a witch and had practiced evil deeds upon family and fellow church members," and that these statements were later repeated to a wider audience at another church service. The "evil deeds" allegedly practiced by the plaintiffs included witchcraft, acts of bodily harm, thievery, causing infertility, stealing United States government files to harm a fellow member, and child abuse. The court concluded that the church could not be liable for defamation: "Although plaintiffs alleged that the church conspired with its members to slander them, the doctrine of respondeat superior [that is, that an organization is responsible for the acts of its agents] does not apply in slander cases. Plaintiffs did not allege or show by any record evidence that the church expressly ordered and directed [its members] to say those very words. . . . [A] corporation is not liable for the slanderous utterances of an agent acting within the scope of his employment, unless it affirmatively appears that the agent was expressly directed or authorized to slander the plaintiff. The same would apply to utterances of a church member. Moreover, the complaint does not state an actionable claim against the church. Allegations of slander by individuals and other leaders of the church do not express a claim against the church itself as a separate entity." The court allowed the members to sue those who had uttered the defamatory words. It rejected the defendant members' claim that they were protected by a qualified privilege. Specifically, the members asserted that their remarks concerning the plaintiffs "were made as testimony or confession during a worship service and thus were a church activity." As a result, the remarks could not be defamatory unless they were made with legal malice, meaning that the members who uttered the remarks either knew that they were false or did so with a reckless disregard as to their truth or falsity. The court disagreed, noting that the statements "were not made in a church tribunal in the course of an investigation of alleged misconduct of church members."*

• *A Georgia court ruled that a $3 million judgment against certain church members for defaming other members of the congregation was not excessive. However, the court ruled that the church was not liable for the defamatory statements made by the members: "Although plaintiffs alleged that the church conspired with its members to slander them, the doctrine of respondeat superior [that is, that an organization is responsible for the acts of its agents] does not apply in slander cases. Plaintiffs did not allege or show by any record evidence that the church expressly ordered and directed [its members] to say those words. . . . [A] corporation is not liable for the*

---

[289] First United Church v. Udofia, 479 S.E.2d 146 (Ga. App. 1996).

slanderous utterances of an agent acting within the scope of his employment, unless it affirmatively appears that the agent was expressly directed or authorized to slander the plaintiff. The same would apply to utterances of a church member."[290]

• An Ohio appeals court ruled that a church could be responsible for defamation as a result of information published in a congregational newsletter about a dismissed secretary. However, the court concluded that a denominational agency could not be liable for the defamation, even though an official had suggested to the church that it publish the defamatory statement. A church secretary claimed that a minister sexually harassed her. A denominational official investigated the charges, but took no action because the minister denied any wrongdoing and there was no other evidence supporting the woman's charges. The minister later dismissed the secretary and published in the parish newsletter a statement that the secretary had been engaging in an open malicious endeavor to discredit him. Following her dismissal, the secretary filed a lawsuit against the church and denomination. She asserted several bases of liability, including defamation. The court allowed the secretary to sue the church for defamation, but not the denomination. It concluded, "However, as to the defamation claim, [the former secretary] contends that the diocese, acting through an archdeacon of the diocese, advised [the minister] what to write in the allegedly defamatory newsletter. Nevertheless, that did not make the publication that of the diocese. The publication was that of [the minister and local church]."

Defenses to Liability

§ 10-16

There are a number of legal defenses that may be available to a church that is sued on the basis of any of the theories of liability addressed in this chapter. Some have been discussed in previous sections, such as the "qualified privilege" defense that is available to a church that is sued for defamation. This section will address several other legal defenses.

Contributory and Comparative Negligence

§ 10-16.1

Key point 10-16.1. *Under the principle of comparative negligence, a church is liable only to the extent of its percentage share of fault for an accident or injury.*

Contributory negligence is conduct on the part of a person injured through the negligence of another that itself falls below the standard to which a reasonable person would conform for his or her own safety and protection. Historically, the contributory negligence of an accident victim operated as a complete defense to

---

[290] Esenyie v. Udofia, 511 S.E.2d 260 (Ga. App. 1999).

negligence. Accordingly, accident victims who themselves were negligent could be denied any damages. To illustrate, a woman who was injured when she fell down the back stairway of a church while carrying a large ice chest was denied any monetary damages on the basis of her own contributory negligence.[291] The court concluded that the member "loses because she was contributorily negligent. [T]he fact is she stepped through a doorway, with her vision at least partially obscured by the ice chest she carried, missed her step, and fell. Reasonable prudence required her to be more careful. . . . She had no right to assume that there was a place to land her foot because she could not see where she was going." The absence of a handrail and the width of the top step in no way contributed to the member's injuries, the court concluded.

Most states have attempted to lessen the severity of the rule denying any recovery to an accident victim who was contributorily negligent through the adoption of *comparative negligence* statutes. Under the so-called pure comparative negligence statutes, accident victims whose contributory negligence was not the sole cause of their injuries may recover damages against another whose negligence was the primary cause of the accident, but their monetary damages are diminished in proportion to the amount of their own negligence. Under a pure comparative negligence statute, victims may recover against a negligent defendant even though their own contributory negligence was equal to or greater than the defendant's negligence.

Many other states have adopted the *equal-to or greater-than rule* or the *fifty-percent rule*. Under these statutes, accident victims whose contributory negligence is equal to or greater than the defendant's negligence are totally barred from recovery. But, accident victims whose contributory negligence is less than the defendant's negligence may recover damages, although their damages are diminished in proportion to the amount of their own negligence.

Other states permit a plaintiff to recover damages for the injuries caused by a negligent defendant if his own contributory negligence was slight in comparison to the negligence of the defendant. To illustrate, a woman was injured when she was struck by a church-owned vehicle that was being driven in a negligent manner. The woman sued the church, and a jury found the church negligent, assessing damages at $300,000. However, the jury also found that 80 percent of the woman's injuries were attributable to her failure to wear a seat belt, and accordingly her damages were reduced by 80 percent (or $240,000) to a total of $60,000. At the trial, the church established that the woman's car had a seat belt. The woman herself testified that she was thankful *not* to have worn the belt because of her belief that a seat belt would have caused additional injuries.[292]

---

[291] Richard v. Church Insurance Company, 538 So.2d 658 (La. App. 1989).

[292] Smith v. Holy Temple Church of God in Christ, Inc., 566 So.2d 864 (Fla. App. 1990). The ruling was reversed on appeal on the basis of a technicality.

Case Studies

• *A Colorado court ruled that a jury erred in finding that a young boy who had been molested by his pastor was partly at fault.*[293] *The jury found the boy to be 4 percent at fault, and reduced the damages it awarded the boy by this amount under the principle of comparative negligence. The court observed, "Here, there was no evidence that would support a finding that the minor unreasonably subjected himself to the risks associated with [the pastor's] counseling. The minor was only seven when he entered counseling, and he continued to see [the pastor] until the time he entered middle school. He entered into the counseling relationship only at [the pastor's] behest and at his mother's direction. Indeed, there was testimony from both the minor and the mother that he was often quite reluctant to see [the pastor] and had to be persuaded to do so. The minor also testified that [the pastor] told him that the counseling was confidential and that the minor should not discuss with others the contents of their sessions. Finally, [the victim's] expert opined that, in situations involving the abuse of a child by an adult in a position of trust, it is common for the child not to report it to others. The church offered no testimony to contradict this view, nor did it offer any testimony respecting the reasonable standard of conduct of a child of the minor's age in such circumstances. We conclude, therefore, that the evidence failed to establish, as a matter of law, any negligence on the part of the minor."*

• *A Pennsylvania court ruled that a church and diocese could be liable for a priest's acts of child molestation. The church defendants argued that the trial court erred in not allowing the defense of comparative negligence. The theory of comparative negligence assigns damages to defendants in proportion to their degree of fault. For example, had the jury determined the priest to be 80 percent at fault, and the church defendants only 20 percent, the church defendants would only have been liable for 20 percent of the jury's verdict. The court stressed that the theory of comparative negligence only applies to negligence. It then observed: "For several reasons, we share the trial court's concern about entering into a comparison of the parties' respective negligence in this case. First, it is problematic that [the priest's] conduct is central to the negligent acts alleged on the part of the [church defendants]. In the context of liability insurance coverage . . . pedophilic sexual abuse is intentional conduct on the part of the abuser, as a matter of law, and is not negligent conduct. . . . [S]ince [the priest's] acts of pedophilic sexual molestation were intentional, the doctrine of comparative negligence has no application here. The acts that directly caused the harm are, in essence, what must be compared. [The priest's] intentional act and the alleged negligence of [the victim] are not equal forms of conduct. . . . [C]omparative negligence is only an appropriate consideration in matters where there is negligence on the part of both the plaintiff and the defendant involved in causing the harm that results, not where the conduct of one is willful."*[294]

---

[293] DeBose v. Bear Valley Church of Christ, 890 P.2d 214 (Colo. App. 1994).

[294] Hutchison v. Luddy, 2000 WL 1585672 (Pa. 2000).

Assumption of Risk

§ 10-16.2

Key point 10-16.2. *Adults who voluntarily expose themselves to a known risk created by a church program or activity generally cannot sue the church if they are injured as a result of that risk.*

Persons who voluntarily expose themselves to a known danger or to a danger that was so obvious that it should have been recognized will be deemed to have assumed the risks of their conduct. As a result, persons who voluntarily expose themselves to the negligent conduct of a defendant with full knowledge of the danger will be barred from recovery for any injuries resulting from the defendant's negligence.

Assumption of risk is closely related to contributory negligence. One court has distinguished the two by noting that assumption of risk connotes "venturousness," whereas contributory negligence connotes a state of carelessness.[295] To illustrate, one court ruled that an adult church member who was seriously injured when he slipped and fell on a wet linoleum floor immediately following his baptism by immersion could sue his church if the church knew or should have known that the floor presented an unreasonable risk of harm. However, the court concluded that the church's negligence might be superseded by the victim's own negligence in carelessly exposing himself to a known hazard.[296]

Case Studies

• An Illinois court ruled that a church board member who was seriously injured when he fell off a ladder while installing a ceiling fan in the church was barred from recovering any damages because of his assumption of a known risk.[297] The court observed, "[I]t is well-established that a landowner is not liable for injuries resulting from open and obvious dangers on the premises, including the open and obvious danger of falling from high places. We determine that [the board member's] attempt to install the ceiling fans in the church's high ceiling by positioning his ladder in the church pews was an open and obvious danger, and his injuries are therefore not recoverable . . . ."

• The Kansas Supreme Court ruled that a minor who had been rendered a quadriplegic as a result of injuries sustained while playing football for a church-operated high school could not sue the church.[298] "We feel sympathy for the severe injuries suffered by this

---

[295] Cross v. Noland, 190 S.E.2d 18 (W. Va. 1972).

[296] Huston v. First Church of God, 732 P.2d 173 (Wash. App. 1987).

[297] Coates v. W.W. Babcock Co., 560 N.E.2d 1099 (Ill. App. 1990). However, the court concluded that the board member had presented enough evidence to sue the church for a violation of the state "Structural Work Act," which protects any person employed or engaged on a ladder while undertaking the repair of a building. The court ordered the case to proceed to trial on this basis.

[298] Wicina v. Strecker, 747 P.2d 167 (Kan. 1987). *But see* Locilento v. John A. Coleman Catholic High School, 523 N.Y.S.2d 198 (1987), in which a New York court concluded that voluntary participation in an athletic contest, without more, amounts to only an implied assumption of risk that is not a complete bar to recovery in the event of an accident. It is, however, a factor to be considered in assessing fault.

plaintiff," the court concluded. "However, there are dangers and risks inherent in the game of football and those who play the game encounter these risks voluntarily."

Intervening Cause § 10-16.3

Key point 10-16.3. *A church is not legally responsible for an injury that occurs on its premises or in the course of one of its activities if the injury resulted from the intervention of a new and independent cause that was unforeseeable.*

Many courts have ruled that a person's negligence is not the legal cause of an injury that results from the intervention of a new and independent cause that is (1) neither anticipated nor reasonably foreseeable, (2) not a consequence of his or her negligence, (3) not controlled by him or her, and (4) the actual cause of the injury in the sense that the injury would not have occurred without it. If an intervening cause meets these conditions, it is considered a "superseding" cause that eliminates the original wrongdoer's liability.

To illustrate, a superseding, intervening cause was found to have insulated the original wrongdoer from liability for his negligence in the following situations: a bus driver ran a stop sign, causing a car approaching from an intersecting street to abruptly stop, resulting in the car being struck by another car that had been following it too closely;[299] a motorist's negligent driving resulted in a collision with a second vehicle, and a third motorist, whose attention was distracted by the scene of the accident, struck a pedestrian;[300] and a motorist's negligent operation of his automobile caused an accident, and a police officer investigating the scene of the accident was injured when struck by another vehicle being operated in a negligent manner.[301]

Case Studies

• *A Georgia court ruled that a public school was not legally responsible for the murder of a child who was released by school officials prior to the end of the school day.[302] While the case involved a school, it is directly relevant to churches as well. The school had a written policy addressing early dismissals of students. The policy specified that no student could be released prior to the end of the school day without the consent of a parent. On the day of the murder, the school received two calls from a person with a male voice requesting that the victim be released early. The caller was informed that this was not possible without the consent of a parent. A short time later the school received a call from a person identifying herself as the victim's mother. This person requested that the victim be released early due to a "family emergency." A school secretary authorized the early release of the victim based on this call, and on her way*

---

[299] Seeger v. Weber, 113 N.W.2d 566 (Wis. 1962).

[300] Lewis v. Esselman, 539 S.W.2d 581 (Mo. 1976).

[301] Schrimsher v. Bryson, 130 Cal. Rptr. 125 (1976).

[302] Perkins v. Morgan County School District, 476 S.E.2d 592 (Ga. App. 1996).

home the victim was abducted and murdered. The victim's parents sued the school, claiming that it was responsible for their daughter's death as a result of its negligent supervision. A state appeals court ruled that the school was not liable for the girl's death. The court conceded that the school may have been negligent, but it concluded that this negligence was not the cause of the girl's death. Rather, the death was caused by an unforeseeable "intervening cause"—the criminal activity of an outsider—which relieved the school from liability. The court observed, "Generally, an intervening criminal act of a third party, without which the injury would not have occurred, will also be treated as the [cause] of the injury thus breaking the causal connection between the defendant's negligence and the injury unless the criminal act was a reasonably foreseeable consequence of the defendant's conduct." The court noted that (1) school officials had no reason to suspect that the murderer posed a risk of harm to the victim; (2) school officials were aware of no threats ever directed to the victim by the murderer or anyone else; (3) no student had ever before been abducted or assaulted after being released before the end of the school day; and (4) the victim expressed no concern for her safety. Based on this evidence, the court concluded that "it was not foreseeable that [the victim] would be murdered after being released from school early." The court concluded that even if the school had been negligent in properly supervising the victim, its negligence "did nothing more than give rise to the occasion which made her injuries possible." The murder was caused by the intervening criminal act.

• The New York Court of Appeals court ruled that a school was liable on the basis of negligent supervision for the rape of a 12-year-old girl that occurred when she left a school outing without permission.[303] A lower court ruled that the school was not responsible for the victim's injuries. It concluded that even if the school had negligently supervised the outing it could not be responsible for the victim's injuries since "the unforeseeable conduct of [the two rapists] constituted a superseding tortious act that absolved the [school] of any culpability for [the victim's] injuries." The victim appealed this decision, and the state's highest court reversed the lower court's decision and ruled in favor of the victim. The court concluded, "[W]e cannot say that the intervening act of rape was unforeseeable as a matter of law. A rational jury hearing the trial testimony could have determined, as the jury did in this case, that the foreseeable result of the danger created by [the school's] alleged lack of supervision was injury such as occurred here. A [jury] could have reasonably concluded that the very purpose of the school supervision was to shield vulnerable schoolchildren from such acts of violence. As we have previously recognized, when the intervening, intentional act of another is itself the foreseeable harm that shapes the duty imposed, the defendant who fails to guard against such conduct will not be relieved of liability when that act occurs."

• A New York court ruled that a church was not legally responsible for the death of a parishioner who was struck and killed by a car while he was standing on the front steps of his church. The court noted that "a landowner has a duty to maintain his or her property in reasonably safe condition," but it also pointed out that "there will ordinarily be no duty imposed on a defendant to prevent a third party from causing harm to another unless the intervening act which caused the plaintiff's injuries was a normal and foreseeable consequence of the situation created by the defendant's negligence. Liability may not be imposed upon a party who merely furnished the condition or

---

[303] Bell v. Board of Education, 687 N.Y.S.2d 1325 (A.D. 1997).

occasion for the occurrence of the event but was not one of its causes. Here, the accident was not a normal and foreseeable consequence of any actions of the church. The church merely provided an area to drop off passengers, thereby furnishing the condition for the accident, but not a cause."[304]

Statutes of Limitations

§ 10-16.4

Key point 10-16.4. *The statute of limitations specifies the deadline for filing a civil lawsuit. Lawsuits cannot be brought after this deadline has passed. There are a few exceptions that have been recognized by some courts: (1) The statute of limitations for injuries suffered by a minor begins to run on the minor's eighteenth birthday. (2) The statute of limitations does not begin to run until an adult survivor of child sexual molestation "discovers" that he or she has experienced physical or emotional suffering as a result of the molestation. (3) The statute of limitations does not begin to run until an adult with whom a minister or church counselor has had sexual contact "discovers" that his or her psychological damages were caused by the inappropriate contact. (4) The statute of limitations is suspended due to fraud or concealment of a cause of action.*

1. In General

Statutes of limitation specify the deadline for filing a civil lawsuit. Most states have several of these statutes, with each pertaining to designated kinds of claims. For example, there often are different statutes of limitation for bringing contract, personal injury, and property damage claims, with different deadlines for each kind of claim. Persons who do not file a lawsuit by the deadline specified by law generally have no legal recourse.

Key point. *This chapter does not address statutes of limitations for criminal prosecutions of persons whose actions violate state or federal criminal law.*

2. Extending the Statute of Limitations—Injuries to Minors

The statute of limitations does not begin to "run" in the case of injuries to a minor until the minor's eighteenth birthday. To illustrate, if the statute of limitations for personal injuries is three years in a particular state, and a minor is injured in an automobile accident, the minor has until his or her twenty-first birthday to file a lawsuit seeking damages. The three-year statute of limitations period begins to run on the minor's eighteenth birthday.

Example. *A four-year-old child is molested by a volunteer worker at church. The statute of limitations for personal injuries is three years. The child has until her twenty-first birthday to file a lawsuit seeking damages for her injuries—a period of nearly 17 years.*

Key point. *Some states have enacted special statutes of limitation for victims of child molestation, and these supersede the statute of limitations for personal injuries.*

---

[304] Bun Il Park v. Korean Presbyterian Church, 1999 WL 1214620 (N.Y.A.D. 1999).

State legislatures and courts have come up with a variety of ways to extend the statute of limitations for injuries to minors (including cases of child molestation). These include:

- The general rule is that the statute of limitations does not begin to run until a minor reaches the age of majority (18). To illustrate, if a five-year-old child is injured at church, and the applicable statute of limitations is three years, then the child will have until his or her twenty-first birthday to file a lawsuit. This is because the three-year statute of limitations does not begin to run until the victim's eighteenth birthday.

- Several states have enacted statutes that extend the statute of limitations in cases of child molestation.

- The legislatures and courts in several states have adopted the so-called "discovery rule" in cases of child molestation. According to this rule, the statute of limitations in cases of child abuse does not begin to run until the victim's eighteenth birthday, or the date that the victim "discovers" the connection between his or her emotional injuries and the abuse, whichever is later.

- Some courts have suspended ("tolled") the statute of limitations in cases of child molestation on the basis of fraud.

The last three of these grounds for extending the statute of limitations are summarized in the following subsections.

3. Extending the Statute of Limitations—State Statutes

Several states have enacted statutes that extend the statute of limitations in cases of child molestation. Consider the following examples:

Table 10-6 Selected State Statutes Extending the Limitations Period in Cases of Child Sexual Abuse

Note: Statutes are subject to change. Do not rely on the text of any statute without the advice of legal counsel.

state	statute
Alabama	If anyone entitled to commence any of the actions enumerated in this chapter, to make an entry on land or enter a defense founded on the title to real property is, at the time the right accrues, below the age of 19 years, or insane, he or she shall have three years, or the period allowed by law for the commencement of an action if it be less than three years, after the termination of the disability to commence an action, make entry, or defend. No disability shall extend the period of limitations so as to allow an action to be commenced, entry made, or defense made after the lapse of 20 years from the time the claim or right accrued. (Ala. Code § 6-2-8)

Table 10-6 Selected State Statutes Extending the Limitations Period in Cases of Child Sexual Abuse

Note: Statutes are subject to change. Do not rely on the text of any statute without the advice of legal counsel.

state	statute
California	In an action for recovery of damages suffered as a result of childhood sexual abuse, the time for commencement of the action shall be within eight years of the date the plaintiff attains the age of majority or within three years of the date the plaintiff discovers or reasonably should have discovered that psychological injury or illness occurring after the age of majority was caused by the sexual abuse, whichever period expires later, for any of the following actions: (1) An action against any person for committing an act of childhood sexual abuse. (2) An action for liability against any person or entity who owed a duty of care to the plaintiff, where a wrongful or negligent act by that person or entity was a legal cause of the childhood sexual abuse which resulted in the injury to the plaintiff. (3) An action for liability against any person or entity where an intentional act by that person or entity was a legal cause of the childhood sexual abuse which resulted in the injury to the plaintiff. (b)(1) No action described in paragraph (2) or (3) of subdivision (a) may be commenced on or after the plaintiff's 26th birthday. (2) This subdivision does not apply if the person or entity knew or had reason to know, or was otherwise on notice, of any unlawful sexual conduct by an employee, volunteer, representative, or agent, and failed to take reasonable steps, and to implement reasonable safeguards, to avoid acts of unlawful sexual conduct in the future by that person, including, but not limited to, preventing or avoiding placement of that person in a function or environment in which contact with children is an inherent part of that function or environment. For purposes of this subdivision, providing or requiring counseling is not sufficient, in and of itself, to constitute a reasonable step or reasonable safeguard. (CAL. CODE OF CIVIL PROCEDURE § 340.1. This section was held unconstitutional in Perez v. Richard Roe, 52 Cal.Rptr.3d 762 (Cal. App. 2006), when applied retroactively to an existing judgment)

Table 10-6 Selected State Statutes Extending the Limitations Period in Cases of Child Sexual Abuse

Note: Statutes are subject to change. Do not rely on the text of any statute without the advice of legal counsel.

state	statute
Florida	An action founded on alleged abuse . . . may be commenced at any time within 7 years after the age of majority, or within 4 years after the injured person leaves the dependency of the abuser, or within 4 years from the time of discovery by the injured party of both the injury and the causal relationship between the injury and the abuse, whichever occurs later. (FLA. STATS. § 95.11(7))
Illinois	(a) Notwithstanding any other provision of law, an action for damages for personal injury based on childhood sexual abuse must be commenced within 10 years of the date the limitation period begins to run under subsection (d) or within 5 years of the date the person abused discovers or through the use of reasonable diligence should discover both (i) that the act of childhood sexual abuse occurred and (ii) that the injury was caused by the childhood sexual abuse. The fact that the person abused discovers or through the use of reasonable diligence should discover that the act of childhood sexual abuse occurred is not, by itself, sufficient to start the discovery period under this subsection (b). Knowledge of the abuse does not constitute discovery of the injury or the causal relationship between any later-discovered injury and the abuse. . . . (d) The limitation periods under subsection (b) do not begin to run before the person abused attains the age of 18 years; and, if at the time the person abused attains the age of 18 years he or she is under other legal disability, the limitation periods under subsection (b) do not begin to run until the removal of the disability. (735 ILCS 5/13-202.2)
Minnesota	(a) An action for damages based on personal injury caused by sexual abuse must be commenced within six years of the time the plaintiff knew or had reason to know that the injury was caused by the sexual abuse. (b) The plaintiff need not establish which act in a continuous series of sexual abuse acts by the defendant caused the injury. (c) The knowledge of a parent or guardian may not be imputed to a minor. (MINN. STATS. § 541.073)

Table 10-6 Selected State Statutes Extending the Limitations Period in Cases of Child Sexual Abuse

Note: Statutes are subject to change. Do not rely on the text of any statute without the advice of legal counsel.

state	statute
Ohio	An action for assault or battery brought by a victim of childhood sexual abuse based on childhood sexual abuse, or an action brought by a victim of childhood sexual abuse asserting any claim resulting from childhood sexual abuse, shall be brought within twelve years after the cause of action accrues. For purposes of this section, a cause of action for assault or battery based on childhood sexual abuse, or a cause of action for a claim resulting from childhood sexual abuse, accrues upon the date on which the victim reaches the age of majority. If the defendant in an action brought by a victim of childhood sexual abuse asserting a claim resulting from childhood sexual abuse that occurs on or after the effective date of this act has fraudulently concealed from the plaintiff facts that form the basis of the claim, the running of the limitations period with regard to that claim is tolled until the time when the plaintiff discovers or in the exercise of due diligence should have discovered those facts. (Ohio Rev. Code § 2305.111(C))
Pennsylvania	(2) (i) If an individual entitled to bring a civil action arising from childhood sexual abuse is under 18 years of age at the time the cause of action accrues, the individual shall have a period of 12 years after attaining 18 years of age in which to commence an action for damages regardless of whether the individual files a criminal complaint regarding the childhood sexual abuse. (42 Pa. C.S.A. § 5533)

4. Extending the Statute of Limitations—the "Discovery Rule"

Some states have adopted, either through legislation or court decision, a limited exception to the statute of limitations known as the *discovery rule*. Under this rule, the statute of limitations does not begin to run until a person realizes that his or her injuries were caused by a particular event or condition. The discovery rule has been applied most often in the following three contexts:

(1) **Medical malpractice.** In some cases, medical malpractice is difficult if not impossible to recognize until after the statute of limitations has expired. To illustrate, if a surgeon inadvertently leaves a scalpel in a patient's body during an operation, and the patient does not discover this fact until after the statute of limitations for medical malpractice has expired, he should not be denied his day in court. Under the discovery rule, the statute of limitations begins to run not when the malpractice occurred, but when

the patient knew or should have known of it.

(2) **Child molestation.** Some courts have applied the discovery rule in cases of child molestation. These courts have concluded that young children may "block out" memories of molestation, and not recall what happened for many years. The statute of limitations does not begin to run until the victim's eighteenth birthday, or until the victim knew or should have known that his or her emotional or physical injuries were caused by the acts of molestation. Courts that have applied this rule generally have limited it to victims who were very young at the time of the molestation. Adults who claim that they repressed memories of molestation occurring when they were adolescents have had a very difficult time convincing juries that they are telling the truth.

(3) **Seduction of adult counselees.** Some courts have applied the discovery rule in cases of sexual contact between a minister and an adult counselee. These courts have concluded that adults who engage in such acts with a minister may attempt to repress their memory of them, or be so intimated by the authority of the minister that they lack the capacity to file a lawsuit.

Key point. *The discovery rule presents extraordinary difficulties for a church that is sued as a result of an alleged incident of sexual misconduct that occurred many years ago. In some cases, church leaders cannot even remember the alleged wrongdoer, much less the precautions that were followed in selecting or supervising this person. Because of these difficulties, a majority of states have rejected the discovery rule, or interpreted it very narrowly.[305]*

Case Studies

• *The Supreme Court of Alabama ruled that the statute of limitations prevented an adult from suing a church for damages he allegedly suffered as a minor when he was molested by a priest.[306] The victim asserted that he was unaware that his emotional problems were associated with the abuse until he met with a counselor as an adult. He filed a lawsuit within the next year—some fifteen years after the last act of abuse. The victim sued the church, claiming that it was responsible for his injuries on the basis of negligent hiring and supervision of the priest, and breach of a fiduciary duty. At the time, the statute of limitations on such claims was two years under Alabama law, beginning when the victim reached age eighteen. Since that period had long expired before the victim filed his lawsuit, he claimed that the statute of limitations should be suspended until he first became aware that his problems resulted from the abuse. The victim insisted that he suffered from a "post traumatic stress disorder" that caused him to repress all memory of the abuse until he saw a counselor.*

---

[305] *See, e.g.,* Tichenor v. Roman Catholic Church, 32 F.3d 953 (5th Cir. 1994) (applying Mississippi law); Cherepski v. Walters, 913 S.W.2d 761 (Ark. 1996); Hertel v. Sullivan, 633 N.E.2d 36 (Ill. App. 1994).

[306] Travis v. Ziter, 681 So.2d 1348 (Ala. 1996).

A court refused to suspend the statute of limitations, and ruled that the victim's claims against the church had to be dismissed since they were filed too late. It began its opinion by noting that "the controversial question of repressed memory of childhood sexual abuse has been the subject of numerous studies" and that a review of these studies "leads to one conclusion—there is no consensus of scientific thought in support of the repressed memory theory." The court acknowledged that "insanity" may suspend the statute of limitations in some cases, but it rejected the victim's claim that his post traumatic stress disorder and repressed memory qualified as insanity.

The court noted that most other courts have reached this same conclusion. It observed, "At its core, the statute of limitations advances the truth-seeking function of our justice system, promotes efficiency by giving plaintiffs an incentive to timely pursue claims, and promotes stability by protecting defendants from stale claims. The essence of the [victim's] claim is that plaintiffs should be able to [suspend the statute of limitations] in any situation where they can demonstrate an inability to comprehend a specific legal right, or to recall events that happened many years before, notwithstanding the fact that they have been capable of living an independent, normal, and productive life as to all other matters. Such an expansive interpretation would undermine the purpose of the statute of limitations." The court noted that allowing alleged victims to sue for incidents of child abuse many years after the statute of limitations ordinarily would have expired would put them "in subjective control" and raise the risk of allowing persons to "assert stale claims without sufficient justification or sufficient guaranties of accurate fact-finding."

• An Arizona appeals court refused to allow an adult who had been sexually molested as a child by his pastor to sue his church after the statute of limitations expired, and rejected the victim's defense that the statute of limitations should be suspended because he was suffering from "cognitive avoidance." The victim argued that a pedophile should not be rewarded by the protection of the statute of limitations when he did something so outrageous that the victim did not want to remember it. The court countered: "Fundamental policy behind statutes of limitation does not, however, equate a plaintiff who deliberately avoids a memory to a plaintiff who is in a blamelessly uninformed state. Our supreme court has determined that tolling the statute of limitations is an appropriate policy for those whose memories are inaccessible but not for those who can remember. Having found, as a matter of fact, that [the victim] was in the latter category, the trial court was legally compelled to find that the statute had not been tolled."[307]

An adult sued a church alleging that he had been sexually molested when he was a minor by a priest. A psychologist testified during the trial that the best predictors for developing amnesia for incidents of abuse are "(1) young age of onset, (2) multiple incidents of abuse, and (3) severity of abuse." The psychologist concluded that Eric did not fit this profile. She also testified that only 15 to 20 percent of victims have full amnesia after childhood sexual abuse and that, in general, the majority of people retain their memories for traumatic events.[308]

---

[307] Watson v. Roman Catholic Church, 64 P.3d 195 (Ariz. App. 2003).

[308] Id.

Case Studies

• *A federal court in Connecticut dismissed a lawsuit brought against a church and diocese by two adults who had been sexually molested by a priest when they were minors.[309] The church and diocese insisted that the negligence claims against them were barred by the statute of limitations. They pointed out that negligence claims under Connecticut law must be brought within two years from the date when the injury is first sustained or discovered, but in no event more than three years from the date of the negligent conduct. The court noted that another Connecticut statute specifies that "no action to recover damages for personal injury to a minor, including emotional distress caused by sexual abuse, sexual exploitation or sexual assault may be brought by such person later than seventeen years from the date such person attains the age of majority." The court concluded that this seventeen year statute applied, and that the brothers' lawsuit was filed before seventeen years had elapsed since their eighteenth birthdays.*

• *A court in the District of Columbia ruled that three adults were barred by the statute of limitations from suing an archdiocese for injuries they suffered as a result of being molested by a priest when they were minors.[310] The victims alleged that they had no reason to suspect negligent hiring or retention of the priest until they read a series of articles in a local newspaper when they were in their thirties. The victims insisted that the discovery rule applied to their claims and that the archdiocese's "fraudulent concealment" of its wrongdoing delayed the statute of limitations until the publication of the newspaper articles. The appeals court concluded that the statute of limitations barred the victims' claims whether the discovery rule was applied or not. It noted that under both the general rule and the discovery rule exception, the statute of limitations begins to run when a plaintiff either has actual knowledge of a cause of action or is charged with knowledge of that cause of action. The court observed that in the District of Columbia, a plaintiff can be charged with notice of his claims "even if he is not actually aware of each essential element of his cause of action. This court has repeatedly held that a claim accrues when the plaintiff knows of (1) an injury, (2) its cause, and (3) some evidence of wrongdoing."*

The court concluded that "according to their complaints, all three [victims] were aware from the outset that it was the archdiocese that had assigned [the priest] to [their church] and that [the priest's] role was that of a subordinate representative of the archdiocese. It is also undisputed that the alleged acts of abuse occurred on church premises, while [the priest] was functioning as a representative of the archdiocese. In these circumstances, we conclude that a reasonable plaintiff would have investigated his potential claims against the archdiocese at the same time that his claims accrued against its representative. Because there is no evidence of fraudulent concealment by the archdiocese, a reasonably diligent investigation would have revealed at least some evidence of wrongdoing on the part of the archdiocese (assuming arguendo that such wrongdoing had occurred). Consequently, we hold that appellants' claims against the archdiocese accrued simultaneously with their claims against the priest."

The court rejected the victims' claim that the statute of limitations should be suspended because of the actions of the archdiocese in concealing from them its

---

[309] Nutt v. Norwich Roman Catholic Diocese, 921 F. Supp. 66 (D. Conn. 1995). *See also* Martinelli v. Bridgeport Roman Catholic Diocese, 989 F. Supp. 110 (D. Conn. 1997).

[310] Cevenini v. Archbishop of Washington, 707 A.2d 768 (D.C. 1998).

responsibility for their injuries. The court conceded that when the party claiming the protection of the statute of limitations has employed "affirmative acts . . . to fraudulently conceal either the existence of a claim or facts forming the basis of a cause of action," such conduct will suspend the statute. But it concluded that the archdiocese did not engage in concealment, noting that "we are unwilling to hold that a failure to disclose information that has not even been requested constitutes fraudulent concealment."

• A Florida court ruled that a 27-year-old man who had been molested by a priest when he was a minor was barred by the statute of limitations from suing his church.[311] The court agreed with the church and bishop that the victim's lawsuit was barred by the statute of limitations. The court noted that the victim was suing the church and bishop for negligence in the hiring and retention of the priest. Under Florida law, the statute of limitations for negligence lawsuits is four years. Since this period is suspended until a minor plaintiff reaches age eighteen, the victim had until age twenty-two to file a lawsuit against the church and bishop. The victim did not sue until he was twenty-seven, but insisted that the statute of limitations should have been suspended further until he became "aware" of his injuries. The court rejected this argument: "This young man knew the identity of the [priest] and the improper conduct engaged in by the [priest] long before he reached the age of majority. This was sufficient knowledge to file an action against the priest for the wrongful sexual battery committed against him and, again assuming such cause of action is available, against the church and bishop for making such conduct possible because of the negligent retention of the priest. . . . [T]he negligent retention of a priest who would commit child abuse, at least insofar as this young man is concerned, must have occurred while he was still a child. Therefore, when [the victim] turned eighteen, he was aware that a priest had sexually abused him and that the church had permitted the priest to serve in the parish which made the abuse possible. Sexual abuse of a child in and of itself causes sufficient actual damages, as a matter of law, to support both the intentional tort action against the priest and the negligence action, if one exists, against the church and the bishop. . . . The fact that [the victim] in this case was not immediately aware of all of his resulting emotional problems might create uncertainty as to the amount of his damages but it does not toll the period of limitations."

• The Illinois Supreme Court refused to toll the statute of limitations in a case involving the sexual molestation of a minor female. The victim failed to file a lawsuit against various church defendants until after the statute of limitations had expired, but she argued that the discovery rule should have extended the period of time for her to sue. She noted that although she was aware of the abuse from the time it occurred, she was not aware of the connection between the abuse and her injuries. The Illinois Supreme Court held that because she had a reasonable knowledge of the abuse, her "failure to understand the connection between the abuse and other injuries [did] not toll the statute of limitations."[312]

• The Illinois Supreme Court ruled that an adult woman was barred by the statue of limitations from suing a priest and his religious order for injuries she suffered as a result of over 900 separate incidents of sexual abuse committed by the priest when she

---

[311] Doe v. Dorsey, 683 So.2d 614 (Fl. App. 1996).

[312] Parks v. Kownacki, 737 N.E.2d 287 (Ill. 2000).

was a child. The court, in rejecting the application of the discovery rule, concluded: "The allegations of the plaintiff's complaint make it clear that [she] had sufficient information about her injury and its cause to require her to bring suit long before the date of discovery alleged in the complaint. [She] does not argue that she repressed her memories of the abuse, and the allegations in the complaint indicate that [she] was aware of the abuse as it occurred. From the chronology set forth in [her lawsuit] it appears that the abuse began when [she] was eight or nine years old, and that it continued for about seven years, until the plaintiff was 15 or 16. . . . She did not bring the present action until . . . she was nearly 32 years old. Given the allegations in the [lawsuit], which show that the plaintiff was always aware of the misconduct charged, and the absence of any contrary assertion that the plaintiff repressed memories of the abuse, we believe that the plaintiff's action must be considered untimely under the discovery rule. . . . The plaintiff does not contend that she repressed memories of the abuse allegedly committed by [the priest], or that she was not aware that his misconduct was harmful. Rather, [she] asserts that she did not discover, until years later, the full extent of the injuries she allegedly sustained as a result of the childhood occurrences. . . . However, a plaintiff's failure to learn the full extent of the injuries caused by the defendant's acts will not toll the statute of limitations."[313]

• *An Indiana state court ruled that the statute of limitations prevented two adult survivors of childhood sexual abuse from suing the ministers who allegedly abused them.[314] In 1960, two girls (eight and nine years of age) were placed as wards in a children's home affiliated with a church. The girls remained in the home for nearly nine years. While in the home, the girls were repeatedly molested by an ordained minister who served as activities director. The molestation included repeated acts of sexual intercourse. The minister frequently gave the girls quinine pills which caused severe vomiting, bleeding, and diarrhea, in an effort to induce abortions. The girls also were molested by a second ordained minister who was superintendent of the home. The abuse caused the girls to develop severe psychological distress, which manifested itself in the form of shame, guilt, self-blame, denial, depression, nightmares, and ultimately disassociation from their experiences. Through these coping mechanisms, the girls were unable to comprehend that they suffered damages as a result of the abuse. Thirty years later, in 1990, both girls experienced several "flashbacks" of the abuse. It was at this time that the victims began to realize that many of their nightmares were in fact true. The victims separately confronted the ministers. The former activities director admitted to having molested the girls "hundreds of times." The former superintendent also admitted his acts of abuse. The victims filed a lawsuit against the ministers and the children's home in 1990. The ministers and children's home sought to have the lawsuit dismissed on the ground that the statute of limitations had expired many years before. A state appeals court ruled that the statute of limitations did not prevent the victims from suing, even though the abuse occurred thirty years before. The court acknowledged that the statute of limitations for personal injuries under Indiana law requires lawsuits to be commenced within two years "after the cause of action accrues." It noted that this rule is subject to an exception—the statute of limitations does not begin to run in any case involving personal injury until the victim "knew, or in the exercise of ordinary diligence, could have discovered that an injury had been*

---

[313] Clay v. Kuhl, 727 N.E.2d 217 (Ill. 2000).

[314] Shultz-Lewis Child & Family Services, Inc. v. Doe, 604 N.E.2d 1206 (Ind. App. 1992). *See also* Doe v. United Methodist Church, 673 N.E.2d 839 (Ind. App. 1996); Konkle v. Henson, 672 N.E.2d 450 (Ind. App. 1996).

sustained as a result of the tortious act of another." The court observed, "In the case before us the plaintiffs have asserted both that they had repressed knowledge that a number of the acts had occurred such that they had no memory of the act having happened until 1990, and that while they were aware of other acts and of feelings of guilt, depression, low self-esteem, etc. they were without knowledge of any causative connection between their psychological and personality problems and the alleged molestations until 1990." The court found the victims' allegations of repressed memory sufficient to overcome the statute of limitations. However, it did acknowledge that "what knowledge each [victim] might be charged with based upon the exercise of ordinary care remains a disputed question of fact." That is, the case was sent back to the trial court where the women would have to prove that they in fact could not have known prior to 1990, through the exercise of reasonable care, that they had suffered emotional injuries as a result of the acts of molestation that occurred when they were children.

• A Kentucky court ruled that a 24-year-old adult was barred by the statute of limitations from suing a priest who allegedly molested him when he was a minor.[315] The court also ruled that the victim was barred from suing his church. The statute of limitations in Kentucky for both battery negligence is one year. However, under Kentucky law (as is true in most states) the statute of limitations does not begin to run for injuries suffered by a minor until the minor's eighteenth birthday. In other words, the statute of limitations for battery and negligence expired one year after the victim's eighteenth birthday, some six years before the lawsuit was filed. The victim argued that there are certain exceptions to the statute of limitations that applied in this case. First, Kentucky law provides that the statute of limitations is suspended if a person is of "unsound mind" when a cause of action accrues. The victim claimed that he had suffered from post-traumatic stress disorder, and that he had repressed the memory of the abuse until shortly before he filed the lawsuit. The court disagreed, noting that the term "unsound mind" under Kentucky law means that a person has been rendered incapable of managing his or her own affairs and accordingly "[t]he mere fact that [the victim] experienced a repression syndrome is not synonymous with being of unsound mind." Second, the victim claimed that the statute of limitations should not begin to run until he "discovered" his injuries, and this did not occur until the day of his suicide attempt (which occurred less than one year before he filed the lawsuit). The court acknowledged that Kentucky has adopted a "discovery rule" in the context of medical malpractice, but "[n]either the Supreme Court nor the General Assembly has further extended the discovery rule." Further, the court observed, "It should again be noted that at the time [the victim's] cause of action accrued, and for sometime thereafter, he was both aware of the abuse and past the age of reason. The fact that his memory of these events was thereafter suppressed, only to return years later, would not seem to present a circumstance falling within the discovery rule which relates to injuries which cannot be discovered with reasonable diligence."

• A Louisiana court ruled that the statute of limitations prevented an adult woman from suing a Catholic diocese for a priest's acts of molestation when the woman was a minor.[316] The woman sued the diocese claiming that it was responsible for a priest's molestation of her in 1961 when she was fifteen years of age. The applicable Louisiana statute of limitations for incidents of child abuse is one year beginning on the child's

[315] Rigazio v. Archdiocese of Louisville, 853 S.W.2d 295 (Ky. App. 1993).

[316] Doe v. Roman Catholic Church, 656 So.2d 5 (La. App. 1995). *Accord* J.A.G. v. Schmaltz, 682 So.2d 331 (La. App. 1996); Harrison v. Gore, 660 So.2d 563 (La. App. 1995).

eighteenth birthday. The woman claimed that this period should not begin until she discovered that her emotional suffering was caused by the prior act of molestation. The court declined the woman's request. It concluded, "It is clear to us from the testimony that [the woman] recalled the events giving rise to the [lawsuit against the diocese] and knew that it was wrong for [the priest] to engage in such activities. Although the alleged mental and physical abuse administered to [the woman] while under the control of [the priest] may have affected a clear, precise recollection of specific acts of sexual abuse, [the woman] was admittedly aware and cognizant of the abuse once she was out of the control of [the priest]. However, suit was not filed until . . . some 25 years after [her] last contact with [the priest]." The court also pointed out that the woman discussed with others the possibility of filing a lawsuit more than a year before doing so, and this further demonstrated that she was aware of her injuries more than a year before the lawsuit was filed. The court concluded, "[The woman] clearly remembered the alleged abuses suffered at the hands or direction of [the priest]. She was not unable to act, but chose not to do so and allowed her claim to [lapse]. Sympathy we share for the victim of [the priest's] misconduct. The suffering she endured and will continue to endure as a consequence of his unholy acts warrants retribution. With heavy hearts, however, we must affirm the trial court's judgment [dismissing the case]."

• The Maryland Court of Appeals (the highest state court) ruled that an adult's "repression" of memories associated with childhood sexual abuse is not a sufficient basis for suspending or delaying the statute of limitations.[317] Two female students at a Catholic high school alleged that they were subjected to severe and repeated acts of sexual molestation by a priest to whom they had been sent for counseling. They alleged that the molestation began when they were in ninth grade and continued all the way up until their graduation. The victims claimed that following their graduation from high school, they "ceased to recall" the abuse due to the process of "repression." It was not until twenty years later, during counseling, that they "recovered" their memories of the abuse. They filed a lawsuit against the priest, their former school, and the archdiocese. A state appeals court ruled that the lawsuit had to be dismissed on the basis of the statute of limitations. Maryland law requires such lawsuits to be filed within three years after a minor attains her eighteenth birthday. The court acknowledged that in some cases the "discovery rule" has been applied—meaning that the statute of limitations does not begin to run until the victim "discovers" that his or her injuries were caused by a particular event. However, the court refused to apply the discovery rule to cases of recovered memories of childhood sexual abuse. It reached the following conclusions: (1) The concept of repression is defined as the selective and involuntary forgetting of information that causes pain. Repressed information is not forgotten, but instead is stored in the unconsciousness and may be recovered at a later time if the anxiety associated with the memory is removed. (2) Several professional studies attempt to validate the concept of repression. (3) Several other professional studies discredit the concept of repression. These studies assert that there is absolutely no scientific evidence to support the claim that repression exists. (4) It is impossible to distinguish between repression and "faking." (5) Since serious disagreement exists within the psychological community regarding the validity of repression theory, it would be inappropriate for a court to recognize it. The court concluded that "we are unconvinced

---

[317] Doe v. Maskell, 679 A.2d 1087 (Md. 1996). *See also* Doe v. Archdiocese of Washington, 689 A.2d 634 (Md. App. 1997).

that repression exists as a phenomenon separate and apart from the normal process of forgetting." And, because the discovery rule does not help those who merely forget their injuries or legal claims, it should not help those who claim that their memories were repressed and later recovered.

• A Minnesota court ruled that a woman's lawsuit against a denominational agency for her molestation by a priest when she was a minor was barred by the statute of limitations.[318] *The woman claimed that a priest sexually abused her over a period of 11 years beginning when she was 15. As their relationship progressed, the priest expressed to the victim his internal conflict over choosing between his love for her and his love for the church. Throughout their relationship, the victim knew that the priest had taken a vow of celibacy and that his conduct with her was inappropriate. As an adult, the victim learned that the priest was engaging in similar behavior with other women. She met another victim, and they shared their experiences. This information was devastating to the victim. She immediately sought professional counseling and experienced radical personality changes. The victim sued the priest and her archdiocese. A state appeals court ruled that the woman's lawsuit was barred by the statute of limitations. Minnesota law provides that "[a]n action for damages based on personal injury caused by sexual abuse must be commenced within six years of the time the plaintiff knew or had reason to know that the injury was caused by the sexual abuse." The victim claimed that not until she received counseling as an adult did she see the situation clearly and recognize that she had been a victim of abuse. Accordingly, she asserted that the statute of limitations began running when she began counseling. The court rejected the victim's argument on the basis of several facts including the following: the victim was aware that priests were unable to marry and must remain celibate; she knew that their relationship violated these rules and therefore she tried to keep their relationship secret; she frequently cried after sexual relations or out of town trips with the priest because she was struggling with the situation; and she informed several friends, and eventually her husband, about the priest's actions. The court concluded that this evidence "establishes overwhelmingly that, under a reasonable person standard, [the victim] should have known . . . that she had been abused as a minor and as an adult."*

• A federal appeals court, applying Nebraska law, ruled that the statute of limitations prevented an adult male from suing a church as a result of injuries he allegedly suffered as a result of being sexually molested by a teacher at a church-operated school when he was a minor. The court ruled that the discovery rule did not extend the statute of limitations in this case: "The undisputed evidence demonstrates that [the victim] drew a direct connection between the abuse and his negative behaviors in 1990, when he disclosed the abuse to his wife and parents as an explanation for his marital discord and homosexual activity. . . . The remaining undisputed evidence indicates that he was aware of sufficient facts by 1995 at the latest, from which he could have, with reasonable diligence, discovered the causal connection. By that time, he had told not only his family, but also friends, counselors, and the school principal about the abuse he had suffered; he was aware of his emotional and behavioral

---

[318] ABC & XYZ v. Archdiocese of St. Paul and Minneapolis, 513 N.W.2d 482 (Minn. App. 1994). *Accord* S.E. v. Shattuck-St. Mary's School, 533 N.W.2d 628 (Minn. App. 1995); M.L. v. Magnuson, 531 N.W.2d 831 (Minn. App. 1995); Roe v. Archbishop of St. Paul and Minneapolis, 518 N.W.2d 629 (Minn. App. 1994). *Contra* Winkler v. Magnuson, 539 N.W.2d 821 (Minn. App. 1995); Doe v. Redeemer Lutheran Church, 531 N.W.2d 897 (Minn. App. 1995); Blackowiak v. Kemp, 528 N.W.2d 247 (Minn. App. 1995).

problems; and [his counselor] had expressly suggested to him in counseling that there was a strong possibility that the sexual abuse he had suffered contributed to his current problems. These undisputed facts, all known to him by 1995, were sufficient to put a person of ordinary intelligence and prudence on an inquiry which, if pursued, would have led to the discovery of the connection between the abuse and the injuries. The fact that he may not have actually drawn the connection at that point or may not have understood the extent of his damages did not prevent the statute of limitations from running. [319]

• *A New Mexico court ruled that a Catholic diocese could not be sued by a 33-year-old woman who claimed to have been sexually molested by a priest when she was a minor.* [320] *The woman alleged that her priest initiated sexual contact with her when she began working in the church office at age 15, and that she had sex with the priest weekly thereafter for the next four years. During this time the priest informed the girl that he had a venereal disease. She contracted the disease and sought treatment from her family physician. When she was 18, the girl became pregnant and obtained an abortion. The girl quit attending church and began to experience depression and suicidal tendencies. She saw a psychiatrist at this time, but said nothing of her affair with the priest. While the girl often protested to the priest about their relationship, the relationship persisted until the girl was nearly 21. At this time the girl fell in love with the man she would later marry. The priest became furious when she informed him that they no longer could have a sexual relationship. In several emotional conversations she asked him to continue a nonsexual relationship, but he responded that there would be no friendship without sex. She later testified that terminating the relationship was "hideously painful" for her. When she was 21, the woman saw a psychologist for disabling depression. When she was 33 years old, she began seeing another psychologist to whom she disclosed her relationship with the priest. The psychologist identified the relationship as the source of the woman's severe psychological problems. The woman sued her diocese, church, and the former priest that same year. A trial court dismissed the case on the ground that it was barred by the state "statute of limitations." Under New Mexico law, a lawsuit generally must be brought within three years of the date of an injury. The court rejected the woman's argument that the statute of limitations did not begin to run until she "discovered" that her psychological problems were caused by the relationship with the priest, and that this did not occur until she began counseling. The woman appealed, and a state appeals court agreed with the trial court that the lawsuit had been brought too late. The court observed, "[The woman's] acquisition of a venereal disease and her pregnancy leading to an abortion were sufficiently substantial injuries that once she knew that they were caused by [the priest] the [statute of limitations] period would no longer be delayed by the discovery rule." The court concluded, "The limitations period is not tolled simply because a plaintiff does not know the full extent of her injuries; the statute begins to run once she knows or should know the sufficient facts to constitute a cause of action."*

• *A federal court in New York refused to find a pastor guilty of malpractice on the basis of his alleged sexual seduction of a church member he had counseled for*

---

[319] Kraft v. St. John's Church, 414 F.3d 943 (8th Cir. 2005).

[320] Martinez-Sandoval v. Kirsch, 884 P.2d 507 (N.M. App. 1994).

several years.[321] The court noted that neither the legislature nor the courts of New York had ever recognized clergy malpractice as a basis of legal liability. Further, to do so would violate the First Amendment guaranty of religious freedom. The court also refused to hold the pastor's church and denomination liable on the basis of "negligent placement, retention, or supervision" and ruled that the woman's lawsuit was barred by the statute of limitations. It noted that the statute of limitations for negligence and malpractice, under New York law, is three years. Since the alleged malpractice first occurred nearly 30 years ago, the woman's claims obviously were barred by the statute of limitations. The woman attempted to avoid the application of the statute of limitations in three ways, each of which was rejected by the court. First, she asked the court to apply the "delayed discovery" doctrine. By this she meant that the statute of limitations should not start until a person "knows or should have known of the injury and the defendant's role in causing that injury." The court acknowledged that some states have adopted such a rule, particularly in the context of child sexual abuse cases. It noted that "the argument for a delayed discovery rule in this context, simply stated, is that victims of child sexual abuse often do not realize until years later either that they have been abused at all or the scope of their injuries." However, the court rejected this view: "Persuasive though this argument may be, there is not authority for the adoption of such a rule in child sex abuse cases in New York. . . . [The New York courts] have steadfastly declined to alter the traditional New York rule that the statute of limitations commences to run when a cause of action accrues, even though the plaintiff is unaware that he has a cause of action." Next, the woman argued that the pastor should be prohibited from relying on the statute of limitations because of his "misrepresentations." The court agreed that the statute of limitations can be suspended if a party's fraud or "active concealment" prevents a plaintiff from filing a timely claim. However, it disagreed that this rule applied in the present case, since the pastor had done nothing to prevent the woman from filing a timely lawsuit. Third, the woman argued that the statute of limitations should be suspended because she was "under duress." The court rejected this claim as well: "This requirement has been applied strictly; courts confronted by facts which might suggest to the layman that duress is present have routinely refused to apply the doctrine. . . . Indeed, the cases are replete with statements . . . to the effect that the statute begins to run irrespective of whether the party seeking to avoid it has enough courage and independence to resist a hostile influence and assert his rights or not. . . . In light of these authorities, it appears that duress is not an element of [the woman's] claims. Even if it were, it is extremely doubtful whether any reasonable juror could find that [she] was under constant legal duress for a 31-year period, during most of which she lived half a continent away from the [pastor]."

• *The Ohio Supreme Court dismissed a lawsuit brought by a 25-year-old man who had been repeatedly molested as a minor by a church choir director.[322] The victim had been molested by his church choir director on nearly 300 occasions over a period of three years when he was between 15 and 18 years of age. Shortly after his 25th birthday, the victim filed a lawsuit against the choir director and his church. He alleged that the director was guilty of assault and battery, and that the church had been negligent in the selection and supervision of the choir director. Ohio has a one-year statute*

---

[321] Schmidt v. Bishop, 779 F. Supp. 321 (S.D.N.Y. 1991). *Accord* Bassile v. Covenant House, 575 N.Y.S.2d 233 (Sup. 1991); Gallas v. Greek Orthodox Archdiocese, 587 N.Y.S.2d 82 (Sup. 1989).

[322] Doe v. First United Methodist Church, 629 N.E.2d 402 (Ohio 1994).

of limitations for assault and battery, meaning that a lawsuit alleging assault and battery must be brought within one year following the alleged wrongdoing. Ohio has a two-year statute of limitations for bodily injury resulting from negligence. Obviously, these statutes had expired long before the victim brought his lawsuit. However, the victim insisted that the statutes had not expired since he did not "discover" the nature and extent of his injuries until he sought psychological help shortly before filing his lawsuit. The court disagreed. It observed, "Given the facts of this case, even if this court were to adopt, now or in the future, a rule of discovery for cases of sexual abuse, the rule would not apply to toll the periods of limitations beyond [the victim's] eighteenth birthday. Here, the facts clearly establish that at the time [he] reached the age of majority, [he] knew that he had been sexually abused by [the choir director]. [The choir director] allegedly initiated homosexual conduct with [the victim] on two hundred to three hundred separate occasions without [his] consent. During the period of sexual abuse, [the victim] was fourteen to seventeen years of age. Apparently, the last act of sexual battery occurred just months prior to [the victim's] eighteenth birthday. After graduating from high school, [he] became preoccupied with his sexual identity and suffered from depression, guilt, anger and anxiety. [He] eventually sought psychological help . . . and told his psychologist of the prior sexual encounters with [the choir director]. . . . [U]pon reaching the age of majority, [the victim] knew that he had been sexually abused, and he knew the identity of the perpetrator. Although [he] may not have discovered the full extent of his psychological injuries . . . the fact that [he] was aware upon reaching the age of majority that he had been sexually abused by [the choir director] was sufficient to trigger the commencement of the statute of limitations . . . ."

• *A Pennsylvania court ruled that a 27-year-old adult was barred by the statute of limitations from suing a priest and his church on account of the priest's alleged acts of molestation.[323] The victim alleged that the priest had molested him when he was an adolescent on numerous occasions. In explaining the delay in filing the lawsuit, the victim claimed that he did not "become aware" of or discover the psychological and emotional injuries he suffered as a result of the abuse for several years after he became an adult. A trial court dismissed the lawsuit, concluding that it was barred by a Pennsylvania statute of limitations which requires that lawsuits be filed within two years of the date of injury. The victim appealed, arguing that the statute of limitations should not begin to run until the date that he "discovered" that he had been injured by the priest's molestation. A state appeals court disagreed, and refused to apply the "discovery" rule in this case. It observed, "In our view . . . it is perfectly clear that this case does not fall within the extremely limited applicability of the Pennsylvania discovery rule. This is simply not a case where the plaintiff, despite the exercise of objectively measured reasonable diligence, could not know of his injury and its cause within the limitations period. [The victim] admits that he knew the abuse was occurring and who was inflicting it, both when it happened and throughout the eight years after the abuse ended and before appellant sued. What he did not know, i.e., that the physical acts allegedly performed on him by [the priest] were abuse and were causing psychological harm, is not relevant to a discovery rule analysis. . . . [The victim] need not have known that what was happening to him was abuse, i.e., was wrongful, or precisely what type of psychological or emotional harm he would suffer as a result. Once he knew what was happening and who was doing it, he had the duty to investigate these questions and to institute suit within the limitations period. Moreover,*

---

[323] E.J.M. v. Archdiocese of Philadelphia, 622 A.2d 1388 (Pa. Super. 1993).

the affidavit submitted by [the victim] in opposition to summary judgment . . . clearly reveals that he was aware, if not that he had been abused, nevertheless that something very troubling and extraordinary was happening to him. He states that he felt confused about what [his priest] was doing to him, thought 'something was wrong with me,' and 'felt guilty and sinful.' Clearly, he not only knew all the relevant facts regarding the abuse and the abuser, but he also knew that something was very wrong with the situation in which he found himself. . . . [The victim] did recognize that something was amiss, and although he allegedly blamed himself for these feelings, that alone does not relieve him of the duty to investigate and bring suit within the limitations period."

• *The South Carolina Supreme Court ruled that an adult woman who claimed that she had been molested as a child at a church-operated preschool was not barred by the statute of limitations from suing the church for the psychological injuries she sustained. The victim claimed that she had "repressed" all memory of the acts of molestation until she was an adult, and that the statute of limitations should not have begun to run until she "discovered" that her psychological injuries were caused by the abuse. The court concluded that the statute of limitations "begins to run on the date that the jury believed the repression ended and the resurfacing memories would have put a reasonable person on sufficient notice." The court conceded that allowing victims to sue long after the statute of limitations has expired as a result of a recovery of repressed memories creates the "horrific possibility of false accusations." As a result, it stressed that a victim "must present independently verifiable, objective evidence that corroborates a repressed memory claim in order to assert the discovery rule," and that such evidence may include any one or more of the following: (1) an admission by the abuser; (2) a criminal conviction; (3) documented medical history of childhood sexual abuse; (4) contemporaneous records or written statements of the abuser, such as diaries or letters; (5) photographs or recordings of the abuse; (6) an objective eyewitness's account; (7) evidence the abuser had sexually abused others; or (8) proof of a chain of facts and circumstances having sufficient probative force to produce a reasonable and probable conclusion that sexual abuse occurred.*[324]

• *The Rhode Island Supreme Court ruled that the statute of limitations barred a woman's claims against her church and denomination as a result of a sexual relationship that her pastor allegedly initiated with her. The court noted that "when the fact of the injury is unknown to the plaintiff when it occurs, the applicable statute of limitations will be tolled and will not begin to run until, in the exercise of reasonable diligence, the plaintiff should have discovered the injury or some injury-causing wrongful conduct. . . . If a reasonable person in similar circumstances should have discovered that the wrongful conduct of the defendant caused her injuries as of some date before the plaintiff alleged that she made this discovery, then the earlier date will be used to start the running of the limitations period."*[325]

• *A Texas court ruled that a 23-year-old male who was molested by a church music director when he was a minor was barred by a two-year statute of limitations from suing his church.*[326] *The court noted that under the applicable statute of limitations*

---

[324] Moriarty v. Garden Sanctuary Church of God, 534 S.E.2d 672 (S.C. 2000).

[325] Martin v. Howard, 784 A.2d 291 (R.I. 2001). *See also* Ryan v. Roman Catholic Bishop, 941 A.2d 174 (R.I. 2008).

[326] Marshall v. First Baptist Church, 949 S.W.2d 504 (Tex. App. 1997). *See also* Rendon v. Roman Catholic Diocese, 60 S.W.3d 389 (Tex. App. 2001).

the victim had to bring a lawsuit no later than two years after the date his cause of action accrued. The court noted that in general a cause of action "accrues" when a wrongful act causes a legal injury, even if the injury is not "discovered" until later. However, the statute of limitations does not begin to "run" for a person who was a minor at the time of an injury until his or her eighteenth birthday. Since the victim in this case was a minor when the injuries occurred, he had until his twentieth birthday to file a lawsuit. And, since he did not file his lawsuit until he was twenty-three years old, his claims were barred by the statute of limitations. The court noted that the discovery rule does not apply unless "the alleged wrongful act and resulting injury were inherently undiscoverable at the time they occurred." The court did not believe that this requirement was met in this case: "Whether or not [the victim] made the complicated connection between the church's conduct and his psychological condition is of no moment because neither the wrongful acts nor the injuries asserted in this case are inherently undiscoverable. In fact, both had rather obvious manifestations long before the limitations period expired. Moreover [the victim] does not argue that he was unaware of the wrongful acts. In addition, he does not contend he was unaware of the psychological and emotional injuries which resulted from those acts. Because [he] was clearly aware of both the wrongful acts and the injury in this case, the [discovery rule does not apply]." The court also rejected the victim's argument that the church's conduct constituted a "continuing tort." Specifically, the victim alleged that because the church failed to report his abuse to the civil authorities, it violated the state's child abuse reporting law. The victim insisted that each day church officials failed to report the abuse constituted "a new wrongful act," initiating a new limitations period. The court disagreed, noting that "the statute only creates a duty to report the abuse or neglect of a child. Thus, the church's duty to report the molestation of [the victim] no longer existed as of the day he turned eighteen."

• A federal court in Vermont ruled that an adult who claimed to have been sexually abused by a nun some 40 years earlier could sue a Catholic diocese for his alleged injuries.[327] An adult male (the plaintiff) began receiving intensive psychotherapy for what he alleges were severe emotional problems. As a result of this therapy, the plaintiff claimed that he discovered he was the victim of "childhood sexual abuse, physical abuse and psychological abuse" allegedly occurring forty years ago when he was a resident of a church orphanage. The plaintiff filed a lawsuit against "Sister Jane Doe," the alleged perpetrator (whose identity was unknown) and various religious organizations allegedly responsible for hiring and supervising Sister Jane Doe. The plaintiff alleged in his lawsuit that he had "used all due diligence, given the nature, extent, and severity of his psychological injuries and the circumstances of their infliction, to discover the fact that he has been injured by the sexual abuse." The diocese urged the court to dismiss the case on the ground that the statute of limitations had expired long before. Under Vermont law, when a plaintiff sues to recover damages for injuries "suffered as a result of childhood sexual abuse," the lawsuit must be brought within "six years of the act alleged to have caused the injury or condition, or six years of the time the victim discovered that the injury or condition was caused by that act, whichever period expires later." The diocese claimed that since the alleged abuse occurred over forty years ago it is reasonable to assume that the plaintiff should have discovered the cause of his injuries long ago. It also argued that forcing it to defend against an alleged injury occurring so long ago violates the

---

[327] Barquin v. Roman Catholic Diocese, 839 F. Supp. 275 (D. Vt. 1993).

very purpose of a statute of limitations—relieving defendants of the difficult if not impossible task of defending against such claims. The court rejected these arguments, and ruled that the statute of limitations had not expired on any of the plaintiff's claims (except for assault and battery, which the court deemed to be unrelated to childhood sexual abuse). The court observed that under Vermont law, the test is when the plaintiff in fact discovered that his injuries were caused by childhood abuse, and not when he reasonably could have made this discovery.

• *A Washington state court ruled that the statute of limitations prevented an adult male from suing his church and a denominational agency for injuries he suffered as a child when he was molested by his pastor.[328] The court noted that under Washington law the victim had until his twenty-first birthday to sue the church and denominational agency for the sexual abuse that occurred while he was a minor. Since the lawsuit was not filed until the victim was twenty-two, it was filed too late. The court noted that even if it applied the discovery rule, the lawsuit was still filed too late: "The common law discovery rule would not apply to [the victim's] claims against the local church and the state office because the record clearly shows, and the trial court so found, that while still a minor [he] clearly knew the facts of the abuse relevant to establish a claim. . . . [He] knew he was being sexually molested by [his pastor]. . . . He knew the molestation was wrong, knew it was causing him substantial harm, as he attempted suicide." The court conceded that the statute of limitations may be suspended or postponed when "plaintiffs could not have immediately known of their injuries due to . . . concealment of information by the defendant." The victim's parents claimed that the statute of limitations did not begin to run on their claims until their son told them the pastor had molested him. The parents argue that before this conversation they could not have learned of their cause of action. The court disagreed, noting that while there was substantial evidence that the pastor concealed important information from the parents and from the church, "there is no evidence that the local church or the state office concealed anything from the [parents]."*

• *The Wisconsin Supreme Court ruled that the statute of limitations prevented a woman from suing a Catholic archdiocese for the alleged acts of molestation by a priest nearly 40 years before.[329] The woman claimed that the priest entered into a sexual relationship with her when she was a high school student, and that as a result of the priest's behavior she "has suffered and continues to suffer from severe emotional distress, causing and contributing to the break-up of her marriage, separation from her children, loss of jobs and other difficulties." The court began its opinion by noting that the applicable statute of limitations in this case was three years. It ruled that the woman filed her lawsuit after this period of time expired, even if the so-called "discovery rule" were applied. Under the discovery rule, the statute of limitations does not begin to run until the victim discovers that his or her injuries were caused by the misconduct of a particular person or organization. The woman in this case argued that she had "suppressed and been unable to perceive the existence, nature or cause of her psychological and emotional injuries" until she sought the assistance of a professional counselor. Therefore, she claimed that her lawsuit was not barred by the statute of*

---

[328] E.R.B. v. Church of God, 950 P.2d 29 (Wash. App. 1998). *See also* Funkhouser v. Wilson, 950 P.2d 501 (Wash. App. 1998).

[329] Pritzlaff v. Archdiocese of Milwaukee, 533 N.W.2d 780 (Wis. 1995). *Accord* Doe v. Archdiocese, 700 N.W.2d 180 (Wis. 2005); Joseph W. v. Catholic Diocese, 569 N.W.2d 795 (Wis. App. 1997); Doe v. Archdiocese of Milwaukee, 565 N.W.2d 94 (Wis. 1997).

limitations. The court concluded that the discovery rule did not help the woman in this case, since the woman by her own admission knew the identity of the priest and was aware of the conduct of the priest. The court pointed out that under the discovery rule the statute of limitations begins to run when a person "has sufficient evidence that a wrong has indeed been committed by an identified person." The court further observed that extending the discovery rule to this case would cause unfairness to a defendant who is forced to attempt to defend a suit for emotional and psychological injuries in which the alleged conduct took place over 40 years ago.

5. Extending the Statute of Limitations—Fraud and Other Grounds

Some courts have permitted the statute of limitations to be suspended in limited circumstances, including fraud or the "active concealment" of the existence of a civil claim by a wrongdoer.

Case Studies

• *A Georgia court dismissed a lawsuit brought by a woman against her church and a denominational agency as a result of injuries she allegedly sustained during a sexual relationship with her pastor.[330] The court concluded that the woman's claims were barred by the statute of limitations. The woman had two years to file her lawsuit under the Georgia statute of limitations, yet the lawsuit was not filed for nearly three years after the pastor left the church to accept a new assignment. The court also noted that the woman admitted that for more than two years prior to the time the lawsuit was filed she had progressed in her therapy to the point where she was able to tell the associate pastor "no" if he approached her about sexual relations. The court concluded that any acts of sexual intercourse occurring after this time were by her own admission consensual. The court rejected the couple's argument that the statute of limitations was "suspended" due to the woman's depression, noting that "this is not evidence of incompetency sufficient to toll the statute of limitation."*

• *A Kentucky court ruled that an adult who had been sexually molested as a minor by a teacher at a parochial school could sue the diocese that operated the school for negligent hiring, supervision, and retention. The victim never reported the incidents nor discussed them with anyone until he was 32 years old. It was at that time that he learned from television reports that the teacher had sexually abused other students. These reports brought back memories of his own abuse, and he was hospitalized three days for emotional trauma several months after the programs aired. The programs also prompted him to have several conversations with the diocese concerning the incidents and how they could have occurred. A criminal investigation resulted in the teacher being arrested and convicted of twenty-eight counts of sexual abuse of minors, as well as the filing of several civil suits by the victim and others. The diocese asked the trial court to dismiss the lawsuit on the ground that it was barred by the statute of limitations since it had been brought some seventeen years after the teacher's last act of molestation. The victim insisted that his lawsuit was filed on time due to the "discovery rule," and the fact that the diocese "fraudulently concealed" relevant information. Kentucky law specifies that a personal injury action must be commenced within one year "after the cause of action accrued." Generally, a cause of action is said*

---

[330] Alpharetta First United Methodist Church v. Stewart, 473 S.E.2d 532 (Ga. App. 1996).

to accrue when the injury occurs. However, in certain cases, a cause of action does not necessarily accrue when the injury occurs, but rather when the plaintiff first discovers the injury or should have reasonably discovered it. However, the court declined to apply the discovery rule to repressed memories of child molestation. It noted that the victim had not alleged memory loss but was well aware of his injury. Kentucky law also specifies that the statute of limitations is extended during the time that one party through concealment or otherwise "obstructs the prosecution" of a lawsuit. The victim claimed that the diocese should be barred from relying on the statute of limitations due to its failure to report the teacher's multiple acts of child abuse to the authorities, as well as its failure to inform students, faculty, and staff of the teacher's behavior. The diocese vigorously disagreed. It insisted that concealment alone is not enough to suspend the statute of limitations. Rather, the concealment must mislead or deceive the plaintiff so that he or she is lulled into inaction or is otherwise obstructed from investigating or instituting a lawsuit during the limitations period. The court noted that the diocese knew prior to the time when the victim was abused that the teacher had sexually abused students and would continue to be "a problem" and continued to receive reports of his sexually abusing students during at least part of the time period in which the victim was being abused. Nevertheless, the diocese took no action to discipline or sanction him, to inform other students, parents, or employees, or to report the incidents to state authorities. The information was kept secret and confidential in a personnel file, and the victim had no idea that the diocese had prior knowledge of the teacher's propensities until he watched the television programs. Until that time, the victim neither knew nor had reason to know that he had a potential cause of action against the diocese for causing injury to him due to its concealment of its knowledge of the teacher's actions toward other students. The court concluded, "The diocese clearly obstructed the prosecution of [the victim's] cause of action against it by continually concealing the fact that it had knowledge of [the teacher's] problem well before the time [the victim] was abused as well as the fact that it continued to receive reports of sexual abuse of other students during part of the time period in which [the victim] was abused. Furthermore, where the law imposes a duty of disclosure, a failure of disclosure may constitute concealment . . . ." The child abuse reporting statute in effect when these incidents occurred imposed a legal duty on "any person" to report child abuse to law enforcement authorities. The diocese failed to comply with this duty, "and such failure constitutes evidence of concealment."

• An Oregon court ruled that a denominational agency was not legally responsible for a priest's acts of child molestation occurring more than twenty years ago.[331] The victim alleged that when he was a minor he was molested on at least twenty occasions by the priest. However, the victim claimed that it was not until nearly twenty years later that he discovered the connection between the molestation and his emotional damages. He sued his archdiocese, claiming that it was legally responsible for the priest's acts on the basis of negligent selection and supervision. The court dismissed all of the victim's negligence claims on the ground that they were barred by the statute of limitations. While Oregon has an "extended" statute of limitations that applies to conduct "knowingly allowing, permitting or encouraging" child abuse, this statute did not apply in this case since the victim failed to prove that the archdiocese had any prior knowledge of the priest's behavior. The court rejected the victim's claim that the archdiocese "knew enough about child abuse in the church generally that it should have known that [the priest in this case] actually presented a risk to children."

---

[331] Fearing v. Bucher, 936 P.2d 1023 (Or. App. 1997).

• The South Dakota Supreme Court ruled that the statute of limitations barred an adult from suing a parochial school and various church defendants for the abuse he suffered 30 years before when he was a minor attending the school. The court noted that the victim's "knowledge of the abuse, coupled with his psychological treatment for his condition, was sufficient to establish constructive knowledge of the abuse and that his injury was caused by that abuse. He was therefore . . . required to seek out further information and pursue his claim following his discoveries." The court rejected the victim's claim that the statute of limitations was tolled or suspended as a result of the church defendant's fraudulent concealment. Again, the court disagreed: "Fraudulent concealment does not toll the statute of limitations, no matter the nature of the concealment if a plaintiff is already on notice of facts sufficient to give rise to a claim."[332]

• The Utah Supreme Court ruled that the statute of limitations barred former students at a church-controlled school from suing the church and school for injuries they received as a result of a teacher's acts of child molestation. In rejecting the victims' claim that the discovery rule extended the statute of limitations in their case, the court noted that "if a party has knowledge of some underlying facts, then that party must reasonably investigate potential causes of action because the limitations period will run." The court noted that the victims knew they had been molested, and they knew the identity of the molester. This knowledge "was sufficient to trigger a duty to inquire into potential claims against the defendants. Because they failed to do so, they cannot now allege that they lacked knowledge of their claims." The court also rejected the victims' claim that the statute of limitations should have been tolled due to the church defendants' fraudulent concealment: "In order to qualify for application of the fraudulent concealment doctrine, a plaintiff must demonstrate either (1) that the plaintiff neither knew nor reasonably should have known of the facts underlying his or her cause of action before the fixed limitations period expired; or (2) that notwithstanding the plaintiff's actual or constructive knowledge of the facts underlying his or her cause of action within the limitations period, a reasonably diligent plaintiff may have delayed in filing his or her complaint until after the statute of limitations expired. The court concluded that "before a plaintiff may rely on the fraudulent concealment doctrine, he must have actually made an attempt to investigate his claim and that such an attempt must have been rendered futile as a result of the defendant's fraudulent or misleading conduct." This requirement was not satisfied in this case.[333]

Charitable Immunity   § 10-16.5

Key point 10-16.5. *The legal liability of churches and their officers, directors, and volunteers, is limited by state and federal "charitable immunity" laws.*

In most states, religious organizations are subject to being sued for the negligence of their employees just like any commercial organization. However, the view that religious organizations should be completely immune from liability was once common. It gradually was rejected by all of the states that had adopted

---

[332] Zephier v. Catholic Diocese, 752 N.W.2d 658 (S.D. 2008). *See also* One Star v. Sisters of St. Francis, 752 N.W.2d 668 (S.D. 2008); Koenig v. Lambert, 527 N.W.2d 903 (S.D. 1995).

[333] Colosimo v. Roman Catholic Bishop, 156 P.3d 806 (Utah 2007).

it. The principle of total immunity frequently was criticized. One court observed, "Even the most cursory research makes it apparent that there is no ground upon which this doctrine of nonliability has rested . . . that has not been assailed and criticized at length by some other court . . . ."[334]

While the view that charities should be completely immune from civil liability has been rejected, it is important to recognize that charities are given limited immunity under both state and federal law. The major forms of limited immunity are addressed in this section.

1. Limited Liability of Uncompensated Officers and Directors

This form of charitable immunity is addressed in section § 6-08, as well as in the following subsection addressing the limited liability of volunteers.

2. Limited Liability of Volunteers

Many states have enacted statutes conferring limited liability upon persons who perform uncompensated volunteer work on behalf of a charity. In addition, Congress enacted the federal Volunteer Protection Act[335] in 1997. This legislation provides substantial protection to volunteers who provide services on behalf of churches and other charities. Here is a summary of the Act's provisions:

> • **Congressional "findings."** The Act begins with several "findings," including the following:

>> (1) the willingness of volunteers to offer their services is deterred by the potential for liability actions against them; (2) as a result, many nonprofit public and private organizations and governmental entities, including voluntary associations, social service agencies, educational institutions, and other civic programs, have been adversely affected by the withdrawal of volunteers from boards of directors and service in other capacities; (3) the contribution of these programs to their communities is thereby diminished, resulting in fewer and higher cost programs than would be obtainable if volunteers were participating . . . (6) due to high liability costs and unwarranted litigation costs, volunteers and nonprofit organizations face higher costs in purchasing insurance, through interstate insurance markets, to cover their activities . . . .

> • **Effect on state laws.** Prior to the enactment of the Volunteer Protection Act, many states had enacted similar laws. What is the legal status of these state laws? The Act addresses this question as follows:

>> This Act preempts the laws of any state to the extent that such laws are inconsistent with this Act, except that this Act shall not preempt

---

[334] Gable v. Salvation Army, 100 P.2d 244, 246 (Okla. 1940).

[335] 42 U.S.C. § 14501

any state law that provides additional protection from liability relating to volunteers or to any category of volunteers in the performance of services for a nonprofit organization or governmental entity.

• **Liability protection for volunteers.** The purpose of the Act is to limit the liability of volunteers. This purpose is accomplished through the following provision:

[N]o volunteer of a nonprofit organization . . . shall be liable for harm caused by an act or omission of the volunteer on behalf of the organization or entity if—(1) the volunteer was acting within the scope of the volunteer's responsibilities in the nonprofit organization or governmental entity at the time of the act or omission; (2) if appropriate or required, the volunteer was properly licensed, certified, or authorized by the appropriate authorities for the activities or practice in the State in which the harm occurred, where the activities were or practice was undertaken within the scope of the volunteer's responsibilities in the nonprofit organization or governmental entity; (3) the harm was not caused by willful or criminal misconduct, gross negligence, reckless misconduct, or a conscious, flagrant indifference to the rights or safety of the individual harmed by the volunteer; and (4) the harm was not caused by the volunteer operating a motor vehicle, vessel, aircraft, or other vehicle for which the state requires the operator or the owner of the vehicle, craft, or vessel to—(A) possess an operator's license; or (B) maintain insurance.

• **Definitions.** The Act defines a *nonprofit organization* to mean "any organization which is described in section 501(c)(3) of the Internal Revenue Code of 1986 and exempt from tax under section 501(a) of such Code and which does not practice any action which constitutes a hate crime," or "any not-for-profit organization which is organized and conducted for public benefit and operated primarily for charitable, civic, educational, religious, welfare, or health purposes and which does not practice any action which constitutes a hate crime . . . ."

The Act defines a *volunteer* as "an individual performing services for a nonprofit organization . . . who does not receive—(A) compensation (other than reasonable reimbursement or allowance for expenses actually incurred); or (B) any other thing of value in lieu of compensation, in excess of $500 per year, and such term includes a volunteer serving as a director, officer, trustee, or direct service volunteer."

• **No effect on a charity's liability.** The Act clarifies that it does not "affect the liability of any nonprofit organization . . . with respect to harm caused to any person." In other words, the limited immunity provided by the Act extends only to volunteers, and not to charities themselves.

• **Punitive damages.** The Act specifies that punitive damages "may not be awarded against a volunteer in an action brought for harm based on the action of a volunteer acting within the scope of the volunteer's responsibilities to a nonprofit organization or governmental entity unless the claimant establishes by clear and convincing evidence that the harm was proximately caused by an action of such volunteer which constitutes willful or criminal misconduct, or a conscious, flagrant indifference to the rights or safety of the individual harmed."

• **Exceptions.** The "immunity" provided by the Act is limited, meaning that it is not absolute. The Act specifies that it confers no immunity upon volunteers whose misconduct (1) is a crime of violence or act of international terrorism for which the volunteer has been convicted in any court; (2) is a hate crime; (3) is a sexual offense, as defined by state law, for which the volunteer has been convicted in any court; (4) is a violation of a federal or state civil rights law; or (5) occurred while the volunteer was under the influence of intoxicating alcohol or any drug at the time of the misconduct.

• **Amount of liability.** In the event that a volunteer is found liable in any civil action, the Act limits the amount of "noneconomic" damages that can be assessed. Noneconomic damages are defined by the Act as "losses for physical and emotional pain, suffering, inconvenience, physical impairment, mental anguish, disfigurement, loss of enjoyment of life, loss of society and companionship, loss of consortium . . . hedonic damages, injury to reputation and all other nonpecuniary losses of any kind or nature." The Act specifies that a volunteer "shall be liable only for the amount of noneconomic loss allocated to that defendant in direct proportion to the percentage of responsibility of that defendant . . . for the harm to the claimant with respect to which that defendant is liable." In other words, if a volunteer is found to be ten percent at fault, he or she cannot be assessed more than ten percent of the noneconomic damages awarded by a jury.

Examples

• *A child drowns during a church youth activity at a lake. The parents of the victim sue the church, and also a volunteer worker who allegedly was negligent. The volunteer received no compensation for her services. She is protected by the federal Volunteer Protection Act, and cannot be liable unless her actions amounted to "criminal misconduct, gross negligence, reckless misconduct, or a conscious, flagrant indifference to the rights or safety of the individual harmed." The Act does not provide the church with any protection.*

• *Same facts as the previous example, except that the volunteer was paid an "honorarium" of $250 each year by the church. The Act only protects uncompensated volunteers, but it defines "uncompensated" to include volunteers who do not receive annual compensation in excess of $500.*

• *A woman sues her church, claiming that an associate pastor to whom she had gone for counseling engaged in inappropriate sexual contact. Because the church has very* limited insurance coverage for such a claim, the woman also sues the members of the church board individually. She claims that they were guilty of negligent supervision. The board members are protected from personal liability by the federal Volunteer Protection Act, unless their actions amounted to "criminal misconduct, gross negligence, reckless misconduct, or a conscious, flagrant indifference to the rights or safety of the individual harmed." The Act does not provide the church with any protection.

• Same facts as the previous question, except that the church provides the board with a dinner twice each year in recognition of the services they provide. The value of the meals is approximately $50 per year for each board member. The board receives no other form of remuneration. The Act only protects uncompensated volunteers, but it defines "uncompensated" to include volunteers who do not receive annual compensation in excess of $500. The board members clearly meet the definition of uncompensated, and so are protected against personal liability by the Act.

• Same facts as the previous example, except that the church pays each board member an honorarium of $1,000 at the end of each year. The board members do not meet the definition of uncompensated, and as a result are not protected by the Act.

• A child is molested by a youth worker while at church. The parents sue the church and members of the board. They allege that the board refused to screen volunteer youth workers, despite numerous requests by parents, because they considered it a waste of time. The Act may not protect the board members, since their actions in refusing to implement any procedures for reducing the risk of child molestation may be viewed by a jury as "gross negligence, reckless misconduct, or a conscious, flagrant indifference to the rights or safety of the individual harmed."

• A volunteer church worker causes an accident while driving a church vehicle on church business. An occupant of another car is injured. The victim sues the church, and also sues the volunteer individually. The volunteer is not protected by the Act, since the Act does not extend to harm caused by a volunteer operating a motor vehicle.

• A church uses a volunteer "lay counselor" to provide counseling services to members of the church. The counselor also provides services to members of the community as an outreach. The counselor is not licensed. A counselee sues the church and counselor, claiming that she was injured by the counselor's services. The counselor is not protected by the Act if she was required to be licensed by the state to engage in the counseling services she provided.

3. Injuries to beneficiaries

Some states immunize religious organizations from liability for the negligence of agents and employees committed against "beneficiaries" of the organization. This view ordinarily is based upon one of the following grounds: (1) the funds of religious organizations are held in trust for charitable purposes and may not be diverted to the payment of damages; (2) the misconduct of employees should not be imputed to a religious organization when their services are for the benefit of humanity and not for the economic gain of the organization that employs them; (3) a religious organization is engaged in work highly beneficial to the state and to humanity, and its funds should not be diverted from this important purpose to the payment of damages; or, (4) those accepting the benefits of a religious organization implicitly agree not to hold it liable for injuries that they may receive at the hands of its employees.[336]

To illustrate, a woman who visited a church to view the sanctuary and its stained-glass windows was deemed to be a beneficiary of the church and therefore incapable of recovering damages for injuries she suffered in the church.[337] Other examples of beneficiaries include a church Sunday school teacher,[338] a nonmember who attended a church social,[339] a member of a Girl Scout troop that met on church property,[340] a person attending a religious service,[341] and a guest at a church wedding.[342]

Case Studies

• *A New Jersey court ruled that a state charitable immunity law prevented a woman from suing a church as a result of injuries she suffered when she tripped on a sidewalk adjacent to the church. A church member (the "plaintiff") was driven to church by a friend to attend Sunday morning services. When they arrived at church, the plaintiff got out of the car carrying a Bible and began walking along a sidewalk next to the church. As she neared the front of the church, she tripped on a raised metal grate and fell, suffering a knee injury. She later sued the church for negligence. The church claimed that the lawsuit was barred by the New Jersey Charitable Immunity Act which provides that nonprofit corporations (including churches) are not liable for injuries suffered by any "beneficiary, to whatever degree, of the works of such nonprofit corporation." The plaintiff insisted that when the accident occurred she was not a beneficiary of the church because she had not yet entered the church. The court disagreed, noting that a church member is "a beneficiary, to whatever degree" of the church's religious mission "not only during the period when church services are actually being conducted, but also while the member is entering or leaving the church to obtain the benefit of those services."[343]*

• *A New Jersey court ruled that a state charitable immunity law prevented a church from being sued by the family of a boy who was injured seriously while attending a*

---

[336] Egerton v. R.E. Lee Memorial Church, 273 F. Supp. 834 (W.D. Va. 1967), *aff'd,* 395 F.2d 381 (4th Cir. 1968).

[337] *Id.*

[338] Wiklund v. Presbyterian Church, 217 A.2d 463 (N.J. 1966).

[339] Burgie v. Muench, 29 N.E.2d 439 (Ohio 1940).

[340] Bianchi v. South Park Presbyterian Church, 8 A.2d 567 (N.J. 1939).

[341] Cullen v. Schmit, 39 N.E. 2d 146 (Ohio 1942).

[342] Anasiewicz v. Sacred Heart Church, 181 A.2d 787 (N.J. 1962), *appeal denied,* 184 A.2d 419 (1962).

[343] Thomas v. Second Baptist Church, 766 A.2d 816 (N.J. Super. 2001). *See also* Loder v. The Church, 685 A.2d 20 (N.J. Super. 1996); Monaghan v. Holy Trinity Church, 646 A.2d 1130 (N.J. Super. A.D. 1994); George v. First United Presbyterian Church, 639 A.2d 1128 (Super. A.D. 1994); Pelaez v. Rugby Laboratories, Inc., 624 A.2d 1053 (N.J. Super. L. 1993).

church day camp.[344] *A church operated a summer day camp for grade school children that was designed to "integrate biblical truth into the lives of children through formal teaching and informal activities such as crafts and games." A boy was injured while participating in a camp activity. Though his parents had registered him in the camping program, neither the parents nor the boy attended the church or had any other contact with it. The parents sued the church, alleging that their son's injuries were caused by the church's negligence. The church asked the court to dismiss the lawsuit against it on the basis of a state "charitable immunity" law that prevented charitable organizations from being sued on the basis of negligence by "beneficiaries" of their charitable activities. The New Jersey statute specifies: "No nonprofit corporation . . . organized exclusively for religious, charitable [or] educational . . . purposes shall . . . be liable to respond in damages to any person who shall suffer damage from the negligence of any agent or servant of such corporation . . . where such person is a beneficiary, to whatever degree, of the works of such nonprofit corporation . . . ." The trial court rejected the church's request to dismiss the case, and the church appealed. A state appeals court agreed with the church that the charitable immunity statute prevented the victim's parents from suing the church, and accordingly it dismissed the lawsuit against the church. The court observed that the statute provides legal immunity to nonprofit organizations with respect to injuries caused to their "beneficiaries" by their agents or representatives. The court concluded that these two requirements were satisfied in this case. Clearly, the church was a nonprofit religious organization. And second, the victim was a beneficiary. The court reasoned that one is a beneficiary who participates in an activity of a charity that furthers its charitable objectives. Since the victim was participating in a camp that existed to further the religious objectives of the church, he was a beneficiary of the church and therefore could not sue it on the basis of its alleged negligence.*

• *A Maryland appeals court reaffirmed that state's adherence to the charitable immunity doctrine, and as a result dismissed a lawsuit against a charitable organization seeking money damages for its alleged negligence.*[345] *An adult was injured during a basketball game at a Jewish Community Center. He sued the center alleging that its negligent supervision of the game resulted in his injury. The center claimed that it was immune from liability as a result of the state's charitable immunity law. A state appeals court agreed with the charity and dismissed the lawsuit. It began its opinion by observing that Maryland has long recognized the doctrine of charitable immunity. While the state legislature enacted a statute permitting charities that carry liability insurance to be sued, "[i]n the absence of such insurance, a negligence action cannot be maintained against a charitable institution." Since the center had no liability insurance coverage, this exception did not apply. The injured basketball player urged the court to follow the lead of most of the other states and reject the doctrine of charitable immunity. The court declined to do so, insisting that it is up to the state legislature to abolish the doctrine. The court noted that the legislature in recent years has expressed no interest in repudiating the doctrine. Quite to the contrary, it has expanded it by*

---

[344] Rupp v. Brookdale Baptist Church, 577 A.2d 188 (N.J. Super. 1990). In defending the statute, the court observed, "The principle of charitable immunity was deeply rooted in the common law of New Jersey. The principle is premised on the fact that charitable associations are created to pursue philanthropic goals and the accomplishment of those goals would be hampered if they were to pay tort judgments in cases similar to this matter. . . . [A] person who makes a charitable contribution expects his donation to further the goals of the organization, and not to be used to satisfy lawsuits which bear no direct relationship to those goals."

[345] Abramson v. Reiss, 638 A.2d 743 (Md. 1994).

granting limited immunity from liability to the directors, employees, and volunteers of charitable organizations. This ruling illustrates the special status enjoyed by churches and other charities in Maryland. While immunity from liability is not absolute (it only applies to acts of ordinary negligence), it is nevertheless a significant protection that is available to churches and other religious organizations in few other states.

• The Supreme Court of Virginia ruled that a volunteer performing services on behalf of a charity cannot be sued as a result of injuries that occur as a result of those services.[346] A Red Cross volunteer was driving a woman in a Red Cross vehicle to a hospital for medical services. On the way the car was involved in an accident with another vehicle and the woman passenger was injured. The woman later died, and her estate sued the volunteer for negligent driving. The volunteer defended himself by asserting that Virginia recognized the principle of charitable immunity, and that under this doctrine he could not be liable for the woman's injuries since they occurred while he was performing charitable services. Under these circumstances, the volunteer claimed that he was "cloaked with the immunity of the charity." A trial court agreed with the volunteer, and the estate appealed. The state supreme court agreed that the volunteer was not liable for the woman's injuries. The court began its opinion by noting that "[t]he doctrine of charitable immunity adopted in Virginia precludes a charity's beneficiaries from recovering damages from the charity for the negligent acts of its servants or agents if due care was exercised in the hiring and retention of those agents and servants." The woman's estate argued that cloaking a volunteer with charitable immunity would unfairly protect charitable activities at the expense of compensating persons who are injured by those volunteers. The court disagreed, noting that "[w]e struck this balance in favor of charitable institutions when the doctrine of charitable immunity was adopted and applied in Virginia years ago." This choice, noted the court, was based upon the belief that "it is in the public interest to encourage charitable institutions in their good work." The court observed, "Like any organization, a charity performs its work only through the actions of its servants and agents. Without a charity's agents and servants, such as the volunteer here, no service could be provided to beneficiaries. Denying these servants and agents the charity's immunity for their acts effectively would deny the charity immunity for its acts. If the charity's servants and agents are not under the umbrella of immunity given the institution itself and they are exposed to negligence actions by the charity's beneficiaries, the "good work" of the charity will be adversely impacted. That result is inconsistent with the Commonwealth's policy underlying the doctrine of charitable immunity." The court concluded that "under the doctrine of charitable immunity, a volunteer of a charity is immune from liability to the charity's beneficiaries for negligence while the volunteer was engaged in the charity's work."

4. State Laws Imposing "Caps" on Damages

Three states have enacted laws limiting the liability of churches (and other charitable organizations). In addition, the federal Civil Rights Act of 1991 places caps on employer damages in some discrimination cases. This section will review these laws, and court rulings applying them.

(1) The Civil Rights Act of 1991

---

[346] Moore v. Warren, 463 S.E.2d 459 (Va. 1995).

The federal Civil Rights Act of 1991 imposes limits on the amount of monetary damages that can be assessed against employers in discrimination lawsuits. Employers with more than 14 but fewer than 101 employees cannot be liable for more than $50,000 to any one person; for employers with more than 100 but fewer than 201 employees, the maximum damages available to any one person is $100,000; for employers with more than 200 but fewer than 500 employees, the maximum damages available to any one person is $200,000; and for employers with more than 500 employees the maximum damages available to any one person is $300,000. Some exceptions apply. The Civil Rights Act of 1991 is addressed further in section 8-12.9.

(2) Massachusetts

In 1971 the Massachusetts legislature enacted a law limiting the liability of charitable organizations. The statute specifies:

> It shall not constitute a defense to any cause of action based on tort brought against a corporation, trustees of a trust, or members of an association that said corporation, trust, or association is or at the time the cause of action arose was a charity; provided, that if the tort was committed in the course of any activity carried on to accomplish directly the charitable purposes of such corporation, trust, or association, liability in any such cause of action shall not exceed the sum of twenty thousand dollars exclusive of interest and cost. Notwithstanding any other provision of this section, the liability of charitable corporations, the trustees of charitable trusts, and the members of charitable associations shall not be subject to the limitations set forth in this section if the tort was committed in the course of activities primarily commercial in character even though carried on to obtain revenue to be used for charitable purposes.[347]

Note the following significant provisions of this law: (1) the liability of charitable organizations for activities carried on to further the organization's charitable purposes is limited to $20,000; (2) there is no $20,000 limit for activities carried on by charitable organizations for "commercial" purposes.

The Massachusetts Supreme Judicial Court unanimously upheld the validity of the Massachusetts law in 1989.[348] The case involved a lawsuit filed against a hospital for its alleged negligent treatment of a minor. A jury awarded the minor $350,000 in damages, and the hospital appealed on the ground that its liability was limited to $20,000 under the Massachusetts law. The minor's attorneys argued that the $20,000 limitation violated the constitutional guarantees of due process, equal protection of the laws, and trial by jury. The Supreme Court conceded that "we are not without misgivings about the paltriness of the $20,000 cap, especially in light of the decline of the dollar since 1971," but it ruled that the law was valid.

---

[347] Mass. General Laws c. 231, § 85K.

[348] English v. New England Medical Center, 541 N.E.2d 329 (Mass. 1989). See also In re Boston's Regional Medical Center, Inc., 328 F.Supp.2d 130 (D. Mass. 2004); St. Clair v. Trustees of Boston University, 521 N.E.2d 1044 (Mass. App. 1988).

The court reasoned that statutes generally should be upheld by the courts so long as they are "rationally related to the furtherance of a legitimate state interest." A statue ordinarily "only needs to be supported by a conceivable, rational basis." The court concluded that the $20,000 limitation was related to a legitimate state interest: "The objective of [the statute] clearly is to protect the funds of charitable institutions so they may be devoted to charitable purposes. That objective is . . . clearly legitimate. If a charity's property were depleted by the payment of damages its usefulness might be either impaired or wholly destroyed, the object of the founder or donors defeated, and charitable gifts discouraged."

The court rejected the claim that the Massachusetts law violated the constitutional guarantees of due process and equal protection of the laws by denying accident victims the ability to recover damages. If also rejected the claim that the law violated the right to a trial by jury. In responding to the argument that the expenses involved in litigating serious personal injury cases often far exceed the $20,000 limit, the court observed that it was "not the court's prerogative to determine whether a more equitable distribution of the burden of negligently inflicted personal injuries could be devised. We cannot say that there is no rational relationship between the cap on damages and the statute's legitimate objective of preserving charitable assets."

(3) South Carolina

Section 33-56-180 of the South Caroline Code contains the following provision:

(A) A person sustaining an injury or dying by reason of the tortious act of commission or omission of an employee of a charitable organization, when the employee is acting within the scope of his employment, may recover in an action brought against the charitable organization only the actual damages he sustains in an amount not exceeding the limitations on liability imposed in the South Carolina Tort Claims Act in Chapter 78 of Title 15 [generally, the Act limits liability to $300,000 per person, and $600,000 in total in cases of multiple plaintiffs]. An action against the charitable organization pursuant to this section constitutes a complete bar to any recovery by the claimant, by reason of the same subject matter, against the employee of the charitable organization whose act or omission gave rise to the claim unless it is alleged and proved in the action that the employee acted in a reckless, willful, or grossly negligent manner, and the employee must be joined properly as a party defendant. A judgment against an employee of a charitable organization may not be returned unless a specific finding is made that the employee acted in a reckless, willful, or grossly negligent manner. If the charitable organization for which the employee was acting cannot be determined at the time the action is instituted, the plaintiff may name as a party defendant the employee, and the entity for which the employee was acting must be added or substituted as party defendant when it reasonably can be determined.

(B) If the actual damages from the injury or death giving rise to the action arose from the use or operation of a motor vehicle and exceed two hundred fifty thousand dollars, this section does not prevent the injured person from recovering benefits pursuant to section 38-77-160 but in an amount not to exceed the limits of the uninsured or underinsured coverage.[349]

Here is a summary of the important features of this law:

First, it applies to "charitable organizations," a term that covers most churches and religious organizations.

Second, persons injured as a result of the negligence (or other wrongful activity) of a church employee may not sue the employee. They must sue the church itself—unless the employee "acted recklessly, wantonly, or grossly negligent," or unless the identity of the church cannot be established.

Third, and most significantly, *the church is liable only for actual damages up to but not exceeding $300,000* (for one plaintiff, or a maximum of $600,000 for multiple plaintiffs).

Fourth, churches are not liable for speculative or punitive damages, and their liability for actual damages (i.e., out-of-pocket expenses that can be substantiated by receipts and other written evidence) cannot exceed $600,000.

Fifth, a special rule applies in the case of injuries caused by the use of motor vehicles.

The South Carolina Supreme Court unanimously upheld the constitutionality of the statute in a case challenging its validity.[350] In 1985, a woman undergoing routine gall bladder surgery was given a unit of blood containing the AIDS virus. A Red Cross office had collected the infected blood from a volunteer donor four months before a test for detecting the AIDS virus in blood supplies was developed. The victim sued the Red Cross for negligence, and the Red Cross asserted that its liability was limited to $200,000 on the basis of the state law limiting the liability of charitable organizations. The victim argued that the state law violated the "equal protection clause" of the state constitution, which specifies simply that "no person shall be denied the equal protection of the laws." Specifically, she argued that the law impermissibly established a distinction or classification between charitable organizations and non-charitable organizations by limiting

[349] *See* Smith ex rel. Estate of Smith v. Church Mutual Insurance Company, 375 F.Supp.2d 451 (D.S.C. 2005).

[350] Doe v. American Red Cross Blood Services, 377 S.E.2d 323 (S.C. 1989). This case involved the original cap of $200,000.

the liability of charitable organizations while leaving non-charitable organizations subject to unlimited liability. Further, she argued that the law would affect charities differently depending on their size—i.e., a $200,000 limit on liability would not be of much help to smaller charities (a $200,000 judgment would be catastrophic), but it would be of significant benefit to larger charities.

The South Carolina Supreme Court ruled that a law which treats different classes of persons or organizations differently will satisfy the equal protection clause of the state constitution if the following three requirements are satisfied: "(1) the classification bears a reasonable relation to the legislative purpose sought to be effected; (2) the members of the class are treated alike under similar circumstances and conditions; and (3) the classification rests on some reasonable basis." The court concluded that the law limiting the liability of charitable organizations satisfied all three requirements, and accordingly was constitutional. As to the first requirement, the court noted that the purpose of the law in question was "to encourage the formation of charitable organizations, to promote charitable donations, and to preserve the resources of the charitable organizations." The legislature sought to accomplish this purpose by insulating charitable organizations from liability in excess of $200,000. "It was rational," concluded the court, "for the government to make distinctions between those in business for profit and those who have [nonprofit or charitable] motives. We therefore hold that the limitation on liability [contained in the law] bears a rational relationship to the legislative goal."

The court also concluded that the law satisfied the second requirement: "We find that although the impact of a $200,000 damage judgment may vary according to the size of the charitable organization, the varying impact does not violate the equal protection clause [since] we find that potential plaintiffs are not treated disparately because the same monetary cap applies equally to the entire class of plaintiffs."

The court further concluded that the law satisfied the third requirement— that the classification contained in the law rested on a reasonable basis. The statute's classification between charitable and non-charitable organizations "is not arbitrary," the court concluded, "and there is a reasonable relationship between promoting charitable activities and limiting the liability of entities that engage in such activities."

Case Study

• *The South Carolina Supreme Court ruled that a church member could sue his unincorporated church for injuries sustained while repairing the church sound system, but he could not recover more than the $200,000 "cap" allowed by state law.[351] The member volunteered to enter the church attic to repair the sound system. While in the attic, he fell through the ceiling and landed on a concrete floor some ten feet below. His injuries required him to miss work for nearly a year. The victim sued his church, pastors, and church board members, alleging that they were all negligent and responsible for his injuries. A jury awarded him $300,000, and the defendants*

---

[351] Crocker v. Barr, 409 S.E.2d 368 (S.C. 1992). This case involved the original cap of $200,000.

appealed. The supreme court ruled that the injured member could sue his church, even though it was unincorporated. But it reduced the jury's award from $300,000 to $200,000 on the basis of a state law that provides: "Any person sustaining an injury or dying by reason of the tortious act . . . of an employee of a charitable organization, when the employee is acting within the scope of his employment, may only recover in any action brought against the charitable organization in an amount not exceeding two hundred thousand dollars." The court concluded that a church fit "squarely within the definition of a charitable organization" for purposes of this law.

(4) Texas

The Texas legislature has enacted a law limiting the legal liability of charitable organizations. Section 84.006 of the Texas Code of Civil Procedure specifies:

> Except as provided in section 84.007 of this Act, in any civil action brought against a nonhospital charitable organization for damages based on an act or omission by the organization or its employees or volunteers, the liability of the organization is limited to money damages in a maximum amount of $500,000 for each person and $1,000,000 for each single occurrence of bodily injury or death and $100,000 for each single occurrence for injury to or destruction of property.

The Act defines "charitable organization" to include charitable and religious organizations exempt from federal income taxation under section 501(c)(3) of the Internal Revenue Code. Churches and most religious organizations will satisfy this definition. The Act permits employees of "charitable organizations" to be sued as a result of injuries caused by their negligence in the course of their employment, but their liability is limited to "money damages in a maximum amount of $500,000 for each person and $1,000,000 for each single occurrence of bodily injury or death and $100,000 for each single occurrence for injury to or destruction of property" (i.e., the same limitations that apply to charitable organizations themselves). "Volunteers" (those serving without compensation, including officers and directors) are totally immune from liability (they cannot be sued) for injuries or death resulting from their conduct on behalf of a charitable organization so long as they were acting "in good faith and in the course or scope of [their] duties or functions within the organization." The immunity of volunteers does not cover injuries caused by the negligent use of motor vehicles, to the extent of any existing insurance coverage.

The Texas law does *not* apply to (1) "an act or omission that is intentional, willfully or wantonly negligent, or done with conscious indifference or reckless disregard for the safety of others"; or (2) any charitable organization that does not have liability insurance coverage in an amount of at least "$500,000 for each person and $1,000,000 for each single occurrence of bodily injury or death and $100,000 for each single occurrence for injury to or destruction of property."

Here is a summary of the more important features of the Texas law.

- **"Cap" on church liability.** The statute limits the liability of charitable organizations to "money damages in a maximum amount of $500,000 for each person and $1,000,000 for each single occurrence of bodily injury or death and $100,000 for each single occurrence for injury to or destruction of property."

- **"Cap" on personal liability.** Church employees can be sued personally as a result of injuries or damages caused by their negligence in the course of their duties, but their personal liability is subject to the same dollar limitations that apply to charitable organizations.

- **Definition of "charitable organization."** The term *charitable organization* is defined broadly, and includes most churches and many religious organizations.

- **Definition of "volunteer."** Volunteers (uncompensated workers) cannot be sued personally as a result of injuries or damages caused by their negligent activities, except in the case of negligent operation of a motor vehicle (and then only to the extent of existing liability insurance coverage).

- **Exceptions.** The dollar limits do not apply in the case of "intentional, willfully or wantonly negligent" acts or omissions, or to conduct that shows a conscious indifference or reckless disregard for the safety of others.

- **Necessity of having insurance coverage.** The dollar limits do not apply to a charitable organization that does not have liability insurance coverage in an amount of at least "$500,000 for each person and $1,000,000 for each single occurrence of bodily injury or death and $100,000 for each single occurrence for injury to or destruction of property."

Limiting a Church's Liability for Money Damages

Ministers and lay leaders of churches should be aware of the following considerations:

(1) **Legislative initiatives.** There is a litigation epidemic in this county, and it is impacting churches. Church leaders can no longer afford to sit back and passively wait to be sued. There are meaningful steps that can be taken that will either reduce the amount of damages for which churches will be liable, or that will reduce the risk of being sued in the first place. One such step, for churches not located in Massachusetts, South Carolina, or Texas, is to encourage state legislators to sponsor legislation imposing dollar caps on damages that can be assessed against charities. The fact that three states have enacted such laws (two of which have been upheld unanimously by the state supreme court) should increase the likelihood of finding sympathetic legislators. The assistance of other charities (*e.g.*, Red Cross, Boy Scouts and Girl Scouts, the Salvation Army, Catholic Charities, hospitals, schools, libraries, museums) as well as church insurance companies and other churches and denominations should also be sought.

Limiting a Church's Liability for Money Damages

Ministers and lay leaders of churches should be aware of the following considerations:

(2) **Locating a religious or parachurch ministry.** There are many factors that should be considered in establishing a location for a parachurch ministry or denominational agency. One of those factors is the existence of a charitable immunity law in states under consideration. Any religious organization planning the location of a regional or national office should seriously consider Massachusetts, South Carolina, and Texas as a result of the laws in those states limiting the liability of charitable organizations.

(3) **"Charitable" organizations.** While churches and religious organizations generally are considered to be "charitable" organizations, it would be prudent for churches and religious organizations in the states of Massachusetts, South Carolina, and Texas to ensure that their charters define their purposes to include *charitable* as well as religious activities.

(4) **Insurance coverage.** Should churches in Massachusetts, South Carolina, and Texas reduce their liability insurance coverage to match the maximum amount of liability allowed under state law? This is a difficult question that must be answered by a local attorney and a church's insurance agent. Churches in Texas have much less reason to reduce their insurance coverage than churches in South Carolina and Massachusetts, since (1) the validity of the Texas statute has not been upheld by the state supreme court, and (2) churches and other charitable organizations may be subject to liability in excess of the statute's limitations if their employees cause injury to other persons as a result of willful or wanton conduct. Further, the Texas statute only protects charities that maintain the specified amount of insurance. Even in South Carolina and Massachusetts, the state supreme courts simply found that the state laws limiting the liability of charitable organizations did not violate specific constitutional protections. It is possible that these laws will be attacked in the future on the basis of other provisions in the state or federal constitutions. And, it is conceivable that courts may conclude that churches are religious rather than charitable organizations, and therefore outside the protection of these laws.

> ### Are Limitations on the Liability of Churches and other Charitable Organizations Fair?
>
> It certainly could be argued that it is unfair to limit the liability of an innocent person who is seriously injured by the negligence of a church employee. After attorneys' fees and medical expenses are deducted, a $20,000 (or even a $300,000 or $500,000) judgment would be of little value to a person who is rendered a quadriplegic because of the negligence of a church employee. The fact is, however, that serious injuries caused by the negligence of church employees and agents are relatively rare, and that a limitation on liability is necessary to protect churches from the excessive and often meritless claims for damages that divert time and resources from the prosecution of the church's mission. Further, a church in Massachusetts, South Carolina, or Texas is free to voluntarily compensate (over and above the legal limitations) a victim of the church's negligence in the event that the congregation feels that the victim would not otherwise be adequately compensated.

Release Forms

§ 10-16.6

Key point 10-16.6. *A release form is a document signed by a competent adult that purports to relieve a church from liability for its own negligence. Such forms may be legally enforceable if they are clearly written and identify the conduct that is being released. However, the courts look with disfavor on release forms, and this has led to several limitations, including the following: (1) release forms will be strictly and narrowly construed against the church; (2) release forms cannot relieve a church of liability for injuries to minors, since minors have no legal capacity to sign such forms and their parents' signature does not prevent minors from bringing their own personal injury claim after they reach age 18; (3) some courts refuse to enforce any release form that attempts to avoid liability for personal injuries on the ground that such forms violate public policy; and (4) release forms will not be enforced unless they clearly communicate that they are releasing the church from liability for its negligence.*

Many churches use "release forms," which purport to release the church from legal responsibility for injuries inflicted by the negligence of its employees and volunteers. Besides being of dubious legal value,[352] such forms primarily protect the church's insurance company. If injuries are caused by the negligence of a church worker, then the liability insurer will pay for such damages up to the policy limits. If the church is not negligent, then it ordinarily will not be assessed any damages. A release form, even if deemed legally valid by a court, would have the effect of excusing the church's liability insurer from paying damages to a victim of the church's negligence. Imagine, for example, an adult who signs a valid release form as a condition to participating in a church activity. The adult breaks a leg as a result of the negligence of a church worker, and incurs $20,000 of medical bills only to discover that the release form he signed prevents him from obtaining insurance benefits under the church's insurance policy that would have been available to him had he not signed the release. The pastor of this church will have a very unhappy member.

---

[352] *See, e.g.,* Note, *The Quality of Mercy: "Charitable Torts" and Their Continuing Immunity,* 100 Harv. L. Rev. 1382, 1394-95 (1987).

Release forms that purport to excuse a church or other organization from liability for injuries to a minor are the most likely to be invalidated by the courts, often on the ground that they violate public policy. However, the courts have been less reluctant to recognize release or "assumption of risk" forms signed by competent adults, but even these forms are viewed with disfavor and some courts will go to great lengths to invalidate them, especially if they seek to relieve an organization of liability for personal injuries as opposed to property damage.

There are two exceptions to the enforceability of releases that often are recognized by the courts. First, releases generally will not prevent an organization from being liable for its gross negligence. Second, releases will be scrutinized closely by the courts, and must clearly point out exactly what is being released. This is a very exacting standard that many release forms that are used by churches will not meet. There are other exceptions to the enforceability of release forms that have been recognized by other courts, including the fact that the person signing the release is a minor. Churches should not use releases without discussing them with their insurance agent and a local attorney.

▶ *Churches that send groups of adults to other locations for short-term missions projects should consider having each participating adult sign an assumption of risk form. So long as these forms clearly explain the risks involved, and leave no doubt that the signer is assuming all risks associated with the trip, they may be enforced by the courts. This assumes that the signer is a competent adult. Churches should consult with an attorney about the validity of such forms under state law.*

Parental Permission and Medical Consent Forms

Churches should not allow a minor child to participate in any church activity (such as camping, boating, swimming, hiking, or some sporting events) unless the child's parents or legal guardians sign a form that (1) consents to their child participating in the specified activity; (2) certifies that the child is able to participate in the event (e.g., if the activity involves boating or swimming, the parents or guardians should certify that the child is able to swim); (3) lists any allergies or medical conditions that may be relevant to a physician in the event of an emergency; (4) lists any activities that the parents or guardians do not want the child to engage in; and (5) authorizes a designated individual to make emergency medical decisions for their child in the event that they cannot be reached.

Ideally, the form should be signed by both parents or guardians (if there are two), and the signatures should be notarized. If only one parent or guardian signs, or the signatures are not notarized, the legal effectiveness of the form is diminished. Having persons sign as witnesses to a parent's signature is not as good as a notary's acknowledgment, but it is better than a signature without a witness. The form should require the parent or guardian to inform the church immediately of any change in the information presented, and it should state that it is valid until revoked by the person who signed it. The parent or guardian should sign both in his or her own capacity as parent or guardian, and in a representative capacity on behalf of the minor child.

Case Studies

• *A Michigan court ruled that a release form signed by a competent adult prior to participating in a dangerous activity prevented him from suing as a result of injuries he sustained.[353] As part of an annual historic festival, a city sponsored a "rope climb" contest. A rope was stretched across a river and participants would hang onto the rope with their hands and attempt to cross the river. The winner was the participant who crossed the river in the shortest period of time. Various cash prizes were awarded to the winner and runners-up, and there was a one dollar entry fee paid by all participants. One participant lost his grasp of the rope and fell head first into the river, sustaining permanent and disabling injuries. He sued the city and the individuals who organized the festival. The city and festival organizers claimed that the victim could not sue because he signed a liability release form. Before participating in the rope climb, each participant was required to sign a "waiver of liability" form. A state appeals court ruled that the release prevented the victim from suing. The court rejected the victim's claim that the release was invalid since it did not specifically name every person or organization that was being released from liability. It observed simply that "[i]t was not necessary for the release to individually name each person or entity to be released from liability. The scope of the applicability of the waiver is clear: it waived liability with respect to any person or group responsible for the rope climb event." The court also rejected the victim's claim that the release was unenforceable because he had failed to read it before signing it.*

• *A New York court ruled that a church could not avoid liability for personal injuries suffered by a construction worker on church premises on the basis of a release form that did not specifically release the worker.[354] A church hired a contractor to repair its bell tower and spire, and had the contractor sign an agreement that contained the following "hold harmless" agreement: "The contractor agrees that he undertakes all repairs and renovations as detailed in the proposal at his own risk and he agrees to indemnify and save the church and all its members and officers for damage to property or injury to, or the death of any person, including employees, of any actions arising out of the acts of the contractor and at his own cost and expense; defend any action brought against either the contractor or the church; and promptly pay any adverse judgment in any such action, and hold the church and its members and officers harmless from and against any loss or damage and expense claimed by the church and its members and officers by reason of such claim." The contractor hired a worker who was seriously injured when he fell nearly 30 feet when the scaffolding on which he was working collapsed. The worker sued the church, and the church defended itself by citing the "hold harmless" agreement quoted above. A court ruled that the church could not escape liability on this basis. It noted that New York law imposes absolute liability upon owners and contractors for a failure to furnish and erect safe scaffolding, and that this liability was not avoided by the hold harmless agreement since only the contractor (and not the worker he hired) agreed to release the church from liability.*

• *A New York court ruled that a release form signed by a high school student and his parents did not relieve a church-operated school from liability for injuries sustained by the student when he was sexually assaulted by other students while on*

---

[353] Dombrowski v. City of Omer, 502 N.W.2d 707 (Mich. App. 1993).

[354] Bain v. First Presbyterian Church and Society, 601 N.Y.S.2d 535 (Sup. 1993).

a school-sponsored trip to Europe. The court concluded that the release form was "unenforceable because it does not clearly and unequivocally express the intention of the parties to relieve the [defendants] from liability for injuries sustained as the result of their negligence."[355]

• An Ohio court enforced an indemnification clause in a "facility use agreement" that required a charity that used a nonprofit camp to reimburse the camp for any legal judgments or settlements arising out of injuries occurring at the camp. The court noted that an indemnification clause is a clause obligating one party to pay any judgment or settlement assessed against another party. Such clauses are usually included in facility use agreements, and specify that organizations using the landowner's property must indemnify the landowner against any expenses incurred as a result of accidents occurring on the property. The court noted that "an agreement may exculpate a person from negligence only where the language doing so is clear and unambiguous." The court concluded that both parties were "sophisticated long-standing corporations" equal in bargaining position, and therefore the indemnification clause was enforceable. It conceded that the clause did not specifically mention "negligence," but it did identify "any and all" claims relating to the use of the camp. The court agreed that "one may not contractually relieve oneself for responsibility for acts constituting willful and wanton misconduct." It concluded that the evidence was not adequate to determine if this exception applied.[356]

• A Washington court ruled that the family of a college student killed during a scuba diving activity was prevented from suing the college or scuba instructor by a release form signed by the student prior to his death.[357] The student also signed an "assumption of risk" form that specified: "In consideration of being allowed to enroll in this course, I hereby personally assume all risks in connection with said course, for any harm, injury or damage that may befall me while I am enrolled as a student of the course, including all risks connected therewith, whether foreseen or unforeseen." During one dive the student panicked when he noticed the air in his tank was low, and died of air embolism resulting from too rapid an ascent. His family sued the college and his instructor. A state appeals court ruled that the family was barred from suing as a result of the release and assumption of risk forms signed by the student. The court acknowledged that "a release is a contract in which one party agrees to abandon or relinquish a claim . . . against another party," and that release agreements "are strictly construed and must be clear if the release from liability is to be enforced." The court also stressed that "the general rule is that a pre-injury release of the employer from liability also releases the employee." As a result, the student's release of the college had the effect of releasing the instructor (even if the instructor had not been specifically named in the release). The court agreed with the family that a release will not be enforced if it violates "public policy." However, the court noted that under Washington law, a release agreement does not violate public policy unless it involves a "public interest." Scuba diving did not involve such an interest. The court acknowledged that a release form only releases organizations and individuals from their ordinary negligence, and not from their gross negligence. However, the court added that "evidence of negligence is not evidence of gross negligence; to raise an issue of

---

[355] John Doe v. Archbishop Stepinac High School, 729 N.Y.S.2d 538 (2001).

[356] Weiner v. American Cancer Society, 2002 WL 1265575 (Ohio 2002).

[357] Boyce v. West, 862 P.2d 592 (Wash. App. 1993).

gross negligence, there must be substantial evidence of serious negligence." The court concluded that there was no evidence of gross negligence in this case other than the unsupported allegations of the family. The court also rejected the family's argument that the assumption of risk form their son signed was unenforceable since he did not specifically assume the risks of negligent instruction and negligent supervision. The court simply noted that the student had signed an assumption of risk form in which he assumed "all risks" associated with his scuba diving class.

• A court in the Virgin Islands ruled that a release form signed by a mother of a minor child who attended a church-operated school did not absolve the school from liability for injuries the child sustained when injured during an after-school program. The court concluded that the release form was "ambiguous on the issue of whether it releases the liability of the school . . . for negligence in the supervision of the after-school program."[358]

• A West Virginia court refused to recognize a "release form" as a legal defense to an organization's liability.[359] A young woman went whitewater rafting as paying passenger on a raft owned and operated by a commercial outfitter. During the trip, the guide who was operating the raft attempted to dislodge another raft that was stuck among some rocks by ramming it with his raft. This maneuver caused the woman to be thrown violently, causing serious injuries. The woman sued the outfitter that owned the raft. The outfitter defended itself by referring to a release form that the woman had signed prior to her trip. The court ruled that the woman could sue the outfitter despite the release. It acknowledged that a release form may be legally enforceable if a person clearly agrees to accept a specified risk of harm. But there are some very important limitations upon this general rule, including the following: (1) The victim must have been aware of and understood the terms of the release. The court observed, "[F]or an express agreement assuming the risk to be effective, it must appear that the [victim] has given his or her assent to the terms of the agreement" and if the agreement is prepared by another person or organization "it must appear that the terms were in fact brought home to, and understood by, the victim, before it may be found that the victim has agreed to them." (2) The release will be effective only with respect to risks that it specifically mentions. For example, a general release exempting an organization from negligence "will not be construed to include intentional or reckless misconduct or gross negligence, unless such intention clearly appears from the circumstances." (3) A release that violates "public policy" will not be enforced by the courts. The court concluded that a release will violate public policy and be unenforceable if it seeks to exempt a person from liability for failure to conform to a standard of conduct prescribed by statute. In this case, state law prescribed a level of care required of whitewater raft operators, and accordingly it was impossible for that duty to be released.

• A West Virginia court refused to enforce a release agreement signed by the youth pastor of a church on behalf of a 14-year-old girl who drowned while participating on a church-sponsored whitewater rafting trip. The court noted that an "anticipatory release of liability" like the one in this case that "purports to exempt the defendant from liability to the plaintiff for the failure of the defendant to conform to the standard of care expected of members of his occupation is unenforceable." As a result, the release form signed by the youth pastor was unenforceable. The court also refused to

[358] Joseph v. Church of God (Holiness) Academy, 2006 WL 1459505 (V.I. Super. 2006).
[359] Murphy v. North American River Runners, Inc., 412 S.E.2d 504 (W. Va. 1991).

enforce an indemnification clause in the release agreement on the ground of ambiguity. The indemnification clause stated that "the undersigned parent and/or guardian of the minor, for themselves and on behalf of the minor, join in the foregoing waiver and release and stipulates and agrees to save and hold harmless, indemnify, and forever defend [the tour company] from and against any claims and negligence made or brought by the minor or by anyone on behalf of the minor." However, the youth pastor who signed the form was not the parent or guardian of any of the minors.[360]

Insurance   § 10-16.7

Key point 10-16.7. *A liability insurance policy provides a church with a legal defense to lawsuits claiming that the church is responsible for an injury, and it will pay any adverse settlement or judgment up to the limit specified in the policy. Liability insurance policies exclude a number of claims. For example, some policies exclude injuries based on criminal or intentional acts and claims for punitive damages. A church has an obligation to promptly notify its insurer of any potential claim, and to cooperate with the insurer in its investigation of claims.*

Liability insurance may be viewed as a "defense" to church liability in the sense that it will provide the church with a legal defense of a civil lawsuit and pay any portion of a settlement or judgment up to the insurance policy limits. This assumes, of course, that the lawsuit sought damages for an act or occurrence covered by the policy. Listed below are several aspects of church insurance with which church leaders should be familiar:

1. Coverage

An insurance policy will provide a church with a legal defense of a covered claim, and pay any portion of a settlement or judgment up to the policy limit. It is very important for church leaders to be familiar with those claims that are covered under the church's insurance policy or policies.

Churches often engage in activities that are not clearly covered under their insurance policy. Examples include counseling, use of personal vehicles for church-related work, and use of the church facilities by outside groups. Be sure that you check with your insurance agent about coverage for these and other activities.

The issue of directors and officers insurance is addresses in section 6-08.1.

---

[360] Johnson v. New River Scenic Whitewater Tours, Inc., (S.D.W.V. 2004).

Q

How much insurance should we purchase?

A

Unfortunately, there is no simple answer to this question. Here are a few points that may help:

• In general, the amount of coverage should be based on two primary considerations: (1) the nature and frequency of your activities, and (2) the net value of the church's assets. To illustrate, if your church has a youth program that has frequent meetings involving several minors, or your church provides counseling, or hosts community activities, then your liability risks are increased and you should be looking for higher insurance limits. Further, as a general rule, liability insurance should have limits in excess of the net value of the church's assets, so that the assets are protected in the event of litigation.

• Annually review all church insurance coverages to be sure they are adequate.

• Periodically obtain appraisals of church property (real property, personal property, and fixtures) to be sure that you have adequate coverage.

• Be sure that your church is insured for an amount in excess of what is required by a "coinsurance clause" in your insurance policy. A coinsurance clause is often difficult to understand, but the idea is that unless a church is insured for a specified amount (e.g., 80% of market value) then the church becomes a "coinsurer" in the event of a partial loss, and is responsible for paying part of that loss. This is done by a reduction in the amount that the insurer has to pay. The purpose of such clauses is to persuade property owners to insure their property for an amount equal to or approaching its market value. Over time, a church's failure to increase the amount of its property insurance to reflect the current value of the church property will reduce the insured amount to less than the coinsurance amount, and this can result in an unpleasant and unbudgeted expense when the insurer only pays a portion of a substantial partial loss.

Key point. *Church insurance policies generally do not cover employment-related claims, including discrimination, wrongful termination, and sexual harassment. If your church is sued on the basis of such claims, you probably will need to retain and pay for your own attorney, and pay any judgment or settlement amount. This often comes as a shock to church leaders. You should immediately review your policy with your insurance agent to see if you have any coverage for such claims. If you do not, ask how it can be obtained. You may be able to obtain an endorsement for "employment practices." Also, a "directors and officers" policy may cover these claims.*

Key point. *In evaluating whether or not an insurance policy provides coverage for a particular claim, the courts generally apply the following principles: (1) the insurance contract is "construed liberally" in favor of the insured and "strictly" against the insurer; and (2) exclusions are interpreted as narrowly as possible, so as to provide maximum coverage for the insured, and are construed most strongly against the insurance company that drafted and issued the policy.*

▶ *Does your church have insurance that covers losses caused by embezzlement and employee dishonesty? Ask your insurance agent the following questions: (1) Does our church insurance policy cover employee thefts and dishonesty? (2) If so, what is the coverage amount? (3) Is the coverage amount adequate for our church? If not, how much would additional coverage cost? (4) If our church is not insured against employee theft or dishonesty, what would the cost be for different levels of coverage? (5) Would a series of acts of embezzlement, occurring over more than one year, be a single "occurrence" or separate occurrences under our employee dishonesty policy?*

Counseling Insurance

Does your church carry counseling liability insurance for its ministers? If not, you should give serious consideration to obtaining such coverage. At this time, it is still relatively inexpensive. Do not assume that you are covered simply because your church carries general liability insurance. While the risk of a minister being successfully sued for negligent counseling is remote, the risk that a minister may be sued is increasingly possible. If counseling liability insurance covers an alleged incident, then your insurer ordinarily will provide a church with a complete legal defense to the lawsuit, and pay any resulting damages or settlement up to the policy limits. Since the risk of losing such a suit is remote, the availability of counseling liability insurance will have the effect of a "legal defense" policy. It is true that your church may increase its risk of being sued if it obtains counseling liability insurance (it will become a more attractive "target"). Yet, this consideration should not necessarily be controlling. The risk of being sued without adequate insurance coverage is an equally if not more grave concern.

Table 10-7 Insurance Coverages for Churches	
coverage	**description**
property	Covers many major risks to church property, including fire, smoke, lightning, hurricane, tornado. **Checklist:** <ul><li>Check to see if unique items such as stained glass windows, pipe organs, handbells, artwork, and sound equipment require special "endorsements."</li><li>Obtain appraisals of unique items to be sure they are adequately insured.</li><li>Conduct periodic inventories of property to prove claims in the event of loss or destruction.</li><li>Check to see if coverage is limited to the market value of damaged or destroyed property. If so, consider obtaining replacement cost coverage.</li><li>Check on coverage for items of personal property owned by members or employees. Examples include expensive coats left in a coat room, or an employee's own laptop computer.</li><li>Check to see if boilers require a special endorsement.</li><li>Check the exclusions under the policy. Some risks, such as earthquakes, mold, and sewer or drain backup, may be excluded and require special endorsements.</li><li>If your church is located in one of 19,000 communities that participate in the National Flood Insurance Program, you can obtain flood insurance from insurers that participate in the National Flood Insurance Program (NFIP). Coverage amounts are often inadequate.</li><li>Check to see if your policy contains a "coinsurance clause." If so, you are required to insure your property for a specified percentage of its market value. If you don't, you become a "coinsurer," meaning that your policy will pay less than the stated limits in the event of a partial loss. These clauses make it essential for churches to be sure they have adequate coverage. This review should be done annually.</li></ul>

Table 10-7
Insurance Coverages for Churches

coverage	description
liability	Covers many forms of personal injury and damage to the property of others. Common examples includes slips and falls, sexual misconduct (coverage may be limited to the church, and exclude the offender). **Checklist:** • Check to see if sexual misconduct coverage is limited, and if higher amounts can be obtained by complying with specified procedures. • Check to see if liability insurance is provided on an "occurrence" or "claims made" basis. • Some policies provide minimal medical benefits to persons injured on church property. Additional coverage should be considered.
church-owned vehicles	Covers injuries and damages resulting from the use of church-owned vehicles. • Check to see if your property or general liability policy contains coverage for church-owned vehicles. If not, be sure to obtain a separate endorsement for this coverage.
non-owned vehicles	Covers injuries and damages caused by members who use their own vehicle while performing services for their church. The driver's personal car insurance is also available, but if inadequate, the church will likely be sued. Often must be obtained as a separate endorsement. Essential for churches that allow members or employees to drive personal vehicles on church business. **Checklist:** • Check to see if non-owned vehicle coverage applies to rented vehicles.
counseling	Covers injuries caused during counseling activities. Often must be obtained as a separate endorsement. Essential for churches that provide counseling services. **Checklist:** • Check exclusions carefully. For example, some policies exclude sexual misconduct.

Table 10-7 Insurance Coverages for Churches	
coverage	**description**
employment practices	Covers certain employment-related claims such as wrongful dismissal and some forms of discrimination. These are among the most common types of church litigation today. Many church leaders erroneously assume that their general liability policy covers these claims. In most cases it does not. **Checklist:** • If your church has employees, you should consider this coverage. The more employees you have, the more essential this becomes.
directors and officers	Covers several potential legal claims that can be brought against officers and directors directly. "D&O" policies also may cover claims not covered by general liability policies. While uncompensated directors of nonprofit organizations have "limited immunity" from personal liability under both state and federal law, this protection does not cover compensated directors and does not cover acts of "gross negligence." Must be obtained as a separate endorsement or policy. **Checklist:** • If your church does not screen youth workers, lets children ride in fully-loaded 15-passenger vans, or engages in other high-risk activities that may be deemed "grossly negligent," then this coverage is essential.
theft	Covers embezzlement and other misappropriations of church funds and securities by employees and others having access to money or property. Often must be obtained as a separate endorsement. This form of insurance is also referred to as bonding. **Checklist:** • Remember, the opportunity to steal, rather than a need for money, is often the primary reason for employee theft. Institute procedures to minimize unsupervised access to funds.
foreign travel	Provides medical benefits for injuries occurring during foreign travel. Costs of a medical evacuation may also be covered. Often must be obtained as a separate endorsement or policy. **Checklist:** • Most general liability policies exclude any injuries or damages occurring outside of the US. • Essential coverage for churches that send groups on missions trips to foreign countries.

Table 10-7
Insurance Coverages for Churches

coverage	description
umbrella	Covers legal judgments in excess of the limits on other insurance policies. **Checklist:** • Does your church have substantial assets to be protected, or inadequate liability insurance? If so, this coverage is essential to protect against catastrophic damages.
workers compensation	Workers compensation insurance provides benefits to employees who are injured or become ill in the course of (or because of) their employment. Many church leaders erroneously assume that churches are not covered by state workers compensation laws. In most cases this assumption is incorrect, and exposes a church to a substantial uninsured risk. **Checklist:** • Check to see if churches are subject to workers compensation law in your state. If so, obtain insurance to cover potential claims.

2. Exclusions

All church insurance policies contain exclusions. An exclusion is a claim that is not covered under an insurance policy. It is important for church leaders to be familiar with the exclusions set forth in their church's liability insurance policy, since these represent potentially uninsured claims that can expose the church to substantial damages. Further, the church would have to retain and compensate its own attorney if it is sued on the basis of an excluded claim.

Common exclusions include intentional or criminal misconduct, injuries occurring outside of the United States, employment-related claims, and injuries caused by exposure to hazardous substances. Some policies exclude claims arising out of incidents of sexual misconduct. Church leaders may want to discuss with their church insurance agent the possibility of obtaining insurance to cover exclusions.

Case Studies

• A federal appeals court ruled that a church's insurance policy did not cover lawsuits arising from the employment relationship.[361] A pastor dismissed his church's music director. The music director sued the pastor, church, and state denominational agency, claiming that she had been dismissed because she suffered from post-traumatic stress

---

[361] The Parish of Christ Church v. The Church Insurance Company, 166 F.3d 419 (1st Cir. 1999).

disorder and multiple personality disorder. She insisted that her dismissal amounted to unlawful discrimination based on disability. She also claimed that the pastor had defamed her, and invaded her privacy. The church's insurance carrier insisted that the church insurance policy did not cover the woman's claims, and it refused to provide the church with a legal defense or to pay any portion of a jury verdict or settlement. A federal appeals court agreed that the insurance policy did not cover the woman's claims. It noted that the policy indemnifies the church for damages resulting from "personal injury," including injury from defamation. The policy further obligates the company to defend the church in any suit seeking damages covered by the policy. However, the policy excludes from coverage "personal injury sustained by any person as a result of an offense directly or indirectly related to the employment of such person by the named insured." The court noted that the key question was whether the woman's lawsuit was for "personal injury" sustained "as a result of an offense directly or indirectly related to her employment" by the church. If it was, then the exclusion applied, and the company had no duty to defend the church against the lawsuit. The court concluded that "defamatory statements providing an explanation for termination or directed to performance are related to employment. Alleged offenses occurring as part and parcel of an allegedly wrongful termination are plainly related to employment. Post-employment defamations can be directly or indirectly related to employment, and thus can fall within an exclusion of the sort at issue here. The statements to which [the lawsuit] refers are comments as to [the woman's] abilities and job performance. They are explanations as to why [the pastor] terminated [her] employment."

• A federal appeals court ruled that an insurance policy covered two denominational agencies that were sued as a result of the sexual misconduct of an affiliated pastor, despite the fact that the policy excluded sexual misconduct claims.[362] A learning disabled woman claimed that she had been sexual assaulted by an ordained minister on several occasions at a state school for the mentally handicapped. The minister served as a chaplain at the school. The woman sued the minister for injuries she allegedly suffered as a result of these assaults. She also sued the national denomination (the "national church") with which the minister was affiliated, and a regional denominational agency (the "regional church"). She claimed that the national and regional churches had been negligent in training, supervising, placing, and monitoring the chaplain, who eventually was indicted for alleged sexual contact with three mentally handicapped individuals. The chaplain was never an agent or employee of the national or regional churches, but graduated from a seminary affiliated with the national church and was listed in the national church's "clergy roster" as a retired pastor. The national church had an insurance policy containing both comprehensive general liability and "umbrella" liability provisions. The comprehensive general liability provision provided nationwide coverage for the national church. The umbrella liability provision covered the national church and about 40 regional churches. Both the comprehensive general liability and umbrella liability provisions obligated the insurance company to pay "damages because of bodily injury or property damage to which this insurance applies," but the policies explicitly require that "the bodily injury or property damage must be caused by an occurrence." An "occurrence" is defined as "an accident, including continuous or repeated exposure to substantially the same general conditions." Both policies excluded "bodily injury or property damage expected

---

[362] Evangelical Lutheran Church in America v. Atlantic Mutual Insurance Company, 169 F.3d 947 (5th Cir. 1999). *See also* D.E.M. v. Allickson, 555 N.W.2d 596 (N.D. 1996).

or intended from the standpoint of the insured." The insurance company asked a federal district court to dismiss the case on the ground that the chaplain's conduct had been "intended" and therefore was excluded from any coverage under the terms of the policy. The district court declined to do so, and ruled that the policies did provide coverage for the national and regional churches. The insurance company appealed. The federal appeals court concluded that under Illinois law (that law applicable to this case) it was clear that the victim's allegations of negligent hiring fell within the definition of "occurrence." It added that "if a complaint potentially supports a ground for recovery, the insurer must defend the entire complaint." The court, in rejecting the insurance company's argument that the exclusion of intentional acts precluded coverage, observed: "Here, negligent training was not an intentional tort, and [the chaplain's] acts are not the insureds' intentional acts. Thus, the insurance policy did not exclude the acts, and [the insurer] has a duty to defend."

• A federal appeals court ruled that a church insurance policy did not provide for a legal defense of a minister who engaged in sexual relations with two members of his congregation.[363] The minister sued the church's insurance company after it refused to pay for his legal defense. The church's comprehensive general liability policy provides coverage for pastoral counseling liability under a provision defining "personal injury" to include "acts, errors or omissions of ordained clergy, acting within the scope of their duties as employees of the named insured and arising out of the pastoral counseling activities of these individuals." The minister argued that he was entitled to a defense under the policy since the women's allegations arose out of his duties as a pastoral counselor. A federal appeals court disagreed, and ruled that the church's insurance policy did not cover the minister's actions. The critical question, the court concluded, was whether or not the minister was acting within the scope of his employment when he engaged in sexual relations with the two women. It concluded that "a priest does not act in furtherance of the business or interests of his employer when he engages in sexual misconduct with parishioners." As a result, the minister was not entitled to a defense under the policy "as the alleged acts of sexual misconduct do not fall within the scope of his employment."

• A federal appeals court ruled that a church insurance company was under no legal obligation to provide a legal defense to a church or its board of directors in a lawsuit alleging that a church volunteer had sexually molested a young girl.[364] The church's insurance company refused to provide the volunteer, the church, or the church board with a legal defense to the lawsuit, and denied any obligation to pay any judgment rendered in the case. The insurer based its position on the following language in the church's insurance policy: "This policy does not apply . . . to personal injury arising out of the willful violation of a penal statute or ordinance committed by or with knowledge or consent of any insured." The policy defined the term "insured" to include any duly appointed volunteer. The church and church board conceded that the insurance policy did not protect the volunteer, but they insisted that they were being sued solely on the basis of their negligence and accordingly the insurance policy should cover them. The appeals court rejected the position of the church and church board. It observed, "[T]here is conclusive proof [of a willful violation of penal statutes] by guilty pleas and

---

[363] Newyear v. The Church Insurance Company, 155 F.3d 1041 (8th Cir. 1998).

[364] All American Insurance Company v. Burns, 971 F.2d 438 (10th Cir. 1992). *Contra* American Employers Insurance Co. v. Doe 38, 165 F.3d 1209 (8th Cir. 1999).

criminal convictions on both such charges. . . . We cannot agree with the [argument of the church and church board] that the cases can be viewed as involving only the negligence allegations and the negligent entrustment theory. It is, instead, an essential element of [negligence] that [the volunteer] molested the girls and caused them injuries of mind and body. A cause of action for negligence depends not only upon the defendant's breach of duty to exercise care to avoid injury to the plaintiff, but also upon damage or injury suffered by the plaintiff as a consequence of the violation of the duty. The sexual violations and resulting injuries cannot therefore be disregarded. And giving consideration to them, the exclusion in the policy is thus applicable providing that the policy does not apply 'to personal injury arising out of the willful violation of a penal statute or ordinance committed by or with knowledge or consent of any insured.'"

• A federal appeals court ruled that a church's insurance policy did not cover a lawsuit against the church for the negligent hiring and supervision of a minister who engaged in sexual misconduct. The church's insurance policy excluded damages "arising from sexual action." The court concluded that the exclusion applied to the claims against the church, and so there was no coverage available under the policy. It concluded that the term "arising out of" meant that a claim need only bear an "incidental relationship" to the minister's acts of sexual misconduct. "Without [the minister's] sexual misconduct, the victims of the misconduct would have no claims against the church and the four associate ministers. Every alleged harm caused to the victims by the church and the four associate ministers stems from and is integrally related to the minister's acts. Therefore . . . all of the allegations that underlie the victim's claims against the church and the four associate ministers arise out of the minister's sexual actions, thereby precluding coverage."[365]

• A federal appeals court ruled that a camp's general liability insurance policy did not apply to sexual misconduct claims because these claims were specifically excluded by the policy. An adult male (the "plaintiff") sued a camp facility claiming he was subjected to sexual acts by a co-camper when he was ten years old and attending a one-week summer camp for mentally or physically disabled youth. He claimed that the camp was negligent in supervising and training camp counselors, supervising the young campers, and failing to disclose to his parents what had occurred. The camp turned the lawsuit over to its insurance company. The insurance company informed the camp that the policy excluded sexual misconduct claims and therefore the camp would be solely responsible for hiring legal counsel to defend the lawsuit and pay any settlement or verdict. The camp asked a court to rule on the issue of whether the insurance policy excluded sexual misconduct claims. It stressed that it was not guilty of, or being sued for, sexual misconduct. Rather, it was being sued for negligence, and this was a covered claim under the insurance policy. The court noted that the policy's exclusion of sexual misconduct claims was worded broadly: "This insurance does not apply to bodily injury, personal injury or medical payments arising out of . . . the actual or threatened abuse or molestation by anyone of any person while in the care, custody or control of any insured." The court concluded that "the abuse or molestation clause makes it crystal clear that no coverage is provided to employers for their negligence relating to any abuse or molestation."[366]

---

[365] American States Insurance Co. v. Bailey, 133 F.3d 363 (5th Cir. 1998).

[366] *Nautilis Insurance Company v. Our Camp, Inc.*, 136 Fed.Appx. 134 (10th Cir. 2005).

• An Alabama court ruled that a church's "directors and officers" insurance policy covered a lawsuit brought against a pastor for improperly obtaining money from an elderly member.[367] The daughter of an elderly church member was appointed guardian of her mother's property. The daughter sued the minister of her mother's church, claiming that he improperly obtained funds from her mother by means of conversion, fraud, and undue influence. The minister notified the church's "directors and officers" insurer of the lawsuit and asked the insurer to provide him with a legal defense. The insurer asked a court to determine whether or not the minister's actions were covered under the insurance policy. The court concluded that the insurer had a legal duty to provide the minister with a defense of the lawsuit. It noted that the church's insurance policy provided coverage for officers and directors (including the minister in this case) in any lawsuit brought against them by reason of alleged dishonesty on their part unless a court determined that the officer or director acted with deliberate dishonesty. Since the minister had not yet been found guilty of "deliberate dishonesty," he was covered under the insurance policy. The court acknowledged that if the minister was found to have acted with deliberate dishonesty in the daughter's lawsuit, the insurer would have no duty to pay any portion of the judgment or verdict.

• A Georgia court found that a general liability insurance policy covered a sexual assault claim at a church-run children's home, despite several exclusions in the policy.[368] A child resident at a church-operated children's home was sexually assaulted by other residents of the facility. The home was sued by the victim and his parents for its alleged negligence in adequately protecting, supervising, controlling, and caring for the residents of the facility. The children's home forwarded the lawsuit on to its insurance company. The insurance company concluded that the insurance policy in this case did not cover claims based on sexual assaults. It relied primarily on the following exclusion: "It is agreed that such coverage as is provided by the policy shall not apply to any claim, demand and causes of action arising out of or resulting from either sexual abuse or licentious, immoral or sexual behavior intended to lead to, or culminating in any sexual act, whether caused by, or at the instigation of, or at the direction of, or omission by, the insured, his employees, patrons or any causes whatsoever." The insurance company also relied on two other exclusions that denied any coverage for "bodily injury or property damage arising out of assault and battery" and "claims, accusations or charges of negligent hiring, placement, training or supervision arising from actual or alleged assault or battery." The court acknowledged that the insurance policy in this case could be construed to exclude any coverage for the victim's claims. However, it concluded that the policy also could be interpreted to require coverage of the victim's claims. With regard to the general sexual abuse exclusion, the court noted that it clearly applied to sexual assaults by "employees and patrons," but it did not necessarily apply to assaults by minor residents. The court concluded that "we do not believe that children residents of [the home] may reasonably be included in the group of individuals specified in the exclusion." The court also rejected the applicability of the other two exclusions relied upon by the insurance company. It noted that the specific sexual abuse exclusion prevented application of the two more general exclusions in deciding the question of insurance coverage for any claims involving sexual abuse, since "a limited or specific provision of a contract will prevail

---

[367] Graham v. Preferred Abstainers Insurance Company, 689 So.2d 188 (Ala. App. 1997).

[368] Georgia Baptist Children's Homes & Family Ministries, Inc. v. Essex Insurance Company, 427 S.E.2d 798 (Ga. App. 1993).

over one that is more broadly inclusive." The court concluded, "[I]nsurance policies are prepared and proposed by insurers. Thus, if an insurance contract is capable of being construed two ways, it will be construed against the insurance company and in favor of the insured. Construing the ambiguity in the sexual abuse exclusion in this case against [the insurance company], the policy did not exclude coverage for sexual abuse perpetrated by the children residents against another resident in the . . . facility."

• *A federal district court in Minnesota resolved a dispute between a church-operated school and its liability insurance company regarding payment of a claim.*[369] *The school had purchased a policy insuring against wrongful acts of its employees. While the insurance was in force, a female employee notified the school principal that she intended to resign. The principal informed her that her husband (who also was an employee of the school) would be fired if she quit. Soon after this conversation, the wife resigned and the husband was fired. The husband filed a "marital discrimination" claim against the school under a Minnesota human rights law, and the school eventually settled the claim with the husband for $15,000. The insurance company refused to reimburse the school for the amount of the settlement on the grounds that (1) the settlement did not constitute an insurable loss under the policy, (2) the school should not able to insure itself against unlawful actions by its employees, and (3) employers should not be permitted to "shift" their labor costs onto their insurers. The court rejected all of these claims. It concluded that the school's settlement of the discrimination claim was a "loss" under the insurance policy since it was a liability resulting from an employee's wrongful act. It further noted that the insurance company had "failed to show that unlawful acts relating to termination of employment are uninsurable."*

• *A Minnesota court ruled that a church insurance policy did not require the insurance company to defend a pastor who was sued by a woman he had seduced.*[370] *The court also ruled that the insurance company would not have to pay any portion of a jury verdict against the pastor. The court noted that the church's insurance policy specified that the insurer was liable for any personal injury "caused by an occurrence to which this insurance applies." The policy defined the term occurrence as an act that "results in bodily injury . . . neither expected nor intended." The court concluded that the pastor's repeated sexual exploitation of the victim resulted in personal injuries that were both "expected and intended," and accordingly they did not constitute an "occurrence" for which insurance coverage was available. The court observed, "We conclude [that the victim's] allegations that [the pastor] used his authority as a pastor and counselor to facilitate his sexual abuse of a psychologically vulnerable person creates an inference of an intent to injure and relieves [the insurance company] of its duty to defend." The court also relied on a provision in the church's insurance policy denying any coverage "to liability resulting from any actual or alleged conduct of a sexual nature, [or] to any dishonest, fraudulent or criminal act or omission of any insured."*

• *The Ohio Supreme Court ruled that a church's liability insurance policy covered allegations that the church was responsible, on the basis of negligence, for the sexual misconduct of a church employee. An adult male claimed that he contracted the*

---

[369] Convent of the Visitation School v. Continental Casualty Co., 707 F. Supp. 412 (D. Minn. 1989).

[370] Houg v. State Farm Fire and Casualty Company, 481 N.W.2d 393 (Minn. App. 1992).

human immunodeficiency virus ("HIV") after having been sexually molested by a church employee. He sued the church, claiming that it was legally responsible for his condition on the basis of negligent hiring and supervision. The church's insurance company claimed that there was no coverage under the church's insurance policy for such a claim since the coverage of intentional or criminal acts, including sexual molestation, are not covered. The supreme court disagreed, and ruled that the negligence claims against the church were covered by the church's insurance policy. The court noted that the "societal condemnation that animates the public policy forbidding insurance for the intentional tort of sexual molestation does not exist for the tort of negligence." And, since the claims against the church were all based on negligence rather than intentional or criminal conduct, there was no basis for denying insurance coverage.[371]

• A federal court in Rhode Island ruled that a diocese's insurance company had a legal duty to defend diocesan officials who were sued as a result of the sexual molestation of several children by Catholic priests.[372] Nine lawsuits were brought against the Roman Catholic Diocese of Providence, Rhode Island, and various of its officials, by persons who claimed that they were sexually assaulted by priests of the diocese. The lawsuits were brought against the individual priests accused of perpetrating the assaults, the diocese, and various diocesan officials. The victims claimed that the diocese and its officials were liable for their injuries on the ground that they were negligent in hiring and supervising the priests and that they failed to take appropriate preventive action after learning of the priests' propensities. The diocese's insurance company asked a federal court to rule that it had no duty to defend the diocese or its officials, or to pay any damages awarded to the victims as a result of their lawsuits. The insurance company claimed that it had no duty to defend the diocese or pay any judgments since (1) the diocese had violated the insurance policy by not providing it with timely notice of the claims; (2) the priests' actions were intentional, and the policy excluded any coverage for intentional acts; and (3) the victims sought punitive damages which were excluded under the policy. The court rejected the insurance company's position, and ordered it to defend the diocese and its officials in the lawsuits brought by the alleged molestation victims. The court pointed out that under Rhode Island law "an insurer's duty to defend is broader than its duty to indemnify," and that "a duty to defend arises if the factual allegations contained in the complaint raise a reasonable possibility of coverage. An insurer is not relieved of its duty to defend . . . on the ground that the claim against the insured lacks merit. In short, determining whether an insurer has a duty to defend requires nothing more than comparing the allegations in the complaint with the terms of the policy. If the facts alleged in the complaint fall within the risks covered by the policy, the insurer is obligated to defend. Otherwise, it is not."

---

[371] Doe v. Shaffer, 738 N.E.2d 1243 (Ohio 2000).

[372] Aetna Casualty & Surety Company v. Kelly, 889 F. Supp. 535 (D.R.I. 1995).

DID YOU KNOW?
A Potentially Significant Uninsured Risk

These cases suggest that sexual misconduct exclusions in church insurance policies may apply even though a church is being sued for negligence. Other courts have disagreed with this conclusion. Church leaders should examine their insurance policies to see if a sexual misconduct exclusion exists. If so, do not assume that it will not apply to negligence claims brought against the church resulting from the sexual misconduct of an employee or volunteer. Church leaders should discuss this coverage issue with their insurance agent. If the policy does not provide coverage in the event the church is sued on the basis of negligence for the sexual misconduct of an employee or volunteer, then this represents a potentially significant uninsured risk that needs to be addressed either through a separate endorsement with the current insurer, if available, or by switching to another insurer that will insure against this risk.

3. Duty to Cooperate

Most insurance policies impose a "duty to cooperate" on the insured. This means that a church must cooperate with its insurance company in any investigation, or in responding to reasonable requests for information. Church leaders should be aware of this requirement and understand that a failure to cooperate may result in the denial of insurance benefits. There are limits to the authority of an insurance company to investigate. However, churches should never decline an insurance company's request for information without the advice and consent of a local attorney.

Case Studies

• *A church building and its contents were totally destroyed in a fire of suspicious origin. The loss was covered by an insurance policy, and the church promptly filed a claim against its insurance company. The insurance company launched an investigation into the facts and circumstances surrounding the fire. It notified the church that it wanted numerous documents, including (1) a list of monthly expenses for the church, (2) a listing of all income of the church, including the names of donors and the amounts they individually contributed, (3) copies of tax returns filed by the church, (4) copies of tax returns filed by the directors and officers of the church, and (5) a list of the salaries of the directors and officers (from their secular employment). The basis for this request for information was a provision in the insurance policy specifying that the insurance company "may examine and audit the named insured's books and records at any time during the policy period and extensions thereof and within three years after the final termination of this policy, as far as they relate to the subject matter of this insurance." Despite being warned by the insurance company's attorney that a refusal to provide the requested information might lead to a refusal to a denial of any coverage under the policy, the church refused to provide the requested information. A*

New York court ruled that the church had to provide the documents that were "material and relevant to the issue of [its] financial status at the time of the fire," if the fire loss was to be covered under the insurance policy. However, the court emphasized that "the circumstances presented do not provide a basis for [the insurance company] to be granted access to personal financial information pertaining to [the church's] board of directors and officers, or to the names of church donors . . . ."[373]

• *A church sustained a $100,000 fire loss, and promptly notified its insurance company. However, the insurance company refused to pay for any portion of the loss because of the church's alleged failure to cooperate in the investigation of the claim. In particular, the insurance company complained that the church refused to allow certain individuals to be examined under oath. The church sued its insurance company, and a state appeals court has ordered the case to proceed to trial. A jury will now decide if the insurance company acted properly in denying coverage.[374]*

4. Duty to Notify

Most insurance policies impose on the insured a duty to promptly notify the insurance company of any potential claim. Failure to comply with this condition can result in a loss of coverage. Here are some points to consider:

• **Notifying your broker may not be enough.** Many churches purchase their insurance through a local broker. Sometimes this person is a member of the congregation. Church leaders naturally assume that in the event of an accident or injury they can simply call this individual and everything will be "taken care of." This case illustrates that such a conclusion may not always be correct. A broker may not be deemed to be an "agent" of the insurance companies he or she represents, and accordingly when a church provides its insurance broker with notice of an accident or loss it is not necessarily notifying its insurance company.

▶ *If you notify your insurance broker of a loss, insist on a written assurance that he or she will notify the insurance company in writing within the period of time specified in the insurance policy. If you do not hear back within a week or so, contact the broker again to follow up. Better yet, the church itself should notify both its broker and insurance company. The insurance company's address will be listed on your insurance policy. Ask the insurance company to provide you with written confirmation of receipt of your notice.*

• **Written rather than oral notice.** If your insurance policy requires written notice, then be sure you provide written rather than oral notice of a loss.

▶ *Church leaders should be familiar with the insurance policy's provisions regarding notification of the insurance company. Is written notice required? If so, how soon after a loss? It is essential that these provisions be scrupulously followed in order to prevent a loss of coverage.*

---

[373] Church of St. Matthew v. Aetna Casualty and Surety Co., 554 N.Y.S.2d 563 (A.D. 1 Dept. 1990).

[374] Bethel Baptist Church v. Church Mutual Insurance Company, 924 S.W.2d 494 (Ark. App. 1996).

▶ *If you change insurance companies, be sure to review the new insurance policy. Do not assume that it will contain the same "notice" provisions as your previous policy.*

• **A reasonable time.** How soon does your church insurance policy require that notice be submitted to the insurance company following an accident or loss? Be sure you know, and that this requirement is followed whenever there is an accident, personal injury, or other kind of loss.

▶ *The duty to inform your insurance company of an accident or loss arises when the injury occurs, and not when a lawsuit is filed. The purpose of the notice requirement is to give your insurance company sufficient time to investigate the incident and provide a defense.*

Case Studies

• *The church board at First Church is informed by a parent that her minor child was molested by a church volunteer. The volunteer is questioned, and admits having molested the child. This incident represents a potential "loss" under the church's insurance policy, triggering a duty to inform the church's insurance company of the loss within the period of time specified in the insurance policy. The church should inform its insurance company immediately. It is very important that it not wait until a lawsuit is filed to notify its insurance company. Such a delay not only hinders the insurance company's ability to investigate the incident and defend the case, but it also may result in loss of coverage under the policy. This could have disastrous consequences to the church.*

• *A federal court in Rhode Island ruled that a diocese's insurance company had a legal duty to defend diocesan officials who were sued as a result of the sexual molestation of several children by Catholic priests, despite the insurance company's claim that the diocese had failed to promptly notify it of the potential claims.[375] The court pointed out that for the insurance company to prevail on this claim it would have to prove that the incidents of molestation actually occurred and that the diocese was aware of them. The court noted that these are the very facts that the victims would have to prove to hold the diocese liable for their injuries, and it would be unthinkable for the diocese's own insurance company to attempt to prove the victims' case for them. Such efforts "would be inconsistent with [the insurance company's] obligations as an insurer. The principal purpose of liability insurance is to protect policy holders from claims asserted by third parties based on matters covered by the policy. By taking action that makes a policy holder liable for such claims, an insurer would subvert the purpose of the policy and violate one of the most fundamental duties it owes to its insured."*

• *A church member was injured when he fell on church property during a funeral.[376] At the time of the injury, the church had a general liability insurance policy that required the church to give the insurance company written notice of any accident "as soon as practicable." Immediately following the accident the pastor instructed the chairman of the board of trustees to notify the church's insurance broker about the accident. The*

---

[375] Aetna Casualty & Surety Company v. Kelly, 889 F. Supp. 535 (D.R.I. 1995).

[376] Shaw Temple v. Mount Vernon Fire Insurance Company, 605 N.Y.S.2d 370 (A.D. 2 Dept. 1994)

chairman did so by calling the insurance broker's office. An employee of the broker assured the chairman that the insurance company would be duly notified. In fact, the insurance company was not notified. Nine months later the church received a letter from an attorney for the injured member threatening to sue the church unless it paid the member a large amount of money. The church immediately turned this letter over to its insurance broker, who in turn forwarded it to the church's insurance company. The insurance company refused to provide the church with a defense of the lawsuit or pay any amount of money based on the accident since the church had failed to provide it with written notice of the accident "as soon as practicable" as required by the insurance policy. The church responded by suing its insurance company. It sought a court order requiring the insurance company to defend the church under the terms of the policy and to pay for any damages awarded by a jury. A state appeals court ruled that the insurance company had no legal duty to defend the church or pay for any jury verdict since the church had failed to notify it of the accident "as soon as practicable." The court concluded that when the church gave notice of the accident to its insurance broker it was not giving notice to its insurance company as required by the policy. In addition, the insurance policy required that the church provide the insurance company with written notice of any accident. Even if the broker were an agent of the insurance company, the church still failed to comply with the terms of the insurance policy since it provided the broker with oral rather than written notice of the accident.

5. Coverage Limits

Insurance policies only provide coverage up to the "limits" specified in the policy. Church leaders should be familiar with the limits in their church insurance policy, and be certain that these limits are adequate. The adequacy of policy limits is a complex question that involves an analysis of several conditions. Most importantly, a church should consider its own net worth, and the frequency and relative risk of its programs and activities. Discuss the adequacy of your limits with your insurance agent, or with an insurance broker.

Some church insurance policies have reduced limits for certain risks, including sexual misconduct. This may expose the board to greater risk, as plaintiffs seek to recover damages in excess of the policy limits by suing board members directly.

Case Study

• A federal appeals court ruled that several children who were molested over a number of years by two priests represented multiple "occurrences" under a church insurance policy.[377] Two priests molested 31 children over a 7-year period. The priests were sued along with their diocese, and a question arose as to the number of "occurrences" the numerous incidents of molestation represented under the diocese's insurance policies. These policies provided insurance to the diocese on a "per occurrence" basis. The more occurrences that occurred, the more insurance coverage that was available. The court acknowledged that defining this term in the context of multiple acts of molestation occurring over several years is difficult: "An occurrence could be the church's continuous negligent supervision of a priest, the negligent supervision of a

---

[377] Society of Roman Catholic Church v. Interstate Fire & Casualty Co., 26 F.3d 1359 (5th Cir. 1994).

priest with respect to each child, the negligent supervision of a priest with respect to each molestation, or each time the diocese became aware of a fact which should have led it to intervene, just to name a few possibilities." The court added that "when a term in an insurance policy has uncertain application [the courts] interpret the policy in favor of the insured." The court concluded that "[w]hen a priest molested a child during a policy year, there was both bodily injury and an occurrence, triggering policy coverage. All further molestations of that child during the policy period arose out of the same occurrence. When the priest molested the same child during the succeeding policy year, again there was both bodily injury and an occurrence. Thus, each child suffered an occurrence in each policy period in which he was molested." To illustrate, a child that was molested several times in each of seven different years represented seven different "occurrences" under the insurance policies. On the other hand, several incidents of molestation occurring within the same year represented only one occurrence.

6. Liability for Maintaining Inadequate Insurance Coverage

A few churches have been sued for failing to maintain adequate insurance coverage. Such claims have been rejected by the courts.

Case Study

• The Kansas Supreme Court ruled that a student who was rendered a permanent quadriplegic as a result of injuries sustained while playing football for a church-operated high school could not sue church officials for failing to obtain adequate insurance coverage.[378] The victim alleged that the school and church officials had been negligent in "failing to properly insure students for injury incurred as a result of school activities and in failing to properly advise and inform students and their parents . . . of the insurance protection provided to students." In rejecting this claim, the court cited a state law making the purchase of liability insurance coverage by public schools discretionary rather than mandatory. Such a law, reasoned the court, applied "by implication" to private schools as well. Since private schools were not required to purchase insurance, they could not be liable for failure to have enough coverage to cover catastrophic losses. "We feel sympathy for the severe injuries suffered by this plaintiff," concluded the court. "However, there are dangers and risks inherent in the game of football and those who play the game encounter these risks voluntarily. It is fundamental that before there can be any recovery in tort there must be a violation of a duty owed by one party to the person seeking recovery. . . . It is clear under the facts of this case that no . . . duty existed to properly insure or to advise the plaintiff regarding medical insurance purchased by the defendants for the plaintiff."

7. Punitive Damages

Church insurance policies exclude punitive damages. This means that a jury award of punitive damages represents an uninsured risk. As a result, it is important for church leaders to understand the basis for punitive damages. Punitive damages are damages awarded by a jury "in addition to compensation for a loss sustained, in order to punish, and make an example of, the wrongdoer." They are awarded when a defendant's conduct is particularly reprehensible and outrageous. This does not necessarily mean intentional misconduct. Punitive damages often

---

[378] Wicina v. Strecker, 747 P.2d 167 (Kan. 1987).

are associated with reckless conduct or conduct creating a high risk of harm. Unfortunately, it is not uncommon for church leaders to ignore significant risks. Church leaders must understand that reckless inattention to such risks can lead to punitive damages, and that such damages may not be covered by the church's liability insurance policy.

8. Claims Made or Occurrence Coverage

Many forms of liability insurance come in two varieties: (1) occurrence policies, and (2) claims made policies. It is critical for church leaders to understand the difference. Occurrence policies only cover injuries that occur during the policy period, regardless of when a claim is made. A "claims made" policy covers injuries for which a claim is made during the policy period if the insured has continuously been insured with claims made policies with the same insurer since the injury occurred. Some insurers who offer claims made policies may agree to cover claims made during the current policy period for injuries occurring in the past when the insured carried insurance with another insurer. This is often referred to as "prior acts coverage."

Table 10-8 summarizes the advantages and disadvantages of both forms of coverage.

Table 10-8 Claims Made and Occurrence Coverage

coverage	advantages	disadvantages
claims made	• covers any lawsuit filed during the policy period, regardless of when the injury occurred • coverage limits are the current limits, not the limits in effect when the injury occurred • insurance premiums often are lower than for an occurrence policy	• must have carried "claims made" insurance continuously with the same insurer from the date of the injury to the date of the claim, or have purchased "prior acts coverage" • "prior acts" coverage can be costly • a brief lapse in insurance coverage for any reason can result in no "claims made" coverage • coverage for prior claims is lost if a church switches from a claims made to an occurrence policy • when a policy expires or is terminated, for any reason, coverage ceases (even for claims that are later made for injuries occurring during the policy period) • claims for injuries occurring in more than one year may be filed during the same year, meaning that the policy's "aggregate" coverage limit is more quickly reached (the aggregate limit is the total amount the insurer will pay out during that year for all covered claims) • claims must not only be made during the policy period to be covered—they also must be reported to the insurer (a technicality that is sometimes overlooked)

Table 10-8 Claims Made and Occurrence Coverage

coverage	advantages	disadvantages
occur-rence	• covers any injury that occurs during the policy period regardless of when a lawsuit is filed • no "prior acts" coverage needed if a church maintains a succession of "occurrence" policies	• does not cover lawsuits filed during the policy period for injuries occurring prior to the policy period • insurance premiums usually higher than for a "claims made" policy

Example. *A church purchases "claims made" counseling insurance from Company A each year for several years. It switches to an "occurrence policy" with Company B this year. A lawsuit is brought against the church this year for an alleged act of counseling malpractice that occurred in three years ago. The church's policy with Company A will not cover this claim, since the claim was not "made" during the policy period (even though it occurred during the policy period). Had the church not switched insurers this year, the claim would have been covered. Does the policy with Company B cover the claim? No, since the injury did not occur during the policy period. As a result, there is no coverage for this claim. Note that the result would have been the same had the church purchased a claims made policy from Company B, unless it also purchased "prior acts" coverage. This example illustrates an important point. Churches should not switch from a claims made to an occurrence policy (with the same or a different insurer), or switch claims made insurers, without legal counsel.*

9. Subrogation

Church leaders should be familiar with the principle of subrogation since it may expose church members to unexpected liability. Church members whose negligence causes a loss (injury or property damage) that the church's insurer pays under the church insurance policy may be sued by the insurer to recover the full amount of the loss that it paid. Insurance companies cannot subrogate against persons who are "insureds" under a church insurance policy. Church members and volunteers are specifically listed as insureds under some church insurance policies with respect to actions they perform on behalf of the

Subrogation = the substitution (one person) for another with reference to a claim or right church, but this is not always true. Review your church insurance policy to see if members and volunteers are insureds. If they are not, talk with your insurance agent about including them.

Insurance companies generally can subrogate against volunteers or church members who perform criminal acts, even if the perpetrator is otherwise an "insured" under the church insurance policy. Church staff members or volunteers who engage in criminal acts for which the church insurance company pays a loss should understand that they may be sued personally by the insurance company for the full amount of the loss. For example, church members and volunteers who engage in sexual misconduct, embezzlement, or reckless driving of a vehicle may be sued personally by the church insurer to recover any amounts paid out under the church insurance policy as a result of such acts.

10. Other Matters

Here are some additional points to note about church insurance:

- **Retaining your policies.** It is important for church leaders to keep church insurance policies permanently, since some claims (such as sexual misconduct) may arise years or even decades later, and a church may need to produce a copy of the insurance contract for the year in which the misconduct occurred in order to obtain coverage.

- **Reservation of rights letters.** It is common for churches to receive a "reservation of rights" letter when they report a claim to their insurance company. Under such a reservation, an insurance company agrees to defend an insured, but reserves the right to deny any obligation to pay an adverse judgment as a result of an exclusion in the policy.

- **Periodic insurance review.** Churches should appoint an insurance committee consisting of persons with some knowledge of insurance who periodically review the church's insurance coverages to ensure they are adequate.

Other Defenses § 10-16.8

Key point 10-16.8. *Churches have various defenses available to them if they are sued as a result of a personal injury. One such defense is an arbitration policy. By adopting an arbitration policy, a church can compel members to arbitrate specified disputes with their church rather than pursue their claim in the civil courts.*

The courts have recognized various other defenses that are available to churches in the event of litigation. Here are some of them:

1. Status of the Person Causing the Injury or Damage

Since a church is liable only for the injuries and damages caused by employees and volunteers, a church generally will not be liable for injuries inflicted by independent contractors.

2. Course of Employment

Since a church is liable only for the injuries and damages caused by employees acting in the course of their employment, a church generally will not be liable for injuries inflicted by employees outside of the course of their employment.

3. Arbitration

The arbitration of disputes has many advantages over litigation in the civil courts. Consider the following:

(1) a much faster resolution of disputes;

(2) lower attorneys' fees;

(3) arbitration awards are often less than civil court judgments;

(4) little if any risk of punitive damages, or astronomical verdicts out of proportion to the alleged wrong;

(5) disputes are resolved privately, with little or no media attention;

(6) the spectacle of plaintiffs' attorneys appealing to the emotions of juries through courtroom theatrics is eliminated;

(7) arbitration can reconcile the parties to a dispute unlike civil litigation in which the parties almost always enter and leave court as enemies;

(8) no threatening letters from attorneys demanding exorbitant payoffs in order to avoid litigation;

(9) parties to a dispute can select one or more arbitrators having specialized knowledge concerning the issues involved (unlike civil court judges who often have limited familiarity with applicable law);

(10) arbitration awards are final (no time-consuming appeals).

There are additional reasons for churches to consider the mediation or arbitration of disputes. First, as is obvious from even a casual reading of this text, most lawsuits against churches are brought by "insiders" (i.e., members and adherents). Arbitration is ideal for such disputes. Second, there is scriptural support for arbitration of internal church disputes. In 1 Corinthians 6:1-8 (NIV), the apostle Paul observed:

> If any of you has a dispute with another, dare he take it before the ungodly for judgment instead of before the saints? Do you not know that the saints will judge the world? And if you are to judge the world, are you not competent to judge trivial cases? Do you not know that we will judge angels? How much more the things of this life! Therefore, if you have disputes about such matters, appoint as judges even men of little account in the church! I say this to shame you. Is it possible that there is nobody

among you wise enough to judge a dispute between believers? But instead, one brother goes to law against another—and this in front of unbelievers! The very fact that you have lawsuits among you means you have been completely defeated already. Why not rather be wronged? Why not rather be cheated? Instead, you yourselves cheat and do wrong, and you do this to your brothers.

With these numerous advantages, arbitration is becoming an increasingly common way of resolving disputes. A decision by the United States Supreme Court in 2001 has made the arbitration of disputes even more common, especially for employment disputes.

Two Supreme Court Rulings

The United States issued important decisions in 2001 and 2002 regarding the validity of arbitration policies.

(1) **Circuit City Stores, Inc. v. Adams, 532 U.S. 105 (2001).** The Court ruled that a clause in an employment application requiring disputes to be settled through binding arbitration was legally enforceable. As a result, the Court threw out a lawsuit brought by an employee for alleged violations of a state nondiscrimination law and ordered the dispute to be resolved through arbitration.

(2) **E.E.O.C. v. Waffle House, Inc., 534 U.S. 279 (2002).** The Court held that the EEOC could not be barred from seeking victim-specific relief under Title VII, even where the individual employee signs a mandatory arbitration agreement. The Court noted that "nothing in the statute authorizes a court to compel arbitration of any issues, or by any parties, that are not already covered in the agreement. The Federal Arbitration Act does not mention enforcement by public agencies; it ensures the enforceability of private agreements to arbitrate, but otherwise does not purport to place any restriction on a nonparty's choice of a judicial forum." The Court further observed that "it goes without saying that a contract cannot bind a nonparty." Thus, the Supreme Court concluded that the EEOC (a non-signatory) could not be bound by an employee's arbitration agreement.

Key point. *Employment-related claims are significant not only because of their number, but also because they represent an uninsured risk for most churches. Most church general liability insurance policies contain no coverage for such claims. This means that a church that is sued for such a claim will be compelled to hire and pay its own attorney, and pay any settlement or court judgment. The costs associated with even a single claim can be substantial, and this can force a church to divert funds budgeted for ministry to the payment of attorneys and possibly a settlement or judgment.*

Further, if a discrimination complaint is filed by a current or former employee with the Equal Employment Opportunity Commission (EEOC) or its state or local counterparts, this can lead time-consuming and often unpleasant interaction with government investigators that many church leaders have found to be condescending if not hostile toward religion.

Clearly, it is in the best interests of every church to consider alternatives to civil litigation. The Supreme Court case addressed in this section demonstrates that arbitration is a legally valid alternative.

Here are some points for church leaders to consider:

1. the arbitration of employment claims under state law

In the past, some courts and state legislatures attempted to impose limits on the enforceability of arbitration provisions in employment contracts under state law. The Supreme Court's decision in the Circuit City case (see sidebar) addressed the enforceability of arbitration provisions in the context of state employment or civil rights claims. The Court concluded that (1) arbitration provisions are enforceable, and are not barred by the Federal Arbitration Act (for employees not directly engaged in transportation); and (2) the FAA preempts states laws that seek to impose limits on the enforceability of arbitration provisions in employment contracts. It is now clear that employers can compel employees to arbitrate wrongful dismissal and discrimination claims under state law by inserting valid arbitration provisions in employment contracts and applications.

The Supreme Court concluded in the Circuit City case that arbitration clauses prevent employees from pursuing discrimination or wrongful dismissal claims under state law. And, it is these state law claims that expose employers to the greatest amount of money damages since there are limits on employer liability under Title VII of the federal Civil Rights Act of 1964. The Civil Rights Act of 1991 limits the amount of compensatory and punitive damages that are available to most discrimination victims. Because of these limits, plaintiffs' attorneys who represent current and former employees routinely file claims under state law. It is these state law claims that expose employers to substantial jury verdicts, and it is these that the Supreme Court has said may be pre-empted by arbitration provisions.

2. the arbitration of employment claims under federal law

Can a clause in an employment application or contract calling for binding arbitration of employment disputes pre-empt the jurisdiction of the EEOC under federal employment and civil rights laws? Consider the following example:

Example

• *A church employs Barb as an office secretary. After working for the church for two years, Barb is dismissed because of extramarital sexual relations in violation of the church's religious and moral teachings. Barb files a complaint with the EEOC claiming that her dismissal constituted unlawful sex discrimination in violation of Title VII of the federal Civil Rights Act of 1964 since the church had not dismissed a male youth pastor who was guilty of the same kind of misconduct a year earlier. The church insists that the EEOC must drop its investigation since Barb signed an employment application prior to being hired in which she agreed to resolve all legal disputes with the church, including discrimination claims under Title VII, through binding arbitration.*

Is the EEOC deprived of jurisdiction over this claim by virtue of the arbitration clause in the church's employment application? This issue was addressed by the Supreme Court in the Waffle House case (see sidebar). The Court ruled that arbitration agreements do not divest the EEOC of suing employers for violating federal employment discrimination laws, since the EEOC is not a party to such agreements. However, note that there is still a significant advantage to using arbitration clauses in employment applications and contracts, even with respect to claims under federal law. As the Court noted: "When speculating about the impact this decision might have on the behavior of employees and employers, we think it is worth recognizing that the EEOC files suit in less than one percent of the charges filed each year."

3. should our church compel employees to arbitrate employment claims?

This is a question that every church should consider. In answering this question, there are a number of points that should be considered:

(1) The advantages to arbitration, summarized above, should be reviewed.

(2) Employment claims represent one of the most common grounds for lawsuits against churches.

(3) Is your church subject to state or federal civil rights laws protecting employees against various forms of discrimination? What about other kinds of employment claims, such as wrongful dismissal?

(4) Employment lawsuits generally are not covered under church general liability insurance policies. This means that if your church is sued for such a claim, you may be required to hire and pay your own attorney, and pay any settlement or court judgment. The costs associated with a single claim can be substantial.

(5) Check with your insurance agent to see if your church has insurance to cover employment claims. Remember that such

coverage may be available under a directors and officers insurance policy, if you have one, even if it is not provided under your general liability policy.

Key point. *If you don't have coverage for employment claims, then arbitration may help your church limit the costs associated with such claims. But remember, the costs associated with a single claim may be substantial. As a result, church leaders should discuss with their insurance agent or broker the availability of employment practices insurance coverage. And, they should take steps to minimize or manage the risk of employment-related legal claims.*

(6) If you have insurance to cover employment claims, then check with your insurance company to be sure that an arbitration award would be honored under your insurance policy up to your coverage limits.

(7) Be sure to consult with an attorney concerning the advantages and disadvantages of an arbitration policy. You may want to have an attorney meet with your board or congregation concerning this issue. If possible, use an attorney who specializes in employment law.

(8) Many cite 1 Corinthians 6:1-8 as scriptural support for the arbitration of internal church disputes. This passage is quoted below:

> If any of you has a dispute with another, dare he take it before the ungodly for judgment instead of before the saints? Do you not know that the saints will judge the world? And if you are to judge the world, are you not competent to judge trivial cases? Do you not know that we will judge angels? How much more the things of this life! Therefore, if you have disputes about such matters, appoint as judges even men of little account in the church! I say this to shame you. Is it possible that there is nobody among you wise enough to judge a dispute between believers? But instead, one brother goes to law against another-and this in front of unbelievers! The very fact that you have lawsuits among you means you have been completely defeated already. Why not rather be wronged? Why not rather be cheated? Instead, you yourselves cheat and do wrong, and you do this to your brothers.

4. how do we implement a policy for the arbitration of employment disputes?

In drafting an arbitration policy, keep the following considerations in mind:

- How will the policy be implemented? There are a number of options, including an amendment to the church's bylaws, or a board-adopted policy that is referenced on each new member's membership card. The most effective means of adopting an arbitration policy is for the church membership to adopt one as an amendment to the church bylaws. Since members are bound by the church bylaws (including any amendments),[379] this approach will have the best chance of binding all members.

• What disputes will be referred to arbitration? Only those disputes relating to church affairs? Disputes between members? What about disputes between a minister and other members, or between a minister and either the church board or the church itself? What about disputes between employees and the church? These are very important questions to resolve.

• How will the arbitration process be conducted? Often, each side in a dispute selects an arbitrator, and the two persons so selected choose a third arbitrator. Of course, the third arbitrator must be completely unbiased. Arbitration procedure often is quite informal, and attorneys may or may not be allowed to participate.

• It is essential to consult with the church's liability insurer before implementing any arbitration policy to ensure that it is in complete agreement with the concept and it will honor arbitrators' judgments up to the policy limits. Churches should not change insurers without obtaining the same assurances. The arbitration policy may even contain language conditioning its use on acceptance by the church's liability insurer.

• Given the importance of having a policy that complies with local law, we recommend that any church wanting to adopt an arbitration policy retain the services of a local attorney who specializes in employment law. The last thing you want is a false sense of security based on a home-made and unenforceable arbitration policy. Here are some recommendations you may want to share with your attorney:

(1) Check with other churches in your state and find some that have adopted arbitration policies. Ask if you can see their policies.

(2) Ask your insurance company if it has sample arbitration policies for churches.

(3) Be sure that the arbitration policy covers claims under federal, state, and local civil rights and employment laws. Ideally, you will want to refer to applicable laws by name. If you don't, then employees may be able to avoid arbitration by saying that they did not understand what they were agreeing to arbitrate because the arbitration clause was not specific enough.

---

[379] Watson v. Jones, 80 U.S. 679, 729 (1871) ("all who unite themselves to such a body do so with an implied consent to its government, and are bound to submit to it").

(4) Be sure the arbitration policy contains a "severability" clause. Such a clause states that if any provision of the policy is determined to be invalid by a court of law, the remaining provisions will remain valid. To illustrate, if the Supreme Court reverses the Waffle House case, then employees cannot be compelled to arbitrate claims under federal civil rights laws. A church arbitration clause that covers both federal and state claims will likely remain valid as to state claims, and this conclusion will be reinforced by the presence of a savings clause.

Your attorney will assist you in deciding whether to place the arbitration policy in your employment application, in an employee handbook, or both.

5. what about employment disputes regarding ministers?

There is no reason to exclude ministers from a church's arbitration policy. However, note the following unique rules:

(1) Most courts have ruled that ministers are not protected by federal and state civil rights laws since the First Amendment religious clauses prevent the civil courts from deciding "who will preach from the pulpit." Therefore, you may want to exclude ministers, or those serving in positions that would be deemed "ministerial," from your arbitration policy. In other words, why submit claims to arbitration that the civil courts would not accept? On the other hand, some churches may prefer to arbitrate all employee claims, including those brought by ministers.

(2) Many churches have governing documents (such as bylaws) that prescribe how ministers are selected and removed. If a congregation acts to remove a minister in accordance with its governing document and the minister threatens to challenge the church's decision, you need to decide if this is the kind of claim you want to submit to arbitration. That is, if the church acts consistently with its bylaws in removing the pastor, should the pastor be able to use the church's arbitration policy to challenge the church's decision? Once again, the courts generally have not been willing to resolve such claims.

(3) In some churches, ministers are selected and removed only through action of a parent denominational agency. Employment claims involving ministers may be resolved within the denomination using existing procedures. Arbitrating such claims may conflict with denominational rules. This issue must be clarified with denominational officers before adopting an arbitration policy.

6. what about the arbitration of other claims?

This section is addressing only the arbitration of disputes involving employees. Church leaders may want to consider adopting a separate policy to resolve disputes involving members and the church, or disputes between members.

7. civil court review of arbitration awards

Note that the Federal Arbitration Act cautions that "an agreement in writing to submit to arbitration an existing controversy . . . shall be valid, irrevocable, and enforceable, save upon such grounds as exist at law or in equity for the revocation of any contract." In other words, an agreement to arbitrate is a contract, and like any contract, is subject to challenge on the basis of a number of legal theories. This is why it is so important for churches to have arbitration policies drafted by an attorney who specializes in employment law.

8. what about current employees who have not signed an arbitration agreement?

Let's say that your church has seven employees, and that you decide to adopt an arbitration policy this year. Will your policy be binding on existing employees, or only on new employees hired after implementation of the policy? The courts have reached conflicting answers to this question. Ask your attorney how to best ensure that your policy covers both current and future employees. The basic idea here is that new employment conditions, such as the arbitration of disputes, are not legally enforceable unless employees receive something of value (other then compensation or benefits to which they are already entitled). For example, some courts have ruled that an agreement to arbitrate future employment claims is enforceable if incorporated into current employees' annual performance reviews. Other courts have allowed an arbitration policy to apply to current employees so long as they agree in writing to be bound by the policy at the time they receive a pay raise.

Case Studies

• *An Illinois court upheld the validity of a church arbitration policy despite the alleged "bias" of the arbitrators. The plaintiff pointed out that the procedure called for arbitrators who are either members or employees of the church or parent denomination. He claimed that these people cannot be impartial, and this made the agreement to arbitrate invalid. The court disagreed, noting that "the purpose of the dispute resolution procedure is to resolve disputes within the church," and that the plaintiff had "not pointed to any specific prejudice he would suffer under the bylaws, but only a generalized fear of partiality. This anxiety is insufficient to overturn the arbitration process." Further, the court noted that the plaintiff consented to this procedure when he became a pastor.*[380]

• *A federal appeals court enforced the decision of an arbitrator in an employment dispute between a church-operated school in Louisiana and its principal. The principal of a private Christian school (the "plaintiff") was fired from her position, and she later sued the school for breach of contract and discrimination. The school asked the court to compel the plaintiff to arbitrate her claims pursuant to an arbitration provision in her employment contract. The plaintiff was reluctant at first to pursue arbitration because she was concerned that the process was biased in favor of the school. She ultimately agreed to the arbitration policy with modifications. One modification made the arbitration procedure subject to the Montana Arbitration Act. The court granted this request, and an arbitration was conducted in accordance with the Rules of Procedure for Christian Conciliation ("Rules") of the Institute for Christian Conciliation ("ICC"). In arbitration, the plaintiff prevailed on her breach of contract claim and was awarded $150,000 in damages. In reaching his decision, the arbitrator determined that the school had wrongfully discharged the plaintiff by failing to follow Biblical precepts, as required in her employment contract; specifically, the conflict resolution process described in Matthew 18.*

 The school asked a federal district court to vacate the arbitration on the basis of the Montana Arbitration Act, which empowers the civil courts to vacate arbitration awards under narrow conditions including arbitrator bias and an arbitrator acting outside the scope of his or her authority. A federal district court ruled that none of these exceptions applied, and the school appealed. A federal appeals court agreed that none of the narrow grounds for vacating the arbitrator's award existed in this case. It concluded:

 The parties freely and knowingly contracted to have their relationship governed by specified provisions of the Bible and the Rules of the ICC, and the arbitrator's determination that the school had not acted according to the dictates of Matthew 18 relates to that contract. Further, the Rules of the ICC indisputably contemplate that an arbitrator will have extremely broad discretion to fashion an appropriate remedy; and no language in the parties' contracts expresses their intent to depart from the Rules of the ICC. We hold that the arbitrator's award of damages is rationally derived from Julie's employment contract with the school and is not contrary to any express contractual provisions, either biblical or secular. Consequently, the school is not entitled to a vacating of the arbitrator's decision on this ground.

 The court also rejected the school's claim that the arbitrator's award should be vacated on the basis of the arbitrator's lack of impartiality since the school failed to address or explain this argument in the brief it submitted to the court.[381]

• *Maryland's highest court ruled that an arbitration award addressing the composition of a church's board of trustees was not reviewable by the civil courts since any review would require an interpretation of religious doctrine.*[382] *A dispute arose within a church regarding control of church property. A faction of the church board (the "dissident faction"), headed by the board's president, claimed that the church had become*

---

[380] Jenkins v. Trinity Evangelical Lutheran Church, 825 N.E.2d 1206 (Ill. App. 2005).

[381] Prescott v. Northlake Christian School, 141 Fed.Appx. 263 (5th Cir. 2005).

[382] American Union of Baptists v. Trustees of the Particular Primitive Baptist Church, 644 A.2d 1063 (Md. 1994). *See also* Seat Pleasant v. Long, 691 A.2d 721 (Md. App. 1997).

extinct because its minister had died and there were no living members. This group did not recognize the current congregation to be "members." Another faction of the board opposed the dissidents and called a special business meeting to elect a new board. The dissident faction claimed that this election was invalid because the meeting had not been properly called by the president as required by the church's bylaws. The dissident group later authorized the merger of the church with another congregation, and the resulting church elected new trustees including the dissident members and president. As a result, there were two boards of trustees claiming control of the church and its property. In order to resolve this impasse, the parties submitted the dispute to arbitration pursuant to a provision in the Maryland nonprofit corporation law. This provision specifies that "if any contest arises over the voting rights or the fair conduct of an election," then the matter shall be submitted to arbitration and the arbitrators' judgment will be "final." The arbitrators ruled in favor of the board elected at the special business meeting, and the dissident board members immediately appealed to a civil court. The court refused to adopt a rule preventing civil court review of all arbitration awards involving church elections. While conceding that the civil courts could not review such awards if they involve religious doctrine or polity, it noted that not all disputes fall into this category. The court concluded that this dispute did involve religious doctrine and polity, making any judicial review of the arbitration award impermissible: "The root question, then, is whether the [church] was extinct . . . . The church would be deemed extinct if it had no members; the existence of members, conversely, would keep the church alive. It is well-settled in this state that the determination of a membership in a church is a question well embedded in the theological thicket and one that will not be entertained by the civil courts."

• A New Jersey court upheld an arbitration award entered in a dispute between a synagogue and its rabbi.[383] The synagogue and its rabbi were embroiled in a "lengthy and destructive dispute" that they agreed to submit to binding arbitration by a panel of ecclesiastical experts (a "Beth Din"). The "arbitration agreement" signed by the parties specified, "This is to certify that we the undersigned fully accept upon ourselves the following judgment of the Beth Din of the Union of Orthodox Rabbis of the United States and Canada . . . to adjudicate between us according to their judicious wisdom, we affirm hereby that we have accepted upon ourselves to obey and fulfill the judgment which shall issue forth from this Beth Din whether it be verdict or compromise, according to the determination of the aforementioned judges without any appeal whatsoever before any Beth Din under Jewish law or any civil court, but it is incumbent upon us to obey the verdict of the aforementioned Beth Din without any further complaint. All of the above was entered into voluntarily . . . without any reservations whatsoever in a recognizable and legally binding manner and is entered into in a manner so to be completely and lawfully binding." After an extended hearing involving "voluminous documentary evidence" and "lengthy oral testimony," the Beth Din ordered the synagogue to pay the rabbi $100,000, and asked the rabbi to resign "for the sake of peace" (it found no other basis to remove him). The synagogue appealed this arbitration order to a state civil court. A state appeals court upheld the decision of the Beth Din, and rejected the synagogue's appeal. It observed that the "arbitration agreement" was entered into "freely and voluntarily, with an awareness on the part of both sides as to the meaning and significance of that form of religious

---

[383] Elmora Hebrew Center v. Fishman, 570 A.2d 1297 (N.J. Super. 1990), aff'd, 593 A.2d 725 (N.J. 1991).

dispute resolution." The court noted that the authority of a civil court to review an arbitration award is "extremely limited," and is not permissible "absent proof of fraud, partiality, [or] misconduct on the part of the arbitrators . . . ." The court concluded by noting that "the law favors dispute resolution through consensual arbitration, and so the award is presumed to be valid. So it is here. On this record, the Beth Din's decision and award must be confirmed."

• A New York court ruled that an arbitration clause in an employment contract between a synagogue and a rabbi was legally enforceable, and so the rabbi was barred from suing the synagogue in civil court for discrimination and wrongful termination. The court concluded: "We perceive no public policy reasons for not enforcing anticipatory agreements to arbitrate statutory employment discrimination claims arising under [state law]. Moreover, the broad arbitration clause in [the rabbi's] employment contract encompasses his claim of wrongful discharge based on a physical disability."[384]

Damages—In General   § 10-17

When a jury finds a church liable in a civil lawsuit, it can award monetary damages to the plaintiff. Monetary damages may be either compensatory or punitive in nature. Compensatory damages are awarded to compensate plaintiffs for the actual injuries or harm they have suffered. They are intended to restore plaintiffs, as much as possible, to their condition before they were injured. Punitive damages are addressed in the next subsection.

Punitive Damages   § 10-17.1

Key point 10-17.1. *Punitive damages are monetary damages awarded by a jury "in addition to compensation for a loss sustained, in order to punish, and make an example of, the wrongdoer." They are awarded when a person's conduct is reprehensible and outrageous. Most church insurance policies exclude punitive damages. This means that a jury award of punitive damages represents an uninsured risk.*

Punitive damages are monetary damages awarded by a jury "in addition to compensation for a loss sustained, in order to punish, and make an example of, the wrongdoer." They are awarded when a person's conduct is particularly reprehensible and outrageous. This does not necessarily mean intentional misconduct. Punitive damages often are associated with reckless conduct or conduct creating a high risk of harm. It is critical to note that many church insurance policies exclude punitive damages. This means that a jury award of punitive damages represents an uninsured risk. Accordingly, it is critical for church leaders to understand the basis for punitive damages.

---

[384] South Huntington Jewish Center, Inc. v. Heyman, 723 N.Y.S.2d 511 (App. Div. 2001).

Case Studies

• *A Connecticut court ruled that a church and diocese could be liable for punitive damages based on "reckless indifference" if they were aware of a priest's proclivity to molest children but did not restrict his access to children. The court noted that "reckless indifference" can justify punitive damages. Further, "reckless misconduct exceeds mere negligence. A reckless actor is one who recognizes that his or her behavior involves a risk of injury to others substantially greater than negligence. It requires a conscious choice of a course of action with knowledge that that action will seriously endanger others or with knowledge of facts which would disclose this danger. In the present case, the plaintiff alleges that the diocese and local church knew of [the priest's] proclivity to abuse children sexually and consistently allowed him to have private access to such children, including the plaintiff. Reckless indifference encompasses such conscious behavior, if proven."[385]*

• *A Kentucky court ruled that an adult who had been sexually molested as a minor by a teacher at a parochial school could sue the diocese that operated the school for negligent hiring, supervision, and retention.[386] A jury awarded the victim $50,000 in compensatory damages and $700,000 in punitive damages, and it apportioned fault seventy-five percent to the diocese and twenty-five percent to the teacher. An appeals court rejected the claim of the diocese that the jury erred in awarding $700,000 in punitive damages against it. Kentucky law provides that "[a] plaintiff shall recover punitive damages only upon proving, by clear and convincing evidence, that the defendant from whom such damages are sought acted toward the plaintiff with oppression, fraud or malice." The diocese argued that by the plain language of the statute, punitive damages are available only upon a showing that it acted with fraud, malice, or oppression toward the victim and that there was no evidence that it acted in this manner since it had no way of knowing that the teacher had abused the victim or would likely do so. The court rejected this argument.*

• *A Minnesota appeals court concluded that churches and denominational agencies can be liable for punitive damages (which are meant to punish defendants for shocking and reprehensible conduct).[387] The case involved a Catholic priest who repeatedly was placed by church officials in situations in which he could sexually abuse boys, despite knowledge by church officials of the priest's propensities. A jury awarded a victim $855,000 in compensatory damages and $2,700,000 in punitive damages. The court upheld the trial court's reduction in the punitive damages award to approximately $187,000, based on the church's limited resources and the "total effect" of "other punishment" upon the church, including monetary damages in similar lawsuits and the extent of negative publicity generated by the trial. The court rejected the church's claim that subjecting it to punitive damages violated the state constitution, which prohibits interference with religious freedom. However, the court noted that the state constitution further states: "[T]he liberty of conscience hereby secured shall not be so construed as to excuse acts of licentiousness or justify practices inconsistent with the peace or safety of the state." The court concluded, "The church's actions . . .*

---

[385] Dumais v. Hartford Roman Catholic Diocese, 2002 WL 31015708 (Conn. Super. 2002). *But see* Hayes v. Norwich Roman Catholic Diocese, 2004 WL 2165071 (Conn. Sup. 2004) (no punitive damages without advance notice that a priest would molest minors).

[386] Roman Catholic Diocese v. Secter, 966 S.W.2d 286 (Ky. App. 1998).

[387] Mrozka v. Archdiocese of St. Paul and Minneapolis, 482 N.W.2d 806 (Minn. App. 1992).

fall within this exclusion. The repeated placement of [the priest] in parishes without restriction arguably condoned acts of licentious behavior and justified practices inconsistent with the peace and safety of the state. Awarding punitive damages furthers the state's interest in protecting its citizens from harm by deterring and punishing such conduct. The state is not only concerned with compensating plaintiffs, but also ensuring that similar conduct does not harm others in the future. Here, the unavailability of criminal sanctions and the ineffectiveness of a punitive damages award against the individuals involved support the trial court's determination that an imposition of punitive damages against the church is appropriate because the state's goals cannot be accomplished through less restrictive means." The court rejected the church's claim that there was insufficient evidence to establish a claim for punitive damages.

• *A federal district court in Michigan ruled that a church school and various church agencies were not liable on the basis of negligent hiring, supervision, or retention, for the sexual molestation of a minor student by a priest.[388] The court also noted that neither the school nor any of the church agencies was liable for punitive damages. It noted that under Wisconsin law (the law applicable to the case) punitive damages can be awarded in only two situations: (1) "a defendant desires to cause the harm sustained by the plaintiff, or believes that the harm is substantially certain to follow his conduct"; or (2) the defendant knows, or should have reason to know, not only that his conduct creates an unreasonable risk or harm, but also that there is a strong probability, although not a substantial certainty, that the harm will result, but, nevertheless, he proceeds with his conduct in reckless or conscious disregard of the consequences." The court continued, "Wisconsin courts often use the short-hand term 'outrageous' for the type of conduct which justifies the imposition of punitive damages. This 'outrageous' conduct must be proven by clear and convincing evidence. However, the fact that the conduct on which the suit is based is unlawful and would subject the defendant to criminal prosecution is not itself sufficient to impose punitive damages. Given the 'clear and convincing' evidentiary standard which governs the punitive damages, the court finds that the evidence presented is not sufficient to warrant submitting the punitive damages claims to the jury."*

• *An Ohio court ruled that a church could be liable as a result of the molestation of several young children by two adolescent boys who served as volunteer teachers and caregivers. The court rejected the church's claim that it could not liable for punitive damages. The church insisted that in order to demonstrate conduct worthy of a punitive damage award, a plaintiff must show hatred, ill will, a spirit of revenge, outrageous behavior, or willful indifference to the rights and safety of others. The court concluded that reasonable minds "could differ regarding whether [the church's] conduct demonstrated a conscious disregard for [the victims'] rights and safety having a great probability of substantial harm."[389]*

• *A Pennsylvania court ruled that a church and diocese could be liable for a priest's acts of child molestation. But the court reversed the trial court's award of $1 million in punitive damages against the church defendants. The court explained that punitive damages are designed to punish wrongdoers for reckless or wanton misconduct, and cannot be awarded on the basis of negligence. Therefore, to the extent that the church*

---

[388] Isely v. Capuchin Province, 880 F. Supp. 1138 (E.D. Mich. 1995).

[389] Doe v. First Presbyterian Church (USA), 710 N.E.2d 367 (Ohio App. 1998).

defendants' liability was based on negligence (in hiring, supervising, or retaining the priest), there was no basis for punitive damages.[390]

• *A federal court in Pennsylvania ruled that a church and diocese could be liable for punitive damages as a result of the sexual misconduct of a priest. The court noted that under Pennsylvania law, "punitive damages may be awarded for conduct that is outrageous, because of the defendant's reckless indifference to the rights of others," and that "as the name suggests, punitive damages are penal in nature and are proper only in cases where the defendant's actions are so outrageous as to demonstrate willful, wanton or reckless conduct." In determining whether punitive damages are warranted in a particular case, "the state of mind of the actor is vital. The act, or the failure to act, must be intentional, reckless or malicious. . . . As such, a showing of mere negligence, or even gross negligence, will not suffice to establish that punitive damages should be imposed. However, notwithstanding this heightened standard, punitive damages may be awarded based on a cause of action sounding in negligence if the plaintiff is able to show that the defendant's conduct not only was negligent but that the conduct was also outrageous." The court concluded that a reasonable jury would assess punitive damages against the church defendants, and so it rejected the defendants' request to dismiss the plaintiff's request for such damages. It pointed out that the defendants "knew that the plaintiff was routinely sleeping in [the minor victim's] bedroom and that he had taken [him] on several overnight trips. . . . A reasonable jury could conclude that a minor's sleeping in a priest's bedroom and a priest's taking a minor alone on overnight trips are facts which create a high degree of risk of physical harm to the minor. The failure to end this conduct, with its high degree of risk of physical harm to the plaintiff, could reasonably be viewed by a jury as reckless. As such, the court will deny the defendants' motion for summary judgment as to the plaintiff's claim for punitive damages."*[391]

Duplicate Verdicts § 10-17.2

Key point 10-17.2. *Juries generally cannot assess monetary damages against two or more organizations for the same wrong. If a jury determines that a personal injury victim has suffered damages of a specified amount, it cannot assess this amount separately against more than one defendant since doing so would result in duplicate verdicts.*

Juries generally cannot assess monetary damages against two or more entities for the same wrong. To illustrate, assume that a victim of sexual misconduct sues a church and a denominational agency, and that a jury determines that the victim's damages amounted to $100,000. If the jury then assesses this amount of damages against both the church and denominational agency, it has rendered duplicate verdicts. Such verdicts are subject to reduction by the trial court or an appeals court.

---

[390] Hutchison v. Luddy, 2000 WL 1585672 (Pa. 2000).

[391] Doe v. Liberatore, 478 F.Supp.2d 742 (M.D. Pa. 2007).

Case Study

• A Colorado court addressed the liability of a church and denominational agency for a sexual relationship between a youth pastor and a girl in his youth group. The victim sued the youth pastor, her church, and a denominational agency.[392] *The jury awarded her $187,500 in compensatory damages against the youth pastor on claims of breach of fiduciary duty and outrageous conduct and another $187,500 in punitive damages. It awarded her $37,500 in compensatory damages against the church on claims of negligent hiring and supervision and breach of fiduciary duty. The jury awarded $150,000 in compensatory damages against the denominational agency on claims of negligent hiring and supervision and breach of fiduciary duty, and an additional $150,000 in punitive damages. The church and denominational agency argued that the jury's various awards of damages were inconsistent. In particular, they argued that it was illogical to award damages against both the youth pastor and church defendants on the basis of the same theories of liability. The court agreed, noting that the jury's award of damages against the youth pastor and church defendants for the same alleged wrongs resulted in "duplication of damages" since the actions of the church defendants did not result in any additional harm to the victim beyond what had been caused by the youth pastor.*

Denominational Liability— In General

§ 10-18

Denominational agencies can be liable for their own acts. For example, they may be directly liable for the negligent driving of a denominational official in the course of church business; defamatory statements in denominational publications; or unlawful discrimination or wrongful termination claims involving their own employees.

However, denominational agencies also have been sued for the acts and obligations of affiliated churches and ministers. Such lawsuits often are little more than a search for a "deep pocket" out of which to pay damages when the local church has inadequate insurance coverage or financial resources. Most of these cases fall into one of two categories: (1) incidents of sexual misconduct by clergy or lay church workers, or (2) personal injuries resulting from accidents (on church property, during church activities, or involving a church vehicle).

The alleged basis for denominational liability in such cases generally will be one or more of the theories of liability addressed previously in this chapter in connection with the liability of local churches. To illustrate, if a denominational agency is sued because of the sexual misconduct of a minister, the agency may be sued on the basis of respondeat superior; negligent selection, supervision, or retention of the minister; or breach of a fiduciary duty. Some plaintiffs have asserted that a denominational agency will be liable in such cases on the basis of

---

[392] Bohrer v. DeHart, 943 P.2d 1220 (Colo. App. 1996)

an "agency" relationship with the offending minister.

Plaintiffs who sue denominational agencies for injuries resulting from accidents generally assert that the denomination is liable on the basis of "agency" for the acts and obligations of affiliated churches.

The following subsections will address (1) court rulings finding denominational agencies liable for the acts of affiliated ministers and churches (often referred to as vicarious, secondary or ascending liability); (2) court rulings finding denominational agencies not liable for the acts of affiliated ministers and churches; (3) defenses to liability; and (4) risk management.

Court Decisions Recognizing Vicarious Liability
§ 10-18.1

Key point 10-18.1. *Some courts have found denominational agencies liable for the acts of affiliated ministers and churches on the basis of a number of grounds, including negligence and agency.*

This subsection addresses the "secondary" liability of denominational agencies for the acts and obligations of affiliated churches, ministers, and lay workers. This form of liability is sometimes referred to as "ascending liability." Denominations also are subject to direct liability for their own acts, and this kind of liability is addressed previously in this and other chapters.

In a small number of cases, the civil courts have found denominational agencies liable for the acts and obligations of affiliated churches, agencies, clergy, and lay workers. Most of the earlier cases involved liability based on the negligent driving of affiliated clergy. To illustrate, in 1951 the California Supreme Court ruled that a presbytery was responsible for injuries caused by the negligent driving of the pastor of an affiliated "mission church."[393] The court concluded that the pastor was an "agent" of the presbytery, since "he was not responsible to the local church but only to the presbytery. The presbytery, not the church, had the power to remove him. Furthermore, he could not transfer to another pastorate without permission of the presbytery, and in fact he was a member of the presbytery rather than of the local church." The court concluded:

> The existence of the right of control and supervision establishes the existence of an agency relationship [making the employer legally responsible for the acts of an employee committed within the scope of his or her employment]. The evidence clearly supports the conclusion of the jury that such control existed in the present case. The right of the presbytery to install and remove its ministers, to approve or disapprove their transfer to other jurisdictions, and to supervise and control the

---

[393] Malloy v. Fong, 232 P.2d 241 (Cal. 1951).

activities of the local churches, particularly those in the mission stage, is inconsistent with a contrary conclusion.[394]

The court emphasized that the presbytery exercised significant control over "missions" churches (it held title to all church property, assisted with the churches' finance, and paid a portion of clergy salaries). It cautioned that "we are not here called upon to determine the liability of the presbytery for negligence in the activities of a fully established and independently incorporated Presbyterian church which has passed from the mission stage."

In a similar case, a California appeals court ruled that a trial court had improperly dismissed a lawsuit against a denomination (the International Church of the Foursquare Gospel).[395] The denomination had been sued by a person who was injured as a result of the negligent driving of one of the denomination's pastors (while engaged in church business). The court concluded that there was ample evidence demonstrating that the denomination was legally responsible for the injuries since the pastor was its "agent," and was acting within the scope of church business at the time of the accident. Accordingly, the trial court acted improperly in dismissing the case.

The court based its finding of an agency relationship upon the following factors: (1) The denomination's charter specified that it was incorporated "to supervise the management of the churches of the [denomination]," and to establish and grant charters to churches which would "be subject at all times to the supervision of [the denomination]." (2) The denomination ordained ministers "for the furtherance of the work of the [denomination]." (3) All property or equipment acquired by any local church is required to be held in the name of the denomination. (4) No church is allowed to execute a general contract to build without the written consent of a denominational official. (5) Each church is required to keep books of account and to prepare full and accurate monthly reports of activities in such form as is prescribed by the denomination. (6) The denomination is empowered to remove from office pastors who are not functioning in such a manner as to promote the best interests of their church. (7) Pastors who desire to transfer to a church in another state must secure a letter of transfer from a denominational official. (8) One of the pastor's duties is to see that the local church cooperates in all programs of the denomination.

The court concluded, on the basis of these facts, that "manifestly, this evidence meets every requirement for the establishment of an agency relationship as set forth in *Malloy v. Fong*."[396] Further, the pastor was not only an agent of the denomination, but also was acting within the scope of his duties at the time of the accident. Accordingly, the denomination was legally responsible for his negligence.

In a third California state court ruling, an appeals court ruled that a Catholic bishop was legally responsible for a death caused by the negligent driving of a

---

[394] *Id.* at 249-50.

[395] Miller v. International Church of the Foursquare Gospel, Inc., 37 Cal. Rptr. 309 (Cal. 1964).

[396] *See* note 400, *supra*, and accompanying text.

priest.[397] The priest was a French citizen who was sent to the United States to minister to the religious and cultural needs of Basque Catholics residing in the western United States. The state appeals court concluded that the priest was an agent of the bishop, and was acting within the scope of his agency at the time of the accident. The "significant test of an agency relationship," observed the court, "is the principal's right to control the activities of the agent." While acknowledging that the "evidence of agency is not strong," the court concluded that there was sufficient evidence to establish that the priest's activities were subject to the control of the bishop. It relied primarily upon the following considerations: (1) The bishop, "had he chosen, could have exercised full authority over [the priest] by extending to him an official, written assignment." While the bishop never took this step, the court concluded that he could have, and this was sufficient. (2) The bishop had jurisdiction over the priest's ministry. (3) In a letter to the Immigration and Naturalization Service, the bishop had stated that the priest was "under the direction of the undersigned bishop of this diocese." (4) In ministering to Basque Catholics, the priest "was performing some of the duties the bishop was responsible for."

In a fourth California case, a state appeals court ruled that the United Methodist Church (UMC) could be sued for the alleged misconduct of a subsidiary.[398] The UMC was sued for the alleged improprieties of a subsidiary corporation that operated fourteen nursing homes in California, Arizona, and Hawaii. When the subsidiary encountered financial difficulties, it raised the monthly payments of residents in violation of the terms of their "continuing care agreements" that guaranteed lifetime nursing and medical care for a fixed price. The subsidiary went bankrupt, and a class of nearly 2,000 residents sued the UMC for fraud and breach of contract. Although the case eventually was settled out of court, a California appeals court did rule that the UMC could be sued for the misconduct of its subsidiary. The court emphasized that the UMC was a hierarchical denomination with control over local churches and subsidiary institutions, ranging from restrictions on the purchase or sale of property to the selection of local church pastors. Such control, observed the court, made the UMC responsible for the liabilities of its affiliated churches and subsidiary institutions. The court also found it relevant that the subsidiary organization that operated the nursing homes was engaged in a commercial enterprise.

The court suggested that the First Amendment guaranty of religious freedom might prohibit direct actions against the UMC on account of the actions of subsidiary organizations if the allowance of such actions "would affect the distribution of power or property within the denomination, would modify or interfere with modes of worship affected by Methodists or would have any effect other than to oblige UMC to defend itself when sued upon civil obligations it is alleged to have incurred."[399]

---

[397] Stevens v. Roman Catholic Bishop of Fresno, 123 Cal. Rptr. 171 (Cal. App. 1975).

[398] Barr v. United Methodist Church, 153 Cal. Rptr. 322 (1979), *cert. denied*, 444 U.S. 973 (1979).

[399] *Id.* at 332.

More recent cases involving denominational liability have focused largely on "ascending liability" claims involving sexual misconduct by affiliated clergy or lay workers. Many of these cases are summarized in Table 10-11.

Court Decisions Rejecting Vicarious Liability

§ 10-18.2

Key point 10-18.2. *Most courts have refused to hold denominational agencies liable for the acts of affiliated ministers and churches, either because of First Amendment considerations or because the relationship between the denominational agency and affiliated church or minister is too remote to support liability.*

Most courts have rejected the secondary liability of denominational agencies for the acts and obligations of affiliated churches, ministers, and lay workers. This form of liability is sometimes referred to as vicarious or "ascending liability." The courts generally have declined to impose vicarious liability on denominational agencies on the basis of one or more of the defenses summarized in the next section.

Leading cases addressing denominational liability are summarized in Table 10-11.

Defenses to Liability

§ 10-18.3

Key point 10-18.3. *There are several legal defenses available to a denominational agency that is sued as a result of the acts or obligations of affiliated clergy and churches. These include a lack of temporal control over clergy and churches; a lack of official notice of a minister's prior wrongdoing in accordance with the denomination's governing documents; lack of an agency relationship; the prohibition by the First Amendment of any attempt by the civil courts to impose liability on religious organizations in a way that would threaten or alter their polity; and elimination or modification of the principle of joint and several liability.*

There are a number of legal defenses available to a denominational agency that is sued as a result of the acts or obligations of affiliated ministers or churches. Some of these are the same that are available to local churches, and they are addressed in previous sections of this chapter. Others are more unique to denominational agencies, and they are addressed in this subsection.

Most attempts to hold denominations legally accountable for the activities of clergy or affiliated churches have failed. The courts have relied on a variety of grounds in reaching this conclusion. The more important grounds are summarized in the paragraphs that follow.

1. Ecclesiastical Rather than Temporal Control

A number of courts have recognized that some denominations have authority to exercise only ecclesiastical control over affiliated clergy and churches, and that this form of control is not enough to warrant the imposition of legal liability upon the denomination for the activities of clergy and churches. In one of the earliest cases, the national conference of the Pentecostal Holiness Church was sued for breach of contract when its Florida regional conference defaulted on a life-care contract with two elderly church members who resided in a nursing home owned by the conference.[400] A state appeals court concluded that the national conference could not be sued for the financial improprieties of a local church or regional conference since local churches and regional conferences were totally independent of the national conference with respect to financial matters.

In a similar case, a Florida court made the following observation in a lawsuit attempting to impute liability to the Central Florida Diocese of the Episcopalian Church for injuries sustained on the premises of a local Episcopalian church:

> We perceive the Constitution and Canons of the Diocese to be in the nature of a contract between it and its missions and parishes. In that circumstance, consistent with the well-settled principle that it is a function of the court to construe and interpret contracts, it was error to grant to the jury the power to interpret the Constitution and Canons in the search for an agency relationship . . . between the Diocese and [the local church]. [W]e conclude that where vicarious liability is sought to be imposed upon one of two ostensibly interrelated entities through the ordinary principles of agency, the imposition of such liability is unwarranted in the absence of evidence revealing that one entity controls the other. Our analysis of the Diocese's Constitution and Canons fails to disclose that quantum of diocesan control, let alone domination, over the everyday secular affairs of [the local church] to sustain the imputation of liability to the Diocese. Indeed, we do not gainsay that the Diocese has impressed upon and demands from [the local church] unfailing obedience to ecclesiastical dogma, discipline and authority. We subscribe, however, to the concept that whenever a religious society incorporates, it assumes a dual existence; two distinct entities come into being—one, the church, which is conceived and endures wholly free from the civil law, and the other, the corporation created through the state prescribed method. Each remains separate although closely allied. The components of the ecclesiastical inter-relationship between the parent church and the subordinate body cannot be permitted to serve as a bridge capable of reaching the nonsecular parent in a civil proceeding.[401]

This language illustrates quite well the difference between ecclesiastical relationship and legal agency. To quote the Florida court, "the components of the

---

[400] Pentecostal Holiness Church, Inc. v. Mauney, 270 So.2d 762 (Fla. 1972), *cert. denied,* 276 So.2d 51 (Fla. 1973).

[401] Folwell v. Bernard, 477 So.2d 1060, 1063 (Fla. App. 1985).

ecclesiastical interrelationship between the parent church and the subordinate body cannot be permitted to serve as a bridge capable of reaching the nonsecular parent in a civil proceeding." Further, the Florida court observed that "[w]e find no evidence from which a jury could conclude that the Diocese controlled or regulated the church [or its agents] in the maintenance of its grounds or the manner in which the equipment used to maintain the grounds was either operated or kept in repair." In other words, the Diocese could not be liable on an agency theory for injuries occurring on a local church's premises during mowing activities since the Diocese had no authority to control the church's maintenance activities or the instrumentalities that allegedly caused the injuries in question.

The Alabama Supreme Court ruled that a Catholic religious order was not responsible for the misconduct of a priest.[402] The court noted that "the relationship between [the priest] and the society was ecclesiastical and did not necessarily create a . . . principal/agent relationship." The court further observed that

> the law with regard to ecclesiastical orders and religious societies [is] that the relationship is essentially ecclesiastical in nature. I would analogize this to situations where a young man may be in a seminary and the seminary is asked to supply a preacher or a minister for a congregation. The fact that the young minister may have some alma mater does not make the seminary responsible for his behavior in the event he elects to commit a burglary or some other act . . . . [T]he plaintiff must have evidence in addition to the fact that [the priest] was a member of the Benedictine Society of monks.[403]

The Kansas Supreme Court ruled that the fact that a priest was subject to the "ecclesiastical control" of his diocese was not relevant in determining the issue of legal control for purposes of imputing liability to the diocese on the basis of agency or respondeat superior.[404]

In another case, the United States Tax Court addressed the question of whether a minister (Rev. Shelley), who was ordained by the International Pentecostal Holiness Church (IPHC), was an employee or self-employed for federal income tax reporting purposes.[405] The IRS argued that the fact that Rev. Shelley was expected to comply with the provisions of the IPHC Manual indicated that he was an employee. While the Court conceded that the Manual imposed certain requirements on Rev. Shelley, it viewed these as "more in the nature of an outline of his responsibilities than directions on the manner in which he was to perform his duties. We do not find the Manual or its contents to be determinative of an employer-employee relationship." The IRS noted that the Manual described

---

[402] Wood v. Benedictine Society of Alabama, Inc., 530 So.2d 801 (Ala. 1988).

[403] *Id.* at 806 (quoting from the trial judge's opinion).

[404] Brillhart v. Scheier, 758 P.2d 219 (Kan. 1988).

[405] Shelly v. Commissioner, T.C. Memo. 1994-432 (1994). *See also* Weber v. Commissioner, 103 T.C. 378 (1994), *aff'd*, 60 F.3d 1104 (4th Cir. 1995). In *Weber*, a case involving the correct reporting status of a Methodist minister, the Tax Court observed that "[w]e recognize that there may be differences with respect to ministers in other churches or denominations, and the particular facts and circumstances must be considered in each case."

pastors as "amenable to the quadrennial conference and the conference board," and it insisted that this proved an employer-employee relationship. The Tax Court disagreed:

> While this language suggests an employee-employer relationship, we are not persuaded that it fully defines the relationships between the parties. The Manual provides little guidance as to how this amenability is exercised so as to give this description significance. In addition, testimony and other evidence indicate that the relationships between the parties are more complicated than the statement suggests. A chart included in the Manual depicts the local church board as amenable or accountable to the pastor. But, similarly, an examination of the record reveals that the relationship between those parties is less hierarchical and more interwoven than the chart indicates. While Rev. Shelley had a place in the structure of the IPHC, that structure was a looser affiliation than the strict hierarchy suggested by the term "amenable."

A federal appeals court reached the same conclusion in a case involving the question of whether an Assemblies of God minister (Rev. Alford) was an employee or self-employed for federal income tax reporting purposes.[406] The IRS insisted, based on language in the Constitution and Bylaws of the national church (the "General Council") and a state agency (the "District Council") that Rev. Alford was an employee. In rejecting this conclusion, the court observed:

> The General Council's and District Council's right to control Alford during the relevant years extended primarily to their function in awarding credentials to ministers like himself. Generally, the church has established certain criteria that must be met for an individual such as Alford to obtain credentials initially and to renew that status annually. . . . Thus it is apparent that, while the regional and national churches had doctrinal authority to exercise considerable control over Alford as regards his beliefs and his personal conduct as a minister of the church, they did not have "the right to control the manner and means by which the product [was] accomplished."
>
> The [trial court] and the United States make much of the fact that Alford, as a minister holding credentials, was "amenable" to the General Council and to the District Council in matters of doctrine and conduct. But this is not unusual in such a profession, and actually is merely a shorthand way of describing the parent church's doctrinal and disciplinary control discussed above. The control exercised by the regional and national organizations, and their right to control Alford, was no more nor less than most professions require of individuals licensed or otherwise authorized to work in the profession. State bar associations, for example, have certain education requirements and demand a certain level of performance on a bar examination before an individual can be licensed to practice law. On an

---

[406] Alford v. Commissioner, 116 F.3d 334 (8th Cir. 1997).

annual basis, such associations require the payment of dues and often the completion of continuing legal education in order for an attorney to retain his license. State bar associations are empowered to monitor attorneys' behavior and to discipline them as they see fit, including the revocation of an attorney's license to practice law (disbarment). Yet no one would suggest that, by virtue of this right to control an attorney's working life, the bar association is his employer, or even one of his employers.

Further, we are somewhat concerned about venturing into the religious arena in adjudicating cases such as this one, and interpreting what really are church matters as secular matters for purposes of determining a minister's tax status. The doctrinal and disciplinary control exercised by the General and District Councils, or available for their exercise, "is guided by religious conviction and religious law, not by employment relationships, and . . . should be considered impermissible or immaterial in determining the employment status of a religious minister."

Such cases are significant. They recognize that the mere presence of authority to exercise control over some ecclesiastical activities of a minister or church is not enough of a relationship to impose legal liability on the denomination. Unfortunately, the bylaws or other internal rules of many denominations define the relationship with local churches and clergy in a way that suggests far more "control" than actually exists. For example, many denominational documents speak generally of an almost unlimited authority to "control" or "supervise" the activities of affiliated churches or clergy, when in fact no such control was intended. Using unlimited language of "control" or "supervision" should be scrupulously avoided, if such authority does not exist. Words such as *control* or *supervision* have legal connotations, and should not be used without qualification unless unlimited authority in fact exists.

> "... the mere presence of authority to exercise control over some ecclesiastical activities of a minister or church is not enough of a relationship to impose legal liability on the denomination."

2. Notice of Wrongful Conduct

In many cases victims of sexual misconduct involving clergy have argued that a denominational agency is legally responsible for a minister's actions because it was aware of, or should have been aware of, the minister's wrongful conduct. Some courts have noted that denominations often have clearly prescribed internal rules for bringing charges against ministers who engage in inappropriate conduct, and that the only way for such denominations to be "on notice" of a minister's dangerous propensities is if a charge is filed and processed under the denomination's system of clergy discipline. Without a formal charge or complaint being brought, the denomination is not officially on notice and cannot be liable for the minister's subsequent acts.

Case Study

• *An Indiana court ruled that a denominational agency was not liable on the basis of negligent supervision or negligent retention for the molestation of a minor by a pastor.[407] When the victim was an adult, she sued her church and denomination, claiming that they were responsible for the pastor's actions on the basis of several theories, including negligence. The court concluded that the national church was not liable for the pastor's acts of molestation, even if it had some knowledge of them, if the disciplinary procedure outlined in its bylaws was not activated by the victim. It concluded, "The [national church], which is only affiliated with the local church and [regional agency] through its constitution and judicial procedures, was not informed. The evidence . . . does not indicate that [the woman] invoked the judicial procedures, which is the only mechanism by which the [national church] could have taken action against [the pastor]. According to the judicial procedures, the [regional agency] forms a committee to investigate alleged misconduct upon the submission of a complaint signed by two or more persons. Only after this investigation is completed and the [regional agency] determines that the evidence warrants a trial does the [national church] become involved. [The woman] has not alleged . . . that she or anyone else ever filed a complaint against [the pastor] with the [regional agency]. Therefore, the [national church] could not have disciplined [the pastor]. Accordingly, we conclude that because the evidence does not show that the [national church] was aware of [the pastor's] actions, summary judgment in favor of the [national church] is proper on [the woman's] claims for negligent hiring, supervision, and retention."*

3. Lack of an Actual Agency Relationship

One of the principal grounds cited by plaintiffs' attorneys in seeking access to the "deep pockets" of a denomination is agency. If a minister or lay worker can be classified as an "agent" of a denomination, then the denomination may be legally responsible for his or her acts occurring within the scope of employment. The courts have consistently rejected agency as a basis for making denominational agencies accountable for accidents occurring in local churches.

Section 1 of the *Restatement of Agency* (an authoritative legal treatise) specifies that "agency is the fiduciary relation which results from the manifestation of consent by one party to another that the other shall act on his behalf and subject to his control, and consent by the other so to act." The *Restatement* further specifies that "the one for whom action is taken is the principal," and "the one who is to act is the agent."

Section 219 of the *Restatement of Agency* specifies that an employer is subject to liability "for the torts of his servants committed while acting in the scope of their employment." This form of vicarious liability was discussed fully earlier in this chapter. The important point here is that clergy serving local churches rarely will be considered to be agents or "servants" (i.e., employees) of a parent denomination, since they will satisfy few if any of the factors indicating an agency relationship enumerated in the *Restatement of Agency*.[408] To illustrate, a Missouri

---

[407] Konkle v. Henson, 672 N.E.2d 450 (Ind. App. 1996).

[408] *See* note 31, *supra*, and accompanying text, for a listing of the factors to be considered in determining whether or not a particular individual is a servant of another.

court ruled that a Catholic priest was not an agent of the Archdiocese of St. Louis with respect to his anti-abortion torts. The court observed:

> When questioned about the duty of a priest in the Archdiocese concerning protesting abortions at abortion clinics, the Archbishop stated "there's no such duty prescribed of any priest." Neither was it a priest's duty to "trespass unlawfully on property to express opposition to abortion. . . ."
>
> [The priest's] activities were not within the direction of his superiors or the Church. Moreover, they were neither authorized, usual, customary, incidental, foreseeable, nor fairly and naturally incidental to his duties. . . . There is nothing in the . . . directions or authorizations of the Archbishop . . . nor under canon law to indicate that it is or was a priest's duty to engage in such activities.[409]

Can a denomination be legally responsible for the obligations of an affiliated church on the ground that the church is its "agent"? Such a conclusion is highly unlikely for many denominations. One authority has observed:

> Generally, absent fraud or bad faith, a corporation will not be held liable for the acts of its subsidiaries. There is a presumption of separateness the plaintiff must overcome to establish liability by showing that the parent is employing the subsidiary to perpetrate a fraud and that this was the proximate cause of the plaintiff's injury. Merely showing control, in the absence of an intent to defraud or escape liability, is insufficient to overcome that presumption. Further, although wrongdoing by the parent need not amount to plain fraud or illegality, the injured party must show some connection between its injury and the parent's improper manner of doing business—without that connection, even when the parent exercises domination and control over the subsidiary, corporate separateness will be recognized. Thus, under ordinary circumstances, a parent will not be liable for the obligations of its subsidiary.[410]

Under general principles of agency law, an agency relationship requires (1) a manifestation of consent by a denomination to its affiliated churches that they shall act on its behalf and subject to its control, (2) consent by the affiliated churches to act as the denomination's agents, and (3) control exerted by the denomination. A fourth requirement that is implicit in the *Restatement's* definition of agency is some direct benefit to the principal.[411]

Those national and regional denominational agencies that have no authority

---

[409] Maryland Casualty Co. v. Huger, 728 S.W.2d 574 (Mo. App. 1987). *See also* Brillhart v. Scheier, 758 P.2d 219 (Kan. 1988); Wood v. Benedictine Society of Alabama, Inc., 530 So.2d 801 (Ala. 1988).

[410] Fletcher Cyc. Corp. § 43 (perm. ed. 2008).

[411] *See generally* E. Gaffney & P. Sorensen, Ascending Liability in Religious and Other Nonprofit Organizations (1984), in which the authors assert that benefit to the principal is implicit in the definition of agency, presumably because of the fiduciary nature of the relationship.

to supervise the activities of affiliated churches obviously cannot be liable for the churches' obligations or activities on the basis of agency. As noted in the preceding section, some denominations retain a limited authority with regard to specified ecclesiastical functions of affiliated churches. This limited "authority" clearly is not an adequate basis for denominational liability for the activities of affiliated churches. As one authority has observed: "Whether the parent so dominates the activities of the subsidiary as to establish an agency relationship is a question of fact determined primarily by the degree of control the parent has over the subsidiary. Generally, for the parent to be held liable for the subsidiary's acts *this control must be actual, participatory, and total.*"[412] Few if any denominations exercise this degree of control over affiliated churches.[413]

A number of courts have rejected the allegation that churches are "agents" of the denomination with which they are affiliated. To illustrate, a federal appeals court rejected the claim that the Assemblies of God denomination exerted sufficient "control" over affiliated churches to warrant denominational liability for the activities of its churches.[414] The national offices and a regional office of the Assemblies of God were sued in 1981 for failure to supervise the fund-raising activities of an affiliated church. The church had created a trust fund in 1973 as a means of financing a new church building and related facilities. The fund consisted of unsecured deposits solicited from both church members and nonmembers. According to the trust agreements and certificates of deposit used in connection with the fund, the deposits could be withdrawn after one year, with interest. Eventually, the fund had assets of over $7,000,000 which had been deposited by some 1,100 persons. In 1978, state banking authorities served the fund with a cease and desist order for operating a bank without a license. A subsequent run on the fund resulted in its collapse. In 1979, the church filed a petition for relief under Chapter 11 of the Bankruptcy Code.

In 1981, a class action suit was filed in federal district court naming the national Assemblies of God offices (the "General Council") and one of its regional divisions ("District Council") as defendants. The suit was brought against the national and regional offices because of an automatic stay by the bankruptcy court prohibiting the plaintiffs from suing the church directly. Specifically, the class action complaint alleged that the church had committed securities fraud in violation of state and federal law by selling securities without proper registration, and that the national and regional offices were derivatively responsible for the securities fraud as "control persons" under section 20(a) of the Securities Exchange Act. Section 20 provides:

---

[412] Fletcher Cyc. Corp. § 43 (2008 perm. ed.).

[413] The most that could be said in such cases is that the denomination may have a limited liability commensurate with its limited authority. In other words, the local church may be a limited agent of the denomination for purposes of those specific activities over which the denomination reserves a right of control. The denomination would have liability, based on agency, only with respect to those activities of the church that the denomination has authority to control. For example, if a denomination's sole authority with respect to affiliated churches is to hold title to real property, then the denomination should have no liability for accidents involving church vehicles.

[414] Kersh v. The General Council of the Assemblies of God, 804 F.2d 546 (9th Cir. 1986).

Every person who, directly or indirectly, controls any person liable under any provision of this title or any rule or regulation thereunder shall also be liable jointly and severally with and to the same extent as such control person to any person to whom such control person is liable, unless the controlling person acted in good faith and did not directly or indirectly induce the act or acts constituting the violation or cause of action.

To substantiate their allegation of control person liability, the plaintiffs cited several factors, including the following: (1) the General Council and District Council issued ministerial credentials to the church's pastor; (2) the General Council and District Council retained control over the pastor's activities by their power to discipline him and withdraw his credentials; (3) the General Council could withdraw the church's certificate of affiliation for improper conduct, and, by failing to do so, it ratified the church's securities fraud; (4) the General Council and District Council and their missionary activities were beneficiaries of some church contributions; (5) by permitting the church to affiliate itself with the Assemblies of God, the General Council and District Council permitted the church to hold itself out as being under their general supervision; and (6) the church was covered by the group federal income tax exemption issued by the IRS to the General Council and all its "subordinate units."

The plaintiffs conceded that the General Council and District Council did not participate in or even know of the church's activities until the state banking authorities issued the cease and desist order in 1978, and therefore were not liable under a strict reading of section 20(a). However, they relied on cases in which the courts have concluded that "broker-dealers" participate in the securities fraud of agents by failing to enforce a reasonable system of supervision.

The General Council and District Council filed motions for summary judgment on a variety of grounds, included the following: (1) they were not "control persons" within the meaning of section 20(a) since (a) under the organizational documents, practice, and theology of the Assemblies of God, they were powerless to exercise control over local churches, (b) their lack of knowledge and participation constituted a "good faith" defense, (c) the stringent broker-dealer standard had no application to religious organizations, and (2) the First Amendment's free exercise of religion clause prohibited a civil court from requiring a religious denomination to exercise a degree of control over its affiliated churches contrary to its practices, organization, and theology. The General Council noted that judicial imposition of a duty to supervise the financial affairs of its 11,000 churches in the United States, despite long-established practice and theology to the contrary, would force it to change its polity in order to avoid unlimited liability for the obligations of all of its churches. It noted that the Supreme Court has frequently observed that judicial manipulation of the polity or internal organization of church bodies violates the First Amendment.[415]

---

[415] This contention is discussed in detail later in this chapter.

In 1985, a federal district court granted the motion for summary judgment filed by the General Council and District Council.[416] The court concluded that the defendants could not be guilty as control persons under section 20(a) of the Securities Exchange Act since they did not know of or participate in the activities of the church. The court was not willing to extend the more stringent "broker-dealer" standard (i.e., failure to adequately supervise constitutes participation) to the defendants "since there are some significant differences between the broker-dealer context and the church structure at issue here." In particular, the court observed that "it is generally recognized that broker-dealers have a high degree of control over their agents," unlike the relationship between the defendants and local Assemblies of God churches. Further, the defendants were nonprofit entities and thus significantly differed from the typical broker-dealer. Most importantly, however, the court stressed that "the Assemblies of God . . . was founded on the principle that local churches would be sovereign, self-governing units, and are given wide discretion in operating their affairs." This relationship falls short of the "control" contemplated by section 20(a). The plaintiffs appealed this decision, and a federal appeals court agreed with the district court that the Assemblies of God national and regional offices were not responsible for the activities of an affiliated church. The court observed:

> [W]e find the evidence that [plaintiffs] present regarding the power or influence of General Council insufficient to establish "control" under section 20(a). [Plaintiffs] argue that the General Council maintains control by licensing ministers; however, there is no evidence indicating how such control is exercised once a minister has been licensed. [Plaintiffs] contend that the General Council exercises control over a minister's "promotion" to larger congregations; however, each local church has independent power to select its ministers. Moreover, the General Council was not required to approve the [church's] fundraiser. Indeed, there are no facts at all suggesting a nexus between [the church] and General Council regarding the transaction.[417]

The court further noted that the local church "did not act as the agent of the national church in this transaction. [The local church] did not receive compensation from the national church for the sale. More importantly, the sale was solely for the benefit of [the local church] with no direct benefit going to the national church."

The case is important, for it illustrates that a principal may have liability only for those specific activities of an agent over which the principal has the authority to exert control. It also suggests that an agency relationship requires some element of direct benefit to the principal. This is an important observation, since in many cases the activity allegedly creating denominational liability on the basis of agency

---

[416] Kersh v. The General Council of the Assemblies of God, No. C 84-0252 (N.D. Cal., May 17, 1985).

[417] 804 F.2d at 549.

is of no direct benefit to the denomination.[418]

Several other courts have rejected the contention that local churches or other institutions are agents of a denomination.[419]

4. Lack of an "Apparent Agency" Relationship

Even if a church or minister is not an actual agent of a national or regional denominational agency, it is possible for the denomination to be liable for their activities on the basis of *apparent agency*. Most states recognize the theory of apparent agency. Under this theory, a person or organization can become the "agent" of another though no actual agency relationship in fact exists. Section 267 of the *Restatement of Agency*, which has been adopted by many states, specifies:

One who represents that another is his servant or other agent and thereby causes a third person justifiably to rely upon the care or skill of such apparent agent is subject to liability to the third person for harm caused by the lack of care or skill of the one appearing to be a servant or other agent as if he were such.

An official comment to this section further specifies that

[t]he mere fact that acts are done by one whom the injured party believes to be the defendant's servant is not sufficient to cause the apparent master to be liable. There must be such reliance upon the manifestation as exposes the plaintiff to the negligent conduct.

Some persons injured by the activities of a local church or pastor have sued a parent denomination on the basis of apparent agency. The argument is that the denomination has "held out" the local church or pastor as its agent, and thus is responsible for injuries or damages that are caused by their activities. This argument has been rejected by a number of courts.[420] To illustrate, an Indiana state appeals court ruled that 65 plaintiffs who brought a class action lawsuit against a federation of Lutheran churches failed as a matter of law to establish apparent agency.[421] The plaintiffs all had purchased "life-care" contracts in a "Lutheran" nursing home organized as a separate nonprofit corporation but actively supported and promoted by the federation of churches. The corporate board consisted of 15 members, including 9 laypersons and 6 ministers—all of whom had to be members of federation churches. The corporate charter stated

[418] *See* note 411, *supra.*

[419] *See, e.g.,* Folwell v. Bernard, 477 So.2d 1060 (Fla. App. 1985); Pentecostal Holiness Church, Inc. v. Mauney, 270 So.2d 762 (Fla. 1972), *cert. denied,* 276 So.2d 51 (Fla. 1973); Hope Lutheran Church v. Chellew, 460 N.E.2d 1244 (Ind. App. 1244).

[420] *See generally* E. GAFFNEY & P. SORENSEN, ASCENDING LIABILITY IN RELIGIOUS AND OTHER NONPROFIT ORGANIZATIONS (1984); Hotz, *Diocesan Liability for Negligence of a Priest,* 26 CATH. LAW. 228 (1981); Note, *Will Courts Make Change for a Large Denomination? Problems of Interpretation in an Agency Analysis in Which a Religious Denomination Is Involved in an Ascending Liability Tort Case,* 72 IOWA L. REV. 1377 (1987).

[421] Hope Lutheran Church v. Chellew, 460 N.E.2d 1244 (Ind. App. 1984).

that the corporation was a "joint agency" of federation churches. Federation churches became members of the corporation, and they approved the articles of incorporation, bylaws, and initial board. The venture never attracted sufficient funding, and the corporation eventually declared bankruptcy.

The court concluded that the individual Lutheran churches in the federation were not legally responsible for the bankrupt corporation's liabilities on the basis of "apparent agency." It noted that the "essential element" of apparent agency is "some form of communication, direct or indirect, by the principal, which instills a reasonable belief in the mind of the third party" that another individual is an agent of the principal. The plaintiffs argued that apparent agency was established by use of the name "Lutheran" in the nursing home title and in promotional literature. Such conduct "led life membership purchasers to believe the [nursing] home had the support and financial backing of the Lutheran Church in general and the participating congregations in particular." In rejecting the application of apparent agency, the court observed that

> use of the word "Lutheran" in the name of the retirement home did not exhibit the degree of control by the churches necessary to create an apparent agency. While delegates from the churches may have been involved in the formation of [the nursing home corporation], it was ultimately the decision and responsibility of [the corporation] and its board of directors to use the word "Lutheran" in the name of the home. The same is true of the promotional materials . . . . Therefore, not only was the evidence insufficient to establish a manifestation by the churches to the plaintiffs, it was devoid of proof that [the nursing home corporation's] operations were controlled by the churches.[422]

In another significant ruling, a Texas state appeals court concluded that the Assemblies of God was not responsible for the activities of local churches or clergy on the basis of apparent authority.[423] An injured plaintiff had alleged that apparent agency was established by the denomination's "holding out" of local churches and clergy as its agents. The plaintiff claimed that this "holding out" occurred through "the ordination and licensing of ministers, accepting money from local churches, use of the 'Assembly of God' name by local churches, and publishing [a denominational magazine]." The court acknowledged that a national church can be legally accountable for the acts of a local minister or church on the basis of "apparent agency" if the national church "holds out" the church or minister as its agent or otherwise causes third parties to reasonably believe that the local church or minister is in fact an agent of the national church. The court concluded that the alleged methods by which the Assemblies of God "held out" its churches and ministers as its "agents" did *not* establish liability on the basis of apparent agency. With regard to the denomination's ordination and licensing of clergy, the court noted that the authority to ordain and discipline ministers was limited, and that

---

[422] *Id.* at 1251.

[423] Eckler v. The General Council of the Assemblies of God, 784 S.W.2d 935 (Tex. App. 1990).

"by plaintiff's close association with the local church and the Assembly of God religion, it is reasonable to believe that she had notice of these limitations on the [national church's] power to ordain and license."

The court rejected the plaintiff's claim that the financial contributions of local churches to the national church demonstrated that the national church was involved in an apparent agency relationship with the local churches (and was therefore responsible for their misconduct). It emphasized that the financial contributions were voluntary, and "would not reasonably lead a prudent person to believe that the local church was an agent of the [national church]." Further, there was no evidence whatever that the plaintiff was even aware that the local church made contributions to the national church, and therefore it was not possible to say that she "relied" on such conduct as indicating an agency relationship.

The court rejected the plaintiff's claim that the local church's use of the "Assembly of God" name demonstrated an apparent agency relationship. The sovereignty granted local churches in the General Council's bylaws rendered it impossible that a reasonable person would conclude that a local church was an agent of the General Council. The court observed that "the local church's autonomy is not affected by the authorized use of 'Assembly of God,' and no apparent agency arises from this use." Similarly, the court rejected the claim that the national church's denominational magazine created an apparent agency relationship with its local churches, since "the bylaws do not indicate that the [magazine] makes representations about the local church in any way, but only publicizes the doctrine of the Assembly of God religion. This does not constitute a sufficient 'holding out' which would generate a reasonable belief that the local church was an agent of [the national church]."

Further, in rejecting the plaintiff's claim that the denomination used "less than ordinary care" in discharging its "continuing duty" to monitor and supervise its clergy, the court observed that the national church "exercises no supervisory powers over the local ministers" and "is not responsible for the day-to-day oversight of the ministers." Since the national church had no duty to supervise clergy, "it is impossible that lack of supervision . . . was a substantial factor in causing plaintiff's injuries."

5. Lack of an Alter Ego Relationship

A few attempts have been made to establish denominational liability for the activities of affiliated churches on the basis of the *alter ego* theory. One court, in rejecting the application of this theory to the Catholic Church, described it as follows:

The requirements for applying the "alter ego" principle are thus stated:
It must be made to appear that the corporation is not only *influenced and governed* by that person [or other entity], but that there is such a *unity of interest and ownership* that the individuality, or separateness, of such person and corporation has ceased, and the facts are such that an adherence to the fiction of the separate existence of the corporation would, under the particular circumstances, sanction a *fraud or promote injustice.* . . . Among the factors to be considered in applying the doctrine are commingling of

funds and other assets of the two entities, the holding out by one entity that it is liable for the debts of the other, identical equitable ownership in the two entities, use of the same offices and employees, and use of one as a mere shell or conduit for the affairs of the other.[424]

One authority states that the alter ego theory requires " . . . complete domination, not only of the finances, but of policy and business practice with respect to the transaction so that the corporate entity as to this transaction had at the time no separate mind, will or existence of its own; and (2) such control must have been used by the defendant to commit fraud or wrong, to perpetrate the violation of the statutory or other positive legal duty, or dishonest and unjust act in contravention of the plaintiff's legal rights; and (3) the aforesaid control and breach of duty must proximately cause the injury or unjust loss."[425]

Obviously, few if any churches would be deemed an "alter ego" of an affiliated denomination under these tests. One court rejected an attempt to hold a denomination liable for the activities of an affiliated church on the ground that the denomination and its churches were "inextricably intertwined."[426]

6. Parent-Subsidiary Relationship

There is considerable confusion regarding the liability of a "parent" corporation for the actions of a "subsidiary" corporation. The courts have generally ruled that separately incorporated "subsidiaries" of a parent corporation are independently liable for their own actions, and this liability cannot be imputed to the parent. To illustrate, the United States Supreme Court issued a ruling in 1996 that addressed directly the liability of parent corporations for the acts of subsidiaries.[427] The Court noted that "it is a general principle of corporate law deeply ingrained in our economic and legal systems that a parent corporation is not liable for the acts of its subsidiaries," and that "the mere fact that there exists a parent-subsidiary relationship between two corporations [does not make the parent] liable for the torts of its affiliate."

Similarly, a leading treatise on corporation law contains the following statement with regard to the liability of one corporation for the actions of another corporation:

---

[424] Roman Catholic Archbishop v. Superior Court, 93 Cal. Rptr. 338, 341-42 (Cal. App. 1971).

[425] Fletcher Cyc. Corp. § 41.10 (2008). This authority lists the following factors to consider in applying the alter ego theory:

> The factors include whether: (1) the parent and subsidiary have common stock ownership; (2) the parent and subsidiary have common directors and officers; (3) the parent and subsidiary have common business departments; (4) the parent and subsidiary file consolidated financial statements and tax returns; (5) the parent finances the subsidiary; (6) the parent caused the incorporation of the subsidiary; (7) the subsidiary operates with grossly inadequate capital; (8) the parent pays the salaries and other expenses of the subsidiary; (9) the subsidiary receives no business except that given to it by the parent; (10) the parent uses the subsidiary's property as its own; (11) the daily operations of the two corporations are not kept separate; and (12) the subsidiary does not observe the basic corporate formalities, such as keeping separate books and records and holding shareholder and board meetings. *Id.* at § 43.

[426] Eckler v. The General Council of the Assemblies of God, 784 S.W.2d 935 (Tex. App. 1990).

[427] United States v. Bestfoods, 524 U.S. 51 (1996).

Generally, absent fraud or bad faith, a corporation will not be held liable for the acts of its subsidiaries. There is a presumption of separateness the plaintiff must overcome to establish liability by showing that the parent is employing the subsidiary to perpetrate a fraud and that this was the proximate cause of the plaintiff's injury. Merely showing control, in the absence of an intent to defraud or escape liability, is insufficient to overcome that presumption. Further, although wrongdoing by the parent need not amount to plain fraud or illegality, the injured party must show some connection between its injury and the parent's improper manner of doing business—without that connection, even when the parent exercises domination and control over the subsidiary, corporate separateness will be recognized. Thus, under ordinary circumstances, a parent will not be liable for the obligations of its subsidiary.[428]

The Supreme Court has acknowledged that a parent corporation may be liable for the actions of a subsidiary corporation (the corporate "veil" can be "pierced") "when the corporate form would otherwise be misused to accomplish certain wrongful purposes, most notably fraud." Many other courts have concurred that one corporation may be liable for the actions of another corporation in exceptional circumstances. These include the following:

A federal appeals court provided a useful list of factors to consider in determining whether or not a "parent" corporation is legally responsible for the liabilities and obligations of a "subsidiary" or affiliate.[429] While this case involved a parent and subsidiary business corporations, the court's conclusion will be directly relevant to denominational agencies that are sued as a result of liabilities of subsidiary or affiliated corporations. Here is the list of twelve factors to be considered:

(1) the parent corporation owns all or a majority of the stock of the subsidiary

(2) the corporations have common directors or officers

(3) the parent and the subsidiary have common business departments

(4) the parent and the subsidiary file consolidated financial statements and tax returns

(5) the parent corporation finances the subsidiary

(6) the parent corporation caused the incorporation of the subsidiary

---

[428] FLETCHER CYC. CORP. § 43 (perm. ed. 2008).

[429] Gundle Lining Construction Corp. v. Adams County Asphalt, Inc., 85 F.3d 201 (5th Cir. 1996). *See also* In re Catfish Antitrust Litigation, 908 F. Supp. 400 (N.D. Miss. 1996) ("we must remember that the alter ego doctrine and piercing of the corporate veil are truly exceptional doctrines, reserved for those cases where the officers, directors or stockholders utilized the corporate entity as a sham to perpetuate a fraud, to shun personal liability, or to encompass other truly unique situations").

(7) the subsidiary has grossly inadequate capital

(8) the parent corporation pays the salaries or expenses or losses of the subsidiary

(9) the subsidiary has substantially no business except with the parent corporation

(10) the parent uses the subsidiary's property as its own

(11) The daily operations of the two corporations are not kept separate

(12) the subsidiary does not observe the basic corporate formalities, such as keeping separate books and records and holding shareholder and board meetings

Denominational agencies are routinely sued as a result of the actions or obligations of affiliated churches. It is important to recognize that ascending liability in such cases is not automatic. The person bringing the lawsuit must establish a legal basis for imposing liability on the parent organization. The twelve factors mentioned in this case demonstrate that finding a parent organization legally responsible for the acts or liabilities of a subsidiary can be very difficult.

Table 10-9
Ascending Liability Using the OFCCP 27-Factor Analysis
Note: Set forth below is the 27-factor test used by the Office of Federal Contract Compliance Programs (OFCCP) to determine if the nondiscrimination rules that apply to government contractors apply to their subsidiaries. This same analysis is useful in evaluating the potential liability of religious organizations for the acts of their subsidiaries and affiliates since it is more comprehensive than the tests usually applied by the courts in ascending liability cases. The OFCCP states that "an organization need not meet all five factors to be considered a single entity with a covered Federal contractor," and that "there is growing recognition that centralized control over personnel functions is the most important factor."

factor 1: common ownership	
1	Percentage of stock of subsidiary owned by parent corporation?
factor 2: common directors and officers	
2	Names of directors of parent?
3	Names of directors of subsidiary?
4	Names of directors on boards of both parent and subsidiary?
5	Names of officers of both parent and subsidiary?

Table 10-9
Ascending Liability Using the OFCCP 27-Factor Analysis

Note: Set forth below is the 27-factor test used by the Office of Federal Contract Compliance Programs (OFCCP) to determine if the nondiscrimination rules that apply to government contractors apply to their subsidiaries. This same analysis is useful in evaluating the potential liability of religious organizations for the acts of their subsidiaries and affiliates since it is more comprehensive than the tests usually applied by the courts in ascending liability cases. The OFCCP states that "an organization need not meet all five factors to be considered a single entity with a covered Federal contractor," and that "there is growing recognition that centralized control over personnel functions is the most important factor."

6	What positions do the individuals in no. 5 hold in each corporation?

factor 3: de facto control

7	Does the parent pay the wages of the subsidiary's employees?
8	Does the parent pay any other expense of the subsidiary? If so, which ones?
9	Does the parent negotiate or provide health insurance, pension, or other employee benefits for subsidiary's employees?
10	In advertising, is the subsidiary referred to as part of the parent?
11	In financial statements of either corporation is the subsidiary described as a department or division of the parent?
12	Does the same in-house legal staff serve both the parent and subsidiary?
13	Are any services provided by the parent for the subsidiary, or vice versa? If so, which services?
14	The books and financial records of the two corporations are combined.

factor 4: unity of personnel policies from a common source

15	Does the parent control the hiring or compensation practices of the subsidiary (i.e., hiring standards, compensation ranges, nondiscrimination policy)?
16	Does the parent review or control the labor practices of the subsidiary?
17	Is there ever an exchange of personnel between parent and subsidiary? If yes, does the individual who transfers retain the same seniority date used at the transferor corporation for the purposes of benefits, promotions, layoffs and/or recall?
18	Does the parent recruit personnel for the subsidiary, or vice versa?
19	Does the parent hire the subsidiary's top management officials?

Table 10-9 Ascending Liability Using the OFCCP 27-Factor Analysis	

Note: Set forth below is the 27-factor test used by the Office of Federal Contract Compliance Programs (OFCCP) to determine if the nondiscrimination rules that apply to government contractors apply to their subsidiaries. This same analysis is useful in evaluating the potential liability of religious organizations for the acts of their subsidiaries and affiliates since it is more comprehensive than the tests usually applied by the courts in ascending liability cases. The OFCCP states that "an organization need not meet all five factors to be considered a single entity with a covered Federal contractor," and that "there is growing recognition that centralized control over personnel functions is the most important factor."

20	Are minority employees of the subsidiary listed on EEO-1 reports of the parent?

factor 5: dependency of operations

21	Has there ever been an infusion of capital from parent to subsidiary? If so, when and in what amount?
22	What percent of the subsidiary's business is with the parent?
23	What percentage of the parent's business is with the subsidiary?
24	Does either the parent or subsidiary use any of the property of the other?
25	Is the product or service of either the parent or subsidiary essential to the conduct of the other's business?
26	Does the parent or subsidiary provide any marketing service for the other?
27	Would the parent or subsidiary be unable to function if the other ceases operation?

7. First Amendment Prohibition of Civil Court Manipulation of Ecclesiastical Polity

As formidable as the preceding defenses are, the most significant defense available to many denominations is provided by the First Amendment to the United States Constitution. Judicial recognition of a duty on the part of a denomination to supervise the activities of affiliated churches, clergy, and lay workers, where no such authority exists, would violate the First Amendment religion clauses since it would amount to governmental manipulation of the polity of a sovereign religious organization. The ultimate question in such cases is whether a civil court, consistently with the First Amendment's religion clauses, can impose a duty on a denomination to supervise and control affiliated churches, clergy, or lay workers when the theology, history, practice, and organizational documents of the denomination forbid such control. Stated simply: Can a court "connectionalize" an essentially congregational association of churches? The answer to both questions is no. The United States Supreme Court has often stated that the civil courts may not affect ecclesiastical doctrine or polity:

> • But it is a very different thing where a subject-matter of dispute, strictly and purely ecclesiastical in its character—a matter over which the civil courts exercise no jurisdiction—a matter which concerns theological controversy, church discipline, ecclesiastical government or the conformity of the members of the church to the standard of morals required of them—becomes the subject of its action. It may be said here, also, that no jurisdiction has been conferred on the tribunal to try the particular case before it, or that, in its judgment, it exceeds the powers conferred upon it.[430]

> • Legislation that regulates church administration, the operation of the churches, the appointment of clergy . . . prohibits the free exercise of religion. . . . Watson v. Jones . . . radiates, however, a spirit of freedom for religious organizations, and independence from secular control or manipulation, in short, power to decide for themselves, free from state interference, matters of church government as well as those of faith and doctrine.[431]

> • First Amendment values are plainly jeopardized when church property litigation is made to turn on the resolution by civil courts of controversies over religious doctrine and practice. If civil courts undertake to resolve such controversies in order to adjudicate the property dispute, the hazards are ever present of inhibiting the free development of religious doctrine and of implicating secular interests in matters of purely ecclesiastical concern.[432]

> • To permit civil courts to probe deeply enough into the allocation of power within a church so as to decide where religious law places control over the use of church property would violate the First Amendment in much the same manner as civil determination of religious doctrine. Similarly, where the identity of the governing bodies that exercises general authority within the church is a matter of substantial controversy, civil courts are not to make the inquiry into religious law and usage that would be essential to the resolution of the controversy. In other words, the use of the Watson approach is consonant with the prohibitions of the First Amendment only if the appropriate church governing body can be determined without the resolution of doctrinal questions and without extensive inquiry into religious polity.[433]

> • The fallacy fatal to the judgment of the Illinois Supreme Court is that it . . . impermissibly substitutes its own inquiry into church polity . . . . To permit civil courts to probe deeply enough into the allocation of power within a hierarchical

---

[430] Watson v. Jones, 80 U.S. 679, 733 (1871) (emphasis added).

[431] Kedroff v. St. Nicholas Cathedral of the Russian Orthodox Church, 344 U.S. 94, 105-106, 116 (1952).

[432] Presbyterian Church in the United States v. Mary Elizabeth Blue Hull Memorial Presbyterian Church, 393 U.S. 440, 449 (1969).

[433] Maryland and Virginia Eldership of the Churches of God v. The Church of God at Sharpsburg, 396 U.S. 367, 369-70 (1970).

church so as to decide religious law governing church polity would violate the First Amendment . . . . For where resolution of disputes cannot be made without extensive inquiry by civil courts into religious law and polity, the First and Fourteenth Amendments mandate that civil courts shall not disturb the decisions of the highest ecclesiastical tribunal within a church of hierarchical polity, but must accept such decisions as binding on them in their application to the religious issues of doctrine of policy before them. . . . In short, the First and Fourteenth Amendments permit hierarchical religious organizations to establish their own rules and regulations for internal discipline and government . . . .[434]

The implication of the above-cited precedent is unequivocal—government action that seeks to manipulate or distort the internal organization and government of a religious denomination violates the constitutional guarantee of free exercise of religion. A civil court is therefore without power to impose a duty of supervision and control upon a congregational association of churches over its affiliated entities contrary to the doctrine, history, and organizational documents of the association in order to redress injuries allegedly caused by the activities of an affiliate. In many cases, a judicial "connectionalizing" of denominational polity would be particularly repugnant since it would present a denomination with the following alternatives: (1) continue to honor its practice of not supervising or interfering with the activities of local churches, even though it will be legally responsible for all such local churches activities; or (2) in fact conform its polity to that of a hierarchical denomination and begin scrutinizing the activities of churches and clergy. Surely no court could be so insensitive to the constitutional guarantee of free exercise of religion or the principle of separation of church and state.

8. "De Novo" Review for Violations of Constitutional Rights

The United States Supreme Court ruled in 1964 that the courts have a duty to "make an independent examination of the whole record" when constitutional rights are at stake, to be sure that there is no "forbidden intrusion" on the field of First Amendment protections.[435] The Court reiterated this principle in a 1984 ruling,[436] in which it observed:

The simple fact is that First Amendment questions of "constitutional fact" compel this Court's de novo review. . . . The requirement of independent appellate review . . . is a rule of federal constitutional law. It emerged from the exigency of deciding concrete cases; it is law in its purest form under our common law heritage. It reflects a deeply held conviction that judges—and particularly members of this Court—must exercise such review in order to preserve the precious liberties established and ordained by the Constitution. . . . Judges, as expositors of the Constitution, must

---

[434] Serbian Eastern Orthodox Diocese v. Milivojevich, 426 U.S. 696, 708-09, 724 (1976).

[435] New York Times v. Sullivan, 376 U.S. 254, 285 (1964).

[436] Bose Corporation v. Consumers Union, 466 U.S. 485, 509-10 (1984).

independently decide whether the evidence in the record is sufficient to cross the constitutional threshold that bars the entry of any judgment that is not supported by clear and convincing proof . . .[437]

This precedent may be more appropriate at the appellate court level. But the implication is clear—courts (presumably even state trial judges) must independently review the record before them and make whatever rulings are required to protect federal constitutional rights. Such rights should not be left to the whim of juries.

9. The "Bar Association" Analogy

In recent years, a number of lawsuits have attempted to hold denominational agencies legally accountable for the acts of ministers that they ordain or license. The argument is that the act of issuing credentials to a minister, and the retention authority to discipline or dismiss a minister for misconduct, constitutes sufficient "control" to make the denomination liable for the minister's actions. In most cases, such efforts will fail. It is true that many denominational agencies ordain or license ministers; require ministerial credentials to be renewed annually; and reserve the authority to discipline or dismiss clergy whose conduct violates specified standards. In some cases, ministers are required or expected to provide annual contributions to the denomination. However, in most cases, the denomination retains no authority to supervise or control the day-to-day activities of ordained or licensed ministers. It may be authorized to discipline or dismiss a minister following an investigation, but ordinarily it has it has no authority to independently monitor or supervise the day-to-day conduct of ministers, and no such authority is ever exercised. It is important to point out that most denominations are "delegated powers" institutions, meaning that they can only exercise those powers that have been delegated to them by their constituent members in their governing documents. If these documents confer no authority to monitor and supervise the day-to-day activities of clergy, the denomination is prohibited from doing so.

The authority of many denominations to license and ordain clergy, require annual renewals of ministerial credentials, and discipline or dismiss clergy found guilty of specified misconduct, is precisely the same authority that is exercised by state professional accrediting organizations such as the bar association. Like such denominational agencies, the bar association has the authority to license attorneys, require annual renewals, and discipline or dismiss attorneys for proven misconduct in violation of professional standards. In addition, many require annual contributions. However, this limited authority does not give the bar association any right to control or supervise the day-to-day activities of attorneys, and it is for this reason that no bar association has ever been sued on account of the malpractice or misconduct of a licensed attorney. State bar associations have never been sued or found liable for the numerous incidents of attorney misconduct and malpractice that occur each year, and religious organizations should be treated no differently.

---

[437] *Id.* at 508 n.27, 510-11.

An identical analogy can be made to any professional licensing organization (*e.g.*, physicians, CPAs, veterinarians, dentists, nurses, morticians), since they all exercise about the same degree of control—they license and retain the right to discipline or dismiss for violations of a professional code of conduct, but they have no authority to supervise the day-to-day activities of licensees.

The civil courts are beginning to recognize this principle. In a leading case, a federal appeals court has recognized the "bar association analogy" directly.[438] The court, in addressing the question of whether Rev. Alford, an Assemblies of God minister, was an employee of the national church ("General Council") and one of its regional agencies ("District Council"), made the following observation:

> The General Council's and District Council's right to control Alford during the relevant years extended primarily to their function in awarding credentials to ministers like himself. Generally, the church has established certain criteria that must be met for an individual such as Alford to obtain credentials initially and to renew that status annually. There are standards for the education a minister must acquire (which he must obtain and pay for himself) and for his performance on certain tests. Other requirements include subscribing to the doctrinal statement of the Assemblies of God, which sets forth the religious beliefs of the church, its ministers, and its members, and to the form of church government. Ordained ministers must preach thirteen times a year, but topics are not decreed by the regional or national organizations. Ministers holding credentials cannot preach in churches other than Assemblies of God churches without permission of the District Council. Ministers may be disciplined for what the church considers failure to follow church doctrine and for lapses in personal conduct, and may, in fact, have their credentials revoked. With some exceptions not relevant here, a minister must tithe to both the regional and national organizations. Attendance at certain meetings is expected, but not required. Thus it is apparent that, while the regional and national churches had doctrinal authority to exercise considerable control over Alford as regards his beliefs and his personal conduct as a minister of the church, they did not have "the right to control the manner and means by which the product [was] accomplished."
>
> The [trial court] and the United States make much of the fact that Alford, as a minister holding credentials, was "amenable" to the General Council and to the District Council in matters of doctrine and conduct. But this is not unusual in such a profession, and actually is merely a shorthand way of describing the parent church's doctrinal and disciplinary control discussed above. The control exercised by the regional and national organizations, and their right to control Alford, was no more nor less than most professions require of individuals licensed or otherwise authorized to work in the profession. State bar associations, for example, have certain education requirements and demand a certain level of performance on a

---

[438] Alford v. Commissioner, 116 F.3d 334 (8th Cir. 1997).

bar examination before an individual can be licensed to practice law. On an annual basis, such associations require the payment of dues and often the completion of continuing legal education in order for an attorney to retain his license. State bar associations are empowered to monitor attorneys' behavior and to discipline them as they see fit, including the revocation of an attorney's license to practice law (disbarment). Yet no one would suggest that, by virtue of this right to control an attorney's working life, the bar association is his employer, or even one of his employers.

Obviously, the importance of this case cannot be overstated. It will effectively refute, in many cases, attempts by plaintiffs to hold denominational agencies accountable for the acts of their ordained and licensed ministers.

Case Studies

• *A Minnesota appeals court applied the bar association analogy in concluding that a regional and national church (the "church defendants") were not liable for the sexual misconduct of a pastor since the relationship between them and credentialed clergy (which resembled the relationship between state bar associations and licensed attorneys) was too attenuated to justify the imposition of liability on the church entities for clergy misconduct. The court concluded that the fact that the church defendants "set certain standards for ministers, and can be involved in disciplinary proceedings, does not automatically mean a true employment relationship exists" that would support the imposition of liability on the church entities for the misconduct of ministers. The court drew an analogy to the relationship between attorneys and the state supreme court. In Minnesota, the supreme court "through the Rules of Professional Conduct, sets forth the rules and standards by which lawyers must adhere. If these rules are violated, the court may discipline the responsible attorney. But this relationship between the supreme court and the disciplined attorney is not an employment relationship. There has to be something more." Similarly, the church defendants in this case had "limited control over the pastor." But, "the congregation, not the umbrella entity, has the responsibility for hiring and firing the pastor, setting forth the terms and conditions of employment, supplying the pastor with parsonage, vacation and supplies, and paying the pastor. [It] is the congregation, not the [church defendants] which employs the minister."[439]*

• *The Alabama Supreme Court compared an attempt to impute legal liability to a denomination as a result of the misconduct of a minister "to situations where a young man may be in a seminary and the seminary is asked to supply a preacher or a minister for a congregation. The fact that the young minister may have some alma mater does not make the seminary responsible for his behavior in the event he elects to commit a burglary or some other act which he might consider to be ordained by divine aegis or providence. It would not in and of itself make the seminary responsible for his behavior."[440]*

---

[439] *C.B. ex rel. L.B. v. Evangelical Lutheran Church in America*, 726 N.W.2d 127 (Minn. App. 2007).

[440] Wood v. Benedictine Society of Alabama, Inc., 530 So.2d 801 (Ala. 1988).

The Bar Association Analogy

In recent years several plaintiffs have attempted to hold denominational agencies liable for the acts of ministers that they ordain or license. The argument is that the act of ordaining or licensing to a minister, and the retention of authority to discipline or dismiss a minister for misconduct, constitutes sufficient "control" to make the denomination liable for the minister's actions.

It is true that many denominational agencies ordain or license ministers; require ministerial credentials to be renewed annually; and reserve the authority to discipline or dismiss ministers whose conduct violates specified standards. In some cases, ministers are required or expected to provide annual contributions to the denomination. However, in most cases, the denomination retains no authority to supervise or control the day-to-day activities of ministers. It may be authorized to discipline or dismiss a minister following an investigation, but ordinarily it has no authority to independently monitor or supervise the day-to-day conduct of ministers, and no such authority is ever exercised.

The authority of many denominations to license and ordain clergy, require annual renewals of ministerial credentials, and discipline or dismiss clergy found guilty of specified misconduct, is precisely the same authority that is exercised by state professional accrediting organizations, such as bar associations. Like denominational agencies, the bar association (or, in some states, the state supreme court) has the authority to license attorneys, require annual renewals, and discipline or dismiss attorneys for violations of professional standards. In addition, many require annual contributions. However, this limited authority does not give the bar association any right to control or supervise the day-to-day activities of attorneys, and it is for this reason that no bar association has ever been sued on account of a licensed attorney's malpractice, much less been found liable, and religious organizations should be treated no differently.

An identical analogy can be made to any professional licensing organization (e.g., physicians, CPAs, veterinarians, dentists, nurses, morticians), since they all exercise about the same degree of control—they issue licenses and retain the right to discipline or dismiss licensees for violations of a professional code of conduct, but they have no authority to supervise licensees' day-to-day activities.

Obviously, the importance of this case cannot be overstated. It will effectively refute, in many cases, attempts by plaintiffs to hold denominational agencies accountable for the acts of their ordained and licensed ministers.

Key point. *Any regional or national church that issues ministerial credentials, and that disciplines ministers who violate a code of conduct, can use the bar association analogy. It is a powerful and compelling argument. The bottom line is this—no bar association has ever been sued, much less found liable, for the malpractice of an attorney; why should religious organizations be treated differently? The First Amendment would be a bar to any such disparate treatment.*

10. The Single Employer Doctrine

Some courts have applied the "single employer" theory to impute liability to a parent organization for the acts and liabilities of a subsidiary. One of the first courts to recognize this theory noted that "superficially distinct entities may be exposed to liability upon a finding they represent a single, integrated enterprise: a single employer."[441] The court gave the following definition, which has since been applied by many other courts:

> Factors considered in determining whether distinct entities constitute an integrated enterprise are (1) interrelation of operations, (2) centralized control of labor relations, (3) common management, and (4) common ownership or financial control.

One court noted that "a finding that the corporations are a single employer requires evidence of control suggesting a significant departure from the ordinary relationship between a parent and its subsidiary—domination similar to that which justifies piercing the corporate veil. Plaintiff only makes a conclusory statement that the evidence presented in the [exhibits] establishes material and genuine issues of fact. That fails to meet the requirement to identify specific evidence in the record and to articulate the precise manner in which that evidence supports his or her claim."[442] The court then addressed each of the four factors mentioned in the Trevino test (see above), and provided helpful clarification:

> With respect to the first factor, interrelation of operations, the court notes that [the parent and affiliate] had separate offices and employees. [The parent] was headquartered in Atlanta, Georgia while [the affiliate] was based in Fort Worth, Texas. . . . The court found no indication that operations were more interrelated than is normal for a parent and subsidiary. The first factor therefore provides no support for a finding that [the parent and affiliate] were a single employer.
>
> The second factor concerns centralized control of labor relations, and particularly the parent's involvement in the employment decision that gives rise to the cause of action. Plaintiff makes a conclusory allegation that [the parent] "was a final decisionmaker in the daily employment decisions of [the affiliate] but supports this only with a generic reference to the summary judgment record as a whole. By contrast [the parent company] provides an affidavit that asserts that it "did not involve itself in the day-to-day employment practices or decisions" of [the affiliate] including reviewing applications for employment, hiring/termination decisions, and performance evaluations. Further, the summary judgment record does not show any involvement by [the parent company] in terminating plaintiff—the key employment decision in this action. . . . The second factor therefore provides strong evidence that [the parent and affiliate] were not a "single employer."

---

[441] Trevino v. Celanese Corp., 701 F.2d 397 (5th Cir. 1983).

[442] Kirshner v. First Data Corporation, 2000 WL 1772759 (N.D. Tex. 2000).

The third factor, common management, also provides no support for plaintiff's position. . . . The fact that officers of a subsidiary eventually report, through several intermediate steps in the chain of command, to an officer of the parent is the corporate norm, rather than "a significant departure from the ordinary relationship between a parent and its subsidiary." Further [the parent company] provides evidence that [it and its affiliate] have never had common directors and had only one officer in common (out of thirteen) at the time of the events that gave rise to this action. This level of "common management" is certainly no more than "the ordinary relationship between a parent and its subsidiary," and quite likely less. The third factor does not help establish plaintiff's theory that [the parent company and its affiliate] were a "single employer."

The last factor to be considered is common ownership or financial control. Because [the affiliate] was a wholly-owned subsidiary of [the parent company] this factor supports plaintiff's contention. Common ownership or financial control, however, is insufficient by itself to support a finding that two corporations constitute a single employer.

Only one court has applied the "single employer" concept to religious organizations.[443] The case involved a disability discrimination complaint brought against a church and its affiliated private school by a woman who claimed that she was not hired as a music director because of her disability. The issue was whether enough employees (15) existed to trigger application of the Americans with Disabilities Act. The church and school each had fewer than 15 employees, but the EEOC claimed that the two entities, and a church-operated preschool, should be treated as a "single entity" for purposes of counting employees and assessing liability.

In deciding whether or not the church, school, and preschool were a "single, integrated enterprise," a federal district court applied a four-part test announced by the Supreme Court in a 1965 ruling.[444] This test focuses on the following four factors: (1) interrelation of operations; (2) common management; (3) centralized control of labor relations; and (4) common ownership or financial control. This is virtually identical to the four factors applied by the federal appeals court in the Trevino case (see above). The court clarified that "the absence or presence of any single factor is not conclusive," and that "control over the elements of labor relations is a central concern." The court cautioned that a plaintiff "must make a substantial showing to warrant a finding of single employer status," and that "there must be sufficient indicia of an interrelationship between the immediate corporate employer and the affiliated corporation to justify the belief on the part of an aggrieved employee that the affiliated corporation is jointly responsible for the acts of the immediate employer." The court referred to an earlier federal appeals court case finding that the entities must be "highly integrated with respect

---

[443] Equal Employment Opportunity Commission v. St. Francis Xavier Parochial School, 117 F.3d 621 (D.C. Cir. 1997).

[444] Radio Union v. Broadcast Services, 380 U.S. 255 (1965).

to ownership and operations" in order for single employer status to be found.

The district court concluded that the three entities should not be treated as single employer or entity because they were not sufficiently interrelated. The case was appealed, and a federal appeals court reversed the district court's ruling on the ground that there was insufficient evidence to support the trial court's conclusion that the church, school, and preschool should not be treated as a single employer in applying the 15 employee requirement. Of most significance to the appeals court was the fact that the record did not reveal whether or not the church, school, and preschool were one corporate legal entity, or three separate entities.

The appeals court acknowledged that no other court has ever addressed the application of the Supreme Court's 4 factor test to religious organizations:

> The cases in which we have applied the [4 factor test] have all involved business corporations. We have found no cases in this circuit or elsewhere applying the test to a religious corporation. Because a religious corporation can possess unique attributes . . . it may be the case that even where there are multiple religious entities, aggregation (or non-aggregation) of employees in employment discrimination cases should not be resolved under [this test]. Although we express no opinion on the question, we note that the question to be answered by the [trial] court on remand may be [the first time any court has addressed this question].

This case is important for two reasons. First, the court noted that no other case has applied the Supreme Court's four factor test of single entity status to religious organizations. This test is essentially identical to the Trevino test described above. Second, the court suggested that applying the single entity concept to religious organizations may implicate constitutional concerns.

11. Joint and Several Liability

One of the most unfair aspects of our legal system is the principle of "joint and several liability." Under this principle, which is recognized by most states, any defendant in a lawsuit may be liable for the entire amount of a plaintiff's damages regardless of the degree of fault. This principle often is directed at churches and denominational agencies. To illustrate, assume that Bob drives a church van to a church activity and that several members of the youth group join him. Assume further that Bob's negligent driving results in an accident in which several persons are injured. A lawsuit is filed naming Bob, his church, and a parent denomination as defendants. A jury determines that Bob was 98 percent at fault, and the church and denomination each 1 percent at fault. The jury awards a total of $1 million to the victims. If Bob has no money to pay such an award, the church and the denomination are each individually (or jointly) liable for the entire $1 million judgment even though their respective degree of fault was only 1 percent each. This system is unfair, since legal liability is assigned solely on the basis of the ability to pay without regard to the degree of fault.

The morally inappropriate basis for the rule of joint and several liability has been recognized by several courts. To illustrate, the Kansas Supreme Court observed:

> There is nothing inherently fair about a defendant who is 10 percent at fault paying 100 percent of the loss, and there is no social policy that should compel defendants to pay more than their fair share of the loss. Plaintiffs now take the parties as they find them. If one of the parties at fault happens to be a spouse or a governmental agency and if by reason of some competing social policy the plaintiff cannot receive payment for his injuries from the spouse or agency, there is no compelling social policy which requires the codefendant to pay more than his fair are of the loss. The same is true if one of the defendants is wealthy and the other is not.[445]

The good news is that several states have limited the principle of joint and several liability. In fact, most states have either eliminated joint and several liability, or have limited it significantly.[446]

12. Policy Reasons for Limiting Vicarious Liability of Nonprofit Defendants

As discussed earlier in this chapter,[447] the policy considerations supporting vicarious liability (under both respondeat superior and agency) rest upon the fundamental principle of risk allocation. That is, a principal or employer has the unique ability to allocate the risks of inevitable injuries suffered by the consumers of its products and services through price adjustments. By increasing its prices, the employer allocates the risk of injuries to the consumers of its products and services. As reasonable as this policy may be in the context of "for-profit" employers, it has no application whatever to most nonprofit employers who have no ability to allocate risk to consumers through price increases. Certainly this is true of religious organizations, which obviously cannot "adjust their prices" to allocate risks to the "consumers" of their products or services. Further, as mentioned earlier in this chapter, religious organizations cannot effectively allocate risks through obtaining liability insurance, since such insurance is increasingly difficult for religious organizations to afford or obtain, and many risks are excluded from coverage or have limited coverage.

Risk Management §10-18.4

Key point 10-18.4. *Denominational agencies can reduce the risk of liability for the acts and obligations of affiliated churches, agencies, clergy, and lay workers by adopting risk management policies and procedures.*

---

[445] Brown v. Keill, 580 P.2d 867 (Kan. 1978).

[446] Many states abolish joint and several liability for defendants whose fault is less than a specified percentage, or permit joint and several liability only up to a specified amount.

[447] *See* § 10-02.4, *supra.*

There are many ways for denominational agencies to reduce the risk of legal liability. Many of these are the same risk management strategies that may be employed by local churches, and they are addressed in previous sections of this chapter. Other risk management strategies are suggested in the previous subsection in which legal defenses available to denominational agencies are reviewed.

There are some risk management strategies that are unique to denominational agencies. Consider the following:

1. The Discipline of Ministers

Many denominational agencies ordain or license ministers, and reserve the authority to discipline ministers for violations of prescribed standards. Deciding whether or not to discipline ministers, and restore them to pastoral ministry, can be difficult questions because imprudent decisions may expose a denominational agency to liability for future misdeeds. Here are some factors that denominational agencies should consider in deciding whether or not to restore a disciplined minister to pastoral ministry:

- **Type of misconduct.** The type of misconduct is an important consideration. Some kinds of misconduct are more severe than others.

- **Duration of misconduct.** The duration of a minister's misconduct is a relevant consideration. The longer the duration, the less likely rehabilitation will be effective.

- **Number of incidents.** The more separate incidents of misconduct, the less likely rehabilitation will be effective.

- **Number of victims.** The more victims, the less likely rehabilitation will be effective.

- **Subsequent misconduct.** Denominational leaders must recognize that the risk of liability increases significantly when a denomination disciplines and restores to pastoral ministry a minister who was previously disciplined for the same kind of misconduct.

- **How the misconduct was discovered.** Did the minister come forward and confess voluntarily? Or was the confession prompted by some external inducement, such as an awareness that the misconduct was about to be revealed.

- **When the incident occurred.** In some cases, the misconduct occurred many years ago and has not recurred. This is a relevant, but not conclusive, factor to consider.

- **Restitution.** If there is a "victim" to the minister's misconduct, has the minister apologized to the victim and made appropriate restitution?

- **Criminal nature of misconduct.** A decision to rehabilitate an employee should take into account the potential for criminal prosecution.

• **The strength of the evidence.** In some cases the evidence of misconduct is not conclusive. In general, the legal risk associated with rehabilitating or reinstating a minister increases if the evidence of guilt is weak and conflicting.

• **A counselor's opinion.** In some cases, denominational agencies have conditioned the discipline of ministers on the receipt of an opinion by a licensed psychologist or counselor that the minister no longer poses a risk of repeating the same kind of misconduct.

• **Limited disclosure agreement.** A number of courts have stated that denominational agencies can avoid legal liability for a disciplined minister's repeat misconduct by disclosing to local churches the minister's prior behavior at the time he or she is employed. To illustrate, one court ruled that a denominational agency was legally responsible for a pastor's sexual misconduct since it was aware of a previous incident and failed to communicate this knowledge to the pastor's employing church.[448] It concluded that "[t]he failure to communicate this knowledge to the [church board] and subsequent placement of [the pastor] in the role of counselor breached the diocese's duty of care to [the victim]." Of course, disclosing information regarding a minister's previous discipline to a local church may expose a denominational agency to liability. This risk can be reduced by having disciplined ministers, as a condition of discipline, sign a "limited disclosure agreement" authorizing designated denominational officials to share with local church boards and pastoral search committees the nature and basis of the disciplined minister's prior discipline. Such an agreement enables a local church to make an informed judgment on whether or not to call a pastor who has completed a rehabilitation program. Lay leaders in a local church are justifiably upset when their minister engages in inappropriate behavior and they later discover that a denominational agency failed to inform them that the minister had committed similar behavior at a previous church. There is no doubt that rehabilitated ministers will have a much more difficult if not impossible time finding employment if churches are advised of the nature of prior discipline. This is one unfortunate consequence of a minister's misconduct. But denominational agencies are under no duty to "protect" a minister's employability by concealing relevant information from local churches. The question is whether a denominational agency should protect a rehabilitated minister's future employment prospects by concealing from prospective churches his or her past, or reduce its own risk of liability through full disclosure.

2. Accepting Ministers from other Organizations

Denominational leaders must scrutinize carefully any applicant for ministry that comes from another denomination. In some cases, ministers who are disciplined or dismissed in one denomination apply for ministry in another denomination. If such a minister later engages in the same type of misconduct for which he or she was previously disciplined or dismissed, the new denomination may be legally responsible for such misconduct on the basis of negligent selection.

---

[448] Moses v. Diocese of Colorado, 863 P.2d 310 (Colo. 1993).

The Legal Effect of a Group Exemption Ruling

§ 10-18.5

Key point 10-19.5. *The tax code permits denominational agencies to obtain a "group exemption" for affiliated churches and organizations that establishes their exemption from federal income tax. While such rulings require the denominational agency to exercise "control" over its affiliates, the IRS and the courts have concluded that this "control" is ecclesiastical in nature and as a result a group exemption ruling does not make a denominational agency liable for the obligations of its affiliates.*

Recognition of exemption from federal income tax under section 501(c)(3) of the Internal Revenue Code may be obtained on a group basis for "subordinate organizations" affiliated with and under the supervision or control of a "central organization."[449] This procedure relieves each of the subordinates covered by a group exemption letter of the necessity of filing its own application for recognition of exemption. To be eligible for a group exemption ruling, a central organization must obtain recognition of its own exempt status. It must also submit to the IRS information on behalf of those subordinates to be included in the group exemption letter. The required actions are summarized in Table 10-10.

Table 10-10	Group Exemption Requirements
require-ment	action
1	"central organization . . . must establish that the subordinates to be included in the group exemption letter are affiliated with it . . . ."
2	"central organization . . . must establish that the subordinates to be included in the group exemption letter are . . . subject to its general supervision or control . . . ."
3	"central organization . . . must establish that the subordinates to be included in the group exemption letter are . . . all exempt under the same paragraph of section 501(c) of the Code . . . ."
4	"central organization . . . must establish that the subordinates to be included in the group exemption letter are . . . not private foundations . . . ."
5	"central organization . . . must establish that the subordinates to be included in the group exemption letter are . . . all on the same accounting period . . . ."
6	"each subordinate must authorize the central organization to include it in the application for the group exemption letter"
7	the application for a group exemption must include "a sample copy of a uniform governing instrument (charter, trust indenture, articles of association, etc.) adopted by the subordinates . . . ."

[449] Rev. Proc. 80-27, 1980-1 C.B. 677.

Table 10-10 Group Exemption Requirements

require-ment	action
8	the application for a group exemption must include "a detailed description of the purposes and activities of the subordinates . . . ."
9	the application for a group exemption must include "an affirmation that . . . the purposes and activities of the subordinates are as set forth" in #8 and #9
10	the application for a group exemption must include "a list of subordinates to be included in the group exemption letter . . . ."
11	the application for a group exemption must include "the information required by Revenue Procedure 75-50" (pertaining to racially nondiscriminatory policies of schools)
12	the application for a group exemption must include "a list of the . . . employer identification numbers of subordinates to be included in the group exemption letter . . . ."
13	"The central organization must submit with the exemption application a completed Form SS-4 on behalf of each subordinate not having" an employer identification number
14	each year the central organization must provide the IRS with lists of "(a) subordinates that have changed their names or addresses during the year, (b) subordinates no longer to be included in the group exemption letter because they have ceased to exist, disaffiliated, or withdrawn their authorization to the central organization, and (c) subordinates to be added to the group exemption letter . . . ."

The group exemption procedure technically is available only to "connectional," or hierarchical, church organizations consisting of a "central organization" that exerts "general supervision or control" over "subordinate" local churches and church agencies. There are many conventions and associations of churches, however, that exert little if any "general supervision or control" over "subordinate" churches. Up until now, these "congregational" conventions and associations of churches have had to construe the group exemption requirements very loosely in order to obtain the benefits of a group exemption. Many have done so. A potential problem with such an approach is that the association or convention of churches itself may increase its potential liability for the misconduct and improprieties of affiliated churches and clergy, since in pursuing the group exemption the association or convention must affirm that it does in fact exercise "general supervision or control" over its affiliates. Such an affirmation could serve as a possible basis of legal liability.

Any attempt to use a group exemption ruling as evidence of denominational liability for the obligations of affiliated churches faces formidable obstacles, including the following:

1. **No court has recognized such a basis of liability**. No court in the history of this country has found a denominational agency liable on the basis of a group exemption ruling.

2. **One court has rejected this basis of liability**. There has been only one reported case in which a group exemption ruling was cited as evidence in support of an ascending liability claim.[450] A federal appeals court upheld a district court's summary judgment in favor of the national Assemblies of God church (the "General Council of the Assemblies of God") in a case claiming that the national church was legally responsible for the alleged securities fraud of an affiliated church.

3. **The IRS Tax Guide for Churches and "ecclesiastical" control.** In 1994 the IRS issued a "Tax Guide For Churches." The Tax Guide clarifies that "a church or other organization with a parent organization may wish to contact the parent to see if the parent has a group exemption letter." The Tax Guide further explains:

An organization has a parent if, for example, another organization manages, financially or ecclesiastically, the first organization. If the parent holds a group exemption letter, then the organization seeking exemption may already be recognized as exempt by the IRS. Under the group exemption process, one organization, the parent organization, becomes the holder of a group exemption ruling naming other affiliated churches as included within the ruling. Under these rules, a church is recognized as exempt if it is included in the annual update of the parent organization. If the church is included on such a list, it need take no further action in order to obtain such recognition.

This language is significant, since the IRS concedes that the "control" that is needed to qualify for a group exemption may be *ecclesiastical*. Certainly, it could be said that many national and regional denominational agencies exercise some degree of "ecclesiastical" control over affiliated churches. But this kind of control certainly cannot support legal liability. Unfortunately, this language was dropped from subsequent editions of the Guide. However, the language in the original edition is still useful.

4. **IRS bias in favor of hierarchical churches.** "Congregational" associations and conventions of churches are forced to interpret the "control" language loosely because of the discrimination by the IRS against such organizations in favor of connectional, or hierarchical, church organizations. The current group exemption procedure, granting favored status only to connectional church organizations, is suspect under the Supreme Court's interpretation of the First Amendment's nonestablishment of religion clause. In 1982, the Court invalidated

---

[450] Kersh v. The General Council of the Assemblies of God, 804 F.2d 546 (9th Cir. 1986).

a Minnesota law that imposed certain registration and reporting requirements upon religious organizations soliciting more than 50 percent of their funds from nonmembers.[451] The Court observed that "when we are presented with a state law granting a denominational preference, our precedents demand that we treat the law as suspect and that we apply strict scrutiny in adjudging its constitutionality." The Court concluded that any law granting a denominational preference must be "invalidated unless it is justified by a compelling governmental interest, and unless it is closely fitted to further that interest."

Similarly, a federal appeals court, in construing section 6033 of the Internal Revenue Code, observed: "If 'church' were construed as meaning only hierarchical churches such as the Catholic Church—[this] would result in an unconstitutional construction of the statute [IRC 6033] because favorable tax treatment would be accorded to hierarchical churches while being denied to congregational churches, in violation of the First Amendment."[452]

There is no conceivable governmental interest that would justify the government's stated preference for connectional church organizations in the present group exemption procedure.

5. **Noncompliance with the group exemption requirements.** Many denominational agencies that have obtained group exemptions have not fully complied with the requirements summarized in Table 10-10. Some do not even meet a majority of them. Obviously, these "requirements" do not mean much. As a result, little if anything can be made of the "general supervision or control" language.

Table 10-11 Liability of Denominational Agencies for the Sexual Misconduct of Affiliated Clergy and Lay Workers— A State-By-State Review of Selected Cases

STATE	SUMMARY
Alabama	no directly relevant precedent in recent years
Alaska	no directly relevant precedent in recent years
Arizona	no directly relevant precedent in recent years
Arkansas	no directly relevant precedent in recent years
California	• A religious denomination was not responsible for the sexual molestation of a 13-year-old boy by his pastor, or for the boy's subsequent molestation of his 6-year-old sister. *Evan F. v. Hughson United Methodist Church, 10 Cal. Rptr.2d 748 (Cal. App. 1992).* • An archdiocese could be sued on the basis of negligence and breach of fiduciary duty for a priest's sexual acts. *Richelle L. v. Roman Catholic Archbishop, 130 Cal.Rptr.2d 601 (Cal. App. 2003).*

[451] Larson v. Valente, 410 U.S. 437 (1982).

[452] Lutheran Social Service of Minnesota v. United States, 758 F.2d 1283 (8th Cir. 1985).

Table 10-11 Liability of Denominational Agencies for the Sexual Misconduct of Affiliated Clergy and Lay Workers— A State-By-State Review of Selected Cases

STATE	SUMMARY
Colorado	• A denominational agency could be sued on the basis of negligent supervision for the sexual misconduct of a minister if it had reason to know that the minister was likely to harm others. *Destefano v. Grabian, 763 P.2d 275 (Colo. 1988)*. • The state supreme court found a diocese and bishop legally responsible for a pastor's sexual misconduct with a female parishioner. *Moses v. Diocese of Colorado, 863 P.2d 310 (Colo. 1993)*. • A denominational agency was not liable on the basis of negligence for a minister's acts of sexual harassment. *Van Osdol v. Vogt, 892 P.2d 402 (Colo. App. 1994)*. • A denominational agency could be sued on the basis of negligent hiring and supervision, and a breach of a fiduciary duty, as a result of a pastor's sexual relationship with a member of his congregation. *Winkler v. Rocky Mountain Conference of United Methodist Church, 923 P.2d 152 (Colo. App. 1995)*. • A denominational agency was liable on the basis of negligent hiring and negligent supervision for a pastor's sexual molestation of a minor. *Bohrer v. DeHart, 943 P.2d 1220 (Colo. App. 1997)*.
Connecticut	• A church and diocese were not responsible on the basis of respondeat superior or negligence for the sexual misconduct of a pastor. The court cautioned that churches and denominational agencies are potentially liable on the basis of negligence for injuries sustained by victims of sexual molestation if they have knowledge of prior sexual misconduct by the molester. However, since the victims could not prove that church officials either knew or should have known of any previous sexual misconduct by the offending priest, the negligence claims had to be dismissed. The court ruled that the First Amendment guaranty of religious freedom does not necessarily protect a church or denominational agency from liability in a lawsuit based on negligent hiring, retention, or supervision if the victim's claims do not implicate issues of ecclesiastical concern. *Nutt v. Norwich Roman Catholic Diocese, 921 F. Supp. 66 (D. Conn. 1995)*. • A federal court in Connecticut ruled that the statute of limitations did not necessarily prevent an adult from suing a diocese for injuries he allegedly suffered as a minor when he was molested by a priest. The court noted that the statute can be suspended if a defendant "fraudulently conceals" the existence of a cause of action, and the diocese may have done so by breaching a "fiduciary duty" to warn potential victims of the priest's dangerous propensities. *Martinelli v. Bridgeport Roman Catholic Diocese, 989 F. Supp. 110 (D. Conn. 1997)*. • A Connecticut court ruled that a religious order could not be sued on the basis of respondeat superior for the sexual misconduct of a priest. *Mullen v. Horton, 700 A.2d 1377 (Conn. App. 1997)*. • A diocese was not liable on the basis of ratification for a priest's molestation of minors. *Beach v. Jean, 746 A.2d 228 (Conn. App. 1999)*. • A denominational agency was not liable on the basis of negligent supervision for a priest's sexual misconduct. *Ahern v. Kappalumakkel, 903 A.2d 266 (Conn. App. 2006)*. • A diocese was not liable on the basis of respondeat superior for the sexual misconduct of a priest. *Doe v. Norwich Roman Catholic Diocese, 909 A.2d 983 (Conn. App. 2006)*.
Delaware	no directly relevant precedent in recent years
Dist. Col.	• A court in the District of Columbia ruled that three adults were barred by the statute of limitations from suing an archdiocese for injuries they suffered as a result of being molested by a priest when they were minors. *Cevenini v. Archbishop of Washington, 707 A.2d 768 (D.C. 1998)*.
Florida	• The First Amendment did not prevent the civil courts from resolving negligent hiring and supervision claims against a denominational agency by a victim of sexual misconduct. *Doe v. Evans, 814 So.2d 370 (Fla. 2002); Jane Doe I v. Malicki, 771 So.2d 545 (Fla. App. 2000)*. • A denominational agency could be liable, based on negligent supervision but not emotional distress or breach of a fiduciary duty, for the sexual misconduct of a pastor. *Elders v. United Methodist Church ex rel. Florida Conference, 793 So.2d 1038 (Fla. App. 2001)*.

Table 10-11 Liability of Denominational Agencies for the Sexual Misconduct of Affiliated Clergy and Lay Workers— A State-By-State Review of Selected Cases

STATE	SUMMARY
Georgia	• A court dismissed a negligent hiring claim against a denominational agency as a result of a sexual relationship that a pastor initiated with a woman during marital counseling. The court noted that the plaintiff "points to nothing in the record showing that during the hiring process either [the local church or denominational agency] became aware of anything in the pastor's background indicating he was unsuited for employment as a minister or which put them on notice that further investigation was warranted." *Poole v. North Georgia Conference of Methodist Church, Inc., 615 S.E.2d 604 (Ga. App. 2005).*
Hawaii	no directly relevant precedent in recent years
Idaho	no directly relevant precedent in recent years
Illinois	• A federal appeals court ruled that a denominational agency was not responsible for the alleged seduction of a female parishioner by a Catholic priest. *Doe v. Cunningham, 30 F.3d 879 (7th Cir. 1994).*
	• A federal appeals court ruled that a church and denominational agency were not legally responsible for a pastoral counselor's sexual contacts with a female counselee. The court stressed that the woman's lawsuit failed "to adequately allege that the church defendants knew or should have known of the improper counseling conduct of [the pastor]." The court also ruled that the church defendants were not liable on the basis of negligent supervision since the lawsuit was "devoid of any allegation that the church defendants were aware or had any knowledge that [the pastor] made improper sexual advances either before or during the time in question." *Dausch v. Rykse, 52 F.3d 1425 (7th Cir. 1994).*
	• An Illinois court ruled that evidence regarding a priest's prior acts of sexual misconduct were not relevant and therefore were not admissible in proving that the priest molested a young boy. The court pointed out that evidence of prior "bad acts" is generally not admissible to prove that a person committed a particular offense—unless the prior bad acts "show a method of behavior that is so distinct that separate wrongful acts are recognized to be the handiwork of the same person." This test was not met in this case. *Doe v. Lutz, 668 N.E.2d 564 (Ill. App. 1996).*
	• An Illinois court ruled that a husband whose wife was seduced by her pastor could not sue the pastor or denominational agencies for malpractice or breach of a fiduciary duty. *Amato v. Greenquist, 679 N.E.2d 446 (Ill. App. 1997).*
	• The First Amendment did not prevent adults from suing a denominational agency for injuries they suffered as a result of having been sexually molested by a priest when they were minors. *Softcheck v. Imesch, 855 N.E.2d 941 (Ill. App. 2006).*

Table 10-11 Liability of Denominational Agencies for the Sexual Misconduct of Affiliated Clergy and Lay Workers— A State-By-State Review of Selected Cases

STATE	SUMMARY
Indiana	• A federal appeals court ruled that a denominational agency was not responsible for the alleged seduction of a female parishioner by a Catholic priest. *Doe v. Cunningham, 30 F.3d 879 (7th Cir. 1994).* • A federal appeals court ruled that a church and denominational agency were not legally responsible for a pastoral counselor's sexual contacts with a female counselee. The court stressed that the woman's lawsuit failed "to adequately allege that the church defendants knew or should have known of the improper counseling conduct of [the pastor]." The court also ruled that the church defendants were not liable on the basis of negligent supervision since the lawsuit was "devoid of any allegation that the church defendants were aware or had any knowledge that [the pastor] made improper sexual advances either before or during the time in question." *Dausch v. Rykse, 52 F.3d 1425 (7th Cir. 1994).* • The First Amendment does not prevent a woman from suing her church and a denominational agency on account of injuries she suffered as a result of being molested by her pastor when she was a minor. The court concluded that neither the church nor the regional or national denominational agency could be sued on the basis of negligent selection of the pastor. The court ruled that the national church was not liable on the basis of negligent supervision or retention for the actions of the pastor. It observed, "The [national church], which is only affiliated with the local church and [regional agency] through its constitution and judicial procedures, was not informed. The evidence . . . does not indicate that [the woman] invoked the judicial procedures, which is the only mechanism by which the [national church] could have taken action against [the pastor]. . . . [The woman] has not alleged . . . that she or anyone else ever filed a complaint against [the pastor] with the [regional agency]. Therefore, the [national church] could not have disciplined [the pastor]." The court concluded that there was evidence that the local church and a regional denominational agency were aware of the pastor's actions, and therefore they could be sued for negligent supervision and retention. *Konkle v. Henson, 672 N.E.2d 450 (Ind. App. 1996).*
Iowa	• A federal court in Iowa ruled that a woman who had been seduced by a priest could not sue her church and diocese for violating the federal Violence Against Women Act. *Doe v. Hartz, 134 F.3d 1339 (8th Cir. 1998).* • A denominational agency was not liable on the basis of negligence or respondeat superior for the sexual misconduct of a priest. *Walderbach v. Archdiocese of Dubuque, Inc., 730 N.W.2d 198 (Iowa 2007).*
Kansas	no directly relevant precedent in recent years
Kentucky	• A state appeals court ruled that an adult was barred by the statute of limitations from suing a priest and his church on account of the priest's alleged acts of molestation. The court acknowledged that Kentucky has adopted a "discovery rule" in the context of medical malpractice, but "[n]either the Supreme Court nor the General Assembly has further extended the discovery rule." Further, the court observed, "It should again be noted that at the time [the victim's] cause of action accrued, and for sometime thereafter, he was both aware of the abuse and past the age of reason." *Rigazio v. Archdiocese of Louisville, 1993 WL 153206 (Ky. App. 1993) (unpublished opinion).* • A Kentucky court ruled that an adult who had been sexually molested as a minor by a teacher at a parochial school could sue the diocese that operated the school for negligent hiring, supervision, and retention. In extending the applicable statute of limitations, the court observed, "The diocese clearly obstructed the prosecution of [the victim's] cause of action against it by continually concealing the fact that it had knowledge of [the teacher's] problem well before the time [the victim] was abused as well as the fact that it continued to receive reports of sexual abuse of other students during part of the time period in which [the victim] was abused. Furthermore, where the law imposes a duty of disclosure, a failure of disclosure may constitute concealment . . . ." The child abuse reporting statute in effect when these incidents occurred imposed a legal duty on "any person" to report child abuse to law enforcement authorities. The diocese failed to comply with this duty, "and such failure constitutes evidence of concealment." The court rejected the claim of the diocese that the jury erred in awarding $700,000 in punitive damages against it. *Roman Catholic Diocese v. Secter, 966 S.W.2d 286 (Ky. App. 1998).* • A denominational agency was not liable on the basis of respondeat superior for the sexual misconduct of a minister. *Osborne v. Payne, 31 S.W.3d 911 (Ky. 2000).* • A denominational agency was not liable on the basis of negligence for the molestation of a minor by a missionary. *Olinger v. Corporation of the President, 521 F.Supp.2d 577 (E.D. Ky. 2007).*

Table 10-11 Liability of Denominational Agencies for the Sexual Misconduct of Affiliated Clergy and Lay Workers— A State-By-State Review of Selected Cases

STATE	SUMMARY
Louisiana	• A Louisiana appeals court reversed a trial judge's decision that a church and religious denomination were legally responsible for the sexual assaults committed by a volunteer youth worker. The court ruled that the church defendants were not responsible for the offender's actions since a "master-servant" relationship did not exist between him and the church defendants. *Doe v. Roman Catholic Church, 602 A.2d 129 (La. App. 4 Cir. 1992); Doe v. Roman Catholic Church, 615 So.2d 410 (La. App. 1993).*
	• A federal appeals court ruled that an archdiocese was not responsible for the alleged molestation of a minor by a priest. The court observed: (1) "The record, however, permits of no conclusion that the [archdiocese] suspected that [the priest] had engaged in sexual improprieties or might do so in the future. It is doubtful that the archdiocese . . . knew anything about [his] darker side." (2) "Employers do not have a duty to supervise their employees when the employees are off-duty or not working. Employers also are not liable for failure to supervise when the employee engages in independent criminal conduct which results in the plaintiff's injuries. Moreover, an employer's duty to supervise does not include a duty to uncover his employees' concealed, clandestine, personal activities." *Tichenor v. Roman Catholic Church, 32 F.3d 953 (5th Cir. 1994).*
	• A state appeals court ruled that a diocese was not legally responsible for the suicide of a woman allegedly caused by a sexual relationship with a priest. The court observed, "What it comes down to is that the secular state is not equipped to ascertain the competency of counseling when performed by those affiliated with religious organizations." And, since the priest could not maintain a lawsuit against the priest, "there can be no claim against the Episcopal Diocese based on any theory of responsibility for [the priest's] actions." The court also rejected any liability based on negligent selection, since such a basis of liability when applied to a religious organization would violate the First Amendment. *Roppolo v. Moore, 644 So.2d 206 (La. App. 4 Cir. 1994).*
	• A state appeals court ruled that the statute of limitations prevented an adult woman from suing a Catholic diocese for a priest's acts of molestation when the woman was a minor. *Doe v. Roman Catholic Church, 656 So.2d 5 (La. App. 3 Cir. 1995).*
	• A Louisiana court ruled that a 32-year-old adult's lawsuit against a diocese and a priest who molested him when he was a minor was barred by the statute of limitations. *J.A.G. v. Schmaltz, 682 So.2d 331 (La. App. 1996).*
Maine	• The Maine Supreme Court ruled that the First Amendment prevented a couple from suing their church as a result of a priest's sexual relationship with the wife. The court observed that it had never recognized "negligent supervision" as a basis for liability, and that even if it did, the First Amendment barred its application to the church in this case. The court also rejected denominational liability on the basis of agency. *Swanson v. Roman Catholic Bishop, 692 A.2d 441 (Maine 1997).*
	• A diocese could be liable on the basis of a breach of fiduciary duty for the sexual misconduct of a priest. *Fortin v. Roman Catholic Bishop, 871 A.2d 1208 (Me. 2005).*
Maryland	• A Maryland court ruled that a 34-year-old adult's lawsuit against a diocese and two priests who molested him when he was a minor was barred by the statute of limitations. *Doe v. Archdiocese of Washington, 689 A.2d 634 (Md. App. 1997).*
Mass.	• A Massachusetts court ruled that a diocese probably was not liable for the sexual molestation of a child by a priest more than twenty years ago. The court noted that "the only shred of evidence" that the diocese had notice of the priest's pedophiliac propensities before the time of the victim's molestation was a response to a question in a 1963 confidential investigation of the priest. The question asked, "has he conducted himself with persons of the other sex in such a way as to cause scandal, criticism or suspicion?" The answer to this question was "yes." The court concluded that "it is doubtful that the questionnaire's answer to this question alone would be sufficient to permit a jury to reasonably infer that the diocese had notice in regard to possible molestation of a young female child prior to the incidents alleged in this case." *Yerrick v. Kelley, 1998 WL 374941 (Mass. Super. 1998).*

Table 10-11 Liability of Denominational Agencies for the Sexual Misconduct of Affiliated Clergy and Lay Workers— A State-By-State Review of Selected Cases

STATE	SUMMARY
Michigan	• A federal district court ruled that a seminary and denominational agency were not liable on the basis of negligent hiring, supervision, or retention for the sexual molestation of a seminarian by a priest. The court observed, (1) "Questions of hiring and retention of clergy necessarily will require interpretation of church canons, and internal church policies and practices. It is well-settled that when a court is required to interpret canon law or internal church policies and practices, the First Amendment is violated because such judicial inquiry would constitute excessive government entanglement with religion. . . . [An] inquiry into the decision of who should be permitted to become or remain a priest necessarily would involve prohibited excessive entanglement with religion. Therefore [the victim's] claims of negligence predicated upon a negligent hiring theory will be dismissed." (2) Few states have recognized "negligent supervision" as a basis of liability. *Isely v. Capuchin Province, 880 F. Supp. 1138 (E.D. Mich. 1995).* • A denominational agency was not liable on the basis of a breach of a fiduciary duty or clergy malpractice for a pastor's sexual relationship with an adult counselee. *Teadt v. Lutheran Church Missouri Synod, 603 N.W.2d 816 (Mich. App. 1999).*

Table 10-11 Liability of Denominational Agencies for the Sexual Misconduct of Affiliated Clergy and Lay Workers— A State-By-State Review of Selected Cases

STATE	SUMMARY
Minnesota	• Churches and denominational agencies can be liable for punitive damages. The case involved a Catholic priest who repeatedly was placed by church officials in situations in which he could sexually abuse boys, despite knowledge by church officials of the priest's propensities. *Mrozka v. Archdiocese of St. Paul and Minneapolis, 482 N.W.2d 806 (Minn. App. 1992).*
	• A church and denominational organization were not legally responsible on the basis of negligent hiring for a pastor's acts of child molestation. The court pointed out that "there is no evidence [the church] had actual knowledge of [the pastor's] propensities to commit sexual abuse before he was hired." In rejecting liability based on negligent supervision, the court observed, "Even assuming that [the pastor's] abuse of [the victim] occurred within his scope of employment, there was insufficient evidence for the jury to conclude that [the church] failed to exercise ordinary care in supervising [him]. By the nature of the position, a clergyperson has considerable freedom in religious and administrative leadership in a church. The clergy also require privacy and confidentiality in order to protect the privacy of parishioners. There was no evidence that the supervision provided by [the church] differed from the supervision a reasonable church would provide. Nor was there any evidence of further reasonable supervision that could have prevented [the pastor] from abusing [the victim]. There was not enough evidence from which a reasonable jury could conclude that [the church] negligently supervised [the pastor]. *M.L. v. Magnuson, 531 N.W.2d 831 (Minn. App. 1995).*
	• A church and pastor could be sued as a result of the pastor's acts of child molestation. However, state and national denominational bodies were found not to have been negligent. *Doe v. Redeemer Lutheran Church, 531 N.W.2d 897 (Minn. App. 1995).*
	• A Catholic church was not an "agent" of its diocese and accordingly the diocese was not legally responsible for an injury that occurred on church property. *Plate v. St. Mary's Help Church, 520 N.W.2d 17 (Minn. App. 1994).*
	• A 38-year-old man's lawsuit against a pastor who had molested him when he was a minor may not be barred by the statute of limitations. The court refused to allow the victim to pursue his lawsuit against the church and denominational agency because the victim "has failed to produce any evidence of negligence. It is uncontroverted that no member or employee of the church knew of [the pastor's] abusive conduct with this or any other victim until after the incidents with [the victim] had ended. [The victim] admits that the incidents took place in private and that he himself told no one." *Winkler v. Magnuson, 539 N.W.2d 821 (Minn. App. 1995).*
	• A denominational agency that operated a school was guilty of sexual harassment as a result of its failure to address its principal's offensive behavior with several female employees. The court upheld the trial court's award of $300,000. It referred to the "long-term, ostrich-like failure" by denominational and school officials to "deal forthrightly with [the principal's] treatment of female employees." The court observed that "the jury was entitled to conclude that [the agency] not only looked the other way for many years but that its corrective action was woefully inadequate, as demonstrated by [the principal's] later conduct." *Jonasson v. Lutheran Child and Family Services, 115 F.3d 436 (7th Cir. 1997).*
	• A denominational agency could be liable on the basis negligent hiring, retention and supervision, and respondeat superior, for the sexual misconduct of a pastor with an adult female counselee. *Odenthal v. Minnesota Conference of Seventh-Day Adventists, 657 N.W.2d 569 (Minn. App. 2003).*
	• A denominational agency was liable on the basis of negligent hiring for the sexual misconduct by a pastor with an adult counselee. *J.M. v. Minnesota Dist. Council of Assemblies of God, 658 N.W.2d 589 (Minn. App. 2003).*
	• A denominational agency could be sued on the basis of negligent retention and respondeat superior for a pastor's sexual relationship with an adult female counselee. *Olson v. First Church of Nazarene, 661 N.W.2d 254 (Minn. App. 2003).*
	• A denominational agency was not liable on the basis of respondeat superior, negligent supervision, or ratification, for a pastor's molestation of a minor. *C.B. ex rel. L.B. v. Evangelical Lutheran Church in America, 726 N.W.2d 127 (Minn. App. 2007).*

Table 10-11 Liability of Denominational Agencies for the Sexual Misconduct of Affiliated Clergy and Lay Workers— A State-By-State Review of Selected Cases

STATE	SUMMARY
Mississippi	• A federal appeals court ruled that an archdiocese was not responsible for the alleged molestation of a minor by a priest. The court observed: (1) "The record, however, permits of no conclusion that the [archdiocese] suspected that [the priest] had engaged in sexual improprieties or might do so in the future. It is doubtful that the archdiocese . . . knew anything about [his] darker side." (2) "[E]mployers do not have a duty to supervise their employees when the employees are off-duty or not working. Employers also are not liable for failure to supervise when the employee engages in independent criminal conduct which results in the plaintiff's injuries. Moreover, an employer's duty to supervise does not include a duty to uncover his employees' concealed, clandestine, personal activities." *Tichenor v. Roman Catholic Church, 32 F.3d 953 (5th Cir. 1994).* •The First Amendment did not prevent a diocese from being sued on the basis of negligent hiring and assignment, negligent retention, and breach of a fiduciary duty, for a priest's molestation of three minor girls. *Diocese v. Morrison, 905 So.2d 1213 (Miss. 2005).* •The First Amendment prevented a diocese from being sued on the basis of negligent supervision and retention for a pastor's sexual relationship with an adult counselee, and no fiduciary relationship existed that would support liability based on a breach of a fiduciary duty. *Mabus v. St. James Episcopal Church, 884 So.2d 747 (Miss. 2004).*
Missouri	•The Missouri Supreme Court ruled that the First Amendment barred it from resolving a lawsuit in which a Catholic diocese was sued on the basis of respondeat superior, agency, negligence, and breach of fiduciary duty as a result of a priest's acts of sexual molestation. *Gray v. Ward, 950 S.W.2d 232 (Mo. 1997).* • The Missouri Supreme Court ruled that a diocese could not be liable for the sexual misconduct of a priest. The court concluded that the First Amendment barred the civil courts from imputing liability to the diocese on the basis of a fiduciary duty, conspiracy, agency, negligent hiring, negligent ordination, negligent retention, negligent supervision, or emotional distress. However, the court allowed the diocese to be sued on the basis of intentional failure to supervise clergy—if the victim could prove that a "supervisor" knew that the priest was likely to harm others but disregarded the risk. *Gibson v. Brewer, 952 S.W.2d 239 (Mo. 1997).* • A federal court ruled that a religious order was not liable on the basis of a breach of a fiduciary duty for a priest's sexual misconduct, but it could be liable on the basis of negligent retention or supervision, and intentional infliction of emotional distress. The court noted that federal courts generally are required to follow state court rulings regarding the meaning of state law, but it noted that this was not true for state court decisions interpreting the federal Constitution. It therefore was not bound by the Gray and Gibson decisions (above) since they were based on an interpretation of the First Amendment. The court ruled that imposing liability on a religious entity on the basis of negligent retention and supervision would not violate the First Amendment. *John Doe v. Capuchin Franciscan Friars, 520 F.Supp.2d 1124 (E.D. Mo. 2007).*
Montana	no directly relevant precedent in recent years
Nebraska	•The state supreme court ruled that a Catholic Archdiocese was not legally responsible for damages allegedly suffered by a woman who engaged in sexual relations with a priest. *Schieffer v. Catholic Archdiocese, 508 N.W.2d 907 (Neb. 1993).*
Nevada	no directly relevant precedent in recent years
New Hamp.	no directly relevant precedent in recent years
New Jersey	no directly relevant precedent in recent years
New Mexico	• A state appeals court ruled that a Catholic diocese could not be sued by a 33-year-old woman who claimed to have been sexually molested by a priest when she was a minor. The court observed, "[R]egardless of whether [the woman] knew or should have known of the severe psychological damage caused by [the priest's] alleged misconduct [she] knew and should have known well before the limitations expiration date that the alleged misconduct had caused her other substantial injury. The limitations period is not tolled simply because a plaintiff does not know the full extent of her injuries; the statute begins to run once she knows or should know the sufficient facts to constitute a cause of action." *Martinez-Sandoval v. Kirsch, 884 P.2d 507 (N.M. App. 1994).*

Table 10-11 Liability of Denominational Agencies for the Sexual Misconduct of Affiliated Clergy and Lay Workers— A State-By-State Review of Selected Cases

STATE	SUMMARY
New York	• A federal court in New York refused to find a pastor guilty of malpractice on the basis of his alleged sexual seduction of a church member he had counseled for several years. The court also refused to hold the pastor's church and denomination liable on the basis of "negligent placement, retention, or supervision." The court observed, "[A]ny inquiry into the policies and practices of the church defendants in hiring or supervising their clergy raises the same kind of First Amendment problems of entanglement discussed above, which might involve the court in making sensitive judgments about the propriety of the church defendants' supervision in light of their religious beliefs." The court also observed, "It would therefore also be inappropriate and unconstitutional for this court to determine after the fact that the ecclesiastical authorities negligently supervised or retained the [pastor]. Any award of damages would have a chilling effect leading indirectly to state control over the future conduct of affairs of a religious denomination, a result violative of the text and history of the [First Amendment]." The court also observed, "[The New York courts] have steadfastly declined to alter the traditional New York rule that the statute of limitations commences to run when a cause of action accrues, even though the plaintiff is unaware that he has a cause of action." *Schmidt v. Bishop, 779 F. Supp. 321 (S.D.N.Y. 1991)*. • A court refused to extend the "statute of limitations" to allow an alleged victim of child sexual molestation to sue the minister who he claimed was the molester. *Bassile v. Covenant House, 575 N.Y.S.2d 233 (Sup. 1991)*. • A New York state court ruled that the statute of limitations prevented an adult survivor of alleged childhood sexual abuse from suing her church. *Gallas v. Greek Orthodox Archdiocese, 587 N.Y.S.2d 82 (Sup. 1989)*. • A New York appeals court ruled that a Catholic church and diocese could be sued as a result of the sexual molestation of an 11-year-old boy by a Catholic priest. The court rejected the argument of the church and diocese that permitting the civil courts to find religious organizations liable on the basis of negligent hiring or supervision of clergy would constitute excessive governmental interference with church autonomy in violation of the First Amendment guaranty of religious freedom. *Jones by Jones v. Trane. 591 N.Y.S.2d 927 (Sup. 1992)*. • A state appeals court ruled that a church and diocese could not be sued on the basis of "malpractice" or "respondeat superior" for the alleged sexual misconduct of a priest. The court observed simply that "the alleged sexual assault was not within the scope of employment and cannot be said to have been in furtherance of the employer's business." *Joshua S. v. Casey, 615 N.Y.S.2d 200 (A.D. 4 Dept. 1994)*. • A New York court ruled that a Catholic diocese could not be sued on the basis of negligent hiring for a priest's acts of child molestation, but it could be sued for negligent supervision and negligent retention. It noted that "there is no indication that requiring increased supervision of [the priest] or the termination of his employment by the [diocese] based upon [his] conduct would violate any religious doctrine or inhibit any religious practice." The court concluded that there was evidence that the level of supervision exercised over the offending priest, or his retention by the diocese, was dictated by any religious doctrine. It insisted that "religious entities have some duty to prevent injuries incurred by persons in their employ whom they have reason to believe will engage in injurious conduct." *Kenneth R. v. Roman Catholic Diocese, 654 N.Y.S.2d 791 (N.Y.A.D. 1997)*. • A New York court ruled that it was barred by the First Amendment from resolving a woman's claim that she had been injured by a priest's repeated sexual contacts with her. *Langford v. Roman Catholic Diocese, 677 N.Y.S.2d 436 (A.D. 1998)*. • A denominational agency was not liable on the basis of negligent retention or supervision for a minister's sexual assault on a member of the congregation. *Ehrens v. Lutheran Church, 385 F.3d 232 (2nd Cir. 2004)*. • A denominational agency was not liable, on the basis of fiduciary duty, emotional distress, clergy malpractice, or negligent ordination, for a minister's sexual relationship with an adult counselee. *Wende C. v. United Methodist Church, 776 N.Y.S.2d 390 (N.Y.A.D. 2004)*. • A denominational agency could be liable on the basis of breaching a fiduciary duty, and negligent retention and supervision, for a minister's sexual relationship with an adult counselee. *Doe v. Roman Catholic Diocese, 857 N.Y.S.2d 866 (N.Y.A.D. 2008)*.
N. Carolina	no directly relevant precedent in recent years

Table 10-11 Liability of Denominational Agencies for the Sexual Misconduct of Affiliated Clergy and Lay Workers— A State-By-State Review of Selected Cases

STATE	SUMMARY
N. Dakota	• The North Dakota Supreme Court ruled that a denominational agency could not be liable on the basis of respondeat superior for a pastor's sexual misconduct since the victim had entered into an agreement releasing the pastor from liability. The court also ruled that the agency was not liable on the basis of a breach of a fiduciary duty. The victim insisted that the denomination's "Book of Discipline" imposed a fiduciary duty on the denomination and its officials to investigate and confront clergy for sexual misconduct. The court disagreed, noting that the Book of Discipline "defines the duties and responsibilities of [denominational agencies and officials] and local ministers. [Denominational officials] have no responsibility for the direct pastoral care of parishioners in individual congregations. Such functions are the responsibility of the local church minister." *L.C. v. R.P. 563 N.W.2d 799 (N.D. 1997).*
Ohio	• A state appeals court ruled that a minister and his church, but not his denomination, could be sued for the minister's acts of sexual harassment involving a church secretary. The court observed, "Although [the minister] sought advice from the bishop, and the bishop investigated plaintiff's complaints, this does not make the diocese liable for the conduct of [the minister or church]." *Davis v. Black, 70 Ohio App. 359 (Ohio App. 1991).*

• The Ohio Supreme Court dismissed a lawsuit brought against a religious institution for negligent hiring because it failed to identify specific knowledge of prior misconduct. *Byrd v. Faber, 565 N.E.2d 584 (Ohio 1991).*

• A state appeals court ruled that a denominational agency was not responsible for a local church elder's actions even though it exercised ecclesiastical control over him. *Nye v. Kemp, 646 N.E.2d 262 (Ohio App. 10 Dist. 1994).* |
| Oklahoma | • The state supreme court ruled that a married couple could not sue their church and former pastor for damages they allegedly incurred as a result of an adulterous affair between the former pastor and the wife. The court observed, "Neither the claims by the husband nor the wife against the minister are cognizable in Oklahoma. . . . Because their claims against the minister also serve as the basis for the claims against the church for its negligent hiring and supervision of the minister, that claim is also not cognizable." *Bladen v. First Presbyterian Church, 857 P.2d 789 (Okla. 1993).* |
| Oregon | • A state appeals court ruled that a victim of clergy sexual misconduct could sue her minister, and possibly her church and denomination. It acknowledged that the constitutional guaranty of religious freedom "may provide the [denomination] with an affirmative defense at some later stage of the proceeding." *Erickson v. Christenson, 781 P.2d 383 (Or. App. 1989).*

• A denominational agency was not legally responsible for a priest's acts of child molestation occurring more than 20 years ago. *Fearing v. Bucher, 936 P.2d 1023 (Or. App. 1997).*

• A diocese could be liable on the basis of respondeat superior for a priest's acts of child molestation. *Fearing v. Bucher, 977 P.2d 1163 (Or. 1999).*

• A denominational agency was not liable for a priest's acts of sexual abuse on the basis of respondeat superior. *Schmidt v. Archdiocese, 180 P.3d 160 (Or. App. 2008).* |

Table 10-11 Liability of Denominational Agencies for the Sexual Misconduct of Affiliated Clergy and Lay Workers— A State-By-State Review of Selected Cases

STATE	SUMMARY
Pennsylvania	• A state appeals court ruled that an adult was barred by the statute of limitations from suing a priest and his church on account of the priest's alleged acts of molestation. The court observed, "This is simply not a case where the plaintiff, despite the exercise of objectively measured reasonable diligence, could not know of his injury and its cause within the limitations period. [The victim] admits that he knew the abuse was occurring and who was inflicting it, both when it happened and throughout the eight years after the abuse ended and before appellant sued. What he did not know, i.e., that the physical acts allegedly performed on him by [the priest] were abuse and were causing psychological harm, is not relevant to a discovery rule analysis." *E.J.M. v. Archdiocese of Philadelphia, 622 A.2d 1388 (Pa. Super. 1993).* • A Pennsylvania court ruled that a church and diocese could not be legally responsible for a priest's repeated acts of child molestation occurring off of church premises. The court noted that the Restatement of Torts (an authoritative legal text) imposes liability for negligent supervision upon employers only for misconduct occurring on their premises. It pointed out that all of the priest's acts of molestation occurred in motel rooms while on trips, and not on church premises. *Hutchinson v. Luddy, 683 A.2d 1254 (Pa. Super. 1996).* • A diocese was not liable on the basis of negligence for a priest's acts of child molestation. *Hartz v. Diocese, 94 Fed.Appx. 52 (3rd Cir. 2004).* • A diocese could be liable on the basis of negligent supervision and fiduciary duty for a priest's sexual misconduct, but not on the basis of negligent hiring, emotional distress, or respondeat superior. *Doe v. Liberatore, 478 F.Supp.2d 742 (M.D. Pa. 2007).*
Rhode Island	• A federal court in Rhode Island ruled that the First Amendment did not prevent it from resolving a lawsuit brought by victims of clergy sexual misconduct against denominational officials. *Smith v. O'Connell, 986 F.Supp. 73 (D.R.I. 1997).*
S. Carolina	• A South Carolina court ruled that a denominational agency and one of its officials were not liable on the basis of negligence, invasion of privacy, fiduciary duty, emotional distress, or fraud for a pastor's acts of sexual harassment. The women claimed that a denominational agency and official "had a duty to prevent the sexual harassment of its parishioners by a member of the clergy and to help in healing afterward rather than being indifferent." They insisted that the agency and official should be found guilty of negligence for violating this standard. The court disagreed, noting that the women "have cited no precedent and we are aware of none that stands for the proposition a church owes its parishioners a duty of care regarding its handling of their complaints." The court also rejected the women's claim that the agency and official breached a fiduciary duty. *Brown v. Pearson, 483 S.E.2d 477 (S.C. App. 1997).*
S. Dakota	• The state supreme court ruled that the statute of limitations for bringing a lawsuit for acts of sexual molestation may be suspended or delayed through "fraudulent concealment" by a denominational agency of the incidents. *Koenig v. Lambert, 527 N.W.2d 903 (S.D. 1995).*
Tennessee	no directly relevant precedent in recent years

Table 10-11 Liability of Denominational Agencies for the Sexual Misconduct of Affiliated Clergy and Lay Workers— A State-By-State Review of Selected Cases

STATE	SUMMARY
Texas	• A federal appeals court ruled that an archdiocese was not responsible for the alleged molestation of a minor by a priest. The court observed: (1) "The record, however, permits of no conclusion that the [archdiocese] suspected that [the priest] had engaged in sexual improprieties or might do so in the future. It is doubtful that the archdiocese . . . knew anything about [his] darker side." (2) "[E]mployers do not have a duty to supervise their employees when the employees are off-duty or not working. Employers also are not liable for failure to supervise when the employee engages in independent criminal conduct which results in the plaintiff's injuries. Moreover, an employer's duty to supervise does not include a duty to uncover his employees' concealed, clandestine, personal activities." *Tichenor v. Roman Catholic Church, 32 F.3d 953 (5th Cir. 1994).* • A denominational agency was not liable on the basis of negligent selection or supervision, or respondeat superior, for a minister's acts of child molestation. The agency's organizational documents vested control over the hiring of local staff to affiliated churches. *Williams v. United Pentecostal Church Intern. 115 S.W.3d 612 (Tex. App. 2003).* • A diocese was not liable on the basis of respondeat superior for a priest's acts of child molestation. *Soto v. Catholic Diocese of El Paso, 156 S.W.3d 881 (Tex. App. 2005).*
Utah	no directly relevant precedent in recent years
Vermont	• A federal court in Vermont ruled that an adult who claimed to have been sexually abused by a nun some 40 years earlier could sue a Catholic diocese for his alleged injuries. *Barquin v. Roman Catholic Diocese, 839 F. Supp. 275 (D. Vt. 1993).*
Virginia	no directly relevant precedent in recent years
Washington	• A Washington court ruled that a church and a member of the church board could be sued by three women who had been molested by a volunteer youth worker when they were minors. The court noted that "as a general rule, there is no legal duty to protect another from the criminal acts of a third person." However, a church may have a duty to prevent a third person from causing physical harm to another if a "special relationship" exists between the church and the victim which imposes upon the church a duty to "protect" the victim from harm. The court concluded that such a relationship did exist: "[W]e believe that churches and the adult church workers who assume responsibility for the spiritual well being of children of the congregation, whether as paid clergy or as volunteers, have a special relationship with those children that gives rise to a duty to protect them from reasonably foreseeable risk of harm from those members of the congregation whom the church places in positions of responsibility and authority over them." However, no special relationship existed between the victims and a denominational agency. *Funkhouser v. Wilson, 950 P.2d 501 (Wash. App. 1998) aff'd C.J.C. v. Corporation of Catholic Bishop, 985 P.2d 262 (Wash. 1999).* • A Washington state court ruled that the statute of limitations prevented an adult male from suing his church and a denominational agency for injuries he suffered as a child when he was molested by his pastor. *E.R.B. v. Church of God, 950 P.2d 29 (Wash. App. 1998).*
W. Virginia	no directly relevant precedent in recent years

Table 10-11 Liability of Denominational Agencies for the Sexual Misconduct of Affiliated Clergy and Lay Workers— A State-By-State Review of Selected Cases

STATE	SUMMARY
Wisconsin	• A federal appeals court ruled that a denominational agency was not responsible for the alleged seduction of a female parishioner by a Catholic priest. *Doe v. Cunningham, 30 F.3d 879 (7th Cir. 1994)*. • A federal appeals court ruled that a church and denominational agency were not legally responsible for a pastoral counselor's sexual contacts with a female counselee. The court stressed that the woman's lawsuit failed "to adequately allege that the church defendants knew or should have known of the improper counseling conduct of [the pastor]." The court also ruled that the church defendants were not liable on the basis of negligent supervision since the lawsuit was "devoid of any allegation that the church defendants were aware or had any knowledge that [the pastor] made improper sexual advances either before or during the time in question." *Dausch v. Rykse, 52 F.3d 1425 (7th Cir. 1994)*. • A state appeals court ruled that the statute of limitations prevented a woman from suing a Catholic archdiocese for the alleged acts of molestation by a priest nearly 40 years before. The court noted that "extending the discovery rule to this case would cause unfairness to a defendant that is forced to attempt to defend a suit for emotional and psychological injuries in which the alleged conduct took place over [40] years ago and increase the potential for fraud." The court also observed, "To establish a claim for negligent hiring or retention [the woman] would have to establish that the archdiocese was negligent in hiring or retaining [the priest] because he was incompetent or otherwise unfit. But, we conclude that the First Amendment to the United States Constitution prevents the courts of this state from determining what makes one competent to serve as a Catholic priest since such a determination would require interpretation of church canons and internal church policies and practices. Therefore [the suit] against the archdiocese is not capable of enforcement by the courts." *Pritzlaff v. Archdiocese of Milwaukee, 533 N.W.2d 780 (Wis. 1995)*. • The Wisconsin Supreme Court ruled that seven adults who were molested as children by parish priests were barred by the statute of limitations from suing the priests, their churches, and a diocese. *Doe v. Archdiocese of Milwaukee, 565 N.W.2d 94 (Wis. 1997)*. • A Wisconsin court ruled that the statute of limitations barred an adult from suing a church and diocese for injuries he allegedly sustained as a result of a priest's acts of child molestation. The victim argued that he did not "discover" the relationship between his suffering and the priest's assaults until years later, and his claim did not accrue until that date, making his lawsuit timely. The court rejected this attempt to extend the statute of limitations. It concluded, "As a matter of law, [the victim] discovered, or in the exercise of reasonable diligence should have discovered, the cause of his injury at least by the time of the last incident of assault, in May of 1984. Therefore, his claims against the diocese and [church] as well as those against [the priest] accrued no later than the time of the last assault." *Joseph W. v. Catholic Diocese, 569 N.W.2d 795 (Wis. App. 1997)*. • A Catholic Diocese could not be sued as a result of an alleged sexual relationship that began when a woman began a counseling relationship with a priest who served as a hospital chaplain and counselor. The court concluded that the First Amendment prohibited it from resolving the victim's negligent supervision claim. *L.L.N. v. Clauder, 563 N.W.2d 434 (Wis. 1997)*. • A diocese was not liable on the basis of negligent supervision for a priest's acts of child molestation, since it had no knowledge of any facts that would have led it to believe that the priest would engage in such behavior. The court also rejected liability based on breach of a fiduciary duty. *Doe v. Archdiocese, 700 N.W.2d 180 (Wis. 2005)*. • A diocese was not liable on the basis of negligent supervision for a priest's sexual misconduct, because the plaintiffs filed their lawsuit after the statute of limitations had expired. *John Doe 1 v. Archdiocese, 734 N.W.2d 827 (Wis. 2007)*. • A diocese was not liable on the basis of negligence for a priest's sexual misconduct. The court concluded: "The plaintiffs also fail to provide legal authority supporting their arguments. They argue that the duty of ordinary care in this case encompasses a specific obligation to warn all parochial schools and dioceses in this country, as well as future parents of unforeseeable victims, but have cited no cases in which the failure to warn third parties has been described in such sweeping terms." *Hornback v. Archdiocese of Milwaukee 752 N.W.2d 862 (Wis. 2008)*.
Wyoming	no directly relevant precedent in recent years

Instructional Aids to Chapter 10

Key Terms

agency

arbitration

apparent agency

ascending liability

assumption of risk

charitable immunity

common interest privilege

comparative negligence

contributory negligence

course of employment

"discovery" rule

fiduciary duty

intervening cause

invitee

joint and several liability

licensee

Megan's laws

negligence

negligent retention

negligent selection

negligent supervision

punitive damages

qualified privilege

ratification

references, institutional

references, personal

respondeat superior

scope of employment

statute of limitations

trespasser

vicarious liability

Learning Objectives

- Define the term *negligence*.

- Define the term *respondeat superior*, and explain its relevance to churches.

- Understand the potential legal liability of churches for failing to exercise reasonable care in the selection of workers.

- Understand the potential legal liability of churches for failing to exercise reasonable care in the supervision of workers and activities.

- Understand the potential liability of churches for retaining an employee or volunteer after being made aware of information suggesting that the person represents a risk of harm to others.

- Explain the concept of "fiduciary duty," and its relevance to churches.

- Identify several legal defenses to negligence.

- Understand the legal status of "release forms" that purport to relieve a church of liability for the negligence of its employees and volunteers.

- Explain the concept of risk management, and identify risk management strategies that can reduce the risk of church liability based on negligent selection, negligent retention, and negligent supervision.

- Define "defamation," and explain defenses that are available to churches that are sued for alleged defamation.

- Identify legal risks associated with counseling activities, and explain how those risks may be reduced.

- Describe the potential legal liability of religious denominations for the conduct of affiliated churches and clergy, and identify several defenses that are available to denominations.

Short-Answer Questions

1. Define the term respondeat superior, and explain its relevance to churches.

2. Pastor B fails to stop at a red light and collides with another vehicle while driving from the church to visit a church member in the hospital. The driver of the other vehicle was seriously injured. Pastor B has not been charged with a traffic violation in more than ten years. Answer the following questions:

a. On the basis of what legal theory would the church most likely be responsible for the victim's injuries?

b. What is the justification for the legal liability of the church for the victim's injuries?

c. What would the victim have to prove in order for the church to be liable?

d. What if the minister reports his income taxes as a self-employed person? Would this affect the liability of the church? Explain.

e. What if the accident occurred on a Friday evening while Pastor B was on his way to buy groceries? Would this affect the liability of the church? Explain.

f. What if the accident occurred while Pastor B was on his way to watch his daughter participate in a sporting event? Would this affect the liability of the church? Explain.

g. What if the accident occurred while Pastor B was on his way home from church? Would this affect the liability of the church? Explain.

h. Assuming that the church is sued by the victim, what legal defenses could the church assert?

i. Can the victim sue Pastor B personally? Explain.

3. A church hires D to mow its lawn on a weekly basis. D spends about three hours at the church each week during the mowing season. While mowing the yard one day, D's tractor runs over a rock that is thrown across the street and strikes a neighbor. The neighbor sues the church, claiming that it is responsible for her injuries on the basis of respondeat superior. How will a court likely rule? Explain.

4. Some courts refuse to apply the principle of respondeat superior to churches and other charities. Why?

5. G is a volunteer youth worker at a church. He sexually assaults an adolescent female while driving her home following a church activity. The victim sues her church, claiming that it is legally responsible for G's actions on the basis of respondeat superior. Answer the following questions:

    a. Will a court find the church liable for G's actions on the basis of respondeat superior? Why or why not?

    b. What other theories of liability could be asserted against the church?

6. The text states that sexual molestation of minors and adults is one of the greatest legal risk facing churches today. Why? Do you agree or disagree?

7. The text lists several risks associated with incidents of sexual misconduct in churches. List five of them.

8. After attending a church for 2 weeks, M volunteers to work as a Sunday School teacher. He begins teaching a class a few weeks later. The church did not ask M to complete any application form and did not ask for or contact any references. Shortly after beginning to teach the class, M is accused of molesting a child on church premises following a class. The child's parents sue M and the church. It is later discovered that M was convicted of the sexual molestation of a minor in another community five years previously. Answer the following questions:

    a. On the basis of what legal theory would the church most likely be responsible for the victim's injuries?

    b. Church leaders claim that they had no knowledge of the previous conviction, or of any other information suggesting that M would pose a risk of harm to anyone. Would this constitute an effective defense? Why or why not?

    c. List ways that the church could have reduced the risk of this incident occurring.

    d. Will the church's liability insurance policy cover the church? What about M?

9. Assume the same facts as the previous question, except that M had not been convicted in the past of sexually molesting a minor. Answer the following questions:

    a. Would the church be legally responsible for the child's injuries? Explain.

b. How should church leaders respond to inconclusive or unresolved criminal records on the part of applicants for youth work in the church?

10. What is the difference between a personal and an institutional reference? Which is more effective? Why?

11. A church decides to implement a procedure for "screening" persons who work with children. One aspect of its screening procedure is an application form to be completed by all workers. Answer the following questions:

a. Should such a form be completed by current workers? Or, should it be completed only by those workers hired in the future?

b. Should such a form be completed by paid employees? Uncompensated volunteers? Both?

c. Should the church ask applicants whether or not they have been arrested or convicted of a crime? If so, which crimes should be included?

d. What other questions would be appropriate on a screening application form?

12. A church decides to begin screening volunteers who work with minors in any capacity. Church leaders decide to streamline the process by only doing criminal records checks. They believe that such checks are the most effective and important screening tool, and so no other procedures are necessary. How would you evaluate this approach?

13. An individual begins attending a church and expresses interest in working with the children's program. He mentions that he was convicted of sexually molesting a child and served a 3-year term in a state penitentiary. However, he insists that he no longer presents a risk of harm because of a religious conversion that he experienced while in prison. He is interviewed by several church leaders, who all agree that he seems to have experienced a genuine conversion. They would like to give the person the benefit of the doubt and use him in a volunteer capacity in a children's program. Answer the following questions:

a. Should the church use this person in a children's program? Why or why not?

b. Would it matter how long ago the previous conviction occurred? What if the criminal conviction was 10 years ago, and the person has had no other charges or convictions? What if the person was released from prison within the past year?

c. Are there any other alternatives available to the church in responding to such a person's desire to volunteer his services?

14. Assume that you have been asked by your church to recommend procedures to reduce the risk of child molestation occurring on church premises or in the course of church activities. How would you respond?

15. Many churches use adolescents to assist with children's programs. Can a church be liable on the basis of negligent selection for sexual assaults committed by such persons on younger children? If so, how might this risk be reduced?

16. Many incidents of child molestation have occurred in church restrooms. What are some steps that church leaders can take to reduce this risk?

17. Answer the following questions regarding criminal records checks:

a. What is a criminal records check?

b. Has a church ever been found liable for not obtaining a criminal records check on an employee or volunteer?

c. Should a church ever obtain a criminal records check on an employee or volunteer? If so, under what circumstances, and what kind of check?

d. Summarize the Volunteers for Children Act and its significance to churches.

18. What are the advantages and disadvantages of each of the following kinds of criminal records checks:

a. County records checks.

b. State records checks.

c. Sex offender registry checks.

d. FBI database checks.

19. A church conducts criminal records checks, in addition to other procedures, for every volunteer who wants to work with minors. K applies for a volunteer youth worker position, but a criminal records check reveals a 10-year-old conviction for resisting arrest. Does this disqualify the applicant from any position involving access to minors? Explain.

20. Same facts as the previous question, except that applicant had been convicted of embezzlement ten years ago.

21. Which of the following crimes should disqualify a person from working as a volunteer in a church youth program:

a. Embezzlement.

b. Possession of a narcotic drug.

c. Burglary.

d. Forgery.

e. Driving while intoxicated.

f. Rape of an adult.

g. Armed robbery.

22. A church performs a criminal records check on an applicant for a children's ministry position, and learns of two 30-year-old convictions for sexually molesting young children. The individual served a brief prison sentence for his offenses, and has lived an exemplary life ever since. Can the church disregard the prior convictions due to the fact that they happened so many years ago? Explain.

23. A church board member insists that the church cannot use known homosexuals as volunteers in the church's youth ministry, since they are pedophiles. Evaluate this claim.

24. A church selects Pastor J as its minister. Church leaders do not investigate the background of Pastor J, and do not discover that Pastor J was guilty of sexually seducing a church member in a previous church. Pastor J sexually seduces a member of his current church during marital counseling. The member sues the church as well as Pastor J. Answer the following questions:

a. On the basis of what legal theory would the church most likely be responsible for the member's alleged injuries?

b. Church leaders claim that they had no knowledge of the previous incident of misconduct, or of any other information suggesting that Pastor J would pose a risk of harm to anyone. Would this constitute an effective defense? Why or why not?

c. How could the church have reduced the risk of this incident occurring?

25. Same facts as the previous question. Assume that Pastor J's denomination was aware of the previous misconduct, but did nothing to advise the church at the time it employed Pastor J, and did nothing to supervise or monitor Pastor J's activities.

a. On the basis of what legal theory would the denomination most likely be responsible for the member's alleged injuries?

b. What steps could the denomination have taken to reduce its risk of liability?

26. A church lets D drive several members of the church youth group in a church vehicle on a church-sponsored activity. D's reckless driving results in an accident that injures some of the members of the youth group. The victims sue the church, as well as D. They reveal that D had been convicted of several traffic offenses in the year preceding the accident, and that his drivers license had been suspended. Answer the following questions:

a. On the basis of what legal theory would the church most likely be responsible for the victims' injuries?

b. Church leaders claim that they had no knowledge of D's poor driving record, or of any other information suggesting that D would pose a risk of harm to anyone. Would this constitute an effective defense? Why or why not?

c. How could the church have reduced its risk of liability?

27. Several courts have refused to find churches liable on the basis of negligent selection or negligent supervision for the sexual misconduct of ministers. Why?

28. Churches can be liable on the basis of negligent supervision for the sexual molestation of children on church premises. Name five precautions that a church can adopt that will reduce this risk.

29. What is negligent retention? Give an example of how a church may be liable on this basis for the molestation of a child by volunteer church worker.

30. An adolescent boy is injured while playing in a church-sponsored basketball game. The minor's parents sue the church, claiming that it is responsible for their child's injuries on the basis of negligent supervision. They claim that the molestation never would have occurred had the church exercised proper supervision over its workers and activities. What factors will a jury consider in reaching a decision in this case?

31. A 10-year-old boy is injured when he falls off a cliff while participating in a church-sponsored camping trip. The minor's mother sues the church, claiming that it is responsible for her child's injuries on the basis of negligent supervision. She claims that the accident never would have occurred had the church exercised proper supervision over its workers and activities. What factors will a jury consider in reaching a decision in this case?

32. Pastor S, a youth minister at First Church, takes 23 children swimming at a nearby lake. There were no other adult supervisors and no life guards were on duty. One of the children drowns. Answer the following questions:

    a. On the basis of what legal theory would the church most likely be responsible for the victim's injuries?

    b. What is the probable outcome of such a lawsuit?

    c. What steps could the church have taken to reduce its risk of liability?

33. A church operates a preschool. Children often are taken to a neighboring park for recreation. A four-year-old child is injured when she falls off a slide while her class is at the park. Is the church responsible for her injuries? Explain.

34. A church's organized children's activity ("children's church") is released prior to the end of the adult worship service. A 6-year-old child wanders out of the church building and is struck by a car while crossing a nearby street. Answer the following questions:

    a. On the basis of what legal theory would the church most likely be responsible for the victim's injuries?

    b. What is the probable outcome of such a lawsuit?

    c. What steps could the church have taken to reduce its risk of liability?

35. A church operates a nursery during morning worship services. During one service, the nursery is staffed by two 13-year-old girls. An infant breaks her leg when she falls off a diaper changing table during a diaper change. Answer the following questions:

    a. On the basis of what legal theory would the church most likely be responsible for the victim's injuries?

    b. What is the probable outcome of such a lawsuit?

    c. What steps could the church have taken to reduce its risk of liability?

36. A youth pastor takes his church youth group to an activity in another city. The group travels in a bus. On the way, the group stops at a fast food restaurant for lunch. A few of the children ask if they can go to another restaurant across the street where they will not have to wait so long to be served. The youth pastor agrees. As they cross the street, one of the children is struck by a car. The child's parents sue the church. What is the most likely basis of liability? Explain.

37. A mother brings her infant child to the church nursery before a morning worship service. During the service, an adult male comes to the nursery and asks a teenage nursery attendant for the same child. The attendant is reluctant, because she has never seen the man before. He assures her that he is an "uncle" visiting from out-of-town. The attendant is satisfied with this explanation and gives the child to the man. Following the morning service the mother goes to the nursery and is

shocked to learn that her child is not there. It is later determined that the "uncle" in fact was a former husband who was seeking custody of the child. Answer the following questions:

a. On the basis of what legal theory would the church most likely be responsible for the victim's injuries?

b. What is the probable outcome of such a lawsuit?

c. What steps could the church have taken to reduce its risk of liability?

38. A church has a policy requiring two adults to work in the nursery. However, the policy does not prohibit children from being in the custody of less than two adults. On a Sunday morning during worship services, one adult temporarily leaves the nursery for ten minutes to speak with another church member. A few days later the parents of one of the infants in the nursery suspect that their child has been molested. Suspicion is focused on the church nursery. Since the two nursery workers cannot prove that they both were present with the child throughout the entire worship service, they cannot "prove their innocence." The worker who was present in the nursery while the other worker was temporarily absent is suspected of wrongdoing, even though she is completely innocent. What steps could the church have taken to prevent this from happening?

39. A pastor learns that a registered sex offender is attending the church. Should the person be barred from attending the church? If not, should his activities be limited, and if so, how?

40. A church sponsors several small groups that meet in members' homes. Parents of young children often bring their children with them to such meetings. Children typically are placed in a room separate from their parents, and supervised by a teenage worker. On one occasion, a five-year-old child is molested by a teenage supervisor at a small group meeting. Answer the following questions:

a. Can the church be liable for the victim's injuries? If so, what is the most likely theory of church liability?

b. What steps could the church have taken to prevent this incident from occurring?

41. T was a Sunday School teacher for several years. T resigned his position and had no further position in the church involving minors. A few years later it is disclosed that T invited a child from the church to his home and molested her. Church leaders were not aware that T had ever invited a child to his home, or that he ever had any social contacts with children from the church. T's parents sue the church, claiming that it was negligent in supervising T. What is the probable outcome of such a lawsuit?

42. Same facts as the previous example, except that T had been asked to resign as a Sunday School teacher after the pastor learned that he had engaged in inappropriate sexual conduct with another minor. Church leaders were not aware of any contacts or socializing between T and children from the church. What is the probable outcome of the lawsuit?

43. A church adopts a policy requiring reference checks on all persons who volunteer to work in any youth program. B is allowed to work as a volunteer in a youth activity without any reference checks. If B engages in inappropriate sexual contacts with a minor and the church is sued, what is the most likely basis of liability?

44. Pastor J accepts a position as pastor of a church. He plans on counseling church members in his office, but is concerned about reducing the risk of false allegations of inappropriate behavior during counseling sessions. What precautions can Pastor J take to reduce or eliminate the risk of inappropriate behavior and false allegations?

45. A church wants to start a counseling ministry that will be staffed by volunteers. The volunteers are not licensed counselors or psychologists, but they have attended a 3-day training event. List several legal concerns that are associated with this counseling ministry.

46. A 30-year-old woman sues a church, claiming that when she was a 15 years old a youth pastor sexually molested her on church premises. Answer the following questions:

a. On the basis of what legal theory would the church most likely be responsible for the victim's injuries?

b. What is the most likely legal defense available to the church? What is the likelihood that this defense will be successful?

47. Same facts as the previous question. Assume that the woman claims that she has suffered severe emotional problems since being molested by the youth pastor, but that she did not "discover" that her problems were caused by the youth pastor's misconduct until she went to a counselor shortly before filing her lawsuit. Will these allegations affect the outcome of the case? Explain.

48. Same facts as the previous question, except that the woman claims that the molestation occurred when she was 3 years old, and that she had "repressed" all memory of it until she went to a counselor shortly before filing her lawsuit. Will this allegation affect the outcome of the lawsuit? Explain.

49. What is "ratification"? Give an example of how a church might be liable on this basis.

50. A pastor announces to the congregation following a worship service that the church board dismissed T from membership in the church because of adultery. T sues the church for defamation. How would a court most likely resolve this case under each of the following assumptions:

a. T was guilty of adultery.

b. T was not guilty of adultery.

c. There were nonmembers present in the congregation when the pastor made the announcement.

d. There were no nonmembers present in the congregation when the pastor made the announcement.

51. A denominational publication lists ministers who have been "dismissed" as a result of discipline. A dismissed minister sues the denomination for defamation. What is the likely outcome of such a case? Explain.

52. Explain the "qualified privilege" defense that may be available to churches that are sued for defamation.

53. What is charitable immunity? Is it recognized in any states? Explain.

54. A church requires all parents to sign a "release form" before their children can participate in swimming and other sports activities and out-of-town trips. Answer the following questions:

a. What is a release form?

b. Assume that the youth group goes on a trip to another city in a church-owned vehicle, and that several children are injured when the driver loses control because of a tire blowout. It is later determined that the tire had been driven for 70,000 miles and had little if any tread left. Several parents threaten to sue the church on behalf of their injured children. Would the release form prevent them from doing so?

c. How do the courts generally view release forms? Why?

55. What is comparative negligence? Why would this concept be relevant in the event someone is injured on church property or during a church activity?

56. A parent informs two board members at her church that her 5-year-old child was sexually molested by a volunteer children's worker during a church activity. The board members share this information with the entire board, and the board removes the accused worker from his position. However, no one notifies the church's liability insurance company of the potential claim. Two years later, the parent sues the church. The lawsuit claims that the victim has suffered

severe psychological problems as a result of the molestation, and that the church is legally responsible for the injuries on the basis of negligent selection and negligent supervision. The church sends the lawsuit to its insurance agent. The insurance company refuses to provide the church with a defense of the case, or pay any judgment or settlement, on the ground that the church failed to provide it with timely notice of the potential claim after the incident occurred. The church asks a court for a ruling on the coverage of this claim under its insurance policy. What is the likely outcome of such a claim?

57. A minister of a local church injures the driver of another car while driving negligently. Answer the following questions:

a. On the basis of what legal theory would the church most likely be responsible for the victim's injuries?

b. On the basis of what legal theory would a parent religious denomination most likely be responsible for the victim's injuries?

c. What defenses are available to the denomination in the event it is sued by the victim?

58. What are punitive damages? Why should church leaders be familiar with this term?

59. The legal doctrine of joint and several liability is being restricted or eliminated in several states. Why is this development of interest to denominational agencies?

60. A woman who is sexually seduced by a minister sues a denomination with which the church is affiliated. The woman argues that the denomination is liable for the conduct of affiliated churches and clergy, since they are all "one big family." Specifically, she alleges that the denomination "held out" affiliated churches to be its agents through (1) local church use of the denominational name, (2) ordination of ministers by the denomination, and (3) denominational authority to discipline clergy. Answer the following questions:

a. On the basis of what legal theory would the church most likely be responsible for the victim's injuries?

b. On the basis of what legal theory would a parent religious denomination most likely be responsible for the victim's injuries?

c. What defenses are available to the denomination in the event it is sued by the victim?

61. A minister confesses to sexual relations with a church member. The minister is disciplined by his denomination, but he is allowed to remain in the active ministry. The minister accepts a call at a church in another community. Does this situation impose any risk for the denomination? Explain.

62. Same facts as the previous question, except that the minister is dismissed by his denomination. He applies for ordination in another denomination, which ordains him. The other denomination did not ask the minister if he had previously been ordained with another church, and did not discover that he had been dismissed for inappropriate sexual relations with a church member. Assume that the minister engages in inappropriate sexual relations with a member of his new church. Answer the following questions:

   a. The woman sues the former denomination, claiming that it negligently failed to warn the other denomination of the minister's misconduct. What is the likely outcome of such a claim? Explain.

   b. The woman sues the second denomination. What is the most likely basis of liability? Explain.

   c. Identify any legal defenses that may be available to the second denomination.

   d. What steps could the second denomination have taken to reduce the risk of liability in such a case?

63. A parent informs church leaders that her child was molested by a volunteer youth worker at the church. The church leaders remove the volunteer from his position, but do not inform the church insurance company. Answer the following questions:

   a. Is the church's failure to promptly notify the insurer of any legal significance? Explain.

   b. The church's liability insurance policy excludes any intentional or criminal acts. Does this mean that the church is uninsured if the victim or her parent decides to sue the church? Explain.

64. Explain the difference between claims made and occurrence insurance policies.

65. Answer the following questions about arbitration:

   a. What is arbitration?

   b. What is the difference between arbitration and mediation?

   c. What are the advantages of arbitration?

   d. Should churches adopt arbitration policies? If so, for what disputes, and on what terms?

   e. On what grounds might the validity of an arbitrator's award be legally challenged?

Essay Questions

1. Why do you suppose that churches once were immune from legal liability in many states? Do you agree with the prevailing view that churches should be responsible like any other organization for injuries caused by their employees or by dangerous conditions on their premises?

2. Some argue that the existence of liability insurance only encourages lawyers to file lawsuits, and that the lack of insurance will discourage litigation. Do you agree with this logic? Should churches be uninsured? Explain.

3. Some male clergy have adopted a policy of not counseling with unaccompanied females without a third person being present. Evaluate the effectiveness of such a procedure in reducing the risk of seduction, as well as the risk of false claims of seduction. Is such a procedure going too far? Are there less restrictive means that would be as effective?

4. Many courts have ruled that churches and denominational agencies cannot be liable on the basis of negligent selection or negligent supervision for the sexual misconduct of clergy, since any attempt by the civil courts to resolve such claims would violate the First Amendment religion clauses. Do you agree with this position? What considerations support the opposite view?

5. How should church leaders respond when they learn that one or more registered sex offenders is attending the church? Should such persons be permanently excluded? Should they be allowed unrestricted access to church property and activities? How are the principles of mercy and protection reconciled?

A Summary of
Constitutional History

Legal Briefs

"Congress shall make no law respecting an establishment of religion, or prohibiting the free exercise thereof." So begins the First Amendment to the United States Constitution. The meaning of these words is apparent to even a casual reader: Congress, our national legislature, can neither establish a religion nor prohibit its free exercise. These provisions were incorporated into the Constitution because of the fear that the new federal government would create an established church, as many of the colonies had done.

Since Congress never attempted to establish a church, these constitutional provisions were all but forgotten at the beginning of the twentieth century. Prayers, Bible readings, and religious instruction in the public schools; rental of public facilities by church groups; religious symbols on public property; tax exemptions for religious organizations; and state assistance to religious education were seldom if ever challenged since such practices were plainly far from the congressional establishment of a national religion prohibited by the First Amendment. However, since 1940, the religion clauses have taken on a new and expanded meaning that is foreign to the objectives of its drafters. This story is the focus of chapter 11.

> "... since 1940, the religion clauses have taken on a new and expanded meaning that is foreign to the objectives of its drafters."

The continuing frustration by the Supreme Court and lower federal courts of voluntary religious practices that are perceived as legitimate by a substantial majority of the public may one day prompt a reassessment of the meaning of First Amendment religion clauses. Until then, chapter 11 focuses on constitutional history and our courts' views on First Amendment freedoms.

Congress shall make no law respecting an establishment of religion, or prohibiting the free exercise thereof . . . .[1]

The First Amendment religion clauses were the product of the egalitarian fervor of the fledgling Republic. The federal government—"Congress"—would never be able to commit the sin of many of the colonies: establishment of an official religion. Correlatively, the right of each citizen to "freely exercise" his or her religion was protected from federal encroachment. Justice Stewart, dissenting in the *Schempp* case, observed:

> As a matter of history, the First Amendment was adopted solely as a limitation upon the newly created National Government. The events leading to its adoption strongly suggest that the Establishment Clause was primarily an attempt to insure that Congress not only would be powerless to establish a national church, but would also be unable to interfere with existing state establishments.[2]

Justice Reed, dissenting in the *McCollum* case,[3] observed:

> The phrase "an establishment of religion" may have been intended by Congress to be aimed only at a state church. When the First Amendment was pending in Congress in substantially its present form, Mr. Madison said, he apprehended the meaning of the words to be, that Congress should not establish a religion, and enforce the legal observation of it by law, nor compel men to worship God in any manner contrary to their conscience." Passing years, however, have brought about acceptance of a broader meaning . . . .[4]

Similarly, Justice Powell noted:

> At this point in the 20th century we are quite far removed from the dangers that prompted the Framers to include the Establishment Clause in the Bill of Rights. The risk of significant religious or denominational control over our democratic processes—or even of deep political division along religious lines—is remote.[5]

---

[1]   U.S. CONST. amend. 1 (1791).

[2]   School District of Abington v. Schempp, 374 U.S. 203, 309-10 (1963). The *Schempp* case is discussed in chapter 12, *infra. See also* Jaffree v. Board of School Commissioners, 554 F. Supp. 1104 (S.D. Ala. 1983) (extensive historical analysis), *rev'd*, Wallace v. Jaffree, 472 U.S. 38 (1985) (extensive historical analysis by Justice Rehnquist, in a dissenting opinion, is summarized in chapter 16, *infra*); R. CORD, SEPARATION OF CHURCH AND STATE: HISTORICAL FACT AND CURRENT FICTION (1982); Kurland, *The Irrelevance of the Constitution: The Religion clauses of the First Amendment and the Supreme Court*, 24 VILLANOVA L. REV. 3 (1978); McClellan, *The Making and the Unmaking of the Establishment Clause*, in A BLUEPRINT FOR JUDICIAL REFORM (P. McGuigan & R. Rader eds. 1982).

[3]   People of State of Illinois ex rel. McCollum v. Board of Education, 333 U.S. 203, 244 (1948).

[4]   Justice Douglas, concurring in Engel v. Vitale, 370 U.S. 421, 442 (1962), remarked, "I cannot say that to authorize this prayer is to establish a religion in the strictly historic meaning of those words. A religion is not established in the usual sense merely by letting those who choose to do so say the prayer that the public school teacher leads."

[5]   Wolman v. Walter, 433 U.S. 229, 263 (concurring in part and dissenting in part). This statement was quoted with approval by a majority of the Supreme Court in Mueller v. Allen, 463 U.S. 388 (1983).

After a comprehensive analysis of the history of the establishment clause, Chief Justice Rehnquist concluded:

> It seems indisputable from these glimpses into Madison's thinking, reflected by actions on the floor of the House in 1789, that he saw the amendment as designed to prohibit the establishment of a national religion, and perhaps to prevent discrimination among sects. . . . The framers intended the Establishment Clause to prohibit the designation of any church as a "national" one.[6]

Justice Story, writing early in our nation's history, noted that "the real object of the [First] Amendment was . . . to prevent any national ecclesiastical establishment, which would give to an hierarchy the exclusive patronage of the national government."[7]

This construction of the intent of the framers of the religion clauses is supported by the absence of federal court decisions interpreting these clauses for the first one and a half centuries following their enactment. Prayers, Bible readings, and religious instruction in the public schools; rental of public facilities by church groups; religious symbols on public property; tax exemptions for religious organizations; and state assistance to religious education were seldom if ever challenged since such practices were plainly far from the congressional establishment of a national religion prohibited by the First Amendment. In a related context, the Supreme Court has observed that "[i]f a thing has been practiced for two hundred years by common consent, it will need a strong case for the Constitution to affect it."[8]

Thomas Cooley, an eminent 19th-century authority on constitutional history, observed that "[n]o principle of constitutional law is violated when thanksgiving or fast days are appointed; when chaplains are designated for the army and navy; when legislative sessions are opened with prayer or the reading of the Scriptures; or when religious teaching is encouraged by a general exemption of the houses of religious worship from taxation for the support of state government."[9]

In more recent years, other judges have interpreted the historical precedent as supporting a much broader interpretation of the establishment clause.[10] Many would concur with Justice Brennan's conclusion that a too literal quest for the advice of the founding fathers upon these issues is futile and misdirected since "the historical record is at best ambiguous, and statements can readily be found to support either side of the proposition."[11] Nevertheless, Justice Brennan conceded that the framers of the First Amendment were "preoccupied" with the "imminent

---

[6]   Wallace v. Jaffree, 472 U.S. 38 (1985) (dissenting opinion).

[7]   J. STORY, COMMENTARIES ON THE CONSTITUTION 630 (5th ed. 1891).

[8]   Jackman v. Rosenbaum Co., 260 U.S. 22, 31 (1922). See also Coler v. Corn Exchange Bank, 250 N.Y. 136, 138 (1928) (Cardozo, J.) ("[n]ot lightly vacated is the verdict of quiescent years").

[9]   T. COOLEY, CONSTITUTIONAL LIMITATIONS 471 (1851).

[10] Everson v. Board of Education, 330 U.S. 1, 31 (1947) (Rutledge, J., dissenting); People of State of Illinois ex rel. McCollum v. Board of Education, 333 U.S. 203, 212 (Frankfurter, J., concurring).

[11] School District of Abington v. Schempp, 374 U.S. 203, 237 (Brennan, J., concurring).

question of established churches."[12]

Three factors have considerably broadened the meaning and effect of the First Amendment's religion clauses, and particularly the establishment clause. The first occurred in 1803 when the United States Supreme Court ruled that "an act of the legislature, repugnant to the Constitution, is void," and that the federal judiciary is the ultimate interpreter of the Constitution.[13] Thereafter, federal judges had the power—nowhere given in the Constitution itself—to invalidate legislation they deemed inconsistent with the Constitution. A law that established a religion, violated an individual's right to freely exercise his or her religion, or contravened any other provision of the Constitution could be invalidated by a federal court. The nature of the American polity had been redefined.

The second factor that considerably extended the scope of the First Amendment was the judge-made doctrine of *incorporation* expressed in 1937 in the landmark case of *Palko v. Connecticut*.[14] The Supreme Court ruled in *Palko* that those provisions of the Bill of Rights—the first ten amendments to the federal Constitution—that were "implicit in the concept of ordered liberty" were incorporated into the Fourteenth Amendment's "due process clause" and accordingly became applicable to the states.[15] This decision was of fundamental significance, for the framers of the Bill of Rights never intended these amendments to apply to the states. Chief Justice Marshall himself, the author of *Marbury v. Madison*,[16] observed over a century prior to *Palko* that the provisions of the Bill of Rights "contain no expression indicating an intention to apply them to the state governments. This court cannot so apply them."[17] Marshall's admonition was ignored by a majority of the Supreme Court in *Palko*. In 1940, the Court concluded that the religion clauses of the First Amendment were "implicit in the concept of ordered liberty," and so were limitations upon state as well as federal action.[18] As a result, since 1940 the states have been prohibited from making any law "respecting an establishment of religion, or prohibiting the free exercise thereof . . . ." And, significantly, the term *state* has been construed to mean any

---

[12] *Id.*

[13] Marbury v. Madison, 1 Cranch 137 (1803).

[14] 302 U.S. 319 (1937).

[15] The Fourteenth Amendment provides in part, "nor shall any State deprive any person of life, liberty, or property, without due process of law . . . ." It is important to note that the Fourteenth Amendment is a limitation on the power of "States." By comparison, the Bill of Rights, including the First Amendment, was intended to be a limitation solely upon the power of Congress.

[16] See note 13, *supra*, and accompanying text.

[17] Barron v. Mayor and City Council, 32 U.S. (7 Pet.) 243 (1833). *See also* Adamson v. California, 332 U.S. 46 (1947), in which Justice Frankfurter observed:

> Those reading the English language with the meaning which it ordinarily conveys, those conversant with the political and legal history of the concept of due process, those sensitive to the relations of the States to the central government as well as the relation of some of the provisions of the Bill of Rights to the process of justice, would hardly recognize the Fourteenth Amendment as a cover for the various explicit provisions of the first eight amendments. . . . The notion that the Fourteenth Amendment was a covert way of imposing upon the States all the rules which it seemed important to Eighteenth Century statesmen to write into the Federal Amendments, was rejected by judges who were themselves witnesses of the process by which the Fourteenth Amendment became part of the Constitution. *Id.* at 63-4.

[18] Cantwell v. Connecticut, 310 U.S. 296 (1940).

subdivision or agency of a state. The First Amendment thereby applies to cities, counties, boards of education, and every other level, department, office, or agency of government.

A federal district court judge, in a notable if futile opinion, openly condemned the Supreme Court for its unwarranted extension of the First Amendment religion clauses to the states.[19] Ironically, the Supreme Court publicly derided this lower court ruling as "remarkable" and "aberrant."[20]

A third factor that has extended the reach of the First Amendment's establishment clause is the willingness of the federal courts, since 1948, to liberalize the concept of "establishment" to such a degree as to prohibit conduct that had been deemed consistent with the First Amendment for over a century and a half.

But the establishment clause is not the only religion clause contained in the First Amendment. There is another: "Congress shall make no law . . . prohibiting the free exercise [of religion]." This latter clause—the free exercise clause"—is undamentally incompatible with the philosophy of disestablishment contained in the establishment clause: disestablishment necessarily restricts the free exercise of religion. Thus, the recent judicial emphasis upon disestablishment has at times collided with free exercise interests and with other express and implied rights (speech, assembly, association) contained in the First Amendment. Chief Justice Burger, in *Walz v. Tax Commission*,[21] commented on this underlying tension: "The Court has struggled to find a neutral course between the two religion clauses, both of which are cast in absolute terms, and either of which, if expanded to a logical extreme, would tend to clash with the other." Similarly, Justice Stewart, dissenting in *Schempp*,[22] observed, "[T]here are areas in which a doctrinaire reading of the establishment clause leads to irreconcilable conflict with the free exercise clause." The Supreme Court has attempted to synthesize the religion clauses by emphasizing the concepts of "neutrality" and "accommodation." To illustrate, the Court has observed:

> The general principle deductible from the First Amendment and all that has been said by the Court is this: that we will not tolerate either governmentally established religion or governmental interference with religion. Short of those expressly prescribed governmental acts there is room for play in the joints productive of a benevolent neutrality which will permit religious exercise to exist without sponsorship and without interference.[23]

---

[19] Jaffree v. James, 554 F. Supp. 1130 (S.D. Ala. 1983).

[20] Wallace v. Jaffree, 472 U.S. 38 (1985).

[21] 397 U.S. 664, 668-69 (1970).

[22] See note 11, *supra*, at 309.

[23] Walz v. Tax Commission, 397 U.S. 664, 669 (1970).

The Court has also stated:

> [T]his Court repeatedly has recognized that tension inevitably exists
> between the Free Exercise and the Establishment Clauses . . . and that it
> may often not be possible to promote the former without offending the
> latter. As a result of this tension, our cases require the State to maintain an
> attitude of "neutrality," neither "advancing" nor "inhibiting" religion.[24]

In *Zorach v. Clauson*,[25] the Court spoke of the need of "accommodating" the
religious needs of the people.

Notwithstanding the emphasis upon "neutrality" and "accommodation,"
there is a marked judicial preference for the establishment clause over the free
exercise clause. Chief Justice Rehnquist observed:

> The Court apparently believes that the establishment clause of the
> First Amendment not only mandates religious neutrality on the part of
> government but also requires that this Court go further and throw its
> weight on the side of those who believe that our society as a whole should
> be a purely secular one. Nothing in the First Amendment or in the cases
> interpreting it requires such an extreme approach to this difficult question,
> and any interpretation of the establishment clause and constitutional values
> it serves must also take account of the free exercise clause and the values it
> serves.[26]

Chief Justice Burger observed: "One can only hope that, at some future
date, the Court will come to a more enlightened and tolerant view of the First
Amendment's guarantee of free exercise of religion . . . ."[27]

Ironically, the Supreme Court, in the same decision that outlawed voluntary,
school-sponsored Bible readings on the ground that they violate the establishment
clause, acknowledged that "the state may not establish a 'religion of secularism' in
the sense of affirmatively opposing or showing hostility to religion, thus preferring
those who believe in no religion over those who do believe."[28]

The continuing frustration by the Supreme Court and lower federal courts
of voluntary religious practices that are perceived as legitimate by a substantial
majority of the public may one day prompt a reassessment of the meaning of First
Amendment religion clauses.

---

[24] Committee for Public Education & Religious Liberty v. Nyquist, 413 U.S. 756, 788 (1973).

[25] 343 U.S. 306 (1952).

[26] Meek v. Pittinger, 421 U.S. 349, 395 (1975) (Rehnquist, J., dissenting).

[27] Meek v. Pittinger, 421 U.S. 349, 387 (1975) (Burger, C.J., dissenting).

[28] School District of Abington v. Schempp, 374 U.S. 203, 225 (1963).

Instructional Aids to Chapter 11

Key Terms

benevolent neutrality

Congress

establishment clause

free exercise clause

incorporation doctrine

judicial review

Marbury v. Madison

state

Learning Objectives

- Understand the original purpose of the First Amendment's "nonestablishment of religion" clause.

- Explain the three factors that have led to the enormous expansion and revision of the original intent of the First Amendment's "nonestablishment of religion" clause.

- Understand the significance of the Supreme Court's decision in *Marbury v. Madison*.

- Understand what is meant by the *incorporation doctrine*.

Short-Answer Questions

1. The manager of a large apartment complex prohibits non-residents from entering the premises for evangelistic purposes. The minister of a neighboring church contacts the manager, and suggests that the manager's behavior violates the First Amendment right of religious freedom. Is the minister correct? Explain.

2. How can the First Amendment, which prevents "Congress" from establishing a religion, be relied on by the courts in striking down the actions of state legislatures and public school boards that promote religion?

3. The author of this text states that the nature of the American system of government was altered by the Supreme Court's 1803 decision of M*arbury v. Madison.* Do you agree or disagree with this statement? Explain.

4. Explain the "incorporation doctrine." What is its relevance to churches?

5. What do you believe was the original purpose for the First Amendment religion clauses?

6. Massachusetts was the last state to disestablish an established religion. This occurred nearly a half a century after the ratification of the First Amendment. How is this fact relevant in interpreting the original purpose of the First Amendment's nonestablishment of religion clause?

7. The Supreme Court has called for a "benevolent neutrality" on the part of government toward religion. What does this mean, and why is this necessary?

Essay Questions

1. How would the framers of the Constitution and Bill of Rights have viewed the "incorporation doctrine"? Do you believe that it is relevant today to determine the intention of the framers?

2. The Supreme Court has observed that an emphasis on one of the First Amendment's two religion clauses inevitably leads to a clash with the other. What did the Court mean?

CHAPTER TWELVE

Landmark Supreme Court Decisions Interpreting the First Amendment Religion Clauses

Legal Briefs

Charles Evans Hughes, a former Chief Justice of the United States Supreme Court, once remarked that "we are under a Constitution, but the Constitution is what the judges say it is." These words reflect the holding of the Supreme Court's 1803 decision of Marbury v. Madison, in which the Court ruled that the Constitution is the supreme law of the land, that any act of government in conflict with the Constitution is void, and that the federal judges are entrusted with the responsibility of interpreting the Constitution. Since the United States Supreme Court is the highest court in the federal judicial system, its pronouncements have the ultimate authority. An interpretation of the Constitution by the Supreme Court becomes the supreme law of the land until the court reverses itself or until a constitutional amendment is ratified that alters the Court's interpretation. The importance of Supreme Court interpretations of the First Amendment religion clauses should thus be apparent.

In this chapter, several Supreme Court decisions will be reviewed. Through a careful study of these decisions, you will acquire an understanding of how the Supreme Court interprets the religion clauses. Such interpretations are binding on all other courts, and upon every other organ of government.

> "Since the United States Supreme Court is the highest court in the federal judicial system, its pronouncements have the ultimate authority."

The United State Supreme Court in *Marbury v. Madison*[1] concluded that the United States Constitution is the "paramount," or supreme law of the land, and that "it is emphatically the province and duty" of the federal courts to construe the Constitution.[2] Since the United States Supreme Court is the highest federal court, its interpretations of the Constitution in effect become the supreme law of the land, and must be followed by all state and lower federal courts until the Supreme Court reverses itself and overrules the earlier decision, or until the Court's ruling is invalidated by ratification of an amendment to the Constitution. The importance of Supreme Court interpretations of the First Amendment's "religion clauses"[3] should be apparent.

The Supreme Court seldom discussed the religion clauses in the first century and a half following their enactment. Since 1947, however, the Court has construed the religion clauses on a number of occasions. Some of the more significant of these decisions are summarized in this chapter.[4]

Everson v. Board of Education[5]

§ 12-01

A New Jersey statute authorized local school districts to make arrangements for the transportation of children to and from schools. One township board of education, acting pursuant to this statute, adopted a resolution authorizing reimbursement to parents of money expended by them for the bus transportation of their children on buses operated by the public transportation system. Part of this money was for the payment of transportation of some children in the community to Catholic

---

[1] 1 Cranch 137 (1803). See chapter 11, note 13, and accompanying text.

[2] "We are under a Constitution, but the Constitution is what the judges say it is." Charles Evans Hughes, Speech, May 3, 1907.

[3] The First Amendment provides in relevant part that "Congress shall make no law respecting an establishment of religion or prohibiting the free exercise thereof . . . ." The first phrase of the amendment—"Congress shall make no law respecting an establishment of religion"—is referred to as the *establishment clause*. The second phrase—"or prohibit the free exercise thereof"—is referred to as the *free exercise clause*.

[4] Some important Supreme Court decisions interpreting the First Amendment religion clauses are discussed in other chapters. See, e.g., Corporation of the Presiding Bishop of the Church of Jesus Christ of Latter-Day Saints v. Amos, 483 U.S. 327 (1987) (chapter 8); Tony and Susan Alamo Foundation v. Secretary of Labor, 471 U.S. 290 (1985) (chapter 8); Larson v. Valente, 456 U.S. 228 (1982) (chapter 9); Village of Schaumburg v. Citizens for a Better Environment, 444 U.S. 620, 632 (1980) (chapter 9); Jones v. Wolf, 443 U.S. 595 (1979) (chapter 7); NLRB v. Catholic Bishop of Chicago, 440 U.S. 490 (1979) (chapter 8); Serbian Eastern Orthodox Diocese v. Milivojevich, 426 U.S. 696 (1976) (chapters 2 and 9); Maryland and Virginia Eldership of the Churches of God v. Church of God, 396 U.S. 367 (1970) (chapter 7); Presbyterian Church in the United States v. Mary Elizabeth Blue Hull Memorial Presbyterian Church, 393 U.S. 440 (1969) (chapter 7); Kedroff v. St. Nicholas Cathedral, 344 U.S. 94 (1952) (chapters 2 and 9); Cantwell v. Connecticut, 310 U.S. 296 (1940) (chapter 11); Gonzalez v. Roman Catholic Archbishop, 280 U.S. 1 (1928) (chapter 2); Watson v. Jones, 80 U.S. (13 Wall.) 679 (1871) (chapters 2, 7, and 9).

[5] 330 U.S. 1 (1947). See Justice Rehnquist's dissenting opinion in Wallace v. Jaffree, 472 U.S. 38 (1985), for a critique of the historical accuracy of this ruling. The *Wallace* case, and Justice Rehnquist's dissent, are discussed later in this chapter.

parochial schools. A taxpayer filed suit against the board of education, alleging that the state law and board of education resolution constituted a violation of the First Amendment to the United States Constitution insofar as they forced taxpayers to pay for the transportation of children to Catholic schools.

The New Jersey Court of Errors and Appeals concluded that the statute and resolution did not violate the First Amendment, and the taxpayer appealed directly to the United States Supreme Court. In upholding the statute and school board resolution, the Supreme Court rendered the first modern interpretation of the First Amendment's "establishment clause." After briefly describing the colonial experience of established religions and persecution of religious dissenters that "found expression in the First Amendment," the Court observed:

> The "establishment of religion" clause of the First Amendment means at least this: Neither a state nor the Federal Government can set up a church. Neither can pass laws which aid one religion, aid all religions, or prefer one religion over another. Neither can force nor influence a person to go or to remain away from church against his will or force him to profess a belief or disbelief in any religion. No person can be punished for entertaining or professing religious beliefs or disbeliefs, for church attendance or nonattendance. No tax in any amount, large or small, can be levied to support any religious activities or institutions, whatever they may be called, or whatever form they may adopt to teach or practice religion. Neither a state nor the Federal Government can, openly or secretly, participate in the affairs of any religious organizations or groups and vice versa. In the words of Jefferson, the clause against establishment of religion by law was intended to erect "a wall of separation between church and state."[6]

Measured by this standard, the Court concluded that the First Amendment did not prohibit New Jersey from spending tax revenues to pay the bus fares of parochial school pupils as a part of a general program under which it paid the fares of pupils attending public and other schools. "We must be careful," observed the Court, in protecting the citizens of New Jersey against state-established churches, to be sure that we do not inadvertently prohibit New Jersey from extending its general state law benefits to all its citizens without regard to their religious beliefs."[7] The Court acknowledged that payment of the bus fares of parochial school students as well as the protection of parochial school pupils by means of state-paid police officers and firefighters and the use of public streets and sidewalks by parochial school pupils did provide some assistance to such pupils, but the Court insisted that

> cutting off church-schools from these services, so separate and so indisputably marked off from the religious function, would make it far more difficult for the schools to operate. But such is obviously not the purpose of

[6] *Id.* at 15-16.
[7] *Id.* at 16.

the First Amendment. That amendment requires the state to be neutral in its relations with groups of religious believers and non-believers; it does not require the state to be their adversary. State power is no more to be used so as to handicap religions, than it is to favor them.[8]

Finally, the Court observed that the free exercise of religion, also protected by the First Amendment, would be abridged by a state law excluding certain citizens on the basis of their religion from receiving the benefits of public welfare legislation.

People of State of Illinois ex rel. McCollum v. Board of Education[9]

§ 12-02

In 1940, interested members of the Jewish, Roman Catholic, and a few of the Protestant faiths formed a voluntary association in Champaign, Illinois, called the Champaign Council on Religious Education. The council obtained permission from the local board of education to offer classes in religious instruction to public school pupils in grades four to nine inclusive. Classes were made up of pupils whose parents signed printed cards requesting that their children be permitted to attend. Classes were held weekly, 30 minutes for the lower grades and 45 minutes for the higher. The council employed the religious teachers at no expense to the school authorities, but the instructors were subject to the approval and supervision of the superintendent of schools. The classes were taught in three separate groups by Protestant teachers, Catholic priests, and a Jewish rabbi. Classes were conducted in the regular classrooms of the school building. Students who did not choose to take the religious instruction were not released from public school duties; they were required to leave their classrooms and go to some other place in the school building for the pursuit of their secular studies. Students who were released from secular study for the religious instruction were required to be present at the religious classes.

The constitutionality of this "released time" program was challenged by the parent of a public school student on the ground that it violated the First Amendment's prohibition of the establishment of a religion. The state courts of Illinois upheld the constitutionality of the program, and the case was appealed directly to the United States Supreme Court. The Supreme Court struck down the released time program on the ground that it was "beyond all question a utilization of the tax-established and tax-supported public school system to aid religious groups to spread their faith" and thus "falls squarely under the ban of the First

8   *Id.* at 18.
9   333 U.S. 203 (1948).

Amendment."[10] The Court noted in particular that the state's tax-supported public school buildings were used for the dissemination of religious doctrine, and that the state materially aided religious groups by providing pupils for their religious classes through use of the state's compulsory school machinery. "This is not separation of Church and State," the Court concluded.

The Court rejected the argument that the First Amendment was intended to forbid only governmental preference of one religion over another, and not impartial governmental assistance of all religions. The Court also rejected the contention that forbidding the use of public school property to aid all religious faiths in the dissemination of their doctrine constituted an impermissible governmental hostility to religion. A manifestation of governmental hostility to religion would be impermissible, the Court agreed, but it found no such hostility under the facts of this case. The Court concluded:

> [T]he First Amendment rests upon the premise that both religion and government can best work to achieve their lofty aims if each is left free from the other within its respective sphere. . . . [T]he First Amendment has erected a wall between Church and State which must be kept high and impregnable.[11]

Justice Jackson, in a concurring opinion, cautioned that it may be unnecessary if not impossible to cast out of secular education all that some people may reasonably regard as religious instruction:

"I should suppose it is a proper, if not an indispensable, part of preparation for a worldly life to know the roles that religions have played in the tragic story of mankind."

Music without sacred music, architecture minus the cathedral, or painting without the scriptural themes would be eccentric and incomplete, even from a secular point of view. Yet the inspirational appeal of religion in these guises is often stronger than in forthright sermon. Even such a "science" as biology raises the issue between evolution and creation as an explanation of our presence on this planet. Certainly a course in English literature that omitted the Bible and other powerful uses of our mother tongue for religious ends would be pretty barren. And I should suppose it is a proper, if not an indispensable, part of preparation for a worldly life to know the roles that religions have played in the tragic story of mankind. The fact is that, for good or ill, nearly everything in our culture worth transmitting, everything which gives meaning to life, is saturated with religious influences, derived from paganism, Judaism, Christianity—both Catholic and Protestant—and other faiths accepted by a large part of the world's peoples. One can hardly

---

10 *Id.* at 210.

11 *Id.* at 212.

respect a system of education that would leave the student wholly ignorant of the currents of religious thought that move the world society for a part in which he is being prepared.[12]

In a dissenting opinion, Justice Reed insisted that the First Amendment was never intended to prohibit religious instruction of public school children during school hours. He agreed that government cannot "aid" all or any religions, but he construed the word *aid* to mean purposeful assistance directly to a church or religious organization itself. Justice Reed recounted many examples of government accommodation of religious practices, and observed:

> The prohibition of enactments respecting the establishment of religion does not bar every friendly gesture between church and state. It is not an absolute prohibition against every conceivable situation where the two may work together any more than the other provisions of the First Amendment—free speech, free press—are absolutes.[13]

Justice Reed concluded that "[t]his Court cannot be too cautious in upsetting practices embedded in our society by many years of experience" and that devotion to the great principle of religious liberty "should not lead us into a rigid interpretation of the constitutional guarantee that conflicts with accepted habits of our people."[14]

Zorach v. Clauson[15] §12-03

Shortly after deciding that released time programs allowing public school students to receive religious instruction on school property were unconstitutional, the Supreme Court was faced with the task of deciding the constitutionality of released time programs that permitted public school children to leave school property to receive religious instruction.

New York City developed a program that permitted its public schools to release students during the school day so that they could leave the school buildings and grounds and go to religious centers for religious instruction or devotional exercises. Students were released upon written request of their parents. Those not released stayed at school. The churches and other religious centers made weekly reports to the schools. All costs of the program were paid by religious organizations.

A group of parents challenged the constitutionality of the program. In particular, the parents argued that the program constituted an establishment

---

12   *Id.* at 236.

13   *Id.* at 255-56.

14   *Id.* at 256.

15   343 U.S. 306 (1952).

of religion in violation of the First Amendment since the weight and influence of the school was put behind a program of religious instruction; public school teachers policed the program, keeping track of students who had been released; and classroom activities came to a halt while students who had been released were on leave.

The Court rejected the parents' challenge. While acknowledging that "there cannot be the slightest doubt that the First Amendment reflects the philosophy that Church and State should be separated," the Court held that the First Amendment "does not say that in every and all respects there shall be a separation of Church and State."[16] A strict separation, observed the Court, would cause the state and religion to be aliens—hostile, suspicious, and even unfriendly. Municipalities would not be permitted to render police or fire protection to religious groups; police officers who helped parishioners to their places of worship would violate the Constitution; and prayers in the nation's legislative halls, the proclamations making Thanksgiving Day a holiday, and the words "so help me God" in courtroom oaths—these and all other references to the Almighty that run through our laws and ceremonies would flout the First Amendment.

In one of its most eloquent descriptions of the meaning of *establishment*, the Court observed:

> We are a religious people whose institutions presuppose a Supreme Being.
> We guarantee the freedom of worship as one chooses. We make room
> for as wide a variety of beliefs and creeds as the spiritual needs of man
> deem necessary. We sponsor an attitude on the part of government that
> shows no partiality to any one group and that lets each flourish according
> to the zeal of its adherents and the appeal of its dogma. When the state
> encourages religious instruction or cooperates with religious authorities
> by adjusting the schedule of public events to sectarian needs, it follows
> the best of our traditions. For it then respects the religious nature of our
> people and accommodates the public service to their spiritual needs. To
> hold that it may not would be to find in the Constitution a requirement
> that the government show a callous indifference to religious groups. That
> would be preferring those who believe in no religion over those who do
> believe. Government may not finance religious groups nor undertake
> religious instruction nor blend secular and sectarian education nor use
> secular institutions to force one or some religion on any person. But we find
> no constitutional requirement which makes it necessary for government
> to be hostile to religion and throw its weight against efforts to widen the
> effective scope of religious influence. The government must be neutral
> when it comes to competition between sects. It may not thrust any sect on
> any person. It may not make a religious observance compulsory. It may not
> coerce anyone to attend church, to observe a religious holiday, or to take
> religious instruction. But it can close its doors or suspend its operations
> as to those who want to repair to their religious sanctuary for worship or

---

[16] *Id.* at 312.

instruction. No more than that is undertaken here.[17]

The released time program of New York City was found to be valid under this test. The Court distinguished *McCollum* on the ground that classrooms were used in that case for religious instruction, and the force of the public school was used to promote that instruction. In the present case, the public schools did no more than accommodate their schedules to a program of outside religious instruction. "We follow the *McCollum* case," concluded the Court. "[B]ut we cannot expand it to cover the present released time program unless separation of Church and State means that public institutions can make no adjustments of their schedules to accommodate the religious needs of the people. We cannot read into the Bill of Rights such a philosophy of hostility to religion."[18]

Engel v. Vitale[19] §12-04

The New York Board of Regents, a governmental agency having broad supervisory power over the state's public schools, recommended that the following nondenominational prayer be recited in each public school at the start of every school day: "Almighty God, we acknowledge our dependence upon Thee, and we beg Thy blessings upon us, our parents, our teachers, and our country."

A group of parents whose children attended a public school in which the "Regents' prayer" was recited challenged the constitutionality of the practice in state court. The New York state courts upheld the constitutionality of the practice on the condition that no child be compelled to join in the prayer over his own or his parents' objection. The parents appealed to the United States Supreme Court, which ruled that the practice constituted an establishment of religion in violation of the First Amendment:

> [W]e think that the constitutional prohibition against laws respecting an establishment of religion must at least mean that in this country it is no part of the business of government to compose official prayers for any group of the American people to recite as a part of a religious program carried on by government.[20]

The Court rejected the contention that the prayer was permissible because it was nondenominational and voluntary, since the establishment clause "does not depend upon any showing of direct governmental compulsion and is violated by the enactment of laws which establish an official religion whether those laws

---

[17] *Id.* at 313-14.

[18] *Id.* at 313-14.

[19] 370 U.S. 421 (1962).

[20] *Id.* at 425.

operate directly to coerce nonobserving individuals or not."[21] Furthermore, the Court refused to concede that the Regents' prayer was in fact "voluntary" since when the power and prestige of government is placed behind a particular religious belief "the indirect coercive pressure upon religious minorities to conform to the prevailing officially approved religion is plain."[22]

In rejecting the contention that its decision evidenced a hostility toward religion which itself contravened the First Amendment, the Court observed:

> [T]here grew up a sentiment that caused men to leave the cross-currents of officially established state religions and religious persecution in Europe and come to this country filled with that hope that they could find a place in which they could pray when they pleased to the God of their faith in the language they chose. And there were men of this same faith . . . who led the fight for adoption of our Constitution and also for our Bill of Rights with the very guarantees of religious freedom that forbid the sort of governmental activity which New York has attempted here.[23]

The Court acknowledged that governmental endorsement of the Regents' prayer was insignificant in comparison to the encroachments upon religion which were uppermost in the minds of those who ratified the First Amendment, but it reasoned that "it is proper to take alarm at the first experiment with our liberties" in order to preclude more substantial violations.

In dissent, Justice Stewart traced the many spiritual traditions of our nation, including the recitation of prayer before legislative and judicial sessions, the references to God in the Pledge of Allegiance and the national anthem, presidential proclamations of national days of prayer, the provision of military and institutional chaplains at government expense, and imprinting the words "In God We Trust" on coins and currency. He concluded that it was arbitrary to deny school children the right to share in this spiritual heritage by forbidding them to voluntarily recite a prayer at the start of each school day.

School District of Abington v. Schempp[24] § 12-05

The State of Pennsylvania enacted a law that stipulated, "At least ten verses from the Holy Bible shall be read, without comment, at the opening of each public school on each school day. Any child shall be excused from such Bible reading, or attending such Bible reading, upon the written request of his parent or guardian."

---

[21] *Id.* at 430.

[22] *Id.* at 431.

[23] *Id.* at 434-35.

[24] 374 U.S. 203 (1963).

A family having two children in the public schools filed suit to halt enforcement of the Pennsylvania law on the ground that it constituted an impermissible establishment of religion in violation of the First Amendment. A federal district court agreed that the law violated the establishment clause, and the state appealed directly to the United States Supreme Court. The Supreme Court, in affirming the lower court ruling, stated that "to withstand the strictures of the establishment clause there must be a secular legislative purpose and a primary effect that neither advances nor inhibits religion."[25] The Court concluded that the reading of the Bible at the start of each school day was indisputably a religious practice and as such it violated the First Amendment. It did not matter that participation in the readings was voluntary, or that the readings themselves were relatively minor encroachments on the First Amendment, since "[t]he breach of neutrality that is today a trickling stream may all too soon become a raging torrent."[26]

The Court agreed that the state "may not establish a 'religion of secularism' in the sense of affirmatively opposing or showing hostility to religion," but it did not believe that its decision in any sense had that effect.[27] The Court also acknowledged that

> one's education is not complete without a study of comparative religion or the history of religion and its relationship to the advancement of civilization. It certainly may be said that the Bible is worthy of study for its literary and historic qualities. Nothing we have said indicates that such study of the Bible or of religion, when presented objectively as part of a secular program of education, may not be effected consistently with the First Amendment.[28]

Finally, the Court rejected the contention that its decision collided with the majority's right to the free exercise of their religion:

> The very purpose of a Bill of Rights was to withdraw certain subjects from the vicissitudes of political controversy, to place them beyond the reach of majorities and officials and to establish them as legal principles to be applied by the courts. One's right to . . . freedom of worship . . . and other fundamental rights may not be submitted to vote; they depend on the outcome of no elections.[29]

Justice Stewart, in dissent, argued that the neutrality mandated by the First Amendment required that school children be permitted, on a voluntary basis, to start their day with Bible reading since "a refusal to permit religious exercises is

---

[25] *Id.* at 222.

[26] *Id.* at 225.

[27] *Id.*

[28] *Id.*

[29] *Id.* at 226, quoting West Virginia Board of Education v. Barnette, 319 U.S. 624, 638 (1943) (Justice Jackson).

thus seen, not as the realization of state neutrality, but rather as the establishment of a religion of secularism, or at the least, as government support of the beliefs of those who think that religious exercises should be conducted only in private."[30] Justice Stewart also maintained that readings from the Bible unaccompanied by comments and addressed only to those children who chose to be present did not represent the type of support of religion barred by the establishment clause.

Walz v. Tax Commission[31]   § 12-06

The New York legislature enacted a property tax law that exempted real property owned by nonprofit corporations and associations that were organized exclusively for religious, charitable, benevolent, educational, scientific, or literary purposes. A taxpayer filed suit in the New York state courts to prevent the New York City Tax Commission from granting property tax exemptions to religious organizations for properties used solely for religious worship on the ground that such exemptions required the government to make "contributions" to religious organizations in violation of the principle of separation of church and state embodied in the First Amendment. The New York state courts upheld the constitutionality of the exemption, and the case was appealed to the United States Supreme Court.

The Supreme Court, with only one dissenting vote, affirmed the constitutionality of the New York law. After noting that the purpose of the establishment clause is the prevention of "sponsorship, financial support, and active involvement of the sovereign in religious activity,"[32] the Court concluded that the exemption of properties used exclusively for religious purposes did not constitute sponsorship or financial support of religious organizations by the state. "The grant of a tax exemption is not sponsorship," noted the Court, "since the government does not transfer part of its revenue to churches but simply abstains from demanding that the church support the state."[33] In addition, property used for religious purposes was but one of a wide variety of classifications of property that were exempted from tax. The state had not singled out church-owned property for the exemption, but rather it had included such property in a long list of other exempted properties owned by organizations whose activities the state had decided were socially desirable and deserving of protection through exemption from tax.

Finally, the Court emphasized that any practice that leads to an excessive governmental entanglement with religion is prohibited by the establishment clause. It acknowledged that either taxation of churches or exemption occasioned some governmental involvement with religion. However, it concluded that elimination of the exemption would lead to a greater entanglement "by giving

---

[30] *Id.* at 313.

[31] 393 U.S. 664 (1970).

[32] *Id.* at 668.

[33] *Id.* at 675.

rise to tax valuation of church property, tax liens, tax foreclosures, and the direct confrontations and conflicts that follow in the train of those legal processes."[34] On the other hand, the exemption "creates only a minimal and remote involvement between church and state and far less than taxation of churches."[35] The Court also stressed that "an unbroken practice of according the exemption to churches, openly and by affirmative state action, not covertly or by state inaction, is not something to be lightly cast aside,"[36] and it quoted Justice Holmes' earlier observation that "[i]f a thing has been practiced for two hundred years by common consent, it will need a strong case for the [Constitution] to affect it."[37]

Wisconsin v. Yoder[38]

The *Yoder* case involved the constitutionality of applying a state compulsory attendance law to Old Order Amish children who had completed the eighth grade. The principal significance of the decision lies in the Court's construction of the "free exercise clause" of the First Amendment. After emphasizing that "only those interests of the highest order and those not otherwise served can overbalance legitimate claims to the free exercise of religion,"[39] the Court enunciated a three-pronged test for assessing the constitutionality of governmental action under the free exercise clause:

1. Is the activity interfered with by the state motivated by and rooted in legitimate and sincerely held religious belief?

2. Is the activity interfered with by the state unduly and substantially burdened to the extent of affecting religious practice?

3. Does the state have a compelling interest in limiting or restricting the religiously motivated activity that cannot be accomplished through less restrictive means?

This test served as the basic analysis for assessing the validity of governmental limitations on the free exercise of religion until 1990. In 1990, the Supreme Court altered this analysis, making it easier for governmental limitations on religious practice to be constitutional.[40]

---

[34] *Id.* at 674.

[35] *Id.* at 676.

[36] *Id.* at 678.

[37] *Id.*

[38] 406 U.S. 205 (1972).

[39] 406 U.S. at 215.

[40] *See* Employment Division v. Smith, 110 S. Ct. 1595 (1990), which is discussed later in this chapter.

Lemon v. Kurtzman[41]   § 12-08

In striking down various provisions of a New York law authorizing state aid to nonpublic school teachers who taught secular subjects, the Court articulated a three-pronged test for evaluating the constitutionality of government action under the establishment clause: "First, the statute must have a secular legislative purpose; second, its principal or primary effect must be one that neither advances nor inhibits religion; finally, the statute must not foster 'an excessive governmental entanglement with religion.'"[42] This is the test that the federal courts have applied, almost without exception, in evaluating whether or not a particular governmental accommodation of religion violates the establishment clause.

Chambers v. Marsh[43]   § 12-09

For many years, the Nebraska unicameral legislature has begun each of its sessions with a prayer offered by a chaplain chosen biennially and paid out of public funds. This practice was challenged in 1980 by a state senator who claimed that it constituted an establishment of religion in violation of the First Amendment. A federal district court found the practice to be permissible, but a federal appeals court ruled that the practice violated the establishment of religion clause.

In a six to three decision, the Supreme Court reversed the federal appeals court and upheld the constitutionality of the Nebraska legislative chaplaincy program. The Court surveyed the history of legislative chaplains, observing that "[t]he opening of sessions of legislative and other deliberative public bodies with prayer is deeply embedded in the history and tradition of this country," and that this practice "coexisted with the principles of disestablishment and religious freedom." The Court found it especially relevant that the first Congress, which drafted the First Amendment religion clauses, adopted the policy of selecting a chaplain to open each session with prayer:

> It can hardly be thought that in the same week members of the First Congress voted to appoint and to pay a chaplain for each House and also voted to approve the draft of the First Amendment for submission to the States, they intended the establishment clause of the Amendment to forbid what they had just declared acceptable. In applying the First Amendment . . . it would be incongruous to interpret the clause as imposing more stringent First Amendment limits on the states than the draftsmen imposed on the

---

[41]   403 U.S. 602 (1971).

[42]   *Id.* at 612-13. The Court has observed that the "three-part test that has emerged from our decisions is a product of considerations derived from the full sweep of the establishment clause cases." Committee for Public Education v. Nyquist, 413 U.S. 756 (1973).

[43]   463 U.S. 783 (1983).

Federal Government.[44]

While acknowledging that "no one acquires a vested or protected right in violation of the Constitution by long use," the Court found the historical precedent to unequivocally establish the constitutionality of legislative chaplaincies.

The Court also rejected the claim that the Nebraska practice had to be invalidated since a clergyman of only one religious faith had been selected for 16 consecutive years, the chaplain was compensated at public expense, and the prayers were exclusively in the Judeo-Christian tradition. None of these characteristics, concluded the Court, was materially different from the experience of the first Congress.

The true significance of this decision is the Court's willingness to depart from the three-pronged *Lemon* test in evaluating the constitutionality of a practice challenged on establishment clause grounds. In the *Lemon* case, decided in 1971, the Court had formulated the following test as a device to assist in applying the First Amendment's establishment clause: "First, the statute . . . must have a secular legislative purpose; second, its principal or primary effect must be one that neither advances nor inhibits religion; finally, the statute must not foster an excessive governmental entanglement with religion."[45] This test, unfortunately, was used by many state and federal courts as a cudgel to obliterate many forms of religious expression and practice that were not even remotely considered to be establishments of religion by the framers of the First Amendment. The willingness of the Court to uphold a religious practice without any reference to the *Lemon* test suggests that not every accommodation of the "religious nature of our people"[46] or acknowledgment of religious belief will be summarily invalidated.

Wallace v. Jaffree[47] § 12-10

In 1981, the Alabama legislature enacted a law specifying:

At the commencement of the first class of each day in all grades in all public schools the teacher in charge of the room in which each class is held may announce that a period of silence not to exceed one minute in duration shall be observed for meditation or voluntary prayer, and during any such

---

[44] This evidence would conclusively establish the legitimacy of legislative chaplains to all but the most doctrinaire disestablishmentarians, or to those who adhere to a "progressive understanding" of constitutional provisions. To illustrate, in a dissenting opinion, Justice Brennan urged the Court to disregard history and the original purpose of the First Amendment in favor of a more enlightened view of the proper place of religious exercise. Of course, one of the deficiencies of such an approach is that once the moorings of history are abandoned, any substitute standard is itself immediately vulnerable to revision. Thus, condemnations by Justice Brennan and others of decisions that have departed from the "settled" meaning of the *Lemon* decision are hollow and unprincipled.

[45] Lemon v. Kurtzman, 403 U.S. 602 (1971).

[46] Zorach v. Clauson, 343 U.S. 306 (1952) (Justice Douglas speaking for the Court).

[47] 472 U.S. 38 (1985).

period no other activities shall be engaged in.[48]

This law was challenged in 1982 by a parent who asserted that it was an impermissible establishment of religion in violation of the First Amendment. A federal district court, after a lengthy and accurate historical analysis, concluded that the Supreme Court was misguided in its interpretation and application of the First Amendment, and declined to follow its precedents. In particular, the court concluded, correctly, that the First Amendment religion clauses were not applicable to the states, and therefore the State of Alabama was free to accommodate or even establish a religion if it so desired.[49] Predictably, this decision was reversed by a federal appeals court, and ultimately by the Supreme Court as well. Ironically, characterizing the district court's thorough and historically indisputable analysis as "remarkable" and aberrant, the Supreme Court saw nothing improper in its application of the First Amendment to the states contrary to the expressed intention of the framers of that amendment.[50]

The Court concluded that the Alabama law constituted an impermissible "establishment of religion" since it did not have a clearly secular purpose and therefore failed the first prong of the three-pronged *Lemon* test.

The significance of this decision is not the Court's ruling or its facile "historical analysis." Rather, it is the dissenting opinion of Justice Rehnquist, which presents a compelling and comprehensive historical explication of the establishment clause and in the process calls into question the *Lemon* test, the "wall of separation between church and state" metaphor, and the propriety of applying the First Amendment's proscriptions to state governments.

Justice Rehnquist began his opinion by exposing the impropriety of the "wall of separation" metaphor allegedly coined by Thomas Jefferson. Justice Rehnquist pointed out that Jefferson was in France at the time the First Amendment was debated, enacted, and ratified, and that his metaphor was contained in a brief letter to the Danbury Baptist Association 14 years after the First Amendment was drafted. "He would seem to any detached observer," concluded Justice Rehnquist, "as a less than ideal source of contemporary history as to the meaning of the religion clauses of the First Amendment."

Justice Rehnquist then summarized the debates associated with the enactment of the First Amendment by Congress and demonstrated that the concern was "the establishment of a national church, and perhaps the preference of one religious sect over another. . . ." James Madison, the chief architect of the amendment, saw

---

[48]   ALA. CODE § 16-1-20.1.

[49]   *See* chapter 11, *supra.*

[50]   As noted in chapter 11, the Court has, since 1940, assumed that the Fourteenth Amendment's guaranty of "life, liberty and property" against state interference "incorporated" the First Amendment religion clauses. Therefore, the Court believes that it is justified in invalidating state (and local) legislation even though the First Amendment is by its own terms a limitation solely on the power of the federal government ("Congress"). One can only wonder why it took the Court three-quarters of a century to "discover" that the protections of the First Amendment were "incorporated" into an amendment ratified at the conclusion of the Civil War and designed to protect newly-freed slaves. This construction is addressed in a number of scholarly works on constitutional law. *See e.g.*, R. BERGER, GOVERNMENT BY JUDICIARY: THE TRANSFORMATION OF THE FOURTEENTH AMENDMENT (1977).

no need for it, but proposed it merely as an expedient to satisfy the concerns of those opponents of the Constitution who insisted that without a Bill of Rights the newly-created federal government might become despotic. Justice Rehnquist also cited the early nineteenth-century commentaries of Supreme Court Justice Story and legal historian Thomas Cooley as proof that the purpose of the establishment clause was the prevention of a national religion. He condemned the Court's constitutionalization of the "wall of separation" metaphor in its *Everson* decision in 1947, and suggested that this "theory of rigid separation" be "frankly and explicitly abandoned."

Justice Rehnquist denounced the three-pronged *Lemon* test adopted by the Court in 1971, since it "has no more grounding in the history of the First Amendment than does the wall theory upon which it rests." He observed that the Court itself had moved away from the *Lemon* formulation:

> [W]e soon began describing the test as only a 'guideline,' and lately we have described it as 'no more than [a] useful signpost'. . . . We have noted that the *Lemon* test is 'not easily applied,' under the *Lemon* test we have 'sacrificed clarity and predictability for flexibility' . . . [and] the *Lemon* test has never been binding on the Court. . . . If a constitutional theory has no basis in the history of the amendment it seeks to interpret, and is difficult to apply and yields unprincipled results, I see little use for it.[51]

In place of the "wall of separation" metaphor or the *Lemon* test, Justice Rehnquist proposed that the religion clauses be interpreted consistently with the principles that "the framers inscribed," for "[a]ny deviation from their intentions frustrates the permanence of [the Bill of Rights] and will only lead to the type of unprincipled decision-making that has plagued our establishment clause cases since *Everson*" in 1947. The principles inscribed by the framers on the First Amendment's religion clauses were clear:

> The framers intended the establishment clause to prohibit the designation of any church as a "national" one. The clause was also designed to stop the federal government from asserting a preference of one religious denomination or sect over others. Given the "incorporation" of the establishment clause as against the states via the Fourteenth Amendment in *Everson*, states are prohibited as well from establishing a religion or discriminating between sects. As its history abundantly shows, however, nothing in the establishment clause requires government to be strictly neutral between religion and irreligion, nor does that clause prohibit Congress or the states from pursuing legitimate secular ends through nondiscriminatory means.[52]

Justice Rehnquist concluded that the Court's decision would "come as a

---

[51]   472 U.S. at 112.

[52]   *Id.* at 113.

shock to those who drafted the Bill of Rights" as well as to "a large number of thoughtful Americans today." Noting that George Washington himself, at the request of the very Congress that passed the Bill of Rights, proclaimed a day of public thanksgiving and prayer, Justice Rehnquist observed that "[history] must judge whether it was the father of his country in 1789, or a majority of the Court today, which has strayed from the meaning of the establishment clause."

Employment Division v. Smith[53]

§ 12-11

The First Amendment to the United States Constitution guarantees that "Congress shall make no law . . . prohibiting the free exercise of religion." For many years, the United States Supreme Court has interpreted this language to mean that government cannot impose substantial burdens on the exercise of sincerely-held religious beliefs unless its action is justified by a "compelling state interest" that cannot be served through less restrictive means. In a case of historic proportion, the Supreme Court revised its understanding of the "free exercise" clause. It is unclear at this time what the ramifications will be.

Oregon law prohibits the intentional possession of a "controlled substance," including the drug peyote. Two employees of a private drug rehabilitation organization were fired from their jobs because they consumed peyote for "sacramental purposes" at a ceremony of the Native American Church. The two individuals applied for unemployment benefits under Oregon law, but their application was denied on the grounds that benefits are not payable to employees who are discharged for "misconduct." The two former employees claimed that the denial of benefits violated their constitutional right to freely exercise their religion. The state supreme court agreed with the discharged employees, and the state appealed to the United States Supreme Court.

The Supreme Court reversed the Oregon court's decision, and ruled that (1) the constitutional guaranty of religious freedom did not prohibit a state from criminalizing the sacramental use of a narcotic drug, and (2) the state of Oregon could deny unemployment benefits to individuals who were fired from their jobs for consuming peyote.

The Court began its opinion by noting that "we have never held that an individual's religious beliefs excuse him from compliance with an otherwise valid law prohibiting conduct that the state is free to regulate." On the contrary, the constitutional guaranty of religious freedom "does not relieve an individual of the obligation to comply with a valid and neutral law of general applicability on the ground that the law [prohibits] conduct that his religion prescribes."

The real significance of the Court's ruling was its refusal to apply the "compelling state interest" test as requested by the discharged employees. As noted

---

[53]   110 S. Ct. 1595 (1990).

above, the Supreme Court previously had interpreted the constitutional guaranty of religious freedom to mean that government could not impose substantial burdens on the exercise of sincerely-held religious beliefs unless its action was justified by a "compelling state interest" that could not be served through less restrictive means. The former employees argued that the Oregon law's denial of unemployment benefits to persons using peyote for sacramental purposes was not supported by a "compelling state interest" and accordingly could not be applied without violating the constitution.

The Court justified its refusal to apply the "compelling state interest" test by noting that (1) it had not applied the test in a number of its recent decisions, (2) it had never found a state law limiting religious practices invalid on the ground that it was not supported by a compelling state interest, and (3) the compelling state interest test should never be applied "to require exemptions from a generally applicable criminal law."

The Court also rejected the former employees' suggestion that the "compelling state interest" test be applied only in cases involving religiously-motivated conduct that is "central" to an individual's religion. This would require the courts to make judgments on the importance of religious practices—and this the civil courts may never do. The only options are to apply the "compelling state interest" test to all attempts by government to regulate religious practices, or to not apply the test at all. Applying the test in all cases involving governmental attempts to regulate religious practices would lead to "anarchy," since it would render presumptively invalid every law that regulates conduct allegedly based on religious belief. This would open the floodgates of claims of religious exemption

> from civic obligations of almost every conceivable kind—ranging from compulsory military service to the payment of taxes, to health and safety regulation such as manslaughter and child neglect laws, compulsory vaccination laws, drug laws; to social welfare legislation such as minimum wage laws, child labor laws, animal cruelty laws, environmental protection laws, and laws providing for equality of opportunity for the races. The First Amendment's protection of religious liberty does not require this.[54]

The Court's ruling represents a clear departure from its previously well-established understanding of the constitutional guaranty of religious freedom. No longer will a state need to demonstrate that a "compelling state interest" supports a law that prohibits or restricts religious practices. This is unfortunate, and will tend to make it more difficult to prove that a state's interference with religious practices violates the guaranty of religious freedom. Four of the Court's nine justices disagreed with the Court's analysis, and with the virtual elimination of the "compelling state interest" test. The minority asserted that the Court's ruling diminished the guaranty of religious liberty by making it more difficult for persons to prove a violation of this fundamental constitutional guaranty. One of the dissenting Justices lamented that the Court's decision tilts the scales "in the

---

[54] *Id.* at 1605-06 (citations omitted).

state's favor," and "effectuates a wholesale overturning of settled law concerning the religion clauses of our Constitution. One hopes that the Court is aware of the consequences . . . ."

Board of Education v. Mergens[55]

§ 12-12

May a public high school that allows a variety of student groups to meet on school property before or after regular classroom hours deny the same privilege to a student group wanting to meet for prayer and Bible study? No, said the United States Supreme Court in a 1990 decision.

Westside High School is a public high school in Omaha, Nebraska, with a student enrollment of nearly 2,000. Students are permitted to join various student groups and clubs, all of which meet after school hours on school property. Students may choose from among 30 recognized groups on a voluntary basis. The groups include the school band, chess club, cheerleaders, choir, junior rotarians, debate, drill squad, Future Business Leaders of America, photography, and scuba diving. A school board policy recognizes these groups as a "vital part of the total education" of high school students, and it also forbids "political or religious" clubs. In 1985, a student met with the school principal and requested permission to form a Bible study and prayer group. The principal denied this request on the ground that allowing a religious club to meet on school property would violate the First Amendment's "nonestablishment of religion" clause. The school board later upheld the principal's decision, and the student filed a lawsuit in federal court seeking a court order requiring the school to recognize the religious club. The lawsuit claimed that the school's policy of outlawing religious groups violated the "Equal Access Act," which provides:

> It shall be unlawful for any public secondary school which receives federal financial assistance and which has a *limited open forum* to deny equal access or a fair opportunity to, or discriminate against, any students who wish to conduct a meeting within that limited open forum on the basis of the religious, political, philosophical, or other content of the speech at such meetings.[56]

A "limited open forum" exists whenever a public high school "grants an offering to or opportunity for one or more *noncurriculum related student groups* to meet on school premises during noninstructional time."

The school argued that the Equal Access Act did not apply in this case, since all of its student groups were "curriculum related" and therefore the school had

---

[55]   110 S. Ct. 2356 (1990). The *Mergens* case is discussed further in chapter 14, *infra*.

[56]   20 U.S.C. §§ 4071-4074.

not created a "limited open forum" that would be available to religious groups. Further, the school maintained that if the Act required religious groups to meet, then it was unconstitutional.

A trial court agreed with the school and upheld the ban on student groups. It concluded that the school did not have a "limited open forum" since all of its student groups were curriculum related. A federal appeals court reversed the trial court's decision, and ruled in favor of the student. The appeals court rejected the trial court's conclusion that all student groups were "curriculum related." If the scuba diving club and chess club are "curriculum related" because they are related to logic and physical education (as the school and trial court claimed), then "the Equal Access Act [would be] meaningless" and schools could "arbitrarily deny access to school facilities to any unfavored student club on the basis of its speech." The appeals court concluded that many of the school's student groups were noncurriculum related, and accordingly that the Equal Access Act prohibited the school from banning the proposed Bible club on the basis of the religious content of its speech. The United States Supreme Court agreed to review the decision of the appeals court.

The Supreme Court concluded that the school did have noncurriculum related student groups, and accordingly had created a limited open forum. The Court observed that the term *noncurriculum related student group* "is best interpreted broadly to mean any student group that does not *directly* relate to the body of courses offered by the school."[57] The court emphasized that "groups such as a chess club, a stamp collecting club, or a community service club" ordinarily will be noncurriculum related since they do not directly relate to the body of courses offered by a school. Accordingly, the existence of such groups would create a "limited open forum" under the Act and would prohibit the school from denying equal access to any other student group on the basis of the content of that group's speech.

The school contended that all of its 30 student groups were curriculum related because they furthered the general educational goals of the school. For example, the student government club "advances the goals of the school's political science classes," the scuba club "furthers the essential goals of the physical education department," the chess club "supplements math and science courses," and the junior rotarians "promote effective citizenship—a critical goal of the social sciences department." The Court rejected this analysis, noting:

> Allowing such a broad interpretation of "curriculum related" would make the [Act] meaningless. A school's administration could simply declare that it maintains a closed forum and choose which student clubs it wanted to allow by tying the purpose of those clubs to some broadly defined educational goal. At the same time the administration could arbitrarily deny access to school facilities to any unfavored student club on the basis of its speech content. This is exactly the result that Congress sought to prohibit by enacting the [Act]. A public secondary school cannot simply declare

---

[57]   110 S. Ct. at 2366.

that it maintains a closed forum and then discriminate against a particular student group on the basis of the content of the speech of that group.[58]

The Court concluded that the school had a number of noncurriculum related student groups, including the scuba club and chess club. It did not evaluate any other clubs, but hinted that a number of the other groups also would be noncurriculum related. Because the school clearly allowed one or more noncurriculum related student groups to meet during noninstructional hours, it had created a limited open forum and could not discriminate against students wanting to meet for religious purposes.

Finally, the Court rejected the school's argument that the Equal Access Act violated the First Amendment's nonestablishment of religion clause.

Lee v. Weisman[59]

§ 12-13

For many years it was the policy of the Providence (Rhode Island) School Committee and the Superintendent of Schools to permit principals to invite members of the clergy to give invocations and benedictions at middle school and high school graduations. Many, but not all, of the principals elected to include prayers as part of the graduation ceremonies. A student and her father objected to any prayers at the student's graduation, but to no avail. The school principal invited a rabbi to deliver prayers at the student's graduation exercises. The principal provided the rabbi with a pamphlet entitled "Guidelines for Civic Occasions," prepared by the National Conference of Christians and Jews, and advised him that the invocation and benediction should be nonsectarian. The school board (and the United States government) argued that nonsectarian prayers at graduation exercises are of profound meaning to many students and parents throughout this country who consider that due respect and acknowledgement for divine guidance and for the deepest spiritual aspirations of our people ought to be expressed at an event as important in life as a graduation. The dissenting student and her father sought a court order prohibiting any further prayers at public high school graduation ceremonies in Providence. A federal district court issued such an order, and this decision was affirmed by a federal appeals court. The case was then appealed to the United States Supreme Court.

The Supreme Court, by a majority of five votes to four, ruled that prayers offered at public high school graduation ceremonies violate the First Amendment's "nonestablishment of religion" clause. The Court began its opinion by emphasizing that

[i]t is beyond dispute that, at a minimum, the Constitution guarantees that government may not coerce anyone to support or participate in religion

---

[58] *Id.* at 2369, quoting from the federal appeals court decision in Board of Education v. Mergens, 867 F.2d 1076, 1078 (8th Cir. 1989).

[59] 112 S. Ct. 2649 (1992).

or its exercise, or otherwise act in a way which establishes a state religion or religious faith, or tends to do so. The state's involvement in the school prayers challenged today violates these central principles. That involvement is as troubling as it is undenied. A school official, the principal, decided that an invocation and a benediction should be given; this is a choice attributable to the state, and from a constitutional perspective it is as if a state statute decreed that the prayers must occur. The principal chose the religious participant, here a rabbi, and that choice is also attributable to the state. . . . The state's role did not end with the decision to include a prayer and with the choice of clergyman. [The school principal provided the rabbi] with a copy of the "Guidelines for Civic Occasions," and advised him that his prayers should be nonsectarian. Through these means the principal directed and controlled the content of the prayer. . . . It is a cornerstone principle of our establishment clause jurisprudence that it is no part of the business of government to compose official prayers for any group of the American people to recite as a part of a religious program carried on by government, and that is what the school officials attempted to do.

The Court concluded that a public high school graduation ceremony that includes prayers exerts a "psychological coercion" or pressure on everyone to conform, even those who are personally opposed to prayer. The Court observed:

The undeniable fact is that the school district's supervision and control of a high school graduation ceremony places public pressure, as well as peer pressure, on attending students to stand as a group or, at least, maintain respectful silence during the invocation and benediction. This pressure, though subtle and indirect, can be as real as any overt compulsion. Of course, in our culture standing or remaining silent can signify adherence to a view or simple respect for the views of others. And no doubt some persons who have no desire to join a prayer have little objection to standing as a sign of respect for those who do. But for the dissenter of high school age, who has a reasonable perception that she is being forced by the state to pray in a manner her conscience will not allow, the injury is no less real. There can be no doubt that for many, if not most, of the students at the graduation, the act of standing or remaining silent was an expression of participation in the Rabbi's prayer. That was the very point of the religious exercise. It is of little comfort to a dissenter, then, to be told that for her the act of standing or remaining in silence signifies mere respect, rather than participation. What matters is that, given our social conventions, a reasonable dissenter in this milieu could believe that the group exercise signified her own participation or approval of it.

The Court emphasized that "[r]esearch in psychology supports the common assumption that adolescents are often susceptible to pressure from their peers towards conformity, and that the influence is strongest in matters of social convention."

The Court acknowledged that participation in graduation ceremonies is voluntary, and that students who are opposed to prayers can simply not attend. But it concluded that the voluntary nature of the ceremony did not mean that prayers had to be allowed. It noted:

[T]o say a teenage student has a real choice not to attend her high school graduation is formalistic in the extreme. True, [the student] could elect not to attend commencement without renouncing her diploma; but we shall not allow the case to turn on this point. Everyone knows that in our society and in our culture high school graduation is one of life's most significant occasions. A school rule which excuses attendance is beside the point. Attendance may not be required by official decree, yet it is apparent that a student is not free to absent herself from the graduation exercise in any real sense of the term "voluntary," for absence would require forfeiture of those intangible benefits which have motivated the student through youth and all her high school years. Graduation is a time for family and those closest to the student to celebrate success and express mutual wishes of gratitude and respect, all to the end of impressing upon the young person the role that it is his or her right and duty to assume in the community and all of its diverse parts.

The Court acknowledged that a majority of those attending graduation ceremonies probably have no objection to prayers being offered, and would even prefer that they be. It concluded, however, that "[w]hile in some societies the wishes of the majority might prevail, the establishment clause of the First Amendment is addressed to this contingency and rejects the balance urged upon us. The Constitution forbids the state to exact religious conformity from a student as the price of attending her own high school graduation."

The Court acknowledged that

[w]e do not hold that every state action implicating religion is invalid if one or a few citizens find it offensive. People may take offense at all manner of religious as well as nonreligious messages, but offense alone does not in every case show a violation. We know too that sometimes to endure social isolation or even anger may be the price of conscience or nonconformity. But, by any reading of our cases, the conformity required of the student in this case was too high an exaction to withstand the test of the establishment clause.

> "People may take offense at all manner of religious as well as nonreligious messages, but offense alone does not in every case show a violation."

The Court concluded its opinion with the following statement:

Our society would be less than true to its heritage if it lacked abiding concern for the values of its young people, and we acknowledge the profound belief of adherents to many faiths that there must be a place in the student's life for precepts of a morality higher even than the law we today enforce. We express no hostility to those aspirations, nor would our oath permit us to do so. A relentless and all-pervasive attempt to exclude religion from every aspect of public life could itself become inconsistent with the Constitution. We recognize that, at graduation time and throughout the course of the educational process, there will be instances when religious values, religious practices, and religious persons will have some interaction with the public schools and their students. But these matters, often questions of accommodation of religion, are not before us. The sole question presented is whether a religious exercise may be conducted at a graduation ceremony in circumstances where, as we have found, young graduates who object are induced to conform. No holding by this Court suggests that a school can persuade or compel a student to participate in a religious exercise. That is being done here, and it is forbidden by the establishment clause of the First Amendment.

Mitchell v. Helms[60]   § 12-14

The Supreme Court ruled that the use of federal funds to provide secular and nonideological educational materials (including library materials, computer equipment and software, and textbooks) to both public and church-affiliated schools did not violate the First Amendment's nonestablishment of religion clause. As part of a longstanding school aid program known as "Chapter 2," the federal government distributes funds to state and local governmental agencies, which in turn lend educational materials and equipment to public and private schools. The question addressed by the Court was whether Chapter 2 violates the First Amendment's "nonestablishment of religion" clause if some of the funds are used to provide educational materials to church-affiliated private schools.

Chapter 2 provides funding for a wide variety of educational materials, including library services and materials, reference materials, computer software and hardware for instructional use, and other curricular materials. Several restrictions apply to aid to private schools. For example, the "services, materials, and equipment" provided to private schools must be "secular, neutral, and nonideological." In addition, private schools may not acquire control of Chapter 2 funds or ownership of Chapter 2 materials, equipment, or property. A private school receives the materials and equipment by submitting an application to a local educational agency detailing which items the school seeks and how it will use them. The agency, if it approves the application, purchases those items and then lends them to the school.

---

[60]   530 U.S. 793 (2000).

The Court noted that the First Amendment prevents Congress from making a law "respecting an establishment of religion," and that over the past 50 years it has "consistently struggled to apply these simple words in the context of governmental aid to religious schools." However, the Court noted that in a 1997 case it provided some clarification by holding that government aid to religious schools generally will not violate the First Amendment so long as it (1) has a secular purpose; (2) does not result in governmental indoctrination; (3) does not define its recipients by reference to religion; and (4) does not create an excessive entanglement. Since the parties to the lawsuit never questioned the first or fourth factors, the Court focused on the second and third.

governmental indoctrination

The Court noted that the question "whether governmental aid to religious schools results in governmental indoctrination is ultimately a question whether any religious indoctrination that occurs in those schools could reasonably be attributed to *governmental* action." It continued:

> In distinguishing between indoctrination that is attributable to the state and indoctrination that is not, we have consistently turned to the principle of neutrality, upholding aid that is offered to a broad range of groups or persons without regard to their religion. If the religious, irreligious, and areligious are all alike eligible for governmental aid, no one would conclude that any indoctrination that any particular recipient conducts has been done at the behest of the government. . . . If the government is offering assistance to recipients who provide, so to speak, a broad range of indoctrination, the government itself is not thought responsible for any particular indoctrination. To put the point differently, if the government, seeking to further some legitimate secular purpose, offers aid on the same terms, without regard to religion, to all who adequately further that purpose, then it is fair to say that any aid going to a religious recipient only has the effect of furthering that secular purpose.

The Court also emphasized the importance of determining whether government aid that goes to religious schools does so "only as a result of the genuinely independent and private choices of individuals" as opposed to an act of government: "For if numerous private choices, rather than the single choice of a government, determine the distribution of aid pursuant to neutral eligibility criteria, then a government cannot, or at least cannot easily, grant special favors that might lead to a religious establishment."

The Court concluded that the principles of neutrality and private choice prevented the government aid in this case from being reasonably "attributed" to the government.

defining recipients with reference to religion

Does Chapter 2 define the recipients of government aid by reference to religion? The Court ruled that it did not, since the aid was allocated on the basis of "neutral, secular criteria that neither favor nor disfavor religion, and is made available to both religious and secular beneficiaries on a nondiscriminatory basis."

Santa Fe Independent School District v. Doe[61]

§ 12-15

The Supreme Court ruled that student-led prayers at the start of public high school football games violated the First Amendment's nonestablishment of religion clause.

A public high school adopted a policy permitting, but not requiring, the school's "student council chaplain" to recite a nonsectarian, nonproselytizing prayer at the start of football games. This policy was challenged by two students, and their parents, as a violation of the First Amendment.

The school argued that the prayers were permissible since they were "private student speech" that was beyond the reach of the First Amendment, which is a limitation on government action.

The court agreed that private speech is beyond the reach of the First Amendment, but it concluded that the prayers addressed in this case were not "private speech" but rather had to be attributed to the state (school). It based this conclusion on the following factors: (1) the prayers are authorized by a government policy and take place on government property at government-sponsored school-related events, and are broadcast over the school's public address system which is under the control of school officials; (2) the pregame ceremony, during which the prayer is recited, is "clothed in the traditional indicia of school sporting events, which generally include not just the team, but also cheerleaders and band members dressed in uniforms sporting the school name and mascot; (3) the school's name "is likely written in large print across the field and on banners and flags"; (4) the crowd "will certainly include many who display the school colors and insignia on their school T-shirts, jackets, or hats and who may also be waving signs displaying the school name."

The Court noted that "it is in a setting such as this that the board has chosen to permit the elected student to rise and give the invocation." In this context the members of the listening audience "must perceive the pregame message as a public expression of the views of the majority of the student body delivered with the approval of the school administration." Regardless of the listener's support for, or objection to, the message, an objective student "will unquestionably perceive the inevitable pregame prayer as stamped with the school's seal of approval."

---

[61]   530 U.S. 290 (2000).

The Court listed other factors in support of its conclusion that the prayers were public rather than private speech: (1) the school allows only one student, the same student for the entire season, to give the invocation; (2) the invocation is subject to school regulations that confine the content and topic of the student's message; and (3) the election by the student body of the student council chaplain ensured that "minority" religious views would be "effectively silenced."

The Court concluded:

School sponsorship of a religious message is impermissible because it sends the ancillary message to members of the audience who are nonadherents "that they are outsiders, not full members of the political community, and an accompanying message to adherents that they are insiders, favored members of the political community." The delivery of such a message—over the school's public address system, by a speaker representing the student body, under the supervision of school faculty, and pursuant to a school policy that explicitly and implicitly encourages public prayer—is not properly characterized as "private" speech. . . .

High school home football games are traditional gatherings of a school community; they bring together students and faculty as well as friends and family from years present and past to root for a common cause. Undoubtedly, the games are not important to some students, and they voluntarily choose not to attend. For many others, however, the choice between whether to attend these games or to risk facing a personally offensive religious ritual is in no practical sense an easy one. The Constitution, moreover, demands that the school may not force this difficult choice upon these students for "it is a tenet of the First Amendment that the state cannot require one of its citizens to forfeit his or her rights and benefits as the price of resisting conformance to state-sponsored religious practice."

Zelman v. Simmons-Harris[62] § 12-16

The United States Supreme Court ruled that a state program that provided low-income parents with vouchers that could be used to enroll their children at secular and religious private secondary schools did not violate the First Amendment's "nonestablishment of religion" clause since the aid was being directed to the parents, who in turn could apply it in any manner they chose. The Court noted that "three times we have confronted establishment clause challenges to neutral government programs that provide aid directly to a broad class of individuals, who, in turn, direct the aid to religious schools or institutions of their own choosing. Three times we have rejected such challenges." Those three cases are summarized below.

---

[62]   536 U.S. 639 (2002)

(1) *Mueller v. Allen, 463 U. S. 388 (1983).* In *Mueller,* the Court rejected an establishment clause challenge to a Minnesota program authorizing tax deductions for various educational expenses, including private school tuition costs, even though the great majority of the program's beneficiaries (96 percent) were parents of children in religious schools. The Court found that because the class of potential beneficiaries included *all* parents, including parents with "children [who] attend nonsectarian private schools or sectarian private schools," the program was "not readily subject to challenge under the establishment clause." Then, viewing the program as a whole, the Court focused on the principle of private choice, noting that public funds were made available to religious schools "only as a result of numerous, private choices of individual parents of school-age children." This insured that "no imprimatur of state approval can be deemed to have been conferred on any particular religion, or on religion generally." The Court concluded that it was irrelevant that the vast majority of beneficiaries were parents of children in religious schools, saying: "We would be loath to adopt a rule grounding the constitutionality of a facially neutral law on annual reports reciting the extent to which various classes of private citizens claimed benefits under the law." That the program was one of true private choice, with no evidence that the state deliberately skewed incentives toward religious schools, was sufficient for the program to survive scrutiny under the establishment clause.

(2) *Witters v. Washington Dept. of Servs. for Blind, 474 U. S. 481 (1986).* In *Witters,* the Court used the same reasoning it applied in the *Mueller* case to reject an establishment clause challenge to a vocational scholarship program that provided tuition aid to a student studying at a religious institution to become a pastor. Looking at the program as a whole, the Court observed that "any aid . . . that ultimately flows to religious institutions does so only as a result of the genuinely independent and private choices of aid recipients." The Court further noted that "as in *Mueller,* the program is made available generally without regard to the sectarian-nonsectarian, or public-nonpublic nature of the institution benefited." In light of these factors, the Court ruled that the program was not inconsistent with the establishment clause.

(3) *Zobrest v. Catalina Foothills School Dist., 509 U. S. 1 (1993).* In *Zobrest,* the Court applied *Mueller* and *Witters* to reject an establishment clause challenge to a federal program that permitted sign-language interpreters to assist deaf children enrolled in religious schools. Reviewing its earlier decisions, the Court stated that "government programs that neutrally provide benefits to a broad class of citizens defined without reference to religion are not readily subject to an establishment clause challenge." Looking at the challenged program as a whole, the Court observed that it "distributes benefits neutrally to any child qualifying as disabled." Its primary beneficiaries, the Court concluded, were "disabled children, not

sectarian schools." The Court further observed that "by according parents freedom to select a school of their choice, the statute ensures that a government-paid interpreter will be present in a sectarian school only as a result of the private decision of individual parents." The Court's focus once again was on "neutrality and the principle of private choice, not on the number of program beneficiaries attending religious schools."

The Court summarized these three prior rulings as follows:

Mueller, *Witters*, and *Zobrest* thus make clear that where a government aid program is neutral with respect to religion, and provides assistance directly to a broad class of citizens who, in turn, direct government aid to religious schools wholly as a result of their own genuine and independent private choice, the program is not readily subject to challenge under the establishment clause. A program that shares these features permits government aid to reach religious institutions only by way of the deliberate choices of numerous individual recipients. The incidental advancement of a religious mission, or the perceived endorsement of a religious message, is reasonably attributable to the individual recipient, not to the government, whose role ends with the disbursement of benefits. As a plurality of this Court recently observed: "If numerous private choices, rather than the single choice of a government, determine the distribution of aid, pursuant to neutral eligibility criteria, then a government cannot, or at least cannot easily, grant special favors that might lead to a religious establishment." It is precisely for these reasons that we have never found a program of true private choice to offend the establishment clause.

The Court rejected the argument that the program created a "public perception" that the state was endorsing religious practices and beliefs, noting simply that "we have repeatedly recognized that no reasonable observer would think a neutral program of private choice, where state aid reaches religious schools solely as a result of the numerous independent decisions of private individuals, carries with it the *imprimatur* of government endorsement. . . . Any objective observer familiar with the full history and context of the program would reasonably view it as one aspect of a broader undertaking to assist poor children in failed schools, not as an endorsement of religious schooling in general."

The taxpayers who were challenging the program claimed that the Court should attach constitutional significance to the fact that 96 percent of scholarship recipients enrolled in religious schools. They claimed that this alone proved parents lacked genuine choice, even if no parent had ever said so. Once again, the Court disagreed:

We need not consider this argument in detail, since it was flatly rejected in *Mueller*, where we found it irrelevant that 96 percent of parents taking deductions for tuition expenses paid tuition at religious schools. Indeed, we have recently found it irrelevant even to the constitutionality of a direct aid program that a vast majority of program benefits went to religious schools. The constitutionality of a neutral educational aid program simply does not turn on whether and why, in a particular area, at a particular time, most private schools are run by religious organizations, or most recipients choose to use the aid at a religious school. As we said in *Mueller*, "such an approach would scarcely provide the certainty that this field stands in need of, nor can we perceive principled standards by which such statistical evidence might be evaluated."

The Court concluded: "In sum, the program is entirely neutral with respect to religion. It provides benefits directly to a wide spectrum of individuals, defined only by financial need and residence in a particular school district. It permits such individuals to exercise genuine choice among options public and private, secular and religious. The program is therefore a program of true private choice. In keeping with an unbroken line of decisions rejecting challenges to similar programs, we hold that the program does not offend the establishment clause."

Watchtower Bible and Tract Society v. Village of Stratton[63] § 12-17

The United States Supreme Court ruled that a city ordinance requiring Jehovah's Witnesses and other persons to obtain and display a permit before engaging in door-to-door witnessing violated the First Amendment. A city ordinance prohibited "canvassers" and others from "going in and upon" private residential property for the purpose of promoting any "cause" without first having obtained a "solicitation permit." Residents may prohibit solicitation even by holders of permits by posting a "No Solicitation" sign on their property.

Jehovah's Witnesses refused to obtain a solicitation permit because they derive their authority to preach from Scripture, and to seek a permit to preach from the city would be an "insult to God." They claim to follow the example of the Apostle Paul, teaching "publicly, and from house to house" (Acts 20:20). They take literally the mandate of the Scriptures, "Go ye into all the world, and preach the gospel to every creature." Mark 16:15. In doing so they believe that they are obeying a commandment of God. Moreover, because they lack significant financial resources, the ability to proselytize is seriously diminished by regulations that burden their efforts to canvass door-to-door.

The Supreme Court concluded that the city ordinance, as applied to the Jehovah's Witnesses, violated the First Amendment guaranty of free speech. The city claimed that the permit requirement was justified by the legitimate interests of preventing fraud and crime, and protecting residents' privacy. The Court conceded that cities have a legitimate interest in protecting these interests, but in

[63] 536 U.S. 150 (2002).

this case they went too far. It observed,

> Central to our conclusion that the ordinance does not pass First Amendment scrutiny is that it is not tailored to the city's stated interests. Even if the interest in preventing fraud could adequately support the ordinance insofar as it applies to commercial transactions and the solicitation of funds, that interest provides no support for its application to [church members], to political campaigns, or to enlisting support for unpopular causes. The city, however, argues that the ordinance is nonetheless valid because it serves the two additional interests of protecting the privacy of the resident and the prevention of crime. With respect to the former, it seems clear that the ordinance, which provides for the posting of "No Solicitation" signs . . . coupled with the resident's unquestioned right to refuse to engage in conversation with unwelcome visitors, provides ample protection for the unwilling listener. . . . With respect to the latter, it seems unlikely that the absence of a permit would preclude criminals from knocking on doors and engaging in conversations not covered by the ordinance. . . .

The Court concluded: "The mere fact that the ordinance covers so much speech raises constitutional concerns. It is offensive—not only to the values protected by the First Amendment, but to the very notion of a free society— that in the context of everyday public discourse a citizen must first inform the government of her desire to speak to her neighbors and then obtain a permit to do so. . . . A law requiring a permit to engage in such speech constitutes a dramatic departure from our national heritage and constitutional tradition."

McCreary County v. American Civil Liberties Union[64]

§ 12-18

In 1999 two county courthouses in Kentucky hung large, gold-framed copies of an abridged text of the King James version of the Ten Commandments (including a citation to the Book of Exodus), on a courthouse wall. In one county, the placement of the Commandments responded to an order of the county requiring "the display to be posted in a very high traffic area of the courthouse." In the other county, the Commandments were hung in a ceremony presided over by a judge, who called them "good rules to live by" and who recounted the story of an astronaut who became convinced "there must be a divine God" after viewing the Earth from the moon. The judge was accompanied by the pastor of his church, who called the Commandments "a creed of ethics" and told the press after the ceremony that displaying the Commandments was "one of the greatest things the judge could have done to close out the millennium."

---

[64]   545 U.S. 844 (2005).

In each county, the hallway display was "readily visible to county citizens who use the courthouse to conduct their civic business, to obtain or renew driver's licenses and permits, to register cars, to pay local taxes, and to register to vote."

In 1999 the American Civil Liberties Union (ACLU) of Kentucky sued the two counties in federal court, seeking an order barring the displays which the ACLU claimed were violations of the First Amendment's nonestablishment of religion clause. Before the court issued a ruling, each county authorized a second, expanded display, stating that the Ten Commandments are "the precedent legal code upon which the civil and criminal codes of Kentucky are founded," and stating several grounds for taking that position, including that:

> The Ten Commandments are codified in Kentucky's civil and criminal laws"; that the Kentucky House of Representatives had in 1993 "voted unanimously to adjourn in remembrance and honor of Jesus Christ, the Prince of Ethics"; that the "County Judge and magistrates agree with the arguments set out by Judge [Roy] Moore" in defense of his "display of the Ten Commandments in his courtroom"; and that the "Founding Fathers had an explicit understanding of the duty of elected officials to publicly acknowledge God as the source of America's strength and direction."

The expanded displays of the Ten Commandments included eight other documents in smaller frames, each either having a religious theme or excerpted to highlight a religious element. The documents were the "endowed by their Creator" passage from the Declaration of Independence; the Preamble to the Constitution of Kentucky; the national motto, "In God We Trust"; a page from the Congressional Record of February 2, 1983, proclaiming the Year of the Bible and including a statement of the Ten Commandments; a proclamation by President Abraham Lincoln designating April 30, 1863, a National Day of Prayer and Humiliation; an excerpt from President Lincoln's "Reply to Loyal Colored People of Baltimore upon Presentation of a Bible," reading that "the Bible is the best gift God has ever given to man"; a proclamation by President Reagan marking 1983 the Year of the Bible; and the Mayflower Compact.

A federal district court ordered the displays at both county courthouses removed "immediately," and warned county officials not to "erect or cause to be erected similar displays." A federal appeals court affirmed, and the case was appealed to the United States Supreme Court.

The Court began its opinion by observing,

> The touchstone for our analysis is the principle that the "First Amendment mandates governmental neutrality between religion and religion, and between religion and nonreligion." When the government acts with the ostensible and predominant purpose of advancing religion, it violates that central establishment clause value of official religious neutrality, there being no neutrality when the government's ostensible object is to take sides. Manifesting a purpose to favor one faith over another, or adherence to religion generally, clashes with the "understanding, reached . . . after decades

of religious war, that liberty and social stability demand a religious tolerance that respects the religious views of all citizens. By showing a purpose to favor religion, the government "sends the message to nonadherents 'that they are outsiders, not full members of the political community, and an accompanying message to adherents that they are insiders, favored members"

The Court continued: "This is not to deny that the Commandments have had influence on civil or secular law; a major text of a majority religion is bound to be felt. The point is simply that the original text viewed in its entirety is an unmistakably religious statement dealing with religious obligations and with morality subject to religious sanction. When the government initiates an effort to place this statement alone in public view, a religious object is unmistakable."

The Court conceded that the expanded display included eight other historical documents in addition to the Ten Commandments. However, this did not render the posting of the Ten Commandments permissible, since the expanded display included other documents "with highlighted references to God as their sole common element. The display's unstinting focus was on religious passages, showing that the counties were posting the Commandments precisely because of their sectarian content. That demonstration of the government's objective was enhanced by serial religious references and the accompanying resolution's claim about the embodiment of ethics in Christ. Together, the display and resolution presented an indisputable, and undisputed, showing of an impermissible purpose."

The Court stressed that it was not outlawing all exhibitions of the Ten Commandments on government property:

Nor do we have occasion here to hold that a sacred text can never be integrated constitutionally into a governmental display on the subject of law, or American history. We do not forget, and in this litigation have frequently been reminded, that our own courtroom frieze was deliberately designed in the exercise of governmental authority so as to include the figure of Moses holding tablets exhibiting a portion of the Hebrew text of the later, secularly phrased Commandments; in the company of 17 other lawgivers, most of them secular figures, there is no risk that Moses would strike an observer as evidence that the National Government was violating neutrality in religion. The dissent notes that another depiction of Moses and the Commandments adorns this Court's east pediment. But as with the courtroom frieze, Moses is found in the company of other figures, not only great but secular.

The Court concluded that

the principle of neutrality has provided a good sense of direction: the government may not favor one religion over another, or religion over irreligion, religious choice being the prerogative of individuals under the free exercise clause. The principle has been helpful simply because it responds to one of the major concerns that prompted adoption of the religion clauses. The framers and the citizens of their time intended not only to protect the integrity of individual conscience in religious matters, but to guard against the civic divisiveness that follows when the government weighs in on one side of religious debate; nothing does a better job of roiling society, a point that needed no explanation to the descendants of English Puritans and Cavaliers (or Massachusetts Puritans and Baptists). A sense of the past thus points to governmental neutrality as an objective of the establishment clause, and a sensible standard for applying it. To be sure, given its generality as a principle, an appeal to neutrality alone cannot possibly lay every issue to rest, or tell us what issues on the margins are substantial enough for constitutional significance, a point that has been clear from the founding era to modern times. But invoking neutrality is a prudent way of keeping sight of something the framers of the First Amendment thought important.

Justice Scalia's dissenting opinion, which was joined by three other justices, begins with an overview of the place of religion in public life (some of his conclusions were challenged by the Court's majority):

On September 11, 2001 I was attending in Rome, Italy an international conference of judges and lawyers, principally from Europe and the United States. That night and the next morning virtually all of the participants watched, in their hotel rooms, the address to the Nation by the President of the United States concerning the murderous attacks upon the Twin Towers and the Pentagon, in which thousands of Americans had been killed. The address ended, as Presidential addresses often do, with the prayer "God bless America." The next afternoon I was approached by one of the judges from a European country, who, after extending his profound condolences for my country's loss, sadly observed "How I wish that the Head of State of my country, at a similar time of national tragedy and distress, could conclude his address 'God bless _____.' It is of course absolutely forbidden."

That is one model of the relationship between church and state—a model spread across Europe by the armies of Napoleon, and reflected in the Constitution of France, which begins "France is a secular Republic." Religion is to be strictly excluded from the public forum. This is not, and never was, the model adopted by America. George Washington added to the form of Presidential oath prescribed by . . . the Constitution, the concluding words "so help me God." The Supreme Court under John Marshall opened its sessions with the prayer, "God save the United States and this Honorable Court." The First Congress instituted the practice of beginning its legislative sessions with a prayer. The same week that Congress submitted the establishment clause as part of the Bill of Rights for ratification by the states, it enacted legislation providing for paid chaplains in the House and Senate. The day after the First Amendment was proposed, the same Congress that had proposed it requested the President to proclaim "a day of public thanksgiving and prayer, to be observed, by acknowledging, with grateful hearts, the many and signal favours of Almighty God." President Washington offered the first Thanksgiving Proclamation shortly thereafter, devoting November 26, 1789 on behalf of the American people "to the service of that great and glorious Being who is the beneficent author of all the good that is, that was, or that will be," thus beginning a tradition of offering gratitude to God that continues today. The same Congress also reenacted the Northwest Territory Ordinance of 1787, 1 Stat. 50, Article III of which provided: "Religion, morality, and knowledge, being necessary to good government and the happiness of mankind, schools and the means of education shall forever be encouraged." And of course the First Amendment itself accords religion (and no other manner of belief) special constitutional protection.

> "Our Constitution was made only for a moral and religious people. It is wholly inadequate to the government of any other."

These actions of our First President and Congress and the Marshall Court were not idiosyncratic; they reflected the beliefs of the period. Those who wrote the Constitution believed that morality was essential to the well-being of society and that encouragement of religion was the best way to foster morality. The "fact that the Founding Fathers believed devotedly that there was a God and that the unalienable rights of man were rooted in Him is clearly evidenced in their writings, from the Mayflower Compact to the Constitution itself." President Washington opened his Presidency with a prayer, and reminded his fellow citizens at the conclusion of it that "reason and experience both forbid us to expect that National morality can prevail in exclusion of religious principle." President John Adams wrote to the Massachusetts Militia, "we have no government armed with power capable of contending with human passions unbridled by morality and religion. Our Constitution was made only for a moral and religious people. It is wholly inadequate to the government of any other." Thomas Jefferson concluded his second inaugural address by inviting his audience to pray: "I shall need, too, the favor of that Being in whose hands we are, who led our fathers, as Israel of old, from their native land and planted them in a country flowing with all the necessaries and comforts of life; who has covered our infancy with His providence and our riper years with His wisdom and power and to whose goodness I ask you to join in supplications with me that He will so enlighten the minds of your servants, guide their councils, and prosper their measures that whatsoever they do shall result in your good, and shall secure to you the peace, friendship, and approbation of all nations." James Madison, in his first inaugural address, likewise placed his confidence "in the guardianship and guidance of that

Almighty Being whose power regulates the destiny of nations, whose blessings have been so conspicuously dispensed to this rising Republic, and to whom we are bound to address our devout gratitude for the past, as well as our fervent supplications and best hopes for the future."

Nor have the views of our people on this matter significantly changed. Presidents continue to conclude the Presidential oath with the words "so help me God." Our legislatures, state and national, continue to open their sessions with prayer led by official chaplains. The sessions of this Court continue to open with the prayer "God save the United States and this Honorable Court." Invocation of the Almighty by our public figures, at all levels of government, remains commonplace. Our coinage bears the motto "In God We Trust." And our Pledge of Allegiance contains the acknowledgment that we are a Nation "under God." As one of our Supreme Court opinions rightly observed, "We are a religious people whose institutions presuppose a Supreme Being."

With all of this reality (and much more) staring it in the face, how can the Court *possibly* assert that "the First Amendment mandates governmental neutrality between religion and nonreligion," and that "manifesting a purpose to favor adherence to religion generally," is unconstitutional? Who says so? Surely not the words of the Constitution. Surely not the history and traditions that reflect our society's constant understanding of those words. Surely not even the current sense of our society, recently reflected in an Act of Congress adopted *unanimously* by the Senate and with only five nays in the House of Representatives, criticizing a Court of Appeals opinion that had held "under God" in the Pledge of Allegiance unconstitutional. Nothing stands behind the Court's assertion that governmental affirmation of the society's belief in God is unconstitutional except the Court's own say-so, citing as support only the unsubstantiated say-so of earlier Courts going back no farther than the mid-20th century. And it is, moreover, a thoroughly discredited say-so . . . because the Court has not had the courage (or the foolhardiness) to apply the neutrality principle consistently.

Van Orden v. Perry[65]

§ 12-19

The 22 acres surrounding the Texas State Capitol contain 17 monuments and 21 historical markers commemorating the "people, ideals, and events that compose Texan identity." One of the monuments is a 6-feet high portrayal of the Ten Commandments located between the state capitol and state supreme court building. An eagle grasping the American flag, an eye inside of a pyramid, and two small tablets with what appears to be an ancient script are carved above the text of the Ten Commandments. Below the text are two Stars of David and the superimposed Greek letters Chi and Rho, which represent Christ. The bottom

---

[65]   545 U.S. 677 (2005).

of the monument bears the inscription "Presented to the People and Youth of Texas by the Fraternal Order of Eagles of Texas." The other 16 monuments include those depicting the Heroes of the Alamo, Confederate Soldiers, Volunteer Firemen, Texas Rangers, Spanish-American War, Texas National Guard, Texas School Children, Pearl Harbor and Korean War Veterans, Soldiers of World War I, Disabled Veterans, and Texas Peace Officers.

The Fraternal Order of Eagles (a national social, civic, and patriotic organization) paid the cost of erecting the Ten Commandments monument, the dedication of which was presided over by two state legislators. Nearly 50 years after the erection of the Ten Commandments monument, an attorney who frequently walked past the monument on his way to the state supreme court library sued to have the monument removed, claiming that it offended him and that it constituted an establishment of religion in violation of the First Amendment. A federal district court ruled that the monument did not violate the First Amendment, and a federal appeals court affirmed this ruling. The case was appealed to the United States Supreme Court.

The late Chief Justice William Rehnquist, writing for the Court, began his opinion by observing:

> Our cases, Januslike, point in two directions in applying the establishment clause. One face looks toward the strong role played by religion and religious traditions throughout our Nation's history. As we observed in [a previous case]: "It is true that religion has been closely identified with our history and government . . . . The fact that the Founding Fathers believed devotedly that there was a God and that the unalienable rights of man were rooted in Him is clearly evidenced in their writings, from the Mayflower Compact to the Constitution itself . . . . It can be truly said, therefore, that today, as in the beginning, our national life reflects a religious people who, in the words of Madison, are 'earnestly praying, as . . . in duty bound, that the Supreme Lawgiver of the Universe . . . guide them into every measure which may be worthy of his [blessing].' The other face looks toward the principle that governmental intervention in religious matters can itself endanger religious freedom. This case, like all establishment clause challenges, presents us with the difficulty of respecting both faces. Our institutions presuppose a Supreme Being, yet these institutions must not press religious observances upon their citizens. One face looks to the past in acknowledgment of our Nation's heritage, while the other looks to the present in demanding a separation between church and state. Reconciling these two faces requires that we neither abdicate our responsibility to maintain a division between church and state nor evince a hostility to religion by disabling the government from in some ways recognizing our religious heritage

The Court quoted from an earlier case: "We find no constitutional requirement which makes it necessary for government to be hostile to religion and to throw its weight against efforts to widen the effective scope of religious influence." It noted that "fostering a pervasive bias or hostility to religion . . . could undermine the very neutrality the establishment clause requires."

The Court rejected the so-called *Lemon* test for resolving the case before it. The *Lemon* test comes from a 1971 decision of the Supreme Court in which it ruled that a law or practice does not violate the establishment clause if it (1) has a secular legislative purpose; (2) has a principal or primary effect that neither advances nor inhibits religion; and (3) does not foster an excessive government entanglement with religion. The Court concluded that the *Lemon* test was "not useful in dealing with the sort of passive monument that Texas has erected on its Capitol grounds." Instead, our "analysis is driven both by the nature of the monument and by our Nation's history." It observed that "there is an unbroken history of official acknowledgment by all three branches of government of the role of religion in American life from at least 1789." It cited numerous examples, many of which were mentioned by Justice Scalia in his dissenting opinion in the *McCreary* case (see above).

This recognition of religion in public life back to the founding of the country has led to decisions finding that the establishment clause permits some public accommodations of religion. It noted that "acknowledgments of the role played by the Ten Commandments in our Nation's heritage are common throughout America," and that "we need only look within our own Courtroom. Since 1935, Moses has stood, holding two tablets that reveal portions of the Ten Commandments written in Hebrew, among other lawgivers in the south frieze. Representations of the Ten Commandments adorn the metal gates lining the north and south sides of the Courtroom as well as the doors leading into the Courtroom. Moses also sits on the exterior east facade of the building holding the Ten Commandments tablets." The Court continued,

> Similar acknowledgments can be seen throughout a visitor's tour of our Nation's Capital. For example, a large statue of Moses holding the Ten Commandments, alongside a statue of the Apostle Paul, has overlooked the rotunda of the Library of Congress' Jefferson Building since 1897. And the Jefferson Building's Great Reading Room contains a sculpture of a woman beside the Ten Commandments with a quote above her from the Old Testament (Micah 6:8). A medallion with two tablets depicting the Ten Commandments decorates the floor of the National Archives. Inside the Department of Justice, a statue entitled "The Spirit of Law" has two tablets representing the Ten Commandments lying at its feet. In front of the Ronald Reagan Building is another sculpture that includes a depiction of the Ten Commandments. So too a 24-foot-tall sculpture, depicting, among other things, the Ten Commandments and a cross, stands outside the federal courthouse that houses both the Court of Appeals and the District Court for the District of Columbia. Moses is also prominently featured in the Chamber of the United States House of Representatives.

The Court concluded: "Texas has treated her Capitol grounds monuments as representing the several strands in the state's political and legal history. The inclusion of the Ten Commandments monument in this group has a dual significance, partaking of both religion and government. We cannot say that Texas' display of this monument violates the establishment clause of the First Amendment."

Justice Breyer, in a concurring opinion, made the following observations:

The case before us is a borderline case. It concerns a large granite monument bearing the text of the Ten Commandments located on the grounds of the Texas State Capitol. On the one hand, the Commandments' text undeniably has a religious message, invoking, indeed emphasizing, the Deity. On the other hand, focusing on the text of the Commandments alone cannot conclusively resolve this case. Rather, to determine the message that the text here conveys, we must examine how the text is *used*. And that inquiry requires us to consider the context of the display. In certain contexts, a display of the tablets of the Ten Commandments can convey not simply a religious message but also a secular moral message (about proper standards of social conduct). And in certain contexts, a display of the tablets can also convey a historical message (about a historic relation between those standards and the law)—a fact that helps to explain the display of those tablets in dozens of courthouses throughout the Nation, including the Supreme Court of the United States.

Here the tablets have been used as part of a display that communicates not simply a religious message, but a secular message as well. The circumstances surrounding the display's placement on the capitol grounds and its physical setting suggest that the State itself intended the latter, nonreligious aspects of the tablets' message to predominate. And the monument's 40-year history on the Texas state grounds indicates that that has been its effect. . . .

The physical setting of the monument, moreover, suggests little or nothing of the sacred. The monument sits in a large park containing 17 monuments and 21 historical markers, all designed to illustrate the "ideals" of those who settled in Texas and of those who have lived there since that time. The setting does not readily lend itself to meditation or any other religious activity. But it does provide a context of history and moral ideals. It (together with the display's inscription about its origin) communicates to visitors that the state sought to reflect moral principles, illustrating a relation between ethics and law that the state's citizens, historically speaking, have endorsed. That is to say, the context suggests that the state intended the display's moral message—an illustrative message reflecting the historical "ideals" of Texans—to predominate.

If these factors provide a strong, but not conclusive, indication that the Commandments' text on this monument conveys a predominantly secular message, a further factor is determinative here. As far as I can tell, 40 years passed in which the presence of this monument, legally speaking, went unchallenged (until the single legal objection raised by petitioner). And I am not aware of any evidence suggesting that this was due to a climate of intimidation. Hence, those 40 years suggest more strongly than can any set of formulaic tests that few individuals, whatever their system of beliefs, are likely to have understood the monument as amounting, in any significantly detrimental way, to a government effort to favor a particular religious sect, primarily to promote religion over nonreligion . . . . Those 40 years suggest that the public visiting the capitol grounds has considered the religious aspect of the tablets' message as part of what is a broader moral and historical message reflective of a cultural heritage. . . .

To reach a contrary conclusion here, based primarily on the religious nature of the tablets' text would, I fear, lead the law to exhibit a hostility toward religion that has no place in our establishment clause traditions. Such a holding might well encourage disputes concerning the removal of longstanding depictions of the Ten Commandments from public buildings across the Nation. And it could thereby create the very kind of religiously based divisiveness that the establishment clause seeks to avoid.

Instructional Aids to Chapter 12

Key Terms

compelling state interest

entanglement

Equal Access Act

judicial review

public welfare legislation

released time

religion of secularism

sponsorship

Learning Objectives

- Understand the Supreme Court's interpretation of the First Amendment religion clauses in a variety of contexts, including

  - aid to religious schools

  - released time programs

  - prayer and Bible readings in public schools

  - church property tax exemptions

  - compulsory attendance requirements

  - tax credits to parents with children in private schools

Short-Answer Questions

1. Your state legislature is considering a bill that would reimburse parents for the cost of transporting their children to public and private elementary and secondary schools. A taxpayer claims that such a law would constitute the establishment of a religion in violation of the First Amendment. Will a court agree with the taxpayer?

2. Your public school board adopts a "released time" program whereby students are released from school for one hour each week to receive religious instruction at churches and other facilities located away from school property. A parent claims that the program constitutes the establishment of a religion in violation of the First Amendment. Is this claim correct?

3. Same facts as question 2, except that students are permitted to meet in vacant classrooms in the school building. Does this affect your answer?

4. A public school adopts a course entitled "The Bible—Its Literary and Cultural Significance." Several books in both the Old and New Testaments are read for purposes of literary and cultural appreciation. No proselytizing occurs. Is this class constitutionally permissible?

5. All of our coins and currency are required by law to bear the inscription "In God We Trust." Does this practice constitute an impermissible establishment of religion in violation of the First Amendment? Explain.

6. A public high school teacher opens each class with a voluntary prayer. Students not wishing to participate are instructed to remain in the hallway until the prayer is completed. A parent challenges this practice. How would a court rule?

7. A group of 15 public high school students asks their school principal for permission to conduct a Bible study in an empty classroom building one morning each week prior to the start of the school day. The principal denies the request. The students are considering a lawsuit challenging the principal's action. Would such a lawsuit be successful? What factors would be most important in a court's resolution of such a dispute?

8. Does the exemption of church sanctuaries from state property taxes constitute an impermissible establishment of religion? Explain.

9. A state legislature employs a full-time chaplain, who has various duties including the opening of each legislative session with prayer. Is this practice constitutionally permissible? Explain.

10. A state enacts a law permitting each school day to begin with a minute of silence during which students can pray, meditate, do homework, or occupy themselves in any other manner. Is such a law constitutional?

Essay Questions

1. The Supreme Court has outlawed most collective prayers in public elementary and secondary schools, yet Congress continues to open its sessions with prayer. Can you think of a rational basis for this distinction?

2. A substantial majority of the public favors voluntary collective prayer in public elementary and secondary schools. Yet, since 1962, the courts consistently have disallowed such a practice. Can you think of a legitimate justification for this suppression of the will of the majority? How can the majority's rights be accommodated?

3. In 1963, the Supreme Court held that the practice of reading the Bible in public schools at the start of each school day constituted an impermissible establishment of religion in violation of the First Amendment, despite the consistent acceptance of such a practice since the adoption of the First Amendment in 1791. Why did it take the Supreme Court nearly two centuries to decide that the reading of the Bible in public schools violated the First Amendment? Does this delay raise questions about the legitimacy of the Court's interpretation? What else does the delay tell us?

The Present Meaning of the First Amendment Religion Clauses

Legal Briefs

The two previous chapters have addressed the importance of the Supreme Court's interpretation of the First Amendment religion clauses. In this chapter, the Court's current interpretation of the religion clauses is addressed

"In evaluating whether a particular law or government action violates the 'free exercise' clause, the Supreme Court has formulated the following two rules: first, government may never interfere with an individual's right to believe whatever he or she wants. Second, in deciding whether or not a government law, regulation, or practice that burdens religiously motivated conduct violates the free exercise clause, various principles apply."

In 1973, the Court held that a law or government action challenged on the basis of the "establishment clause" will be constitutional only if it meets all of the following three conditions: (1) a clearly secular purpose, (2) a primary effect that neither advances nor inhibits religion, and (3) no excessive entanglement between government and religion. This test often is referred to as the "tripartite" establishment clause test. In more recent rulings the Supreme Court has held that the tripartite test is not the only test available under the establishment clause. It is merely a guide that may be helpful in some contexts but not in others.

To illustrate, in 1984 the Court upheld the constitutionality of a nativity scene on public property during the Christmas season even though such displays might not pass the tripartite test. The Court was satisfied that the display reflected a deeply-held and widely-accepted religious tradition that did not advance or establish religion in a substantial way. In evaluating whether a particular law or government action violates the "free exercise" clause, the Supreme Court has formulated the following two rules: first, government may never interfere with an individual's right to believe whatever he or she wants. Second, in deciding whether or not a government law, regulation, or practice that burdens religiously motivated conduct violates the free exercise clause, various principles apply. For example, "generally applicable criminal prohibitions" that burden religiously motivated conduct do not violate the free exercise clause. Such prohibitions are presumptively valid and need not be supported by a compelling state interest.

In other cases, the courts must consider (i) whether the activity was motivated by and rooted in legitimate and sincerely held religious belief, (ii) whether the activity was unduly and substantially burdened by the government's action, and (iii) whether the government has a compelling interest in limiting the religious activity that cannot be accomplished by less restrictive means.

The Establishment Clause § 13-01

The clearest evidence that the framers of the First Amendment's establishment clause intended only to prohibit the creation of a national church is the virtual absence of any judicial decisions applying the clause in the first century and a half following its adoption despite countless state and federal accommodations of religion.[1] Prior to 1940, the Supreme Court interpreted the establishment clause on only two occasions. In 1890, it rejected a claim that an Idaho law prohibiting polygamy constituted an impermissible establishment of religion.[2] The Court observed that the purpose of the establishment clause was to prohibit federal legislation

for the support of any religious tenets, or the modes of worship of any sect. The oppressive measures adopted, and the cruelties and punishments inflicted, by the governments of Europe for many ages, to compel parties to conform in their religious beliefs and modes of worship, to the views of the most numerous sect, and the folly of attempting in that way to control the mental operations of persons, and enforce an outward conformity to a prescribed standard, led to the adoption of the [first] amendment.[3]

In 1918, the Court summarily dismissed a claim that the exemption of ministers from military conscription constituted the establishment of a religion.[4]

In 1940, the Court reaffirmed that the purpose of the establishment clause was to prevent an established church: "[I]t forestalls compulsion by law of the acceptance of any creed or the practice of any form of worship."[5] However, the Court added that the concept of "liberty" protected against state interference by the Fourteenth Amendment to the federal Constitution "embraces the liberties guaranteed by the First Amendment."

> "The clearest evidence that the framers of the First Amendment's establishment clause intended only to prohibit the creation of a national church is the virtual absence of any judicial decisions applying the clause in the first century and a half following its adoption despite countless state and federal accommodations of religion."

---

[1] This construction is also amply supported by historical evidence. *See, e.g.*, Wallace v. Jaffree, 472 U.S. 38 (1985) (dissenting opinion of Justice Rehnquist); R. CORD, SEPARATION OF CHURCH AND STATE: HISTORICAL FACT AND CURRENT FICTION (1982); chapter 11, *supra*.

[2] Davis v. Beason, 10 S. Ct. 299 (1890).

[3] *Id.* at 300.

[4] Aver v. United States, 245 U.S. 366 (1918).

[5] Cantwell v. Connecticut, 310 U.S. 296 (1940).

The significance of this holding cannot be overstated. The First Amendment's liberties, including the free exercise and nonestablishment of religion, intended by the framers of that amendment as a limitation on the federal government and so interpreted for a century and a half,[6] were now also limitations upon state and local governments. Ironically, shortly after this unwarranted expansion of federal authority over the states, the Court remarked that "[j]udicial nullification of legislation cannot be justified by attributing to the framers of the Bill of Rights views for which there is no historic warrant."[7]

Despite this assurance, the Court largely abandoned the views of the framers of the establishment clause in its landmark *Everson* decision in 1947.[8] In *Everson*, a case involving a constitutional challenge to a state law authorizing bus transportation for parochial school students at public expense, the Court announced the following interpretation of the establishment clause:

> Neither a state nor the Federal Government can set up a church. Neither can pass laws which aid one religion, aid all religions, or prefer one religion over another. Neither can force nor influence a person to go or to remain away from church against his will or force him to profess a belief or disbelief in any religion. No person can be punished for entertaining or professing religious beliefs or disbeliefs, for church attendance or nonattendance. No tax in any amount, large or small, can be levied to support any religious activities or institutions, whatever they may be called, or whatever form they may adopt to teach or practice religion. Neither a state nor the Federal Government can, openly or secretly, participate in the affairs of any religious organizations or groups and vice versa. In the words of Jefferson, the clause against establishment of religion by law was intended to erect a wall of separation between church and state.[9]

Four dissenting justices similarly remarked that the First Amendment's purpose

> was not to strike merely at the official establishment of a single sect, creed or religion, outlawing only a formal relation such as had prevailed in England and some of the colonies. Necessarily, it was to uproot all such relationships. . . . It was to create a complete and permanent separation of the spheres of religious activity and civil authority by comprehensively forbidding every form of public aid or support for religion.[10]

By 1947, the Court not only had expanded the prohibitions of the establishment clause beyond anything contemplated by its framers, but also had

---

[6] *See, e.g.,* chapter 11, *supra. See also* Permoli v. Municipality No. 1 of New Orleans, 44 U.S. 589 (1845) (federal Constitution makes no provision for protecting religious liberties against state interference).

[7] Minersville School District v. Gobitis, 310 U.S. 586 (1940).

[8] Everson v. Board of Education, 330 U.S. 1 (1947).

[9] *Id.* at 15-16.

[10] *Id.* at 31-32.

imposed its interpretation upon state and local governments by means of the Fourteenth Amendment.[11]

The Court found in Jefferson's "wall of separation" metaphor the philosophical basis for its interpretation of the establishment clause in *Everson*. However, as Justice Rehnquist demonstrated convincingly nearly 40 years later, Jefferson's metaphor cannot properly be used as evidence of the meaning of the establishment clause.[12]

In the years following *Everson*, several longstanding accommodations of religious belief and practice fell victim to the new interpretation of the establishment clause. In 1948, the Court, relying on *Everson* and Jefferson's "wall of separation" metaphor, struck down a local school board policy that permitted teachers employed by private religious groups to come weekly into public school buildings during regular school hours and impart religious instruction for 30 minutes to students whose parents requested it.[13]

In 1962, the Court struck down a New York law requiring the following prayer to be said aloud in each public school classroom at the beginning of each school day: "Almighty God, we acknowledge our dependence upon Thee, and we beg Thy blessings upon us, our parents, our teachers and our country."[14] The Court concluded that recitation of this prayer in public schools "breaches the wall of separation between church and state," even though children who were opposed to the prayer were not compelled to participate and could be excused from class until the recitation was completed. Similarly, the Court in 1963 invalidated a Pennsylvania law requiring that "[a]t least ten verses from the Holy Bible shall be read, without comment, at the opening of each public school on each school day."[15] The law permitted children to be excused from attending class during the reading upon the written request of a parent. The Court relied entirely on the expansive interpretation of the establishment clause enunciated in *Everson* in striking down the law.

In 1968, the Court struck down an Arkansas law making it unlawful for public school teachers to "teach the theory or doctrine that mankind ascended or descended from a lower order of animals."[16] The Court, relying on *Everson*, concluded that the First Amendment "does not permit the state to require that teaching and learning must be tailored to the principles or prohibitions of any religious sect or dogma."

---

[11] Wallace v. Jaffree, 472 U.S. 38 (1985) (dissenting opinion of Justice Rehnquist). The dissenting opinion is an extensive historical analysis that seriously undermines the legitimacy of the Court's Everson decision and many subsequent rulings based on that precedent.

[12] *Id. See also* § 12-10, *supra*.

[13] People of State of Illinois ex rel. McCollum v. Board of Education, 333 U.S. 203 (1948). Justice Reed, in dissent, noted that "the 'wall of separation between church and state' that Mr. Jefferson built at the university which he founded [the University of Virginia] did not exclude religious education from that school." *Id.* at 247.

[14] Engel v. Vitale, 370 U.S. 421 (1962). In a dissenting opinion, Justice Steward observed that "the Court's task, in this as in all areas of constitutional adjudication, is not responsibly aided by the uncritical invocation of metaphors like the 'wall of separation,' a phrase nowhere to be found in the Constitution." *Id.* at 445-46.

[15] School District of Abington v. Schempp, 374 U.S. 203 (1963).

[16] Epperson v. Arkansas, 393 U.S. 97 (1968).

The Lemon Test

Key point 13-01.1. *The most commonly applied test for evaluating the validity of a law of government practice under the First Amendment's nonestablishment of religion clause is the three-part "Lemon" test. Under this test, a law or government practice that conveys some benefit on religion will be constitutional if it (1) has a clearly secular purpose; (2) has a primary effect that neither advances nor inhibits religion; and (3) does not foster an excessive entanglement between church and state. All three parts of the test must be met in order for the law or practice to be constitutional. The Supreme Court has recognized limited exceptions to this test.*

" The most commonly applied test for evaluating the validity of a law of government practice under the First Amendment's nonestablishment of religion clause is the three-part "Lemon" test. "

In 1971, the Court held that its establishment clause decisions since *Everson* could be embodied in a three-pronged test: "First, the statute must have a secular legislative purpose; second, its principal or primary effect must be one that neither advances nor inhibits religion; finally, the statute must not foster 'an excessive governmental entanglement with religion.'"[17] This test, known as the three-pronged or "tripartite" *Lemon* test, enshrined the dubious interpretation of the establishment clause announced in *Everson*. The Court, in amplifying on this test, has observed that "[t]he purpose prong of the *Lemon* test asks whether government's actual purpose is to endorse or disapprove of religion. The effect prong asks whether irrespective of government's actual purpose, the practice under review in fact conveys a message of endorsement or disapproval. An affirmative answer to either question should render the challenged practice invalid."[18] With regard to the primary effect prong, the Court has further observed that "not every law that confers an 'indirect,' 'remote,' or 'incidental' benefit upon [religion] is, for that reason alone, constitutionally invalid."[19] "Excessive entanglement" between church and state connotes "comprehensive, discriminating, and continuing state surveillance."[20] The Court suggested in *Lemon* that laws or government practices having the potential for "political divisiveness" may violate the entanglement prong. However, the Court later confined this aspect of entanglement to "cases where direct financial subsidies are paid to parochial schools or to teachers in parochial schools."[21]

Application of the *Lemon* standard resulted, predictably, in the invalidation of many accommodations of religious practice. For example, the Supreme Court

---

[17] Lemon v. Kurtzman, 403 U.S. 602, 612-13 (1971).

[18] Lynch v. Donnelly, 465 U.S. 668 (1984).

[19] Committee for Public Education & Religious Liberty v. Nyquist, 413 U.S. 756, 771 (1973).

[20] Lemon v. Kurtzman, 403 U.S. 602, 619 (1971). *But see* Wallace v. Jaffree, 472 U.S. 38 (1985) (dissenting opinion of Justice Rehnquist).

[21] Mueller v. Allen, 463 U.S. 388, 403 n.11 (1983).

outlawed several programs providing limited assistance to private education;[22] a Kentucky law requiring a copy of the Ten Commandments to be posted in each public school classroom;[23] a state law specifying that each public school day should begin with a minute of silence during which students could pray, meditate, or occupy themselves in any other manner they chose;[24] a state law requiring that public schools present both the theories of evolution and creation science;[25] and a nativity display maintained in a county courthouse building during the Christmas season that was not a part of a larger display containing secular symbols.[26] Lower federal courts invalidated scores of religious practices on the basis of the Lemon test.

The Supreme Court has often expressed misgivings about the *Lemon* formulation. In 1971, the Court called the *Lemon* test a mere "guideline."[27] It later described the test as "no more than [a] useful signpost,"[28] and expressed an unwillingness to be "confined to any single test or criterion."[29] Similarly, the Court has noted that the test "is not easily applied"[30] and "sacrifices clarity and predictability for flexibility."[31] The Court has disregarded the *Lemon* test on at least two occasions. In 1982, the Court deviated from the *Lemon* test in striking down a Minnesota statute requiring certain religious organizations to register with the state prior to soliciting contributions.[32] The Court, observing that the *Lemon* test was "intended to apply to laws affording a uniform benefit to *all* religions," announced the following two-part test to be used in assessing the constitutionality of a law that discriminates "*among* religions": (1) The law must be justified by a compelling governmental interest, and (2) it must be closely fitted to further that interest.

In 1983, the Court again deviated from the *Lemon* test in upholding the practice of legislative chaplains,[33] reversing a federal appeals court ruling that invalidated the practice on the basis of the *Lemon* test. The Court, noting that the very Congress that approved the First Amendment establishment clause also voted to appoint and pay a chaplain for both houses, concluded that "it would be incongruous to interpret that clause as imposing more stringent First Amendment limits on the states than the draftsmen imposed on the federal government." Such cases are a repudiation, at least in part, of the hostility that the Court has shown to religious practice since *Everson.* They suggest that there is hope for a repudiation of

---

[22]   *See, e.g.*, Meek v. Pittinger, 421 U.S. 349 (1975); Wolman v. Walter, 433 U.S. 229 (1977); Levitt v. Committee for Public Education, 413 U.S. 472 (1973).

[23]   Stone v. Graham, 449 U.S. 39 (1980).

[24]   Wallace v. Jaffree, 472 U.S. 38 (1985).

[25]   Edwards v. Aguillard, 482 U.S. 578 (1987).

[26]   County of Allegheny v. American Civil Liberties Union, 109 S. Ct. 3086 (1989).

[27]   Tilton v. Richardson, 403 U.S. 672 (1971).

[28]   Mueller v. Allen, 463 U.S. 388 (1983).

[29]   Lynch v. Donnelly, 465 U.S. 668 (1984).

[30]   Meek v. Pittinger, 421 U.S. 349 (1975).

[31]   Committee for Public Education v. Regan, 444 U.S. 646 (1980).

[32]   Larson v. Valente, 456 U.S. 228 (1982).

[33]   Marsh v. Chambers, 463 U.S. 783 (1983).

Everson and the *Lemon* test, and a return to an interpretation of the establishment clause that is faithful to its history and purpose.[34]

Until the three-part *Lemon* test is repudiated, it likely will continue to be the primary analytical tool employed by the courts in establishment clause cases, with the following limitations:

1. *Laws that discriminate between religious groups.* Laws that discriminate between religious groups will be upheld against a claim that they violate the establishment clause only if (1) they are justified by a compelling governmental interest, and (2) they are closely fitted to further that interest.[35]

2. *Certain accommodations of religious custom and practice.* Certain accommodations of religious custom and practice may be validated by history. For example, in 1984 the Supreme Court upheld the practice of including a nativity scene on public property as part of a Christmas display.[36] While the Court validated the practice on the basis of *Lemon*, its application of the *Lemon* test was influenced if not controlled by historical precedent. Noting that the nativity scene had the secular purpose of depicting the origins of Christmas, did not have a primary effect of advancing religion, and did not create an excessive entanglement between church and state, the Court concluded, "It would be ironic, however, if the inclusion of a single symbol of a particular religious event, as part of a celebration acknowledged in the Western World for 20 centuries, and in this country by the people, by the Executive Branch, by the Congress, and the courts for two centuries, would so taint' the City's exhibit as to render it violative of the establishment clause." Similarly, the court upheld the constitutionality of legislative chaplaincies in 1983 on the basis of historical precedent without any reference to the *Lemon* test.[37] The Court found controlling the fact that the first Congress, which approved the First Amendment establishment clause, also voted to appoint and pay a chaplain for each House.

3. *Public welfare legislation.* The benefits of public welfare legislation cannot be denied to any group of persons "because of their faith, or lack of it."[38] For example, the establishment clause does not require that a law authorizing free transportation of children to school must exclude children attending private religious schools.

---

[34] If the citizens of this country are dissatisfied with the framers' intent, the Constitution itself provides a remedy—amendment. It is the people, through the power to amend the Constitution, that should have determined whether or not the First Amendment should be expanded beyond the original intention to prohibit established churches, and whether the First Amendment's establishment clause should be applied to state and local governments.

[35] Larson v. Valente, 456 U.S. 228 (1982).

[36] Lynch v. Donnelly, 465 U.S. 668 (1984).

[37] Marsh v. Chambers, 463 U.S. 783 (1983).

[38] Everson v. Board of Education, 330 U.S. 1 (1947).

4. *Neutrality.* As noted in the following section of this chapter, the principles underlying the establishment clause can in some cases conflict with the values embodied in the free exercise of religion clause. Therefore, neither clause should be construed in isolation. The establishment clause, properly construed in light of the free exercise of religion clause, mandates governmental neutrality toward religion. Neither sponsorship nor hostility is permissible.

5. *Incidental accommodations religion.* "[N]ot every law that confers an 'indirect,' 'remote,' or 'incidental' benefit upon [religion] is, for that reason alone, constitutionally invalid."[39]

The Free Exercise Clause § 13-02

The First Amendment specifies that "Congress shall make no law . . . prohibiting the free exercise [of religion]." This language generally is referred to as the "free exercise clause." The free exercise clause remained a dormant provision of the Bill of Rights for nearly a century and a half following its adoption. This was based largely on two factors. First, Congress seldom if ever took any action that interfered with the exercise of anyone's religion. Second, in its first decision interpreting the free exercise clause, the Supreme Court ruled in 1878 that while federal laws "cannot interfere with mere religious belief and opinions, they may with practice."[40] According to this interpretation, the free exercise clause would be violated only by congressional legislation that interfered with an individual's religious *beliefs*, and not with religiously-motivated *conduct*.

Two developments significantly increased the relevance and application of the free exercise clause. The first occurred in 1940, when the Supreme Court "incorporated" the First Amendment religion clauses into the Fourteenth Amendment "due process" clause, thereby making the First Amendment a limitation upon state (and local) governments as well as Congress.[41] Prior to 1940, only federal legislation could violate the free exercise clause. Since 1940, the same is true of state and local legislation and regulations. Clearly, this had the effect of greatly expanding the application of the free exercise clause. Second, in 1963 the Supreme Court issued a major reinterpretation of the free exercise clause in the case of *Sherbert v. Verner.*[42] In the *Sherbert* case, the Court departed from the simplistic "belief-conduct" standard that it had enunciated in its earlier *Reynolds* decision and announced that a government statute or regulation that imposes

---

[39] Committee for Public Education & Religious Liberty v. Nyquist, 413 U.S. 756, 771 (1973). *See also* Widmar v. Vincent, 454 U.S. 263, 273 (1981).

[40] Reynolds v. United States, 98 U.S. 145, 166 (1878). The Court upheld the bigamy conviction of a Mormon under a federal statute, and rejected the claim that the statute violated the free exercise clause.

[41] *See* chapter 11, *supra.*

[42] 374 U.S. 398 (1963).

a "burden" on the free exercise of one's religion violates the free exercise clause *unless the statute or regulation is justified by a "compelling state interest."* This test was clarified a few years later in *Wisconsin v. Yoder.*[43] The Supreme Court articulated its understanding of the free exercise clause as follows:

1. Government may never interfere with an individual's right to *believe* whatever he or she wants.

2. In determining whether the government may interfere with or restrict religiously motivated *conduct*, the courts must consider (a) whether the activity was motivated by and rooted in legitimate and sincerely held religious belief, (b) whether the activity was unduly and substantially burdened by the government's action, and (c) whether the government has a compelling interest in limiting the religious activity that cannot be accomplished by less restrictive means.

This general understanding of the free exercise clause was applied by the Court in several cases.[44]

The Smith Case

§ 13-02.1

Key point 13-02.1. *In the* Smith *case (1990) the Supreme Court ruled that a neutral law of general applicability is presumably valid and need not be supported by a compelling government interest to be consistent with the First Amendment, even if it interferes with the exercise of religion.*

Oregon law prohibits the intentional possession of a "controlled substance," including the drug peyote. Two employees of a private drug rehabilitation organization were fired from their jobs because they consumed peyote for "sacramental purposes" at a ceremony of the Native American Church. The two individuals applied for unemployment benefits under Oregon law, but their application was denied on the grounds that benefits are not payable to employees who are discharged for "misconduct." The two former employees claimed that the denial of benefits violated their constitutional right to freely exercise their religion. The United States Supreme Court ruled that (1) the constitutional guaranty of religious freedom did not prohibit a state from criminalizing the sacramental use of a narcotic drug, and (2) the state of Oregon could deny unemployment benefits to individuals who were fired from their jobs for consuming peyote.[45]

The Court began its opinion by noting that "we have never held that an individual's religious beliefs excuse him from compliance with an otherwise valid

---

[43] 406 U.S. 205 (1971). The *Yoder* case is discussed in chapter 12, *supra.*

[44] *See, e.g.,* Hernandez v. Commissioner, 109 S. Ct. 2136 (1989); Hobbie v. Unemployment Appeals Commission, 480 U.S. 136 (1987); United States v. Lee, 455 U.S. 252 (1982).

[45] 110 S. Ct. 1595 (1990). The *Smith* case is discussed in § 12-11, *supra.*

law prohibiting conduct that the state is free to regulate." On the contrary, the constitutional guaranty of religious freedom "does not relieve an individual of the obligation to comply with a valid and neutral law of general applicability on the ground that the law [prohibits] conduct that his religion prescribes."

Key point. *The Court did not throw out the "compelling state interest" requirement in all cases involving governmental restrictions on religious freedom. Rather, the Court stated that this requirement does not apply to restrictions caused by a "neutral law of general applicability." A law or other government act that targets or singles out religious organizations must be supported by a compelling state interest. Further, as noted below, the compelling state interest requirement applies if a second constitutional right is burdened by a law or other government act.*

The real significance of the Court's ruling was its refusal to apply the "compelling state interest" test as requested by the discharged employees. As noted above, the Supreme Court previously had interpreted the constitutional guaranty of religious freedom to mean that the government could not impose substantial burdens on the exercise of sincerely-held religious beliefs unless its actions were justified by a "compelling state interest" that could not be served through less restrictive means. The former employees argued that the Oregon law's denial of unemployment benefits to persons using peyote for sacramental purposes was not supported by a "compelling state interest" and accordingly could not be applied without violating the constitution.

The Court justified its refusal to apply the "compelling state interest" test by noting that

- it had not applied the test in a number of its recent decisions

- it had never found a state law limiting religious practices invalid on the ground that it was not supported by a compelling state interest

- the compelling state interest test should never be applied "to require exemptions from a generally applicable criminal law"

The Court rejected the former employees' suggestion that the "compelling state interest" test be applied only in cases involving religiously-motivated conduct that is "central" to an individual's religion. This would require the courts to make judgments on the importance of religious practices—and this the civil courts may never do. The only options are to apply the "compelling state interest" test to all attempts by government to regulate religious practices, or to not apply the test at all. Applying the test in all cases involving governmental attempts to regulate religious practices would lead to "anarchy," since it would render "presumptively invalid" every law that regulates conduct allegedly based on religious belief. This would open the floodgates of claims of religious exemption "from civic obligations of almost every conceivable kind—ranging from compulsory military service to the payment of taxes, to health and safety regulation such as manslaughter and child neglect laws, compulsory vaccination laws, drug laws; to social welfare legislation such as minimum wage laws, child labor laws, animal cruelty laws, environmental protection laws, and laws providing for equality of opportunity for the races. The First Amendment's protection of religious liberty does not require this."

The Court's ruling represents a clear departure from its previously well-established understanding of the constitutional guaranty of religious freedom. No longer will a state need to demonstrate that a "compelling state interest" supports a law that prohibits or restricts religious practices. This is unfortunate, and will tend to make it more difficult to prove that a state's interference with religious practices violates the guaranty of religious freedom. Four of the Court's nine justices disagreed with the Court's analysis and with the virtual elimination of the "compelling state interest" test. The minority asserted that the Court's ruling diminished the guaranty of religious liberty by making it more difficult for persons to prove a violation of this fundamental constitutional guaranty. One of the dissenting Justices lamented that the Court's decision tilts the scales "in the state's favor," and "effectuates a wholesale overturning of settled law concerning the religion clauses of our Constitution. One hopes that the Court is aware of the consequences . . . ."

The *Smith* case suggests that the Court is moving back towards the old "belief-conduct" analysis articulated more than a century ago in *Reynolds*—religious belief is protected by the free exercise clause, but not religiously-motivated conduct.[46] This shift has generated much criticism and opposition, which will ensure further reinterpretations of the free exercise clause.

The Religious Freedom Restoration Act § 13-02.2

Key point 13-02.2. *Congress enacted the Religious Freedom Restoration Act to prevent the government from enacting any law or adopting any practice that substantially burdens the free exercise of religion unless the law or practice is supported by a compelling government interest. The compelling government interest requirement applies to any law, including neutral laws of general applicability. The objective of the Act was to repudiate the Supreme Court's decision in the Smith case (1990) in which the Court ruled that neutral laws of general applicability that burden the free exercise of religion do not need to be supported by a compelling government interest in order to satisfy the First Amendment. In 1997, the Supreme Court ruled that the Act was unconstitutional. However, other courts have limited this ruling to state and local legislation, and have concluded that the Act continues to apply to federal laws.*

---

[46] Other decisions of the Court support this view. *See, e.g.,* Goldman v. Weinberger, 475 U.S. 503 (1986) (Air Force regulation prohibiting religious headgear upheld despite claim of Jewish officer that it violated the free exercise of his religion); United States v. Lee, 455 U.S. 252 (1982) (Court rejected an Amish farmer's request to be exempt from social security taxes); Bowen v. Roy, 476 U.S. 693 (1986) (government can deny welfare benefits to an individual who refuses to obtain a social security number, even though the individual's actions are based on religious convictions).

The consequences of the Supreme Court's reinterpretation of the First Amendment guaranty of religious freedom were predictable. Scores of lower federal courts and state courts upheld laws and other government actions that directly restricted religious practices. In many of these cases, the courts based their actions directly on the *Smith* case, suggesting that the result would have been different had it not been for that decision.

Congress responded to the *Smith* case in an extraordinary way—by enacting the Religious Freedom Restoration Act ("RFRA") by a unanimous vote of both houses. RFRA was signed into law by President Clinton in 1993. It begins by reciting the following "congressional findings":

(1) the framers of the Constitution, recognizing free exercise of religion as an unalienable right, secured its protection in the First Amendment to the Constitution;

(2) laws "neutral" toward religion may burden religious exercise as surely as laws intended to interfere with religious exercise;

(3) governments should not burden religious exercise without compelling justification;

(4) in Employment Division v. Smith, 494 U.S. 872 (1990) the Supreme Court virtually eliminated the requirement that the government justify burdens on religious exercise imposed by laws neutral toward religion; and

(5) the compelling interest test as set forth in prior federal court rulings is a workable test for striking sensible balances between religious liberty and competing prior governmental interests.

> "Laws "neutral" toward religion may burden religious exercise as surely as laws intended to interfere with religious exercise…"

RFRA next states its purposes as follows: "(1) to restore the compelling interest test . . . and to guarantee its application in all cases where free exercise of religion is burdened; and (2) to provide a claim or defense to persons whose religious exercise is burdened by government."

The key provision of RFRA is section 3, which specifies:

(a) IN GENERAL. Government shall not substantially burden a person's exercise of religion even if the burden results from a rule of general applicability, except as provided in subsection (b) . . . .

(b) EXCEPTION. Government may substantially burden a person's exercise of religion only if it demonstrates that application of the burden to the person—(1) is in furtherance of a compelling governmental interest; and (2) is the least restrictive means of furthering that compelling governmental interest.

(c) JUDICIAL RELIEF. A person whose religious exercise has been burdened in violation of this section may assert that violation as a claim or defense in a judicial proceeding and obtain appropriate relief against the government. Standing to assert a claim or defense under this section shall be governed by the general rules of standing under article III of the Constitution.

Q In practical terms, how did the enactment of RFRA affect local churches and other religious organizations?

A There is little doubt that it provided significant protections to the exercise of religion. Any law or government practice (whether at the local, state, or federal level) that "burdened" the exercise of religion was legally permissible only if the law or practice (1) was in furtherance of a compelling governmental interest, and (2) was the least restrictive means of furthering that compelling governmental interest. These were difficult standards to meet.

As the Supreme Court itself observed in 1993, the concept of a "compelling governmental interest" is a very difficult standard for the government to satisfy:

A law burdening religious practice that is not neutral or not of general application must undergo the most rigorous of scrutiny. To satisfy the commands of the First Amendment, a law restrictive of religious practice must advance interests of the highest order and must be narrowly tailored in pursuit of those interests. The compelling interest standard that we apply once a law fails to meet the Smith requirements is not "watered . . . down" but "really means what it says." A law that targets religious conduct for distinctive treatment or advances legitimate governmental interests only against conduct with a religious motivation will survive strict scrutiny only in rare cases. . . .[47]

In the years following the enactment of RFRA a number of government attempts to regulate or interfere with religious practices were struck down by the courts on the basis of the Act.

The City of Boerne Case   § 13-02.3

Key point 13-02.3. *In the City of Boerne case (1997), the Supreme Court ruled that the Religious Freedom Restoration Act was unconstitutional. Other courts have limited this ruling to state and local legislation, and have concluded that the Act continues to apply to federal laws.*

---

[47]   Church of the Lukumi Babaluaye, Inc. v. City of Hialeah, 508 U.S. 520 (1993).

In the City of Boerne case, in 1997, the Supreme Court struck down the Religious Freedom Restoration Act on the ground that Congress exceeded its authority in enacting the law.[48] The Court's decision will impact virtually every religious organization in America. Some of those impacts are predictable, but others are not. This subsection reviews the facts of this important case, and the Court's conclusions.

Situated on a hill in the city of Boerne, Texas, some 28 miles northwest of San Antonio, is St. Peter Catholic Church. Built in 1923, the church's structure reflects the mission style of the region's earlier history. The church seats about 230 worshippers, a number too small for its growing parish. Some 40 to 60 parishioners cannot be accommodated at some Sunday services. In order to meet the needs of the congregation the Archbishop of San Antonio gave permission to the parish to plan alterations to enlarge the building.

A few months later, the Boerne City Council passed an ordinance authorizing the city's Historic Landmark Commission to prepare a preservation plan with proposed historic landmarks and districts. Under the ordinance, the Commission must pre-approve construction affecting historic landmarks or buildings in a historic district.

Soon afterwards the Archbishop applied for a building permit so construction to enlarge the church could proceed. City authorities, relying on the ordinance and the designation of a historic district (which, they claimed, included the church), denied the application. The Archbishop filed a lawsuit challenging the city's denial of the permit. The lawsuit relied upon RFRA as one basis for relief from the refusal to issue the permit. A federal district court concluded that by enacting RFRA Congress exceeded the scope of its authority. A federal appeals court reversed this decision, and upheld the constitutionality of RFRA. The city appealed to the United States Supreme Court. The appeal addressed the question of the constitutional validity of RFRA.

The Supreme Court ruled that RFRA was unconstitutional since Congress did not have the authority to enact it. The Court began its opinion by noting that the federal government "is one of enumerated powers." That is, each branch (legislative, executive, judicial) can only do those things specifically authorized by the Constitution. The First Amendment specifies that "Congress" cannot enact legislation "prohibiting the free exercise" of religion. Of course, "Congress" refers to the federal legislature, and so the First Amendment guaranty of religious freedom, as originally worded, was not a limitation on the power of state or local governments. In 1868, the Fourteenth Amendment to the Constitution was ratified, which prohibits any state from depriving "any person of life, liberty, or property without due process of law." Then, in 1940, the Supreme Court ruled that the "liberty" protected by the Fourteenth Amendment against state interference included the First Amendment guaranty of religious freedom. For the

---

[48] It is not clear whether the Supreme Court intended to invalidate the Act as applied to federal law, state law, or both. Some courts have concluded that the Supreme Court only intended to invalidate the Act as applied to state and local legislation, and that the Act still applies to federal legislation that burdens the exercise of religion. See, e.g., In re Young, 82 F.3d 1407 (8th Cir. 1996) (the Act prevented federal bankruptcy law from infringing upon the religious beliefs of church members). The Supreme Court will need to resolve this ambiguity.

first time, this limitation upon the power of Congress to prohibit the free exercise of religion now applied to state and local governments as well. The Fourteenth Amendment contained a section (section 5) which gave Congress "power to enforce, by appropriate legislation, the provisions of this [amendment]." Congress pointed to this section as the source of its authority to enact RFRA. Members of Congress insisted that they were only protecting by legislation one of the liberties guaranteed by the Fourteenth Amendment that had been diminished by the Supreme Court's ruling in *Smith*.

The Supreme Court ruled that section 5 of the Fourteenth Amendment did not authorize Congress to enact RFRA. It acknowledged that section 5 authorizes Congress to "enforce" the Fourteenth Amendment, and therefore Congress can enact legislation "enforcing the constitutional right to the free exercise of religion." However, the Court then observed:

> Congress' power under section 5, however, extends only to enforcing the provisions of the Fourteenth Amendment. . . . The design of the amendment and the text of section 5 are inconsistent with the suggestion that Congress has the power to decree the substance of the Fourteenth Amendment's restrictions on the states. Legislation which alters the meaning of the free exercise [of religion] clause cannot be said to be enforcing the clause. Congress does not enforce a constitutional right by changing what the right is. It has been given the power "to enforce," not the power to determine what constitutes a constitutional violation. Were it not so, what Congress would be enforcing would no longer be, in any meaningful sense, the "provisions of [the Fourteenth Amendment] . . . ."
>
> If Congress could define its own powers by altering the Fourteenth Amendment's meaning, no longer would the Constitution be "superior paramount law, unchangeable by ordinary means." It would be "on a level with ordinary legislative acts, and, like other acts . . . alterable when the legislature shall please to alter it." Under this approach, it is difficult to conceive of a principle that would limit congressional power. Shifting legislative majorities could change the Constitution and effectively circumvent the difficult and detailed amendment process contained [therein].

The Court conceded that it is not always clear whether Congress is "enforcing" the Fourteenth Amendment or making unauthorized substantive changes in the Constitution. However, it insisted that there must be a "proportionality between the injury to be prevented or remedied and the means adopted to that end." The Court concluded that this test was not met in this case, since RFRA was not a "proportional" response to the "injury to be prevented or remedied." Rather, RFRA was an expansive law that was enacted to address minimal threats to religious freedom. The Court noted that

> sweeping coverage ensures [RFRA's] intrusion at every level of government, displacing laws and prohibiting official actions of almost every description

and regardless of subject matter. RFRA's restrictions apply to every agency and official of the federal, state, and local governments. RFRA applies to all federal and state law, statutory or otherwise, whether adopted before or after its enactment. RFRA has no termination date or termination mechanism. Any law is subject to challenge at any time by any individual who alleges a substantial burden on his or her free exercise of religion.

Further, this massive response was not warranted by any significant threat to religious freedom:

RFRA's legislative record lacks examples of modern instances of generally applicable laws passed because of religious bigotry. The history of persecution in this country detailed in the [congressional] hearings mentions no episodes occurring in the past 40 years. . . . The absence of more recent episodes stems from the fact that, as one witness testified, "deliberate persecution is not the usual problem in this country." Rather, the emphasis of the [congressional] hearings was on laws of general applicability which place incidental burdens on religion. Much of the discussion centered upon anecdotal evidence of autopsies performed on Jewish individuals and Hmong immigrants in violation of their religious beliefs . . . and on zoning regulations and historic preservation laws (like the one at issue here), which as an incident of their normal operation, have adverse effects on churches and synagogues. . . . It is difficult to maintain that they are examples of legislation enacted or enforced due to animus or hostility to the burdened religious practices or that they indicate some widespread pattern of religious discrimination in this country. Congress' concern was with the incidental burdens imposed, not the object or purpose of the legislation.

The stringent test RFRA demands of state laws reflects a lack of proportionality or congruence between the means adopted and the legitimate end to be achieved. If an objector can show a substantial burden on his free exercise, the State must demonstrate a compelling governmental interest and show that the law is the least restrictive means of furthering its interest. Claims that a law substantially burdens someone's exercise of religion will often be difficult to contest. Requiring a state to demonstrate a compelling interest and show that it has adopted the least restrictive means of achieving that interest is the most demanding test known to constitutional law. If "compelling interest" really means what it says . . . many laws will not meet the test. . . . [The test] would open the prospect of constitutionally required religious exemptions from civic obligations of almost every conceivable kind." Laws valid under Smith would fall under RFRA without regard to whether they had the object of stifling or punishing free exercise. . . . [RFRA] would require searching judicial scrutiny of state law with the attendant likelihood of invalidation. This is a considerable congressional intrusion into the states' traditional prerogatives and general authority to regulate for the health and welfare of their citizens.

The substantial costs RFRA exacts, both in practical terms of imposing a heavy litigation burden on the states and in terms of curtailing their traditional general regulatory power, far exceed any pattern or practice of unconstitutional conduct under the free exercise clause as interpreted in Smith. Simply put, RFRA is not designed to identify and counteract state laws likely to be unconstitutional because of their treatment of religion. In most cases, the state laws to which RFRA applies are not ones which will have been motivated by religious bigotry. . . .

It is a reality of the modern regulatory state that numerous state laws, such as the zoning regulations at issue here, impose a substantial burden on a large class of individuals. When the exercise of religion has been burdened in an incidental way by a law of general application, it does not follow that the persons affected have been burdened any more than other citizens, let alone burdened because of their religious beliefs. (emphasis added)

Conclusions § 13-02.4

The following rules summarize the current interpretation of the First Amendment guaranty of religious freedom, in light of the most recent Supreme Court decisions and other relevant precedent.

RULE #1. *It will be difficult for religious organizations to challenge neutral laws of general applicability that burden religious practices or beliefs, because such laws are presumably valid whether or not supported by a compelling government interest.*

Rule #1 is based on the Supreme Court's decisions in the *Smith* and *City of Boerne* cases. RFRA's attempt to establish a "compelling government interest" requirement in order to justify governmental infringements upon religion was declared unconstitutional by the Court in the City of Boerne ruling.

RULE #2. *Laws that are not "neutral" towards religion, or that are not of "general applicability," will violate the First Amendment guaranty of religious freedom unless supported by a compelling government interest.*

The Court's repeal of the "compelling state interest" requirement in the Smith case applied only in the context of neutral laws of general applicability. In 1993, the Court clarified the meaning of these important terms.[49] It also clarified the meaning of a "compelling state interest."

neutrality

The Court ruled that a law that is not neutral "must be justified by a compelling governmental interest and must be narrowly tailored to advance that interest." It is very important to define neutrality. The Court noted that "[i]f the object of a law is to infringe upon or restrict practices because of their religious motivation, the

---

[49]   Church of the Lukumi Babaluaye, Inc. v. City of Hialeah, 508 U.S. 520 (1993).

law is not neutral." It continued:

> There are, of course, many ways of demonstrating that the object or purpose of a law is the suppression of religion or religious conduct. To determine the object of a law, we must begin with its text, for the minimum requirement of neutrality is that a law not discriminate on its face. A law lacks facial neutrality if it refers to a religious practice without a secular meaning discernible from the language or context.

A law may not be neutral even though it is neutral "on its face." The Court observed:

> The free exercise clause . . . "forbids subtle departures from neutrality," and "covert suppression of particular religious beliefs." Official action that targets religious conduct for distinctive treatment cannot be shielded by mere compliance with the requirement of facial neutrality. The free exercise clause protects against governmental hostility which is masked, as well as overt. The Court must survey meticulously the circumstances of governmental categories to eliminate, as it were, religious gerrymanders.

In evaluating the neutrality of a government action, the courts should consider "the historical background of the decision under challenge, the specific series of events leading to the enactment or official policy in question, as well as the legislative or administrative history, including contemporaneous statements made by members of the decision-making body," to determine if the intent was to single out religious organizations or believers for unfavorable treatment.

general applicability

The Court ruled that a law that is not of general applicability "must be justified by a compelling governmental interest and must be narrowly tailored to advance that interest." This is so even if the law is neutral. Neutrality and general applicability are separate considerations. If a law fails either, then it must be supported by a compelling governmental interest in order to justify a negative impact on religious practices. With regard to the concept of "general applicability," the Court made the following clarification:

> All laws are selective to some extent, but categories of selection are of paramount concern when a law has the incidental effect of burdening religious practice. The free exercise clause "protects religious observers against unequal treatment," and inequality results when a legislature decides that the governmental interests it seeks to advance are worthy of being pursued only against conduct with a religious motivation. The principle that government, in pursuit of legitimate interests, cannot in a selective manner impose burdens only on conduct motivated by religious belief is essential to the protection of the rights guaranteed by the free exercise clause.

The court further observed that "in circumstances in which individualized exemptions from a general requirement are available, the government may not refuse to extend that system to cases of religious hardship without compelling reason." In other words, if a law of general applicability contains some non-religious exceptions, it cannot deny an exemption to religious institutions (in cases of religious hardship) without a compelling reason.

compelling state interest

The Court emphasized the high standard that a law or governmental practice must satisfy that burdens religious practice and that is either not neutral or not generally applicable:

> A law burdening religious practice that is not neutral or not of general application must undergo the most rigorous of scrutiny. To satisfy the commands of the First Amendment, a law restrictive of religious practice must advance interests of the highest order and must be narrowly tailored in pursuit of those interests. The compelling interest standard that we apply once a law fails to meet the Smith requirements is not "watered . . . down" but "really means what it says." A law that targets religious conduct for distinctive treatment or advances legitimate governmental interests only against conduct with a religious motivation will survive strict scrutiny only in rare cases.

The Court then proceeded to give one of its most detailed interpretations of the concept of a "compelling governmental interest":

> Where government restricts only conduct protected by the First Amendment and fails to enact feasible measures to restrict other conduct producing substantial harm or alleged harm of the same sort, the interest given in justification of the restriction is not compelling. It is established in our strict scrutiny jurisprudence that "a law cannot be regarded as protecting an interest of the highest order . . . when it leaves appreciable damage to that supposedly vital interest unprohibited."

RULE #3. *Neutral laws of general applicability that infringe upon a second constitutional right (in addition to religious freedom) will be unconstitutional unless supported by a compelling government interest.*

In the Smith case the Supreme Court observed that the compelling government interest test is triggered if a neutral and generally applicable law burdens not only the exercise of religion, but some other First Amendment right (such as speech, press, or assembly) as well. The Court observed, "The only decisions in which we have held that the First Amendment bars application of a neutral, generally applicable law to religiously motivated action have involved not the free exercise clause alone, but the free exercise clause in conjunction with other constitutional protections, such as freedom of speech and of the press . . . ." In other words, if a neutral and generally applicable law or governmental practice burdens the exercise of religion, then the compelling governmental interest standard can be triggered if the religious institution or adherent can point to some other First Amendment interest that is being violated. In many cases, this will not be hard to do. For example, the First Amendment guaranty of free speech often will be implicated when a law or governmental practice burdens the exercise of religion. The same is true of the First Amendment guarantees of free press and assembly.

RULE #4. *The government may not refuse to extend a system of exemptions to cases of religious hardship without compelling reason.*

In the *Smith* case the Supreme Court observed, "[O]ur decisions in the unemployment cases stand for the proposition that where the state has in place a system of individual exemptions, it may not refuse to extend that system to cases of 'religious hardship' without compelling reason."

RULE #5. *Every state constitution has some form of protection for religious freedom. In some cases, these protections are more comprehensive than under the federal Constitution. State constitutional protections in some cases may provide religious organizations with additional protections.*

Churches and religious adherents whose First Amendment right to the free exercise of religion is not violated by a neutral law of general applicability may claim that their state constitution's guaranty of religious freedom has been violated.

Rule #6. *Government may never interfere with an individual's right to believe whatever he or she wants. Only religiously-motivated conduct may be regulated, in accordance with the previous rules.*

These rules are illustrated by the following examples.

Examples

• *A state law prohibits the issuance of securities by any organization unless the securities are registered with the state securities commissioner. One of the purposes of the law is to prevent fraud. A church would like to sell promissory notes to raise funds for a new sanctuary. When it learns that it cannot do so without registering its securities, it insists that the application of such a law to churches violates the First Amendment's free exercise of religion clause. The church will lose. The securities law is neutral and of general applicability, and accordingly rule #1 controls. The law is presumably valid without the need to prove a compelling governmental interest.*

• *A number of common church practices may violate copyright law. Does the application of copyright law to churches violate the First Amendment's free exercise of religion clause? No. The copyright law is neutral and of general applicability, and accordingly rule #1 controls. The law is presumably valid without the need to prove a compelling governmental interest.*

• *A city enacts a civil rights ordinance that bans any employer (including churches) from discriminating on the basis of sexual orientation in any employment decision.*

A church argues that applying such a law to a church that is opposed on the basis of religious doctrine to hiring homosexuals will violate its constitutional right to freely exercise its religion. Under the Supreme Court's ruling in the Smith case, it is doubtful that the church would prevail. The civil rights law in question clearly is neutral and of general applicability, and accordingly rule #1 applies. This means that the law is presumably valid without the need to prove a compelling governmental interest. However, a number of federal courts (prior to Smith) concluded that the clergy-church relationship is unique and is beyond governmental regulation. Accordingly, it is doubtful that such an ordinance could be applied to clergy. This of course assumes that the Supreme Court, after Smith, would agree with these previous rulings.

• A religious denomination does not ordain women. A female church member sues the denomination, claiming that its ban on female clergy violates a state civil rights law banning discrimination in employment on the basis of gender. Is the denomination's practice legally permissible as a result of the First Amendment's free exercise of religion clause? See the preceding example.

• A city council receives several complaints from downtown business owners concerning homeless shelters that are operated by churches. In response to these complaints, the city council enacts an ordinance banning any church from operating a homeless shelter. This ordinance is neither neutral nor of general applicability, and so rule #2 applies. This means that the city will need to demonstrate that the ordinance is supported by a compelling government interest. It is doubtful that it will be able to do so. First, the law is "underinclusive," meaning that it singles out churches to further its purposes. Further, as the Supreme Court observed in the Hialeah case (discussed above), "[a] law that targets religious conduct for distinctive treatment or advances legitimate governmental interests only against conduct with a religious motivation will survive strict scrutiny only in rare cases."

• Same facts as the previous example, except that the ordinance bans any homeless shelter in the downtown area, whether or not operated by a church. A downtown church sues the city, claiming that the ordinance violates its First Amendment right to freely exercise its religion. The church will lose. The ordinance in this example is a neutral law of general applicability, and so rule #1 controls. This means that the ordinance is presumably valid without the need for demonstrating that it is based on a compelling government interest.

• A state legislature enacts a law that requires teachers at all public and private elementary and secondary schools, including those operated by churches, to be state-certified. A church challenges this law on the basis of the First Amendment guaranty of the free exercise of religion. The church probably will lose. The law in question clearly is neutral and of general applicability, and so rule #1 controls. This means that the law is presumably valid without the need to prove a compelling governmental interest.

• A state legislature enacts a law imposing a sales tax on purchases made by most organizations, including churches. A church challenges this law on the ground that it violates the First Amendment guaranty of the free exercise of religion. It is doubtful that the church will prevail. The law in question clearly is neutral and of general applicability, and so rule #1 controls. This means that the law is presumably valid without the need to prove a compelling governmental interest.

• A city enacts an ordinance establishing a "landmark commission." The commission is authorized to designate any building as an historic landmark. Any building so designated cannot be modified or demolished without the commission's approval. A church is designated as an historic landmark. A few years later, the church asks the commission for permission to enlarge its facility in order to accommodate its growing congregation. The commission rejects this request, despite proof that several persons are "turned away" each Sunday because of a lack of room in the current church facility. These were the facts in the City of Boerne case. If the church relies solely on a violation of its First Amendment right to religious freedom, it will lose because the ordinance is neutral and of general applicability, and so rule #1 controls. This means that the law is presumably valid without the need to prove a compelling governmental interest. However, note that the First Amendment also guarantees the rights of assembly and association, and a strong case can be made that these rights are violated by the commission's action since the right of some members to engage in religious services (assembly and association) is being curtailed. By asserting that these First Amendment rights are being violated in addition to the free exercise of religion, the church invokes rule #3. This will force the city to demonstrate a compelling government interest supporting its decision to deny the church permission to expand its facilities. It is doubtful that the city could meet this requirement.

• A church is located on a major highway. It constructs a billboard on its property that contains religious messages. The city enacts an ordinance prohibiting any billboards along the highway. Since the ordinance is a "neutral law of general applicability" (it applies equally to all property owners and does not single out religious organizations), it is legally valid though it interferes with the church's First Amendment right to freely exercise its religion. There is no need for the city to demonstrate a compelling government interest. However, if the church asserts that its First Amendment right to free speech is being violated by the city ordinance (in addition to its right to freely exercise its religion), then rule #3 is invoked. This will force the city to demonstrate a compelling government interest supporting the ordinance. As noted above, this is a difficult (though not impossible) test to meet. Note, however, that if the church can force the city to demonstrate that the ordinance is based on a compelling government interest, then it has obtained the same legal protection that it would have had under RFRA.

• Federal tax law forbids most tax-exempt organizations from intervening or participating in political campaigns on behalf of or in opposition to any candidate for public office. A church publicly supports a particular candidate during a campaign, and the IRS revokes its exempt status. The church claims that the law violates its First Amendment right to the free exercise of religion. If this is the church's only argument, it will lose since the law is a neutral law of general applicability and therefore need not be supported by a compelling government interest. However, if the church argues that its First Amendment rights to speech and press are also violated by the ban on political participation, then rule #3 is invoked. This will force the government to prove a compelling government interest to justify the law. As noted above, this is a difficult (though not impossible) test to meet. Note, however, that if the church can force the government to demonstrate that the law is based on a compelling government interest, then it has obtained the same legal protection that it would have had under RFRA.

• A public school adopts a policy prohibiting any outside group to rent or use its facilities for any purpose. A church asks for permission to rent the school gymnasium for a special religious service. The school denies this request. The church claims that its First Amendment right to the free exercise of religion has been violated by the school's policy. Since the policy is a neutral law of general applicability, rule #1 controls. The law is presumably valid without the need to prove a compelling governmental interest. However, if the church asserts that its First Amendment rights to free speech, assembly, and association are violated by the school policy (in addition to its right to freely exercise its religion), then rule #3 is invoked. This will force the school to demonstrate a compelling government interest supporting its policy. Other decisions by the Supreme Court suggest that the school will be able to demonstrate a compelling government interest—avoiding the "establishment" of religion (by singling out religious groups for special or favored treatment).

One additional observation must be made about the free exercise clause. The concept of free exercise is fundamentally incompatible with the philosophy of disestablishment contained in the establishment clause.[50] This tension has been aggravated in the past few decades by judicial emphasis upon disestablishment. Chief Justice Burger, in the *Walz* decision, commented on this underlying tension: "The Court has struggled to find a neutral course between the two Religion Clauses, both of which are cast in absolute terms, and either of which, if expanded to a logical extreme, would tend to clash with the other."[51] Similarly, Justice Stewart, dissenting in *Schempp*, observed: "There are areas in which a doctrinaire reading of the establishment clause leads to irreconcilable conflict with the free exercise clause."[52] The Supreme Court in more recent years has attempted to synthesize the religion clauses by emphasizing the concept of neutrality:

> The general principle deducible from the First Amendment and all that has been said by the Court is this: that we will not tolerate either governmentally established religion or governmental interference with religion. Short of those expressly proscribed governmental acts there is room for play in the joints productive of a benevolent neutrality which will permit religious exercise to exist without sponsorship and without interference.[53]

---

[50]   *See generally* chapter 11, *supra.*

[51]   Walz v. Tax Commission, 397 U.S. 664, 669 (1970).

[52]   School District of Abington v. Schempp, 374 U.S. 203, 309 (1963).

[53]   Walz v. Tax Commission, 397 U.S. 664, 669 (1970).

Instructional Aids to Chapter 13

Key Terms

clearly secular purpose

compelling government interest

excessive entanglement

neutral law of general applicability

primary effect

Religious Freedom Restoration Act

Learning Objectives

- Explain the current meaning of the First Amendment's nonestablishment of religion clause.

- Explain the current meaning of the First Amendment's free exercise of religion clause.

- Apply the current meaning of both of the First Amendment's religion clauses to a variety of circumstances.

Short-Answer Questions

1. What three conditions must a law or governmental practice ordinarily satisfy to be consistent with the First Amendment's "establishment clause"?

2. What factors must a court consider in determining whether a particular law or governmental action violates the First Amendment's "free exercise of religion clause"?

3. A public university denies Christian students the right to use campus facilities for group meetings. It permits several other non-religious organizations to use such facilities. Has the university violated the First Amendment's free exercise of religion clause? Explain.

4. A taxpayer is opposed to war on the basis of religious convictions. As a result, she refuses to pay that portion of her federal income taxes that will be allocated to defense. The IRS compels the taxpayer to pay her full income taxes. Has it violated the First Amendment's free exercise of religion clause? Explain.

5. The Supreme Court has observed that the concept of free exercise of religion is fundamentally incompatible with the philosophy of disestablishment contained in the establishment clause. What did the Court mean?

6. A bookstore owner sells a wide variety of books and publications, but he refuses to sell any religious literature. Has he violated the free exercise of religion clause? Explain.

7. A public school permits students to meet on school premises before regular school hours to participate in religious exercises. Does this practice violate the establishment clause? Explain.

8. A new religious sect espouses child sacrifice under certain circumstances. A court grants an injunction prohibiting such a practice. The sect complains that its right to freely exercise its religion has been violated. Evaluate the merits of the sect's claim.

9. A small Jewish sect in New York reintroduces animal sacrifice. The Humane Society seeks a court order prohibiting the practice. The sect counters by claiming that it has a constitutional right to practice its religion. How will the court rule?

10. A person charged with the unauthorized possession and use of narcotic drugs claims that his use of such drugs is a religious exercise that is protected by the First Amendment. He cites as authority Genesis 1:29, which states, "And God said, 'Behold, I have given you every plant yielding seed which is upon the face of the earth.'" How will a court rule on the religious freedom defense?

11. In 1990, the Supreme Court rendered a highly controversial interpretation of the First Amendment's free exercise of religion clause. What did the Court say that was so controversial? Did the decision, as some have suggested, effectively "repeal" the concept of religious freedom? Explain.

Essay Questions

1. The courts have ruled that it is permissible to inscribe the national motto "In God We Trust" on all of our coins and currency, but that it is not permissible to post a copy of the Ten Commandments in public school classrooms. Can you think of a rational basis for this distinction?

2. The courts have relied on the establishment clause in outlawing most collective prayers in public elementary and secondary schools. But does not the prohibition of such prayers violate the First Amendment freedom of certain students to exercise their religion? How should a court balance these competing interests?

Significant First
Amendment Issues

Legal Briefs

Can people engage in religious "witnessing" or proselytizing in residential neighborhoods on a door-to-door basis? Can they use public parks for religious meetings? Under what circumstances can voluntary prayers be uttered on public property? Can a city display a cross or nativity scene on public property during the Christmas season? Can a court display a picture of the Ten Commandments? Can the federal government constitutionally print the national motto "In God We Trust" on all of our nation's currency? Can a public school rent its facilities to a church for religious purposes when the school is not in session? Do Sunday closing laws impermissibly discriminate against religious groups that recognize a Sabbath on another day of the week? Does an adult have the right to refuse medical treatment on the basis of religious beliefs? Can the state compel a sick or an injured child to receive medical treatment against the religious beliefs of his parents? What activities are included within the term "religious"? What activities are excluded?

Such questions present the courts with difficult choices. In this chapter, you will learn how the courts have responded to these questions.

Previous chapters have addressed the application of the First Amendment religion clauses to several issues. Examples include the dismissal of clergy, malpractice, church securities, child abuse reporting, church audits, discipline of church members, judicial review of internal church decisions, church property disputes, the application of various labor and discrimination laws to churches, zoning law, government regulation of church-operated schools, and church tax exemptions. This chapter will review the application of the First Amendment religion clauses in several other contexts.

> "Can a city display a cross or nativity scene on public property during the Christmas season? Can a court display a picture of the Ten Commandments? Can the federal government constitutionally print the national motto "In God We Trust" on all of our nation's currency? "

The Right to Witness §14-01

Key point 14-01. The courts have affirmed the right of persons to disseminate religious literature and doctrine on a door-to-door basis, and in public places. This right may be limited in order to preserve public safety, health, order, and convenience. Strict safeguards, however, must attend any limitations.

1. Door-to-Door Witnessing

The Supreme Court repeatedly has affirmed the right of persons to solicit religious contributions, sell religious books and merchandise, and disseminate religious doctrine on a "door-to-door" basis.[1] Municipal ordinances that condition the exercise of such a right upon the acquisition of a permit or license or upon the payment of a "tax" or fee generally have been found to be unconstitutional.

To illustrate, the Supreme Court struck down a city licensing scheme used by city officials to ban Jehovah's Witnesses from going door-to-door in heavily Catholic neighborhoods playing a phonograph record that attacked the Roman Catholic Church as an "enemy" and the church of the devil.[2] Similarly, the Court invalidated a municipal "license tax" that was imposed upon the door-to-door solicitation and evangelistic activities of Jehovah's Witnesses.[3] The Court observed: "Those who can tax the privilege of engaging in this form of missionary evangelism can close its doors to all those who do not have a full purse. Spreading religious beliefs in this ancient and honorable manner would thus be denied the needy. Those who can deprive religious groups of their colporteurs can take from them a part of the vital power of the press which has survived from the Reformation."[4] The Supreme Court also struck down a municipal ordinance that prohibited anyone engaged in distributing literature to summon the occupants of a home to the door.[5]

The Supreme Court has acknowledged that a city may protect its citizens from fraud by requiring strangers in the community to establish their identity and demonstrate their authority to represent the cause they espouse. Cities also may limit door-to-door proselytizing and solicitation where necessary to preserve public safety, health, order, and convenience. Strict safeguards, however, must attend any such limitations.[6]

---

[1] *See, e.g.*, Murdock v. Pennsylvania, 319 U.S. 105 (1943); Largent v. Texas, 318 U.S. 418 (1943); Jamison v. Texas, 318 U.S. 413 (1943); Cantwell v. Connecticut, 310 U.S. 296 (1940).

[2] Cantwell v. Connecticut, 310 U.S. 296 (1940).

[3] Murdock v. Pennsylvania, 319 U.S. 105 (1943).

[4] *Id.* at 112.

[5] Martin v. City of Struthers, 319 U.S. 141 (1943).

[6] *See* the discussion of witnessing in public places later in this section.

Many lower federal court decisions have protected the rights of persons to engage in door-to-door religious activities.[7]

Example

• The United States Supreme Court ruled that a city ordinance requiring Jehovah's Witnesses and other persons to obtain and display a permit before engaging in door-to-door witnessing violated the First Amendment. A city ordinance prohibited "canvassers" and others from "going in and upon" private residential property for the purpose of promoting any "cause" without first having obtained a "solicitation permit." Residents may prohibit solicitation even by holders of permits by posting a "No Solicitation" sign on their property. The Court concluded that the city ordinance, as applied to the Jehovah's Witnesses, violated the First Amendment guaranty of free speech. The city claimed that the permit requirement was justified by the legitimate interests of preventing fraud and crime, and protecting residents' privacy. The Court conceded that cities have a legitimate interest in protecting these interests, but in this case they went too far. It observed: "Central to our conclusion that the ordinance does not pass First Amendment scrutiny is that it is not tailored to the city's stated interests. Even if the interest in preventing fraud could adequately support the ordinance insofar as it applies to commercial transactions and the solicitation of funds, that interest provides no support for its application to [church members], to political campaigns, or to enlisting support for unpopular causes. The city, however, argues that the ordinance is nonetheless valid because it serves the two additional interests of protecting the privacy of the resident and the prevention of crime. With respect to the former, it seems clear that the ordinance, which provides for the posting of 'No Solicitation' signs . . . coupled with the resident's unquestioned right to refuse to engage in conversation with unwelcome visitors, provides ample protection for the unwilling listener. . . . With respect to the latter, it seems unlikely that the absence of a permit would preclude criminals from knocking on doors and engaging in conversations not covered by the ordinance." The Court concluded: "The mere fact that the ordinance covers so much speech raises constitutional concerns. It is offensive—not only to the values protected by the First Amendment, but to the very notion of a free society—that in the context of everyday public discourse a citizen must first inform the government of her desire to speak to her neighbors and then obtain a permit to do so. . . . A law requiring a permit to engage in such speech constitutes a dramatic departure from our national heritage and constitutional tradition."[8]

> "It is offensive—not only to the values protected by the First Amendment, but to the very notion of a free society—that in the context of everyday public discourse a citizen must first inform the government of her desire to speak to her neighbors and then obtain a permit to do so. . . ."

[7] See, e.g., Troyer v. Town of Babylon, 483 F. Supp. 1135 (E.D.N.Y. 1980), aff'd, 628 F.2d 1346 (2nd Cir. 1980), aff'd, 449 U.S. 988 (1980) ("[r]equiring consent of householders before approaching their homes constitutes, in effect, an indirect unconstitutional imposition of a licensing fee; it generates costs which burden the exercise of First Amendment rights in direct proportion to the number of persons the speaker wants to reach"); Weissman v. City of Alamogordo, 472 F. Supp. 425 (D.N.M. 1979); McMurdie v. Doutt, 468 F. Supp. 766 (N.D. Ohio 1979); Levers v. City of Tullahoma, 446 F. Supp. 884 (D. Tenn. 1978); Murdock v. City of Jacksonville, 361 F. Supp. 1083 (M.D. Fla. 1973).

[8] Watchtower Bible and Tract Society v. Village of Stratton, 536 U.S. 150 (2002).

2. Witnessing In Public Places

The Supreme Court has zealously protected the right to disseminate religious doctrine in public places. The Court has struck down a city ordinance that prohibited the distribution of handbills on city streets as applied to Jehovah's Witnesses who distributed religious handbills to pedestrians in a downtown area.[9] The Court also has invalidated a city ordinance under which a Baptist minister was convicted for holding a religious meeting on city streets without a permit.[10] In striking down the ordinance, the Court held that no ordinance that gives city officials discretionary authority, in advance, to allow or refuse individuals the right to speak publicly on religious matters could ever be constitutionally valid. The Court did emphasize, however, that a carefully worded ordinance that conditions the right to hold public religious meetings in public places on the prior receipt of a municipal permit or license could be constitutionally valid if it (1) removed all discretion on the part of city officials by listing the specific preconditions for issuance of a license, and (2) the specified preconditions were constitutionally permissible, such as the preservation of public peace and order.

In another decision,[11] the Court upheld the conviction of five Jehovah's Witnesses who paraded through a city carrying a sign stating "Religion is a Snare and a Racket" in violation of an ordinance prohibiting "a parade or procession" on a city street without a license. The Court observed that the city officials had no discretion to grant or deny a license since the conditions for obtaining a license were specifically and clearly set forth in the ordinance. Also, the stated purpose of the ordinance and its various conditions were permissible: preserving the public safety, convenience, peace, and order by preventing conflicts in scheduling; controlling the time, place, and manner of each use of the public streets; and enabling the police to oversee each use and thus minimize the risk of disorder.

In conclusion, the following principles should be noted:

1. No law or regulation that gives government officials unbridled discretion to permit or disallow a religious meeting or service or any other religious activity on public property can be consistent with the First Amendment guarantee of free exercise of religion.

2. A law or regulation that requires a license or permit before a religious meeting or activity may be held on public property can be constitutionally valid if

    a. specific guidelines exist for determining whether to grant or disallow a license or permit, and the guidelines remove all discretion from those officials who must evaluate applications

    b. guidelines only ensure public order, peace, health, safety, or convenience

---

[9] Jamison v. Texas, 318 U.S. 413 (1943).

[10] Kunz v. New York, 340 U.S. 290 (1951).

[11] Cox v. New Hampshire, 312 U.S. 569 (1941).

    c. no less restrictive public remedies to protect the peace and order of the community are appropriate or available

3. A permit or licensing scheme is unconstitutional unless it (a) provides for a ruling on an application within a specified brief period of time, (b) places the burden on the government of showing that the law's guidelines are not satisfied, and (c) makes available prompt, final, judicial resolution of the issue.[12]

Numerous lower federal court decisions have protected the rights of persons to engage in religious activities on public property.[13]

Prayer on Public Property Other Than Schools

§ 14-02

Key point 14-02. *The courts have ruled that the First Amendment allows chaplains and other ministers to pray before legislative assemblies.*

The Supreme Court has ruled that it is permissible for state legislatures to select and compensate legislative chaplains,[14] and other courts have approved congressional chaplains[15] and the practice of opening county board meetings with prayer.[16]

Prayer During Public School Activities

§ 14-03

Key point 14-03. *The First Amendment prohibits the recitation of prayers by school officials and clergy in public schools or at public school events, including graduation ceremonies and sports activities. However, some courts have allowed student-initiated prayers during such events.*

---

[12] Freedman v. Maryland, 432 U.S. 43 (1977); Walker v. Wegner, 477 F. Supp. 648 (D.S.D. 1979).

[13] *See, e.g.,* Edwards v. Maryland State Fair and Agricultural Society, Inc., 628 F.2d 282 (4th Cir. 1980); International Society for Krishna Consciousness, Inc. v. Bowen, 600 F.2d 667 (7th Cir. 1979); Bacon v. Bradley-Bourbonnais High School District, 707 F. Supp. 1005 (N.D. Ill. 1989); International Society for Krishna Consciousness, Inc. v. City of New York, 501 F. Supp. 684 (S.D.N.Y. 1980); International Society for Krishna Consciousness v. Eaves, 601 F.2d 809 (5th Cir. 1979); International Society for Krishna Consciousness v. Bowen, 600 F.2d 667 (7th Cir. 1979); International Society for Krishna Consciousness v. Rochford, 585 F.2d 263 (7th Cir. 1978).

[14] Marsh v. Chambers, 463 U.S. 783 (1983). The *Marsh* case is discussed in § 12-09, *supra.*

[15] Murray v. Buchanan, 720 F.2d 689 (D.C. Cir. 1983).

[16] Bogen v. Doty, 598 F. 2d 1110 (8th Cir. 1979). The court upheld this practice since no expenditure of funds was involved and the primary purpose and effect of the prayer was public decorum and solemnity at county board meetings. These requirements would not be necessary after the Supreme Court's decision in the *Marsh* case. See § 12-09, *supra.*

A number of Supreme Court decisions addressing prayer on public property are reviewed in chapter 12. The issue of student-initiated religious activities on public school property is addressed in section 14-07.

1. Prayers at Public School Graduation Ceremonies

A number of federal courts have addressed the question of whether prayers at public school graduation ceremonies violate the First Amendment's nonestablishment of religion clause. Illustrative cases are summarized below. In a 1992 ruling, the United States Supreme Court concluded that such prayers are unconstitutional, at least in some situations.[17] The case involved a challenge to a public high school policy that allowed members of the clergy to give invocations and benedictions at middle school and high school graduations. Clergy were provided with a pamphlet entitled "Guidelines for Civic Occasions," prepared by the National Conference of Christians and Jews, and were advised that the invocation and benediction should be nonsectarian.

The Supreme Court, by a majority of five votes to four, ruled that prayers offered at public high school graduation ceremonies violate the First Amendment's "nonestablishment of religion clause. The Court concluded that a public high school graduation ceremony that includes prayers exerts a "psychological coercion" or pressure on everyone to conform, even those who are personally opposed to prayer. The Court observed:

> The undeniable fact is that the school district's supervision and control of a high school graduation ceremony places public pressure, as well as peer pressure, on attending students to stand as a group or, at least, maintain respectful silence during the invocation and benediction. This pressure, though subtle and indirect, can be as real as any overt compulsion. Of course, in our culture standing or remaining silent can signify adherence to a view or simple respect for the views of others. And no doubt some persons who have no desire to join a prayer have little objection to standing as a sign of respect for those who do. But for the dissenter of high school age, who has a reasonable perception that she is being forced by the state to pray in a manner her conscience will not allow, the injury is no less real. There can be no doubt that for many, if not most, of the students at the graduation, the act of standing or remaining silent was an expression of participation in the Rabbi's prayer. That was the very point of the religious exercise. It is of little comfort to a dissenter, then, to be told that for her the act of standing or remaining in silence signifies mere respect, rather than participation. What matters is that, given our social conventions, a reasonable dissenter in this milieu could believe that the group exercise signified her own participation or approval of it.

---

[17] Lee v. Weisman, 505 U.S. 577 (1992). The *Lee* case is addressed more fully in section 12-13, *supra*.

The Court acknowledged that participation in graduation ceremonies is voluntary, and that students who are opposed to prayers can simply not attend. But it concluded that the voluntary nature of the ceremony did not mean that prayers had to be allowed. It noted:

[T]o say a teenage student has a real choice not to attend her high school graduation is formalistic in the extreme. True, [the student] could elect not to attend commencement without renouncing her diploma; but we shall not allow the case to turn on this point. Everyone knows that in our society and in our culture high school graduation is one of life's most significant occasions. A school rule which excuses attendance is beside the point. Attendance may not be required by official decree, yet it is apparent that a student is not free to absent herself from the graduation exercise in any real sense of the term "voluntary," for absence would require forfeiture of those intangible benefits which have motivated the student through youth and all her high school years. Graduation is a time for family and those closest to the student to celebrate success and express mutual wishes of gratitude and respect, all to the end of impressing upon the young person the role that it is his or her right and duty to assume in the community and all of its diverse parts.

The Court acknowledged that a majority of those attending graduation ceremonies probably have no objection to prayers being offered, and would even prefer that they be. It concluded, however, that "[w]hile in some societies the wishes of the majority might prevail, the establishment clause of the First Amendment is addressed to this contingency and rejects the balance urged upon us. The Constitution forbids the state to exact religious conformity from a student as the price of attending her own high school graduation."

The Court acknowledged that

[w]e do not hold that every state action implicating religion is invalid if one or a few citizens find it offensive. People may take offense at all manner of religious as well as nonreligious messages, but offense alone does not in every case show a violation. We know too that sometimes to endure social isolation or even anger may be the price of conscience or nonconformity. But, by any reading of our cases, the conformity required of the student in this case was too high an exaction to withstand the test of the establishment clause.

The Court concluded its opinion with the following statement:

Our society would be less than true to its heritage if it lacked abiding concern for the values of its young people, and we acknowledge the profound belief of adherents to many faiths that there must be a place in the student's life for precepts of a morality higher even than the law we today enforce. We express no hostility to those aspirations, nor would our oath permit us to do so. A relentless and all-pervasive attempt to exclude religion from every aspect of public life could itself become inconsistent with the Constitution. We recognize that, at graduation time and throughout the course of the educational process, there will be instances when religious values, religious practices, and religious persons will have some interaction with the public schools and their students. But these matters, often questions of accommodation of religion, are not before us. The sole question presented is whether a religious exercise may be conducted at a graduation ceremony in circumstances where, as we have found, young graduates who object are induced to conform. No holding by this Court suggests that a school can persuade or compel a student to participate in a religious exercise. That is being done here, and it is forbidden by the establishment clause of the First Amendment.

The Supreme Court's decision in the Lee case does not necessarily preclude all prayers at public graduation ceremonies, as some of the following cases demonstrate.

Examples

• A federal appeals court ruled that allowing public high school seniors to choose student volunteers to deliver nonsectarian, nonproselytizing invocations at their graduation ceremonies does not violate the First Amendment's nonestablishment of religion clause.[18] A public school district in Texas adopted the following resolution: "The use of an invocation and/or benediction at high school graduation exercises shall rest within the discretion of the graduating senior class, with the advice and counsel of the senior class principal; the invocation and benediction, if used, shall be given by a student volunteer; and consistent with the principle of equal liberty of conscience, the invocation and benediction shall be nonsectarian and nonproselytizing in nature." Pursuant to this resolution, prayers were offered by graduating seniors at public high school graduation ceremonies within the district. A lawsuit was filed challenging the constitutionality of this practice, and a trial court ruled that the practice did not violate the First Amendment. A federal appeals court agreed, concluding that the Supreme Court's decision in the Lee[19] case did not change the result. In the Lee case, the Supreme Court ruled that a public high school principal violated the First Amendment by inviting a local clergyman to deliver a nonsectarian, nonproselytizing invocation at a graduation ceremony. The appeals court acknowledged that it was bound by the Supreme Court's decision in Lee, but concluded that the Lee case did not require that the school district resolution at issue in this case be invalidated. The court noted many

---

[18] Jones v. Clear Creek Independent School District, 977 F.2d 963 (5th Cir. 1992). The United States Supreme Court issued an order declining to review the *Jones* case. This may signal the Court's satisfaction with the lower court's resolution of this controversial issue. Regardless of why the Court declined to review this case, the fact remains that the decision of the federal appeals court remains binding in the fifth judicial circuit, which includes the states of Louisiana, Mississippi, and Texas. Other federal courts have rejected the conclusion of this ruling. *See, e.g.,* Ingebretsen v. Jackson Public School District, 88 F.3d 274 (5th Cir. 1996). *But see* Does 1-7 v. Round Rock Independent School District, 540 F.Supp.2d 735 (W.D. Tex. 2007) (student-initiated prayers at a public school graduation ceremony violated the establishment clause, and the Clear Creek case may not be consistent with the United States Supreme Court's decision in the Santa Fe case, addressed below).

[19] 505 U.S. 577 (1992). *See* §12-13.

critical differences in this case that distinguished it from Lee. First, the graduating seniors themselves decided whether or not they wanted an invocation during their graduation ceremony. In Lee, a high school principal made this decision. Second, the invocation (if desired by the graduating seniors) was offered by a student. In Lee, the invocation was offered by a member of the clergy. Third, the student selected to offer the invocation was free to compose it without any participation by the school (other than the requirement that it be nonsectarian and nonproselytizing). There was no requirement that the invocation mention God or contain any other religious references. In Lee, there was some school involvement in the composition of the prayers, and it was understood that the prayers would be "religious." Fourth, and perhaps most importantly, there was little if any of the "psychological pressure" upon students to participate in the invocation that there was in Lee. The court observed, "We think that the graduation prayers permitted by the resolution place less psychological pressure on students than the prayers at issue in Lee because all students, after having participated in the decision of whether prayers will be given, are aware that any prayers represent the will of their peers, who are less able to coerce participation than an authority figure from the state or clergy."

• A federal appeals court ruled that the spontaneous recitation of the Lord's Prayer at a high school graduation ceremony by a school board member did not violate the First Amendment. The court referred to a ruling in which the United States Supreme Court observed that "there is a crucial difference between government speech endorsing religion, which the establishment clause forbids, and private speech endorsing religion, which the free speech and free exercise clauses protect."[20] The court concluded that the board member's recitation of the Lord's Prayer was private speech due to the "complete lack of school involvement or sponsorship in his remarks," and therefore there was no government promotion of religion and no constitutional violation.[21]

• A federal appeals court ruled that the First Amendment nonestablishment of religion clause would be violated by allowing a prayer to be recited at a public high school graduation ceremony, even though a majority of the graduating class voted to include the prayer in the ceremony and attendance was voluntary.[22] Further, outlawing prayer at the ceremony did not violate the majority's constitutional rights of free speech and freedom of religion, since the ceremony was not an "open forum" and students could exercise their religion outside of the ceremony.

• A federal appeals court ruled that a public school policy permitting high school seniors to vote upon the delivery by a student of a message entirely of that student's choosing as part of graduation ceremonies did not violate the Establishment Clause. The court observed: "Neither the [school district] nor the graduating senior classes decide if a religious prayer or message will be delivered, let alone require or coerce the student audience to participate in any privately-crafted message. While schools may make private religious speech their own by endorsing it, schools do not endorse all speech that they do not censor. We cannot assume that [students] will interpret the school's failure to censor a private student message for religious content as an endorsement of that message—particularly where the students are expressly informed

---

[20] Santa Fe Independent School District v. Doe, 530 U.S. 290 (2000). The *Santa Fe* case is addressed in section 12-15, *supra*.

[21] Doe ex rel. Doe v. School District, 340 F.3d 605 (8th Cir. 2003).

[22] Harris v. Joint School District, 41 F.3d 447 (9th Cir. 1994).

as part of the election process that they may select a speaker who alone will craft any message. No religious result is preordained." The court concluded: "Although it is possible that under [the school's] policy the student body may select a speaker who then chooses on his or her own to deliver a religious message, that result is not preordained, and more to the point would not reflect a majority vote to impose religion on unwilling listeners. Rather, it would reflect the uncensored and wholly unreviewable decision of a single student speaker. . . . The total absence of state involvement in deciding whether there will be a graduation message, who will speak, or what the speaker may say combined with the student speaker's complete autonomy over the content of the message means that the message delivered, be it secular or sectarian or both, is not state-sponsored."[23]

2. Prayers at Public School Athletic Events

The United States Supreme Court has ruled that the practice of reciting prayers at public school athletic events violates the First Amendment.[24]

3. Religious Music Performed by Public School Students

In many cases, students who are barred from performing religious music during public school ceremonies or events claim that their constitutional right to free speech has been violated. Most courts have analyzed these claims by focusing on the "forum" in which the music was to be performed. Generally, the courts have divided government property into four categories: public fora, designated public fora, nonpublic fora, and limited public fora. Table 14-1 defines each of these fora.

Table 14-1 Public and Nonpublic Fora		
Forum where speech occurred	**Definition**	**First Amendment analysis**
Public fora	A place, such as a sidewalk or a park, that has been traditionally open for public expression.	The ability of the government to limit speech is sharply circumscribed. Content-based regulation is justified only when necessary to serve a compelling state interest and when it is narrowly drawn to achieve that end, and content-neutral restrictions that regulate the time, place, and manner of speech are permissible so long as they are narrowly tailored to serve a significant government interest, and they leave open ample alternative channels of communication.

---

[23] Adler v. Duval County School Board, 250 F.3d 1330 (11th Cir. 2001). The court noted that the Supreme Court, in the *Santa Fe* case (see below) "had every opportunity to declare that all religious expression permitted at a public school graduation ceremony violates the Establishment Clause; it did not do so. We could not invalidate [the school's] policy without taking the very step the Court declined to take."

[24] Santa Fe Independent School District v. Doe, 530 U.S. 290 (2000). The *Santa Fe* case is addressed in section 12-15, *supra*.

Table 14-1 Public and Nonpublic Fora		
Forum where speech occurred	**Definition**	**First Amendment analysis**
Designated public fora	The government intentionally opens a nontraditional form to public discourse.	Same as public fora.
Limited public fora	A nonpublic forum that the government intentionally has opened to certain groups or for the discussion of certain topics.	Restrictions governing access to a limited public forum are permitted so long as they are viewpoint neutral and reasonable in light of the purpose served by the forum. In determining whether the restriction is viewpoint neutral, a court must identify whether exclusion of speech is content discrimination, which may be permissible if it preserves the purpose of the limited forum, or viewpoint discrimination, which is presumed impermissible when directed against speech otherwise within the forum's limitations. Content discrimination occurs when the government chooses the subjects that may be discussed, while viewpoint discrimination occurs when the government prohibits speech by particular speakers, thereby suppressing a particular view about a subject.
Nonpublic fora	All remaining public property.	The challenged regulation need only be reasonable, as long as the regulation is not an effort to suppress the speaker's activity due to disagreement with the speaker's view.

Examples

• *A federal court in Washington ruled that a public school acted properly in barring a wind ensemble from performing an instrumental arrangement of "Ave Maria" at a graduation ceremony. The court concluded that the school district created a limited public forum when it allowed the wind ensemble to choose the piece for performance at the graduation. As noted in Table 14-1, a public school's prohibition on the performance of "Ave Maria" was not a violation of the students' free speech rights if the restriction was viewpoint neutral and reasonable in light of the purpose of the forum. In determining whether the restriction is viewpoint neutral, the court noted that it "must identify whether exclusion of Ave Maria is content discrimination, which may be permissible if it preserves the purpose of the limited forum, or viewpoint discrimination, which is presumed impermissible when directed against speech otherwise within the forum's limitations." The court noted that "content discrimination occurs when the government chooses the subjects that may be discussed, while viewpoint discrimination occurs when the government prohibits speech by particular speakers, thereby suppressing a particular view about a subject." The court concluded that the exclusion of "Ave Maria" was based on permissible content restriction, not impermissible viewpoint discrimination since the prohibition "was based on a decision to keep religion out of graduation as a whole, not to discriminate against a specific religious sect or creed. . . . The blanket restriction on the exclusion of religious music that occurred in this case is one based on content, not viewpoint."[25]*

• A federal appeals court ruled that the constitution was not violated when a public high school choir performed religious songs and conducted a few of its concerts in churches.[26] A non-Christian student who was a member of the choir asked a federal court to issue an order banning the choir from singing religious songs and performing concerts in churches. A federal district court refused to do so, and the student appealed. A federal appeals court concluded that the choir's practices were permissible and violated neither the First Amendment's nonestablishment of religion or free exercise of religion clauses. The court applied the Supreme Court's three-part Lemon test in determining whether the choir's practices constituted an impermissible establishment of religion. Under this test, a government practice challenged as an establishment of religion will be valid only if it satisfies the following three conditions—a secular purpose, a primary effect that neither advances nor inhibits religion, and no excessive entanglement between church and state. The court concluded that all of these tests were met.

Display of Religious Symbols on Public Property § 14-04

Key point 14-04. *The display of religious symbols on public property does not violate the First Amendment nonestablishment of religion clause so long as they are part of a larger display that includes secular symbols.*

1. In General

Several courts have ruled on the constitutionality of displaying religious symbols on public property. Many courts have concluded that the maintenance of crosses on public property constitutes an impermissible establishment of religion.[27] One court observed:

The employment of publicly owned and publicly maintained property for a highly visible display of the character of the cross in this case necessarily

---

[25] Nurre v. Whitehead, 520 F.Supp.2d 1222 (W.D. Wash. 2007).

[26] Bauchman v. West High School, 132 F.3d 542 (10th Cir. 1997).

[27] *See, e.g.*, American Civil Liberties Union v. Rabun County Chamber of Commerce, Inc., 678 F.2d 1379 (11th Cir. 1982); ACLU v. Mississippi State General Services Administration, 652 F. Supp. 380 (S.D. Miss. 1987) (state office building created a 22-story tall "cross" during the Christmas season by leaving the lights on in designated offices after hours); Fox v. City of Los Angeles, 587 P.2d 663 (Cal. 1978); Eugene Sand and Gravel, Inc. v. City of Eugene, 558 P.2d 338 (Ore. 1976); Lowe v. City of Eugene, 463 P.2d 360 (Ore. 1969).

creates an inference of official endorsement of the general religious beliefs which underlie that symbol. Accordingly, persons who do not share those beliefs may feel that their own beliefs are stigmatized or officially deemed less worthy than those awarded the appearance of the city's endorsement . . . . The government has no business placing its power, prestige, or property at the disposal of private persons or groups either to aid or oppose any religion.[28]

Other courts have approved of the maintenance of crosses on public property.[29] In one case, a court emphasized that a cross was maintained "to decorate streets and attract holiday shoppers to downtown, rather than establish or create a religious symbol or to promote or establish a religion."[30]

One court ruled that it is constitutionally permissible for public schools to temporarily display children's artwork in school rooms and halls, even though some of the artwork is religious.[31] The court reasoned:

Are school children to be forbidden from expressing their natural artistic talents through media including religious themes? Or, are the results of their efforts to be excluded from display and recognition merely because they choose to adopt a religious, rather than a secular subject? The answer should be obvious. To impose such a restriction would more nearly approach a restraint upon the exercise of religion than does the present practice of the school board in permitting such displays.[32]

The Supreme Court of New Hampshire upheld a state law requiring that all public school classrooms contain a sign stating "In God We Trust."[33] The court observed that such words "appear on all coins and currency, on public buildings, and in our national anthem, and the appearance of these words as a motto on plaques in the public school need not offend the establishment clause . . . ."[34]

2. United States Supreme Court Decisions

The United States Supreme Court has issued a number of rulings addressing the constitutionality of religious symbols on public property.

Lynch v. Donnelly, 465 U.S. 668 (1984)

In 1984, the Supreme Court held that a city's practice of including a nativity creche in an annual Christmas display on public property did not violate the establishment clause. Besides the creche, the city's display contained several

---

[28] Lowe v. City of Eugene, 463 P.2d 360, 363 (Ore. 1969).

[29] *See, e.g.,* Paul v. Dade County, 202 So.2d 833 (Fla. 1967); Meyer v. Oklahoma City, 496 P.2d 789 (Okla. 1972).

[30] Paul v. Dade County, 202 So.2d 833-835 (Fla. 1967).

[31] Chamberlin v. Dade County, 143 So.2d 21 (Fla. 1962).

[32] *Id.* at 35-6.

[33] Opinion of the Justices, 228 A.2d 161 (N.H. 1967).

[34] *Id.* at 164.

"secular" objects, including a Santa Claus house, a talking Christmas tree, reindeer, candy-striped poles, and lights. The Court, applying the three-part Lemon test[35] "in the context of the Christmas season," concluded that inclusion of the creche in the city's display had the secular purpose of depicting the origin of the Christmas holiday, did not have a primary effect of advancing religion, and did not excessively entangle church and state. Acknowledging that the creche "in a sense" advanced religion, the Court concluded that its previous decisions make it "abundantly clear" that not every law or governmental practice that confers an indirect or incidental benefit upon religion is for that reason alone impermissible. Drawing support from the history and context of the display, the Court noted that

> [i]t would be ironic . . . if the inclusion of a single symbol of a particular
> historic religious event, as part of a celebration acknowledged in the
> Western World for 20 centuries, and in this country by the people, by the
> Executive Branch, by the Congress, and the courts for two centuries, would
> so "taint" the City's exhibit as to render it violative of the establishment
> clause.[36]

Board of Trustees v. McCreary, 471 U.S. 83 (1985)

In a similar case, the Court upheld the practice of permitting a nativity scene in a city park during the Christmas season at virtually no expense to the city. Unlike the situation in the Lynch case, the nativity scene was not in the context of a larger display containing numerous "secular" objects. Since the ruling was by an equally divided Court (4-4), it is controlling only in the second federal circuit (New York, Vermont, and Connecticut).

County of Allegheny v. American Civil Liberties Union, 492 U.S. 573 (1989)

In 1989, the Court again addressed the permissibility of nativity scenes on public property. For a number of years, a county government permitted a Roman Catholic group to display a nativity creche on the main staircase of the county courthouse during the Christmas season. The creche included figures of the infant Jesus, Mary, Joseph, farm animals, shepherds, wise men, and an angel bearing a banner proclaiming "Gloria in Excelsis Deo" (glory to God in the highest). The creche bore a plaque stating, "This display donated by the Holy Name Society." The creche was surrounded by poinsettia plants, but otherwise no other seasonal figures or ornaments were located nearby. A municipal building located a few blocks away presented an annual holiday display each December on a public sidewalk outside the main entrance to the building. The display included a large (45-foot) Christmas tree decorated with lights and ornaments, an 18-foot Chanukah menorah (a candleholder with eight branches) owned by a Jewish group, and a sign reading "during this holiday season the City of Pittsburgh salutes liberty. Let these festive lights remind us that we are the keepers of the flame of liberty and our legacy of freedom." The American Civil Liberties Union (ACLU) filed a lawsuit claiming that

---

[35] See § 13-01.1, *supra.*

[36] 465 U.S. at 686.

these displays violated the constitutional ban on any "establishment of religion." A trial court permitted the displays, but a federal appeals court prohibited them.

The Supreme Court agreed to hear the case, and ruled that the nativity creche had to be removed but that the Chanukah menorah was permissible. The Court observed that among other things, the constitutional prohibition of any establishment of religion prevented any governmental "endorsement" of religion. The constitution, noted the Court, "precludes government from conveying or attempting to convey a message that religion or a particular religious belief is favored or preferred." Whether or not a particular display violates the constitution depends upon its context. The Court affirmed its earlier decision in *Lynch* upholding the validity of a Christmas creche that was part of a larger seasonal display that included a Santa Claus, reindeer, a talking wishing well, trees, and lights. Here, however, "the creche stands alone—it is the single element of the display." This, combined with the fact that the creche was located inside the main entrance of the "seat of county government," sent an "unmistakable message that [the county] supports and promotes the Christian praise to God that is the creche's religious message." The Court concluded: "The government may acknowledge Christmas as a cultural phenomenon, but under the First Amendment it may not observe it as a Christian holy day by suggesting that people praise God for the birth of Jesus. . . . [G]overnment may celebrate Christmas in some manner and form, but not in a way that endorses Christian doctrine."

On the other hand, the Court upheld the validity of the Chanukah menorah, since (1) the menorah, being a mere candleholder, was not an "exclusively religious" symbol but rather "has both religious and secular dimensions"; and (2) the menorah stood next to a Christmas tree and a sign saluting liberty and accordingly was part of a "larger display" that detracted from the menorah's religious message. Justice Kennedy, in dissent, criticized the Court's majority for harboring a "latent hostility" and "callous indifference" toward religion. The Court's majority found such a view "as offensive as it is absurd," adding that "there may be some would-be theocrats who wish that their religion were an established creed . . . but this claim gets no relief, for it contradicts the fundamental premise of the establishment clause itself."

McCreary County v. American Civil Liberties Union, 545 U.S. 844 (2005)[37]

In 1999 two county courthouses in Kentucky hung large, gold-framed copies of an abridged text of the King James version of the Ten Commandments (including a citation to the Book of Exodus), on a courthouse wall. In one county, the placement of the Commandments responded to an order of the county requiring "the display to be posted in a very high traffic area of the courthouse." In the other county, the Commandments were hung in a ceremony presided over by a judge, who called them "good rules to live by" and who recounted the story of an astronaut who became convinced "there must be a divine God" after viewing the Earth from the moon. The judge was accompanied by the pastor of his church, who called the Commandments "a creed of ethics" and told the press after the ceremony that displaying the Commandments was "one of the greatest things the judge could have done to close out the millennium."

---

[37] This ruling is addressed more fully in section 12-18, *supra*.

In each county, the hallway display was "readily visible to county citizens who use the courthouse to conduct their civic business, to obtain or renew driver's licenses and permits, to register cars, to pay local taxes, and to register to vote."

In 1999 the American Civil Liberties Union (ACLU) of Kentucky sued the two counties in federal court, seeking an order barring the displays which the ACLU claimed were violations of the First Amendment's nonestablishment of religion clause. Before the court issued a ruling, each county authorized a second, expanded display, stating that the Ten Commandments are "the precedent legal code upon which the civil and criminal codes of Kentucky are founded," and stating several grounds for taking that position, including that:

> The Ten Commandments are codified in Kentucky's civil and criminal laws"; that the Kentucky House of Representatives had in 1993 "voted unanimously to adjourn in remembrance and honor of Jesus Christ, the Prince of Ethics"; that the "County Judge and magistrates agree with the arguments set out by Judge [Roy] Moore" in defense of his "display of the Ten Commandments in his courtroom"; and that the "Founding Fathers had an explicit understanding of the duty of elected officials to publicly acknowledge God as the source of America's strength and direction."

The expanded displays of the Ten Commandments included eight other documents in smaller frames, each either having a religious theme or excerpted to highlight a religious element. The documents were the "endowed by their Creator" passage from the Declaration of Independence; the Preamble to the Constitution of Kentucky; the national motto, "In God We Trust"; a page from the Congressional Record of February 2, 1983, proclaiming the Year of the Bible and including a statement of the Ten Commandments; a proclamation by President Abraham Lincoln designating April 30, 1863, a National Day of Prayer and Humiliation; an excerpt from President Lincoln's "Reply to Loyal Colored People of Baltimore upon Presentation of a Bible," reading that "the Bible is the best gift God has ever given to man"; a proclamation by President Reagan marking 1983 the Year of the Bible; and the Mayflower Compact.

A federal district court ordered the displays at both county courthouses removed "immediately," and warned county officials not to "erect or cause to be erected similar displays." A federal appeals court affirmed, and the case was appealed to the United States Supreme Court.

The Court conceded that the expanded display included eight other historical documents in addition to the Ten Commandments. However, this did not render the posting of the Ten Commandments permissible, since the expanded display included other documents "with highlighted references to God as their sole common element. The display's unstinting focus was on religious passages, showing that the counties were posting the Commandments precisely because of their sectarian content. That demonstration of the government's objective was enhanced by serial religious references and the accompanying resolution's claim about the embodiment of ethics in Christ. Together, the display and resolution presented an indisputable, and undisputed, showing of an impermissible purpose."

The Court stressed that it was not outlawing all exhibitions of the Ten Commandments on government property:

> Nor do we have occasion here to hold that a sacred text can never be integrated constitutionally into a governmental display on the subject of law, or American history. We do not forget, and in this litigation have frequently been reminded, that our own courtroom frieze was deliberately designed in the exercise of governmental authority so as to include the figure of Moses holding tablets exhibiting a portion of the Hebrew text of the later, secularly phrased Commandments; in the company of 17 other lawgivers, most of them secular figures, there is no risk that Moses would strike an observer as evidence that the National Government was violating neutrality in religion. The dissent notes that another depiction of Moses and the Commandments adorns this Court's east pediment. But as with the courtroom frieze, Moses is found in the company of other figures, not only great but secular.

The Court concluded that

> the principle of neutrality has provided a good sense of direction: the government may not favor one religion over another, or religion over irreligion, religious choice being the prerogative of individuals under the free exercise clause. The principle has been helpful simply because it responds to one of the major concerns that prompted adoption of the religion clauses. The framers and the citizens of their time intended not only to protect the integrity of individual conscience in religious matters, but to guard against the civic divisiveness that follows when the government weighs in on one side of religious debate; nothing does a better job of roiling society, a point that needed no explanation to the descendants of English Puritans and Cavaliers (or Massachusetts Puritans and Baptists). A sense of the past thus points to governmental neutrality as an objective of the establishment clause, and a sensible standard for applying it. To be sure, given its generality as a principle, an appeal to neutrality alone cannot possibly lay every issue to rest, or tell us what issues on the margins are substantial enough for constitutional significance, a point that has been clear from the founding era to modern times. But invoking neutrality is a prudent way of keeping sight of something the framers of the First Amendment thought important.

Van Orden v. Perry, 545 U.S. 677 (2005)[38]

The 22 acres surrounding the Texas State Capitol contain 17 monuments and 21 historical markers commemorating the "people, ideals, and events that compose Texan identity." One of the monuments is a 6-feet high portrayal of the Ten Commandments located between the state capitol and state supreme court

---

[38] This ruling is addressed more fully in section 12-19, supra.

building. An eagle grasping the American flag, an eye inside of a pyramid, and two small tablets with what appears to be an ancient script are carved above the text of the Ten Commandments. Below the text are two Stars of David and the superimposed Greek letters Chi and Rho, which represent Christ. The bottom of the monument bears the inscription "Presented to the People and Youth of Texas by the Fraternal Order of Eagles of Texas." The other 16 monuments include those depicting the Heroes of the Alamo, Confederate Soldiers, Volunteer Firemen, Texas Rangers, Spanish-American War, Texas National Guard, Texas School Children, Pearl Harbor and Korean War Veterans, Soldiers of World War I, Disabled Veterans, and Texas Peace Officers.

The Fraternal Order of Eagles (a national social, civic, and patriotic organization) paid the cost of erecting the Ten Commandments monument, the dedication of which was presided over by two state legislators. Nearly 50 years after the erection of the Ten Commandments monument, an attorney who frequently walked past the monument on his way to the state supreme court library sued to have the monument removed, claiming that it offended him and that it constituted an establishment of religion in violation of the First Amendment. A federal district court ruled that the monument did not violate the First Amendment, and a federal appeals court affirmed this ruling. The case was appealed to the United States Supreme Court.

The Court rejected the so-called *Lemon* test for resolving the case before it. The *Lemon* test comes from a 1971 decision of the Supreme Court in which it ruled that a law or practice does not violate the establishment clause if it (1) has a secular legislative purpose; (2) has a principal or primary effect that neither advances nor inhibits religion; and (3) does not foster an excessive government entanglement with religion. The Court concluded that the *Lemon* test was "not useful in dealing with the sort of passive monument that Texas has erected on its Capitol grounds." Instead, our "analysis is driven both by the nature of the monument and by our Nation's history." It observed that "there is an unbroken history of official acknowledgment by all three branches of government of the role of religion in American life from at least 1789." It cited numerous examples, many of which were mentioned by Justice Scalia in his dissenting opinion in the *McCreary* case (see above).

This recognition of religion in public life back to the founding of the country has led to decisions finding that the establishment clause permits some public accommodations of religion. It noted that "acknowledgments of the role played by the Ten Commandments in our Nation's heritage are common throughout America," and that "we need only look within our own Courtroom. Since 1935, Moses has stood, holding two tablets that reveal portions of the Ten Commandments written in Hebrew, among other lawgivers in the south frieze. Representations of the Ten Commandments adorn the metal gates lining the north and south sides of the Courtroom as well as the doors leading into the Courtroom. Moses also sits on the exterior east facade of the building holding the Ten Commandments tablets." The Court continued,

> Similar acknowledgments can be seen throughout a visitor's tour of our Nation's Capital. For example, a large statue of Moses holding the Ten

Commandments, alongside a statue of the Apostle Paul, has overlooked the rotunda of the Library of Congress' Jefferson Building since 1897. And the Jefferson Building's Great Reading Room contains a sculpture of a woman beside the Ten Commandments with a quote above her from the Old Testament (Micah 6:8). A medallion with two tablets depicting the Ten Commandments decorates the floor of the National Archives. Inside the Department of Justice, a statue entitled "The Spirit of Law" has two tablets representing the Ten Commandments lying at its feet. In front of the Ronald Reagan Building is another sculpture that includes a depiction of the Ten Commandments. So too a 24-foot-tall sculpture, depicting, among other things, the Ten Commandments and a cross, stands outside the federal courthouse that houses both the Court of Appeals and the District Court for the District of Columbia. Moses is also prominently featured in the Chamber of the United States House of Representatives.

The Court concluded: "Texas has treated her Capitol grounds monuments as representing the several strands in the state's political and legal history. The inclusion of the Ten Commandments monument in this group has a dual significance, partaking of both religion and government. We cannot say that Texas' display of this monument violates the establishment clause of the First Amendment."

3. Lower Federal Court and State Court Rulings

These decisions indicate that nativity displays will be permissible so long as they are incorporated into a larger "seasonal" display containing secular objects.[39] Nativity displays standing alone on public property violate the Court's present interpretation of the establishment clause. A number of lower courts have attempted to apply this distinction. To illustrate, a federal appeals court ruled (by a 2-1 vote) that the annual display of a nativity scene in Chicago's city hall violated the First Amendment's nonestablishment of religion clause.[40] For 30 years the city of Chicago had displayed the scene, which consisted of 12-inch figures, in the lobby of city hall. The display had been donated to the city, and no public funds were expended in maintaining or installing it. The display contained six disclaimer notices which recited that the display had been donated and that it was in no way sponsored or endorsed by the city government. The American Jewish Congress challenged the display on the ground that it constituted the establishment of religion. In agreeing that the display violated the nonestablishment of religion clause, the court distinguished the Supreme Court's *Lynch* decision. Unlike the Chicago display, the display in *Lynch* was "only one element in a larger display that consisted in large part of secularized symbols and decorations" (e.g., a Santa Claus, reindeer, Christmas trees, lights). The Chicago display was not a part of a larger, secularized display. Further, the display in *Lynch*, while sponsored by the city government, was situated in a park owned by a private nonprofit organization. The Chicago display was situated in "the official

---

[39] *See also* Snowden v. Town of Bay Harbor Islands, 358 F.Supp.2d 1178 (S.D. Fla. 2004); Doe v. Wilson County School System, 2008 WL 2235334 (M.D. Tenn. 2008).

[40] American Jewish Congress v. City of Chicago, 827 F.2d 120 (7th Cir. 1987).

headquarters building of the municipal government." Under these circumstances, the Chicago nativity scene impermissibly "advanced religion by sending a message to the people of Chicago that the city approved of Christianity."

A federal district court in Illinois ruled that a nativity scene on city hall property violated the First Amendment's nonestablishment of religion clause despite the fact that the display was part of a larger display that contained several traditional (and secular) symbols of Christmas and was accompanied by a written notice in which the city disclaimed any endorsement of Christianity or any other religion.[41] The court attempted to distinguish *Lynch* on the ground that the Supreme Court had been addressing the permissibility of a nativity scene located in a private park rather than at the official headquarters of a city government.

A federal appeals court approved the maintenance of a granite monolith bearing the Ten Commandments on public property.[42] The court reasoned that in applying the three-part establishment clause test

> we must strike a balance between that which is primarily religious and that which is primarily secular albeit embodying some religious impact. A tempered approach obviates the absurdity of striking down insubstantial and widely accepted references to the Deity in circumstances such as courtroom ceremonies, oaths of public office, and on national currency and coin . . . Overzealous rigidity may diminish or ultimately destroy the bulwark we have erected against governmental interferences in matters of religion.[43]

The court concluded:

> It does not seem reasonable to require removal of a passive monument involving no compulsion, because its accepted precepts, as a foundation for law, reflect the religious nature of an ancient era . . . . The wholesome neutrality guaranteed by the establishment and free exercise clauses does not dictate obliteration of all our religious traditions . . . . We cannot say that the monument, as it stands, is more than a depiction of a historically important monolith with both secular and sectarian effects.[44]

One court ruled that the Smithsonian Institution's physical illustration of the theory of evolution did not constitute the establishment of a "religion of secular humanism."[45] On the contrary, the court concluded that a ban on all references to evolutionary theory in a public museum would itself constitute a violation of the establishment clause.

Use of a county seal depicting a cross, some sheep, and the motto "Con

---

[41] Mather v. Village of Mundelein, 699 F. Supp. 1300 (N.D. Ill. 1988).

[42] Anderson v. Salt Lake City Corp., 475 F.2d 29 (10th Cir. 1973).

[43] *Id.* at 33.

[44] *Id.* at 34.

[45] Crowley v. Smithsonian Institution, 462 F. Supp. 725 (D.C.D.C. 1978), *aff'd*, 636 F.2d 738 (D.C. Cir. 1980).

Esta Vencemos" (with this we conquer) was upheld against the claim that it constituted an impermissible establishment of religion.[46] The court concluded that the purpose of the seal was to authenticate documents and to commemorate the Christian, Spanish, and sheepherding heritage of the county; that the seal had only a benign reference to religion and thus did not have a primary effect of advancing religion; and that use of the seal resulted in no entanglements between church and state.

In another case, however, a federal district court concluded that a city's corporate seal containing a cross and other religious symbols was unconstitutional.[47] The City of Zion, Illinois, was organized in 1902 by Reverend John Alexander Dowie "for the purpose of the extension of the Kingdom of God on earth where God shall rule in every department of family, industry, commercial, educational, ecclesiastical and political life." Dowie presented a proposed seal to the city council the same year (all of the members of whom were of Dowie's Theocratic Party), and it was unanimously approved. The seal, which contains symbols of a dove, sword, cross, and crown, was explained by Dowie at the time as follows: "Look at that dove, which is the emblem of the Holy Spirit bearing the message of peace and love over the seas. The cross represents everything to us in redemption, salvation, healing, cleansing and keeping power. The sword is the sword of the Spirit, which is the Word of God. The crown is the crown of glory, the crown of joy, the crown of righteousness, the crown of rejoicing." The City of Zion uses its seal on its flag, letterhead, city council chambers, city vehicle stickers, police uniforms, and a city water tower. The seal was challenged on the ground that it violated the First Amendment's "nonestablishment of religion" clause. A federal district court agreed that the seal was unconstitutional, and prohibited its further use.

The court began its opinion by noting that a city practice which allegedly violates the nonestablishment of religion clause will be upheld only if it has a secular purpose, a primary effect that neither advances nor inhibits religion, and does not create any excessive entanglement between church and state.[48] The court concluded that the Zion city seal had a primary effect of advancing religion, and accordingly was unconstitutional. The court rejected the city's claim that the seal merely commemorated the "rich and unique historical heritage of Zion as an experiment in establishing a twentieth century utopian community" and as such had an historical and therefore secular purpose. The court found this theory "not without merit," since "the city was in fact a religious experiment and the seal [recognizes] that origin." However, the court concluded that the religious intent and purpose of the seal was so sectarian that the seal had to be viewed as advancing religion rather than history. It observed, "As Reverend Dowie indicated, each of the symbols [on the seal] has an independent religious significance. The sum of the individual symbols imparts a decidedly religious, in fact sectarian, message." The religious message is enhanced by the words "God Reigns."

Further, the court noted that it could not "impute complete knowledge of the history to the average observer of the seal. We therefore cannot assume the

---

[46] Johnson v. Board of County Commissioners, 528 F. Supp. 919 (D.N.M. 1981).

[47] Harris v. City of Zion, 729 F. Supp. 1242 (N.D. Ill. 1990).

[48] *See* § 13-01.1, *supra.*

average member of Zion's political community will have either general or specific knowledge of Zion's unique history." The court concluded that "it is possible that the majority of Zion's 15,000 inhabitants know little of its unique history." Therefore, the original purpose of the seal—which was the advancement of religion—was not neutralized by its historical significance.

The same court, in a parallel decision, concluded that the corporate seal of another Illinois town (Rolling Meadows) was constitutional despite the presence of a cross. The court emphasized that the seal had been designed in 1960 by an eighth-grade student as part of a school art assignment, and that neither she nor the city council in adopting the seal had any intent of advancing religion. Further, the cross was one of many designs on the seal, all the rest of which were secular. The court found the cross to be one aspect of community life, that was permissible on a city seal in the context of several other secular representations of municipal life. The remaining pictures "neutralized" the impact of the cross. This fact, in addition to the secular intent of the creator of the seal, persuaded the court that it was permissible.

The use of the national motto "In God We Trust" on all United States coins and currency has been upheld on the ground that such use "has nothing whatsoever to do with the establishment of religion" since its use "is of a patriotic or ceremonial character and bears no true resemblance to a governmental sponsorship of a religious exercise."[49]

Example

• *A federal appeals court ruled that a county seal bearing an outline of the Ten Commandments did not violate the nonestablishment of religion clause of the First Amendment. The court noted that the primary purpose of depicting the Ten Commandments on the seal was not the advancement of religion. It stressed that six of the Ten Commandments "deal with honoring one's parents, killing or murder, adultery, stealing, bearing false witness, and covetousness; all of which prescribe rules of conduct for dealing with other people. Much of our private and public law derives from these final six commandments. . . . For this reason, although primarily having a religious connotation, the Ten Commandments can, in certain contexts, have a secular significance." The court noted that the seal is "solely limited to the very narrow context of authenticating legal documents" and therefore there was a "tight connection between a legitimate secular purpose for using the pictograph of the Ten Commandments and sword (using recognizable symbols of secular law, ones that suggest the force of law) and the context in which the seal is used (authentication of legal documents)." In addition, the clerk of the court "has not used the seal in contexts in which a reasonable observer might not understand the relationship between the seal's symbols and its secular purpose." Finally, the court noted that the seal did not contain the text of the Ten Commandments, and that the outline of the Ten Commandments was not the only symbol in the seal. It also has a depiction of a sword intertwined with the tablets. The presence of this additional symbol "increases the probability that observers will associate the seal with secular law rather than with religion."[50]*

---

[49] Aronow v. United States, 432 F.2d 242, 243 (9th Cir. 1970). *Accord* Lambeth v. Board of Commissioners, 407 F.3d 266 (4th Cir. 2005).

[50] King v. Richmond County, 331 F.3d 1271 (11th Cir. 2003).

Recurring Use of Public Property by Religious Congregations for Religious Services

§ 14-05

Key point 14-05. *The First Amendment permits religious congregations to use public property for church services so long as the use is temporary and the congregation pays fair rental value.*

May public property ever be utilized for religious services? In a leading decision, the New Jersey Supreme Court held that "religious groups who fully reimburse school boards for related out-of-pocket expenses may use school facilities on a temporary basis for religious services as well as educational classes."[51] The court concluded that such a practice did not violate the First Amendment's establishment clause. It applied the three-part test announced by the Supreme Court in the *Lemon* case.[52] First, the court observed that "there was a secular purpose in leasing the school facilities. That purpose was to enhance public use of these properties for the common benefit of the residents of East Brunswick."[53] Second, the court noted that the "primary effect" of the rental arrangement was not the advancement of religion: "While we would be naive in refusing to note the obvious advantages to young congregations in the temporary use of school premises, to hold that this scheme primarily benefits religion would be absurd. The community as a whole is benefited when nonprofit organizations of interest to its members prosper." Finally, the court could find no "excessive entanglement" between church and state:

> [N]o significant administrative function is involved. The processing of an application by a clerk is hardly an act of excessive entanglement. Moreover, inasmuch as no use of school premises is made during regular school hours, there is no need for supervision to insure that no religion seeps into secular institutions. The danger of political fragmentation is minuscule, as appropriations are not involved. The mere fact that some persons in the community oppose the use of the schools by sectarian groups should not prevent these groups from enjoying the benefits of premises which the tax dollars of many of their members helped to construct.[54]

The court cautioned that "truly prolonged use of school facilities by a congregation without evidence of immediate intent to construct or purchase its

---

[51] Resnick v. East Brunswick Township Board of Education, 389 A.2d 944, 960 (N.J. 1978).

[52] *See* § 13-01.1, *supra.*

[53] *Id.* at 954.

[54] *Id.* at 958.

own building would be impermissible."[55]

In a similar case, a federal appeals court ruled that a church could use public school facilities on a temporary basis (and during noninstructional hours) during the construction or renovation of its own facilities.[56] A church applied for and was granted permission to use a public school building on four consecutive Sundays while its own church facility was being renovated. During the four week period, the church applied for a permit to use the school facilities for an additional "six to eight months." This permit was denied, and a trial court granted the church's request for an injunction forcing the school district to issue the requested permit.

On appeal, the school district defended its refusal to grant the permit by pointing to a New York law that prohibits public school properties from being used for "meetings . . . where admission fees are charged . . . if such meetings are under the exclusive control, and said proceeds are to be applied for the benefit of . . . a religious sect or denomination." The court acknowledged that this language was inconsistent with church use of public school property. However, it concluded that the school district had "opened this forum to [the church] through a practice of granting permits to use public school facilities to other religious organizations."

The court also rejected the school district's argument that granting the permit to the church would constitute an impermissible "establishment of religion" in violation of the First Amendment. It noted that "the semblance of official support is less evident where a school building is used at night as a temporary facility by religious organizations, under a program that grants access to all charitable groups."

However, some courts have indicated that a church's use of public school facilities must be temporary for the usage to be permissible. To illustrate, one court ruled that public high school officials acted properly in denying a church's request to use school facilities as a *permanent* location.[57] A church of about 100 members had been meeting in a privately-owned auditorium. Its pastor asked local school officials if the church could rent the public high school auditorium on Sunday mornings. The school officials declined this request on the basis of a school policy prohibiting use of school facilities for religious uses. The church immediately filed a lawsuit against the school district, seeking a court order permitting use of the public high school auditorium on Sundays. In support of its case, the church argued that the high school permitted many non-religious groups to rent the auditorium, and it thereby had created an "open forum" that could not be denied to any group (including a church). The school district argued that its policy of denying access to its facilities by religious groups was required by the constitutional principle of "separation of church and state."

The court agreed that the school district had created an "open forum" by permitting various community groups to rent the high school auditorium. However, the court concluded that the district's refusal to rent the auditorium

---

[55] *Id.*

[56] Deeper Life Christian Fellowship v. Board of Education, 852 F.2d 676 (2nd Cir. 1988).

[57] Wallace v. Washoe County School District, 701 F. Supp. 187 (D. Nev. 1988).

to the church was justified, since rental of the facility to the church would "have the primary effect of advancing religion" in violation of the nonestablishment of religion clause of the federal constitution. The court stressed that the church desired to use the school auditorium as the "*permanent* site for its church services and activities." It noted that the church "has no building site nor does it have any present plans to acquire a site or construct a church facility." As a result, the high school "will become the physical embodiment of the church," and in this sense the church's request was "significantly different" from the requests of other community organizations to rent the facility, since no other community group sought to "become permanently institutionalized within the school."

Examples

• *A federal appeals court ruled that a church's constitutional rights were not violated by a public school district rule prohibiting it from conducting religious worship on public school property.[58] The church had asked school officials for permission to use a middle school auditorium for weekly religious services after it outgrew its own facilities. School officials denied this request. School policy allowed school property to be used for a wide variety of outside groups for civic, social, and recreational purposes. However, school property could not be used for religious services. The relevant policy specifies, "No outside organization or group may be allowed to conduct religious services or religious instruction on school premises after school. However, the use of school premises by outside organizations or groups after school for the purposes of discussing religious material or material which contains a religious viewpoint or for distributing such material is permissible." The church challenged the school's denial of its request to use school property for religious services. A federal appeals court upheld the policy. It noted that "freedom to speak on government property is largely dependent on the nature of the forum in which the speech is delivered." The court concluded that the public school in question was a limited public forum since school officials allowed only some groups to use school property for designated purposes. As a result, the exclusion of religious worship from this forum was legitimate only if it was "reasonable in light of the purpose served by the forum" and was "viewpoint neutral." The court concluded that both of these requirements were met, and therefore the school policy was legally permissible. The court noted that religious groups are free to use school property after hours for purposes of discussing religious material or material with a religious viewpoint. It was only the use of school property for religious worship that was excluded.*

• *A federal appeals court ruled that a city's refusal to allow a church to use the town hall for weekly Bible studies violated the First Amendment guaranty of free speech. The court concluded: "It is fundamental First Amendment jurisprudence that where a municipality requires a permit for expressive activity the scheme for issuance of the permit must set objective standards governing the grant or denial of [the permit] in order to ensure that the officials not have the power to discriminate based on the content or viewpoint of speech by suppressing disfavored speech or disliked speakers. Furthermore, discrimination against speech because of its message is presumed to be unconstitutional. However, restrictions on speech in a limited public forum will withstand First Amendment challenge if they are reasonable and viewpoint neutral. The town's written policy created a limited public forum. Because the written policy*

---

[58] Bronx Household of Faith v. Community School District, 127 F.3d 207 (2nd Cir. 1997). *But see* Bronx Household of Faith v. Board of Education, 492 F.3d 89 (2nd Cir. 2007).

itself was utterly silent on the issue of whether the town hall could be used for religious activities of any kind, it could not serve as the basis for a reasonable, viewpoint neutral exclusion from the town hall of religious worship services, such as those conducted by the church. Indeed, in providing that 'the town reserves the right to refuse or terminate permission to use any town facility for any reason,' the written policy constituted an unconstitutional prior restraint on speech that gave [the town commissioner] unfettered discretion to discriminate based on the content or viewpoint of speech. [The commissioner] did precisely that when he, and he alone, decided that, while religious worship services were generally permitted in the town hall, religious worship services involving proselytizing were not permitted. Therefore, we hold that the town's revocation of church's permit to use the town hall for their worship services violated church's First Amendment right to free speech.[59]

• *A federal appeals court ruled that a public school violated the constitutional rights of a church by charging it more rent than it charged other community organizations for the use of school facilities.*[60] *A public school board permitted a wide variety of civic and community groups to use its facilities. Most such groups paid a rental fee substantially less than the commercial rate. Churches were permitted to use school facilities, and they were charged the same rate as other civic and community groups for the first five years they rented school facilities. However, after five years, churches paid a substantially higher rental fee. No other civic or community group paid the higher fee after five years. School officials freely acknowledged that the policy singled out churches for higher rent, but it insisted that the purpose was to encourage churches to go elsewhere out of a concern that continued use by churches of public school facilities might violate the First Amendment's prohibition of an establishment of religion. A church began renting school facilities. For five years it paid the discounted rate, and later began paying the commercial rate. The church estimated that it paid $290,000 in additional rent because of the school board's policy regarding churches. The church sued the school board, claiming that the rental policy for churches violated the First Amendment guarantees of speech and religion. It also demanded a refund of the excess rent it had paid. A trial court agreed with the church that the school board's policy was unconstitutional, but it refused to award the church the excess rent it paid because of the policy. The church appealed. A federal appeals court agreed with the trial court that the policy was unconstitutional, and it ruled that the church was entitled to sue for a return of the excess rent it paid under the policy. The court rejected the school board's suggestion that allowing a church to rent school facilities at a below-market rate for a long period of time automatically violates the First Amendment prohibition of the establishment of religion. Such may be the case, but only if religious use of the public forum is "dominant."*

• *A federal appeals court ruled that a religious group could not use public school property for religious services because the property was not a public forum that had been opened to a wide variety of community groups. A public school district developed a written use policy for non-student groups who wished to use school facilities after hours. That policy permitted buildings to be used for civic, recreational, and entertainment purposes that were open to the public and pertained to the "welfare of the public." It did not permit partisan political activity or for-profit fund-raising. The policy prohibited uses involving "religious services or religious instruction" but*

---

[59] Amandola v. Town of Babylon, 251 F.3d 339 (2nd Cir. 2001).

[60] Fairfax Covenant Church v. Fairfax County School Board, 17 F.3d 703 (4th Cir. 1994).

permits discussions of religious material or material containing a religious viewpoint. A religious organization requested use of school facilities for a prayer meeting at which the group planned "to worship the Lord in prayer and music . . . to discuss family and political issues, pray about those issues, and seek to engage in religious and Biblical instruction with regard to those issues." The school district denied the request, citing the policy, and the religious organization filed a lawsuit in federal court challenging the district's decision. A federal district court ruled that the school district's policy was unconstitutional. A federal appeals court disagreed. It noted that the school district's policy excluded partisan political activity and for-profit fund-raising in addition to religious activities, and therefore "the policy's restrictions indicate that the school's purposes in allowing some public use have not reached the point at which any use—save targeted religious activities—is allowed. We are thus persuaded that the restrictions are minimally sufficient to maintain the school buildings' status as a non-public forum." As a nonpublic forum that allowed limited public access to its property, the school only had to prove that its exclusion of religious groups was "reasonably related to the purposes of the forum and discriminated only on the basis of content, not viewpoint. The government may not exclude a speaker with a religious viewpoint if it has permitted other speakers on similar topics. . . . This does not mean that any ban on religious activities amounts to viewpoint discrimination. Religion may be either a perspective on a topic such as marriage or may be a substantive activity in itself. In the latter case, the government's exclusion of the activity is discrimination based on content, not viewpoint. . . . [We conclude that] religious services and religious instruction are activities which may be excluded as content-based discrimination [since they] are not simply approaches to a topic, but activities whose primary purpose is to teach and experience the subject of religion. These are activities distinct from a topical discussion, a social gathering, or a political meeting. The school district has excluded such religious activities but does not forbid speakers on general topics with a religious perspective—a distinction that viewpoint neutrality permits."[61]

• A federal court in New York ruled that a public school could not bar a church from renting school property on Sunday mornings for religious worship services. The church had asked school officials for permission to use a middle school auditorium for weekly religious services after it outgrew its own facilities. School officials denied this request. School policy allowed school property to be used for a wide variety of outside groups for civic, social, and recreational purposes. However, school property could not be used for religious services. The court concluded that the church's proposed activities included much more than religious worship. They also included other activities "clearly consistent with the type of activities previously permitted in the forum and consistent with activities expressly permitted by the school district's policies" such as "social, civic and recreational meetings and entertainment, and other uses pertaining to the welfare of the community." The court concluded that the church's proposed activities included several that benefited the welfare of the community, including helping the poor with food, clothing, and rent; counseling; friendship; financial advice; encouragement; encouraging people to lead productive lives and leave lives of crime and drugs; and teaching people to "love their neighbors as themselves." Further, the proposed activities included singing, socializing and eating—clearly recreational activities. The court referred to the pastor's testimony that "the Sunday morning meeting provides the theological framework to engage in activities that benefit

---

61   Campbell v. St. Tammany's School Board, 206 F.3d 482 (5th Cir. 2000).

the welfare of the community." Therefore, the church was proposing to engage in permitted activities from a religious viewpoint, and the city's rejection of this use of a public school was an unconstitutional violation of the church's First Amendment right of free speech. The court noted that "the government may not, consistent with the First Amendment, engage in dissecting speech to determine whether it constitutes worship."[62]

• A federal court in South Carolina ordered a public school district to continue allowing a church to rent a school building for weekly worship services, and rejected the school district's arguments for discontinuing the arrangement. A church used a public school building to conduct weekly services pursuant to a school district policy that allowed "recognized nonprofit community organizations" to use school facilities. The school district initially granted the church permission to use the school for a three month period. The church paid a rental fee of $250 per week and $15 per hour for the services of a custodian who was present at the school as required by the policy. At the end of the three month term, the school district granted the church permission to use the school for an additional three months. At the end of this second three month term the church asked for an additional three months since it was still finalizing arrangements to hold services at another location. However, the school district informed the church that its occupancy would not be extended. A school district officer explained that the district did not want to set a precedent by allowing the church to use school facilities for an extended period because then other "undesirable" groups such as religious cults would want to use the facilities. The church asked a court to issue a preliminary injunction allowing it to use the school for an additional three months. The court agreed with the church's position, and ordered the school to allow the church to continue to rent the property. The court noted that all users of school property were charged the same amount, and so no "subsidy" was being provided to religion.[63]

---

[62] Bronx Household of Faith v. Board of Education of the City of New York, 226 F.Supp.2d 401 (S.D.N.Y. 2002). The court quoted from the Supreme Court's *Good News Club* ruling, addressed below: "When the state establishes a limited public forum, the state is not required to and does not allow persons to engage in every type of speech. The state may be justified in reserving its forum for certain groups or for the discussion of certain topics. The state's power to restrict speech, however, is not without limits. The restriction must not discriminate against speech on the basis of viewpoint, and the restriction must be reasonable in light of the purpose served by the forum."

[63] Gracepointe Church v. Jenkins, 2006 WL 1663798 (D.S.C. 2006). See also Child Evangelism Fellowship of South Carolina v. Anderson School District 470 F.3d 1062 (4th Cir. 2006) (school district's policy of charging rent to a religious organization for use of school property after instructional hours, but allowing other groups to use the property at no cost, violated the First Amendment).

Nonrecurring Use of Public Property by Adults for Religious Events and Activities

§ 14-06

Key point 14-06. *Adults may use public property for religious purposes if the property is used by community organizations for non-religious purposes. Excluding religious speech, while allowing other kinds of speech, violates the First Amendment guaranty of free speech.*

Several courts have ruled that public school officials cannot deny use of their facilities to religious groups if nonreligious community groups are permitted to use the facilities. In 1993, the United States Supreme Court unanimously ruled that a public high school that allows various community groups to rent its auditorium for "social, civic and recreational meetings and entertainments, and other uses pertaining to the welfare of the community," cannot deny the same privilege to a church that wants to rent the auditorium to show a religiously-oriented film series on family values.[64] Section 414 of the New York Education Law authorizes local school boards to adopt reasonable regulations for the use of school property for ten specified purposes when the property is not in use for school purposes. Among the permitted uses is the holding of "social, civic and recreational meetings and entertainments, and other uses pertaining to the welfare of the community; but such meetings, entertainment and uses shall be non-exclusive and open to the general public." The list of permitted uses does not include meetings for religious purposes, and a regulation interpreting section 414 specifies that "school premises shall not be used by any group for religious purposes."

Lamb's Chapel (the "church"), an evangelical church, twice applied to a local public school district for permission to use school facilities to show a six-part film series advocating traditional, Christian family values as the only deterrent to the undermining influences of the media. The school district denied the first application, saying that "[t]his film does appear to be church related and therefore your request must be refused."

The church brought suit in federal district court, challenging the school district's denial as a violation of the First Amendment's guarantees of speech, assembly, and religion. The church argued that since school properties could be used for "social, civic, and recreational" purposes, the school district had opened them to such a wide variety of "communicative purposes" that they were in effect "public forums," like public parks and sidewalks in which few restrictions on free speech are tolerated. The district court summarily dismissed the church's lawsuit, rejecting all of the church's claims. The church appealed this ruling, and a federal appeals court affirmed the judgment of the district court "in all respects."

The Supreme Court unanimously reversed the decisions of the district court and appeals court, and ruled in favor of the church. The Court noted that a public school may be a public forum, a limited public forum, or neither, depending on

---

[64] Lamb's Chapel v. Center Moriches Union Free School District, 508 U.S. 384 (1993).

the circumstances of each case. A public school is an *open forum* if its facilities may be used by any outside organization without limitation. However, a public school becomes a *limited forum* if it may be used by only some outside organizations. This, of course, was the case here, since New York law specified that public school property could be used only for designated purposes including "social, civic and recreational meetings and entertainments, and other uses pertaining to the welfare of the community." The Court acknowledged that a public school could prohibit use of its facilities by any outside organization, in which case it would be neither an open forum nor a limited forum. It observed that "there is no question" that a school district "may legally preserve the property under its control for the use to which it is dedicated," and that the school district in this case "need not have permitted" after-hours use of its property by any community group.

The Court noted that the school district's properties in this case were "heavily used by a wide variety of private organizations." These included a New Age religious group known as the "Mind Center," the Southern Harmonize Gospel Singers, the Salvation Army Youth Band, a Council of Churches concert, the humane society's auction, a dance group, a baseball clinic, the chamber of commerce's "town fair day," a drama club, and both boy scouts and girl scouts. When a public school becomes a limited public forum, open to certain types of outside organizations, school officials cannot deny access to school facilities by a permissible group solely on the basis of the content of its speech. It observed:

> [T]he government violates the First Amendment when it denies access to a speaker solely to suppress the point of view he espouses on an otherwise includable subject. The film involved here no doubt dealt with a subject otherwise permissible under [the school district's regulations], and its exhibition was denied solely because the film dealt with the subject from a religious standpoint. The principle that has emerged from our cases "is that the First Amendment forbids the government to regulate speech in ways that favor some viewpoints or ideas at the expense of others."[65] That principle applies in the circumstances of this case . . . .

The Court rejected as "unfounded" the school district's argument that to permit its properties to be used for religious purposes would be an establishment of religion forbidden by the First Amendment. The Court observed:

> The showing of this film would not have been during school hours, would not have been sponsored by the school, and would have been open to the public, not just to church members. The [school district's properties] had repeatedly been used by a wide variety of private organizations. Under these circumstances . . . there would have been no realistic danger that the community would think that the [school district] was endorsing religion or any particular creed, and any benefit to religion or to the church would have been no more than incidental.

---

[65] City Council of Los Angeles v. Taxpayers for Vincent, 466 U.S. 789, 804 (1984).

The Court also rejected the school district's claim that it had justifiably denied use of its property to a "radical" church for the purpose of proselytizing, since to do otherwise would have lead to threats of public unrest and even violence. The Court noted, "There is nothing in the record to support such a justification, which in any event would be difficult to defend as a reason to deny the presentation of a religious point of view about a subject the [school district] otherwise makes open to discussion on [its] property."

Examples

• *A school district opens its facilities for a limited number of specified uses, including "concerts." Several rock concerts (by outside musical groups) are conducted on school property during the current year. A church requests permission to use a public high school auditorium for a concert by a religious group. School officials deny permission on the ground that this would "promote religion." Such a denial would violate the church's constitutional right to free speech according to the Supreme Court's decision in the Lamb's Chapel case.*

• *A school district adopts a policy denying use of its facilities by any community group. A church requests permission to use a public high school auditorium for a religious service. School officials deny permission. Such a denial would be permissible according to the Supreme Court's decision in the Lamb's Chapel case, since the church is not being treated less favorably than other community groups solely on the basis of the religious content of its message.*

• *A school district opens its facilities for a limited number of specified uses, including "civic and cultural" uses. A church requests permission to rent a public high school auditorium for a baccalaureate service for graduating high school students. School officials deny permission on the ground that this would "promote religion." The Court did not address the legality of such a denial in the Lamb's Chapel case. However, an argument could be made that the school officials' actions violate the First Amendment guaranty of free speech based on the following factors: (1) A baccalaureate service is a "civic or cultural" event, and accordingly use of school facilities cannot be denied for such a purpose solely on the basis of the religious content of the speech. (2) If school officials have allowed any religious group to use its facilities in the past, then it would be impermissible to deny use of those same facilities for a baccalaureate service. (3) By creating a limited public forum, public school officials cannot deny access to school facilities solely on the basis of the content of an organization's speech (whether that speech is religious, political, philosophical, or of any other variety). This third argument was not addressed by the Supreme Court in the Lamb's Chapel case, but this does not mean that the Court would not recognize it. Some lower federal courts in fact have recognized this argument. (4) The Court noted in the Lamb's Chapel case that "[a]ccess to a [limited public forum] can be based on subject matter or speaker identity so long as the distinctions drawn are reasonable and viewpoint neutral." An argument could be made that an absolute ban on religious speech does not satisfy this test, particularly if the list of "acceptable" organizations and viewpoints is large. (5) The Court in Lamb's Chapel was impressed with the church's argument that the school district "had opened its property for such a wide variety of communicative purposes that restrictions on communicative uses of the property were subject to the same constitutional limitations as restrictions in traditional public fora such as parks and sidewalks. Hence, its view was that subject-matter or speaker exclusions on district property were required to be justified by a compelling state interest and to be narrowly drawn to achieve that end." While noting that the trial court and appeals court in this case had rejected this argument, the Supreme Court concluded that "[t] he argument has considerable force, for the district's property is heavily used by a wide variety of private organizations . . . ." (6) In Lamb's Chapel, the Court noted that it had previously ruled, in Widmar v. Vincent,[66] that permitting use of public university property for religious services and functions was constitutionally permissible, since the property was open to a wide variety of organizations.*

• A school district opens its facilities for a limited number of specified uses, including "civic and cultural" uses. A church requests permission to rent a public high school auditorium every Sunday for weekly worship services for a period of 18 months while a new church sanctuary is under construction. School officials deny permission on the ground that this would "promote religion." The Court did not address the legality of such a denial in the Lamb's Chapel case. The church had applied to school authorities for such permission, but permission was denied and the church chose not to appeal this denial in court. An argument could be made that the school officials' actions violate the First Amendment guaranty of free speech based on the same factors mentioned in the previous example.

• A school district opens its facilities to a wide variety of community groups, and on several occasions has permitted religious groups to use its facilities. A church requests permission to use a public high school auditorium for a one-time religious service. School officials deny permission on the ground that this would "promote religion." Such a denial would violate the church's constitutional right to free speech according to the Supreme Court's decision in the Lamb's Chapel case. In Lamb's Chapel, the Court noted that it had previously ruled, in Widmar v. Vincent,[67] that permitting use of public university property for religious purposes under the university's "open access" policy was constitutionally permissible.

• A federal appeals court ruled that a public school district violated the First Amendment rights of a religious group by denying it access to school property to distribute literature and conduct meetings. The court noted that the school "created limited public for a" when it opened school property for speech "by a broad array of community groups on matters related to the students and the schools." The school "had no constitutional obligation to distribute or post any community group materials or to allow any such groups to staff tables at Back-to-School nights. But when it decided to open up these fora to a specified category of groups (i.e., non-profit, non-partisan community groups) for speech on particular topics (i.e., speech related to the students and the schools), it established a limited public fora. It may not exclude speech where its distinction is not reasonable in light of the purpose served by the forum, nor may it discriminate against speech on the basis of its viewpoint." The court concluded: "What [the school district] appears to mean when it says that it excludes groups that proselytize is that it rejects religiously affiliated groups that attempt to recruit new members and persuade them to adopt the group's views. This is viewpoint discrimination. . . . The Supreme Court has repeatedly rejected the position that the

---

[66] 454 U. S. 263, 271 (1981).

[67] Id.

Establishment Clause justifies, much less requires, a refusal to extend free speech rights to religious speakers who participate in broad-reaching government programs neutral in design. . . . In sum, we hold, based on undisputed facts in the record and well established Supreme Court precedent, that [the school district] has clearly engaged in a practice of viewpoint discrimination that cannot be justified as an effort to avoid an Establishment Clause violation."[68]

• A federal appeals court ruled that a religious group could use a public library's auditorium for prayer meetings since the auditorium was made available to a variety of other community groups.[69] The religious group requested permission to use the library auditorium, but its request was denied because of a library policy prohibiting use of its auditorium by religious or political groups. The religious group promptly sought a court order forcing the library to permit it to use the auditorium on the ground that the library's policy violated the group's constitutionally protected rights of free speech, assembly, and religion. A trial court issued an injunction compelling the library to permit the religious group to meet, and the library appealed. The federal appeals court for the fifth circuit agreed with the trial court's decision in favor of the religious group. The court noted that the library had permitted various groups to use the auditorium, including the American Association of University Women, an association of retired federal workers, the United States Navy, the United Way, American Legion, an adult AIDS program, and a swimming club. It also allowed a young girl to use the auditorium for a piano recital. The court concluded that the library, by allowing these groups to use the auditorium, had created a "public forum" and accordingly could not deny any other group access to the same facility solely on the basis of the content of its speech. Since the library denied the religious group access to the auditorium solely on the basis of the religious content of its speech, the denial violated the group's constitutional rights. "It is elementary," the court concluded, "that the government may not exclude speech on the basis of its content from . . . a public forum." The court also rejected the library's argument that allowing the religious group to use its auditorium would violate the First Amendment's "nonestablishment of religion" clause. It observed that "in the absence of empirical evidence that religious groups will dominate use of the library's auditorium, causing the advancement of religion to become the forum's `primary effect,' an equal access policy will not offend the [nonestablishment of religion] clause."

• A federal appeals court ruled that a city could not refuse to allow an evangelistic film on the life of Christ to be shown at a city-owned "senior citizen center."[70] A city owns and operates six senior centers. The centers are multipurpose facilities that provide forums for lectures, classes, movies, crafts, bingo, dancing, physical exercise, and other activities. People who use the senior centers do not reside there, and all of the programs are voluntary. Many of the programs at the senior centers are organized and sponsored by private individuals or organizations. Senior center policies permit non-member groups to use the centers for classes and other activities if the subject matter is "of interest to senior citizens." Alternatively, groups may use the centers without regard to this subject matter requirement if they are composed of seventy-five percent or more senior citizens. Nonmembers or persons under fifty-five years of age may conduct classes, and people who deliver lectures or teach classes

---

[68] Child Evangelism Fellowship of New Jersey Inc. v. Stafford Township School District, 386 F.3d 514 (3rd Cir. 2004).

[69] Concerned Women for America v. LaFayette County, 883 F.2d 32 (5th Cir. 1989).

[70] Church on the Rock v. City of Albuquerque, 84 F.3d 1273 (10th Cir. 1996).

are also permitted to distribute literature. The range of subjects that qualify as being "of interest to senior citizens" is quite broad. The senior centers' activities catalogs list many of the programs that meet this requirement, including a number of classes and presentations in which religion or religious matters are the primary focus, such as Bible as Literature, Myths and Stories About the Millennium, Theosophy, and A Passover Commemoration (an oratorio). The catalogs encourage "ideas for new classes and programs" as well. In 1994 a pastor (over the age of fifty-five) requested permission from the supervisor of one of the centers to show a two-hour film entitled "Jesus." A city official denied the pastor's request, stating that city policy prohibited the use of senior centers "for sectarian instruction or as a place for religious worship." A federal appeals court ruled that the city acted improperly in denying the pastor's request to show the religious film. The court began its opinion by noting that the senior centers were limited public forums because the city limited access to these centers in two ways. First, it imposes an age requirement for participation; and second, it limits the subject matter of presentations to topics "of interest to senior citizens." Restrictions on access to such forums based on speaker identity and subject matter "are permissible only if the distinctions drawn are reasonable in light of the purpose served by the forum and are viewpoint neutral." The city claimed that its policy denying religious instruction is a restriction based upon "content," not viewpoint, because it disallows all religious instruction and worship in its senior centers regardless of the particular religion involved. The court disagreed. It pointed out that the city had already "opened the doors" of its senior centers to presentations about religion. The city allowed speakers to discuss the Bible from a "strictly historical" perspective and to address religion as long as such presentations could be characterized as "a literature discussion or a philosophical discussion." The court continued, "The film ran afoul of city policy . . . by advocating the adoption of the Christian faith. In contrast, a film about Jesus's life that ended on a skeptical note and urged agnosticism or atheism would not have contravened the city's policy. Because the prohibited perspective, not the general subject matter, triggered the decision to bar the private expression, the city's policy is properly analyzed as a viewpoint-based restriction on speech." The court noted that "government bears a particularly heavy burden in justifying viewpoint-based restrictions in designated public forums" since viewpoint discrimination is "an egregious form of content discrimination." At a minimum, to survive strict scrutiny the city's policy must be "narrowly drawn to effectuate a compelling state interest." The court concluded that this test was not met. As a result, the city violated the First Amendment guaranty of free speech by refusing to allow the film "Jesus" to be shown.

• Must a public high school rent its auditorium to a church that wants to conduct a baccalaureate service for graduating seniors and their families?[71] Yes, concluded a federal district court in Alabama. The church requested permission to rent the school auditorium since no local church was large enough to accommodate the expected crowd. The school routinely rented its auditorium to a wide variety of community groups at a fee of $200 per day, but the school board rejected the church's request since it would involve a religious service. The church asked a court to issue an order requiring the school to rent its facility to the church for the baccalaureate service. The court agreed. It noted that when public property is opened to a wide range of community groups, it becomes a "public forum," and as such it must be available to any group regardless of the content of its speech. The court concluded that the school

---

[71] Verbena United Methodist Church v. Chilton County, 765 F. Supp. 704 (M.D. Ala. 1991).

had created a public forum by making its auditorium available to a wide range of community groups, and accordingly it could not deny the same privilege to a church solely on the basis of the religious nature of the intended use.

• The Arizona Supreme Court concluded that the rental of a state university stadium to an evangelist for religious services did not constitute the establishment of a religion.[72] The court concluded, "We do not believe that leasing Sun Devil Stadium for an occasional religious service at a fair rental value is an appropriation or application of public property for religious purposes . . . . The twin keys to the use of the stadium are fair rental value and the occasional nature of the use. The lease to a religious group, on a permanent basis, of property on the University campus, for example, would be an entirely different matter because by the permanency of the arrangement, the prestige of the State would be placed behind a particular religion or religion generally. Also, the lease of campus facilities for occasional use, but not for fair rental value, would violate the provision of our Constitution [i.e., of the State of Arizona] as being an appropriation or application of State property for religious purposes."

• A federal court in New York ruled that a church could not be denied use of public school property that was made available to other community groups including at least one other religious organization.[73] A Methodist church asked permission to conduct a magic show on public school property. The church's application to the school indicated that the show would be performed by a Christian illusionist, and would include a religious service. The school board denied this request on the basis of a state law banning use of public school property by religious organizations for religious purposes. The church sued the school board, claiming that its actions violated the constitutional guarantees of speech and religion. The church acknowledged that state law banned the use of public school property for religious purposes, but it noted that the school board had permitted a Pentecostal church to conduct a "Holy Ghost filled concert" on the same public school property that included singing, a sermon by a pastor, and an "altar call." The court concluded that the school board's denial of the church's application to use the school property violated the constitutional guaranty of free speech. The court noted that the guaranty of free speech does not guarantee "unlimited access to government-owned property for purposes of expression" and that "depending on the nature of the property, the government may regulate access." The court also noted that speech may occur in various contexts. The school board claimed that state law had created a limited public forum that was available only to nonreligious groups. However, the court concluded that even if the school board had created a limited open forum, religious services were a permitted use since the board had previously allowed a church choir to use school property for a concert and religious service. As a result, it could not deny access by any group wanting to use the property for religious purposes. The court rejected the school board's argument that allowing the church to use school property for a religious service would violate the First Amendment's nonestablishment of religion clause. It observed: "[The performance] would not have occurred during school hours, would not have been sponsored by the school, and would have been open to the public, not just to church members. In addition, the school facilities have repeatedly been used by a variety of private organizations. [The Supreme Court has ruled] that where a forum is available to a broad class of speakers, allowing religious speech does not confer any imprimatur of state approval on religious sects or practices." The court

---

[72] Pratt v. Arizona Board of Regents, 520 P.2d 514 (Ariz. 1974).

[73] Trinity United Methodist Parish v. Board of Education, 907 F. Supp. 707 (S.D.N.Y. 1995).

concluded that "[t]he gospel concert occurred and it created at least a limited public forum for entertainment events including prayer, religious instruction, music and religious testimony. This means that the school board cannot selectively deny access for activities of the same genre . . . ."

The Supreme Court's Good News Club Case[74]

The United States Supreme Court ruled that a public school violated the free speech rights of a religious club by forbidding the club to meet after hours at the school. The school allowed its facilities to be used for "instruction in any branch of education, learning or the arts" and for "social, civic and recreational meetings and entertainment events, and other uses pertaining to the welfare of the community," provided that the events were open to the general public. The school refused, however, to permit the use of its facilities by a Good News Club, stating that "the kinds of activities proposed to be engaged in by the Good News Club were not a discussion of secular subjects such as child rearing, development of character and development of morals from a religious perspective, but were in fact the equivalent of religious instruction itself."

The Court concluded that the school had engaged in impermissible viewpoint discrimination. It pointed out that the Good News Club sought "to address a subject otherwise permitted under [the school's rules], the teaching of morals and character, from a religious standpoint." The Court rejected the position that "something that is 'quintessentially religious' or 'decidedly religious in nature' cannot also be characterized properly as the teaching of morals and character development from a particular viewpoint." The Court elaborated: "What matters for purposes of the Free Speech Clause is that we can see no logical difference in kind between the invocation of Christianity by the Club and the invocation of teamwork, loyalty, or patriotism by other associations to provide a foundation for their lessons."

The school insisted that its decision to exclude the Club was required by the First Amendment's nonestablishment of religion clause. The court disagreed, based on the following four considerations:

(1) "In distinguishing between indoctrination that is attributable to the state and indoctrination that is not, [this court has] consistently turned to the principle of neutrality, upholding aid that is offered to a broad range of groups or persons without regard to their religion." The Good News Club "seeks nothing more than to be treated neutrally and given access to speak about the same topics as are other groups."

(2) The "community" would feel no coercive pressure to engage in the Club's activities, since the relevant community would be the parents, not the elementary school children. It is the parents who choose whether their children will attend the Good News Club meetings. Because the children cannot attend without their parents' permission, they cannot be coerced into engaging in the Good News Club's religious activities.

---

[74]   Good News Club v. Milford Central School, 533 U.S. 98 (2001).

The Supreme Court's Good News Club Case[74]

(3) "[W]e have never extended our establishment clause jurisprudence to fore-close private religious conduct during nonschool hours merely because it takes place on school premises where elementary school children may be present."

(4) Allowing the Good News Club to meet would not create a misperception by schoolchildren that the school is endorsing religion. "There is no evidence that young children are permitted to loiter outside classrooms after the schoolday has ended. Surely even young children are aware of events for which their parents must sign permission forms. The meetings were held in a combined high school resource room and middle school special education room, not in an elementary school classroom. The instructors are not schoolteachers. And the children in the group are not all the same age as in the normal classroom setting; their ages range from 6 to 12. In sum, these circumstances simply do not support the theory that small children would perceive endorsement here."

(5) "[E]ven if we were to inquire into the minds of schoolchildren in this case, we cannot say the danger that children would misperceive the endorsement of religion is any greater than the danger that they would perceive a hostility toward the religious viewpoint if the Club were excluded from the public forum. . . . We cannot operate . . . under the assumption that any risk that small children would perceive endorsement should counsel in favor of excluding the Club's religious activity. We decline to employ establishment clause jurisprudence using a modified heckler's veto, in which a group's religious activity can be proscribed on the basis of what the youngest members of the audience might misperceive."

Use of Public School Property by Students for Religious Purposes § 14-07

Key point 14-07. *Public school property may be used during noninstructional hours by students for religious purposes if noncurriculum-related student groups are permitted to use school property during noninstructional hours.*

Resource. **In 1998, the federal government issued to every public school in America a document entitled "Religious Expression in Public Schools." This document was designed to inform public school administrators of the religious rights enjoyed by public school students while at school.**

In 1990, the Supreme Court upheld the constitutionality of the "Equal Access Act," which prohibits public high schools from denying any group access during noninstructional hours to school facilities if the same right is given to any noncurriculum related student groups.[75] The Equal Access Act provides:

---

[75] Board of Education v. Mergens, 496 U.S. 226 (1990). The *Mergens* case also is discussed in section 12-12, *supra. See also* Van Schoick v. Saddleback Valley Unified School District, 104 Cal. Rptr.2d 562 (Cal. App. 2001).

It shall be unlawful for any public secondary school which receives federal financial assistance and which has a *limited open forum* to deny equal access or a fair opportunity to, or discriminate against, any students who wish to conduct a meeting within that limited open forum on the basis of the religious, political, philosophical, or other content of the speech at such meetings.[76]

A "limited open forum" exists whenever a public high school "grants an offering to or opportunity for one or more *noncurriculum related student groups* to meet on school premises during noninstructional time." A school is deemed to offer a *fair opportunity* to students wishing to conduct a meeting on school premises during noninstructional hours if it uniformly provides that (1) the meeting is voluntary and student-initiated; (2) there is no sponsorship of the meeting by the school; (3) employees or agents of the school are present at religious meetings only in a nonparticipatory capacity; (4) the meeting does not materially interfere with the orderly conduct of educational activities within the school; and (5) nonschool persons may not direct, conduct, control, or regularly attend activities of student groups.[77] However, the assignment of a teacher, administrator, or other school employee to a meeting for custodial purposes does not constitute impermissible sponsorship. The term *noninstructional time* refers to time set aside by the school before actual classroom instruction begins or after actual classroom instruction ends.

The Supreme Court began its opinion by noting that the critical question is whether or not a public high school permits "noncurriculum related" student groups to use school facilities during noninstructional hours. If it does, then the school has created a "limited open forum," and the Equal Access Act prevents school officials from denying any other student group access to school facilities during noninstructional hours on the basis of the content of its speech. The Court concluded:

> [W]e think that the term "noncurriculum related student group" is best interpreted broadly to mean any student group that does not *directly* relate to the body of courses offered by the school. In our view, a student group directly relates to a school's curriculum if the subject matter of the group is actually taught, or will soon be taught, in a regularly offered course; if the subject matter of the group concerns the body of courses as a whole; if participation in the group is required for a particular course; or if participation in the group results in academic credit. We think this limited definition of groups that directly relate to the curriculum is a common sense interpretation of the Act that is consistent with Congress' intent . . . . For example, a French club would directly relate to the curriculum if a school taught French in a regularly offered course or planned to teach the subject in the near future. A school's student government would generally relate

---

[76] 20 U.S.C. §§ 4071-4074.

[77] 20 U.S.C. § 4071(c).

directly to the curriculum to the extent that it addresses concerns, solicits opinions, and formulates proposals pertaining to the body of courses offered by the school. If participation in a school's band or orchestra were required for the band or orchestra classes, or resulted in academic credit, then those groups would also directly relate to the curriculum. The existence of such groups at a school would not trigger the Act's obligations.

On the other hand, unless a school could show that groups such as a chess club, a stamp collecting club, or a community service club fell within our description of groups that directly relate to the curriculum, such groups would be "noncurriculum related student groups" for purposes of the Act. The existence of such groups would create a "limited open forum" under the Act and would prohibit the school from denying equal access to any other student group on the basis of the content of that group's speech. Whether a specific student group is a "noncurriculum related student group" will therefore depend on a particular school's curriculum, but such determinations would be subject to factual findings well within the competence of trial courts to make.

Public high school officials in the *Mergens* case had attempted to bar religious groups by claiming that the school had not created a limited open forum since all non-religious groups were curriculum related. To illustrate, the school contended that all of its 30 non-religious student groups were curriculum related because they furthered the general educational goals of the school. The student government club "advances the goals of the school's political science classes," the scuba club "furthers the essential goals of the physical education department," the chess club "supplements math and science courses," and the junior Rotarians "promote effective citizenship—a critical goal of the social sciences department." The Court rejected this analysis, noting that

> [a]llowing such a broad interpretation of "curriculum related" would make the [Act] meaningless. A school's administration could simply declare that it maintains a closed forum and choose which student clubs it wanted to allow by tying the purpose of those clubs to some broadly defined educational goal. At the same time the administration could arbitrarily deny access to school facilities to any unfavored student club on the basis of its speech content. This is exactly the result that Congress sought to prohibit by enacting the [Act]. A public secondary school cannot simply declare that it maintains a closed forum and then discriminate against a particular student group on the basis of the content of the speech of that group.[78]

The Court concluded that the school had a number of noncurriculum related student groups under the test that it announced. Examples cited by the Court included the scuba club and chess club. It did not evaluate any other clubs, but

---

[78] *Id.* at 2369, quoting with approval from the appeals court's decision, at 867 F.2d 1076, 1078 (8th Cir. 1989).

hinted that a number of the other groups also would be noncurriculum related. Because the school clearly allowed one or more noncurriculum related student groups to meet during noninstructional hours, it had created a limited open forum and could not discriminate against students wanting to meet for religious purposes.

The Court acknowledged that a school wishing to avoid the obligations of the Equal Access Act could do so by "structuring its course offerings and existing student groups to avoid the Act's obligations." In other words, a school could eliminate all student groups that are not directly related to courses offered at the school. A school that took such action would avoid creating a limited open forum, and accordingly it would have no legal obligation to permit student religious groups to meet. The Court refused to decide whether student groups have a constitutionally protected right to meet on public high school property.

The Act does *not* apply to student groups that meet *during* regular classroom hours. It only applies to schools that permit student groups to meet before or after regular classroom hours.

The Court rejected the school's argument that the Equal Access Act violated the First Amendment's nonestablishment of religion clause. The Court applied its 20-year-old "three-part test" for evaluating the constitutionality of a law challenged under the nonestablishment of religion clause—(1) does it have a clearly secular purpose, (2) does it have a primary effect that neither advances nor inhibits religion, and (3) does it avoid an "excessive entanglement" between church and state? All three of these tests must be satisfied for a challenged law to be constitutional. The Court concluded that all three tests were met—the Act had a "secular purpose" of demonstrating neutrality rather than hostility toward religion, and it did not create an excessive entanglement between church and state. The second test—the primary effect of the law does not advance religion— was the most difficult to answer, but the Court unequivocally ruled that this test was satisfied as well. The school had argued that the Act failed this test since it required public schools to "endorse" religious clubs and provide them with an official platform to proselytize other students. The Court rejected this claim, noting that the message of the Act "is one of neutrality rather than endorsement . . . the [Constitution] does not license government to treat religion and those who teach or practice it . . . as subversive of American ideals and therefore subject to unique disabilities." Further, the Court observed that

> there is a crucial difference between *government* speech endorsing religion, which the establishment clause forbids, and *private* speech endorsing religion, which the free speech and free exercise [of religion] clause protect. We think that secondary school students are mature enough and are likely to understand that a school does not endorse or support student speech that it merely permits on a nondiscriminatory basis. . . . [S]chools do not endorse everything they fail to censor.[79]

---

[79] *Id.* at 2372.

The Supreme Court has recognized the right of students to meet for religious purposes on public university property if the same privilege is granted to non-religious student groups. In 1981, the Court struck down a policy of the University of Missouri at Kansas City that made university facilities available generally to all student groups except those wanting to meet for religious worship and religious teaching.[80] The Court stressed that if a university regulation excludes any group from meeting solely on the basis of the content of the group's speech, the university must show that the regulation is necessary to serve a compelling state interest and that it is narrowly drawn to achieve that end. In rejecting the university's claim that the maintenance of a strict separation of church and state constituted a sufficiently "compelling" interest to justify the abridgment of religious expression, the Court observed:

> Our cases have required the most exacting scrutiny in cases in which a State undertakes to regulate speech on the basis of content. On the other hand, the State interest asserted here—in achieving greater separation than is already ensured under the establishment clause of the Federal Constitution—is limited by the free exercise clause and in this case by the free speech clause as well. In this constitutional context, we are unable to recognize the State's interest as sufficiently "compelling" to justify the content-based discrimination against students' religious speech.[81]

The Court emphasized that a university can impose reasonable regulations affecting the time and place of group meetings, and can exclude any group that violates reasonable campus rules or substantially interferes with the opportunity of other students to obtain an education. It also held that if a school does not make its facilities available to any student group, it is not required to make them available to religious groups.

Similarly, the Supreme Court of Delaware invalidated an absolute ban by the University of Delaware on all religious activities in school buildings.[82] The university's ban barred Christian students from meeting periodically in the "commons" rooms of campus dormitories for religious worship. The Court concluded that

> the University cannot support its absolute ban of all religious worship on the theory that, without such a ban, University policy allowing all student groups, including religious groups, free access to dormitory common areas would necessarily violate the establishment clause. The establishment cases decided by the United States Supreme Court indicate that neutrality is the safe harbor in which to avoid First Amendment violation: neutral "accommodation" of religion is permitted, while "promotion" and

---

[80] Widmar v. Vincent, 454 U.S. 263 (1981). *See also* Clergy and Laity Concerned v. Chicago Board of Education, 586 F. Supp. 1408 (N.D. Ill. 1984).

[81] *Id.* at 277 (citations omitted).

[82] Keegan v. University of Delaware, 349 A.2d 18 (Del. 1975).

"advancement" of religion are not. University policy without the worship ban could be neutral toward religion and could have the primary effect of advancing education by allowing students to meet together in the commons rooms of their dormitory to exchange ideas and share mutual interests. If any religious group or religion is accommodated or benefited thereby, such accommodation or benefit is purely incidental, and would not, in our judgment, violate the establishment clause.[83]

The court distinguished decisions prohibiting religious exercise by public primary and secondary school students on the ground that such decisions did not, like the present case, involve "activity by adult residents of a living complex in common areas generally set aside for the benefit of such residents."[84]

Examples

• A federal appeals court ruled that a public school district violated the constitutional rights of a Christian student group by denying it access to school property after school hours while permitting a secular organization with similar purposes to meet on school property.[85] A public school district adopted a policy prohibiting any group to meet on school premises between 3:00 and 6:00 p.m. other than Scouts and athletic groups. A Christian student group sued the school district claiming that this policy violated the First Amendment guaranty of free speech. The Christian group was organized to foster the moral development of school students from a Christian perspective. Its activities include singing, skits, Bible reading, prayer, and speeches by community role models. The Christian group claimed that both it and the Scouts had the same purpose of fostering the moral development of youth, and that the school district could not deny it access to school property solely on the basis of the religious content of its speech. A federal appeals court ruled in favor of the Christian group. The court began its opinion by referring to a Supreme Court decision holding that a public school district could not deny a Christian group access to school property to show a family film series solely on the basis of the religious perspective of the films, when the same property was available to secular groups to address similar issues from a secular perspective. The Supreme Court concluded that "the government violates the First Amendment when it denies access to a speaker solely to suppress the point of view he espouses on an otherwise includable subject. The film involved here no doubt dealt with a subject otherwise permissible under [the school district's regulations], and its exhibition was denied solely because the film dealt with the subject from a religious standpoint. The principle that has emerged from our cases "is that the First Amendment forbids the government to regulate speech in ways that favor some viewpoints or ideas at the expense of others."[86] The appeals court concluded that this principle required the school district in this case to permit the Christian group to meet. It noted that the school made its facilities available to the Scouts to promote the moral development of youth from a secular perspective, and accordingly it could not deny a Christian group the same privilege solely on the basis of the religious content of its speech. Any other

---

[83] *Id.* at 16 (citations omitted).

[84] *Id.* at 18.

[85] Good News/Good Sports Club v. School District, 28 F.3d 1501 (8th Cir. 1994).

[86] Lamb's Chapel v. Center Moriches Union Free School District, 113 S. Ct. 2141 (1993).

result would permit the school district to prefer some viewpoints on the same subject matter over others, and this is precisely what is prohibited by the First Amendment's guaranty of free speech. In summary, when a public school (or other public entity) creates a "non-public forum" by opening its property to only some groups to address a limited range of issues, it cannot prohibit other groups from using the same property to address similar issues solely on the basis of the religious content of their speech. The court rejected the school district's argument that banning religious groups served a compelling and legitimate governmental interest of avoiding any violation of the First Amendment's prohibition of the establishment of religion.

• A federal appeals court ruled that a public high school that allowed several student groups to meet on school premises during the lunch period could not deny the same opportunity to a student group that wanted to meet for religious purposes.[87] All students at the school had the same lunch period each day, and so no classes were conducted during the lunch period. School officials permitted several student groups to meet during the lunch period, including a surfing club, conservation club, and various ethnic organizations. A student asked a school official for permission to organize a religious club that would meet during the lunch period in an empty classroom. Permission was denied by school officials who insisted that the Equal Access Act did not apply since the lunch period was not "noninstructional time." The student sued the school, and a federal appeals court ruled in favor of the student. The court concluded that a lunch period is "noninstructional time" since the school had "set aside" the lunch period after morning classes ended and before afternoon classes began. The court noted that the United States Supreme Court had ruled that the Equal Access Act reflected a "broad legislative purpose" and must be given a "broad meaning." The court cautioned that the religious club's right to meet "is defined by the extent to which other groups were permitted to meet." It continued, "Our decision today does not necessarily preclude school districts from disallowing religious groups from using school premises for meetings during lunch periods. The Act is about equal access. If a school district wanted to prohibit religious groups from meeting during lunch, the school need only make its prohibition neutral, so that all noncurriculum-related groups are barred from meeting at lunch." The court summarily rejected the school's claim that the First Amendment's nonestablishment of religion clause prohibited public school property from being used for religious purposes. It noted that the Supreme Court rejected this argument in a 1990 ruling.

Sunday Closing Laws   § 14-08

Key point 14-08. *Local ordinances requiring some or all businesses to be closed on Sundays do not violate the First Amendment's nonestablishment of religion clause.*

The Supreme Court has upheld the validity of Sunday closing laws against the claim that they constitute the establishment of the Christian religion.[88] The Court has observed:

---

87 Ceniceros v. Board of Trustees, 106 F.3d 878 (9th Cir. 1997).

88 Braunfeld v. Brown, 366 U.S. 599 (1961); McGowan v. Maryland, 366 U.S. 420 (1961).

[T]he "establishment" clause does not ban federal or state regulation of conduct whose reason or effect merely happens to coincide or harmonize with the tenets of some or all religions. . . . Sunday is a day apart from all others. The cause is irrelevant; the fact exists. It would seem unrealistic for enforcement purposes and perhaps detrimental to the general welfare to require a State to choose a common day of rest other than that which most persons would select of their own accord.[89]

Numerous state and lower federal court rulings have upheld the validity of Sunday closing laws against the contentions that such laws (1) are unconstitutionally vague and uncertain in describing the activities that are either forbidden or allowed,[90] (2) unconstitutionally discriminate against religions that do not observe a Sunday sabbath,[91] (3) "establish" a religion,[92] (4) constitute an impermissible exercise of the police power,[93] (5) arbitrarily discriminate between those commodities that may be sold and those that may not,[94] (6) deny the equal protection of the laws,[95] (7) violate merchants' constitutional right of "commercial speech,"[96] and (8) are invalid due to lax and inconsistent enforcement.[97]

The Virginia Supreme Court ruled that a state Sunday closing law violated the Virginia Constitution's prohibition against "special laws."[98] Virginia enacted its first Sunday closing law in 1610. During the colonial period, this law had a religious purpose, requiring every person "to repair in the morning to the divine service." During the Revolutionary War, in 1779, a Sunday closing law was substituted that had an entirely "secular" purpose—to "prevent the physical and moral debasement which comes from uninterrupted labor." The 1779 law survived until 1960, when the state legislature enacted a new law. In 1974, the legislature completely rewrote the Sunday closing law. The 1974 law generally prohibited commercial establishments to do business on Sunday, but exempted more than 60 "industries and businesses" from the prohibition, and permitted

---

[89] McGown v. Maryland, 366 U.S. 420, 442, 452 (1961).

[90] *See, e.g.*, Mack Paramus Co. v. Borough of Paramus, 549 A.2d 474 (N.J. Super. 1988); Hechinger Co. v. State's Attorney, 326 A.2d 742 (Md. 1974); Voronado, Inc. v. Hyland, 390 A.2d 606 (N.J. 1978), *appeal dismissed*, 439 U.S. 1123 (1978); Charles Stores Co. v. Tucker 140 S.E.2d 370 (N.C. 1965).

[91] *See, e.g.*, Mack Paramus Co. v. Borough of Paramus, 549 A.2d 474 (N.J. Super. 1988); Raleigh Mobile home Sales, Inc. v. Tomlinson, 174 S.E.2d 542 (N.C. 1970); State v. Giant of St. Albans, Inc., 268 A.2d 739 (Vt. 1970).

[92] *See, e.g.*, Discount Records, Inc. v. City of North Little Rock, 671 F.2d 1220 (8th Cir. 1982); Epstein v. Maddox, 277 F. Supp. 613 (N.D. Ga. 1967), *aff'd*, 401 F.2d 777 (1967); Mandel v. Hodges, 127 Cal. Rptr. 244 (Cal. 1976); People v. Acme Markets, Inc., 372 N.Y.S.2d 590 (1975).

[93] *See, e.g.*, Lockwood v. State, 462 S.W.2d 465 (Ark.1971); State v. Underwood, 195 S.E. 2d 489 (N.C. 1973).

[94] *See, e.g.*, Zayre v. City of Atlanta, 276 F. Supp. 892 (N.D. Ga. 1967); Genesco, Inc. v. J. C. Penney Co., Inc., 313 So.2d 20 (Miss. 1975); State v. K Mart, 359 A.2d 492 (N.J. 1976).

[95] *See, e.g.*, Hames Mobile Homes, Inc. v. Sellers, 343 F. Supp. 12 (N.D. Iowa 1972); Southway Discount Center, Inc. v. Moore, 315 F. Supp. 617 (N.D. Ala. 1970); Supermarkets General Corp. v. State, 409 A.2d 250 (Md. 1979).

[96] *See, e.g.*, Mack Paramus Co. v. Borough of Paramus, 549 A.2d 474 (N.J. Super. 1988).

[97] *Id.*

[98] Benderson Development Co. v. Sciortino, 372 S.E.2d 751 (Va. 1988).

cities and counties to exempt themselves entirely from the law by a referendum vote. These exemptions left only about 20 percent of the Virginia workers subject to the law.

Under these facts, the state supreme court concluded that the 1974 law violated a provision in the Virginia Constitution prohibiting "special laws" exempting private companies from the reach of any general law unless the exemption bore "a reasonable and substantial relation to the object sought to be accomplished by the legislation." The court noted that the purpose of the law was to provide the people of Virginia with a common day of rest, and concluded that the exemption of 80 percent of the businesses and employees in the state from the reach of the Sunday closing law clearly indicated that the many exemptions did not bear a reasonable relationship to the object sought to be accomplished by the law. Accordingly, the law violated the ban on special legislation.

The court further held that the Virginia law did not violate the United States Constitution's guaranty of the "equal protection of the laws," since such a standard was more easily satisfied than the state constitution's "special laws" provision. Accordingly, other states will not be able to rely on the Virginia court's decision unless their state constitutions contain a similar ban on special legislation.

In a related matter, one court has held that the establishment clause was violated by an order of the governor of California granting state employees paid time off on Good Friday,[99] although the same court a year later approved the validity of a Good Friday holiday for public school employees.[100] Another court, in upholding the constitutionality of a Hawaii law declaring Good Friday to be a legal holiday, observed:

> [T]he primary purpose of the statute which establishes Good Friday as a legal holiday was to increase the number and frequency of legal holidays. This purpose is clearly secular. The court also finds that the primary effect of the statute is secular. The Good Friday holiday allows the people of Hawaii to play or pray as they see fit. Even the plaintiffs concede that many more people can be found in Hawaii's parks and shopping malls on Good Friday than can be found in its churches. Moreover, this court's finding that Good Friday is similar in nature to Thanksgiving and Christmas provides additional ground for insulating the Good Friday holiday from a successful constitutional challenge. Just as Christmas and Thanksgiving are permissible because of their partially secular observations and because they provide a uniform day of rest and relaxation for Americans, Good Friday has attained a secular position in this nation's traditional fabric and provides citizens of Hawaii with a uniform day of rest.[101]

One court struck down a state law prohibiting the sale of alcoholic liquor

---

[99] Mandel v. Hodges, 127 Cal. Rptr. 244 (1976).

[100] California School Employees Association v. Sequoia Union High School District, 136 Cal. Rptr. 594 (1977).

[101] Cammack v. Waihee, 673 F. Supp. 1524, 1539-40 (D. Hawaii 1987).

on Good Friday on the ground that the law constituted an impermissible establishment of a religion.[102]

The Right to Refuse Medical Treatment

§ 14-09

Key point 14-09. *Competent adults have the right to refuse medical treatment on the basis of their religious beliefs, including potentially life-saving treatment. However, they do not have the right to withhold life-saving medical treatment from their minor children.*

Several courts have dealt with the right of an individual to refuse medical treatment on religious grounds. Such cases often involve treatment that is apparently necessary to save the diseased or injured person's life. In a majority of cases, courts have upheld the right of an adult to refuse potentially life-saving medical treatment on religious grounds, unless the individual is (1) mentally incompetent, (2) the parent and sole provider of young children, or (3) a pregnant woman. The majority rule was well-summarized by a New York court:

> As a general rule, every human being of adult years and sound mind has a right to determine what shall be done with his own body and cannot be subjected to medical treatment without his consent. Specifically, where there is no compelling state interest which justifies overriding an adult patient's decision not to receive blood transfusions because of religious beliefs, such transfusions should not be ordered. Such an order would constitute a violation of the First Amendment's freedom of exercise clause.
>
> However, judicial power to order compulsory medical treatment over an adult patient's objection exists in some situations. It may be the duty of the court to assume the responsibility of guardianship for a patient who is not compos mentis [mentally competent] to the extent of authorizing treatment necessary to save his life even though the medical treatment authorized may be contrary to the patient's religious beliefs. Furthermore, the state's interest, as parens patriae [i.e., protector of its citizens] in the welfare of children may justify compulsory medical care where necessary to save the life of the mother of young children or of a pregnant woman.[103]

Such cases generally involve Jehovah's Witnesses who refuse potentially life-saving blood transfusions, Christian Scientists who refuse any form of medical care, or fundamentalist Christians who rely solely on faith healing. The result

---

[102] Griswold Inn, Inc. v. State, 441 A.2d 16 (Conn. 1981).

[103] In re Melidio, 390 N.Y.S.2d 523, 524 (1976). *Accord* Holmes v. Silver Cross Hospital, 340 F. Supp. 125 (N.D. Ill. 1972); Montgomery v. Board of Retirement, 109 Cal. Rptr. 181 (1973); In re Osborne, 294 A.2d 372 (D.C. App. 1972); People v. Duncan, 205 N.E.2d 443 (Ill. 1965).

generally is the same in all three cases: the courts will honor the individual's desire to refuse medical treatment so long as he or she is mentally competent, even if such a decision will result in what otherwise would have been a preventable death. As the Ohio Supreme Court observed in a case involving a fundamentalist Christian's refusal to receive life-saving medical treatment on the basis of his reliance on prayer, "the state may not compel a legally competent adult to submit to medical treatment which would violate that individual's religious beliefs even though the treatment is arguably life-extending." This is so no matter how "unwise, foolish, or ridiculous" those beliefs may seem to others.[104]

While some courts have limited a competent adult's right to refuse potentially life-saving medical treatment when the individual is a parent of minor children, other courts have rejected such a limitation.

Example

• The Florida Supreme Court ruled that a civil court could not force a mother to receive a life-saving blood transfusion against her will and contrary to her religious beliefs.[105] The woman entered a public hospital suffering from "dysfunctional uterine bleeding," and was informed by doctors that she would die if she did not receive a blood transfusion. The woman, a practicing Jehovah's Witness and mother of two minor children, refused the transfusion on the ground that it would violate her religious beliefs (she was competent at the time of her decision). The hospital asked a civil court to force the woman to undergo a blood transfusion. The court granted the hospital's request and ordered the woman to undergo a transfusion (she was by then unconscious) on the ground that "minor children have a right to be reared by two loving parents, a right which overrides the mother's right of free exercise [of religion] and privacy." Upon regaining consciousness, the woman appealed the court's order to a state appeals court, which ruled in favor of the woman. The hospital appealed the case to the state supreme court, which also ruled in favor of the woman. The court cited four factors to consider in deciding whether or not a patient's constitutional right to religious freedom outweighs the state's interest in requiring potentially life-saving medical treatment: "(1) preservation of life, (2) protection of innocent third parties, (3) prevention of suicide, and (4) maintenance of the ethical integrity of the medical profession." The court disagreed with the hospital's claim that the state's interest in maintaining a home with two parents for minor children outweighed any constitutional right of the mother to terminate her life by refusing medical treatment. It concluded, "[This case involves] a delicate balancing analysis in which the courts weigh, on the one hand, the patient's constitutional right of privacy and right to practice one's religion, as against certain basic societal interests. Obviously, there are no preordained answers to such problematic questions and the results reached in these cases are highly debatable. Running through all of these decisions, however, is the courts' deeply imbedded belief, rooted in our constitutional traditions, that an individual has a fundamental right to be left alone so that he is free to lead his private life according to his own beliefs free from unreasonable governmental interference. Surely nothing, in the last analysis, is more private or more sacred than one's religion or view of life, and here the courts, quite properly, have given great deference to the individual's right to make decisions vitally affecting his private life according to his own conscience. It is difficult to overstate this right because it is, without exaggeration, the very bedrock on which this country was founded."

---

[104] In re Milton, 505 N.E.2d 255 (Ohio 1987).

[105] Public Health Trust v. Wons, 541 So.2d 96 (Fla. 1989). *See also* In re Dubreuil, 603 So.2d 538 (Fla. App.1992).

The courts have consistently held that life-saving medical treatment can be administered to a minor child despite his or her parents' refusal to consent to such treatment on religious grounds, unless the treatment itself poses a significant danger to the child. One court observed:

[P]arents . . . have a perfect right to worship as they please and believe what they please. They enjoy complete freedom of religion. The parents also have the right to use all lawful means to vindicate this right. . . . But this right of theirs ends where somebody else's right begins. Their child is a human being in his own right with a soul and body of his own. He has rights of his own—the right to live and grow up and live without disfigurement. The child is a citizen of the State. While he "belongs" to his parents, he belongs also to his State. Their rights in him entail many duties. Likewise, the fact the child belongs to the State imposes upon the State many duties. Chief among them is the duty to protect his right to live and to grow up with a sound mind in a sound body . . . . When a religious doctrine espoused by the parents threatens to defeat or curtail such a right of their child, the State's duty to step in and preserve the child's right is immediately operative.[106]

Another court has observed that "it does not follow that parents who wish to be martyrs for their religious beliefs have a right to impose such martyrdom upon their offspring . . . ."[107] When a minor child's life is not in danger, some courts have permitted the child's parents to refuse consent to medical treatment on religious grounds. The Supreme Court of Pennsylvania has held, "We are of the opinion that as between a parent and the state, the state does not have an interest of sufficient magnitude outweighing a parent's religious beliefs when the child's life is *not immediately imperiled* by his physical condition."[108] Other courts have reached the opposite conclusion.[109]

Example

• *The Massachusetts Supreme Judicial Court ordered an 8-year-old girl suffering from leukemia to receive blood transfusions despite her parents' claim that such procedures violated their religious beliefs.[110] The parents were Jehovah's Witnesses, a religion that prohibits blood transfusions. The court observed, "The state has three interests in having a dangerously sick child receive medical treatment over her parents' religious objections. First, the state has an interest in protecting the welfare of children within its borders. Second, the state has an interest in the preservation of life, especially*

---

[106] In re Clark, 185 N.E.2d 128, 132 (Ill. 1962). *Accord* In re Karwath, 199 N.W.2d 147 (Iowa 1972); Muhlenberg Hospital v. Patterson, 320 A.2d 518 (N.J. 1974); In re Sampson, 317 N.Y.S.2d 641 (1970); Matter of Hamilton, 657 S.W.2d 425 (Tenn. App. 1983) ("[w]here a child is dying with cancer and experiencing pain which will surely become more excruciating as the disease progresses . . . we believe is one of those times when humane considerations and life-saving attempts outweigh unlimited practices of religious belief").

[107] Muhlenberg Hospital v. Patterson, 320 A.2d 518, 521 (N.J. 1974).

[108] In re Green, 292 A.2d 387, 392 (Pa. 1972).

[109] *See, e.g.,* In re Sampson, 317 N.Y.S.2d 641 (1970).

[110] Matter of McCauley, 565 N.E.2d 411 (Mass. 1991).

when the affliction is curable. Finally, the medical profession is trained to preserve life, and to care for those under its control. The state has an interest in maintaining the ethical integrity of the medical profession." These interests outweighed the parents' religious rights, concluded the court.

Some parents have been prosecuted for manslaughter (or other crimes) when their minor child dies because the parents refused life-saving medical treatment and relied exclusively on divine healing.

Examples

• *The California Supreme Court ruled that a mother could be prosecuted for manslaughter when her child died of meningitis after being treated by prayer instead of medical therapy.*[111] *The victim was a 4-year-old girl who fell ill with flu-like symptoms and a stiff neck. Consistent with the tenets of her religion, the child's mother chose to treat the illness with prayer rather than medical care. Members of the mother's church prayed with the child on two occasions. Nevertheless, the child lost weight, grew disoriented and irritable, and her breathing became heavy and irregular. She died of acute meningitis 17 days after her symptoms first appeared. The child's mother was charged with involuntary manslaughter, and she moved to dismiss the prosecution on the ground that her conduct was protected by law. Specifically, the mother argued that involuntary manslaughter is defined as the unlawful killing of a human being without malice "in the commission of an unlawful act . . . or without due caution or circumspection," and that her child had not died "in the commission of an unlawful act." She pointed out that the only "unlawful act" for which she could have been charged was the criminal neglect of a child, and that California law exempted "treatment by spiritual means through prayer alone" from the definition of criminal neglect. The state supreme court rejected the mother's arguments, concluding that she could be prosecuted for involuntary manslaughter. The court reasoned that the exemption of "treatment by spiritual means by prayer alone" from the definition of criminal neglect did not necessarily exempt such treatment from the crime of manslaughter. The court also rejected the mother's claim that her actions were protected by the constitutional guaranty of religious freedom. It observed that the mother's constitutional rights were outweighed by a "compelling state interest" of "unparalleled significance"—the protection of children. It further noted that "parents may be free to become martyrs themselves . . . but it does not follow that they are free . . . to make martyrs of their children."*

• *A parent was prosecuted for manslaughter when his 5-week-old daughter died from bronchial pneumonia. The parent lived with his wife and 9 children in a small cabin in the mountains. He had been on a "walk of faith," which he described as a total reliance on God for all needs and for healing in times of illness or injury. One of the tenets of his church was healing of the sick through prayer. When the baby developed cold symptoms, her parents and another church member anointed the baby with oil, laid their hands on her head, and prayed for her healing. The next day, the baby's symptoms worsened. Because the mother was exhausted from caring for several sick children, and because the family's wood-burning stove seemed to aggravate the baby's condition, the baby was moved to a neighbor's home. The neighbor (who was a nurse) informed the parents that*

---

[111] Walker v. Superior Court, 253 Cal. Rptr. 1 (Cal. 1988). *Accord* People in Interest of D.L.E., 645 P.2d 271 (Colo. 1982).

the baby might be suffering from pneumonia, and she urged them to take the baby to a hospital at once. The father declined, stating that "we can't, this is our walk and this is our life." The next morning, the baby seemed better. Later in the day, however, the symptoms worsened again, and the baby died that evening. An autopsy revealed that the baby had died from "acute necrotizing bronchial pneumonia." The father was later prosecuted for child abuse resulting in death. At the trial, a pediatrician testified that the baby would have survived had she received proper medical care. The father was convicted, and he was sentenced to 6 years of probation. On appeal, the Colorado Supreme Court reversed the father's conviction on the basis of a technicality, and sent the case back to the trial court for another trial.[112] The court noted that state law provided a defense to child abuse in cases of "treatment by spiritual means," and that the trial court had improperly let the jury decide if this defense were available rather than compelling the prosecutor to establish the crime, and the unavailability of the "treatment by spiritual means" defense, with evidence "beyond a reasonable doubt." The court cautioned that the "treatment by spiritual means" defense to child abuse was not available under state law when a child is suffering from a condition that would create a danger to the child's life if left untreated.

• A Pennsylvania court upheld the criminal convictions of two parents for criminal neglect of their 2-year-old son because of their reliance on prayer and divine healing rather than medical care for a life-threatening medical condition. The parents insisted that they did not commit criminal neglect. To the contrary, they prayed for their son and had him anointed. The court rejected the parents' defense. It observed: "Regardless of the label attached to their course of conduct, their failure to seek medical care constituted a breach of their duties as parents. The law imposes an affirmative duty on parents to seek medical help when the life of a child is threatened, regardless, and in fact despite, their religious beliefs. . . . Every parent . . . has a duty of care to their child, at the very least, to avert the child's untimely death. . . . The validity and sincerity of the religious beliefs of [the parents] were not relevant to the issues presented. They had no choice but to seek help, despite their religious beliefs, when they were faced with a condition which threatened their child's life."[113]

• A Washington state appeals court upheld the first degree manslaughter conviction of a parent who unsuccessfully relied on prayer for the healing of his minor child.[114] The victim's parents were members of a religious group that believed that the medical establishment was "wicked" and that members should rely exclusively upon prayer for healing the sick. A 10-year-old boy whose parents were members of the group began losing weight and exhibiting other abnormal symptoms. A church "elder" determined that the boy's illness was a result of sin, and he ordered the boy to be severely spanked. Following an hour-long session of "ministering" (which consisted of intense interrogation and spanking), the boy's condition continued to worsen. The father continued slapping and spanking the child, and consulting with the elder for guidance. The elder assured the father that the boy would be alright. The boy died the next morning. He was completely emaciated and weighed only 46 pounds. It was determined that he died of untreated juvenile diabetes that had been aggravated by his frequent beatings. The boy's father was prosecuted, and convicted, of first

---

[112] Lybarger v. People, 807 P.2d 570 (Colo. 1991).

[113] Commonwealth v. Foster, 764 A.2d 1076 (Pa. App. 2000).

[114] State v. Norman, 808 P.2d 1159 (Wash. App. 1991).

degree manslaughter. The father appealed, claiming that his conviction violated his constitutional right to religious freedom. A state appeals court rejected the father's claim and upheld his conviction. The court observed, "[The father] was free under the Washington State Constitution to believe [his son] could be healed through prayer. He was not free to act on that belief in a manner jeopardizing the health of his child. We find no constitutional violation."

Another court found a mother guilty of neglect who believed that healing of her son's arthritic knee condition was possible only through prayer.[115]

Definition of "Religion" and "Religious" § 14-10

Key point 14-10. *The courts have defined the terms "religion" and "religious" broadly.*

Occasionally it is important to know how the courts have defined the term *religion*. The First Amendment expressly prohibits the "establishment of religion" and protects its free exercise; the Civil Rights Act of 1964 prohibits discrimination by employers on the basis of an employee's religion; the Internal Revenue Code and several state tax laws exempt certain religious organizations from taxation; and many other federal, state, and local laws and regulations use the term.

The term *religion* is not easily defined.[116] Early court decisions generally limited the term to belief in God. For example, in 1890, the Supreme Court observed that the term *religion* "has reference to one's views of his relations to his Creator, and to the obligations they impose on reverence for his being and character, and of obedience to his will."[117] This view was articulated by numerous lower federal courts and state courts.[118]

The courts eventually interpreted the term *religion* much more broadly. In an early decision expressing the modern view, a prominent judge observed:

Religious belief arises from a sense of inadequacy of reason as a means of relating the individual to his fellow-men and to his universe. . . . It is a belief finding expression in a conscience which categorically requires the believer to disregard elementary self-interest and to accept martyrdom in preference to transgressing its tenets. . . . [Conscientious objection] may justly be regarded as a response of the individual to an inward mentor, call it a conscience or God, that is for many persons at the present time the

---

[115] Mitchell v. Davis, 205 S.W.2d 812 (Tex. App. 1947).

[116] *See generally* Boyan, *Defining Religion in Operational and Institutional Terms*, 116 U. PA. L. REV. 479 (1968); Choper, *Defining "Religion" in the First Amendment*, 1982 U. ILL. LAW REV. 579, Note, *Toward a Constitutional Definition of Religion*, 91 HARV. L. REV. 1056 (1978).

[117] Davis v. Beason, 133 U.S. 333, 342 (1890).

[118] *See, e.g.,* Borchert v. City of Ranger, 42 F. Supp. 577 (N.D. Tex. 1941); Gabrielli v. Knickerbocker, 82 P.2d 391 (Cal. App. 1938); Sunday School Board of the Southern Baptist Convention v. McCue, 293 P.2d 234 (Kan. 1956); Nicholls v. Mayor of Lynn, 7 N.E.2d 577 (Mass. 1937); Taylor v. State, 11 So.2d 663 (Miss. 1943); Kolbeck v. Kramer, 202 A.2d 889 (N.J. Super. 1964); Drozda v. Bassos, 23 N.Y.S.2d 544 (1940).

equivalent of what has always been thought a religious impulse.[119]

This broader definition was adopted by the Supreme Court in a series of rulings. In 1961, the Court observed that "religions" need not be based on a belief in the existence of God: "[N]either [a state nor the federal government] can constitutionally pass laws or impose requirements which aid all religions as against nonbelievers, and neither can aid those religions based on a belief in the existence of God as against those religions founded on different beliefs."[120] The Court added that "among religions in this country which do not teach what would generally be considered as a belief in the existence of God are Buddhism, Taoism, Ethical Culture, Secular Humanism and others."[121]

In two succeeding opinions, the Court defined the term *religion* in the context of section 6(j) of the Universal Military Training and Service Act of 1948, which exempts from combatant training and service in the armed forces persons who by reason of their religious training and belief are conscientiously opposed to participation in war in any form. The Act defines "religious training and belief" as "an individual's belief in a relation to a Supreme Being involving duties superior to those arising from any human relation, but [not including] essentially political, sociological, or philosophical views or a merely personal moral code." In *United States v. Seeger*,[122] the Court surprisingly interpreted this definition of "religious training and belief" to include a sincere and meaningful belief that "occupies a place in the life of its possessor parallel to that filled by the orthodox belief in God of one who clearly qualifies for the exemption. Where such beliefs have parallel positions in the lives of their respective holder we cannot say that one is 'in relation to a Supreme Being' and the other is not."[123]

In *Welsh v. United States*,[124] the Court equated purely moral or ethical convictions with "religious" belief:

> Most of the great religions of today and of the past have embodied the idea of a Supreme Being or a Supreme Reality—a God—who communicates to man in some way a consciousness of what is right and should be done, of what is wrong and therefore should be shunned. If an individual deeply and sincerely holds beliefs that are purely ethical or moral in source and content but that nevertheless impose upon him a duty of conscience to refrain from participating in any war at any time, those beliefs certainly occupy in the life of that individual "a place parallel to that filled by . . . God" in

---

[119] United States v. Kauten, 133 F.2d 703, 708 (2nd Cir. 1943) (Judge Augustus Hand).

[120] Torasco v. Watkins, 367 U.S. 488, 495 (1961). In *Torasco*, the Court ruled that a Maryland law requiring notaries public to take an oath professing their belief in God violated the First Amendment guaranty of freedom of religion.

[121] *Id.* at 495 n.11.

[122] 380 U.S. 163 (1965).

[123] *Id.* at 166. This remarkable interpretation of the plain meaning of the Act apparently was based on the Court's concern that any legislative preference of believers over nonbelievers would be unconstitutional. It is also interesting to note that the Court relied on the writings of several theologians in reaching its decision, including most notably Paul Tillich. P. Tillich, Dynamics of Faith 1-2 (1958).

[124] 398 U.S. 333 (1970).

traditionally religious persons. Because his beliefs function as a religion in his life, such an individual is as much entitled to a "religious" conscientious objector exemption . . . as is someone who derives his conscientious opposition to war from traditional religious convictions.[125]

Lower federal courts and state courts have applied this more liberal definition of *religion* in several cases. To illustrate, one court, in concluding that the Science of Creative Intelligence (Transcendental Meditation) is a religion, observed that "[c]oncepts concerning God or a supreme being do not shed their religiosity merely because they are presented as a philosophy or a science."[126] The court also observed that such elements as "clergy, places of worship or explicit moral code" need not be present for a practice or belief to constitute a religion.[127] The court concluded that "a belief in the existence of a pure, perfect, infinite, and unmanifest field of life" constitutes a religious belief.[128]

Similarly, other courts have found the following beliefs and practices to be religious: witchcraft;[129] pantheistic beliefs of parents upon which they based their opposition to mandatory inoculations of their children;[130] the Black Muslim faith;[131] Krishna Consciousness;[132] the Salvation Army;[133] all aspects of religious observance and practice, as well as belief, whether or not they are acceptable to others;[134] atheism;[135] Alcoholics Anonymous;[136] and the principle of supremacy of conscience.[137]

The concept of religion does have limits. The courts have concluded that the following beliefs and practices are not religious:

- a federal law that prohibits the use of federal funds for nontherapeutic abortions;[138]

- beliefs and practices that tend to mock established institutions and that are obviously shams and absurdities and whose members are patently devoid of

---

[125] *Id.* at 340.

[126] Malnak v. Yogi, 440 F. Supp. 1284, 1322 (D.N.J. 1977).

[127] *Id.* at 1326. *See also* Stevens v. Berger, 428 F. Supp. 896, 900 (E.D.N.Y. 1977) ("neither trappings of robes, nor temples of stone, nor a fixed liturgy, nor an extensive literature or history is required to meet the test of beliefs cognizable under the Constitution as religious, and one person's religious beliefs held for one day are presumptively entitled to the same protection as views of millions which have been shared for thousands of years").

[128] *Id.* at 1324.

[129] Dettmer v. Landon, 799 F.2d 929 (4th Cir. 1986).

[130] Sherr v. Northport-East Northport Union Free School District, 672 F. Supp. 81 (E.D.N.Y. 1987).

[131] Banks v. Havener, 234 F. Supp. 27 (E.D. Va. 1964).

[132] International Society for Krishna Consciousness, Inc. v. Barber, 650 F.2d 430 (2nd Cir. 1981).

[133] McClure v. Salvation Army, 460 F.2d 553 (5th Cir. 1972).

[134] Stormans, Inc. v. Selecky, 524 F.Supp.2d 1245 (W.D. Wash. 2007).

[135] Kaufman v. McCaughtry, 422 F.Supp.2d 1016 (W.D. Wis. 2006).

[136] DeStefano v. Emergency Housing Group, Inc., 247 F.3d 397 (2nd Cir. 2001).

[137] O'Brien v. City of Springfield, 319 F.Supp.2d 90 (D. Mass. 2003).

[138] Woe v. Califano, 460 F. Supp. 234 (D.C. Ohio 1978).

religious sincerity;[139]

• refusal to accept a Social Security number as a precondition to the receipt of government aid;[140]

• the use of marijuana by an individual who claimed that marijuana "was the fire with which baptisms were conducted by John the Baptist";[141]

• the consumption of marijuana by an individual who claimed that it extended and intensified his "ability to engage in meditative communication with the Supreme Being, to attain spiritual peace through union with God the Father and to search out the ultimate meaning of life and nature";[142]

• the consumption of cat food by an individual who claimed that the food was "contributing significantly to [his] state of well-being";[143]

• the sale of golden eagle feathers by an Indian in violation of the Bald Eagle Protection Act;[144]

• deeply rooted convictions of Indian heritage;[145]

• the promotion of a homosexual life-style;[146]

• racist and anti-Semitic ideology;[147]

• publishing and distributing the Bible by an organization without any church affiliation;[148]

• a foundation engaged in the dissemination of religious and philosophical teachings of a Swedish theologian and philosopher;[149]

• a church that denied the existence of God and totally relied on human reason;[150] and

• a foster home controlled by two presbyteries.[151]

---

[139] Theriault v. Silber, 495 F.2d 390 (5th Cir. 1974).

[140] Callahan v. Woods, 479 F. Supp. 621 (D.C. Cal. 1979). *But cf.* Stevens v. Berger, 428 F. Supp. 896 (S.D.N.Y. 1977).

[141] State v. Brashear, 593 P.2d 63 (N.M. 1979). *But cf.* People v. Woody, 40 Cal. Rptr. 69 (1964) (use of peyote by members of the Native American Church held to be a "religious" practice).

[142] People v. Collins, 78 Cal. Rptr. 151 (1969).

[143] Brown v. Pena, 441 F. Supp. 1382 (D.C. Fla. 1977).

[144] United States v. Top Sky, 547 F.2d 486 (9th Cir. 1976).

[145] Matter of McMillan, 226 S.E.2d 693 (N.C. 1976).

[146] Church of the Chosen People v. United States, 548 F. Supp. 1247 (D.C. Minn. 1982).

[147] Bellamy v. Mason's Stores, Inc., 368 F. Supp. 1025 (E.D. Va. 1973).

[148] American Bible Society v. Lewisohn, 386 N.Y.S.2d 49 (1976).

[149] Swedenborg Foundation, Inc. v. Lewisohn, 386 N.Y.S.2d 54 (1976).

[150] Religious Society of Families v. Assessor, 343 N.Y.S.2d 159 (1973).

[151] N.L.R.B. v. Kemmerer Village, Inc., 907 F.2d 661 (7th Cir. 1990).

Instructional Aids to Chapter 14

Key Terms

discretion

proselytize

public safety, convenience, peace and order

religion

Sunday closing law

time, place, and manner restrictions

Learning Objectives

- Understand the extent to which religious "witnessing" is a constitutionally protected practice.

- Understand the extent to which prayer is a permissible activity on public property.

- Distinguish between those religious displays on public property that are permissible under the establishment clause, and those that are not.

- Describe under what circumstances public property can be used for religious purposes.

- Explain the current status of Sunday closing laws.

- Identify those situations in which the state has the legal authority to mandate medical treatment over the religious objections of the patient or the patient's family.

- Define the terms *religion* and *religious.*

Short-Answer Questions

1. A city ordinance requires all outdoor public meetings in city parks to be approved by the parks commissioner. The ordinance does not give the commissioner any criteria to follow. A religious group requests permission to conduct a meeting in a park, but the commissioner denies the request. Is the city ordinance legally valid?

2. A city ordinance permits city officials to deny parade permits if the public safety, convenience, peace, and order would be materially jeopardized. A controversial religious group applies for a parade permit, and its application is rejected on the ground that the proposed parade would be "disruptive of public peace and quiet, and might cause hostilities." The religious group challenges the permit denial in court. How will the court rule?

3. Can a city pass an ordinance prohibiting door-to-door religious evangelism in residential neighborhoods? Explain.

4. A city council opens each session with prayer. Does this practice violate the establishment of religion clause of the First Amendment? Explain.

5. A public courthouse lobby contains a statue of Moses holding the Ten Commandments. Does this display constitute a violation of the establishment of religion clause of the First Amendment?

6. A city maintains the lighted cross on top of city hall during the Christmas season. Is this practice permissible?

7. A city decorates street lamps during the Christmas season with wreaths and colored lights, and it places a large display consisting of Santa Clause, a sleigh, and six large reindeer, on the city hall lawn. Is this practice permissible?

8. Same facts as question 7, except that the display contains a nativity scene showing Mary, Joseph, and the baby Jesus. Does the inclusion of the nativity scene affect the constitutionality of the display?

9. A church's sanctuary is lost in a fire. The congregation would like to use a public school gymnasium for Sunday worship services while its sanctuary is being rebuilt. Determine the constitutionality of this use in each of the following situations:

   a. The school board offers the gymnasium to the congregation without charge.

    b. The school board charges the church the same rental fee it charges other community groups that use the gymnasium.

    c. The school board charges the church more than the rental fee it charges other community groups that use the gymnasium, in order to avoid any violation of the First Amendment's nonestablishment of religion clause.

10. A church's sanctuary becomes too small to accommodate its growing congregation. The church rents public school facilities for worship services and educational classes on Sunday mornings. At first, the church had plans to build a larger sanctuary. However, after several months, the congregation becomes accustomed to using the school facilities, and loses interest in building a new sanctuary. Evaluate the constitutionality of this arrangement.

11. A public high school would like to begin basketball games involving both its boys' and girls' teams with a prayer recited by a local minister. Evaluate the constitutionality of this practice.

12. A church would like to invite a popular Christian author to give a speech on family values as depicted in the Bible. Since the church's sanctuary is too small to accommodate the expected crowd, the church asks public school officials if it can rent a public high school gymnasium for a one-night meeting. School officials reject this request. Evaluate the constitutionality of the school's position in each of the following situations:

    a. The school has allowed a variety of community organizations to rent its gymnasium in recent years, including some religious groups.

    b. The school has never rented its gymnasium to any outside group.

    c. The school permits non-religious community organizations to rent its gymnasium.

13. A group of Christian students at a public high school asks school officials for permission to conduct a Bible study club after school hours in a vacant classroom. The school permits several other student groups to use classrooms after hours for meetings. School officials refuse to permit the Bible club since it would violate the First Amendment's ban on the establishment of religion. Do the Christian students have any recourse? Explain.

14. Federal employees are given a paid holiday at Thanksgiving and at Christmas. Is this practice permissible? Explain.

15. A young woman is seriously injured in an accident. She refuses to receive potentially life-saving medical treatment because of her religious convictions. Can the state compel her to receive medical treatment?

16. Same facts as problem 15, except that the woman's four year old son is also injured in the same accident. Can the woman refuse the administration of medical treatment to her son? Explain.

17. Has the Supreme Court held that secular humanism is a religion?

18. Do the courts restrict the term *religion* to those faiths maintaining a belief in a Supreme Being?

Essay Questions

1. Do you agree with the Supreme Court's definition of religion, or do you find it too expansive or too restrictive? Formulate your own definition.

2. Can you think of a rational basis for permitting public university students to conduct group worship and Bible study in school facilities, but denying the same right to students in public elementary and secondary schools?

3. A city enacts an ordinance banning door-to-door religious evangelism because of the disturbance it causes homeowners. Is disturbance to homeowners a sufficient reason for banning door-to-door evangelism? Should it be?

INDEX